STREET ATLAS
South Yorkshire

Contents

PHILIP'S

First colour edition published 1996
Reprinted in 1997 by

Ordnance Survey®   and   George Philip Ltd.
Romsey Road,   an imprint of Reed Books
Maybush,   Michelin House, 81 Fulham Road,
Southampton SO16 4GU   London SW3 6RB
                                         and Auckland, Melbourne

ISBN 0-540-06330-4 (hardback)
ISBN 0-540-06331-2 (wire-o)

To the best of the Publishers´ knowledge, the information in this atlas
was correct at the time of going to press. No responsibility can be
accepted for any errors or their consequences.

The representation in this atlas of a road, track or path is no evidence
of the existence of a right of way.

**The mapping between pages 1 and 159 (inclusive) in this atlas is
derived from Ordnance Survey® OSCAR® and Land-Line® data,
and Landranger® mapping.**

Ordnance Survey, OSCAR, Land-Line and Landranger are registered
trade marks of Ordnance Survey, the National Mapping Agency of
Great Britain.

Printed and bound in Spain by Cayfosa

Key to map symbols

	Motorway
	Primary Routes (Dual carriageway and single)
	A Roads (Dual carriageway and single)
	B Roads (Dual carriageway and single)
	C Roads (Dual carriageway and single)
	Minor Roads
	Roads under construction
	County boundaries
	All Railways
	Track or private road
	Gate or obstruction to traffic (restrictions may not apply at all times or to all vehicles)
	All paths, bridleways, BOAT's, RUPP's, dismantled railways, etc.

The representation in this atlas of a road, track or path is no evidence of the existence of a right of way

174 Adjoining page indicator

Acad	Academy	Mon	Monument
Cemy	Cemetery	Mus	Museum
C Ctr	Civic Centre	Obsy	Observatory
CH	Club House	Pal	Royal Palace
Coll	College	PH	Public House
Ex H	Exhibition Hall	Resr	Reservoir
Ind Est	Industrial Estate	Ret Pk	Retail Park
Inst	Institute	Sch	School
Ct	Law Court	Sh Ctr	Shopping Centre
L Ctr	Leisure Centre	Sta	Station
LC	Level Crossing	TH	Town Hall/House
Liby	Library	Trad Est	Trading Estate
Mkt	Market	Univ	University
Meml	Memorial	YH	Youth Hostel

	British Rail station
	Private railway station
	Bus, coach station
	Ambulance station
	Coastguard station
	Fire station
	Police station
	Casualty entrance to hospital
	Churches, Place of worship
H	Hospital
i	Information Centre
P	Parking
	Post Office
	Public Convenience
	Important buildings, schools, colleges, universities and hospitals
River Soar	Water Name
	Stream
	River or canal (minor and major)
	Water Fill
	Tidal Water
	Woods
	Sheffield Tramway

0	¼	½	¾	1 mile

0	250 m	500 m	750 m	1 Kilometre

The scale of the maps is 5.52 cm to 1 km (3½ inches to 1 mile)

The small numbers around the edges of the maps identify the 1 kilometre National Grid lines

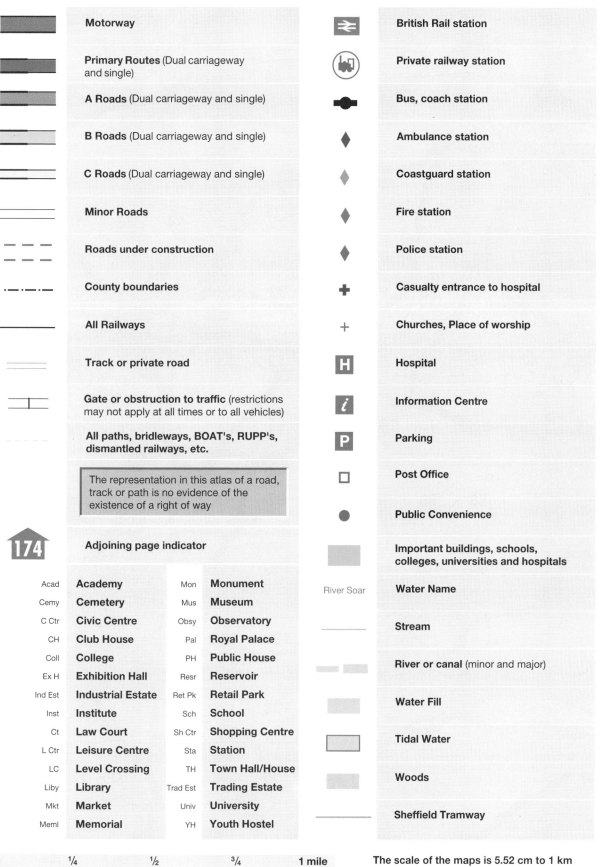

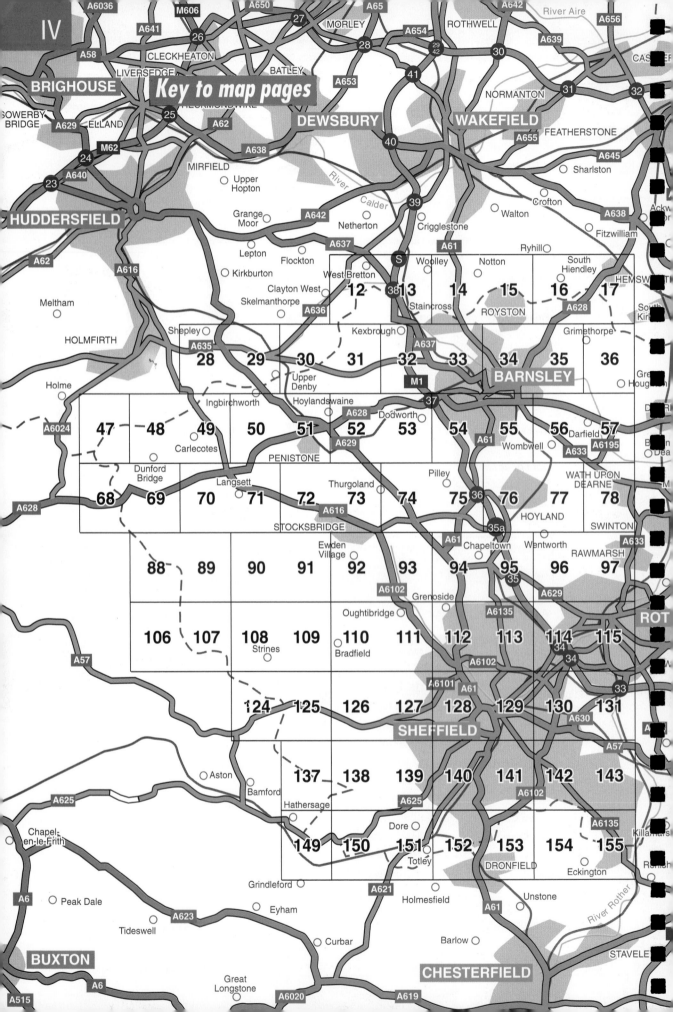

Key to map pages

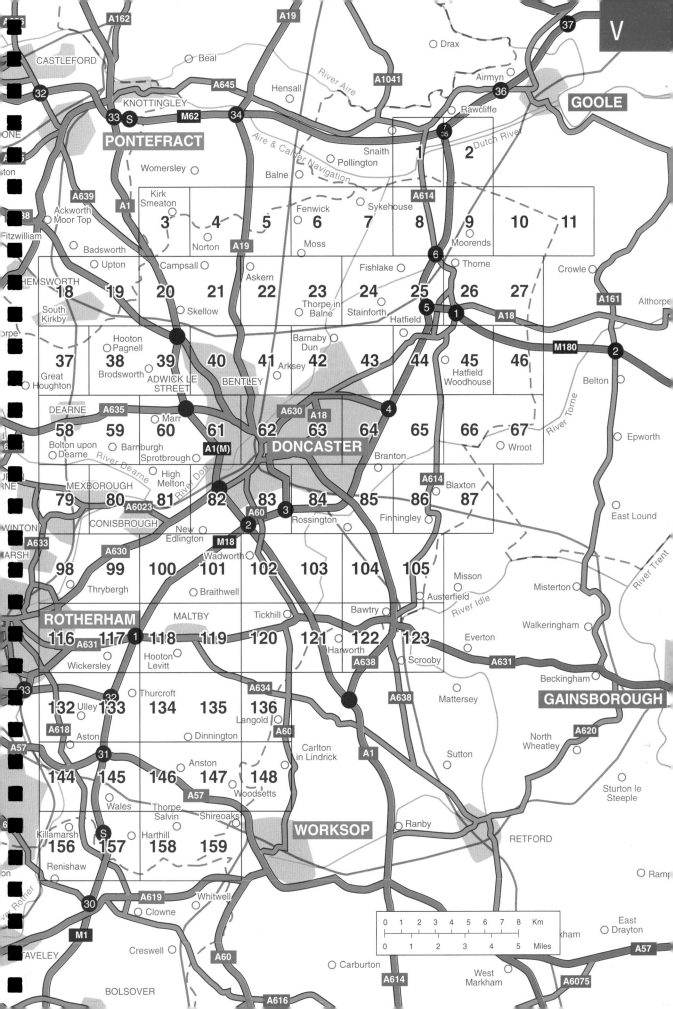

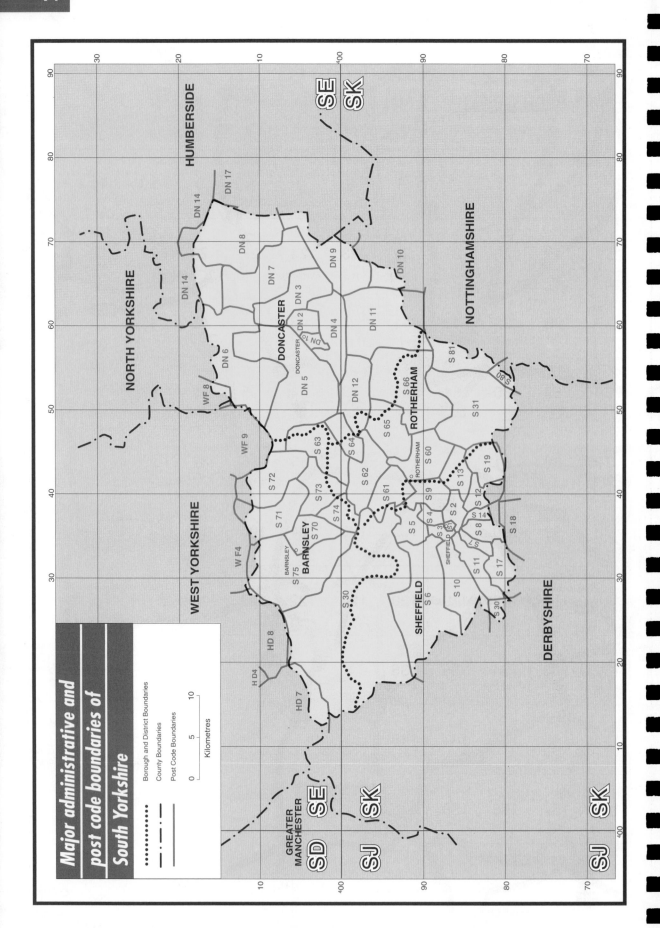

Major administrative and post code boundaries of South Yorkshire

- ••••••••• Borough and District Boundaries
- — · — · — County Boundaries
- ———— Post Code Boundaries

Kilometres
0   5   10

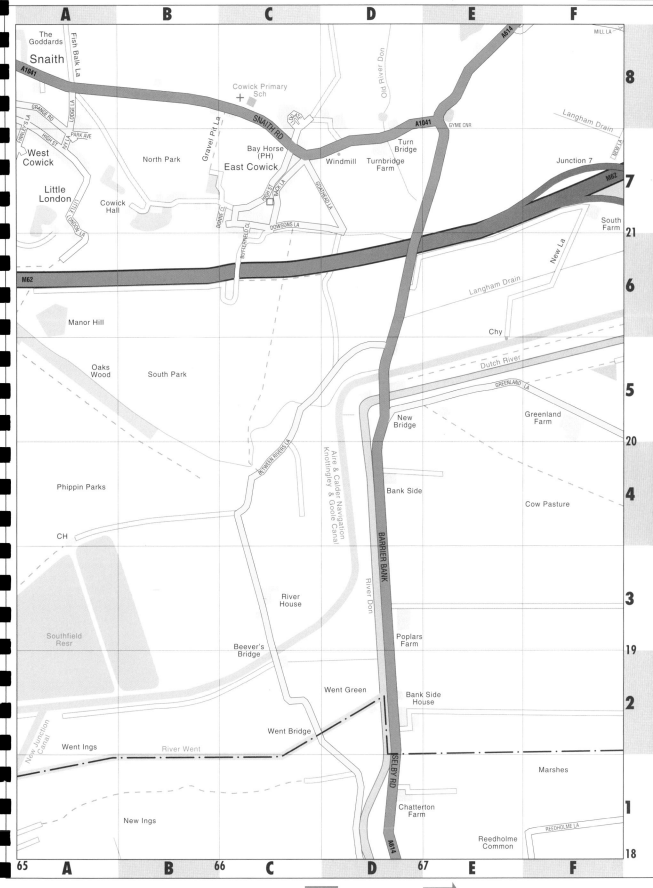

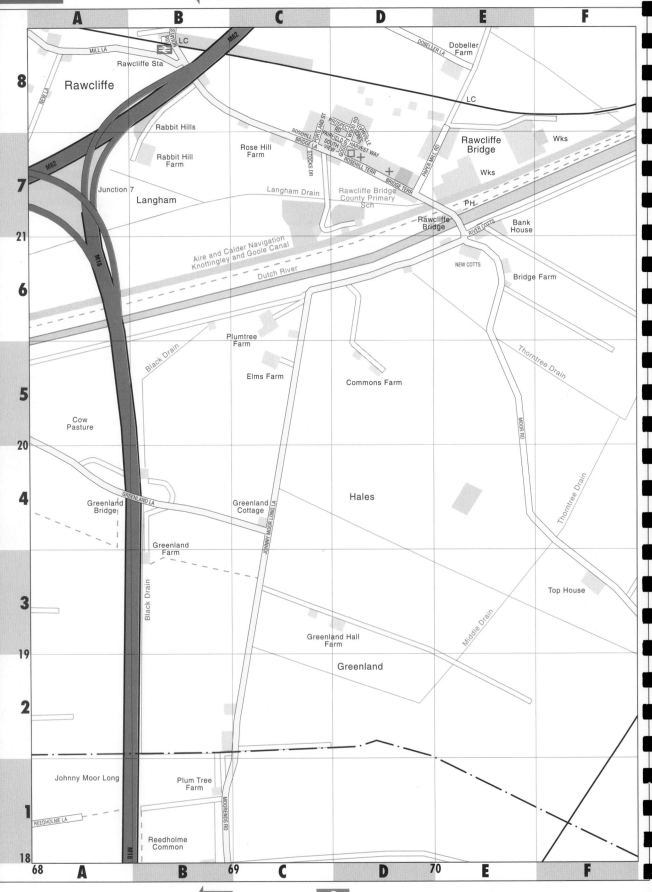

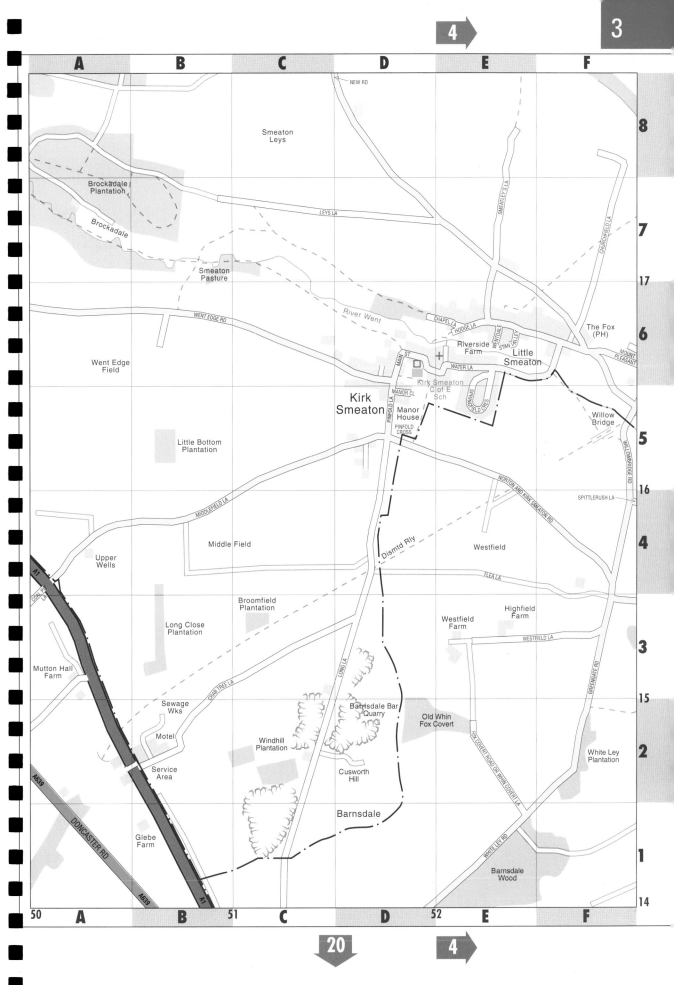

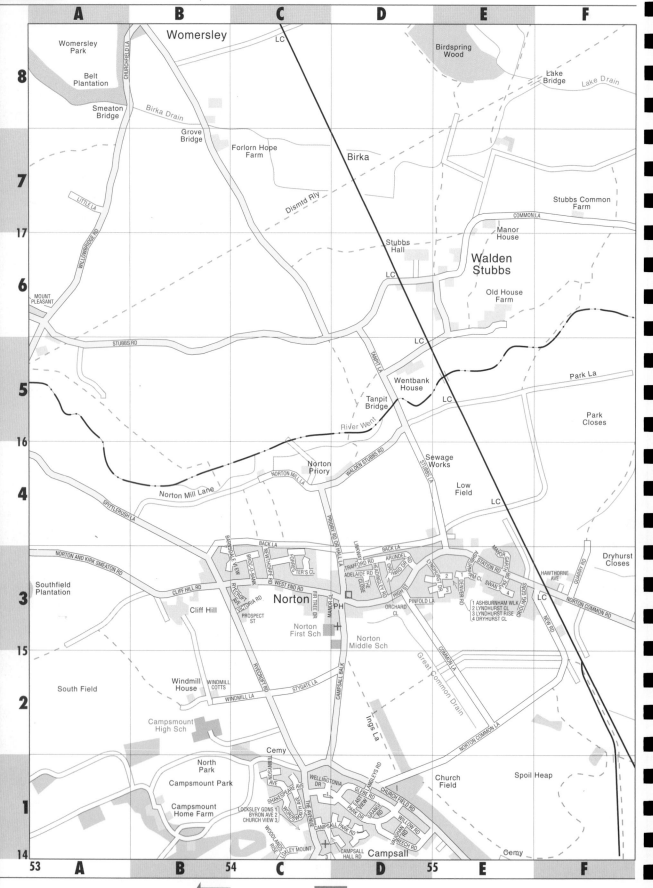

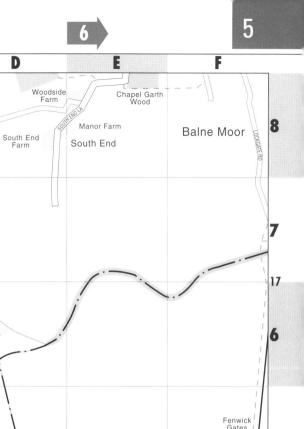

A B C D E F

8

Lake Drain

NEVILLE PITS LA

Woodside Farm

Chapel Garth Wood

South End Farm

Manor Farm

SOUTH END LA

South End

Balne Moor

LOCKGATE RD

Lake Bridge

7

17

BADGER LA

Fox Covert

River Went

6

COMMON LA

Stubbs Grange

Fenwick Gates

Went Farm

Went Bridge

SELBY RD

COMMON LA

Stubbs Common

LC

5

16

River Went (old course)

Fenwick Farm

4

Dryhurst Drain

Moat Hill Farm

Norton Common Farm

Went Lows

Fenwick Common

3

Dryhurst Closes

Moat Hill

FENWICK LA

Cemy

15

Toll Bar

NORTON COMMON RD

CLOUGH LA

Lady Thorpe

Ladythorpe Farm

Moss & Fenwick County Primary Sch

FENWICK COMMON LA

2

Great Common Drain

Norton Common

Elm Field Farm

LC

1

A19

LC

WILLOW GARTH LA

Randall Farm

MOSS RD

Star Inn (PH)

Askern Common Drain

14

56 A B 57 C D 58 E F

A19

A B C D E F

8

Pollington

LC LOWGATE
Cherrytree Farm
Lowgate Farm
Balne Hall Wood

River Went

Topham Ferry Bridge

7

LOCKGATE RD

17

6

Fleet Drain

Fenwick

Riddings Farm

Gate Farm
Baxter Arms (PH)

5

FENWICK LA

Manor Farm

Fenwick Hall

Haggs Farm
LAWN LA

Bungalow Farm

16

SHAW LA

Bunfold Shaw La

Bunfold Shaw

WEST LA

Fenwick London Hill

Lawn

West End

4

Fenwick Common Drain

FENWICK COMMON LA

HAGGS LA

3

Fenwick Common

Fenwick Grange

15

Ell Wood and Fenwick Grange Drain

FLASHLEY CARR LA

Dismtd Rly

2

Jett Hall

Moseley House Farm

Moss London Hill

Flashley Carr

Manor Farm

MOSS RD

LONDON LA

MOSS HAVEN

Moss Farm

Moseley Grange

1

Moss

Star Farm

PINFOLD LA
THRUMPLEFT LA

14

59 A B 60 C D 61 E F

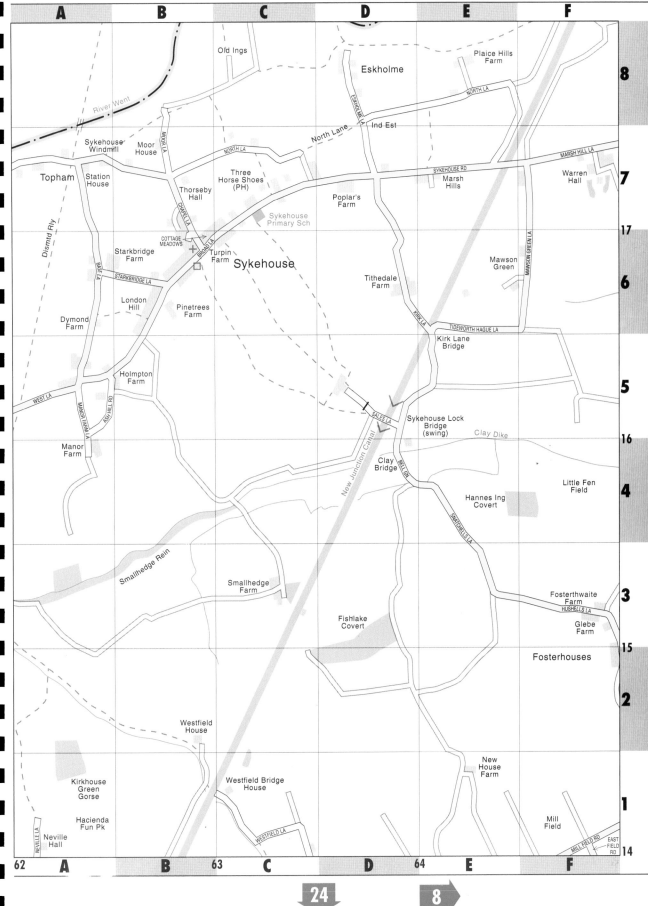

A   B   C   D   E   F

Old Ings

Eskholme

Plaice Hills Farm

North La

River Went

North Lane

Ind Est

Sykehouse Windmill

Moor House

North La

Three Horse Shoes (PH)

Sykehouse Rd

Marsh Hills

Marsh Hill La

Warren Hall

8

Topham

Station House

Thorseby Hall

Poplar's Farm

7

Dismtd Rly

Chapel La

Sykehouse Primary Sch

17

Cottage Meadows

Starkbridge Farm

Broad La

Turpin Farm

Sykehouse

Tithedale Farm

Mawson Green

Mawson Green La

6

Bar La

Starkbridge La

London Hill

Pinetrees Farm

Kirk La

Tideworth Hague La

Dymond Farm

Kirk Lane Bridge

West La

Holmpton Farm

Manor Farm La

Ash Hill Rd

Sales La

Sykehouse Lock Bridge (swing)

Clay Dike

5

New Junction Canal

Manor Farm

Clay Bridge

Bell Dn

16

Little Fen Field

4

Hannes Ing Covert

Smallhedge Rein

Smallhedge Farm

Smatghells La

Fosterthwaite Farm

Hushells La

3

Fishlake Covert

Glebe Farm

15

Fosterhouses

2

Westfield House

New House Farm

Kirkhouse Green Gorse

Westfield Bridge House

1

Neville La

Hacienda Fun Pk

Mill Field

Neville Hall

Westfield La

Mill Field Rd

East Field Rd

14

62   A   B   63   C   D   64   E   F

A B C D E F

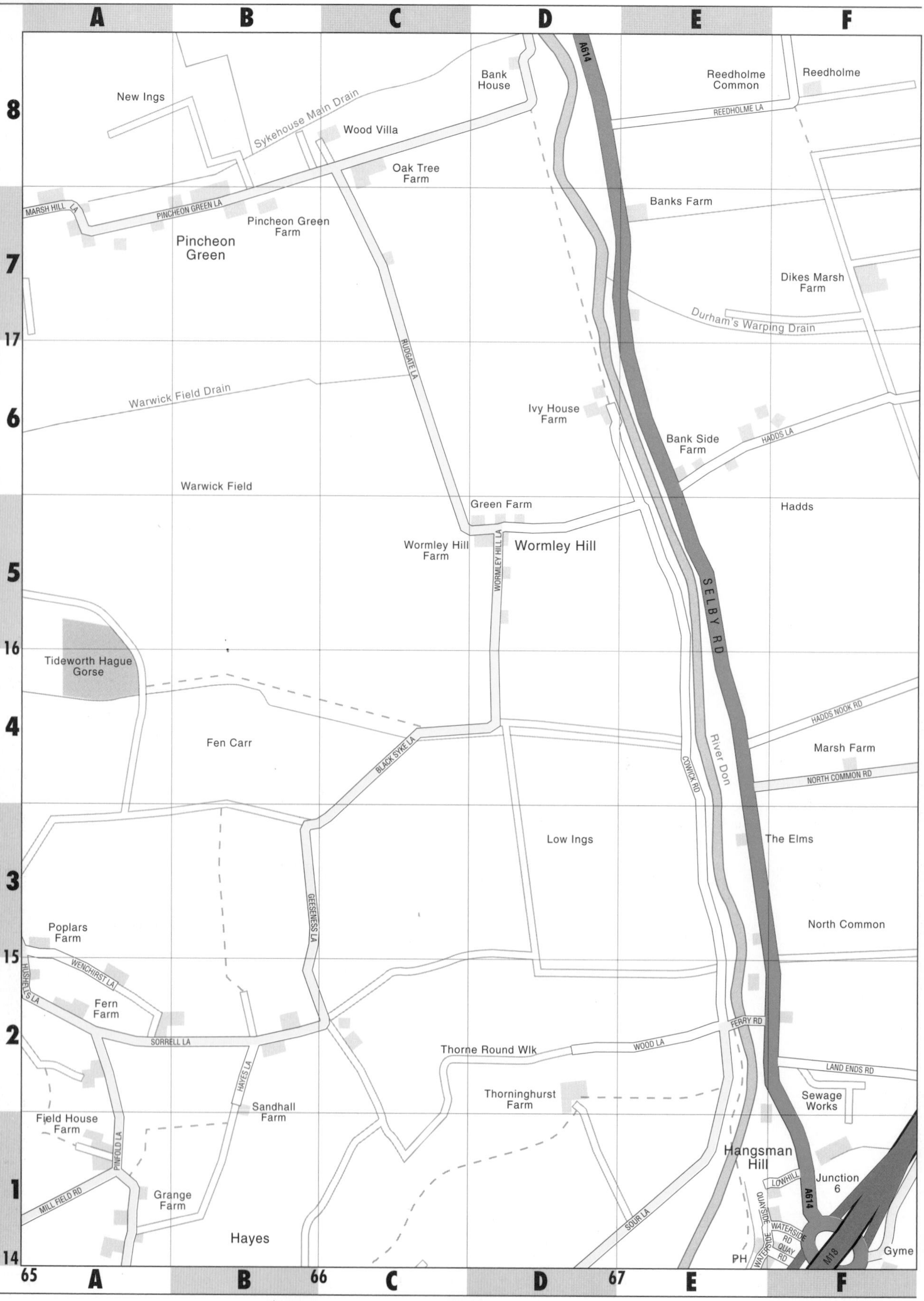

8   New Ings

Sykehouse Main Drain

Bank House

Reedholme Common   Reedholme

REEDHOLME LA

Wood Villa

Oak Tree Farm

MARSH HILL LA

PINCHEON GREEN LA

Pincheon Green Farm

Banks Farm

7   Pincheon Green

Dikes Marsh Farm

17

Durham's Warping Drain

Warwick Field Drain

RUDGATE LA

6   Ivy House Farm

Bank Side Farm

HADDS LA

Warwick Field

Green Farm

Hadds

Wormley Hill Farm

WORMLEY HILL LA

Wormley Hill

5

SELBY RD

16   Tideworth Hague Gorse

4   Fen Carr

BLACK SYKE LA

HADDS NOOK RD

River Don

Marsh Farm

COWICK RD

NORTH COMMON RD

Low Ings

The Elms

3

GEESENESS LA

North Common

Poplars Farm

15

WENCHIRST LA

HUSHEL'S LA

Fern Farm

FERRY RD

2   SORRELL LA

HAYES LA

Thorne Round Wlk

WOOD LA

LAND ENDS RD

Sandhall Farm

Thorninghurst Farm

Sewage Works

Field House Farm

PINFOLD LA

Hangsman Hill

LOWHILL

Junction 6

QUAYSIDE

1   MILL FIELD RD

Grange Farm

SOUR LA

A614

M18

Gyme

Hayes

WATERSIDE RD

QUAY RD

PH

14

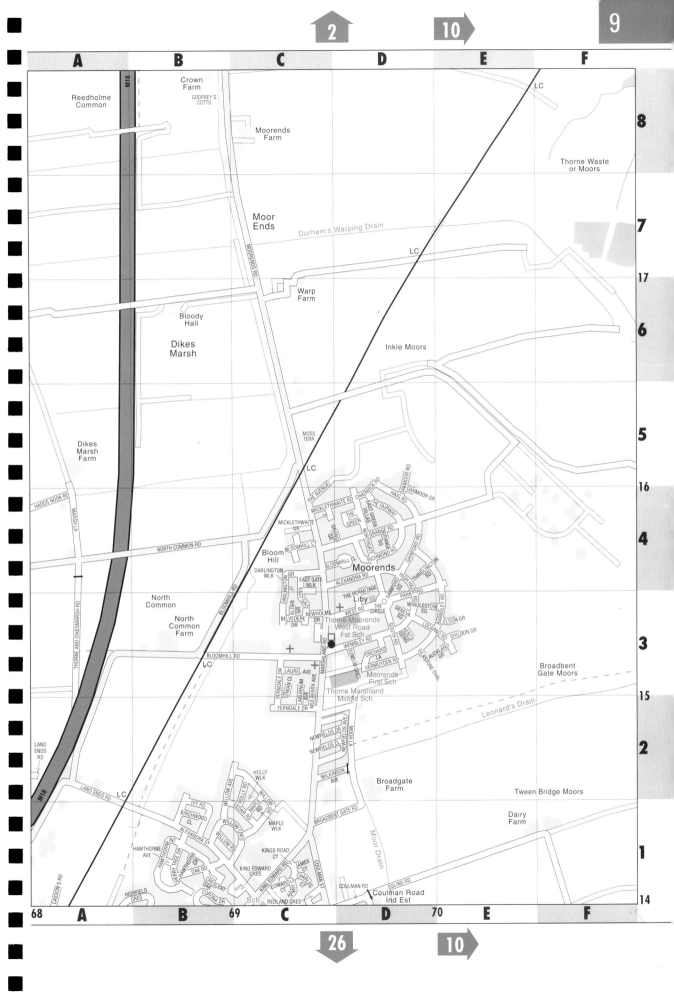

A　B　C　D　E　F

8

Goole Moors

7

Blackwater Dike

17

6

Tramway (dis)

5

Mill Drain

16

4

Cottage Dike

Thorne Waste or Moors

Thousand Acre Drain

3

15

2

Tween Bridge Moors

Thorne Waste Drain

Top Boating Dike

THORNE WASTE DRAIN RD

Angle Drain

1

14

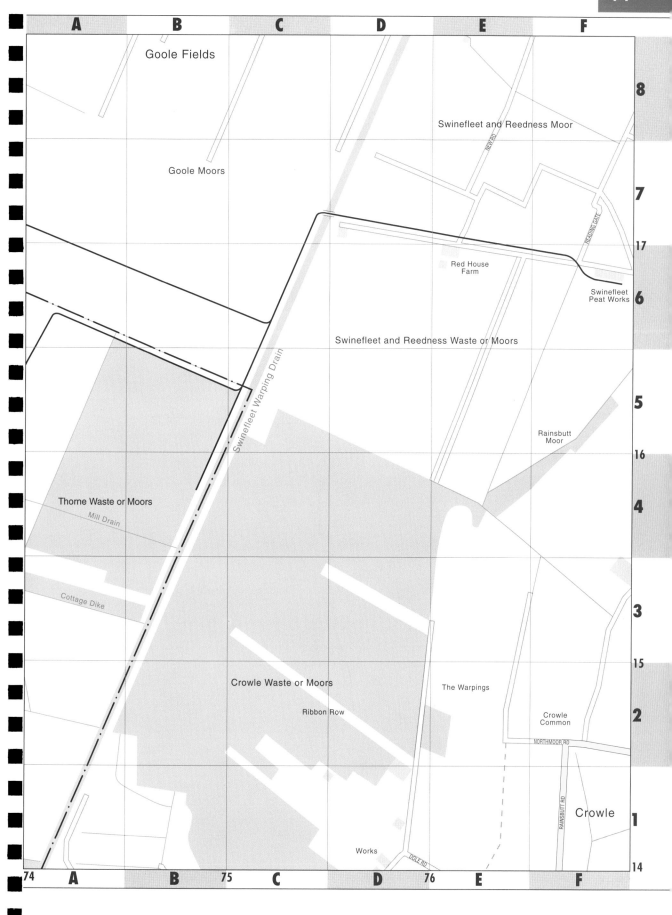

Goole Fields

Swinefleet and Reedness Moor

Goole Moors

Red House
Farm

Swinefleet
Peat Works

Swinefleet and Reedness Waste or Moors

Swinefleet Warping Drain

Rainsbutt
Moor

Thorne Waste or Moors

Mill Drain

Cottage Dike

Crowle Waste or Moors

The Warpings

Crowle
Common

NORTHMOOR RD

Ribbon Row

RAINSBUTT RD

Crowle

Works

DOLE RD

NEW RD

READING GATE

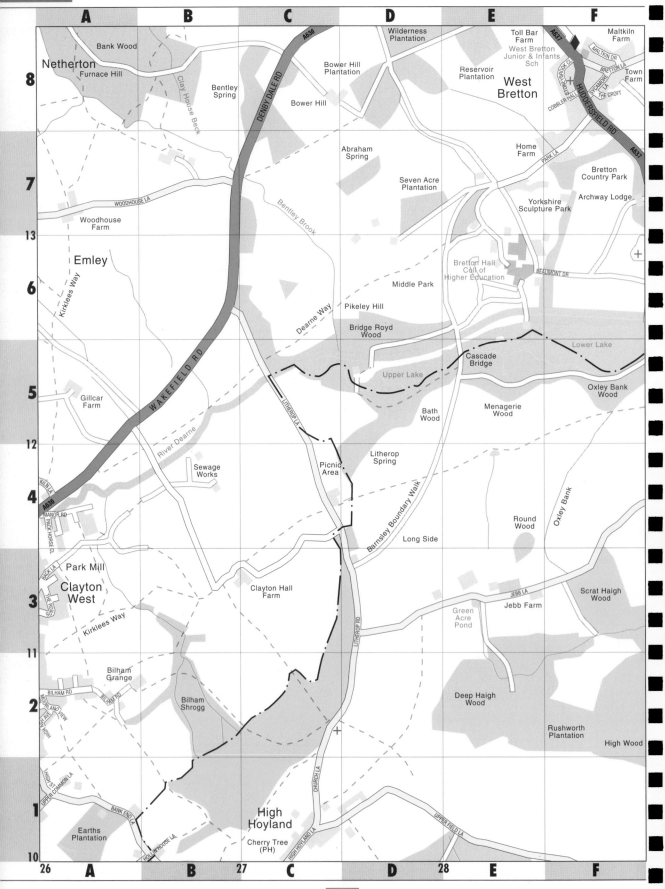

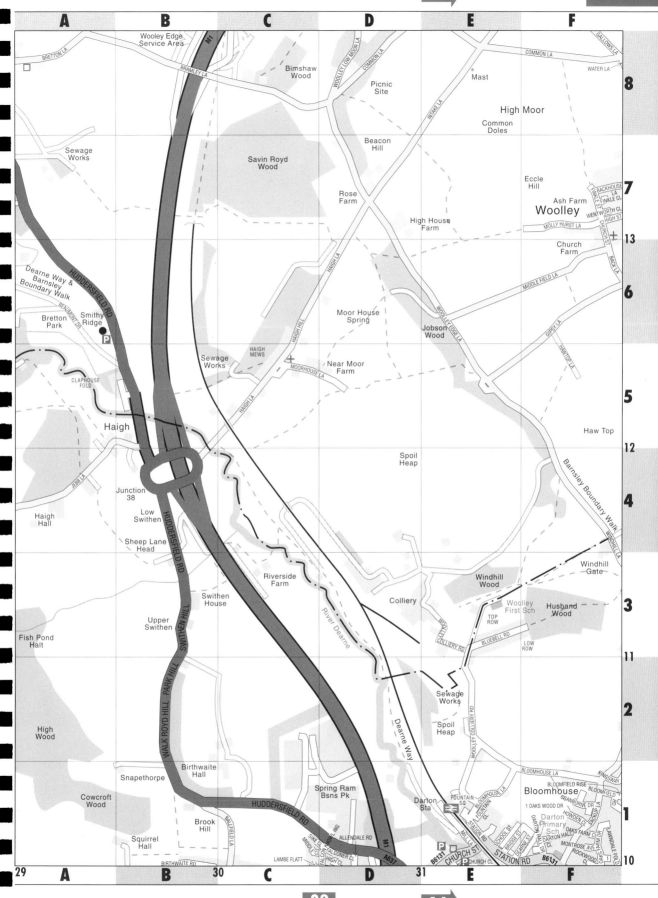

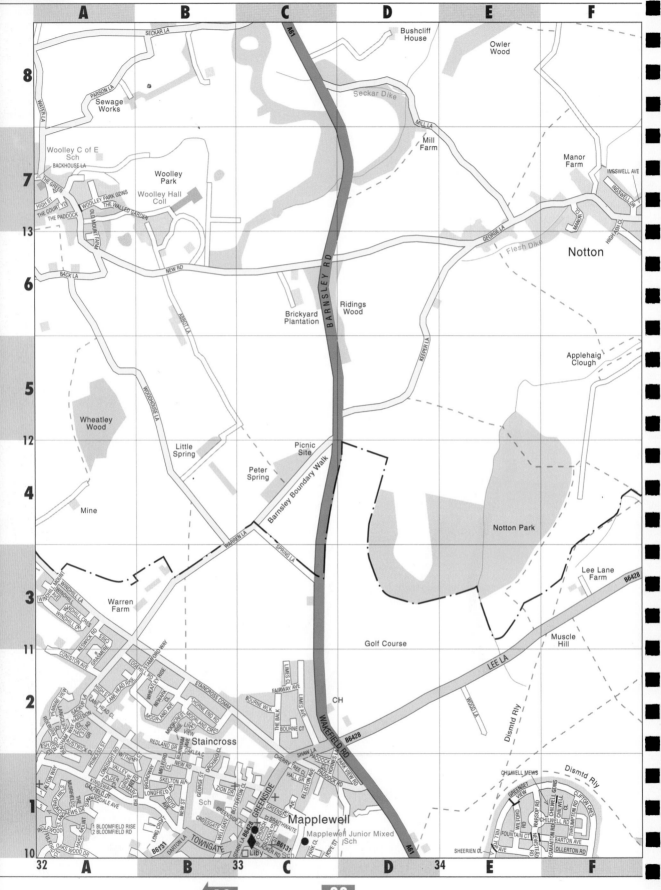

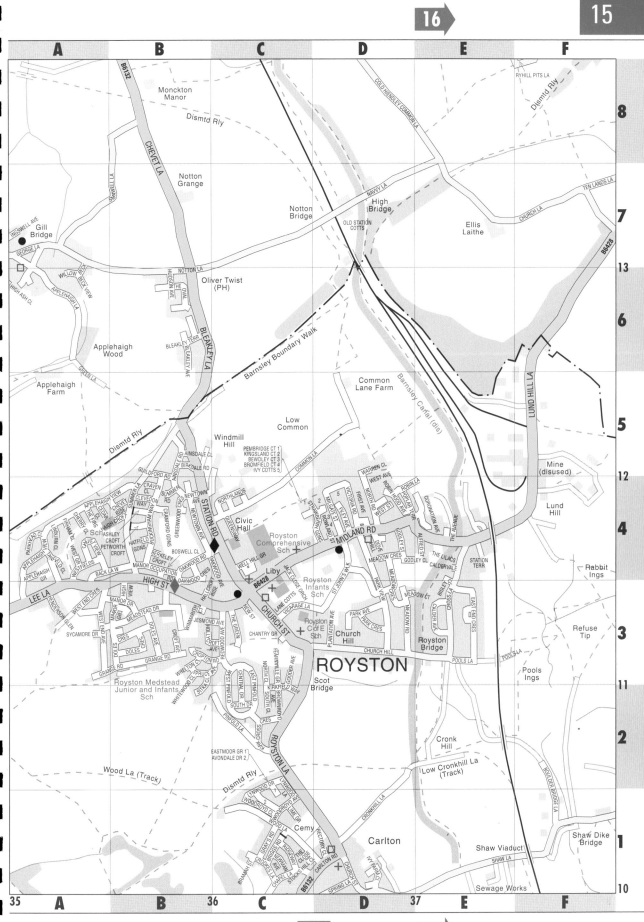

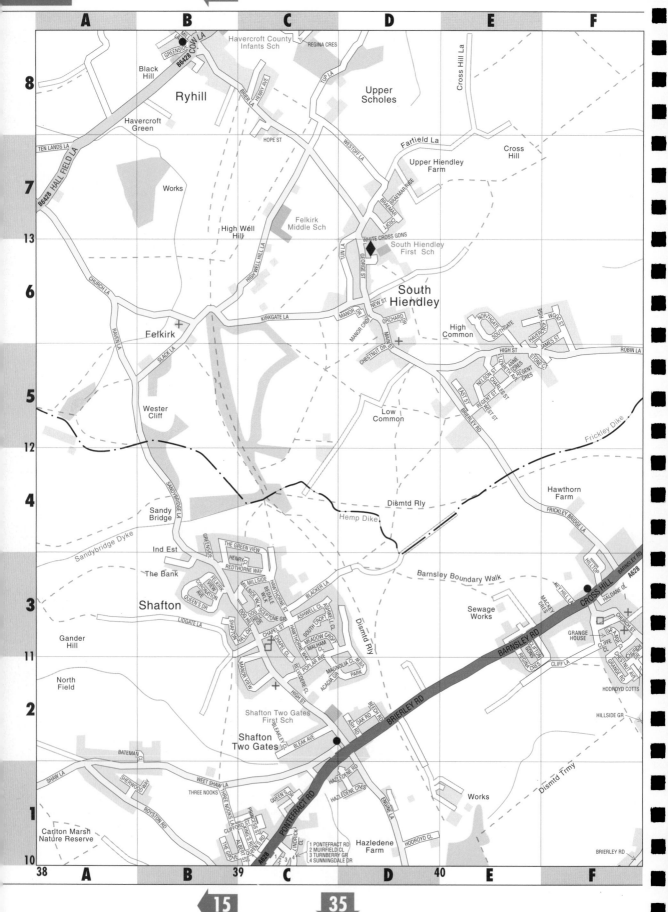

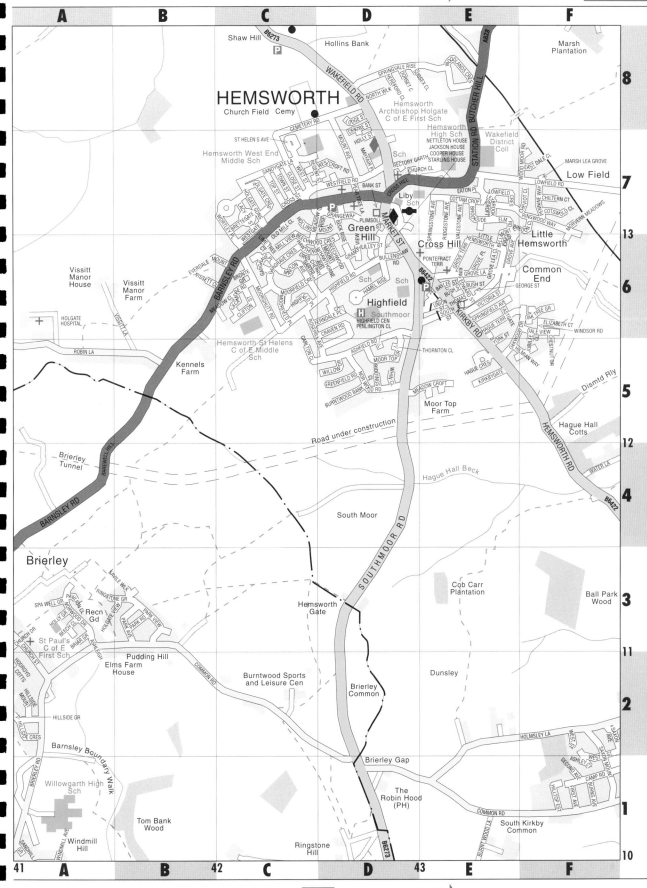

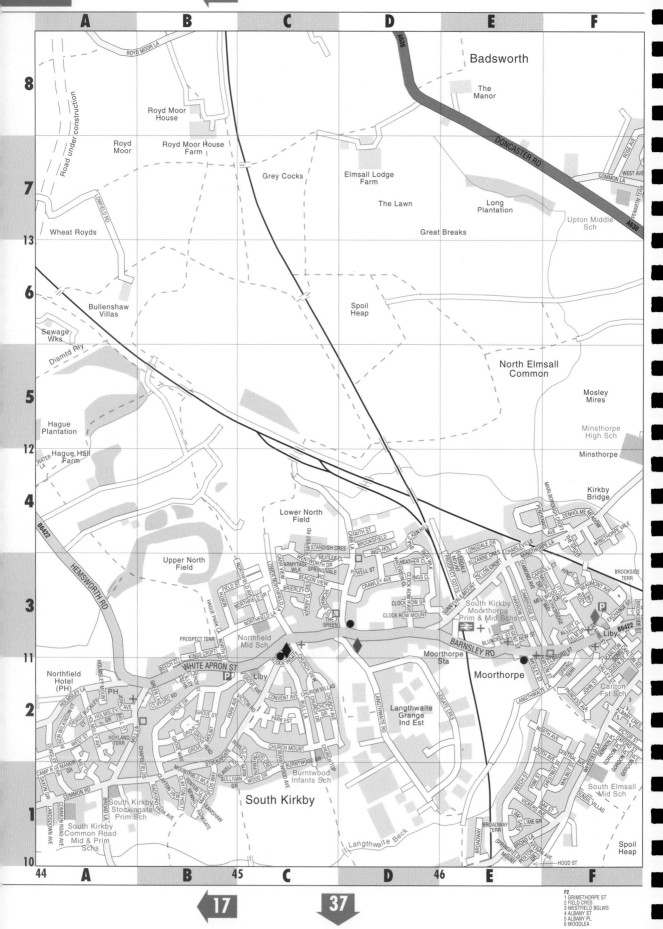

Badsworth

The Manor

DONCASTER RD

Royd Moor House

Royd Moor

Royd Moor House Farm

Grey Cocks

Elmsall Lodge Farm

The Lawn

Long Plantation

Upton Middle Sch

Wheat Royds

Great Breaks

Bullenshaw Villas

Spoil Heap

North Elmsall Common

Mosley Mires

Sewage Wks

Dismtd Rly

Minsthorpe High Sch

Hague Plantation

Minsthorpe

Hague Hall Farm

Kirkby Bridge

Lower North Field

Upper North Field

HEMSWORTH RD

South Kirkby Moorthorpe Prim & Mid Schs

BROOKSIDE TERR

Northfield Mid Sch

WHITE APRON ST

Liby

Moorthorpe Sta

BARNSLEY RD

Moorthorpe

Northfield Hotel (PH)

Liby

Langthwaite Grange Ind Est

Carlton Fst Sch

South Kirkby Stockingate Prim Sch

Burntwood Infants Sch

South Elmsall Mid Sch

South Kirkby

South Kirkby Common Road Mid & Prim Schs

Langthwaite Beck

Spoil Heap

F2
1 GRIMETHORPE ST
2 FIELD CRES
3 WESTFIELD BGLWS
4 ALBANY ST
5 ALBANY PL
6 WOODLEA

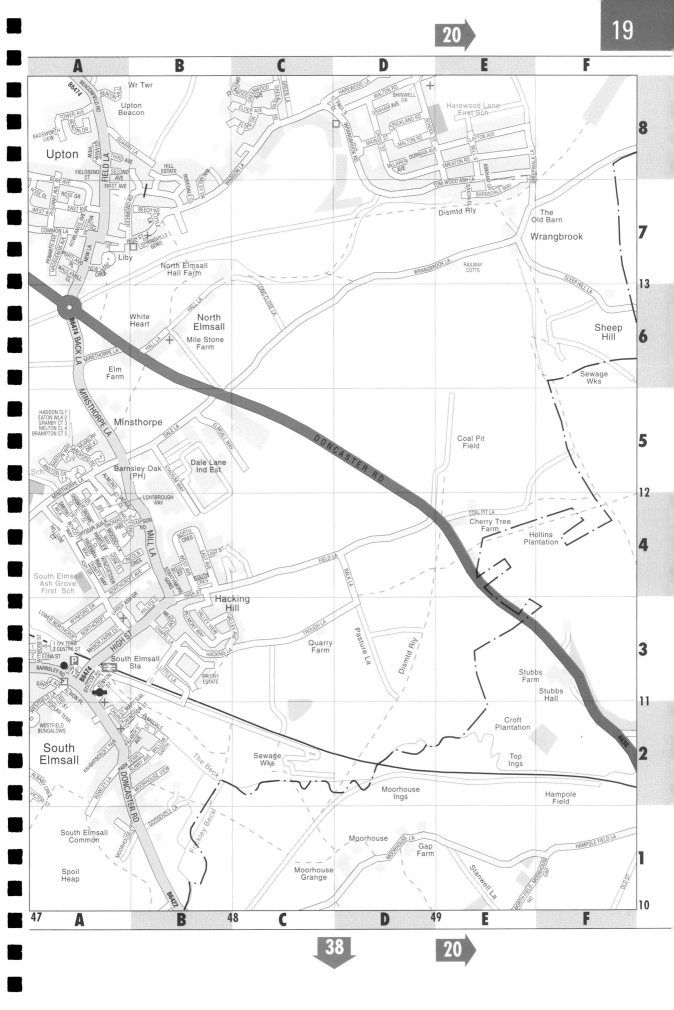

19
3

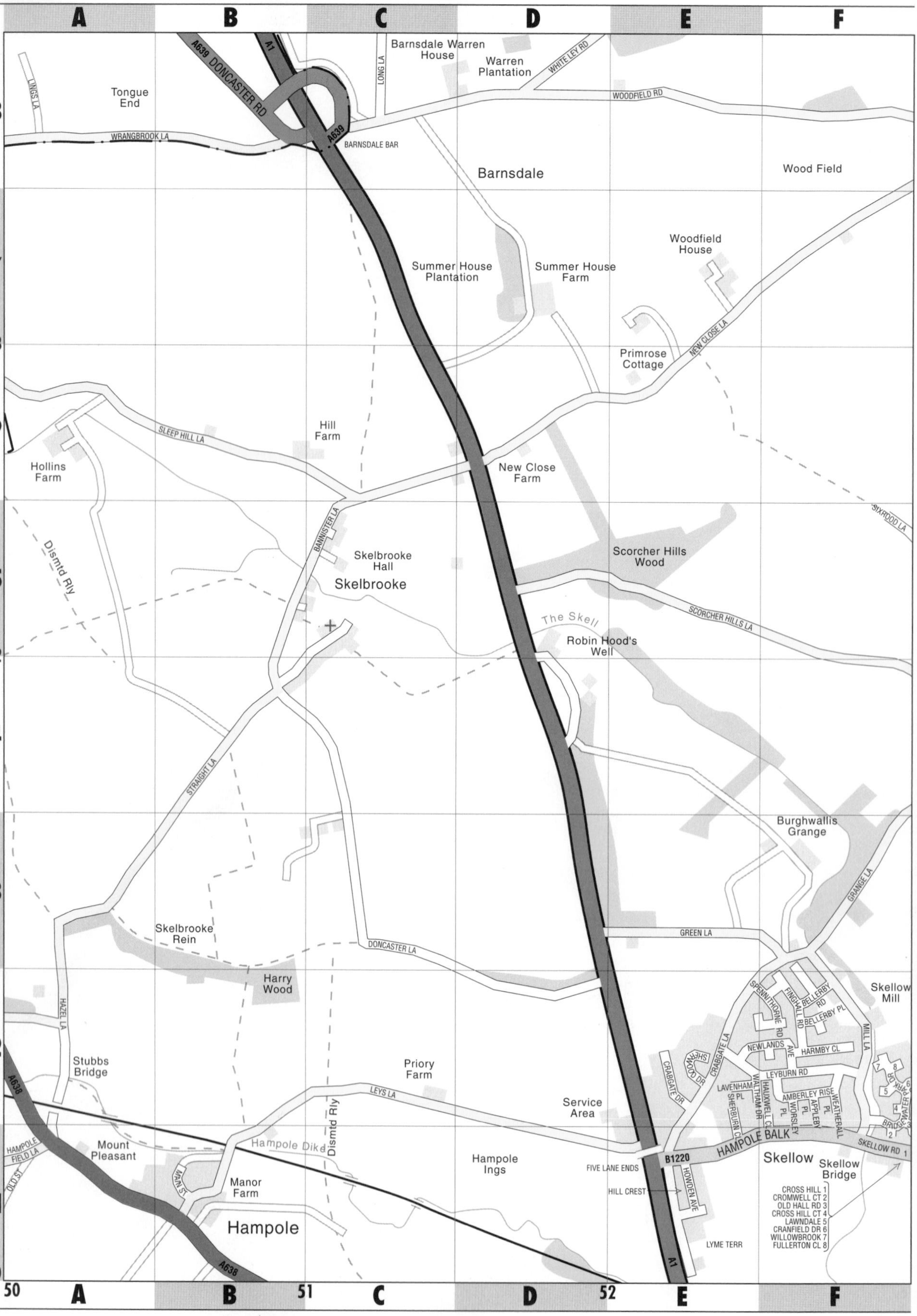

	A	B	C	D	E	F

LINKS LA

A638 DONCASTER RD

A1

Tongue End

Barnsdale Warren House

Warren Plantation

WHITE LEY RD

LONG LA

WOODFIELD RD

8

WRANGBROOK LA

A639

BARNSDALE BAR

Barnsdale

Wood Field

7

Summer House Plantation

Summer House Farm

Woodfield House

NEW CLOSE LA

13

Primrose Cottage

SLEEP HILL LA

Hill Farm

New Close Farm

SIXROOD LA

6

Hollins Farm

Dismtd Rly

BANNISTER LA

Skelbrooke Hall

Scorcher Hills Wood

Skelbrooke

SCORCHER HILLS LA

5

The Skell

Robin Hood's Well

12

STRAIGHT LA

4

Burghwallis Grange

GRANGE LA

3

Skelbrooke Rein

DONCASTER LA

GREEN LA

11

Harry Wood

HAZEL LA

Skellow Mill

MILL A

SPENNITHORNE RD

FINGALL RD

BELLERBY RD

BELLERBY PL

CRAGGATE LA

NEWLANDS

HARMBY CL

HS

2

Stubbs Bridge

Priory Farm

LEYBURN RD

LAVENHAM PL

WALTHAM DR

HAUXWELL PL

SHERBURN CL

AMBERLEY RISE

WORSLEY

APPLEBY PL

WEATHERALL

BROAD WATER WAY

SKELLOW RD 1

LEYS LA

Service Area

Hampole Dike

Dismtd Rly

B1220

HAMPOLE BALK

Skellow

Skellow Bridge

A638

HAMPOLE FIELD LA

OLD ST

Mount Pleasant

MAIN S

Manor Farm

Hampole Ings

FIVE LANE ENDS

HILL CREST

HOWDEN AVE

LYME TERR

1

Hampole

A638

A1

CROSS HILL 1
CROMWELL CT 2
OLD HALL RD 3
CROSS HILL CT 4
LAWNDALE 5
CRANFIELD DR 6
WILLOWBROOK 7
FULLERTON CL 8

10

50	A		B	51	C		D	52	E		F

19
39

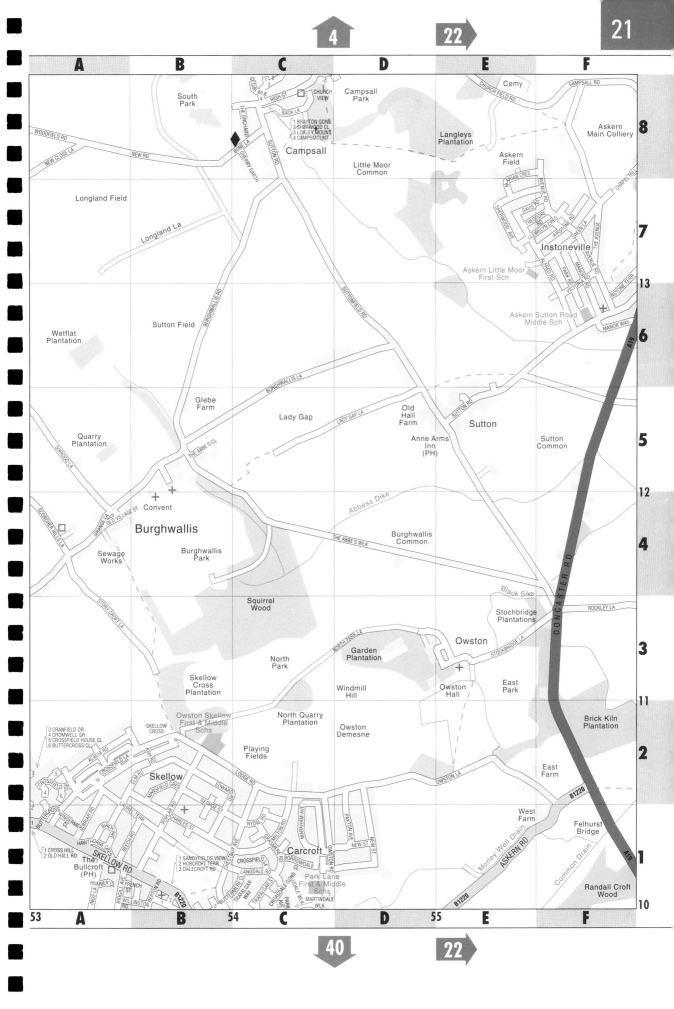

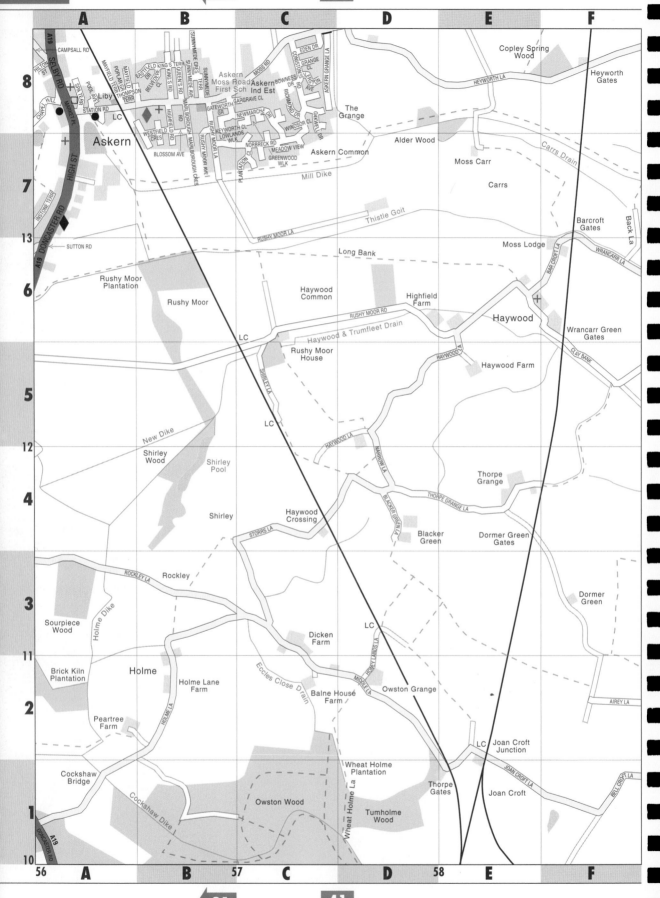

A   B   C   D   E   F

8
7
13
6
5
12
4
3
11
2
1
10

CAMPSALL RD
HILTON ST
SELBY RD
CHAPEL HILL
SPA TERR
POOL AVE
STATION RD
MARKET PL
INSTONE TERR
HIGH ST
DONCASTER RD
A19
SUTTON RD
A19

Liby
LC
Askern

MAYFIELD TERR
POPLAR AVE
MAYFIELD
THOMPSON TERR
SUNNYMEDE CRES
CASTLEFIELD DR
KING'S TERR
BEWERLEY DR
KING'S RD
QUEEN'S RD
SUNNYMEDE AVE
SUNNYMEDE
HIGHFIELD RD
WESTFIELD CRES
BLOSSOM AVE
PLANTATION CL
KEYWORTH CL
NORBRECK RD
RUSHY MOOR LA
RUSHY MOOR AVE
MARLBOROUGH CRES
MARLBOROUGH RD
GATEWORTH GR
LOWLANDS WLK
MEADOW VIEW
GREENWOOD WLK
NEWMARCHE DR
WINDSOR DR
OAKWELL DR
RICHMOND DR
BOWNESS AVE
ULLSWATER AVE
CONISTON RD
GRANGE CL
GRANGE RD
EDEN DR
MOSS RD
ASKERN GRANGE LA
GARGRAVE CL

Askern Moss Road First Sch
Askern Ind Est
Askern Common
The Grange
Alder Wood

Copley Spring Wood
HEYWORTH LA
Heyworth Gates
Carrs Drain
Moss Carr
Carrs

Mill Dike
Thistle Goit
RUSHY MOOR LA
13
Long Bank

Barcroft Gates
Moss Lodge
BARCROFT LA
WRANCARR LA
Back La

Rushy Moor Plantation
Rushy Moor
Haywood Common
RUSHY MOOR RD
Highfield Farm
Haywood
Wrancarr Green Gates

Haywood & Trumfleet Drain
LC
Rushy Moor House
HAYWOOD LA
Haywood Farm
CLAY BANK

SHIRLEY LA
LC
New Dike
Shirley Wood
Shirley Pool
HAYWOOD LA
NARROW LA
Thorpe Grange

Shirley
Haywood Crossing
STORRS LA
BLACKER GREEN LA
THORPE GRANGE LA
Blacker Green
Dormer Green Gates

ROCKLEY LA
Rockley
HOLME DIKE
Dormer Green

Sourpiece Wood
Brick Kiln Plantation
Holme
HOLME LA
Holme Lane Farm
ECCLES CLOSE DRAIN
Dicken Farm
LC
HONEY LANDS LA
MIDDLE LA
Owston Grange
AIREY LA

Peartree Farm
Balne House Farm
LC
Joan Croft Junction

Cockshaw Bridge
COCKSHAW DIKE
Owston Wood
WHEAT HOLME LA
Wheat Holme Plantation
Tumholme Wood
Thorpe Gates
JOAN CROFT LA
Joan Croft
BELL CROFT LA

A19
DONCASTER RD

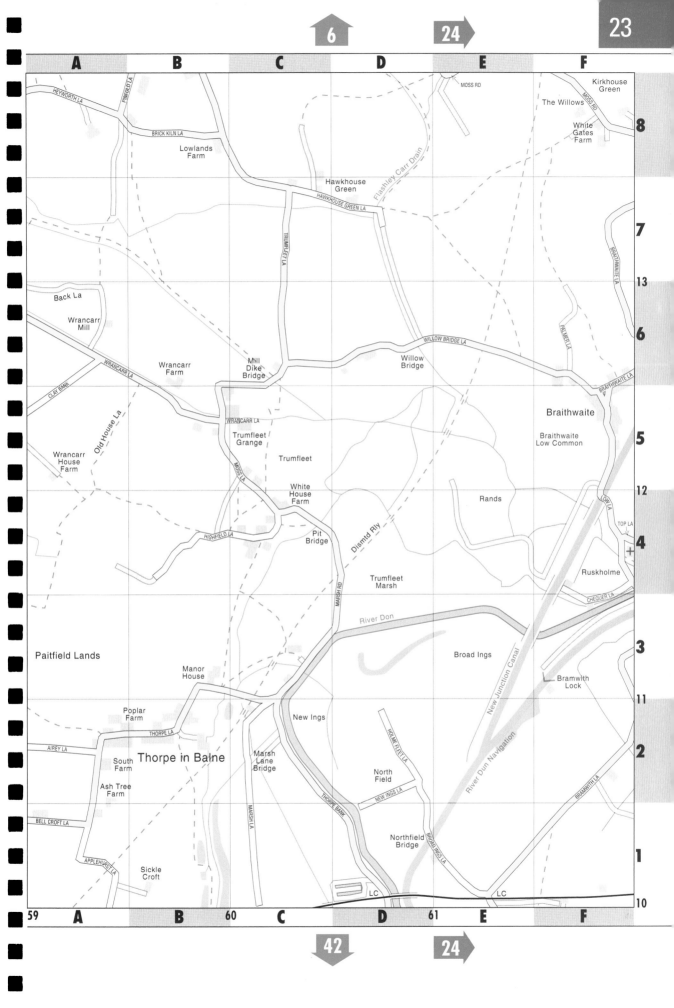

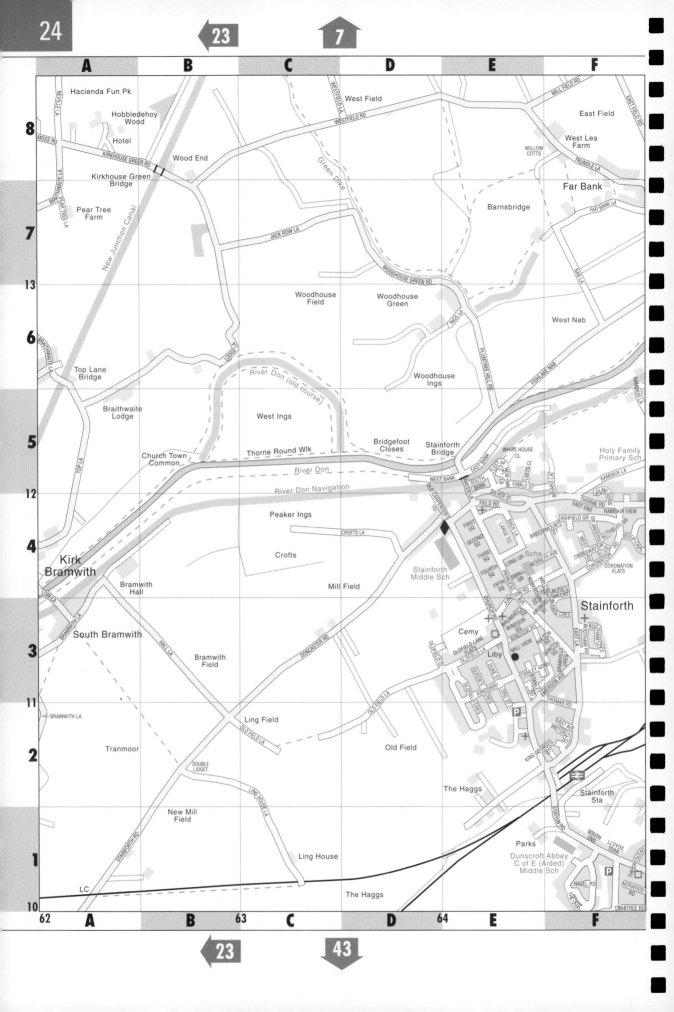

A B C D E F

8

Hacienda Fun Pk
NEVILLE LA
Hobbledehoy Wood
Hotel
MOSS RD
BRAITHWAITE LA
PEAR TREE LA
KIRKHOUSE GREEN RD
Kirkhouse Green Bridge
Wood End
West Field
WESTFIELD LA
WESTFIELD RD
Green Dike
East Field
MILL FIELD RD
FAR FIELD RD
West Lea Farm
WILLOW COTTS
TRUNDLE LA
Far Bank
FAR BANK LA

7

Pear Tree Farm
JACK ROW LA
Barnsbridge
WOODHOUSE GREEN RD

13

New Junction Canal
LODGE LA
Woodhouse Field
Woodhouse Green
INGS LA
PLUMTREE HILL RD
West Nab
FISHLAKE NAB
NAB LA
RAMSKIR LA

6

BRAITHWAITE LA
Top Lane Bridge
River Don (old course)
Woodhouse Ings

5

TOP LA
Braithwaite Lodge
West Ings
Thorne Round Wlk
Bridgefoot Closes
Stainforth Bridge
WHITE HOUSE CL
Holy Family Primary Sch
RAMSKIR LA
Church Town Common
River Don
WEST BANK
EAST BANK
FLEETS CL
NEW INN
FINKLE ST
SOUTH BANK
SILVER ST

12

River Don Navigation
Peaker Ings
OLD CARPENTER YD
WATER
FIELD RD
BACK LA
BREEZEMOUNT
ASHFIELD GR
NUTHOLES GR
THORNE RD
EAST END
RAMSKIR VIEW
DR ANDERSON AVE
WEST
BEECH CRES

4

CROFTS LA
Crofts
Stainforth Middle Sch
FIRST SQ
SECOND SQ
LARGE SQ
THIRD SQ
LONG GR Schs
KENNETH AVE
CROSSWAYS AVE
CORONATION
Coronation Flats
Mill Field
FOURTH SQ
PRINCESS RD
FIFTH SQ
SMALL GR
WELLING SQ
JUNCTION RD
BURN'S VILLAS
Stainforth

Kirk Bramwith
LOW LA
Bramwith Hall
DONCASTER RD
Cemy
OLDFIELD LANE FLATS
CHURCH RD
BRUNSWICK RD
WINDSOR SQ
WINDSOR RD
NELSON
GORDON
GRANVILLE CRES
BOOTHAM RD
BQ2 HAY S63

3

BRAMWITH LA
South Bramwith
HALL LA
Bramwith Field
OLDFIELD LA
OLDFIELD CL
Liby
MILL VIEW
STANLEY GDNS
STANLEY
EMERSON AVE
THOMAS RD
EAST HA
EAST AVE

11

BRAMWITH LA
Ling Field
OLD FIELD LA
OLDFIELD CRES
QUEEN'S
KINGSWAY
DUKE'S ST
LORD ST
VICTORIA
KING GEORGES
P

2

Tranmoor
DOUBLE LIDGET
Old Field
The Haggs
STATION RD
Stainforth Sta

1

STAINFORTH RD
LING HOUSE LA
New Mill Field
LING HOUSE LA
Ling House
Parks
Dunscroft Abbey C of E (Aided) Middle Sch
SOUTH END
LLOYDS TERR
NORWOOD RD
HAZEL RD
THE CRESCENT
THE OVAL

10

LC
The Haggs
CRABTREE RD

62 A B 63 C D 64 E F

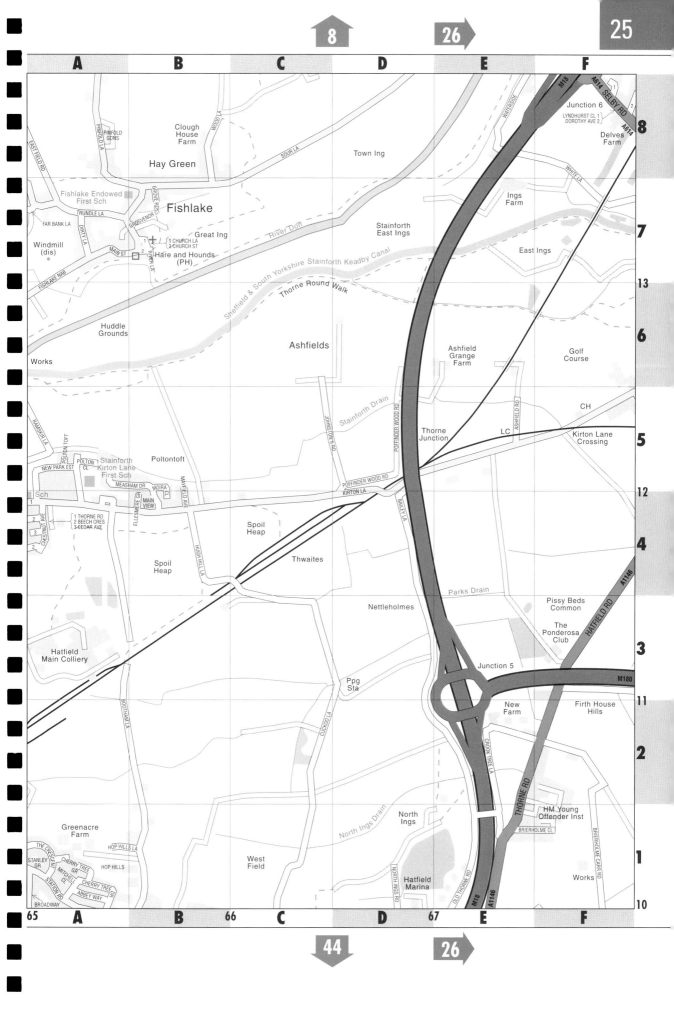

25   9

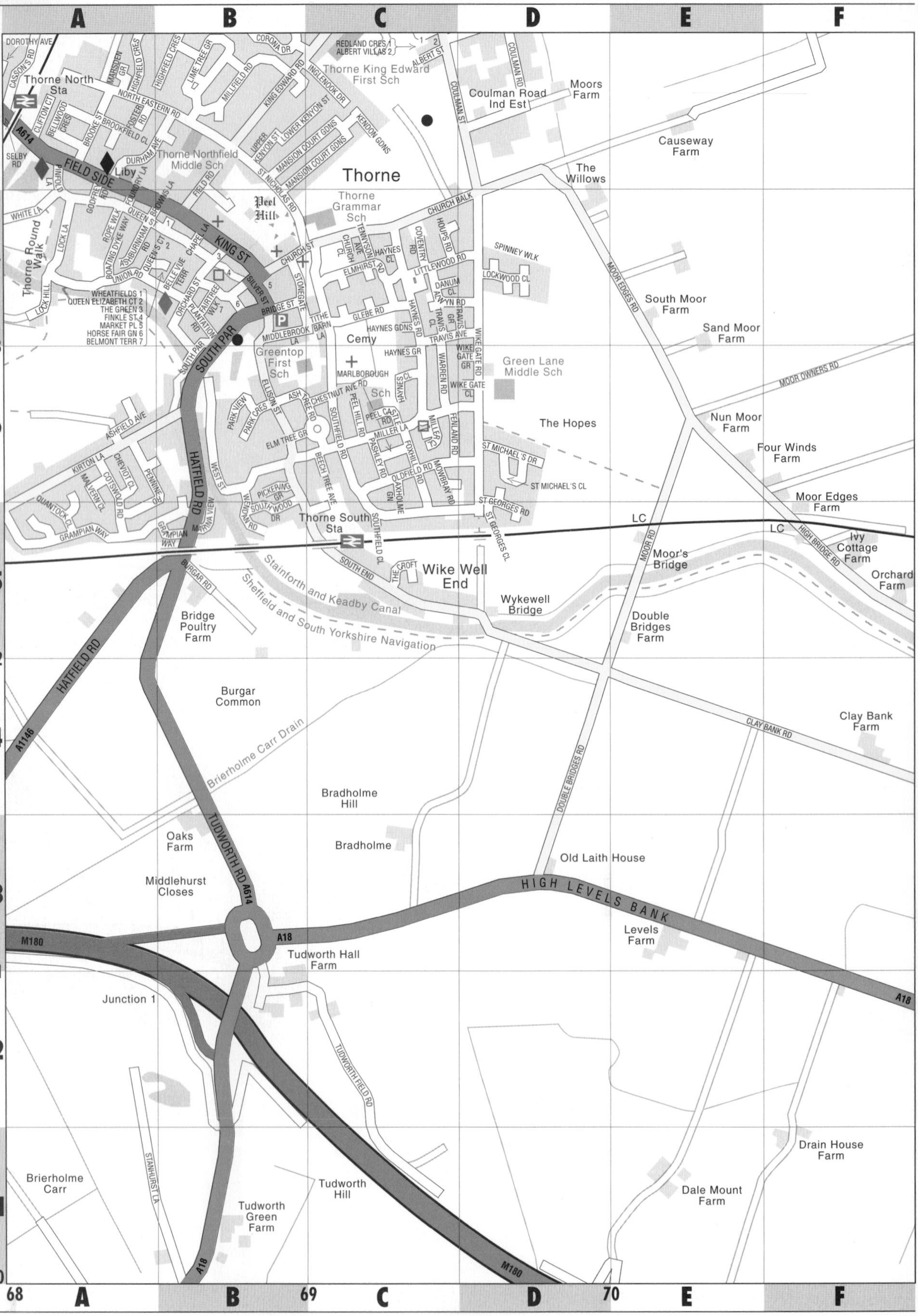

A   B   C   D   E   F

8

DOROTHY AVE
Thorne North Sta
CASSON'S RD
MARSH ST
CLIFTON CT
KELLWOOD CRES
NORTHFIELD CRES
THIRLFIELD RD
LIME TREE GR
COROMA DR
REDLAND CRES 1
ALBERT VILLAS 2
INGLENOOK DR
Thorne King Edward
First Sch
COULMAN RD
Moors Farm
Coulman Road Ind Est

A614
SELBY RD
FIELD SIDE
Liby
WHITE LA
LOCK LA
Thorne Round Walk
LOCK HILL
KIRTON LA
CHEVIOT LA
MALVERN CL
QUANTOCK
COTSWOLD RD
PENNINE
GRAMPIAN WAY
HATFIELD RD
WEST ST
MARSH LA
GRAMPIAN WAY
BURGAR RD

Thorne Northfield
Middle Sch
DURHAM RD
COUNTRY LA
GODNOW RD
QUEEN ST
ROPE WALK
BOATING DYKE WAY
QUEEN'S CT
ANTON RD
ORCHARD RD
KETTLE VUE
KING ST
CHAPEL LA
LADY BALK LA
SILVER ST
STONEGATE
BRIDGE ST
SOUTH PAR
PARK VIEW
PARK CRES
ASHFIELD AVE
ELLISON AVE
ASH TREE RD
CHESTNUT AVE
ELM TREE GR
PICKERING GR
SOUTHWOOD DR
SOUTHFIELD RD
SOUTH END
SOUTH END
THE CROFT

Peel Hill
PEEL HILL
Thorne
Thorne Grammar Sch
St NICHOLAS RD
CHURCH ST
CHURCH BALK
Thorne Grammar Sch
COVENTRY RD
HAYNES CL
TENNYSON
ELMHIRST CL
DANUM RD
LITTLEWOOD RD
LOCKWOOD CL
SPINNEY WLK
Cemy
GLEBE RD
HAYNES GDNS
HAYNES GR
TRAVIS AVE
WIKE GATE RD
WIKE GATE GR
WIKE GATE CL
Green Lane Middle Sch

Greentop First Sch
MARLBOROUGH
Sch
BEECH TREE AVE
FOXHILL RD
PASHLEY RD
OLDFIELD RD
OAKHOLME GRN
MOWBRAN RD
The Hopes
ST MICHAEL'S DR
ST MICHAEL'S CL
ST GEORGES RD
FENLAND RD
MILLER RD

WHEATFIELDS 1
QUEEN ELIZABETH CT 2
THE GREEN 3
FINKLE ST 4
MARKET PL 5
HORSE FAIR GN 6
BELMONT TERR 7
MIDDLEBROOK LA
LITHE BARN

MOOR EDGES RD
MOOR OWNERS RD
South Moor Farm
Sand Moor Farm
Nun Moor Farm
Four Winds Farm
Moor Edges Farm
Ivy Cottage Farm
Orchard Farm
Causeway Farm
The Willows

Thorne South Sta
Wike Well End
SOUTH END
Wykewell Bridge
ST GEORGES CL
Moor's Bridge
Double Bridges Farm
LC   LC
HIGH BRIDGE RD

Stainforth and Keadby Canal
Sheffield and South Yorkshire Navigation
Bridge Poultry Farm

A1146
HATFIELD RD
Burgar Common
Brierholme Carr Drain
TUDWORTH RD A614
Oaks Farm
Middlehurst Closes
Bradholme Hill
Bradholme
Old Laith House
HIGH LEVELS BANK
DOUBLE BRIDGES RD
CLAY BANK RD
Clay Bank Farm
Levels Farm

M180
Junction 1
A18
Tudworth Hall Farm
TUDWORTH FIELD RD
A18

Brierholme Carr
STANHURST LA
Tudworth Green Farm
Tudworth Hill
M180
A18
Dale Mount Farm
Drain House Farm
A18

68   A   B   69   C   D   70   E   F

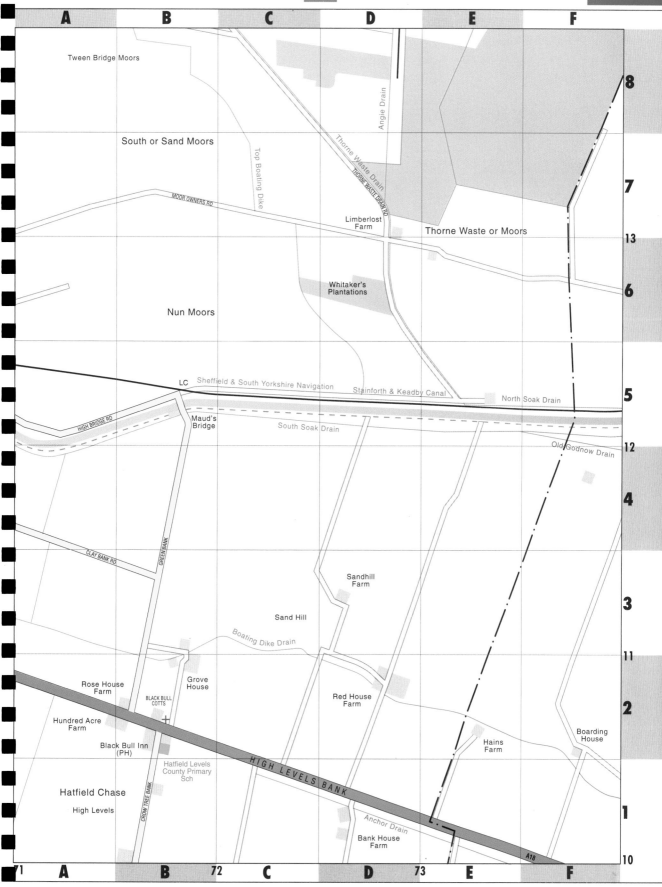

A **B** **C** **D** **E** **F**

8

7

13

6

5

12

4

3

11

2

1

10

Tween Bridge Moors

South or Sand Moors

Top Boating Dike

MOOR OWNERS RD

Angle Drain

Thorne Waste Drain

THORNE WASTE DRAIN RD

Limberlost Farm

Thorne Waste or Moors

Nun Moors

Whitaker's Plantations

LC Sheffield & South Yorkshire Navigation

Stainforth & Keadby Canal

North Soak Drain

HIGH BRIDGE RD

Maud's Bridge

South Soak Drain

Old Godnow Drain

CLAY BANK RD

GREEN BANK

Sandhill Farm

Sand Hill

Boating Dike Drain

Rose House Farm

Grove House

BLACK BULL COTTS

Red House Farm

Boarding House

Hundred Acre Farm

Black Bull Inn (PH)

Hatfield Levels County Primary Sch

Hains Farm

CROW TREE BANK

HIGH LEVELS BANK

Hatfield Chase

High Levels

Anchor Drain

Bank House Farm

A18

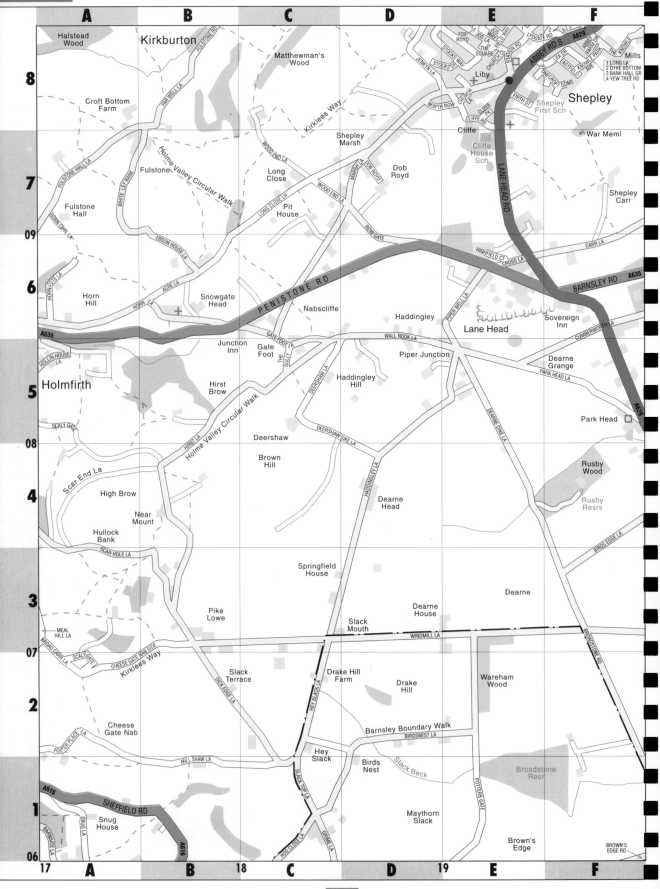

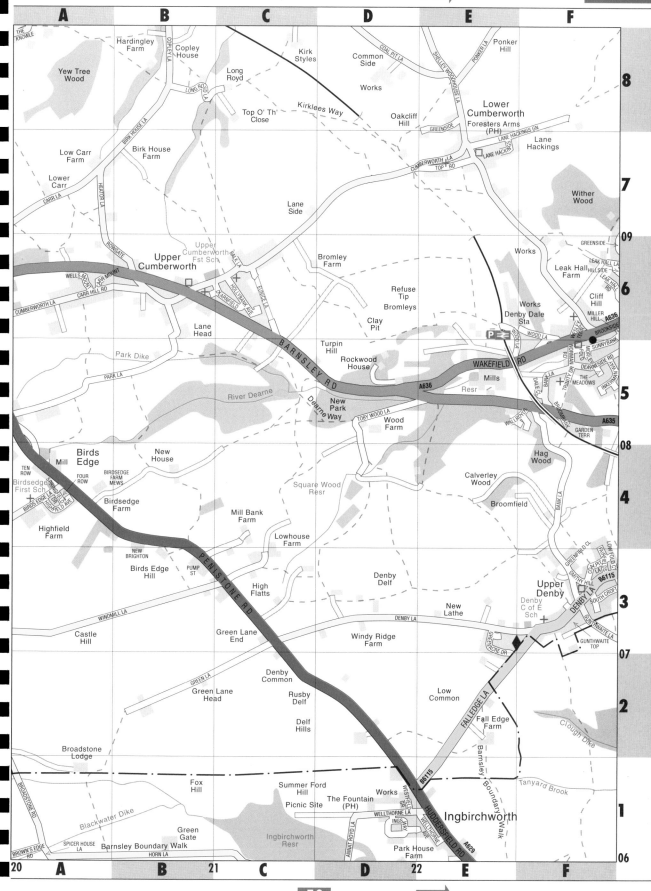

29

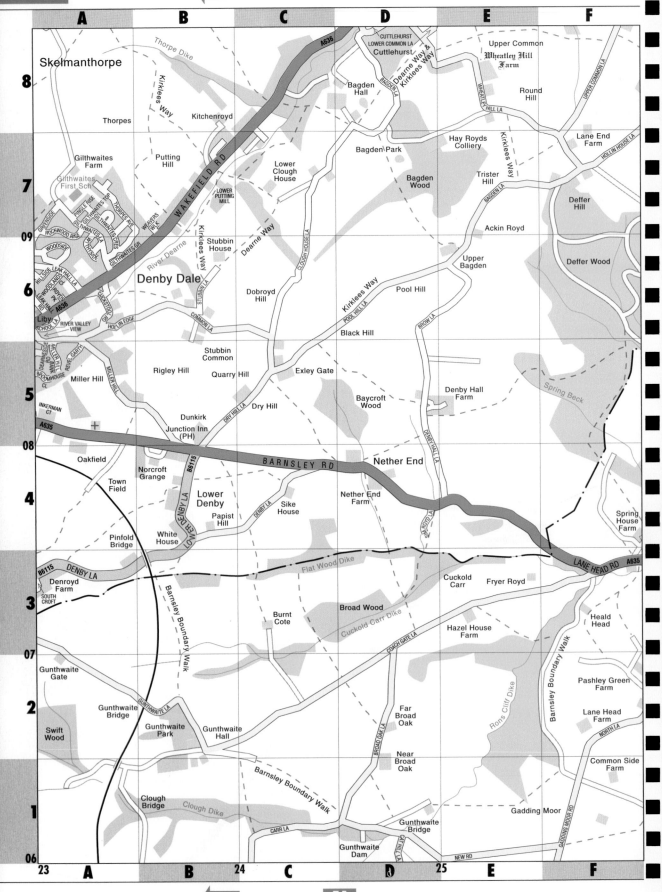

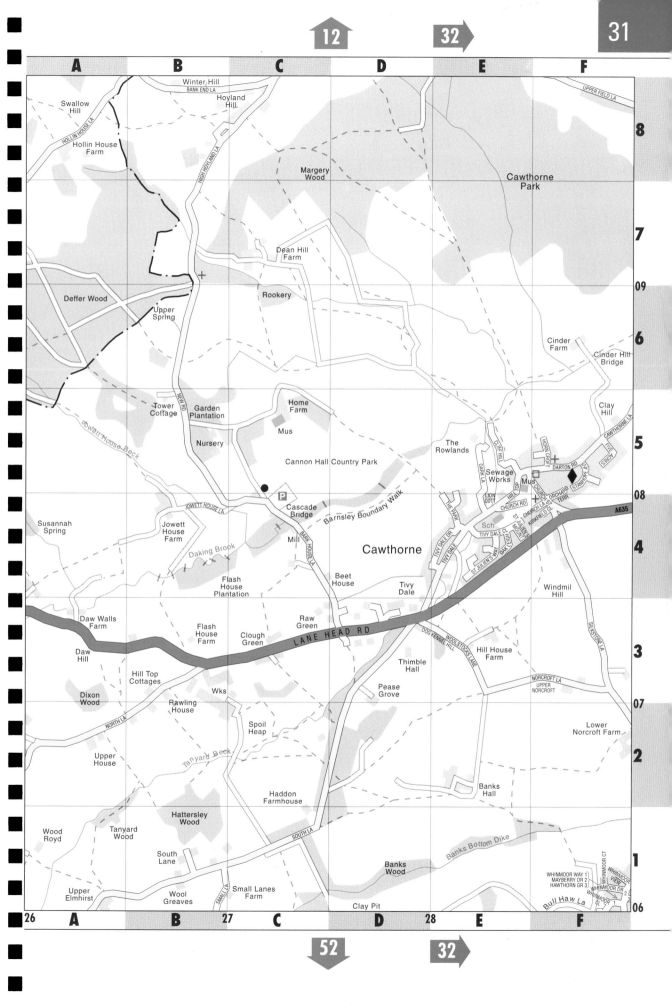

A B C D E F

8

7

09

6

5

08

4

3

07

2

1

06

Winter Hill
BANK END LA
Hoyland Hill
Swallow Hill
HOLLIN HOUSE LA
HIGH HOYLAND LA
Hollin House Farm
Margery Wood
Cawthorne Park
UPPER FIELD LA

Dean Hill Farm
Rookery
Cinder Farm
Cinder Hill Bridge

Deffer Wood
Upper Spring
NEW RD
Clay Hill

Jowett House Beck
Tower Cottage
Garden Plantation
Home Farm
Mus
Nursery
The Rowlands
CLIFF HILL
HORN CROFT
CAWTHORNE LA
FIVE ACRES
DARTON RD
STANHOPE

Cannon Hall Country Park
Sewage Works
Mus
DARK LA
HILL TOP
CHURCH RD

Susannah Spring
JOWETT HOUSE LA
Cascade Bridge
Barnsley Boundary Walk
Cawthorne
LION COTT
THE PARK
CHURCH LA
ST JULIEN'S WAY
KIRKFIELD CL
ORCHARD
TERR
A635

Jowett House Farm
Daking Brook
Mill
BARK HOUSE LA
Sch
TIVY DALE DR
TIVY DALE CL
TIVY DALE
MOUNT
A635

Flash House Plantation
Beet House
Tivy Dale
Windmil Hill

Daw Walls Farm
Flash House Farm
Clough Green
Raw Green
LANE HEAD RD
DOG KENNEL HILL
WOOLSTOCKS LANE
Hill House Farm
SILKSTONE LA
NORCROFT LA
UPPER NORCROFT

Daw Hill
Hill Top Cottages
Wks
Thimble Hall
Pease Grove

Dixon Wood
Rawling House
NORTH LA
Spoil Heap
Lower Norcroft Farm

Upper House
Tanyard Beck
Banks Hall

Wood Royd
Tanyard Wood
Hattersley Wood
Haddon Farmhouse
SOUTH LA
Banks Bottom Dike

South Lane
SMALL LA
Banks Wood
WHINMOOR WAY 1
MAYBERRY DR 2
HAWTHORN GR 3
WHINMOOR DR
WHINMOOR CT
WHINMOOR VIEW

Upper Elmhirst
Wool Greaves
Small Lanes Farm
Clay Pit
Bull Haw La

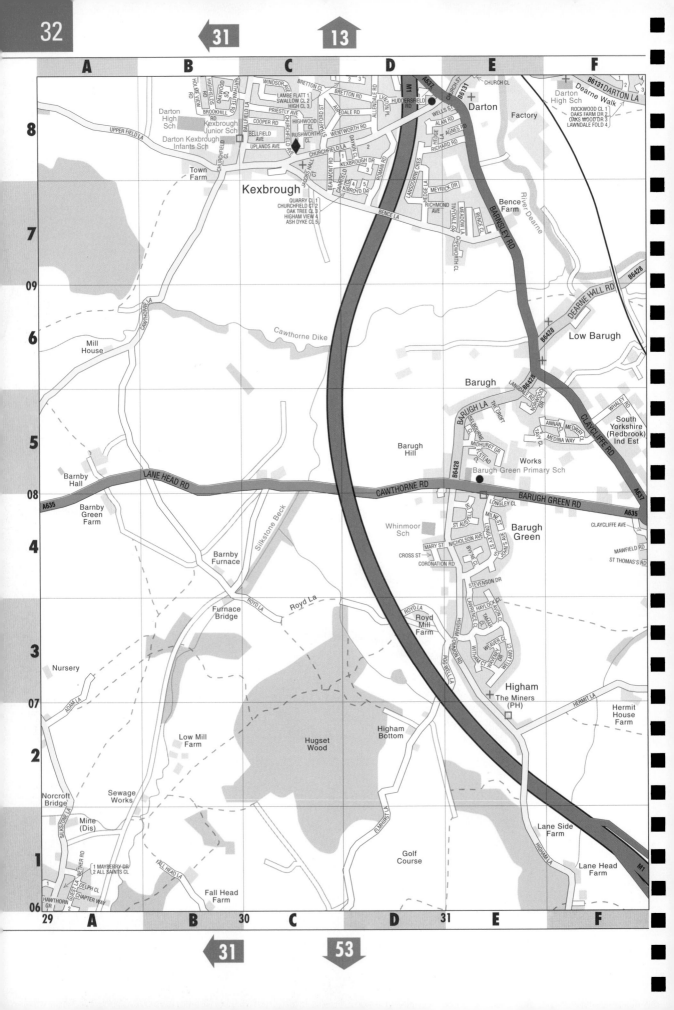

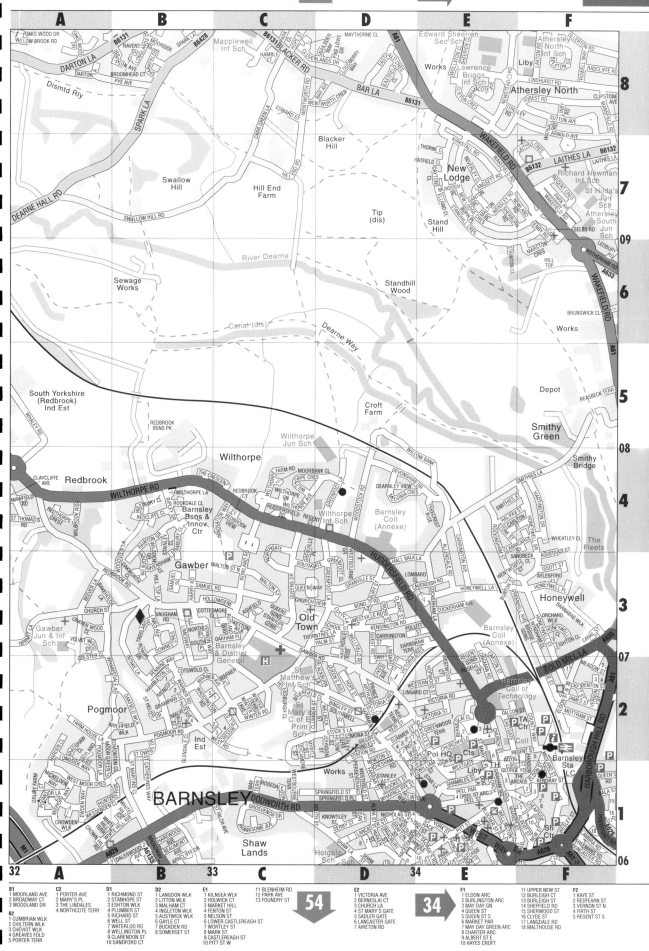

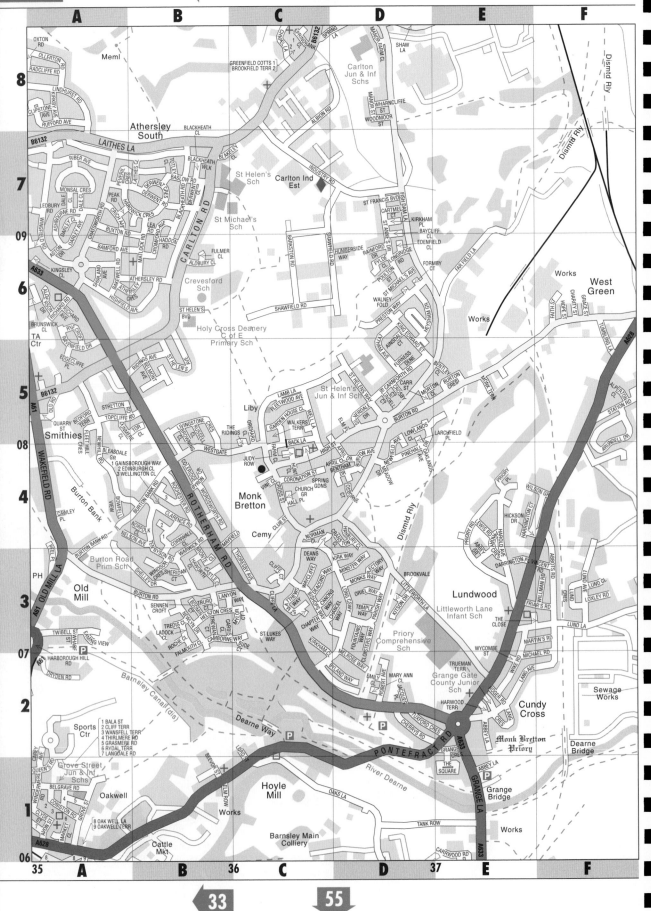

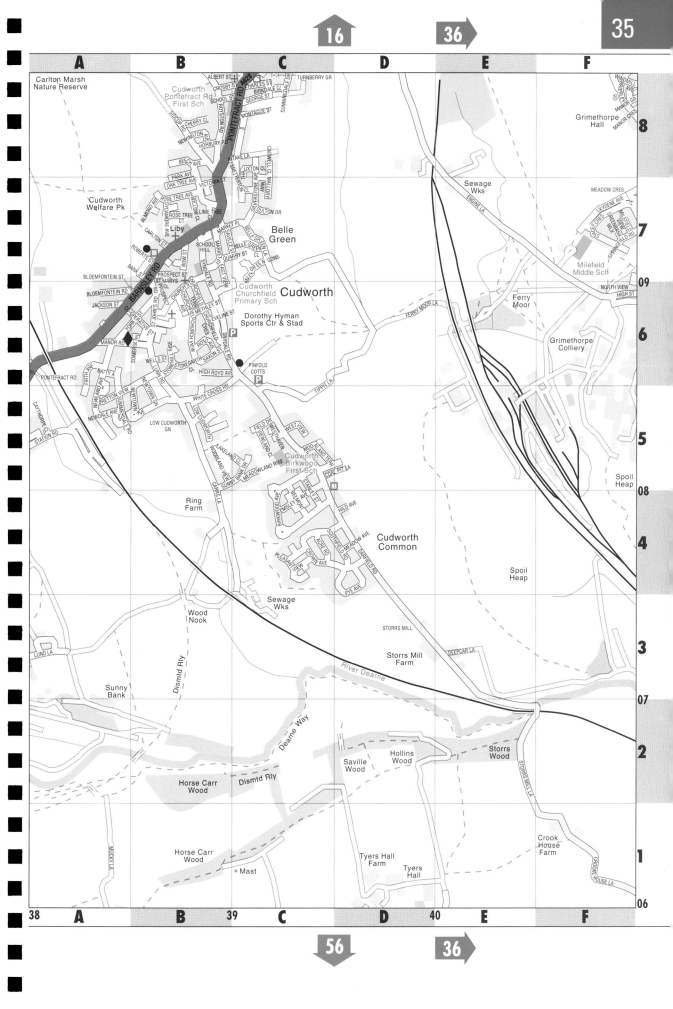

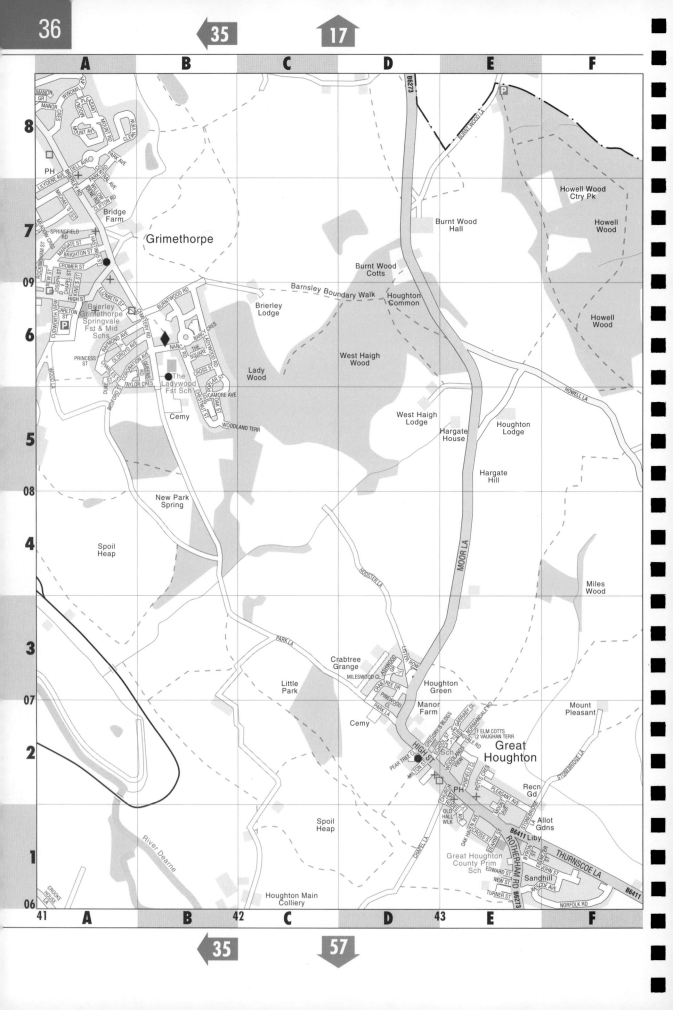

Grimethorpe

Howell Wood Ctry Pk

Howell Wood

Burnt Wood Hall

Burnt Wood Cotts

Barnsley Boundary Walk

Houghton Common

Brierley Lodge

Howell Wood

West Haigh Wood

Lady Wood

Howell La

West Haigh Lodge

Houghton Lodge

Hargate House

Hargate Hill

New Park Spring

Spoil Heap

Moor La

Miles Wood

Park La

Crabtree Grange

Little Park

Hoyster La

Houghton Green

Cemy

Manor Farm

Mount Pleasant

Great Houghton

Spoil Heap

River Dearne

Houghton Main Colliery

Great Houghton County Prim Sch

Sandhill

Recn Gd

Allot Gdns

Thurnscoe La

B6411

Liby

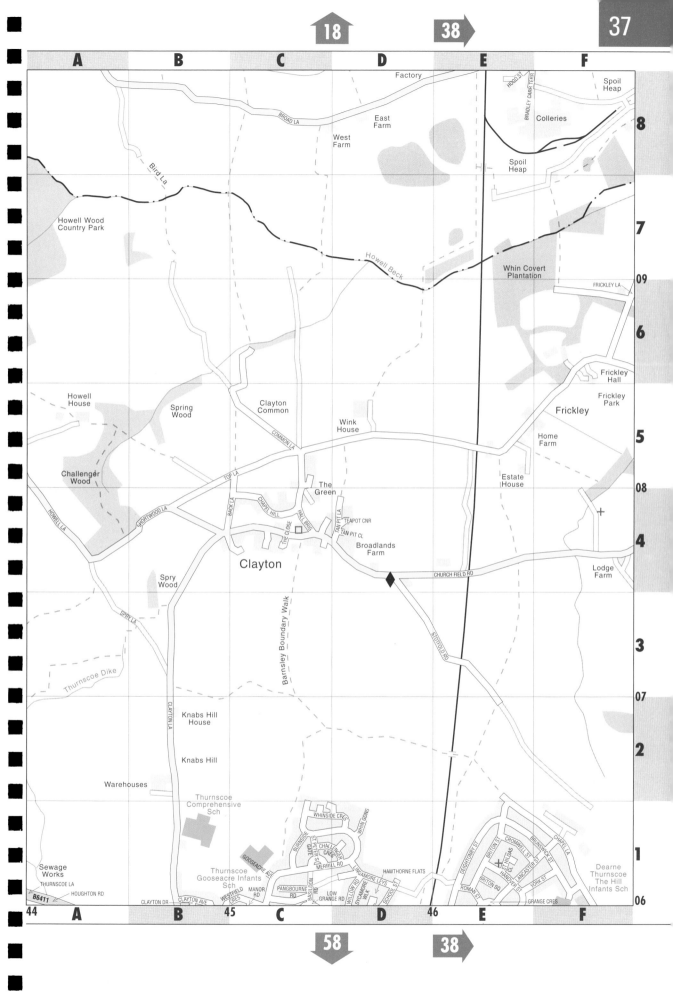

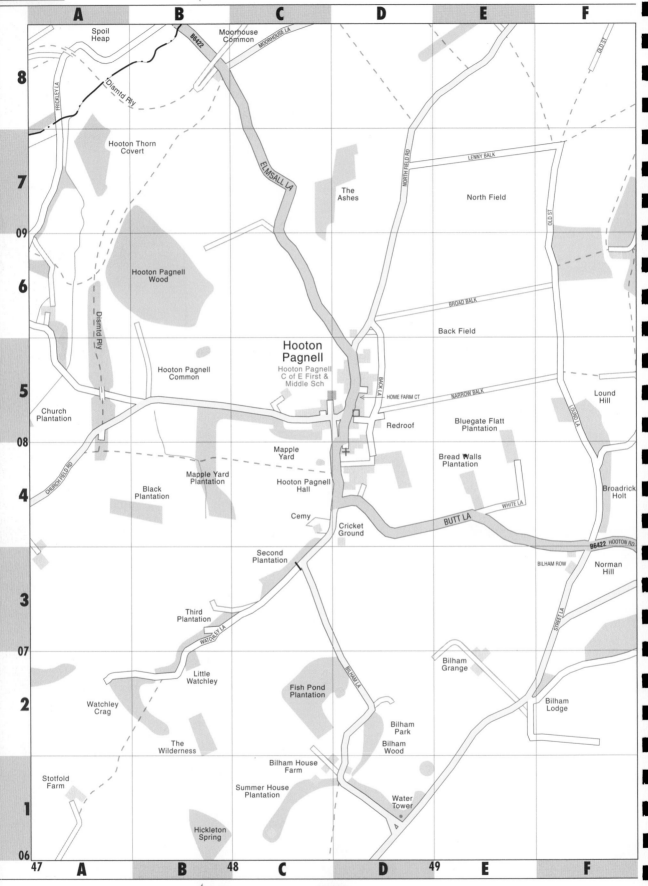

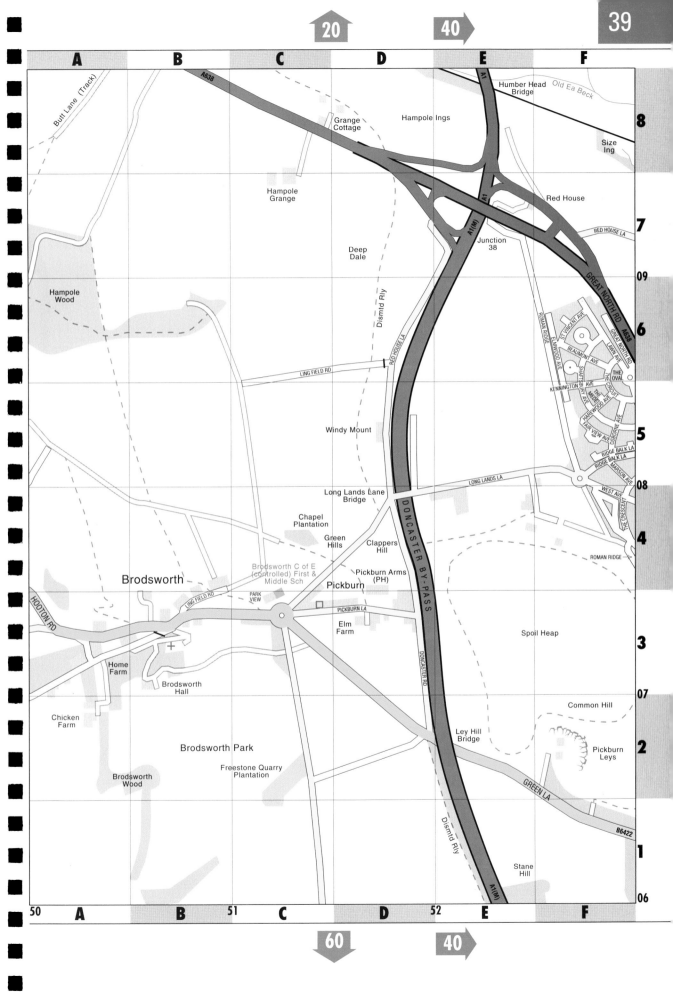

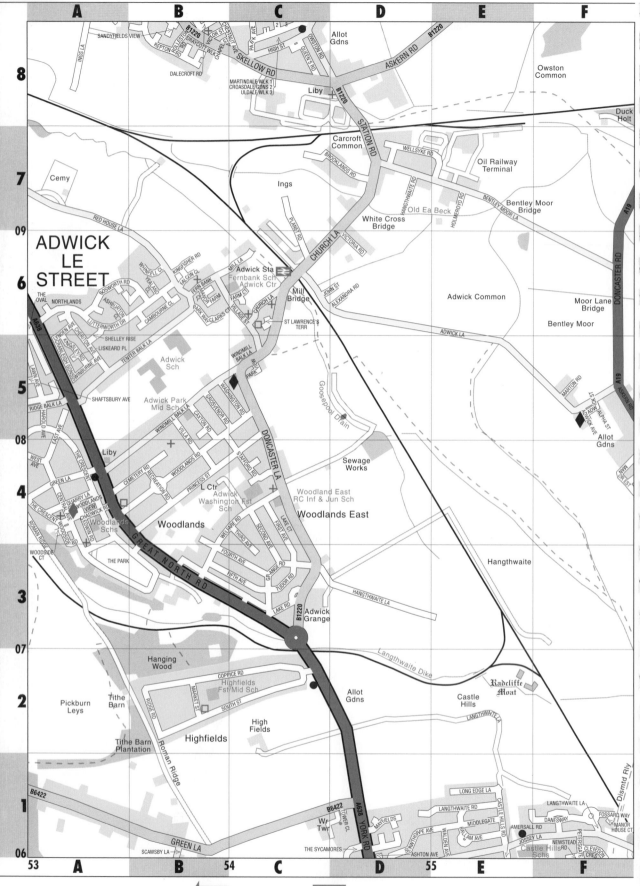

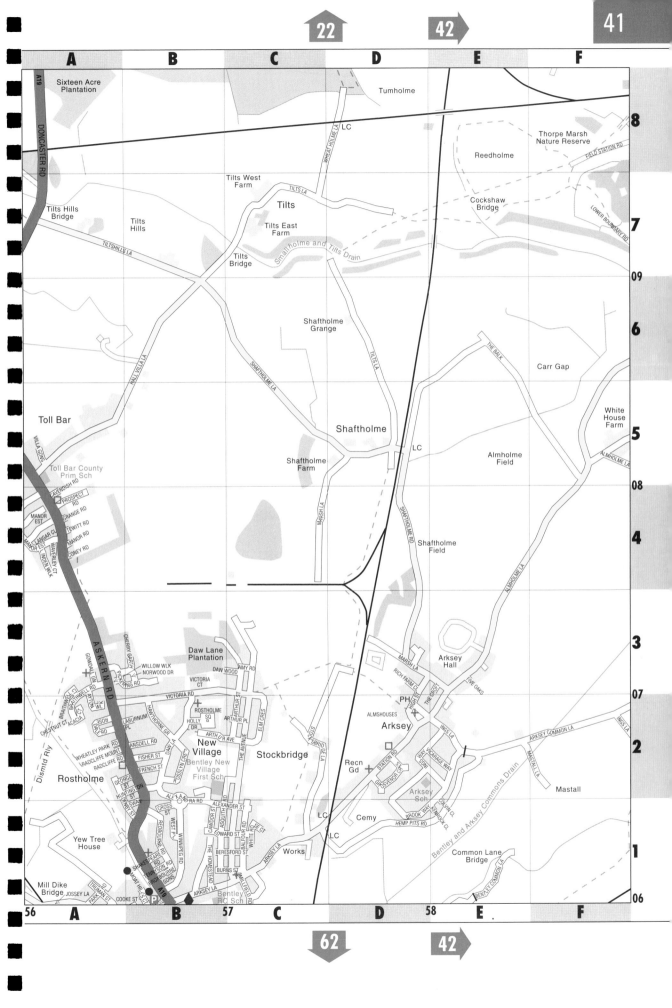

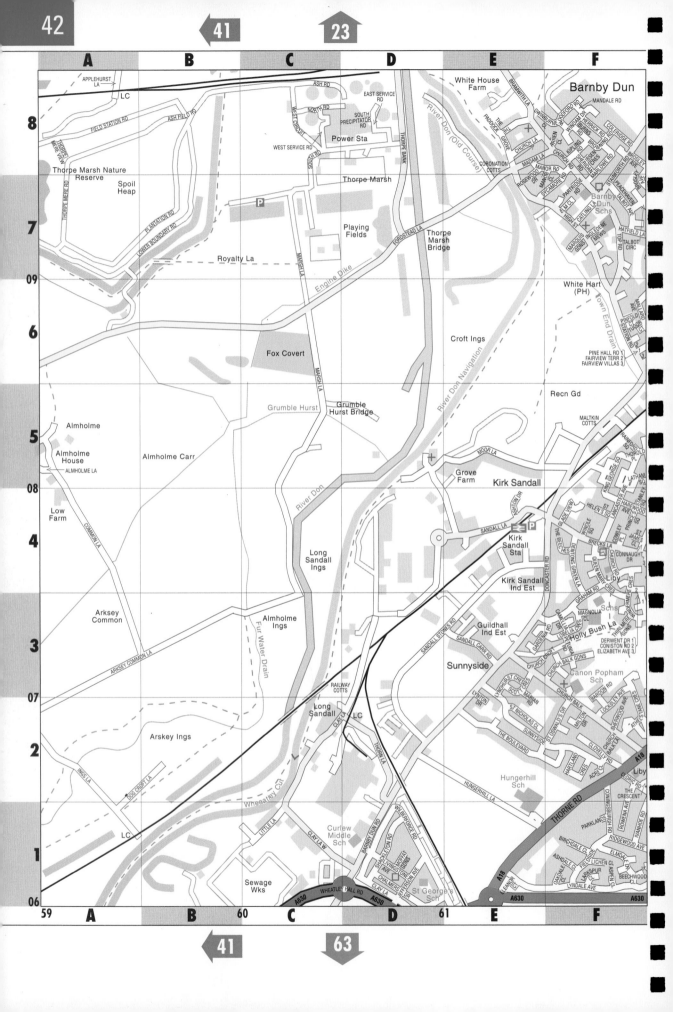

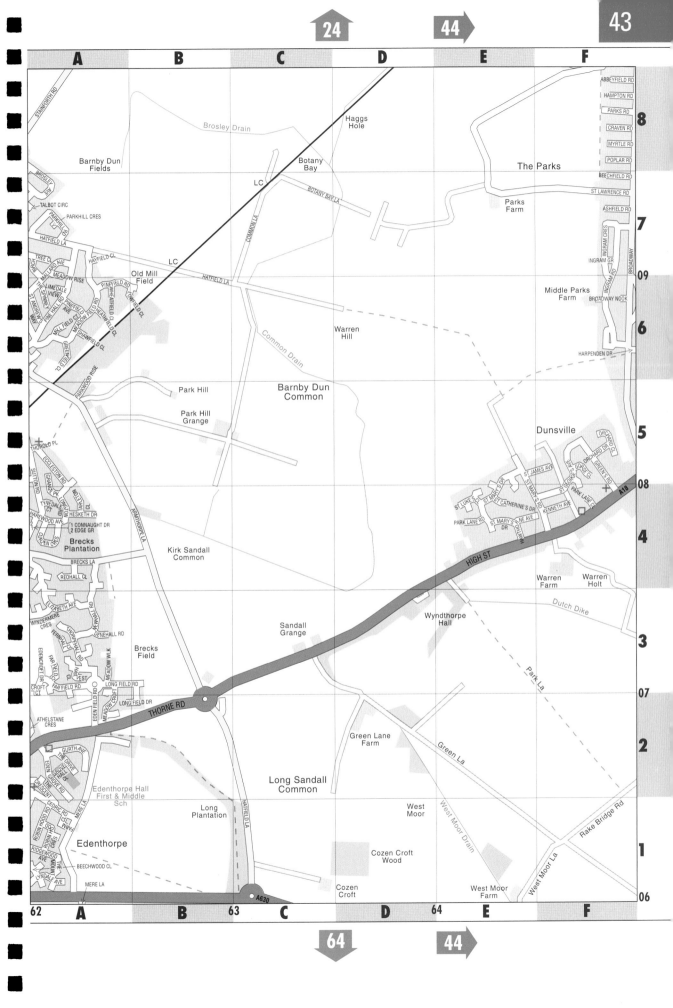

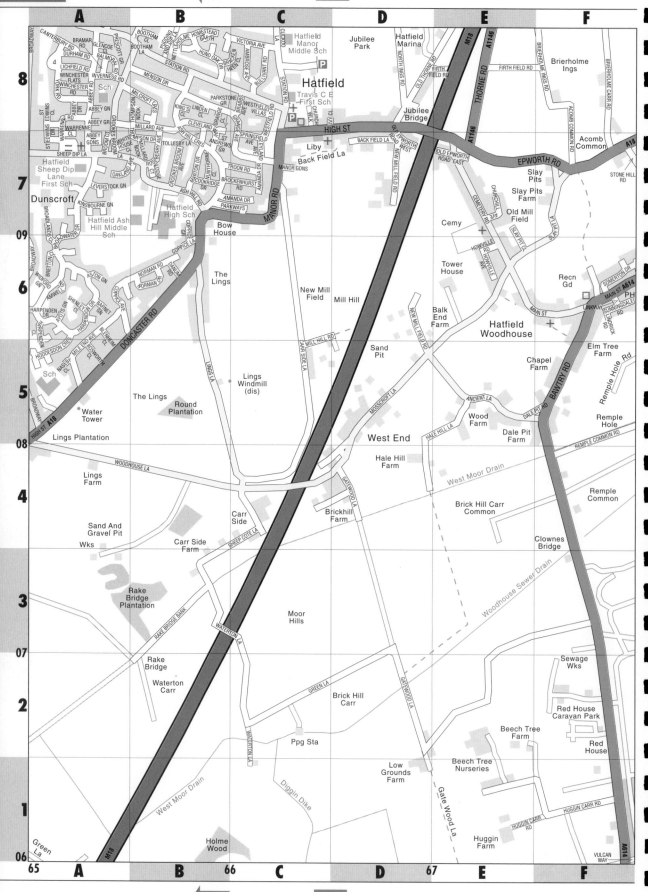

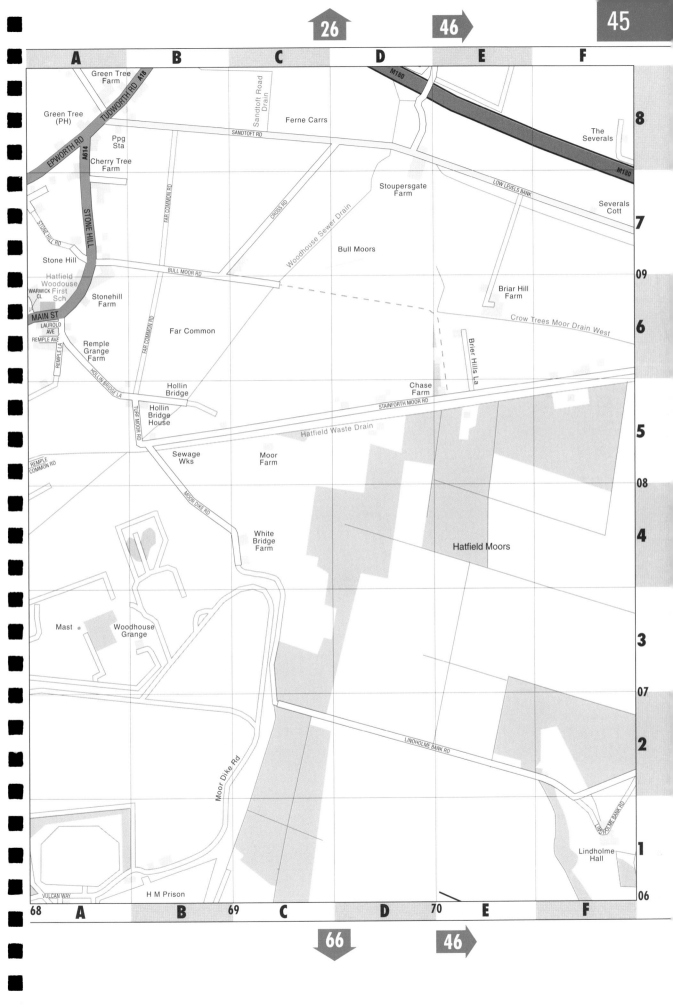

A **B** **C** **D** **E** **F**

8

Crow Tree
Hall

Crow Tree
Farm

Elder Glen
Farm

Elder
House

Elder Gates
Farm

GROW TREE BANK

Anchor Drain

A18
HIGH LEVELS BANK

Plains House
Farm

Plains La

7

M180

Low Bank Drain

09

MOOR LA

M180

Low Levels Bank

6

Crow Trees Moor
Drain West

PLAINS LA

Wks

Crow Trees Moor Drain East

STAINFORTH MOOR RD

Holme
Farm

Briars
Farm

Goodcop
Farm

Ppg
Sta

Park
Farm

5

08

Low
Levels

Willow
Lodge
Farm

Lindholme
Grange
Cotts

Belton

4

Lindholme
Grange
Farm

Old Catline Drain

3

Selby
Farm

07

2

Don
Farm

Hatfield
Moors

Lindholme
Lake

West
Carr

North Idle Drain

1

West
Carr
Houses

IDLE BANK

06

71 **A** **B** 72 **C** **D** 73 **E** **F**

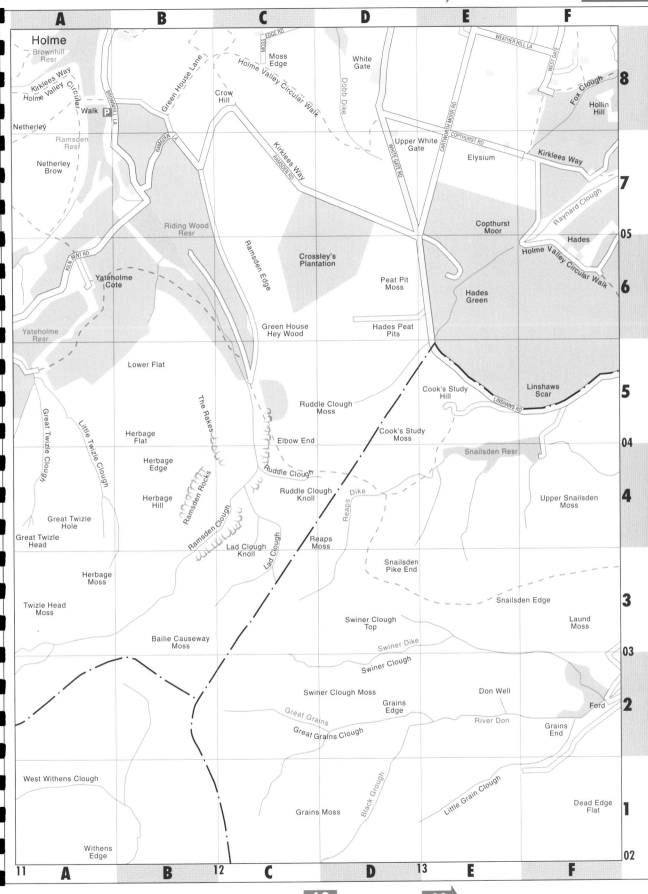

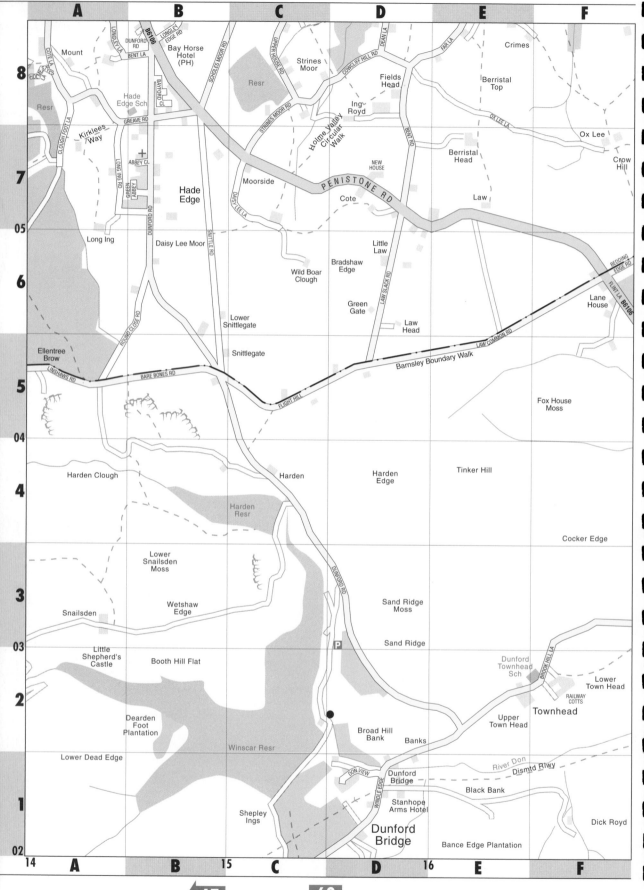

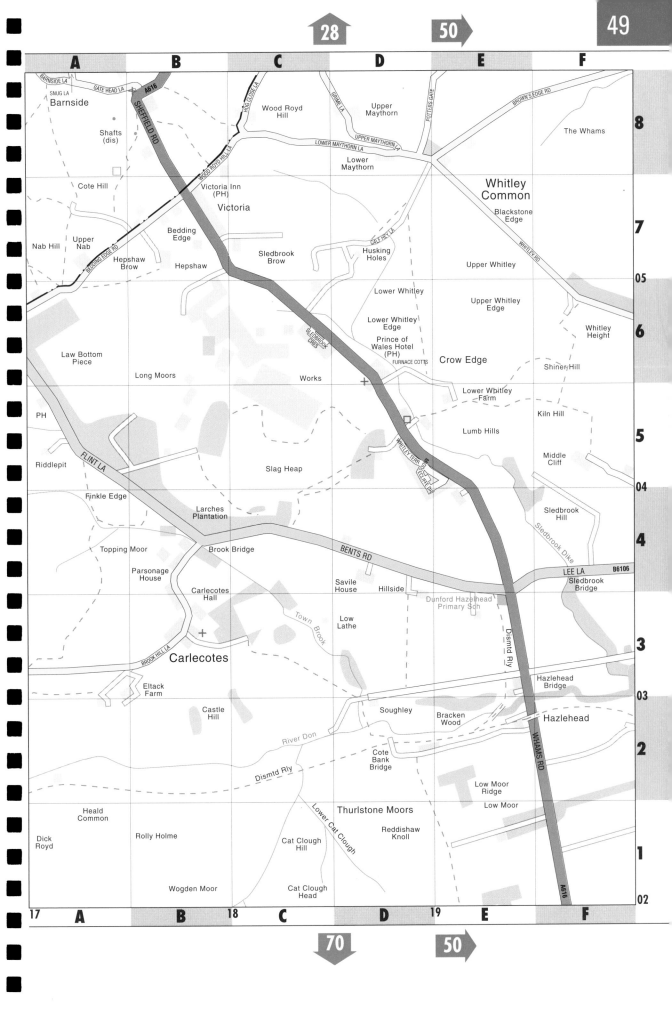

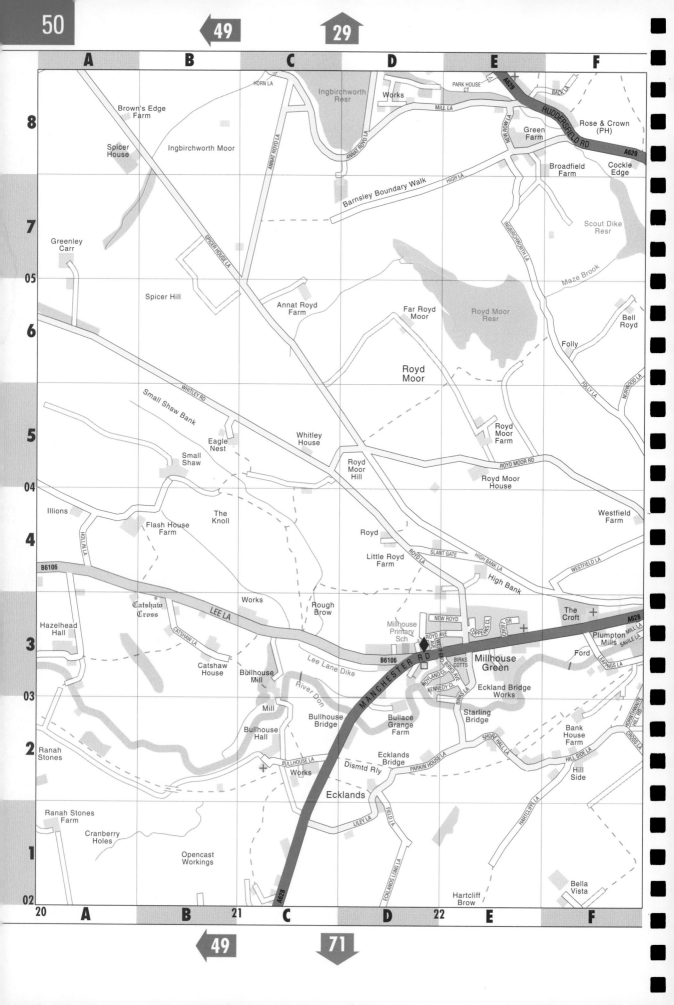

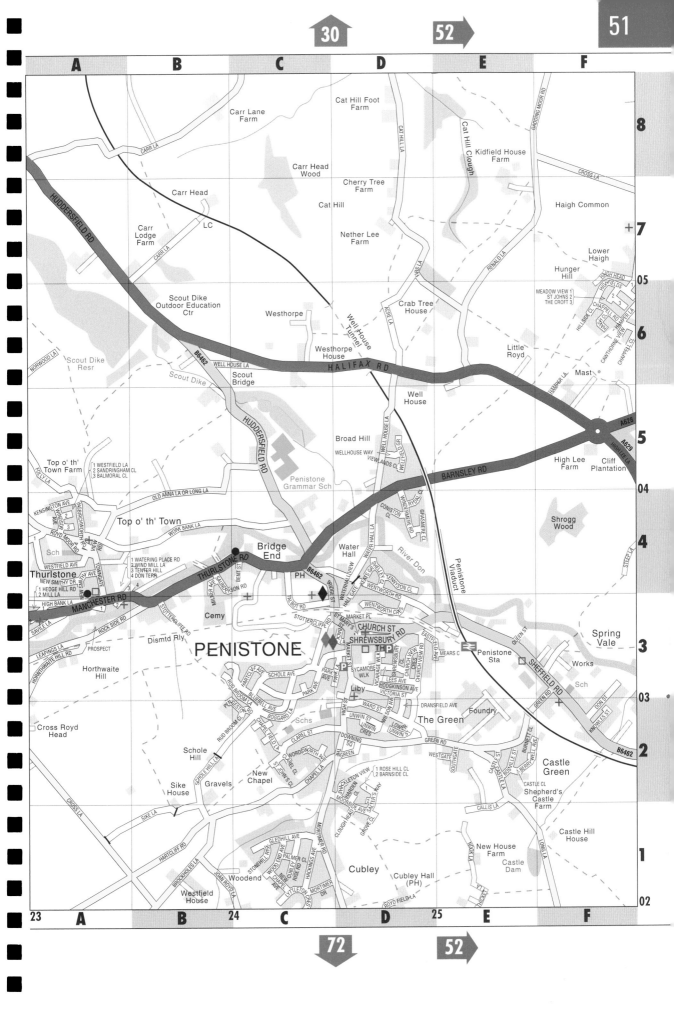

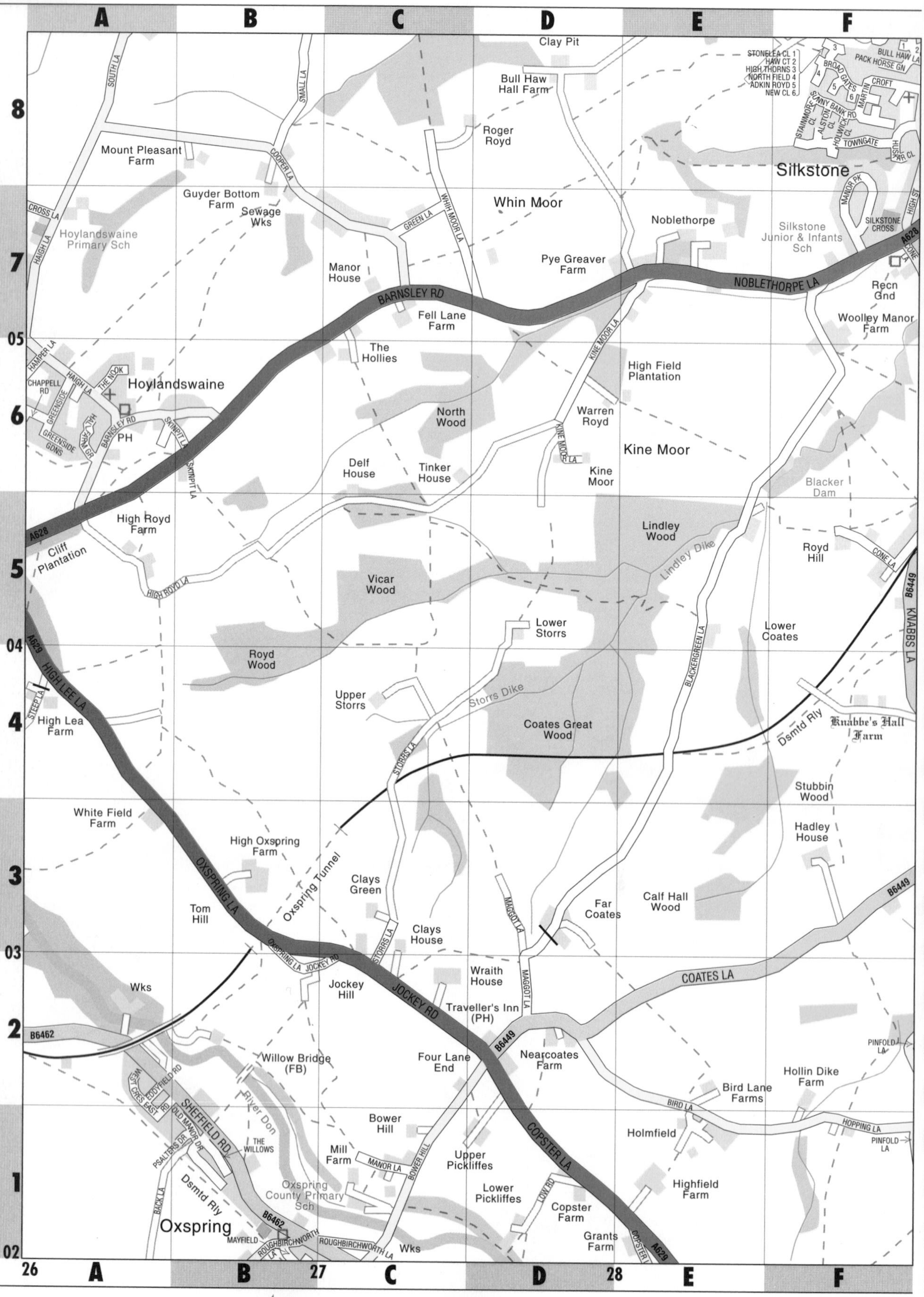

51
31

A B C D E F

8

Clay Pit

Bull Haw
Hall Farm

STONELEA CL 1
HAW CT 2
HIGH THORNS 3
NORTH FIELD 4
ADKIN ROYD 5
NEW CL 6

BULL HAW GN
PACK HORSE GN
BROAD GATES
CARR BANK RD
STANMORE
ALSTON CL
HOLY CL
MARTIN CL
TOWNGATE
MANOR PK
HUSKAR CL

Roger
Royd

Silkstone

Mount Pleasant
Farm

Guyder Bottom
Farm

Sewage
Wks

SMALL LA

CROSS LA

SOUTH LA

COOPER LA

WHIN MOOR LA

GREEN LA

Whin Moor

Noblethorpe

Silkstone
Junior & Infants
Sch

SILKSTONE
CROSS

A628

HIGH HOH LA

Hoylandswaine
Primary Sch

HAIGH LA

7

Manor
House

Pye Greaver
Farm

NOBLETHORPE LA

Recn
Gnd

Woolley Manor
Farm

MANOR PK RD

Fell Lane
Farm

KINE MOOR LA

05

HARPER LA

CHAPPELL
RD

GREENSIDE

HAIGH LA

THE NOK

BARNSLEY RD

The Hollies

Warren
Royd

High Field
Plantation

Hoylandswaine

GREENSIDE GDNS

PH

BARNSLEY RD

SKMPIT LA

North
Wood

KINE MOOR LA

Kine Moor

6

Delf
House

Tinker
House

Kine
Moor

Blacker
Dam

SKMPIT LA

High Royd
Farm

Lindley
Wood

Royd
Hill

CONE LA

A628

Cliff
Plantation

HIGH ROYD LA

Vicar
Wood

Lindley Dike

Lower
Coates

KNABBS LA

B6449

5

04

A629

HIGH LEE LA

Royd
Wood

Lower
Storrs

BLACKERGREEN LA

Dsmtd Rly

Knabbe's Hall
Farm

STEEP LA

High Lea
Farm

Upper
Storrs

Storrs Dike

Coates Great
Wood

Stubbin
Wood

4

STORRS LA

White Field
Farm

High Oxspring
Farm

Hadley
House

3

Oxspring Tunnel

Clays
Green

Far
Coates

Calf Hall
Wood

B6449

OXSPRING LA

Tom
Hill

MAGGOT LA

Clays
House

03

Wks

OXSPRING LA

JOCKEY RD

STORRS LA

Wraith
House

COATES LA

Jockey
Hill

JOCKEY RD

Traveller's Inn
(PH)

MAGGOT LA

PINFOLD
LA

2

B6462

Willow Bridge
(FB)

Four Lane
End

B6449

Nearcoates
Farm

Hollin Dike
Farm

WEST FIELD RD

WEST CLOSE EAST

OLD MANOR DR

SHEFFIELD RD

River Don

THE
WILLOWS

Bower
Hill

BIRD LA

Bird Lane
Farms

HOPPING LA

PINFOLD
LA

1

PSALTERS DR

BACK LA

Dsmtd Rly

Oxspring
County Primary
Sch

Mill
Farm

MANOR LA

BOWER HILL

Upper
Pickliffes

COPSTER LA

Holmfield

Highfield
Farm

Oxspring

B6462

MAYFIELD

ROUGHBIRCHWORTH

ROUGHBIRCHWORTH LA

Wks

Lower
Pickliffes

LOW RD

Copster
Farm

Grants
Farm

A629

COPSTER LA

02

26 A B 27 C D 28 E F

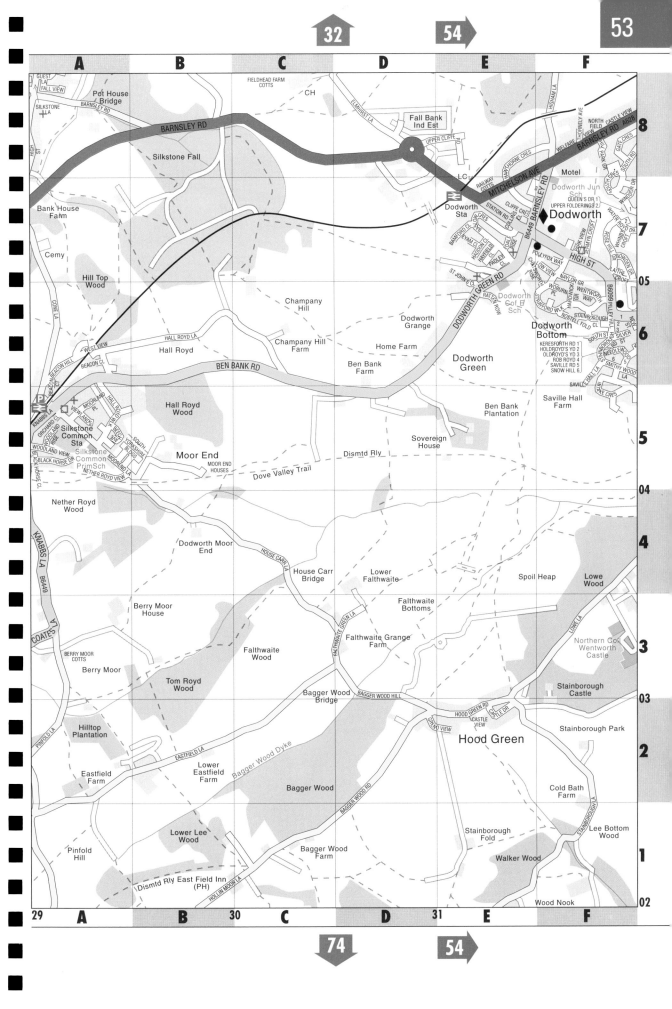

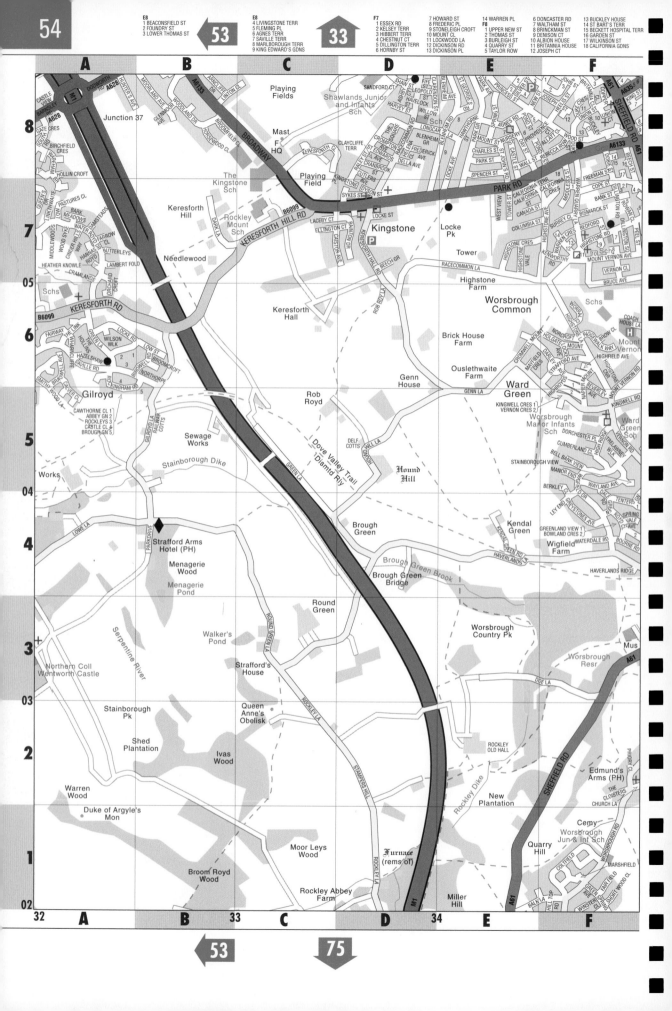

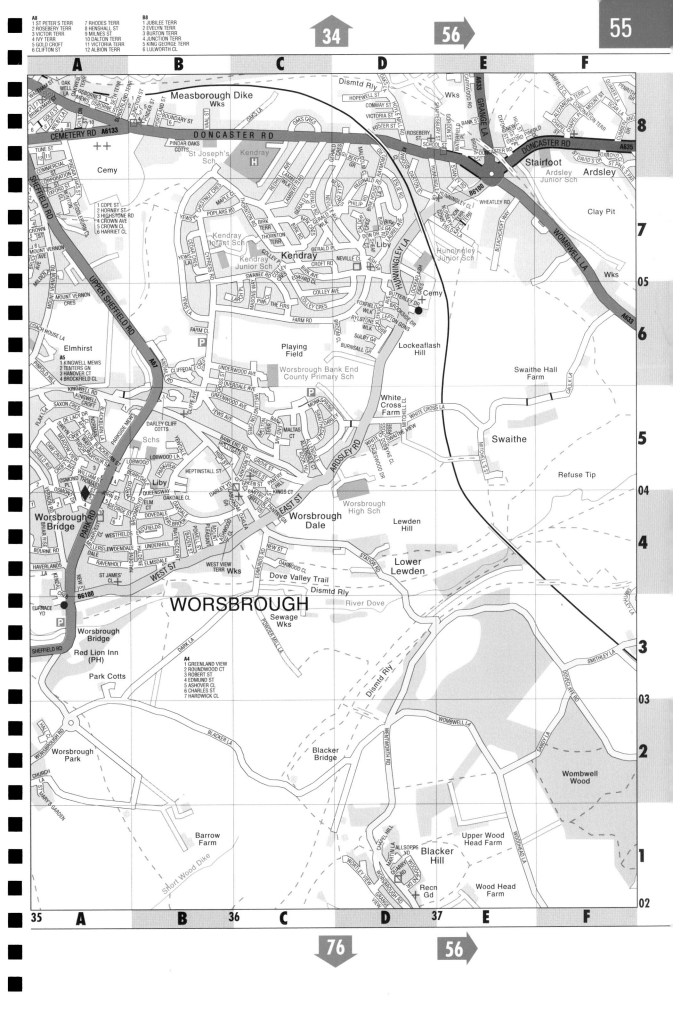

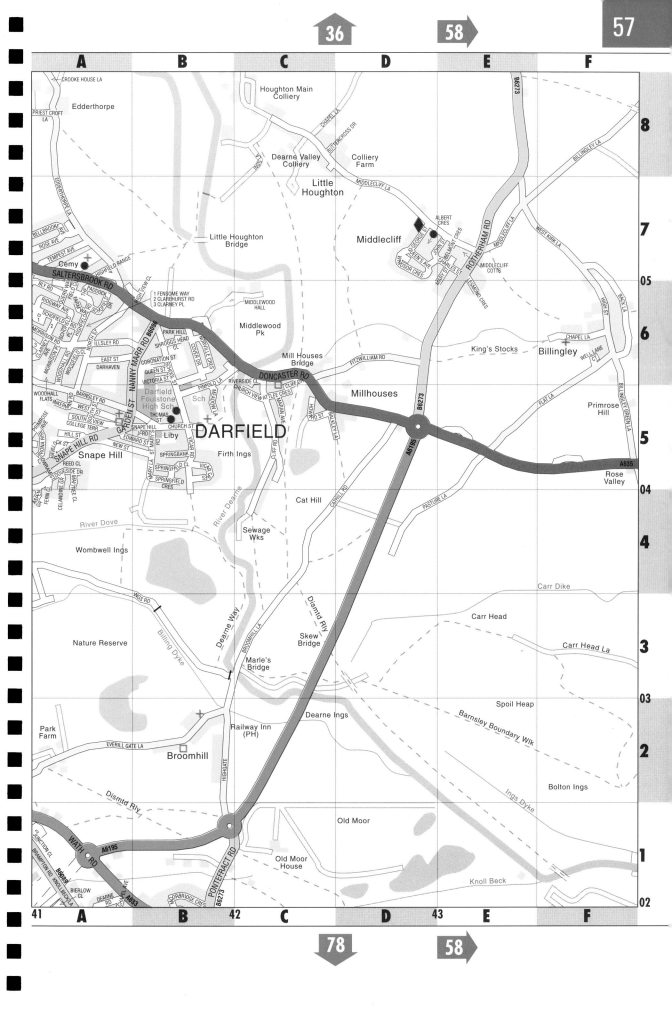

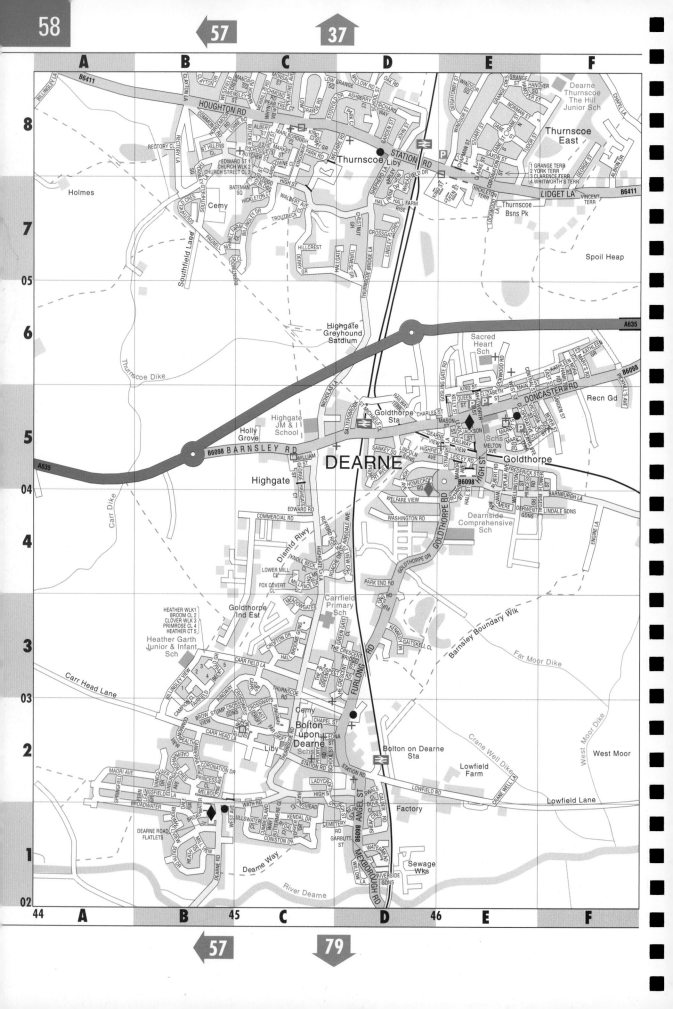

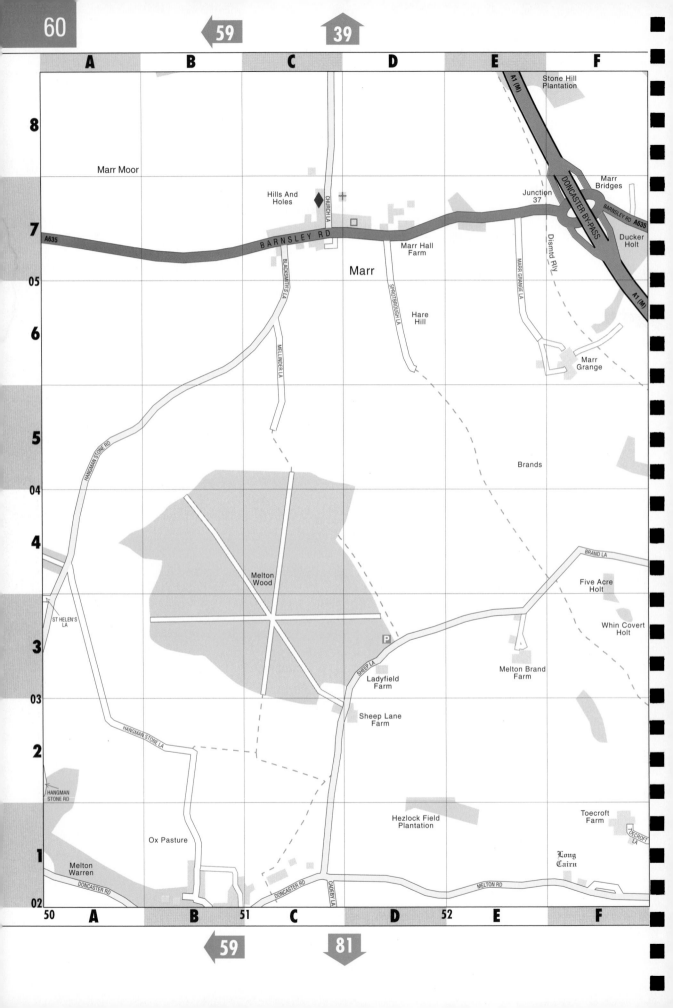

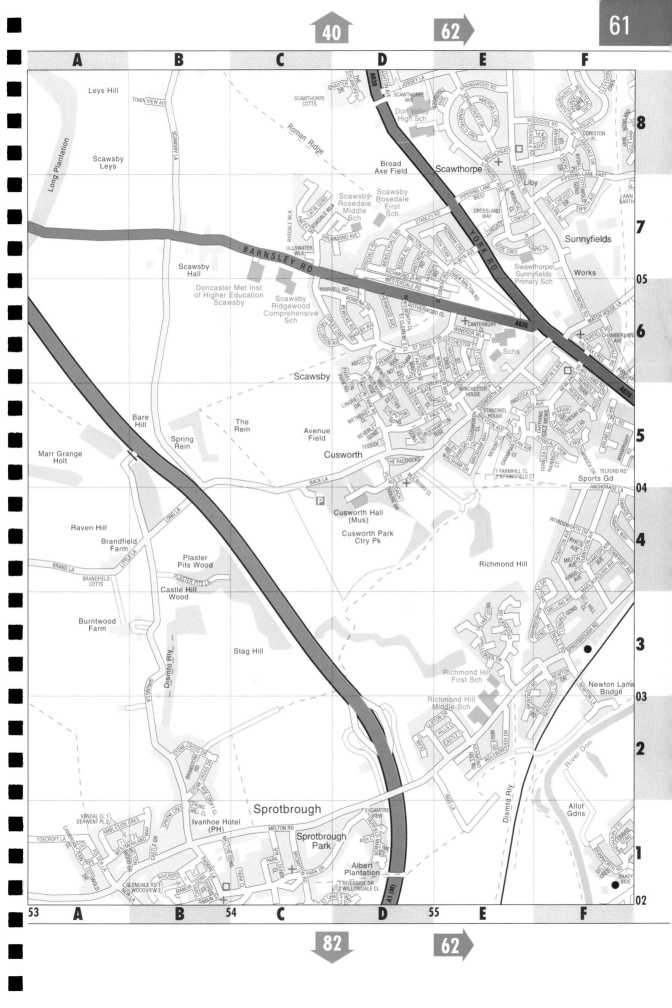

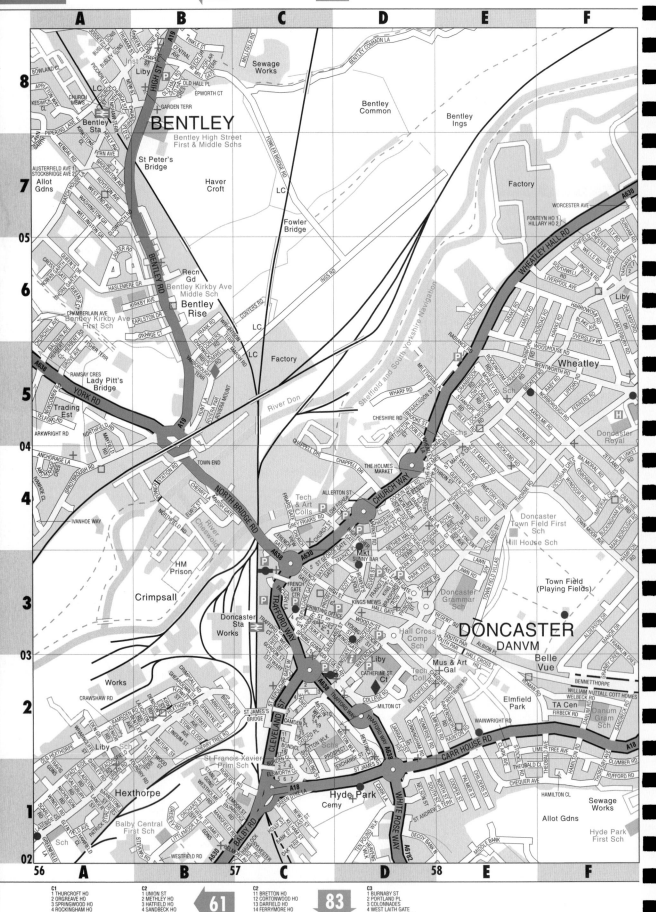

C1
1 THURCROFT HO
2 ORGREAVE HO
3 SPRINGWOOD HO
4 ROCKINGHAM HO
5 ROSSINGTON HO
6 WOOLLEY HO
7 SILVERWOOD HO

C2
1 UNION ST
2 METHLEY HO
3 HATFIELD HO
4 SANDBECK HO
5 FIRBECK HO
6 SERLBY HO
7 CUSWORTH HO
8 EMLEY HO
9 WENTWORTH HO
10 ROWLAND PL

C2
11 BRETTON HO
12 CORTONWOOD HO
13 DARFIELD HO
14 FERRYMORE HO
15 TREETON HO
16 ASKERN HO
17 MALTBY HO
18 LUNDWOOD HO
19 MANTON HO

C3
1 BURNABY ST
2 PORTLAND PL
3 COLONNADES
4 WEST LAITH GATE
5 OLD GUILDHALL YD

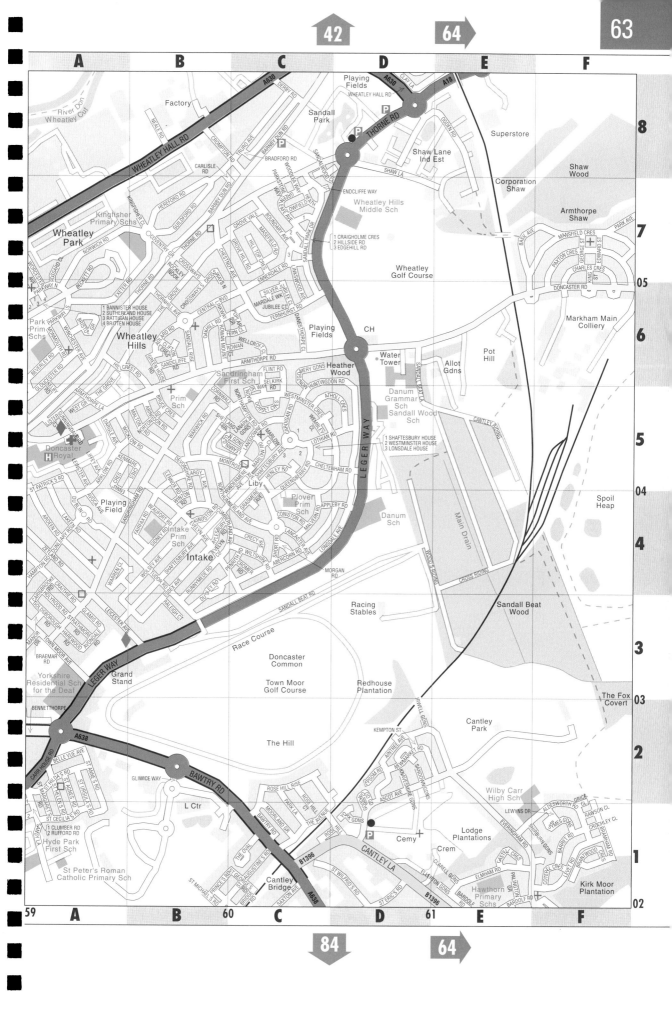

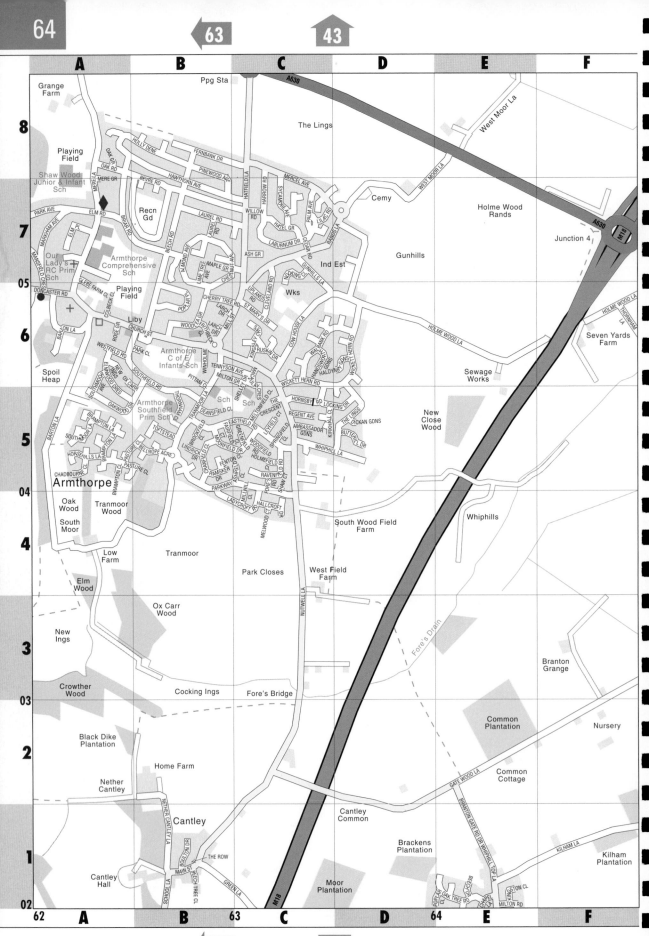

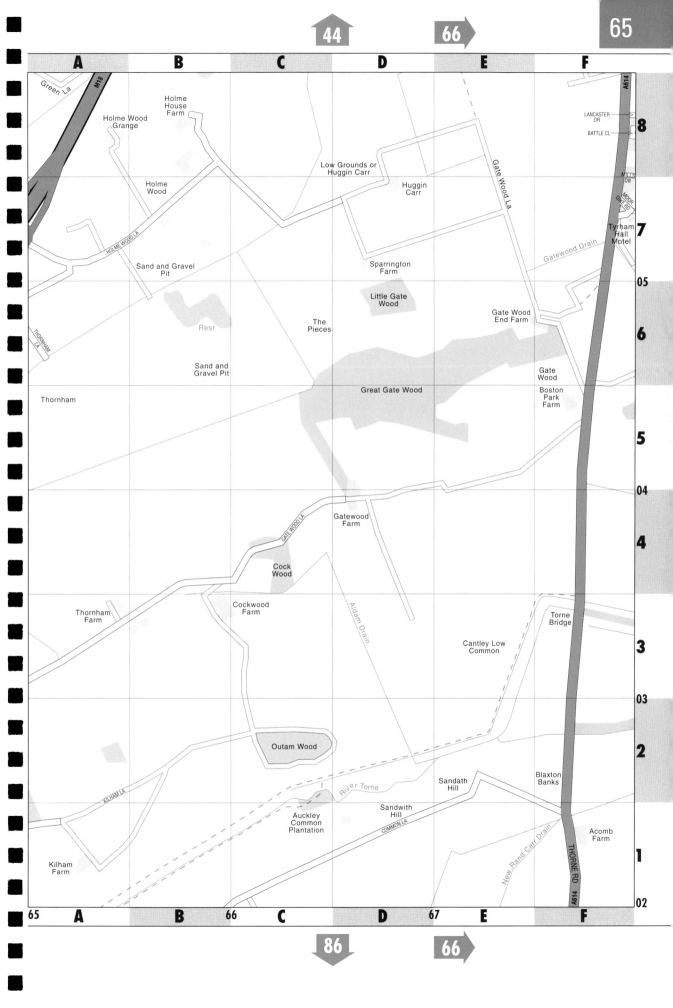

A   B   C   D   E   F

Green La
M18
Holme Wood Grange
Holme House Farm
Holme Wood
HOLME WOOD LA
Sand and Gravel Pit
THORNHAM LA
Thornham
Resr
Sand and Gravel Pit
Thornham Farm
KILHAM LA
Kilham Farm

Low Grounds or Huggin Carr
Huggin Carr
Sparrington Farm
Little Gate Wood
The Pieces
Great Gate Wood

Gatewood Farm
GATE WOOD LA
Cock Wood
Cockwood Farm
Outam Wood
River Torne
Auckley Common Plantation
COMMON LA

Gate Wood La
Gatewood Drain
Gate Wood End Farm
Gate Wood
Boston Park Farm

Aldam Drain
Cantley Low Common
Torne Bridge
Sandath Hill
Sandwith Hill
New Rand Carr Drain

A614
LANCASTER DR
BATTLE CL
MILLS DR
MOOR DIKE RD
Tyrham Hall Motel
Blaxton Banks
THORNE RD
A614
Acomb Farm

8
7
05
6
5
04
4
3
03
2
1
02

A B C D E F

8

HAMPDEN
CRES
LANCASTER DR
BLENHEIM RD
WELLINGTON RD
1 CUNNINGHAM RD
2 GIBSON RD

H M Prison

Playing Fields

MILLS DR
VARSITY CL
CANBERRA AVE
MOOR DIKE RD

Moor Dike Rd

Canberra
Cottage Farm

Hatfield Moors

7

05

Sand &
Gravel Pit

6

Poor
Piece

Old Moor Drain

5

Ellerholme
Farm

04

Middle Ring Drain

North Ring Drain

4

MOOR LA

ACRES LA

Sewage
Wks

SAND LA

Chester
Cottage
Farm

Southlands
Farm

HIGH ST

Dolwood Drain

3

South Ring Drain

Candy
Farm

Glebe
Farm

03

Long Plantation

God's Cross

Godscross Drain

Old Thatch Carr
Drain

2

Long Plantation

River Torne

CANDY BANK

NAN SAMPSON BANK

New Thatch Carr Drain

1

Blaxton
Common

Sand &
Gravel Pit

Thatch Carr
Plantation

02

68   A   B   69   C   D   70   E   F

A B C D E F

8

Hatfield
Moors

Roe
Carr

7

Porters Drain

The
Roe

05

6

Old Moor Drain

Epworth

Moor Bank

Wroot
Acres

Tunnel
Pits

5

East Ring Drain

River Torne

Riverside
Farm

Chestnut
Farm

Ppg
Sta

04

ACRES LA

Common La

IDLE BANK

4

Brook House
Farm

POLES BANK

BROOK TERR

HIGH ST

Wroot

South Engine Drain

Aucklands
Farm

3

Rectory

Cross Keys Inn
(PH)

03

Sandhill
Farm

Woodside

Eastfield
Farm

FIRTH LA

WOODSIDE LA

Woodside
Farm

WOODSIDE
VILLAS

Wroot Travis
Charity Sch
(Junior Mixed
& Infants)

WATER BANK

Thatch Carr
Farm

Franklins Drain

2

South Idle Drain

FIELD LA

Field House
Farm

Load Drain

1

Wroot Church Drain

02

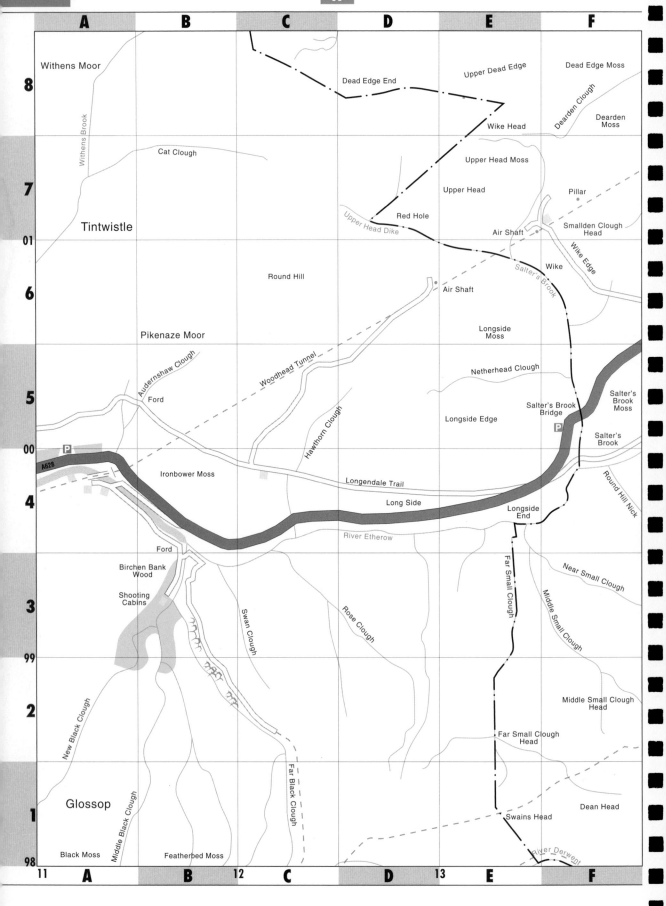

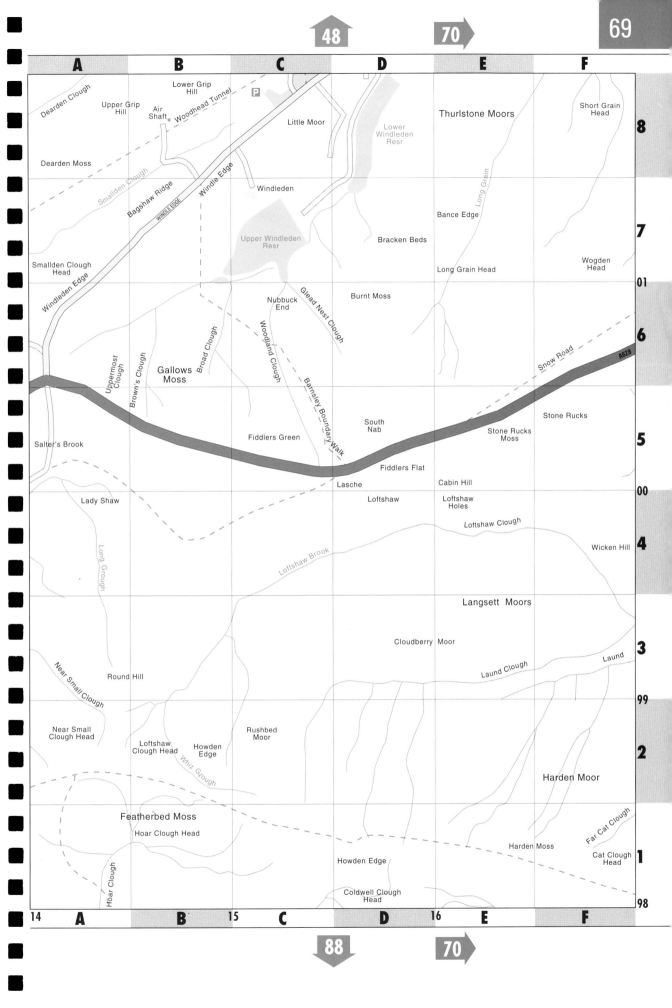

A B C D E F

8

7

01

6

5

00

4

3

99

2

1

98

Dearden Clough

Upper Grip Hill

Lower Grip Hill

Air Shaft

Woodhead Tunnel

P

Little Moor

Lower Windleden Resr

Thurlstone Moors

Short Grain Head

Dearden Moss

Smallden Clough

Bagshaw Ridge

WINDLE EDGE

Windle Edge

Windleden

Upper Windleden Resr

Bance Edge

Long Grain

Smallden Clough Head

Windleden Edge

Nubbuck End

Glead Nest Clough

Burnt Moss

Long Grain Head

Wogden Head

Uppermost Clough

Brown's Clough

Gallows Moss

Broad Clough

Woodland Clough

Barnsley Boundary Walk

Snow Road

A628

Salter's Brook

Fiddlers Green

South Nab

Stone Rucks Moss

Stone Rucks

Fiddlers Flat

Lasche

Cabin Hill

Lady Shaw

Loftshaw

Loftshaw Holes

Loftshaw Clough

Wicken Hill

Long Grough

Loftshaw Brook

Langsett Moors

Cloudberry Moor

Laund

Near Small Clough

Round Hill

Laund Clough

Near Small Clough Head

Loftshaw Clough Head

Howden Edge

Rushbed Moor

Whiz Grough

Harden Moor

Featherbed Moss

Hoar Clough Head

Howden Edge

Harden Moss

Far Cat Clough

Cat Clough Head

Hoar Clough

Coldwell Clough Head

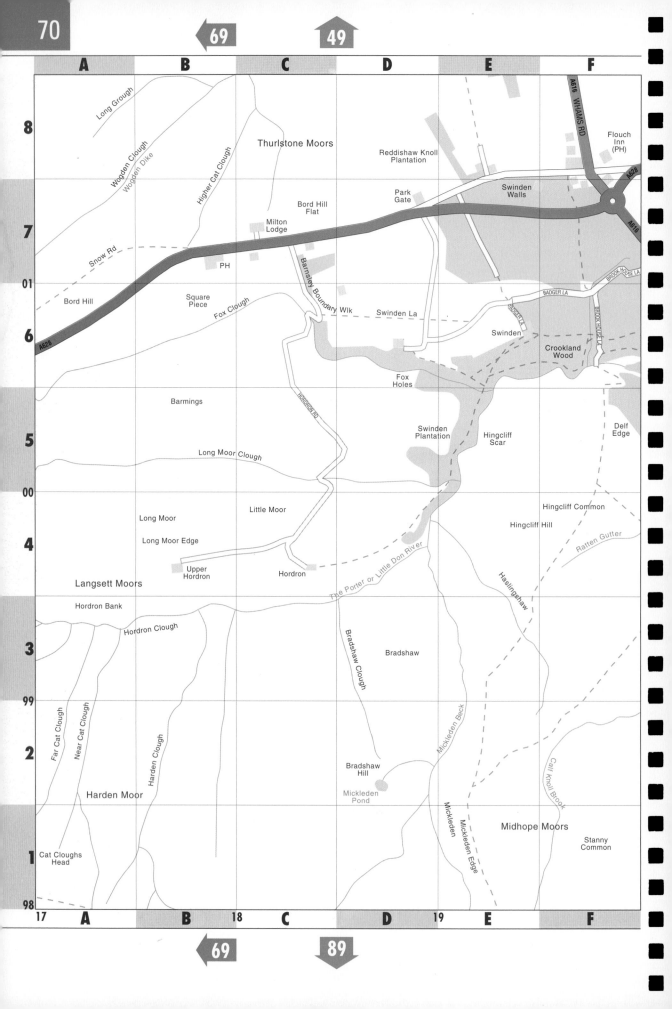

A   B   C   D   E   F

8

Long Grough

Thurlstone Moors

Reddishaw Knoll
Plantation

Flouch
Inn
(PH)

Wogden Clough

Wogden Dike

Higher Cat Clough

Bord Hill
Flat

Park
Gate

Swinden
Walls

7

Milton
Lodge

Snow Rd

PH

Square
Piece

Fox Clough

Barnsley Boundary Wlk

Swinden La

Badger La

01

Bord Hill

6

Swinden

Fox
Holes

Crookland
Wood

Barmings

Hordron Rd

Swinden
Plantation

Hingcliff
Scar

Delf
Edge

5

Long Moor Clough

Hingcliff Common

Little Moor

Hingcliff Hill

00

Long Moor

Ratten Gutter

Long Moor Edge

4

Upper
Hordron

Hordron

The Porter or Little Don River

Haslingshaw

Langsett Moors

Hordron Bank

Bradshaw

3

Hordron Clough

Bradshaw Clough

99

Far Cat Clough

Near Cat Clough

Harden Clough

Mickleden Beck

Call Knoll Brook

2

Bradshaw
Hill

Mickleden
Pond

Harden Moor

Mickleden

Mickleden Edge

Midhope Moors

Stanny
Common

1

Cat Cloughs
Head

98

17   A   18   B   C   19   D   E   F

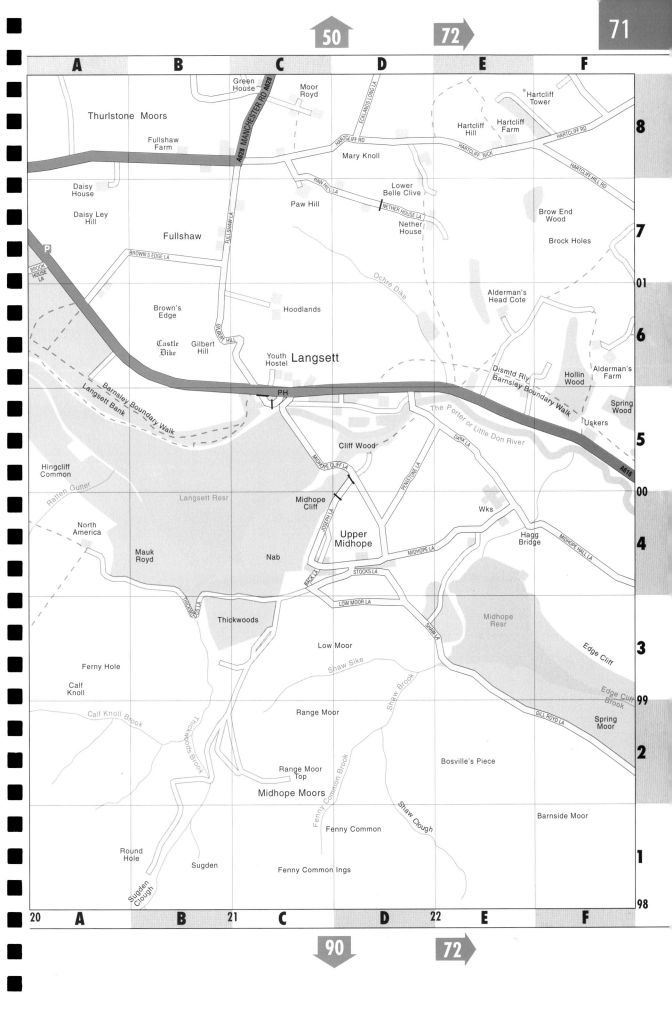

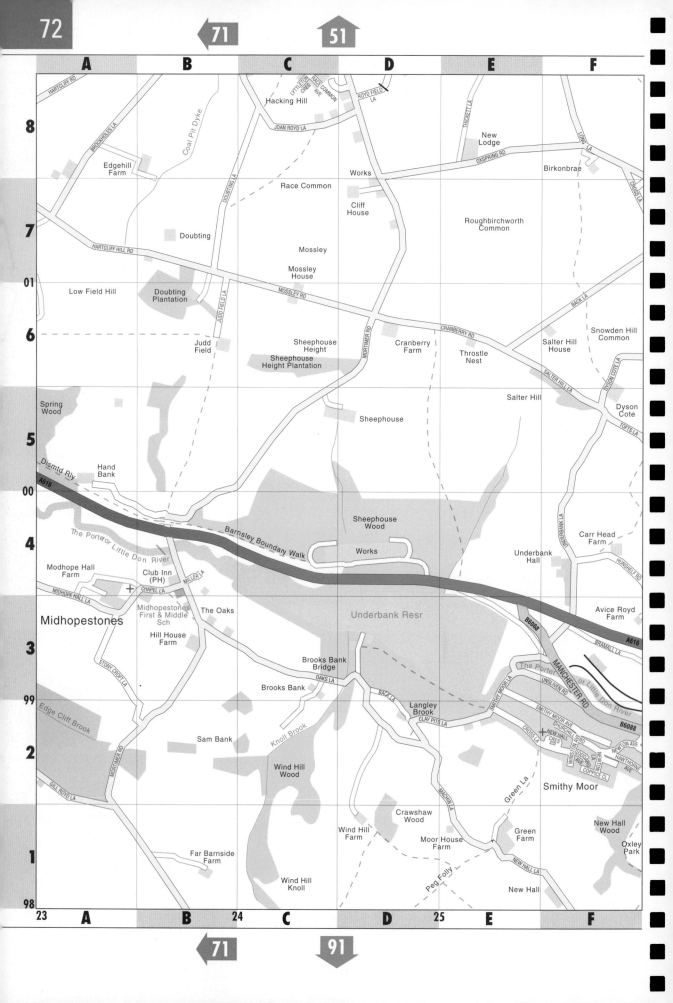

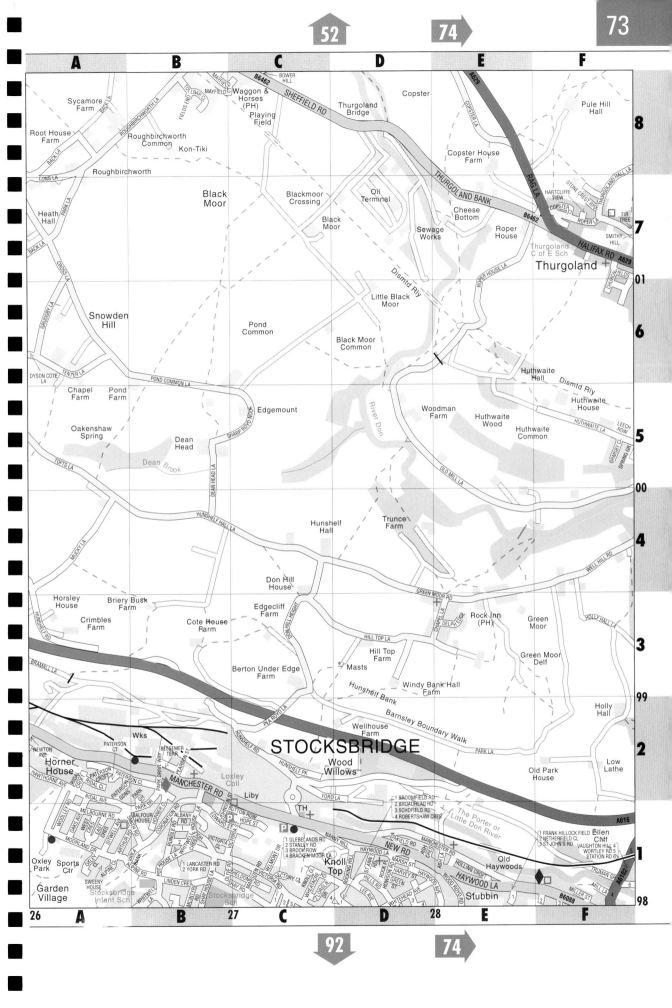

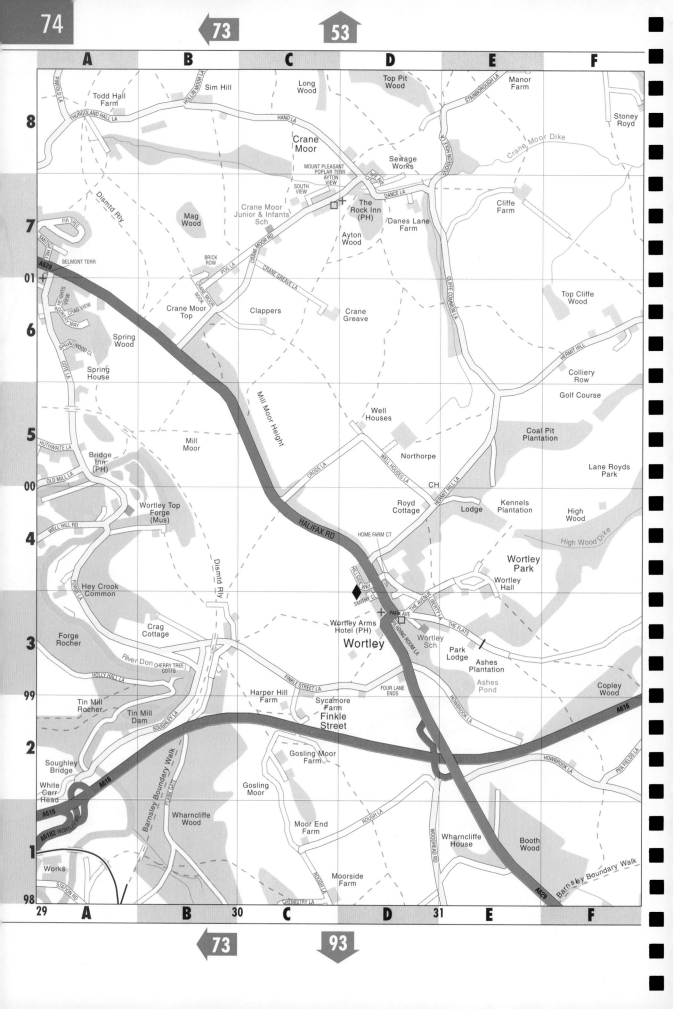

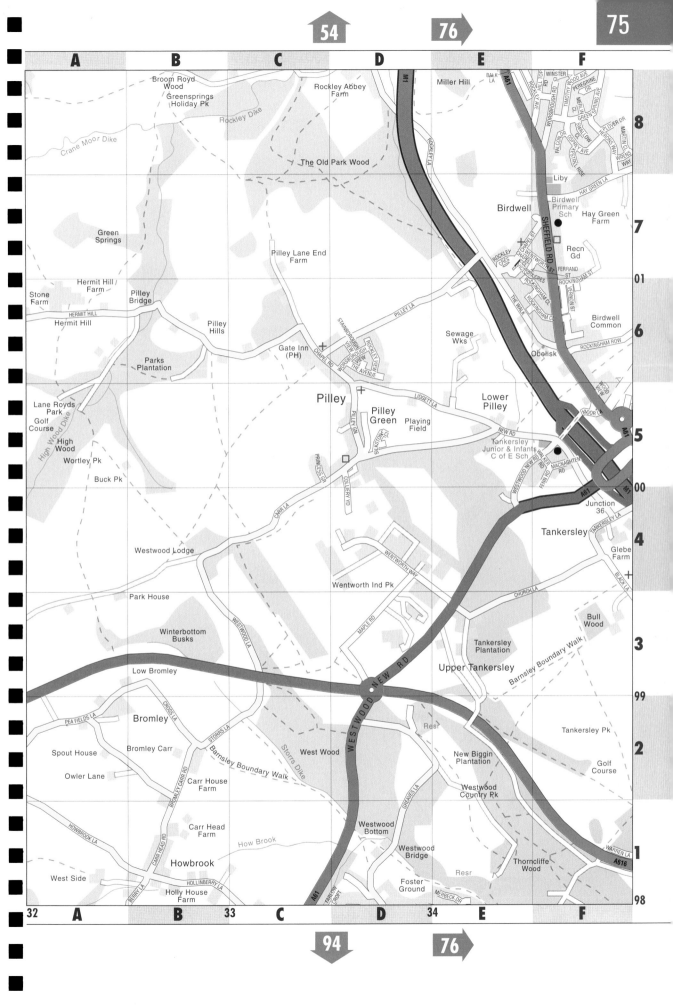

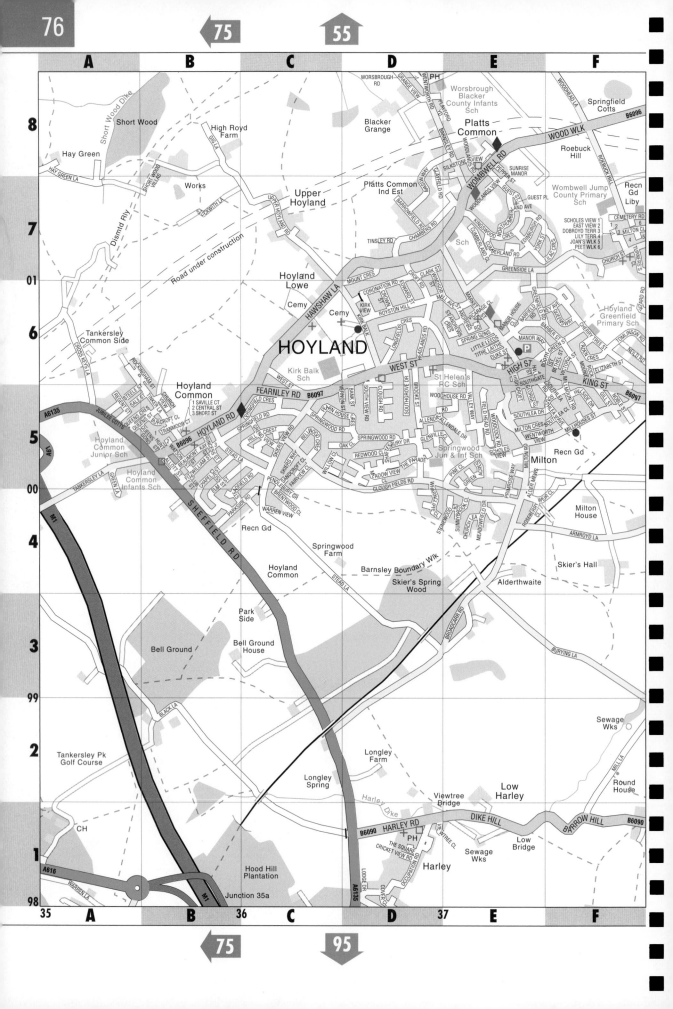

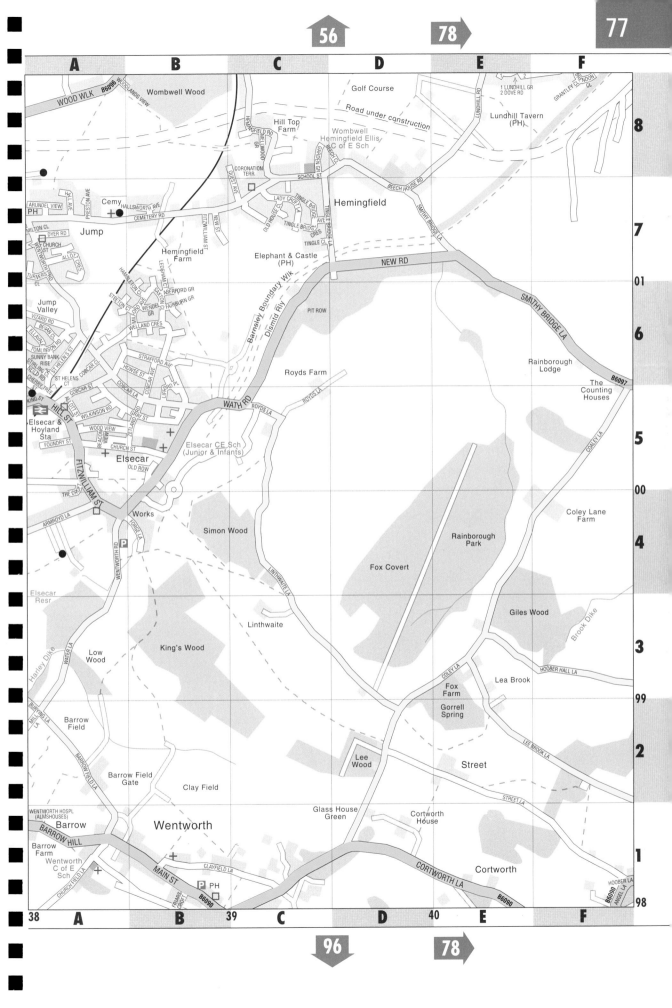

56
78
96
78

A B C D E F

8
7
01
6
5
00
4
3
99
2
1
98

WOOD WLK
B6096
WOODLANDS VIEW
Wombwell Wood
Golf Course
Road under construction
1 LUNDHILL GR
2 DOVE RD
GRANTLEY CL
RENDON CL
LUNDHILL RD
Lundhill Tavern
(PH)
HEMINGFIELD RD
MELLWOOD GR
Hill Top Farm
Wombwell Hemingfield Ellis C of E Sch
GARDEN GR
BEECH CL
ARUNDEL VIEW
PH
HA' AVE
PRESTON AVE
Cemy
Hallsworth Ave
CEMETERY RD
FITZWILLIAM ST
NEW ST
QUEST AVE
CORONATION TERR
SCHOOL ST
LADY CROFT
OLD HOUSE CL
TINGLE BRIDGE
TINGLE BRIDGE CRES
TINGLE BRIDGE AVE
Hemingfield
BEECH HOUSE RD
SMITHY BRIDGE LA
MILTON CL
DYER RD
CHURCH ST
ALLOT CRES
WENTWORTH RD
TURNERS RD CL
Jump
Hemingfield Farm
HAMERTON AVE
LEDHEAM CL
SAXTON GR
ABERFORD GR
FAIRBURN GR
TINGLE CL
Elephant & Castle (PH)
Barnsley Boundary Wlk
NEW RD
SMITHY BRIDGE LA
Jump Valley
VIZARD RD
BEVAR CL
ELLAVALE
TOMLINSON RD
STEETON AVE
MILFORD GR
WENDEL GR
WELLAND CRES
Dismd Rly
PIT ROW
Sunny Bank RISE
STIRLING CL
ENFIELD RD
CHERRY TREE RD
KING ST
St Helens
ST HELENS ST
STRAFFORD AVE
HOWSE ST
LIFORD PL
Royds Farm
Rainborough Lodge
The Counting Houses
B6097
Elsecar & Hoyland Sta
HILL ST
COBCAR CL
COBCAR ST
COBCAR LA
ZETLAND
GRAY ST
WATH RD
ROYDS LA
ROYDS LA
COLEY LA
FOUNDRY ST
ALDITCH
WILKINSON RD
WOOD VIEW
BLACKSMITHS
CHURCH ST
Elsecar CE Sch (Junior & Infants)
Elsecar
Old Row
FITZWILLIAM ST
THE CR
Works
Coley Lane Farm
ARMROYD LA
WENTWORTH RD
FORGE LA
P
Simon Wood
Rainborough Park
Fox Covert
Elsecar Resr
LINTHWAITE LA
Giles Wood
Brook Dike
Low Wood
King's Wood
Linthwaite
COLEY LA
HOOBER HALL LA
Harley Dike
WATER LA
Lea Brook
Fox Farm
Barrow Field
BURYING LA
Gorrell Spring
LEE BROOK LA
BARROW FIELD LA
Barrow Field Gate
Clay Field
Lee Wood
Street
STREET LA
Wentworth Hospl (Almshouses)
Glass House Green
Cortworth House
Barrow
BARROW HILL
Wentworth
Barrow Farm
Wentworth C of E Sch
MAIN ST
CLAYFIELD LA
CHURCH FIELD LA
FRIARS CROFT
P
PH
B6090
CORTWORTH LA
B6090
Cortworth
HOOBER LA
B6090
ANGEL LA

38 A B 39 C D 40 E F

WATH UPON DEARNE

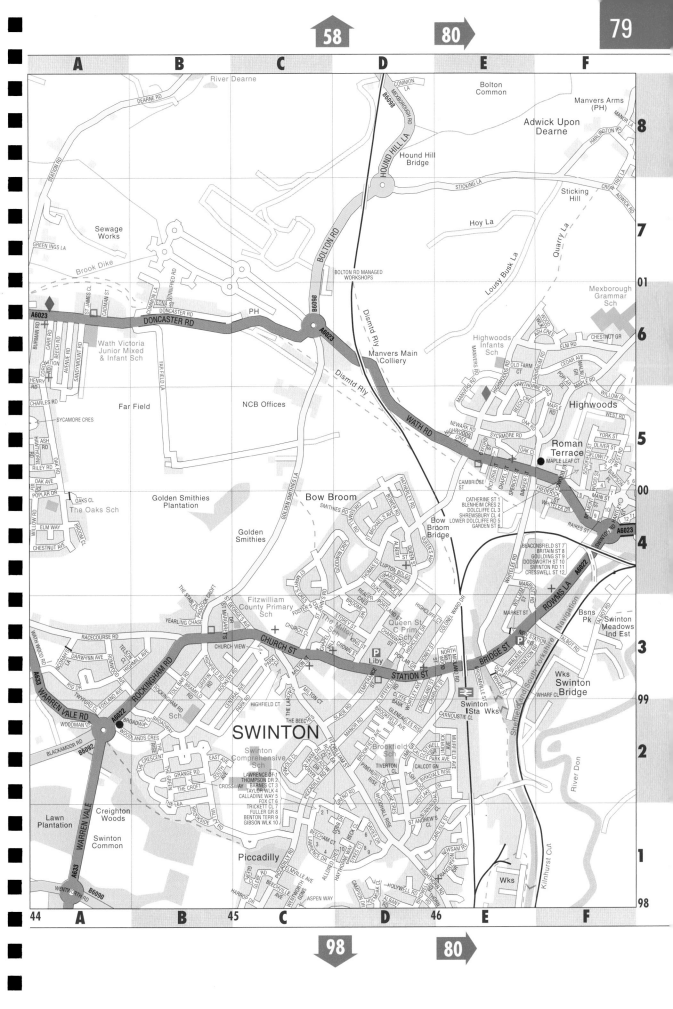

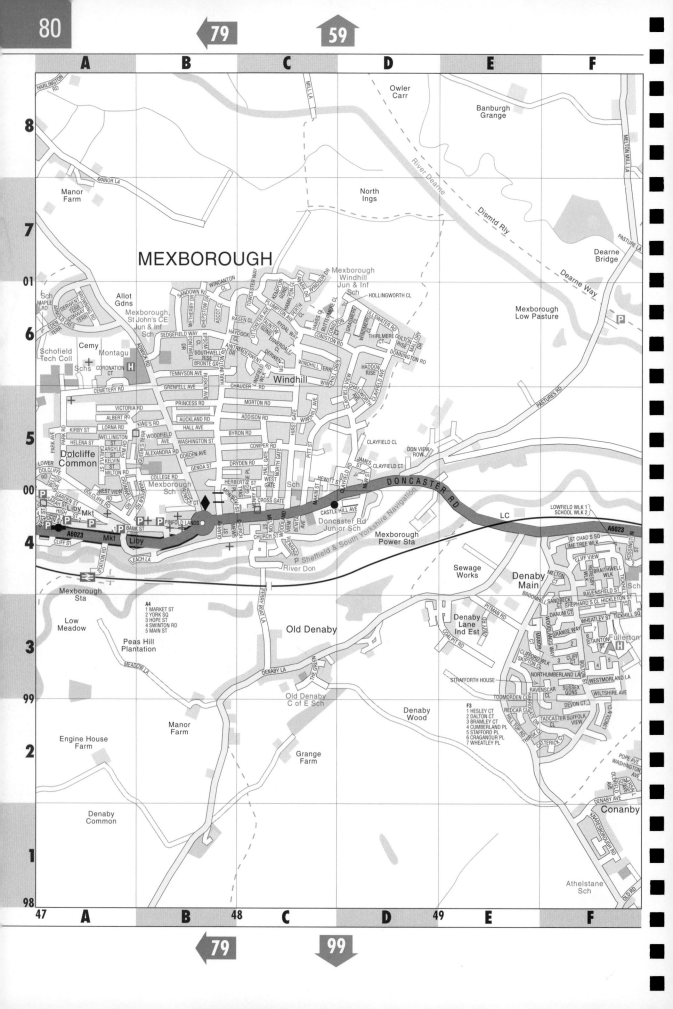

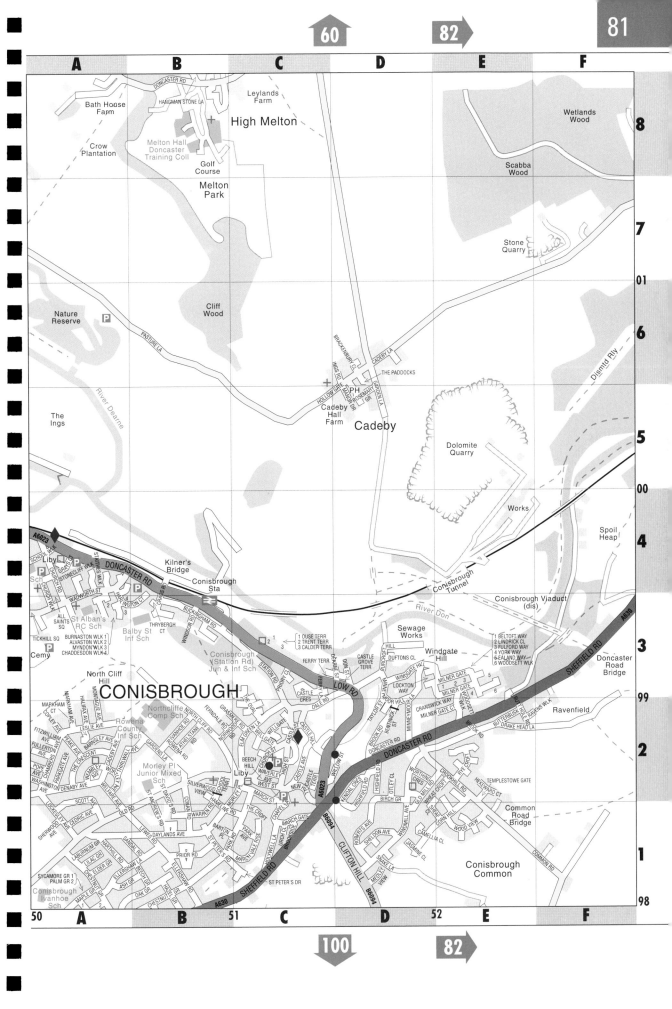

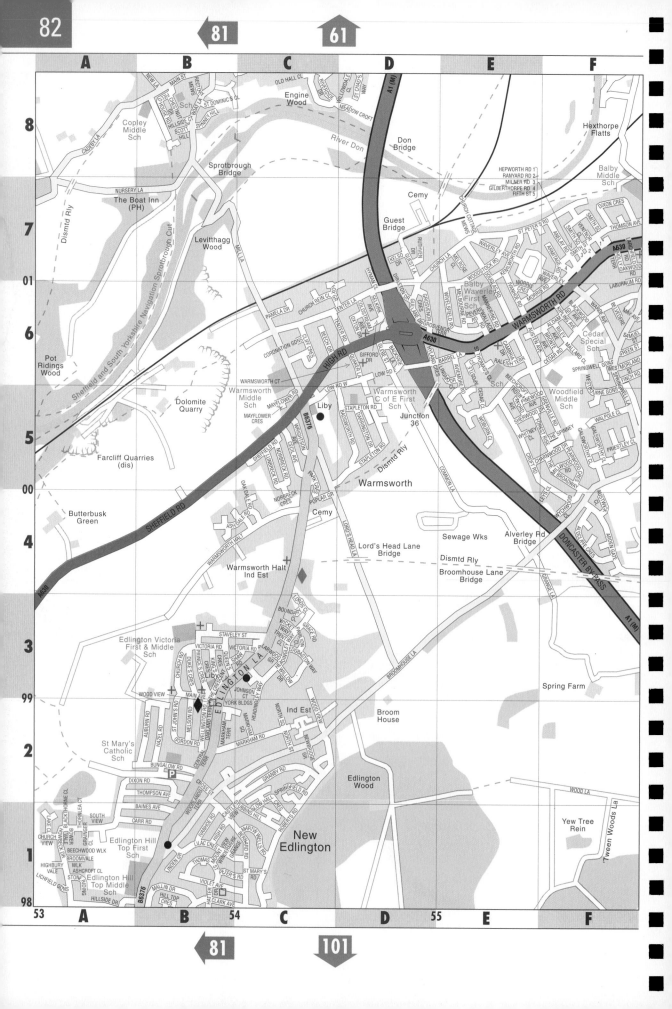

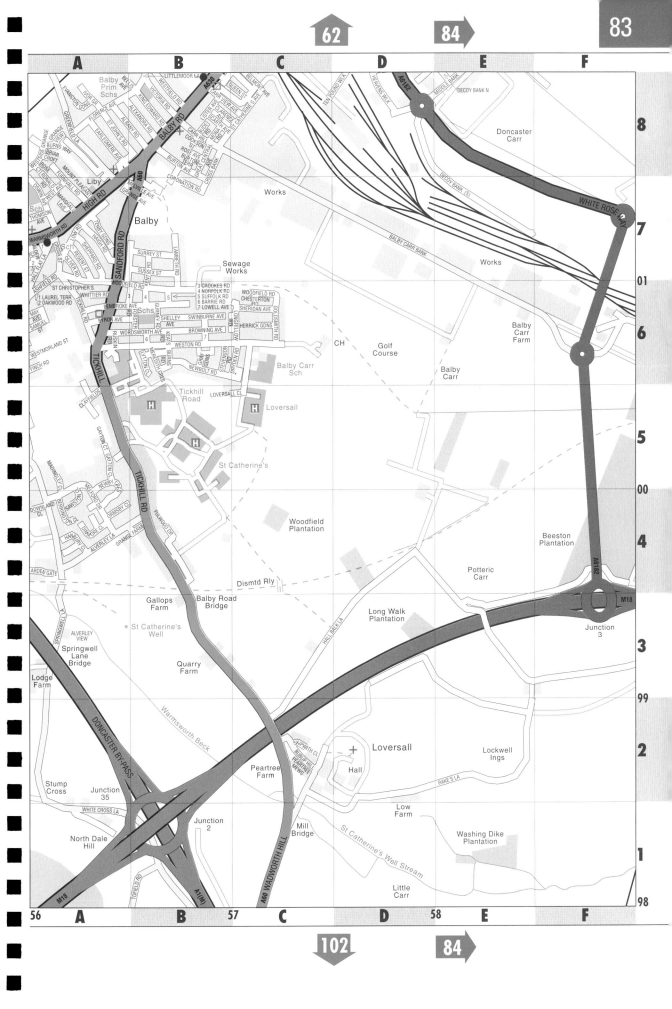

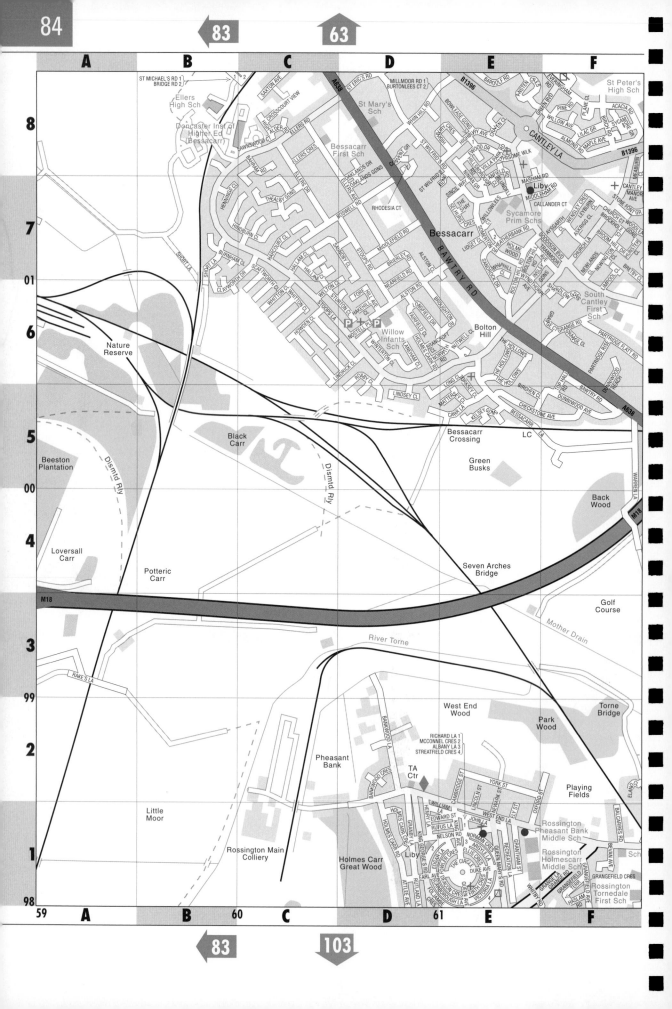

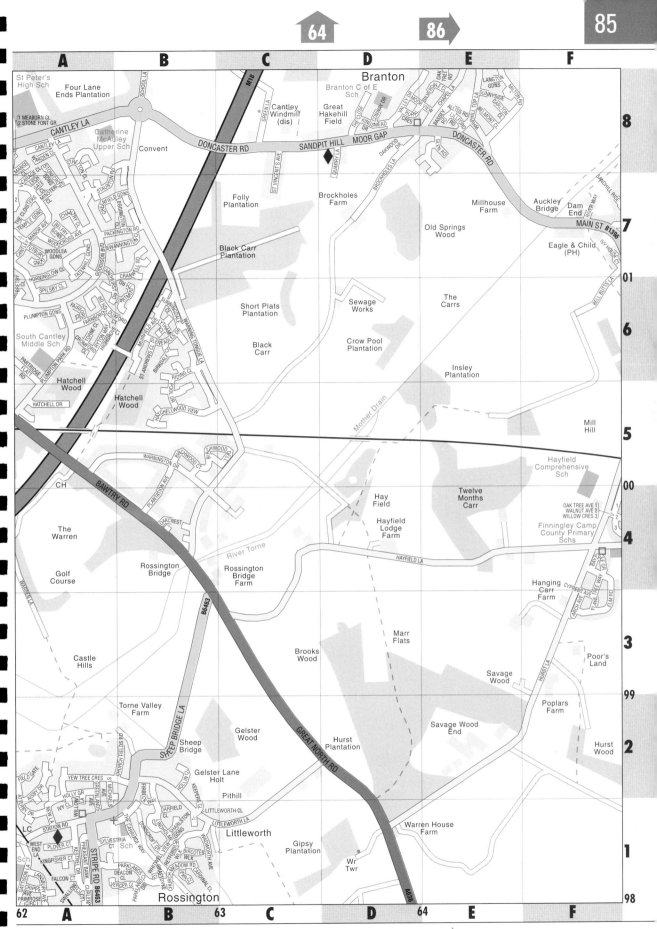

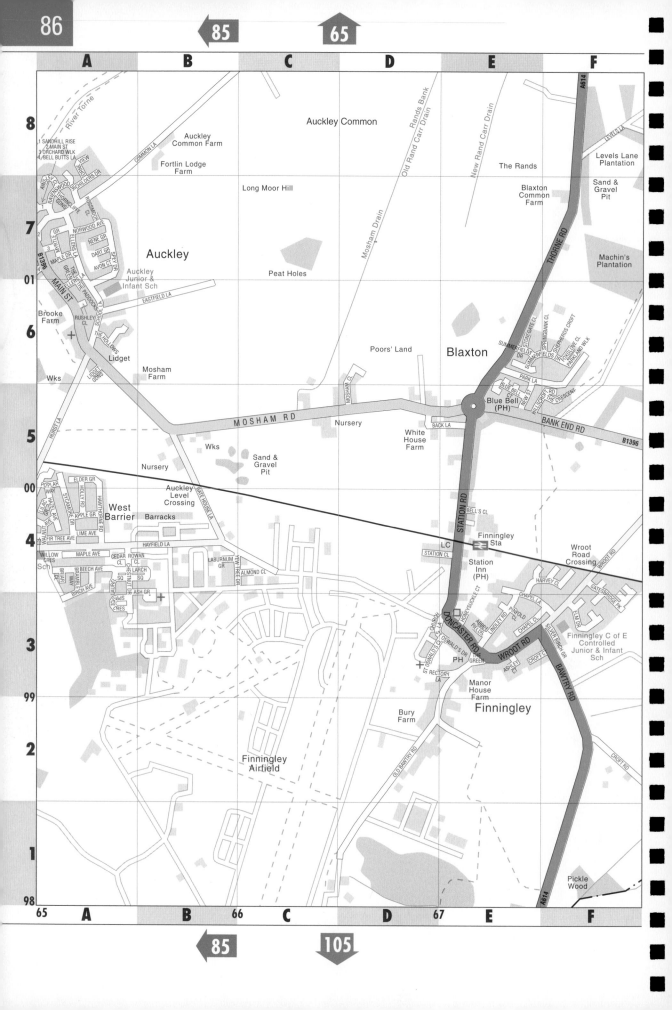

A   B   C   D   E   F

8

River Torne

Auckley Common

Rands Bank

Old Rand Carr Drain

New Rand Carr Drain

The Rands

Levels Lane Plantation

A614

COMMON LA

Auckley Common Farm

Fortlin Lodge Farm

Long Moor Hill

Blaxton Common Farm

LEVELS LA

Sand & Gravel Pit

7

1 SANDHILL RISE
2 MAIN ST
3 ORCHARD WLK
4 BELL BUTTS LA

THORNE RD

Machin's Plantation

Peat Holes

Auckley

Mosham Drain

01

Auckley Junior & Infant Sch

EASTFIELD LA

B1396   MAIN ST

Brooke Farm

6

Lidget

Mosham Farm

Poors' Land

Blaxton

SUMMERFIELD DR   STONEGATE CL   SPRINGBANK CL   SHEPHERDS CROFT   FOXGLOVE CL   PARKLAND WLK

HURST LA

LIDGET GDNS

Wks

Nursery

PARK LA

BLUE BELL ST   VIEW ST   HILLSCROFT   THE CRESCENT

Blue Bell (PH)

5

MOSHAM RD

Nursery

White House Farm

BACK LA

BANK END RD

B1396

MOSHAM CL

Wks

Sand & Gravel Pit

STATION RD

Nursery

00

Auckley Level Crossing

GATE HOUSE LA

BELL'S CL

POPLAR WAY   ELDER GR   HAZEL AVE   SYCAMORE RD   HOLLY RD   APPLE GR   LILAC CL   WALNUT AVE   FIR TREE AVE   LIME AVE

West Barrier

Barracks

Finningley Sta

Wroot Road Crossing

4

HAYFIELD LA

LC

STATION CL

WROOT RD

WILLOW CRES   MAPLE AVE   CEDAR CL   ROWAN CL   CHESTNUT GR   THE LARCH SQ   ASH GR   LABURNUM GR   ALMOND CL

Sch

BIRCH AVE   BRAMBLE CL   BRIAR WAY   BEECH AVE   LAUREL SQ   HOLLY CRES

Station Inn (PH)

HARVEY CL   CHAPEL LA   ELM DR   GATESBRIDGE PK

3

DONCASTER RD

St OSWALD'S CL   St OSWALD'S DR   CHURCH LA   RECTORY LA

PH   St   THE GREEN

HONEYSUCKLE CT   ABBEY FIELDS   LINDLEY RD   PINFOLD CL   CHAPEL CL   SILVER BIRCH GR   ASHLEY CT   CROFT CL

Finningley C of E Controlled Junior & Infant Sch

BAWTRY RD

99

Bury Farm

Manor House Farm

Finningley

2

Finningley Airfield

OLD BAWTRY RD

CROFT RD

1

Pickle Wood

A614

98

65   A   B   66   C   D   67   E   F

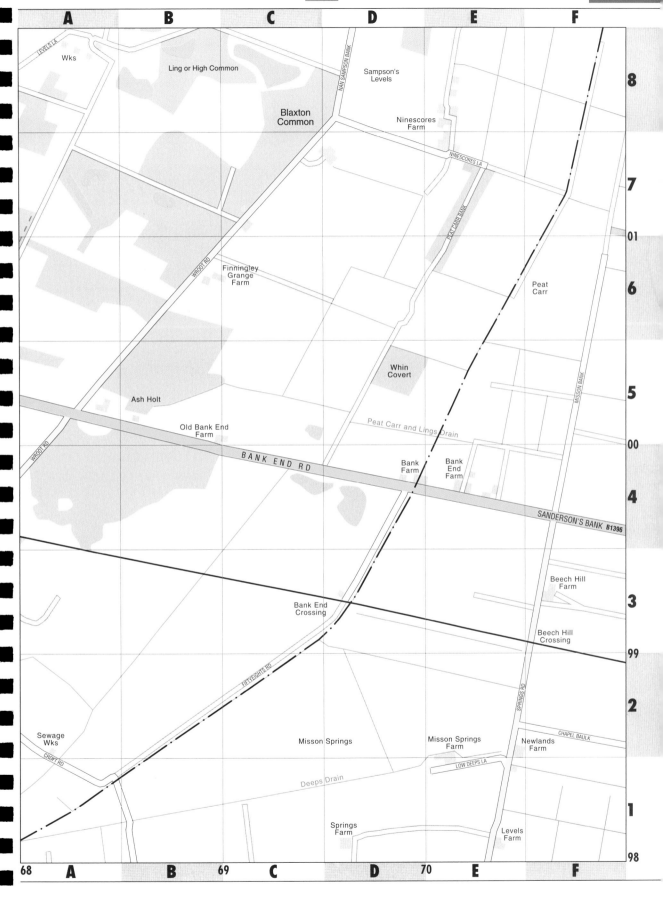

A   B   C   D   E   F

LEVELS LA
Wks
Ling or High Common
NAN SAMPSON BANK
Sampson's Levels
8
Blaxton Common
Ninescores Farm
NINESCORES LA
PEAT CARR BANK
7
01
WROOT RD
Finningley Grange Farm
Peat Carr
6
Whin Covert
MISSON BANK
5
Ash Holt
Old Bank End Farm
Peat Carr and Lings Drain
00
WROOT RD
BANK END RD
Bank Farm
Bank End Farm
4
SANDERSON'S BANK B1396
Beech Hill Farm
3
Bank End Crossing
Beech Hill Crossing
99
FIFTYEIGHTS RD
SPRINGS RD
2
Sewage Wks
Misson Springs
Misson Springs Farm
CHAPEL BAULK
Newlands Farm
CROFT RD
LOW DEEPS LA
Deeps Drain
1
Springs Farm
Levels Farm
98

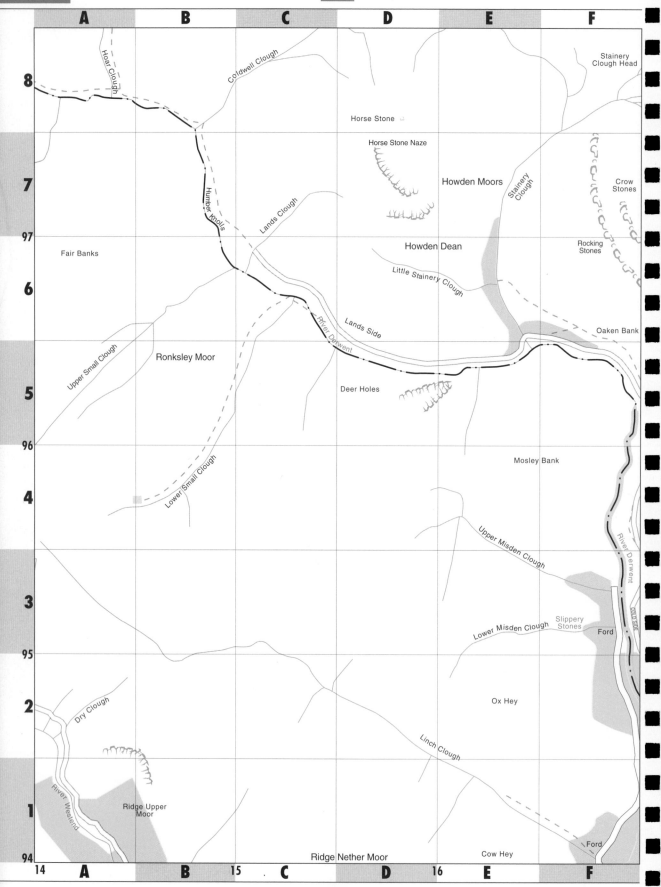

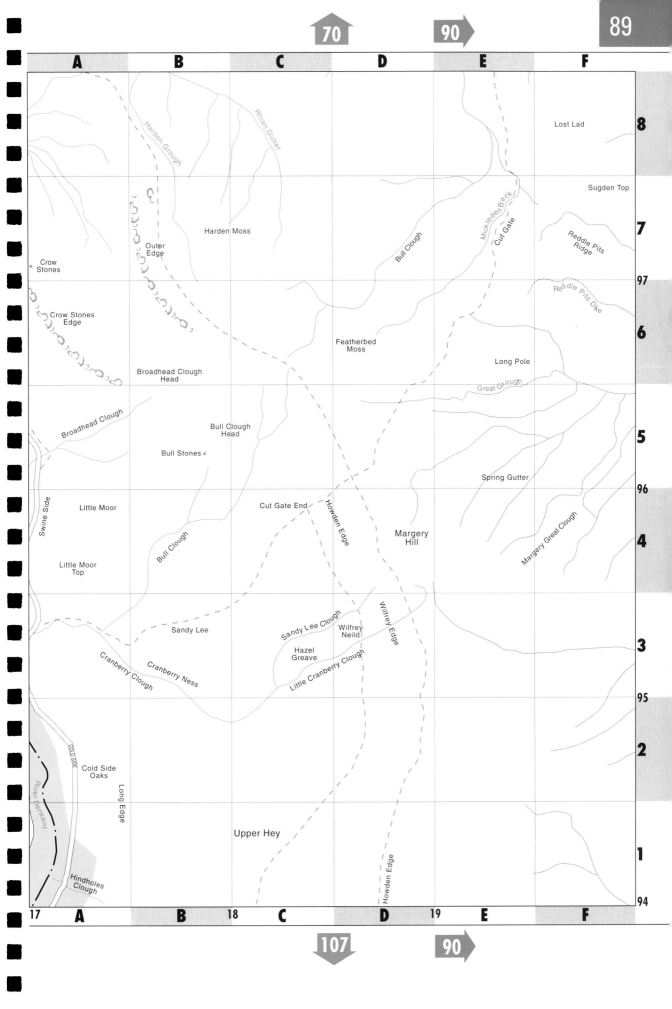

A B C D E F

8

Lost Lad

Sugden Top

7

Harden Moss

Rhian Gutter

Harden Grough

Outer Edge

Bull Clough

Mickleden Beck

Cut Gate

Reddle Pits Ridge

97

Crow Stones

Reddle Pits Dke

6

Crow Stones Edge

Featherbed Moss

Long Pole

Great Grough

Broadhead Clough Head

Broadhead Clough

5

Bull Clough Head

Bull Stones

Spring Gutter

96

Swine Side

Little Moor

Cut Gate End

Howden Edge

Margery Hill

4

Little Moor Top

Bull Clough

Margery Great Clough

Sandy Lee

Sandy Lee Clough

Wilfrey Neild

Wilfrey Edge

3

Cranberry Clough

Cranberry Ness

Hazel Greave

Little Cranberry Clough

95

Cold Side

River Derwent

Cold Side Oaks

Long Edge

2

Upper Hey

Howden Edge

1

Hindholes Clough

94

17 A 18 B C 18 D 19 E F

89
71

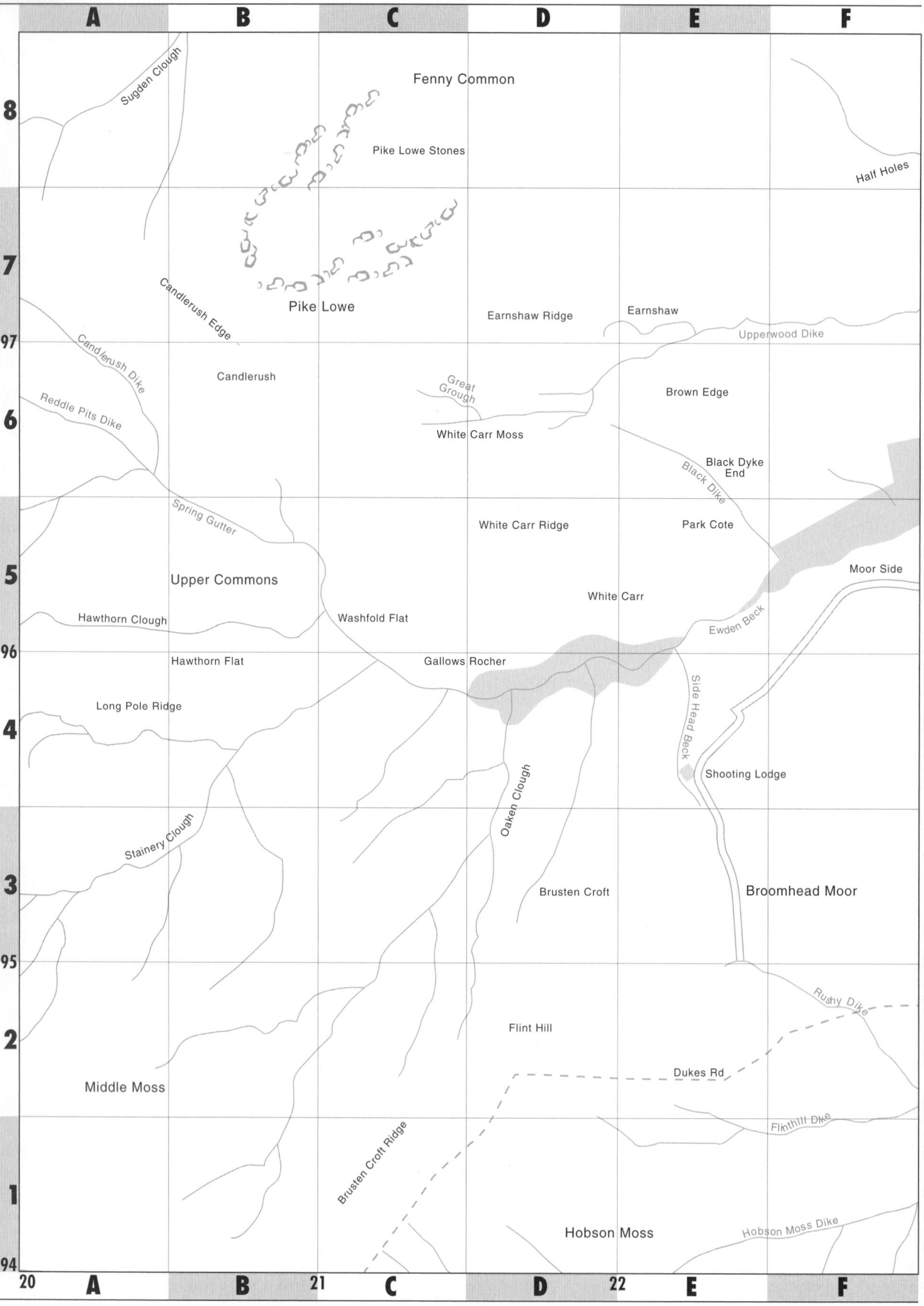

A **B** **C** **D** **E** **F**

8

Sugden Clough

Fenny Common

Pike Lowe Stones

Half Holes

7

Candlerush Edge

Pike Lowe

Earnshaw Ridge

Earnshaw

Upperwood Dike

97

Candlerush Dike

Candlerush

Great Grough

Brown Edge

6

Reddle Pits Dike

White Carr Moss

Black Dyke End

Black Dike

Spring Gutter

White Carr Ridge

Park Cote

5

Upper Commons

White Carr

Moor Side

Hawthorn Clough

Washfold Flat

Ewden Beck

96

Hawthorn Flat

Gallows Rocher

Side Head Beck

Long Pole Ridge

4

Shooting Lodge

Stainery Clough

Oaken Clough

3

Brusten Croft

Broomhead Moor

95

Rushy Dike

2

Flint Hill

Dukes Rd

Middle Moss

Flinthill Dike

Brusten Croft Ridge

1

Hobson Moss

Hobson Moss Dike

94

89
108

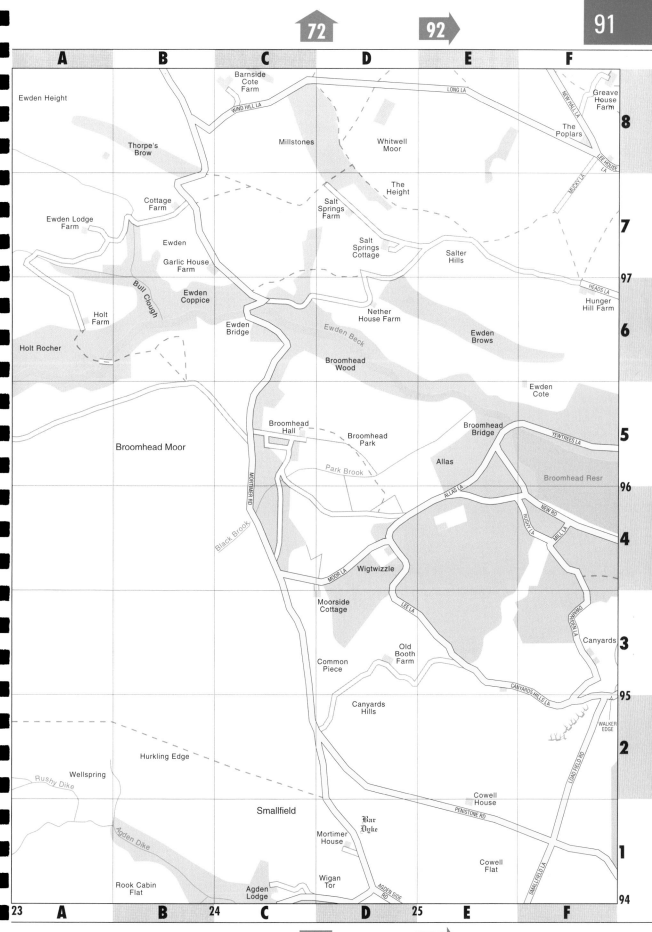

A B C D E F

8
7
97
6
5
96
4
3
95
2
1
94

Ewden Height

WIND HILL LA

Barnside Cote Farm

LONG LA

NEW HALL LA

Greave House Farm

The Poplars

LEE HOUSE LA

Thorpe's Brow

Millstones

Whitwell Moor

MUCKY LA

Cottage Farm

The Height

Ewden

Salt Springs Farm

Ewden Lodge Farm

Garlic House Farm

Salt Springs Cottage

Salter Hills

HEADS LA

Bull Clough

Ewden Coppice

Nether House Farm

Hunger Hill Farm

Holt Farm

Ewden Bridge

Ewden Beck

Ewden Brows

Holt Rocher

Broomhead Wood

Ewden Cote

Broomhead Bridge

YEWTREES LA

Broomhead Moor

Broomhead Hall

Broomhead Park

Broomhead Resr

MORTIMER RD

Park Brook

Allas

ALLAS LA.

NEW RD

RUSSY LA

MILL LA

Black Brook

MOOR LA

Wigtwizzle

LEE LA

DWARIDEN LA

Canyards

Moorside Cottage

Common Piece

Old Booth Farm

CANYARDS HILLS LA

95

Canyards Hills

WALKER EDGE

Hurkling Edge

Rushy Dike

Wellspring

Cowell House

PENISTONE RD

LOADFIELD RD

Smallfield

Bar Dyke

Mortimer House

Cowell Flat

SMALLFIELD LA

Agden Dike

Rook Cabin Flat

Agden Lodge

Wigan Tor

AGDEN SIDE RD

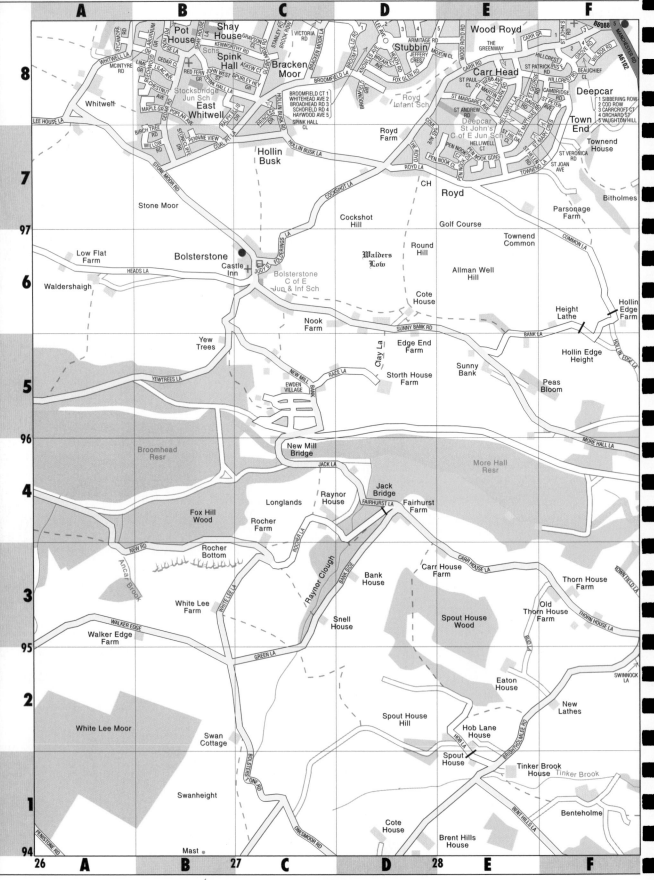

8

97

7

6

5

96

4

95

3

2

94

1

A B C D E F

Whitwell

East Whitwell

Shay House
Pot House
Spink Hall
Bracken Moor
Stocksbridge Jun Sch

Wood Royd
Stubbin
THE GREENWAY
Carr Head
Deepcar
Town End
Townend House

BROOMFIELD CT 1
WHITEHEAD AVE 2
BROADHEAD RD 3
SCHOFIELD RD 4
HAYWOOD AVE 5
SPINK HALL CL

1 SIBBERING ROW
2 COD ROW
3 CARRCROFT CT
4 ORCHARD ST
5 VAUGHTON HILL

Hollin Busk

Royd Infant Sch

Royd Farm

St John's C of E Jun Sch

Stone Moor

Cockshot Hill

Royd

Golf Course

Bitholmes

Parsonage Farm

Low Flat Farm

Bolsterstone

Castle Inn

Bolsterstone C of E Jun & Inf Sch

Walders Low

Cockshot Hill

Round Hill

Townend Common

COMMON LA

Waldershaigh

HEADS LA

Nook Farm

Allman Well Hill

Cote House

Height Lathe

Hollin Edge Farm

Yew Trees

Edge End Farm

Sunny Bank

Hollin Edge Height

YEWTREES LA

Clay La

SUNNY BANK RD

BANK LA

Peas Bloom

New Mill Bank

Ewden Village

RACE LA

Storth House Farm

MORE HALL LA

Broomhead Resr

New Mill Bridge

JACK LA

More Hall Resr

Fox Hill Wood

Longlands

Rocher Farm

Raynor House

Jack Bridge

FAIRHURST LA

Fairhurst Farm

NEW RD

Rocher Bottom

Raynor Clough

BANK SIDE

Bank House

Carr House Farm

CARR HOUSE LA

Thorn House Farm

Ancar Brook

White Lee Farm

WHITE LEE LA

Snell House

Spout House Wood

Old Thorn House Farm

THORN HOUSE LA

TOWNFIELD LA

Walker Edge Farm

WALKER EDGE

GREEN LA

Eaton House

SWINNOCK LA

New Lathes

White Lee Moor

Swan Cottage

BOLSTERSTONE RD

Spout House Hill

Hob Lane House

HOB LA

Spout House

Tinker Brook House

Tinker Brook

Benteholme

Swanheight

OMESMOOR RD

Cote House

Brent Hills House

BRENT HILLS LA

BRIGHTHOLMLEE RD

PENISTONE RD

Mast

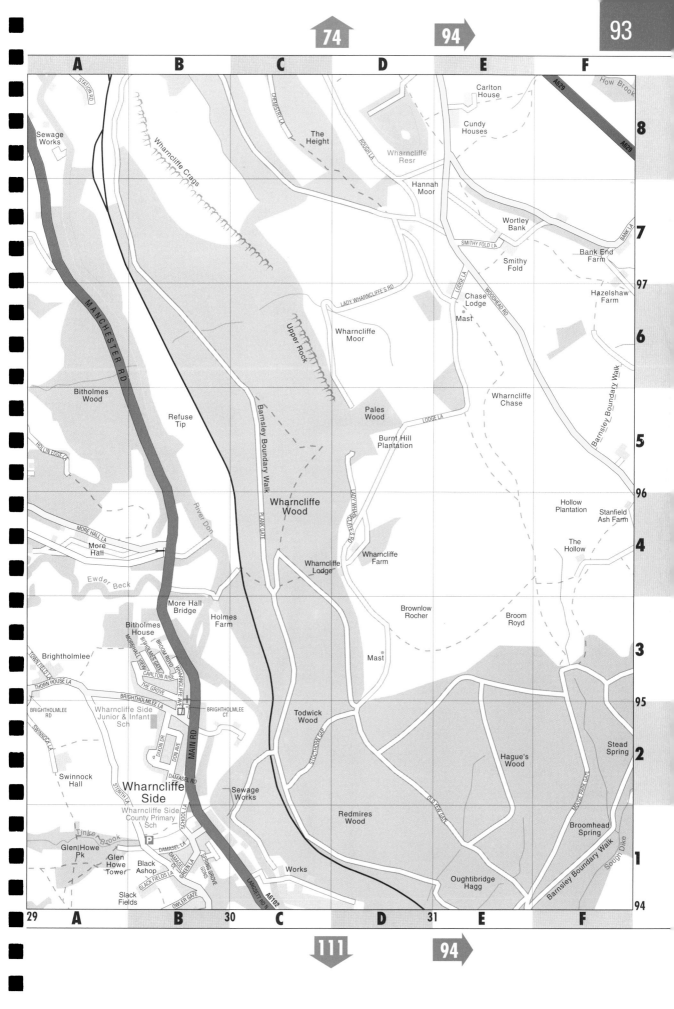

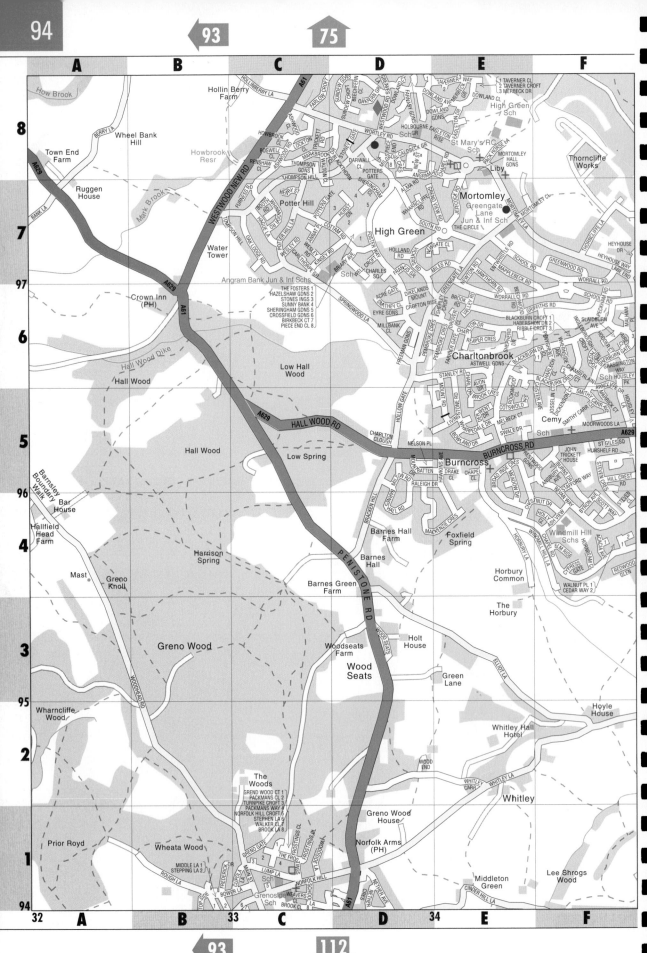

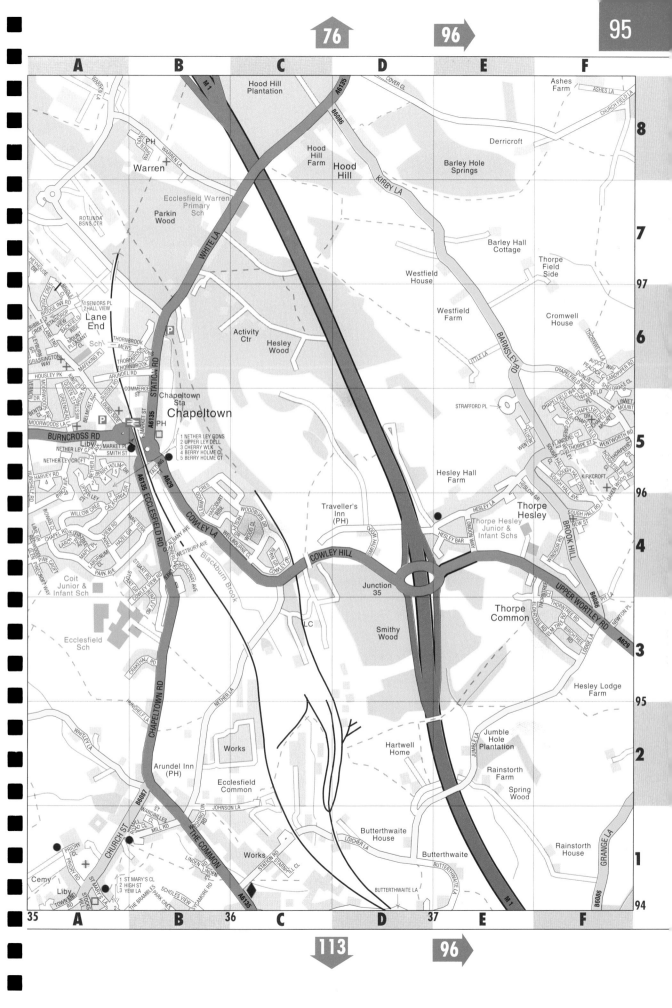

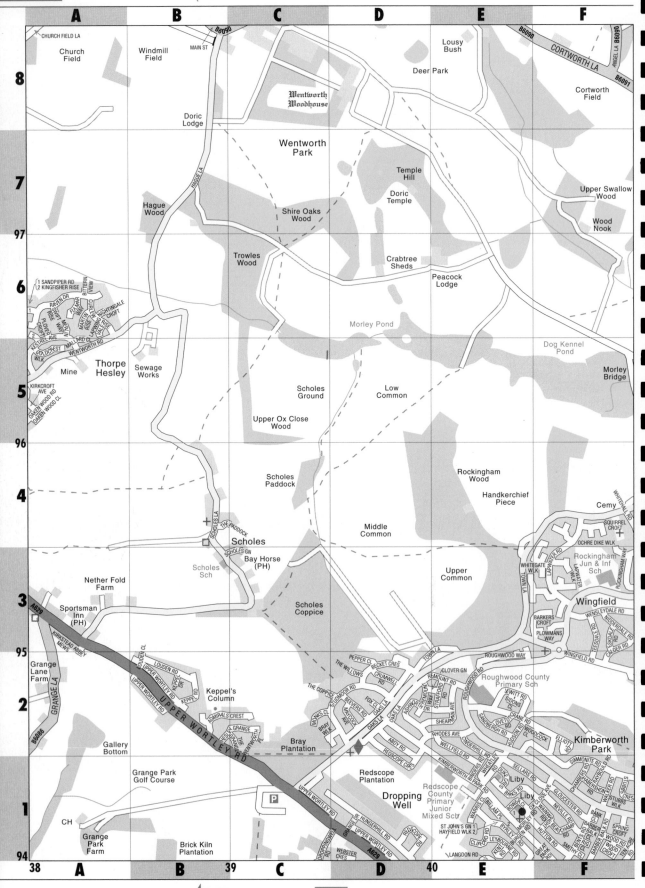

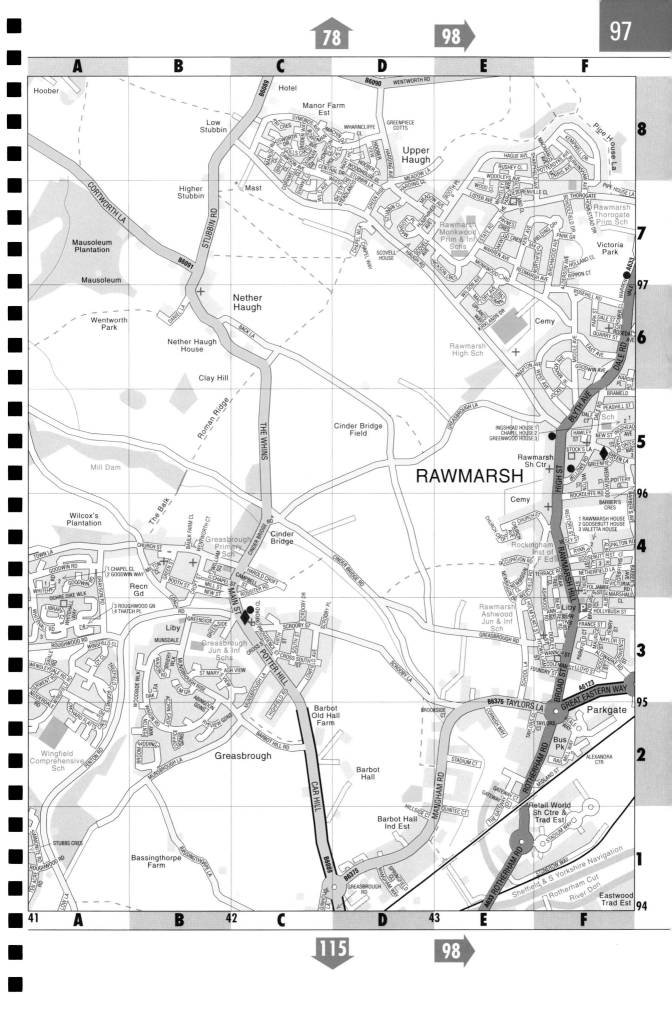

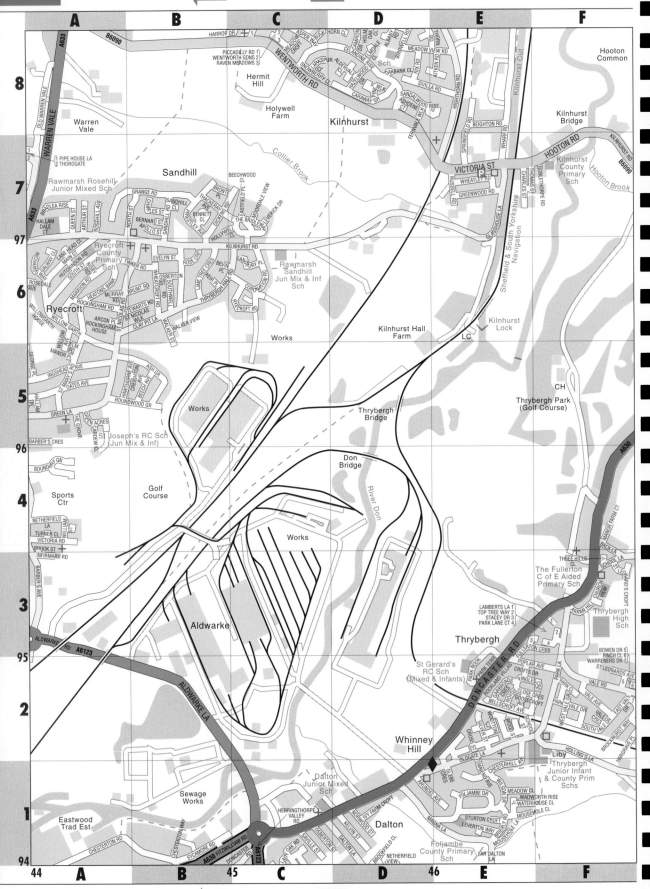

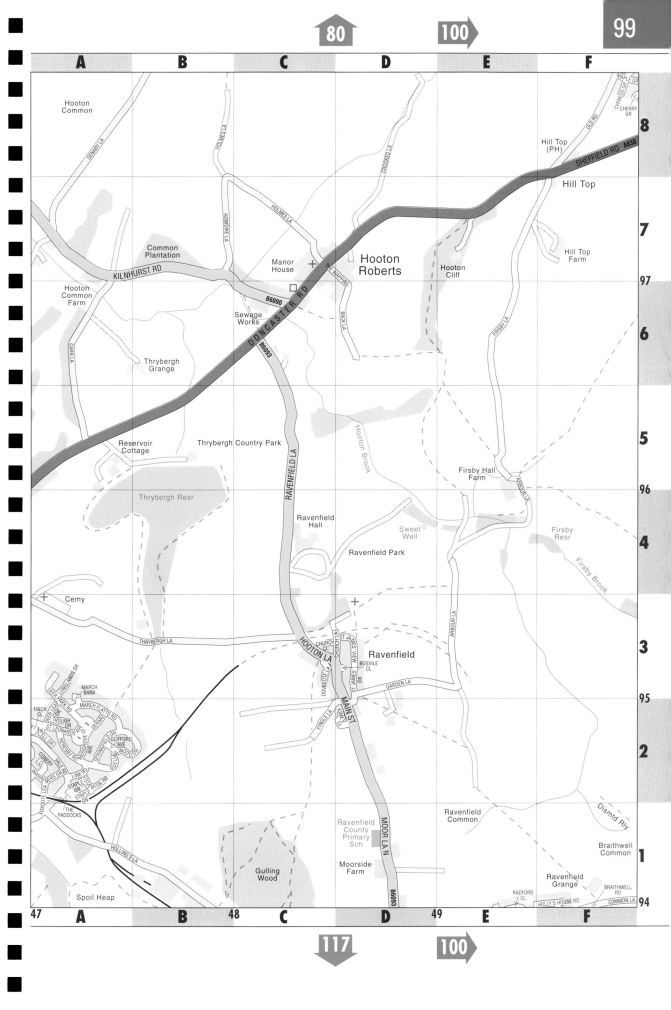

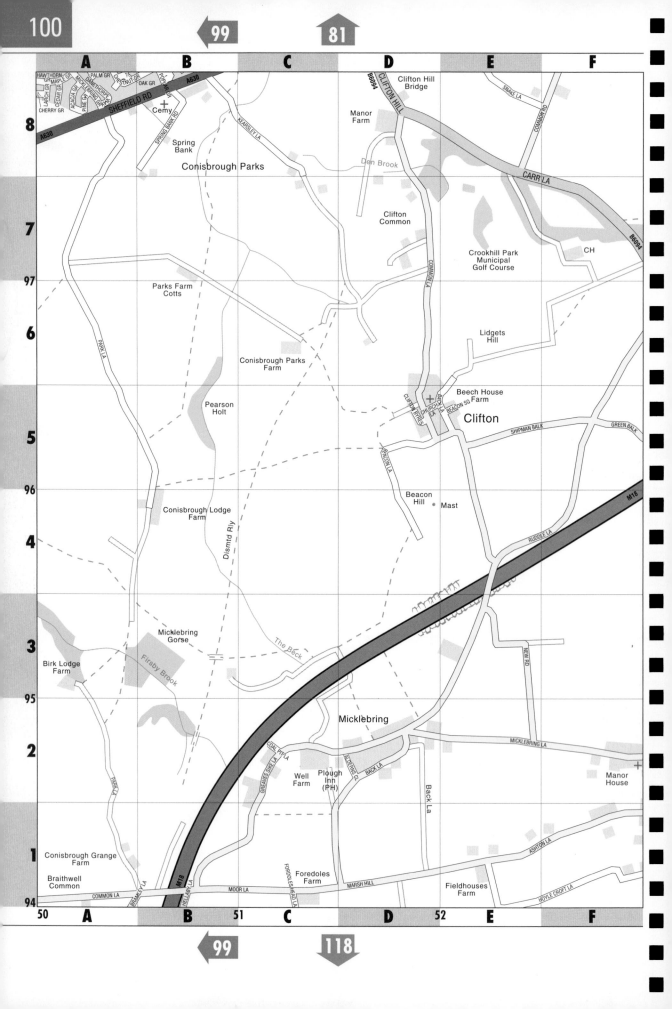

Map labels

A B C D E F

8 7 97 6 96 5 4 3 95 2 1 94

HAWTHORN GR
MAPLE GR
PALM GR
LARCH GR
CEDAR GR
ACACIA GR
PINE GR
MICKLEBRING GR
DAMETHORPE PK
CHESTNUT GR
OAK GR
POPLAR GR
CHERRY GR

SHEFFIELD RD
A630
A630
Cemy
Spring Bank
SPRING BANK RD

KEARSLEY LA

Conisbrough Parks

Spring Bank

B6094
CLIFTON HILL
Clifton Hill Bridge

SNAKE LA
COMMON RD

Manor Farm

Den Brook

CARR LA

Clifton Common

Crookhill Park Municipal Golf Course

CH

B6094

Parks Farm Cotts

COMMON LA

Lidgets Hill

Conisbrough Parks Farm

Pearson Holt

CLIFTON BYPASS
CHURCH LA
BEACON SQ
Beech House Farm

Clifton

SHIPMAN BALK
GREEN BALK

BEACON LA

Conisbrough Lodge Farm

Dismtd Rly

PARK LA

Beacon Hill
• Mast

M18

RUDDLE LA

Micklebring Gorse

The Beck

Firsby Brook

Birk Lodge Farm

NEW RD

Micklebring

MICKLEBRING LA

Manor House

COAL PIT LA
GREAVES SIKE LA

Well Farm

Plough Inn (PH)

ALDERNE CT
BACK LA

BACK LA

PARK LA

Conisbrough Grange Farm

ASHTON LA

Braithwell Common

BRAMLEY LA
M18
HELLABY LA

COMMON LA

MOOR LA

FORDOLES HEAD LA

Foredoles Farm

MARSH HILL

Fieldhouses Farm

HOYLE CROFT LA

50   A   B   51   C   D   52   E   F

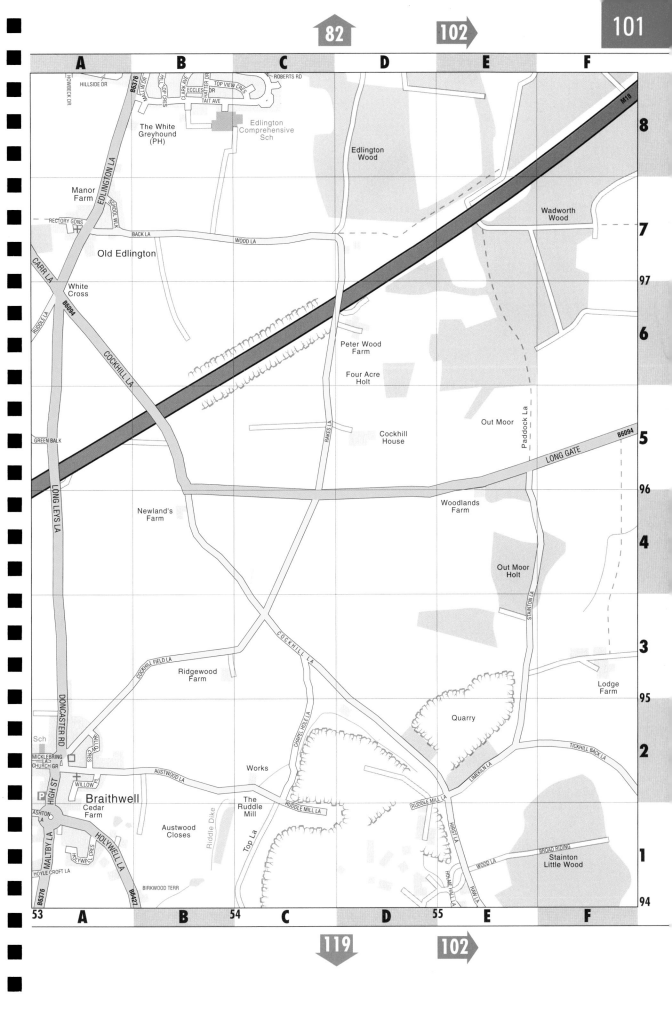

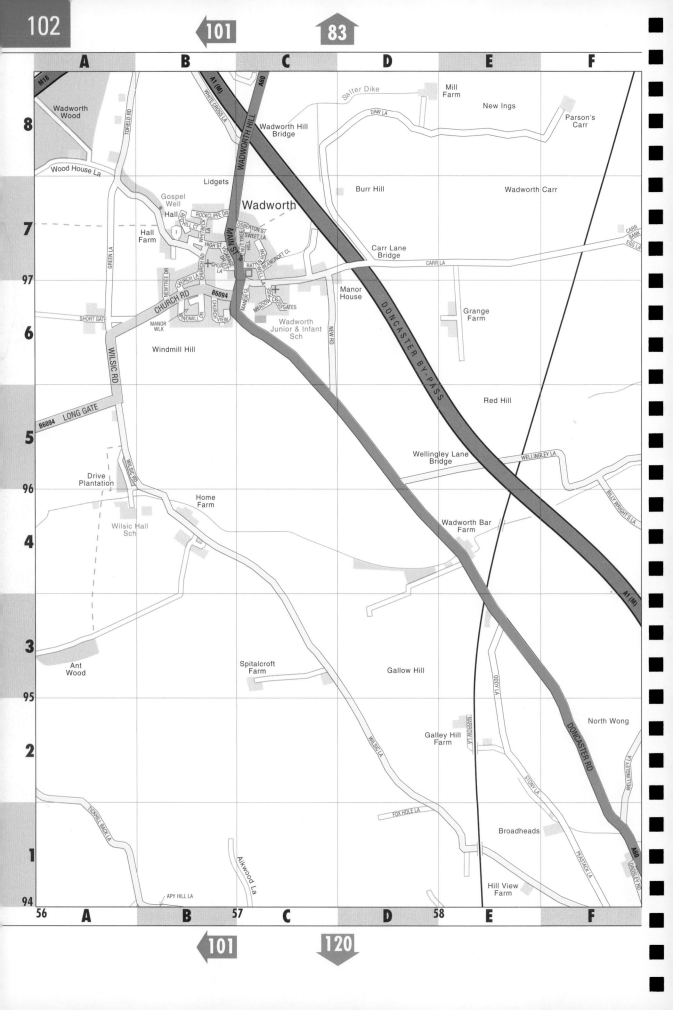

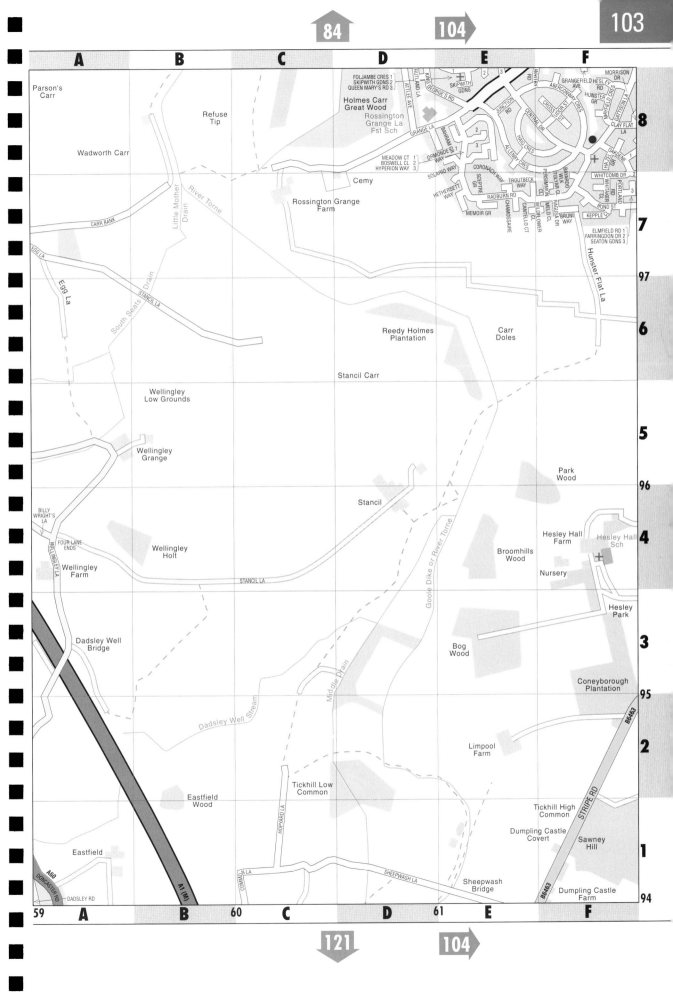

A   B   C   D   E   F

1 PRIMROSE CIRC
2 WILKINSON AVE

KIER
HARDIE AVE
MORRIS DR
BINGWELL DR
LANSBURY AVE
SMILLIE RD
B6463
PASSFIELD RD
SHERWOOD RD
CLAY FLAT LA
ELMFIELD RD
CHERRY GR
BEECH DR
CHESTNUT AVE
REGENT
LIME TREE CRES
HADRIANS
KINGSWAY
HIGHGATE CL
ASHVALE
ALDERSGATE
FARRINGDON DR
LODGATE
BOND ST
BISHOPSGATE
HALL VIEW RD
SPITAL

Church Field

Wr Twr

8

Rossington Comprehensive Sch & Don Valley Institute for Further Education

Stone Hills

7

Gravel Hill Plantation

Whinny Lane Plantation

MOUNT PLEASANT COTTS

Home Farm

A638

Mount Pleasant Hotel

Finningley Park

97

LC

COMMON LA

Sixteen Acre Plantation

Old Park

Park Plantation

HIGH COMMON LA

Hunster Grange

6

Rossington Hall Sch

STRIPE RD

Garden Field Plantation

Partridge Hill Holt

New Lodge

5

GREAT NORTH RD

RSPCA Centre

96

New England Cottage

White Mires Wood

Blackfirs

4

Hesley Park

Hesley Lodge

Martin Common Farm

3

B6463

Bawtry Forest

95

King's Wood

2

Pipers Wood

Martin Beck

Manor Holt

Wr Twr

A638

MARTIN LA

1

Tickhill High Common

MARTIN BECK LA

Martin Hall Cottages

Martin Grange

94

62   A   B   63   C   D   64   E   F

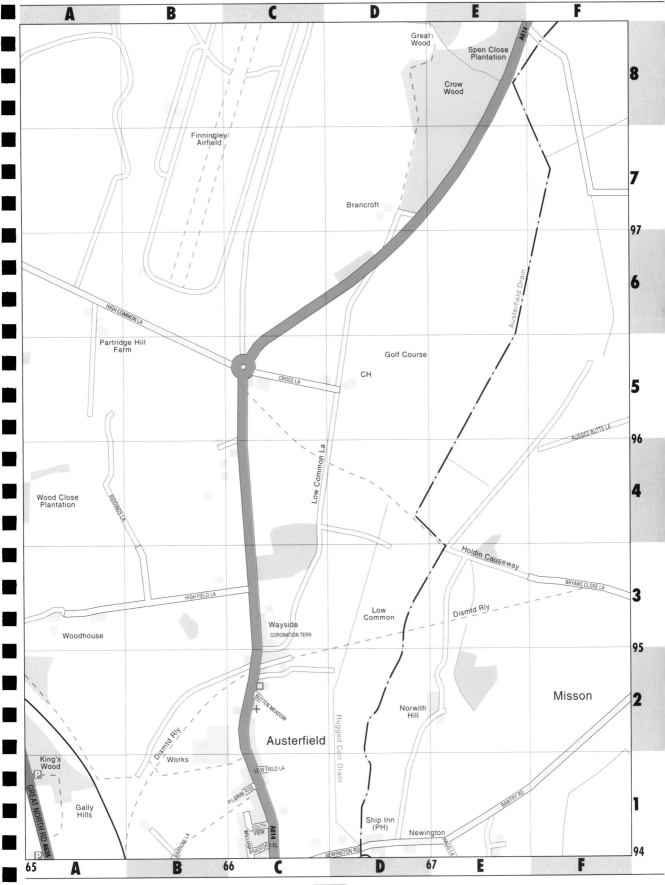

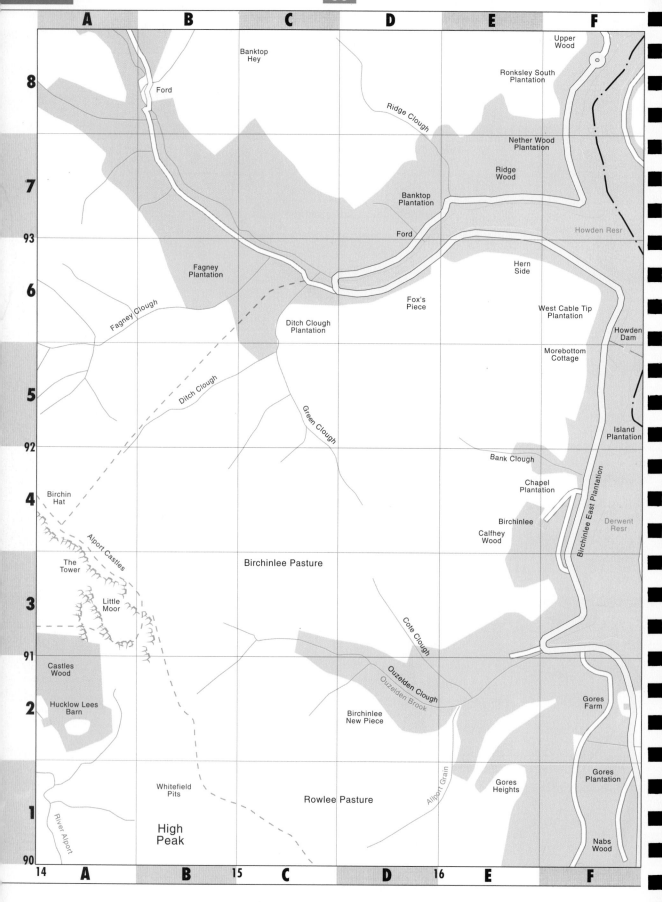

A B C D E F

8

Banktop
Hey

Ford

Ridge Clough

Upper
Wood

Ronksley South
Plantation

Nether Wood
Plantation

Ridge
Wood

7

Banktop
Plantation

93

Ford

Howden Resr

Fagney
Plantation

6

Fox's
Piece

Hern
Side

West Cable Tip
Plantation

Howden
Dam

Fagney Clough

Ditch Clough
Plantation

Morebottom
Cottage

5

Ditch Clough

Green Clough

Island
Plantation

92

Bank Clough

4

Birchin
Hat

Chapel
Plantation

Birchinlee

Calfhey
Wood

Birchinlee East Plantation

Derwent
Resr

Alport Castles

The
Tower

Birchinlee Pasture

3

Little
Moor

Cote Clough

91

Castles
Wood

Ouzelden Clough

Ouzelden Brook

Gores
Farm

2

Hucklow Lees
Barn

Birchinlee
New Piece

Gores
Heights

Gores
Plantation

Whitefield
Pits

Rowlee Pasture

Allport Grain

1

River Alport

High
Peak

Nabs
Wood

90

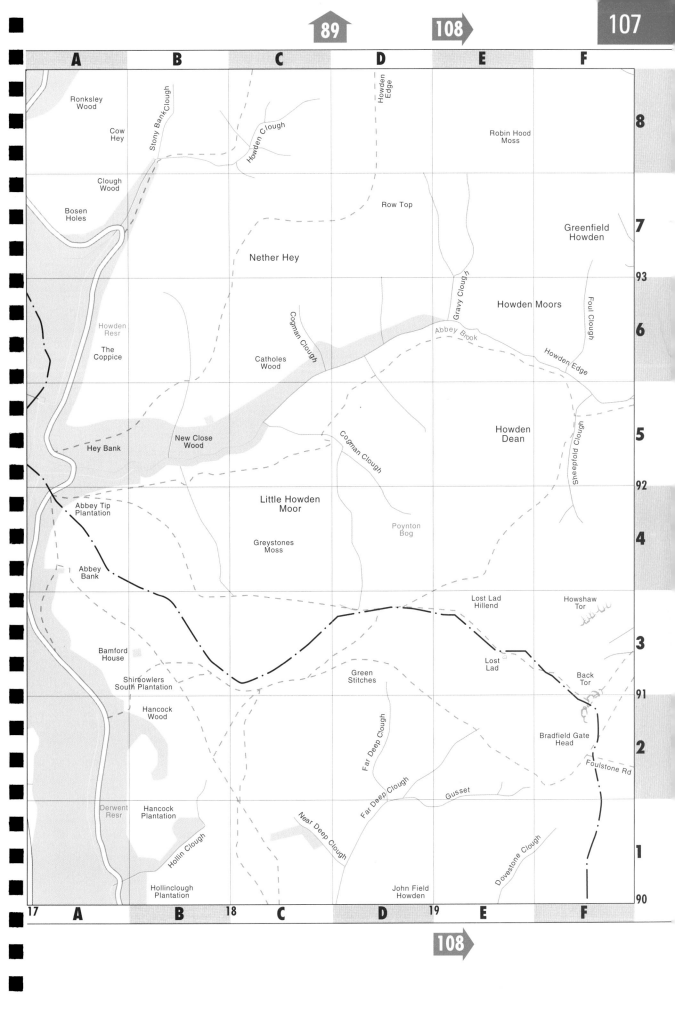

107
90

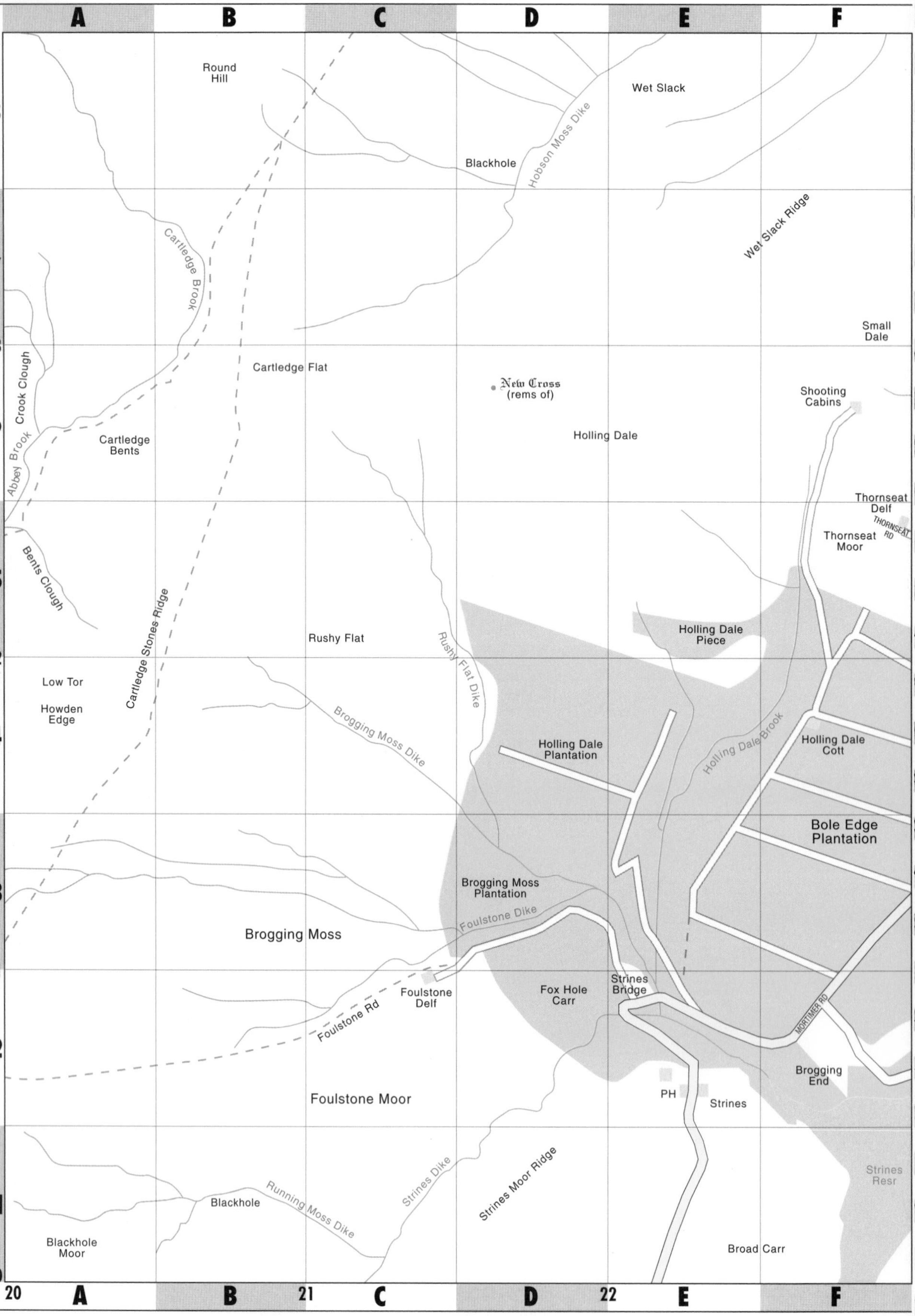
A
B
C
D
E
F
8
7
93
6
5
92
4
3
91
2
1
90
20
21
22
Round Hill
Wet Slack
Hobson Moss Dike
Blackhole
Wet Slack Ridge
Cartledge Brook
Small Dale
Crook Clough
Cartledge Flat
New Cross (rems of)
Shooting Cabins
Abbey Brook
Cartledge Bents
Holling Dale
Thornseat Delf
THORNSEAT RD
Thornseat Moor
Bents Clough
Cartledge Stones Ridge
Rushy Flat
Rushy Flat Dike
Holling Dale Piece
Low Tor
Howden Edge
Brogging Moss Dike
Holling Dale Plantation
Holling Dale Brook
Holling Dale Cott
Bole Edge Plantation
Brogging Moss Plantation
Foulstone Dike
Brogging Moss
Foulstone Delf
Foulstone Rd
Fox Hole Carr
Strines Bridge
MORTIMER RD
Brogging End
PH
Strines
Foulstone Moor
Strines Resr
Strines Dike
Strines Moor Ridge
Running Moss Dike
Blackhole
Blackhole Moor
Broad Carr

107
124

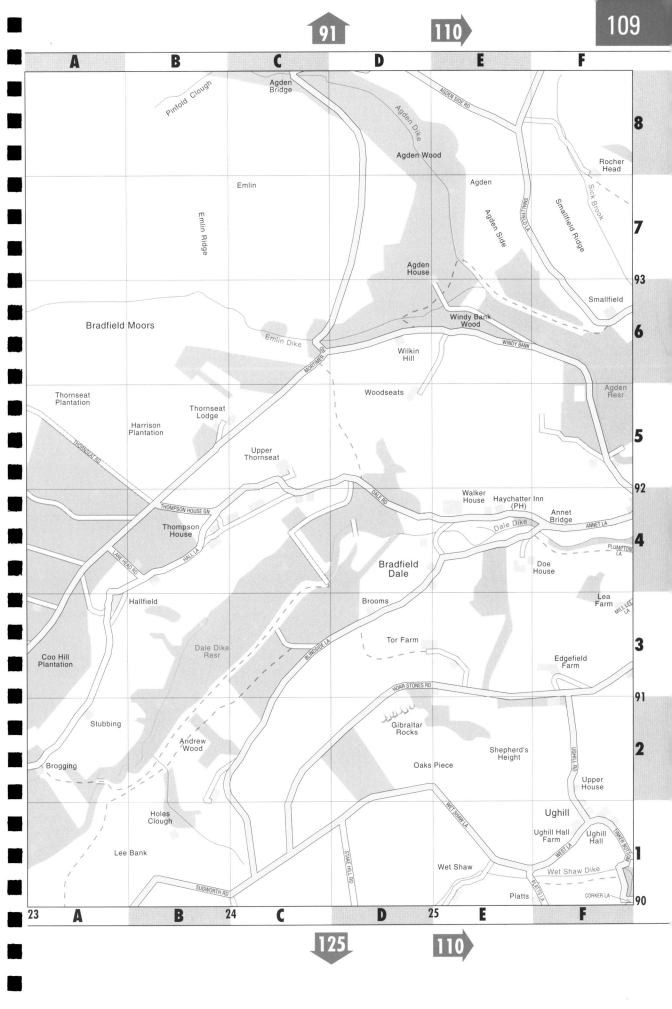

A B C D E F

8

West Nab

Peat Pits Farm
Peat Pits
Bent Hills
Bent Hills Farm
Bentholme
BENT HILLS LA
Hill House

Rocher Flat
ONESMOOR RD
BRIGHTHOLMLEE RD
PEAT PITS LA
LUMB LA
Lumb Bush
Coumes Brook

7

Rocher Wood
Bowsen
Brown House
Kirk Edge
ONESACRE RD
Edge Mount
Brittains Plantation
ONESMOOR BOTTOM

93

PENISTONE RD
WALSTENSMORE RD
BROWN HOUSE LA
Rocher End Brook
DELF RD

6

Bailey Hill
High Bradfield
Onesmoor

Rectory
Old Horns Inn
Castle Hill
Castle Bents
Kirk Edge House
KIRK EDGE RD
Convent of the Holy Ghost
Prospect Farm

5

Agden Resr
SMALLFIELD LA
Bradfield
WOODFALL LA
Watt House
BURNT HILL LA

92

Kirk Bridge
THE SMIDY
Low Bradfield
WINDY BANK
FAIR HOUSE LA
ANNET LA
Low Bradfield County Prim Sch
PLUMPTON LA
MILL RD
DALE CROFT
SMITHY BRIDGE RD
Mill Farm
Nether House Farm
Peck Hall
LOXLEY RD
PECK HALL LA
Cliffe House Farm
New Lathes
Primrose Cottage Farm
MOOR RD
HOLDWORTH LA

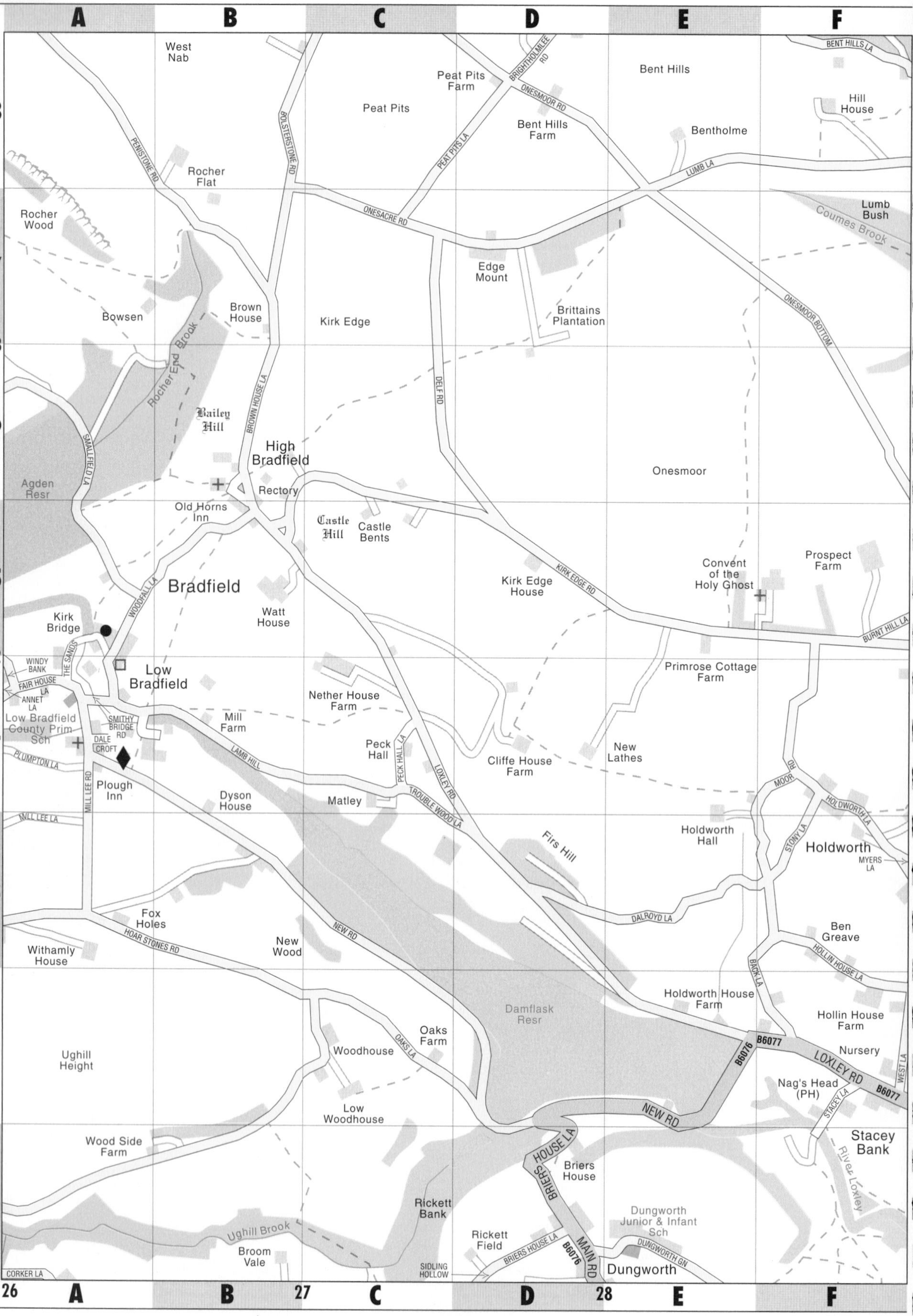

4

Plough Inn
Dyson House
LAMB HILL
Matley
TROUBLE WOOD LA
Firs Hill
Holdworth Hall
STONY LA
Holdworth
MYERS LA

3

MILL LEE LA
Fox Holes
HOAR STONES RD
New Wood
NEW RD
DALROYD LA
Ben Greave
HOLLIN HOUSE LA
BACK LA

Withamly House

91

Ughill Height
Woodhouse
OAKS LA
Oaks Farm
Damflask Resr
Holdworth House Farm
Hollin House Farm
Nursery
WEST LA

2

Low Woodhouse
B6076
B6077
LOXLEY RD
Nag's Head (PH)
STACEY LA
B6077
Stacey Bank
River Loxley

Wood Side Farm
NEW RD
BRIERS HOUSE LA
Briers House
Dungworth Junior & Infant Sch
DUNGWORTH GN

1

Ughill Brook
Rickett Bank
Rickett Field
BRIERS HOUSE LA
MAIN RD
B6076

90

CORKER LA
Broom Vale
SIDLING HOLLOW
Dungworth

26 A B 27 C D 28 E F

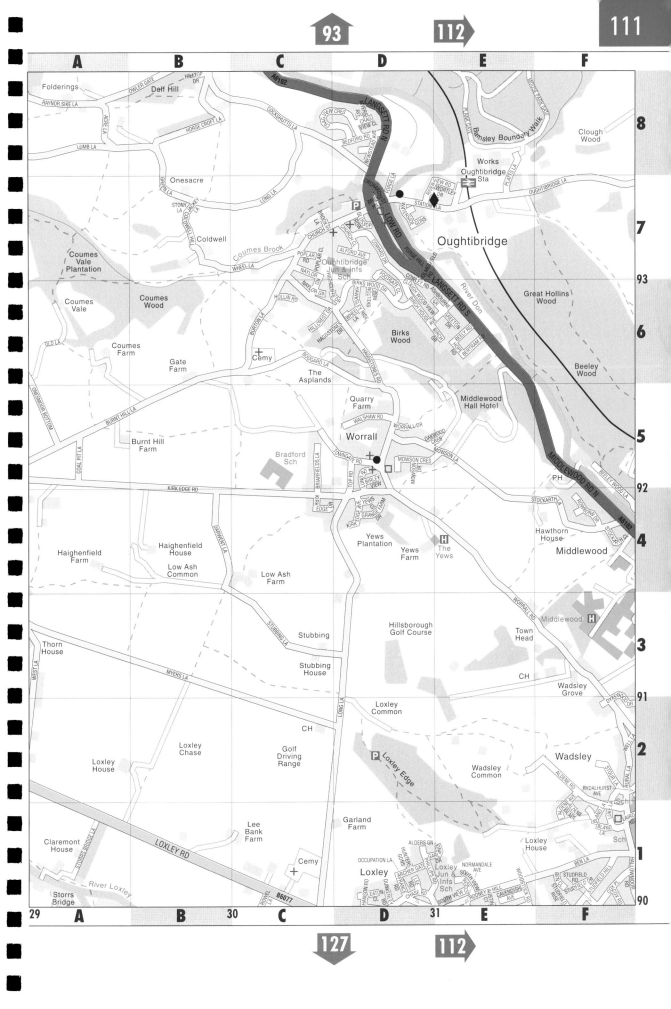

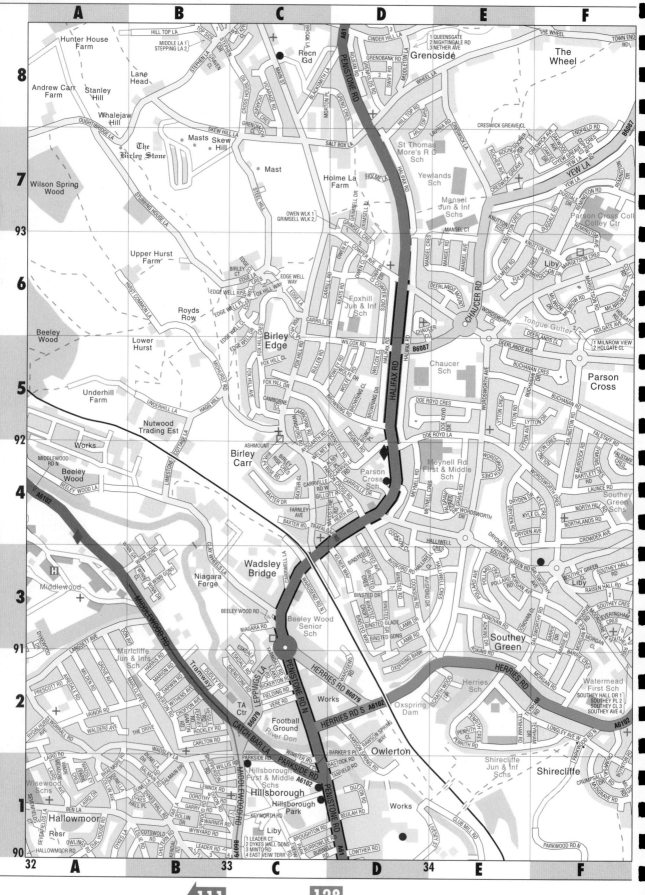

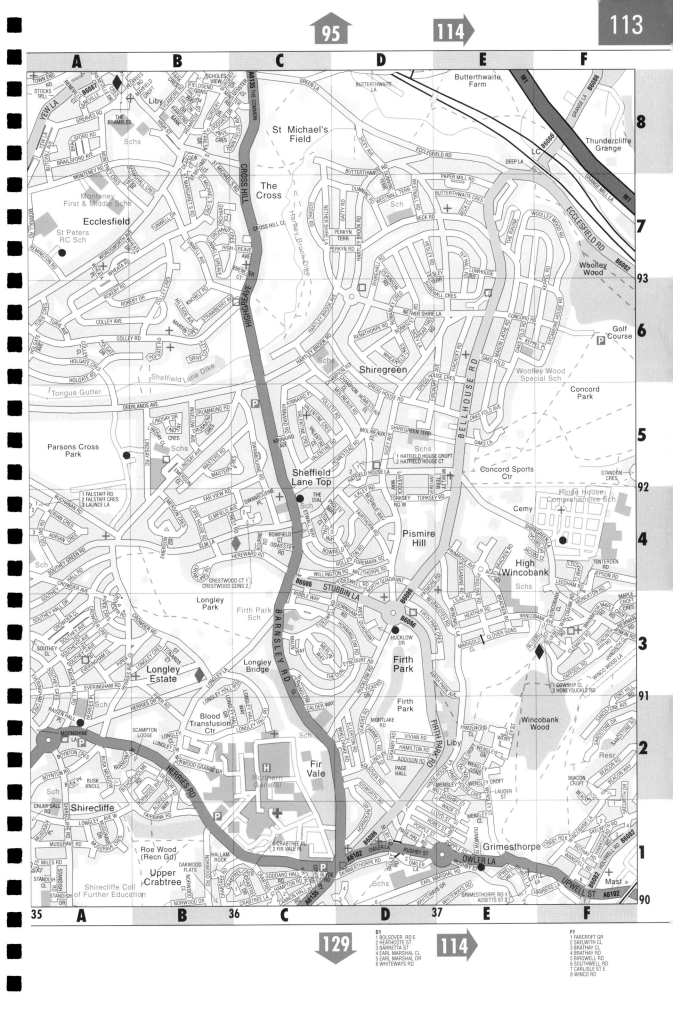

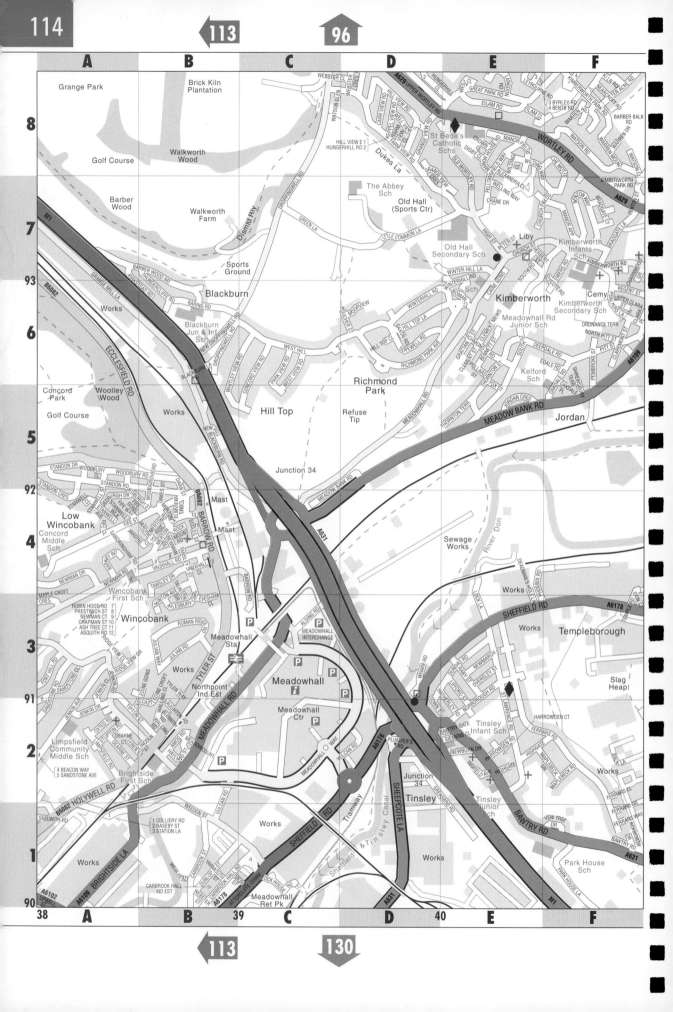

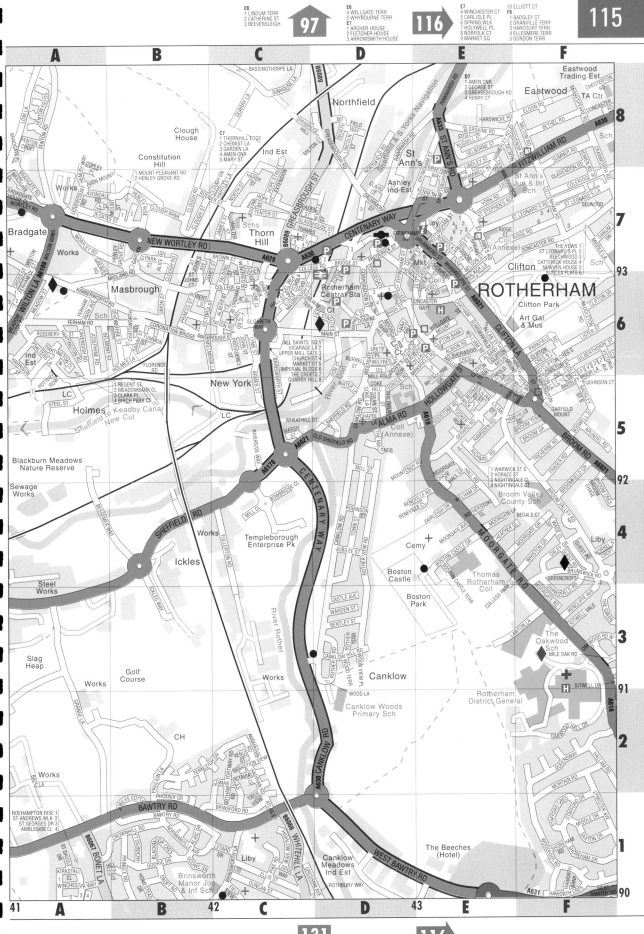

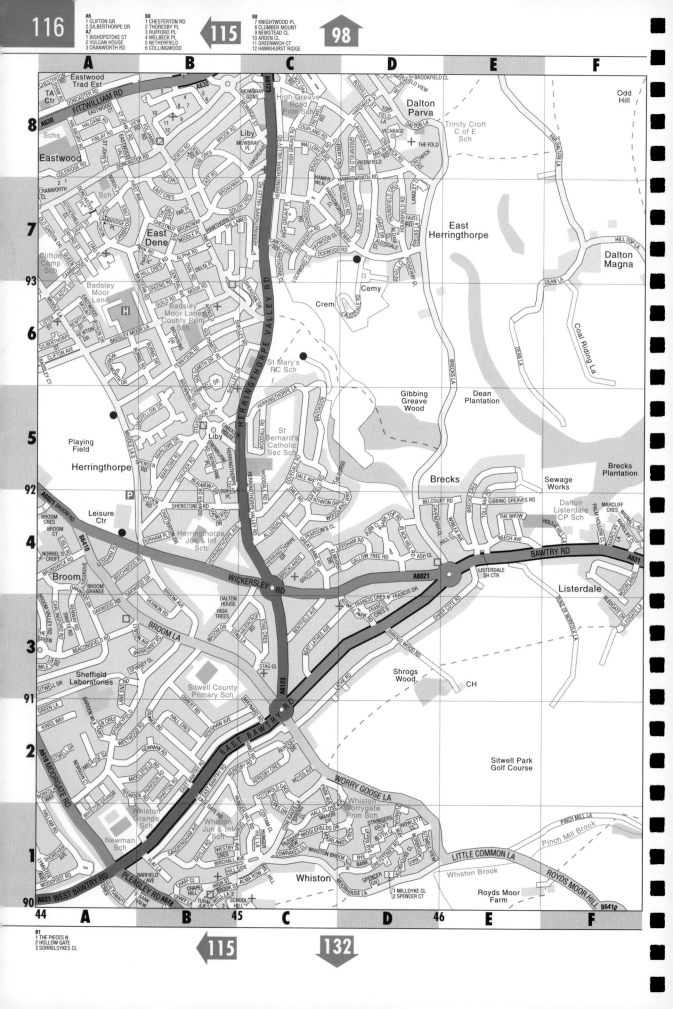

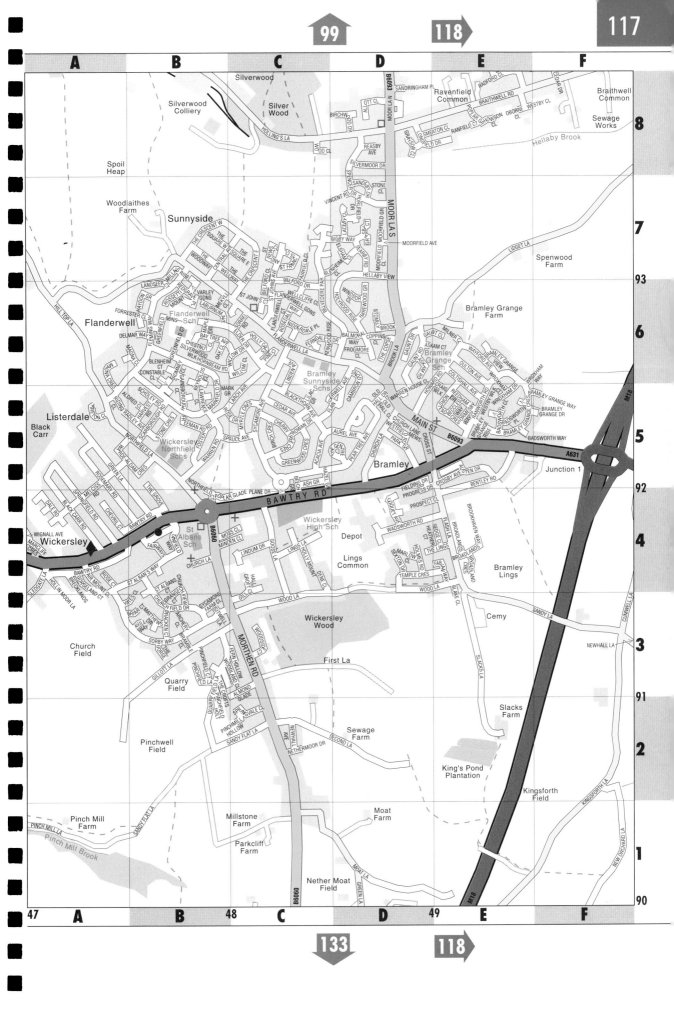

99
118

A   B   C   D   E   F

8
7
93
6
5
92
4
3
91
2
1
90

Silverwood
Silverwood Colliery
Silver Wood

B6093
SANDRINGHAM PL
Ravenfield Common
RADFORD CL
BRAITHWELL RD
CEDAR DR
Braithwell Common
Sewage Works

Hellaby Brook

Spoil Heap
Woodlaithes Farm
Sunnyside

MOOR LA N
MOOR LA S

Spenwood Farm
LIDGET LA

MOORFIELD AVE

Flanderwell
Listerdale
Black Carr

Flanderwell Sch
Wickersley Northfield Schs

Bramley Grange Farm
Bramley Grange Sch

Bramley Sunnyside Schs

MAIN ST
Bramley

M18

A631
Junction 1

Wickersley
St Albans Sch

BAWTRY RD

B6060

Wickersley High Sch
Depot
Lings Common

Bramley Lings

WOOD LA

Cemy
SANDY LA
NEWHALL LA

Church Field
Quarry Field

MORTHEN RD

Wickersley Wood
First La

Slacks Farm

Pinchwell Field

Sewage Farm

King's Pond Plantation

Kingsforth Field
KINGSFORTH LA

Pinch Mill Farm
PINCH MILL LA
Pinch Mill Brook
SANDY FLAT LA

Millstone Farm
Parkcliff Farm

Moat Farm

B6060
Nether Moat Field

M18
NEW ORCHARD LA

133
118

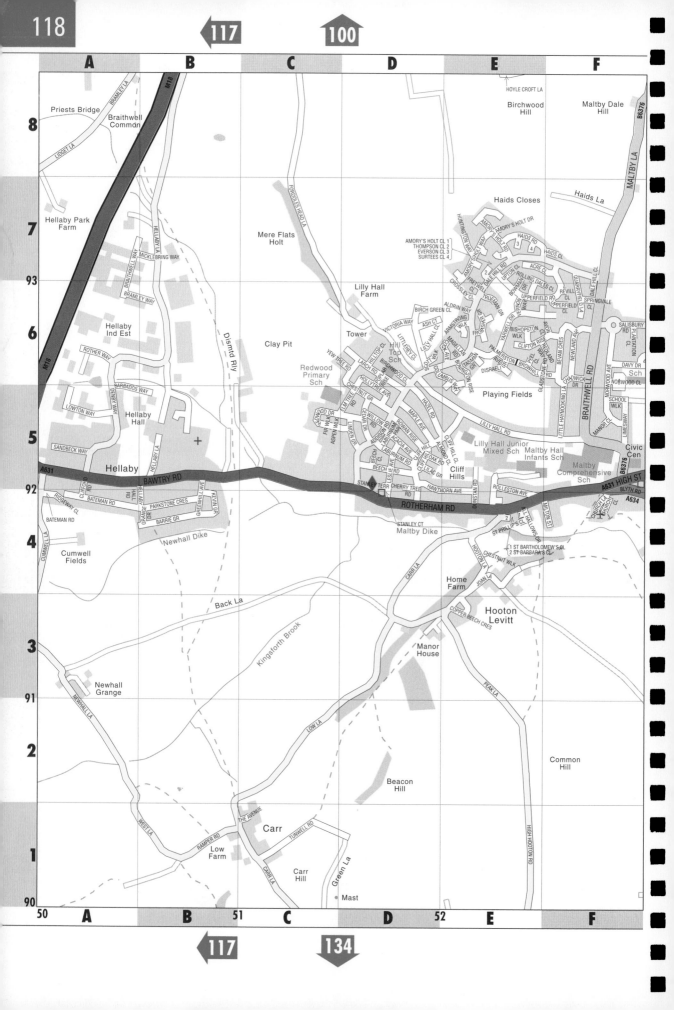

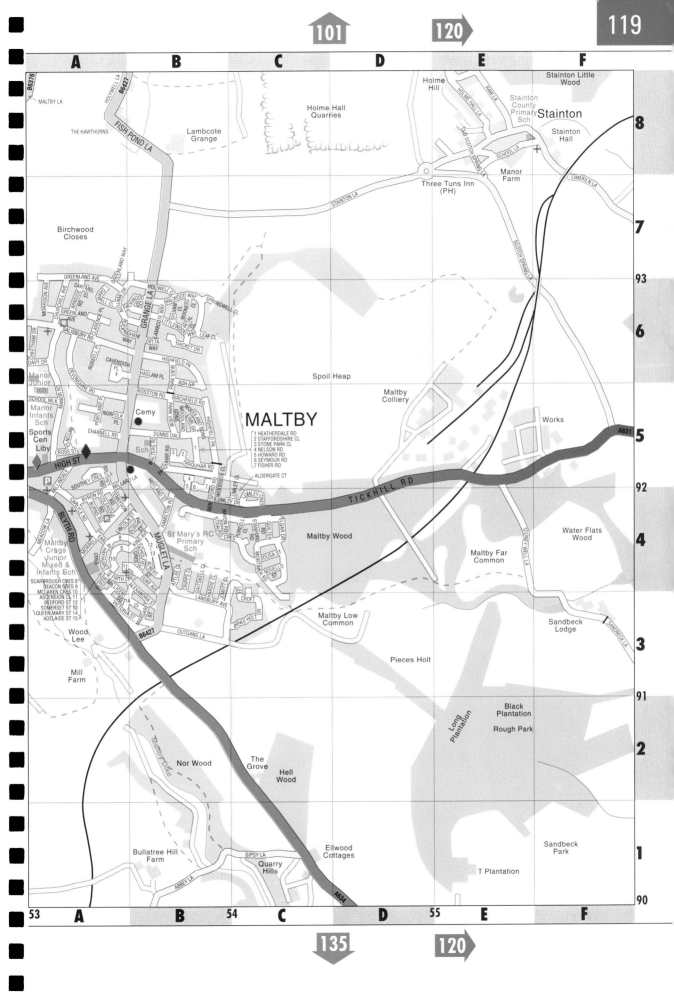

119   102

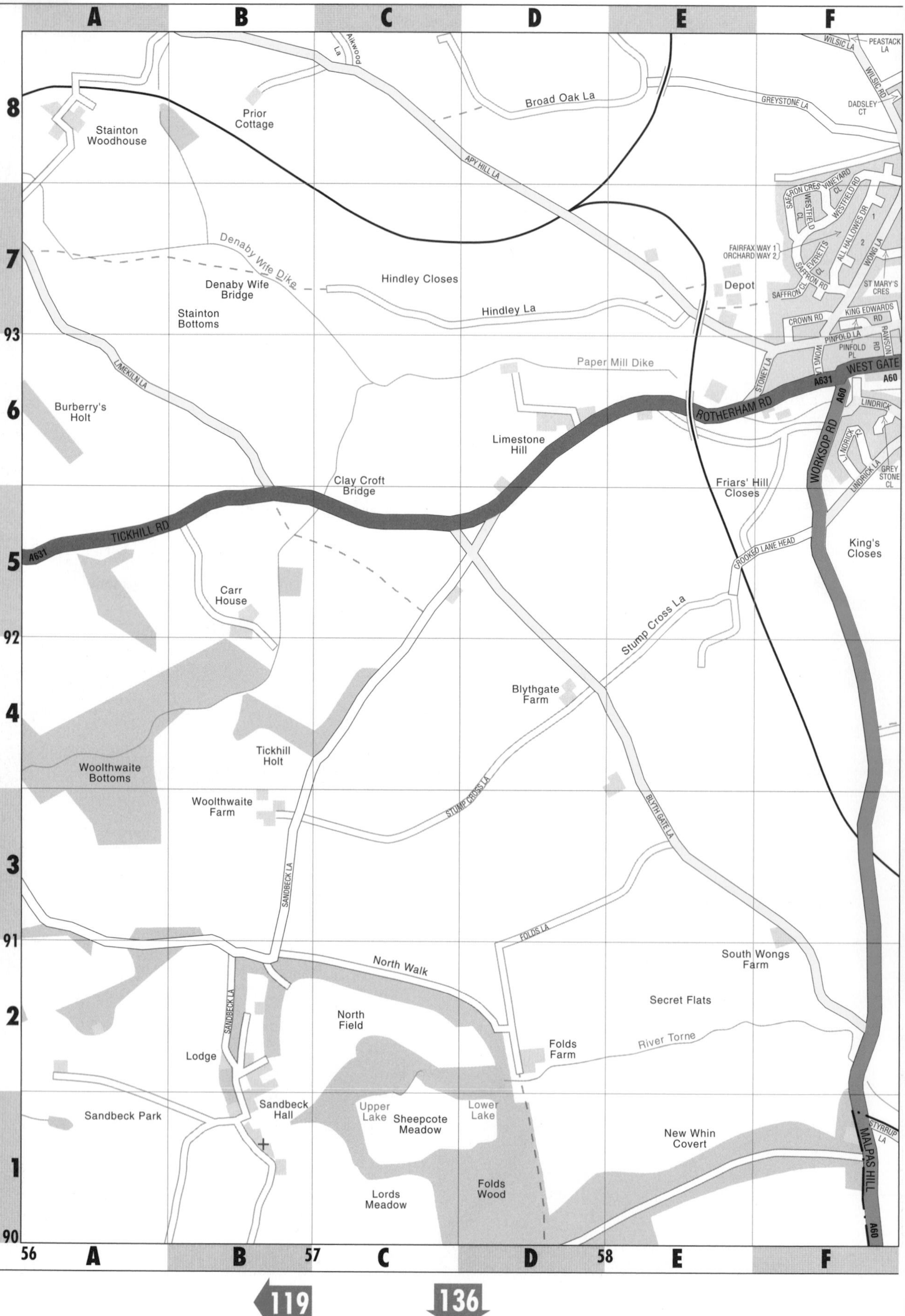

A   B   C   D   E   F

8
Stainton Woodhouse
Prior Cottage
Broad Oak La
WILSIC LA   PEASTACK GATE
GREYSTONE LA
DADSLEY CT
APY HILL LA

SAFFRON CRES   VINEYARD   WESTFIELD RD
WESTFIELD CL   WESTFIELD RD
7
Denaby Wife Dike
Hindley Closes
FAIRFAX WAY 1
ORCHARD WAY 2
ALL HALLOWES DR
Denaby Wife Bridge
Depot
SAFFRON CL
ST MARY'S CRES
Stainton Bottoms
Hindley La
KING EDWARDS
93
L MEKILN LA
CROWN RD
PINFOLD LA
SAFFRON RD
RAWSON RD
Paper Mill Dike
PINFOLD PL
STONEY LA
WEST GATE
A631
A60
6
Burberry's Holt
ROTHERHAM RD
A60
LINDRICK
Limestone Hill
WORKSOP RD
LINDRICK CL
GREY STONE CL
Clay Croft Bridge
Friars' Hill Closes
CROOKSD LANE HEAD
King's Closes
5
A631   TICKHILL RD
92
Carr House
Stump Cross La
4
Blythgate Farm
Woolthwaite Bottoms
Tickhill Holt
91
Woolthwaite Farm
STUMP CROSS LA
BLYTH GATE LA
3
SANDBECK LA
FOLDS LA
South Wongs Farm
North Walk
Secret Flats
2
North Field
SANDBECK LA
River Torne
Folds Farm
Lodge
Sandbeck Hall
Upper Lake
Sheepcote Meadow
Lower Lake
New Whin Covert
STYARUP LA
Sandbeck Park
MALPAS HILL
A60
1
Lords Meadow
Folds Wood
90
56   A   B   57   C   D   58   E   F

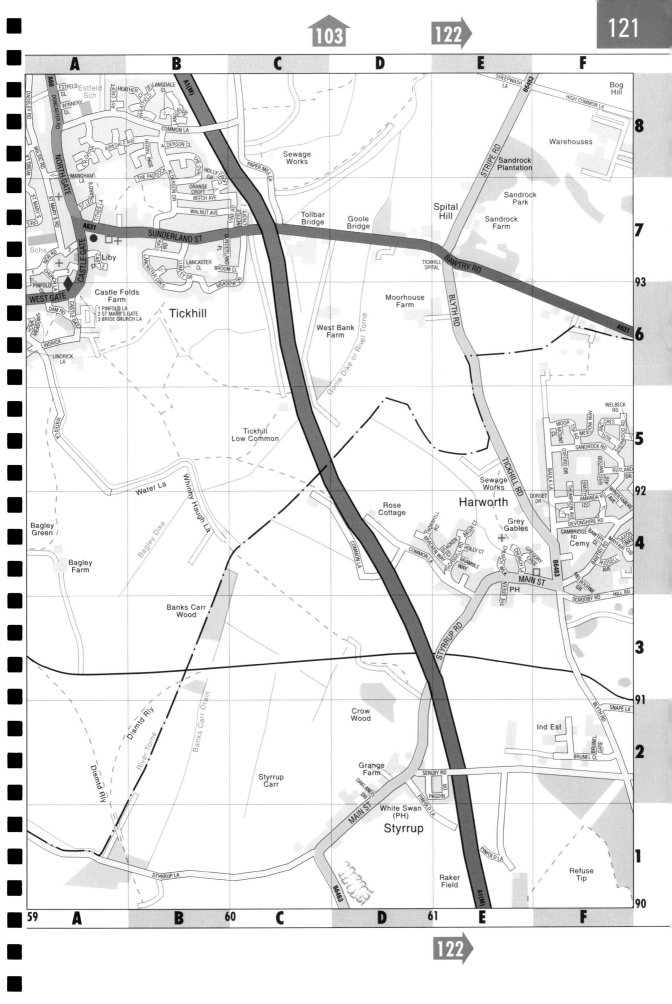

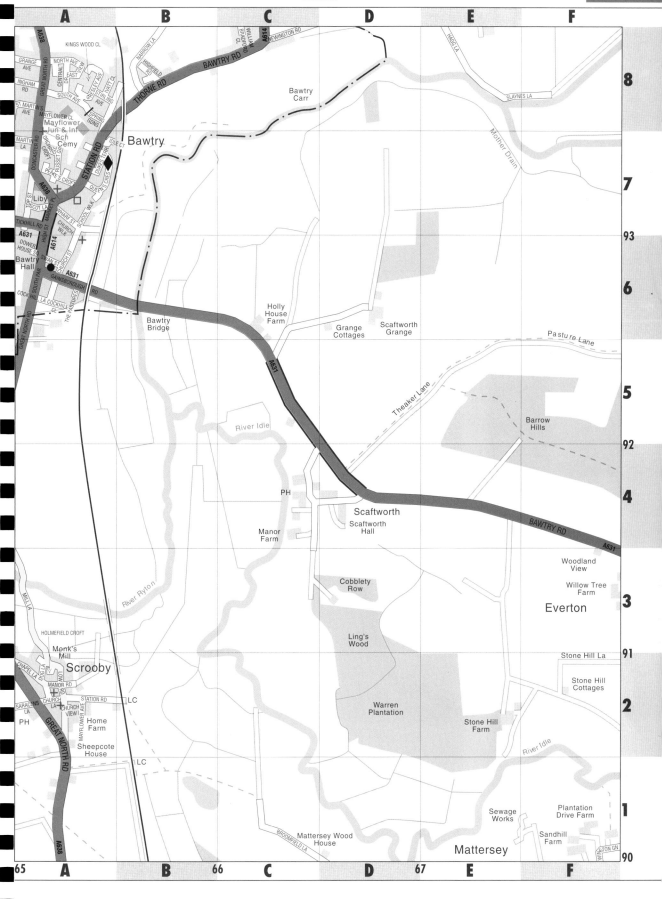

108

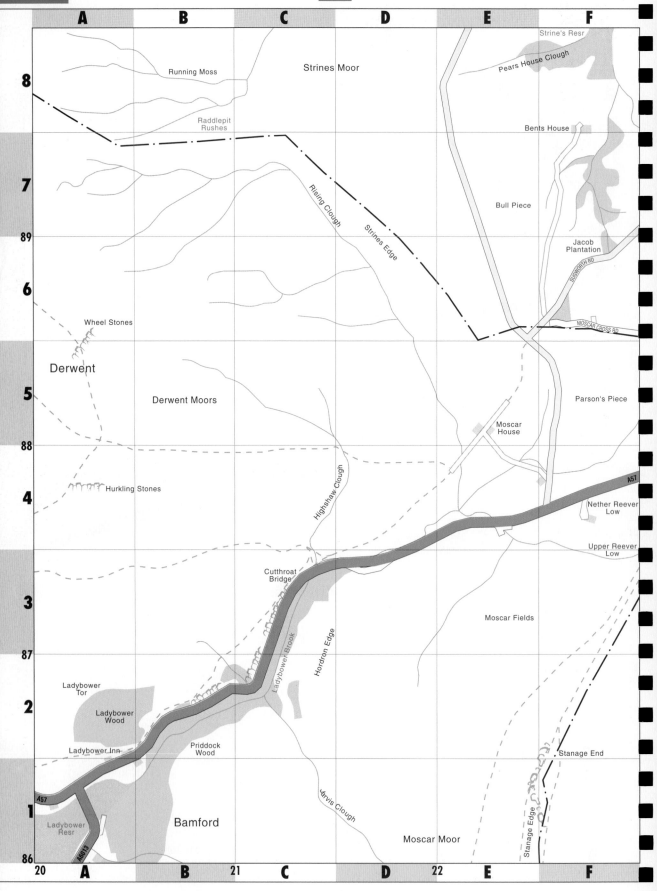

Strine's Resr

Pears House Clough

Running Moss

Strines Moor

Raddlepit
Rushes

Bents House

Rising Clough

Strines Edge

Bull Piece

Jacob
Plantation

SUGWORTH RD

Wheel Stones

MOSCAR CROSS RD

Derwent

Parson's Piece

Derwent Moors

Moscar
House

Hurkling Stones

Highshaw Clough

A57

Nether Reever
Low

Upper Reever
Low

Cutthroat
Bridge

Moscar Fields

Ladybower Brook

Hordron Edge

Ladybower
Tor

Ladybower
Wood

Priddock
Wood

Stanage End

Ladybower Inn

Jarvis Clough

Stanage Edge

A57

Bamford

Moscar Moor

Ladybower
Resr

A6013

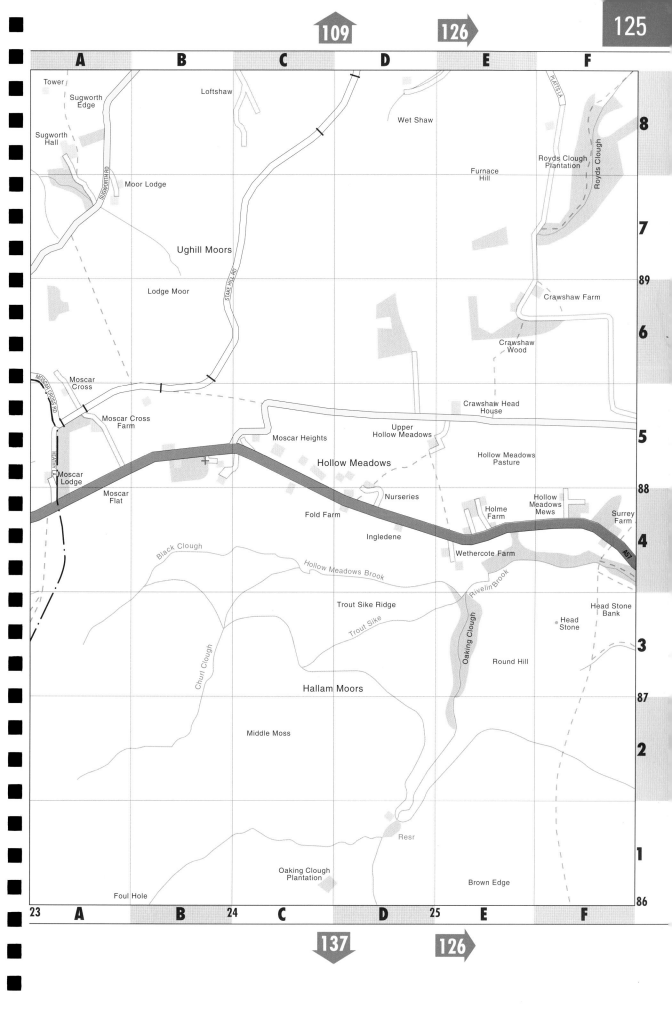

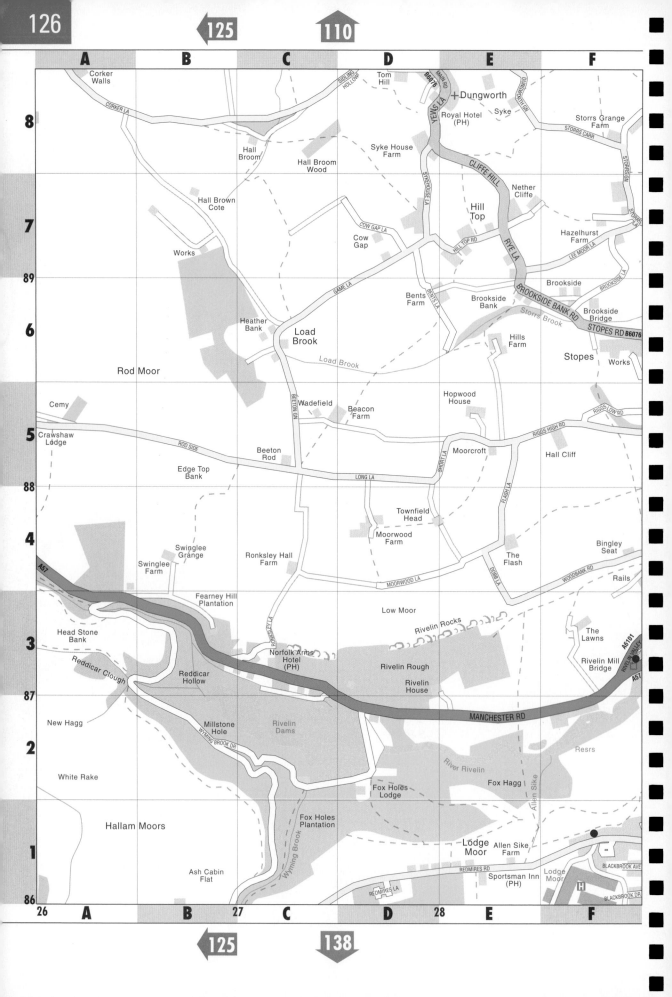

125
110

A   B   C   D   E   F

8

Corker
Walls

CORKER LA

Hall
Broom

Hall Broom
Wood

SIDLING HOLLOW

Tom
Hill

Dungworth

MAIN RD

B6076

YEWS LA

Royal Hotel
(PH)

Syke

Syke House
Farm

CLIFFE HILL

DUCKMANTON

DENTH GN

Storrs Grange
Farm

STORRS CARR

STORRS GN

STORRS LA

7

Hall Brown
Cote

Works

COW GAP LA

Cow
Gap

Hill
Top

HILL TOP RD

RYE LA

LEE MOOR LA

Nether
Cliffe

Hazelhurst
Farm

89

GAME LA

Heather
Bank

Load
Brook

Bents
Farm

BENTS LA

Brookside
Bank

Brookside
Bank

BROOKSIDE BANK RD

Storrs Brook

Brookside

BROOKSIDE LA

Brookside
Bridge

STOPES RD B6076

6

Rod Moor

BEETON GN

Wadefield

Load Brook

Beacon
Farm

Hopwood
House

Hills
Farm

Stopes

Works

RIGGS LOW RD

Cemy

Crawshaw
Lodge

ROD SIDE

Beeton
Rod

Moorcroft

SHORT LA

RIGGS HIGH RD

Hall Cliff

5

Edge Top
Bank

LONG LA

FLASH LA

88

Swinglee
Grange

Ronksley Hall
Farm

Townfield
Head

Moorwood
Farm

The
Flash

COBB LA

Bingley
Seat

4

A57

Swinglee
Farm

Fearney Hill
Plantation

MOORWOOD LA

WOODBANK RD

Rails

Head Stone
Bank

RONKSLEY LA

Low Moor

Rivelin Rocks

The
Lawns

A6101

RIVELIN VALLEY

3

Reddicar Clough

Reddicar
Hollow

Norfolk Arms
Hotel
(PH)

Rivelin Rough

Rivelin
House

Rivelin Mill
Bridge

A57

87

New Hagg

Millstone
Hole

WYMING BROOK DR

Rivelin
Dams

MANCHESTER RD

2

White Rake

Wyming Brook

Resrs

River Rivelin

Fox Hagg

Allen Sike

1

Hallam Moors

Fox Holes
Lodge

Fox Holes
Plantation

Lodge
Moor

Allen Sike
Farm

REDMIRES RD

Sportsman Inn
(PH)

Lodge
Moor

Blackbrook Ave

H

86

Ash Cabin
Flat

REDMIRES LA

BLACKBROOK DR

125
138

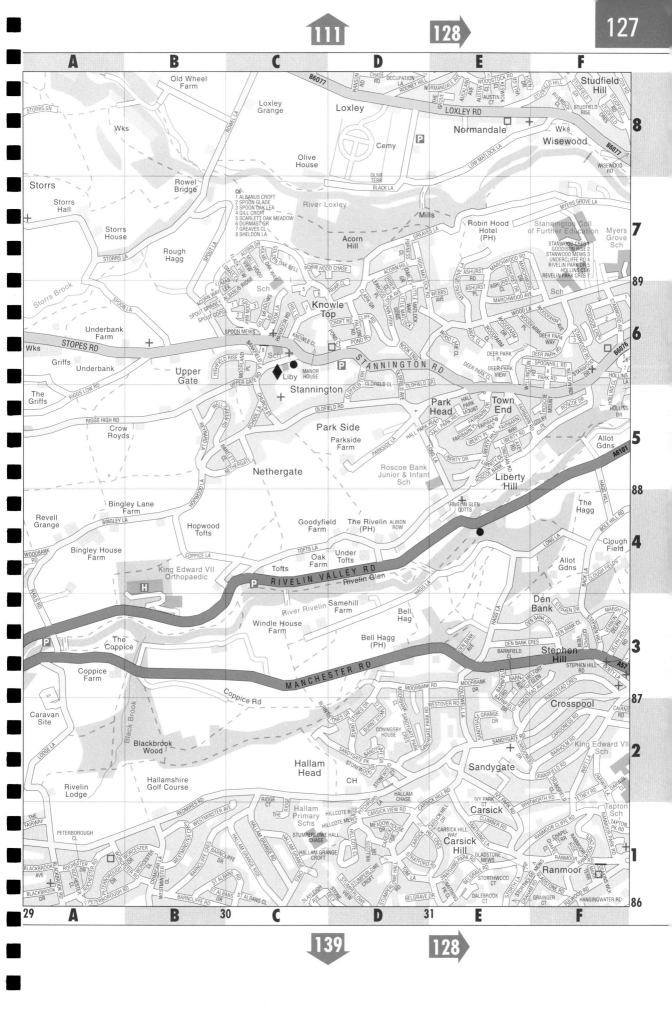

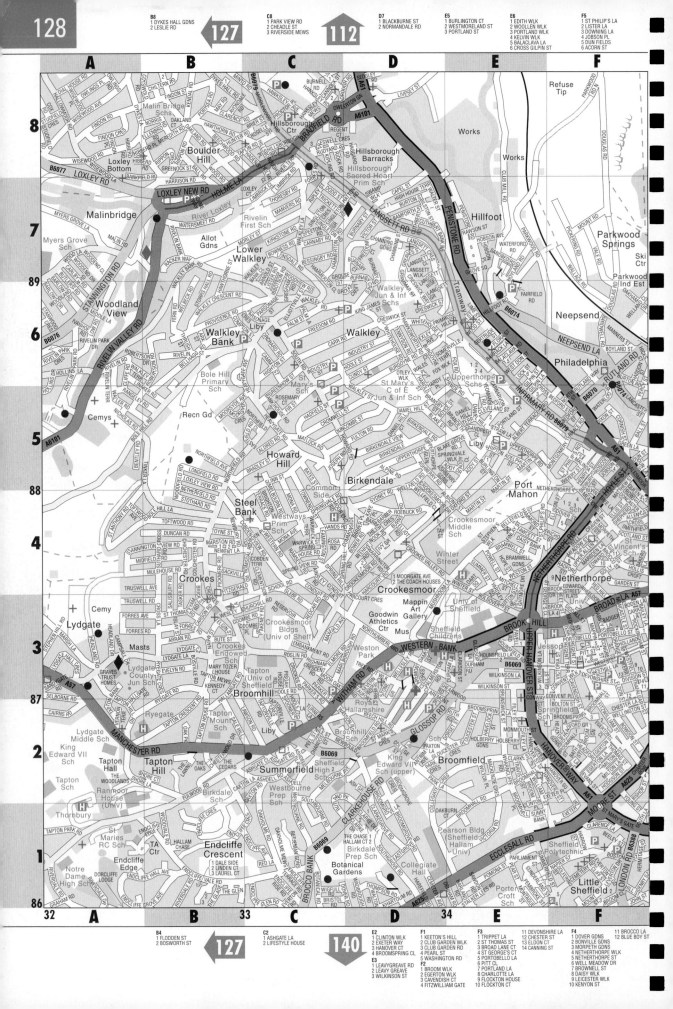

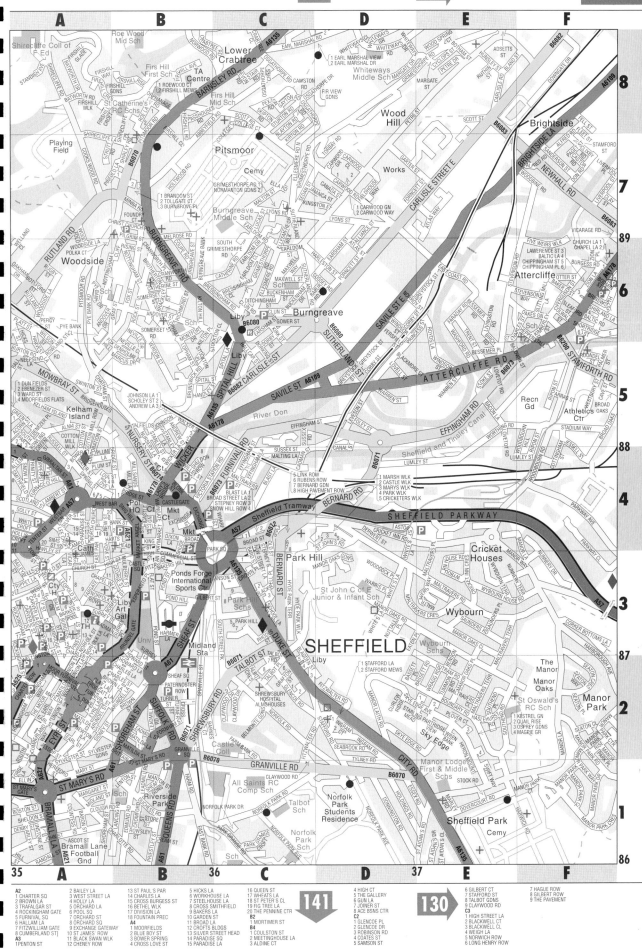

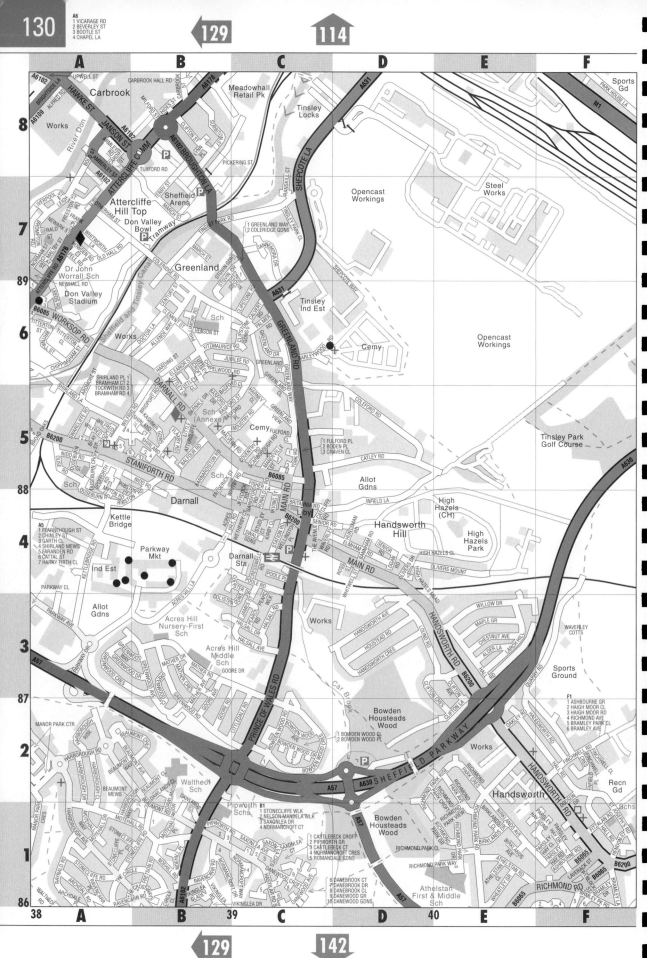

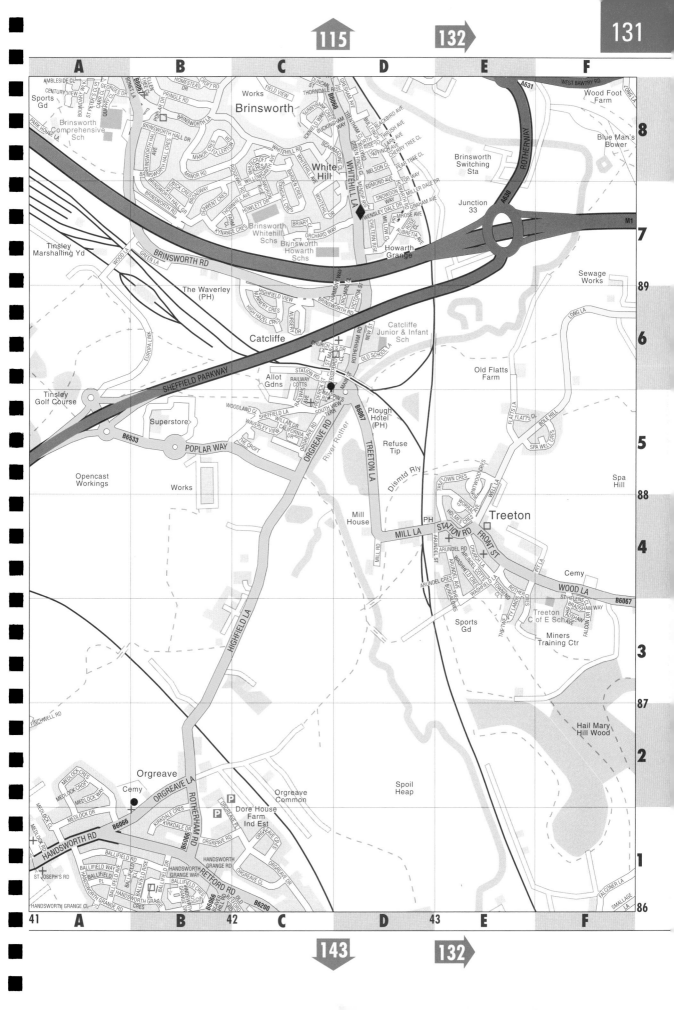

A B C D E F

8

7

89

6

5

88

4

3

87

2

1

86

41 42 43

Sports Gd

Brinsworth Comprehensive Sch

AMBLESIDE CL
CENTURY VIEW
ST GEORGES DR
ST PETER'S CLS
CART CL
QUARRY CL
BOUNDARY WK
HOMESTEAD RD
CROFT RD
POPLAR DR
PRINGLE RD
FELLEN LA
B6067

Works
FIELD VIEW

Brinsworth

DUNCAN ST
THORNDALE RD
GRESHAM AVE
B6066

SUNNYBANK
ICKNIELD WAY
BUCKINGHAM WAY
BLACKBIRD AVE
THRUSH AVE
CLARK AVE
AFFINCH ST
CHERRY TREE CL
PEAR TREE CL

A631
WEST BAWTRY RD
CONGA CL

Wood Foot Farm

Blue Man's Bower

PARK HOUSE LA
Brinsworth Hall Dr
MANOR CR
FLAHERTY
WHITEHILL RD
WHITEHILL RD

White Hill

WHITEHILL LA

NELSON CL
EDMUND AVE
SNOWDON AVE
WILLOW CL
TOR WAY
MILLER DALE AVE
GRAHAM AVE
ROSE AVE
AUBRETIA AVE

Brinsworth Switching Sta

ROTHERWAY

Brinsworth Hall Dr
Brinsworth Hall Gr
BROADWAY
BRICK CRES
DEWENT CRES
THORNHILL AVE
HOWLETT RD
KYNANCE CRES
CRYSTAL CRES
MOY CRES
RIDGEWAY AVE
WILLINGHAM CRES
BARRON CRES
WHITEHILL AVE

Brinsworth Whitehill Schs

BRIARY
ORCHARD WAY

Brinsworth Howarth Schs

WENSLEY DALE DR
CHILTERN RISE
MROSE AVE

Junction 33

A630

M1

Tinsley Marshalling Yd

WOOD LA
GREEN LA

BRINSWORTH RD

The Waverley (PH)

HIGHFIELD VIEW
HIGH HAZEL CRES
NURSERY DR
NUMBERY CRES
HARMONY WAY
VICTORIA ST
NEW ST
BRINSWORTH RD
ORCHARD RD
ROTHERHAM RD

Catcliffe Junior & Infant Sch

Sewage Works

LONG LA

Old Flatts Farm

Catcliffe

CHURCH ST
ST MARY'S DR
FISHPOND RD
OLD SCHOOL LA

SHEFFIELD PARKWAY

EUROPA LINK

Tinsley Golf Course

Allot Gdns

STATION RD
RAILWAY COTTS
RAILWAY TERR
SOUTH VIEW
MAIN ST
MAPPIN'S

WOODLAND RD
SHEFFIELD LA
WILLANS CR
CALIFORNIA DR
WAVERLEY VIEW
FREDERICK ST
ORGREAVE RD

Plough Hotel (PH)

Refuse Tip

FLATTS LA
FLATTS CL
BOLE HILL
SPA WELL CRES

Spa Hill

Superstore

B6533

POPLAR WAY

THE CROFT

River Rother

B6067

TREETON LA

Dismtd Rly

TREE TOWN CRES
GRINYWOOD CRES

WELL LA

Opencast Workings

Works

Mill House

Mill La

WORRALL AVE
HOLMES CRES

Treeton

Cemy

Mill Rd

MILL LA

STATION RD
FRONT ST

PH
ARUNDEL RD
ARUNDEL ST
ARUNDEL CRES
ARUNDEL AVE
WASHFIELD CRES
WASHFIELD LA
CHURCH LA
CHURCH COTTS
TOWEND
ROTHER CRES
PITT LA
ST HELENS CL
BRADSHAW DR
FALCON DR

WOOD LA
B6067

Cemy

HIGHFIELD LA

Sports Gd

THE TWELVE
CITY LANES
BUNGALOWS

Treeton C of E Sch

Miners Training Ctr

FINCHWELL RD

Hail Mary Hill Wood

Orgreave

MEDLOCK CRES
MEDLOCK CROFT
MEDLOCK WAY
MEDLOCK DR
MEDLOCK CL

Cemy

ORGREAVE LA

ROTHERHAM RD
B6066
KIRKDALE CRES
KIRKDALE CL

P
P
ORGREAVE LA
ORGREAVE RD
ORGREAVE DR
ORGREAVE CL
ORGREAVE CA

Dore House Farm Ind Est

Orgreave Common

Spoil Heap

B6066
HANDSWORTH RD

BALLIFIELD RD
BALLIFIELD WAY
BALLIFIELD AVE
BALLIFIELD PL
BALLIFIELD RISE
BALLIFIELD CRES

HANDSWORTH GRANGE RD
HANDSWORTH GRANGE WAY
HANDSWORTH GRANGE CRES
HANDSWORTH GRANGE CL

RETFORD RD

B6200

FALCONER LA
SMALLAGE LA

ST JOSEPH'S RD
ST JOSEPH'S CL

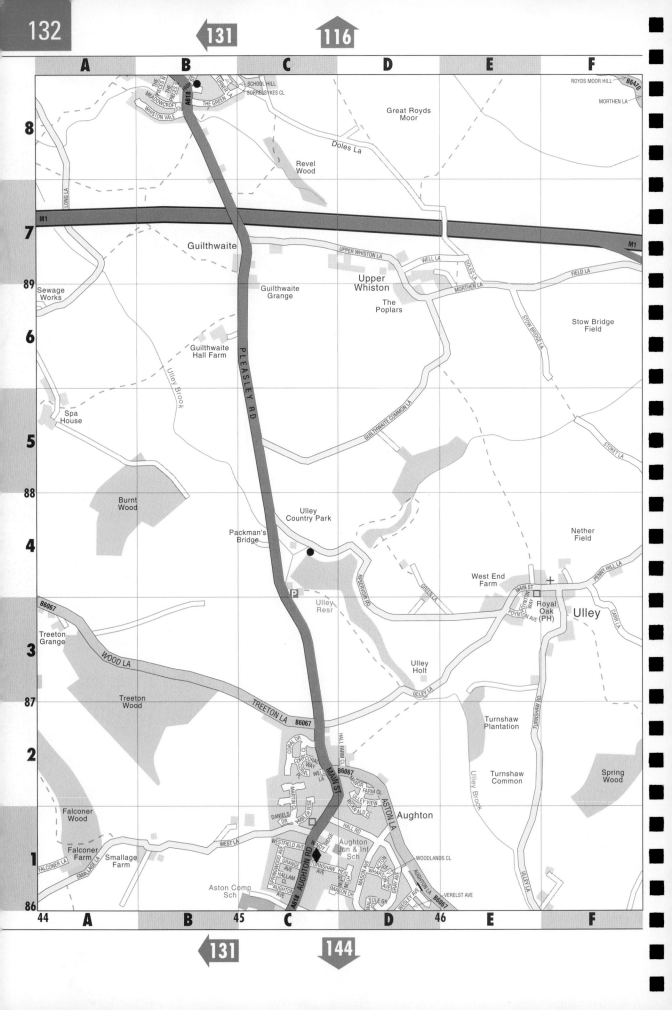

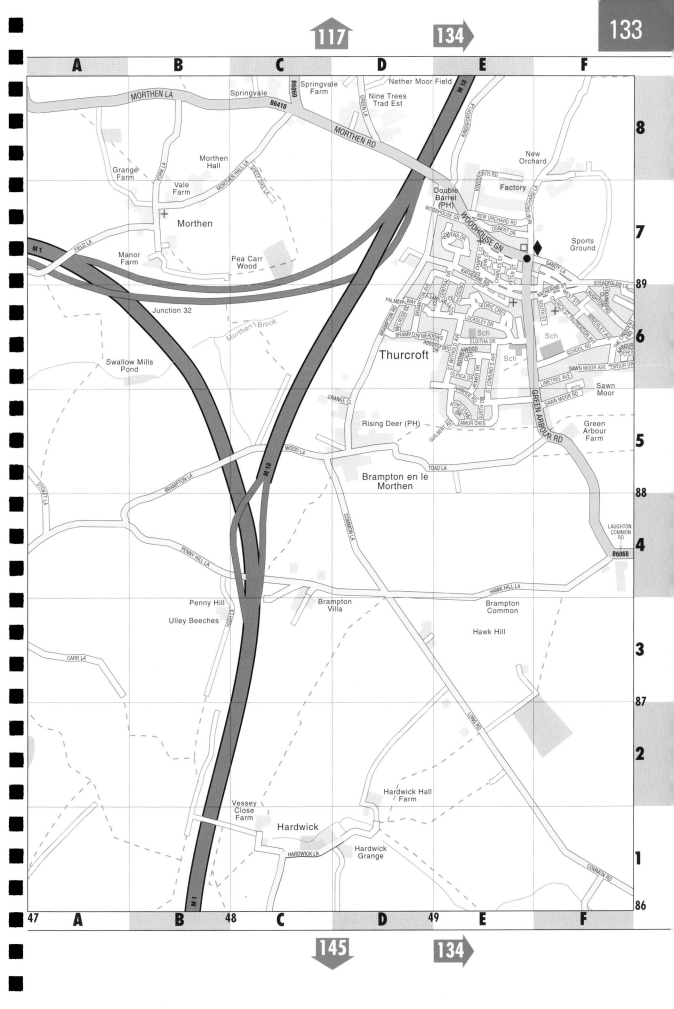

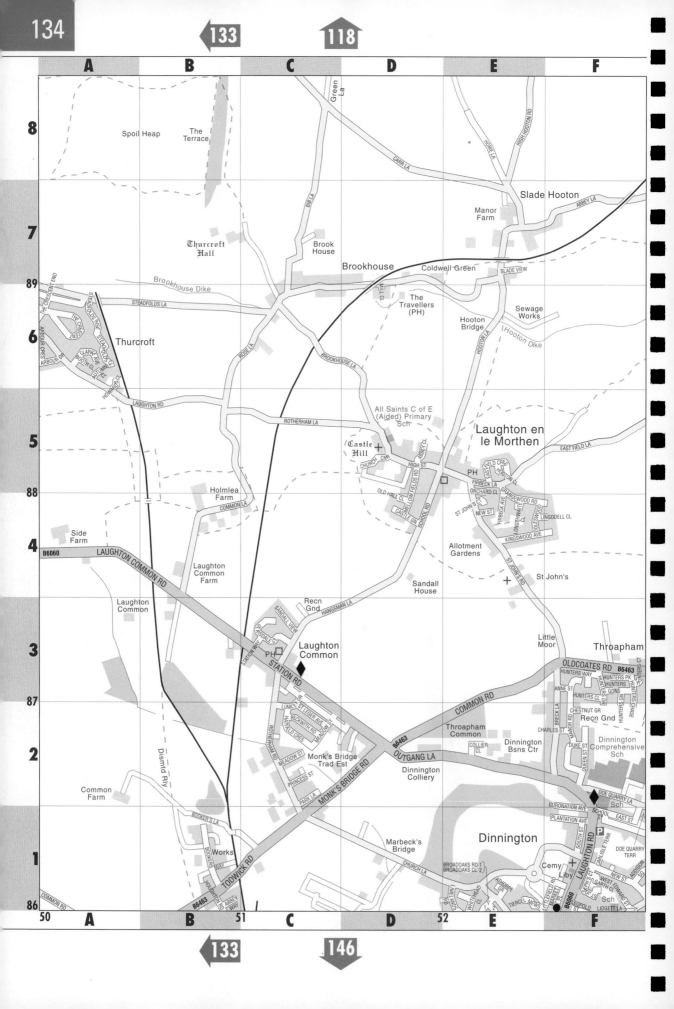

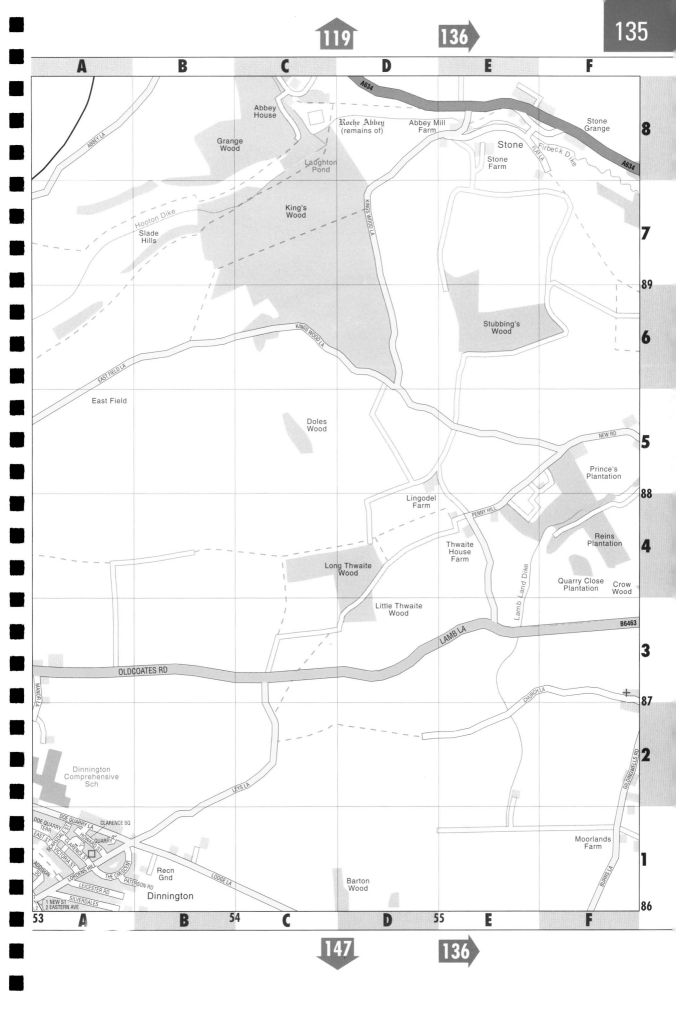

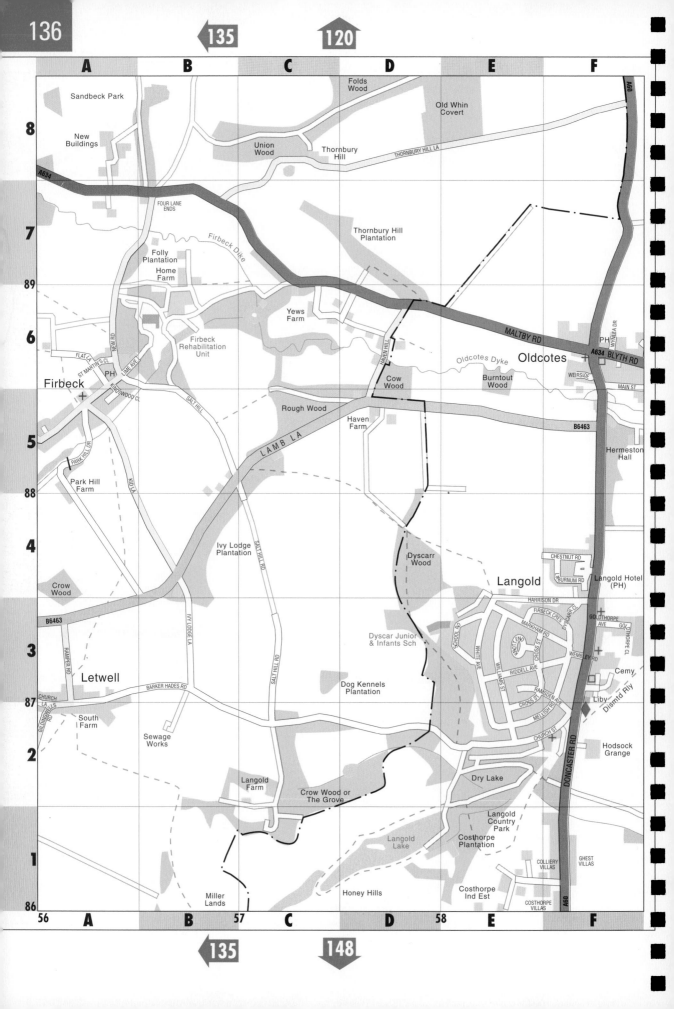

A   B   C   D   E   F

8

Sandbeck Park

New Buildings

Folds Wood

Old Whin Covert

Union Wood

Thornbury Hill

THORNBURY HILL LA

A634

FOUR LANE ENDS

7

Firbeck Dike

Thornbury Hill Plantation

Folly Plantation

Home Farm

89

Yews Farm

6

NEW RD

FLAT LA

ST MARTIN'S CL

PH

LIME AVE

Firbeck Rehabilitation Unit

MALTBY RD

Oldcotes

Oldcotes Dyke

PH

A634 BLYTH RD

WYNLEA DR

WEIRSIDE

MAIN ST

Firbeck

KINGSWOOD CL

SALT HILL

HAVEN HILL

Cow Wood

Burntout Wood

5

PARK HILL DR

Rough Wood

Haven Farm

B6463

Hermeston Hall

LAMB LA

KID LA

Park Hill Farm

88

4

SALT HILL RD

Ivy Lodge Plantation

Dyscarr Wood

CHESTNUT RD

LABURNUM RD

Langold Hotel (PH)

Crow Wood

Langold

HARRISON DR

FIRBECK CRES

DYSCARR CL

B6463

RAMPER RD

IVY LODGE LA

Dyscar Junior & Infants Sch

SCHOOL RD

WHITE AVE

MARKHAM RD

SCOTT RD

CROSS ST

GOLDTHORPE AVE

GOLDTHORPE CL

3

Letwell

BARKER HADES RD

Dog Kennels Plantation

WILLIAMS ST

RIDDELL AVE

RAMSDEN AVE

WEMBLEY RD

Cemy

87

CHURCH LA

GILDINGWELLS RD

South Farm

CROSS ST

MELLISH RD

Liby

Dismtd Rly

2

Sewage Works

Langold Farm

Dry Lake

CHURCH ST

DONCASTER RD

Hodsock Grange

Crow Wood or The Grove

Langold Country Park

Costhorpe Plantation

Langold Lake

COLLIERY VILLAS

GHEST VILLAS

1

Miller Lands

Honey Hills

Costhorpe Ind Est

COSTHORPE VILLAS

A60

86

56   A   57   B   C   57   D   58   E   F

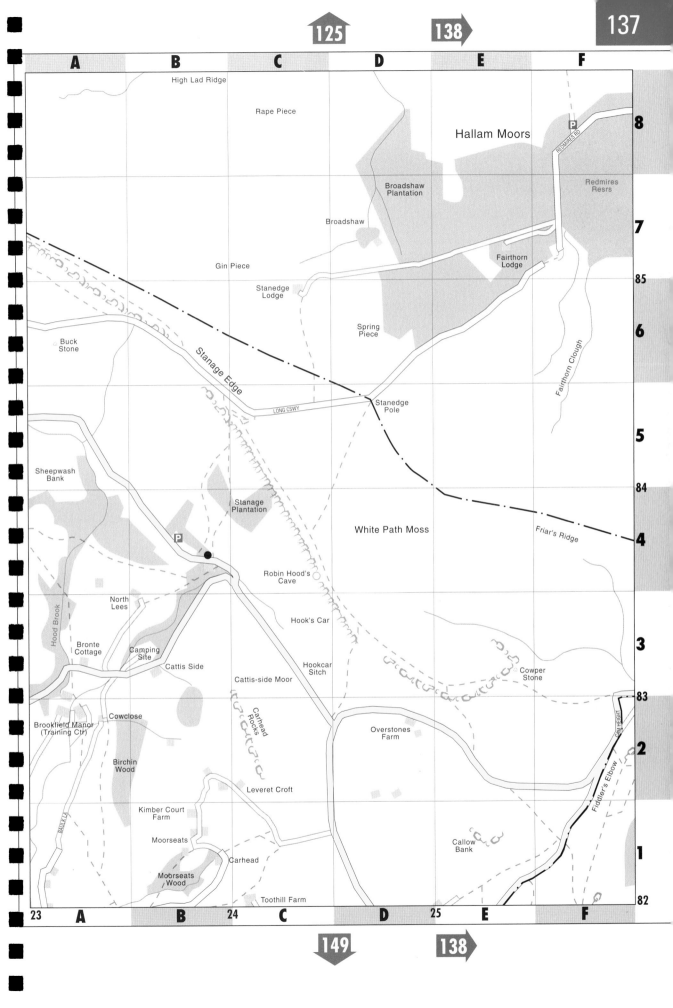

A   B   C   D   E   F

High Lad Ridge

Rape Piece

Hallam Moors

8

Broadshaw
Plantation

Redmires
Resrs

Broadshaw

7

Gin Piece

Fairthorn
Lodge

85

Stanedge
Lodge

Spring
Piece

6

Buck
Stone

Stanage Edge

Fairthorn Clough

Stanedge
Pole

LONG CSWY

5

Sheepwash
Bank

84

Stanage
Plantation

White Path Moss

Friar's Ridge

4

Robin Hood's
Cave

Hook's Car

Cowper
Stone

Hood Brook

North
Lees

Hookcar
Sitch

3

Bronte
Cottage

Camping
Site

Cattis Side

Cattis-side Moor

83

Cowclose

Carhead
Rocks

Overstones
Farm

2

Brookfield Manor
(Training Ctr)

Birchin
Wood

Leveret Croft

BAULK LA

Kimber Court
Farm

Fiddler's Elbow

Moorseats

Callow
Bank

1

Carhead

Moorseats
Wood

Toothill Farm

82

23   A   B   24   C   D   25   E   F

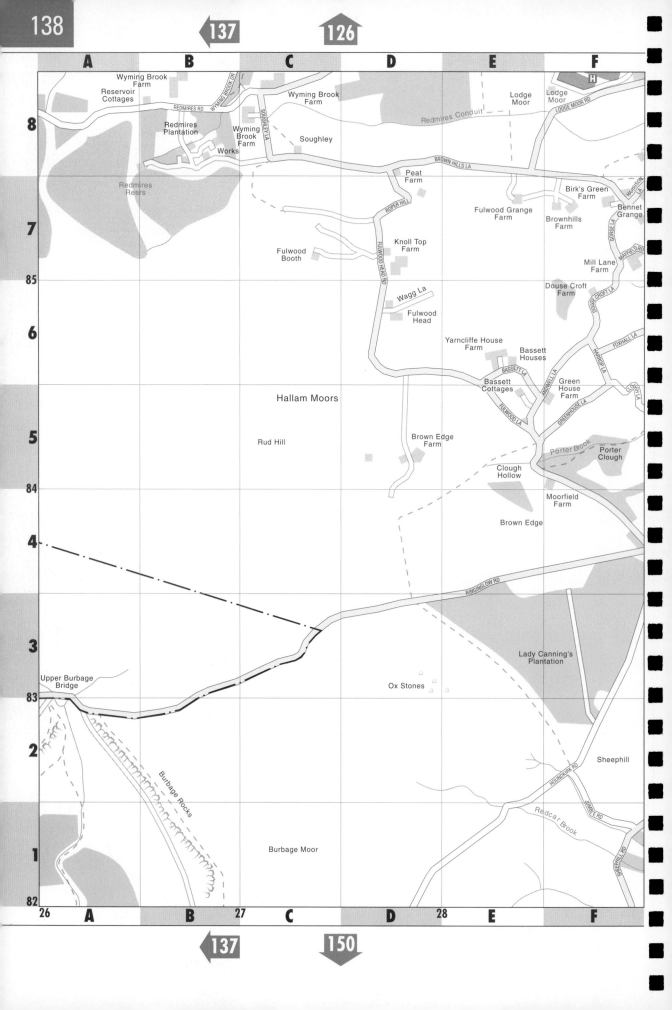

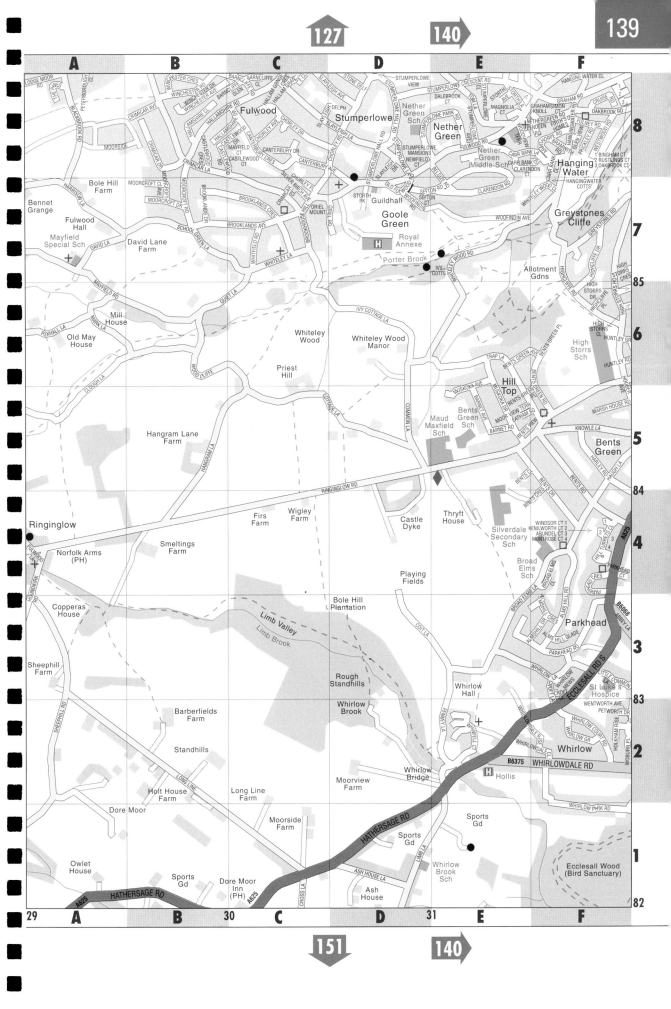

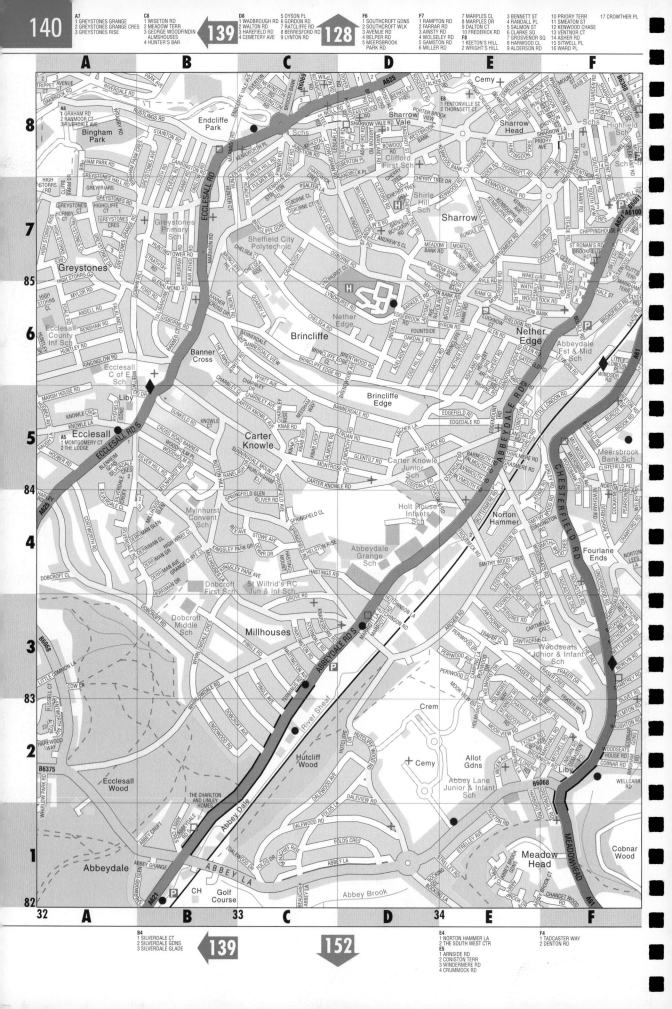

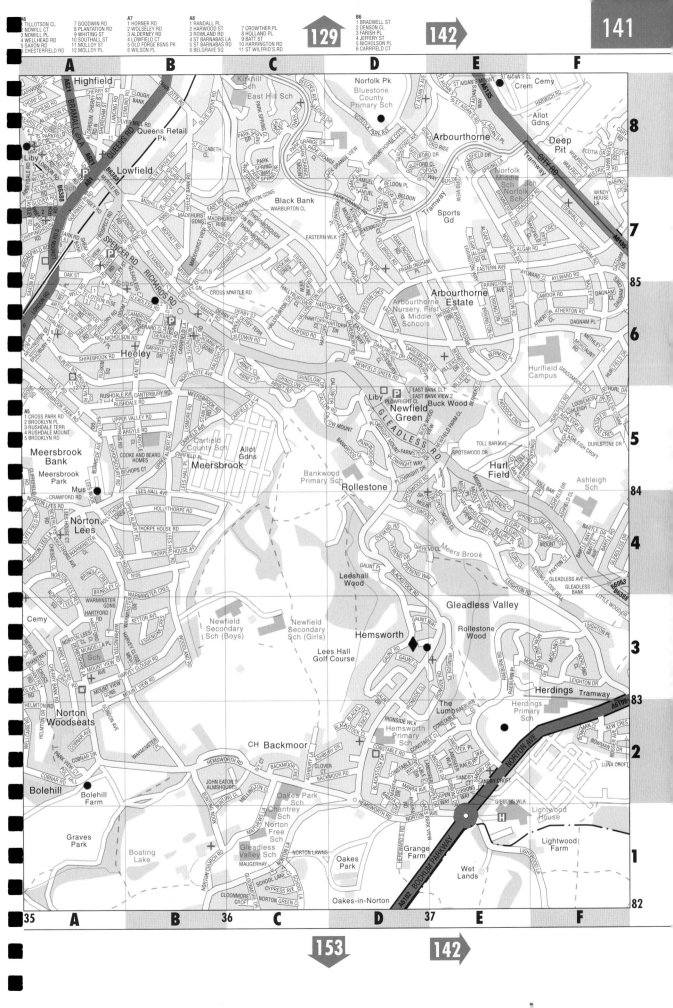

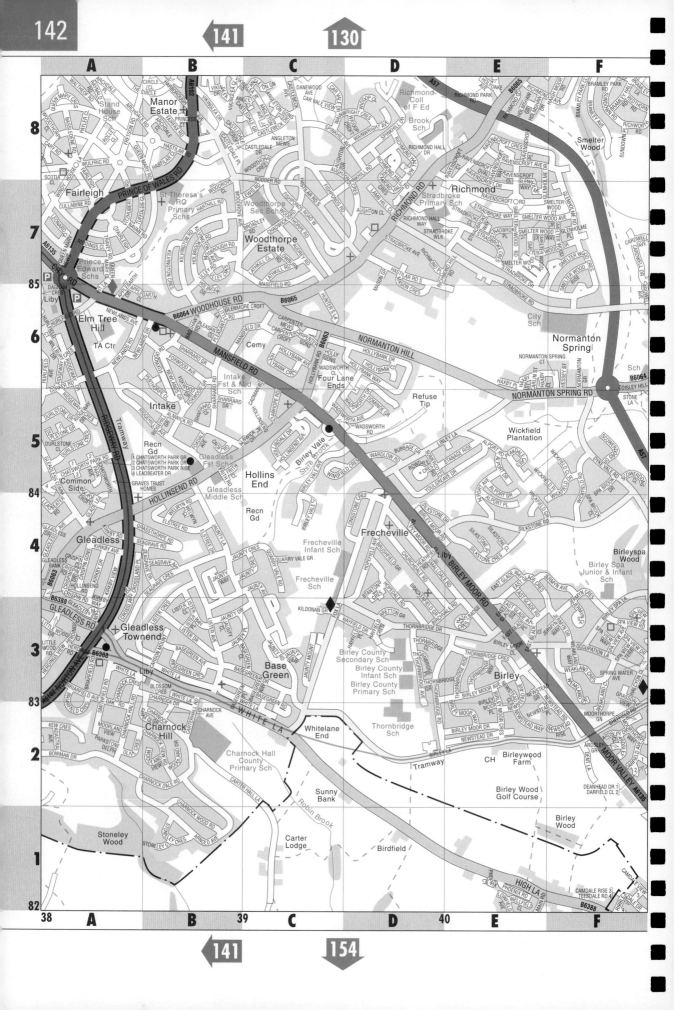

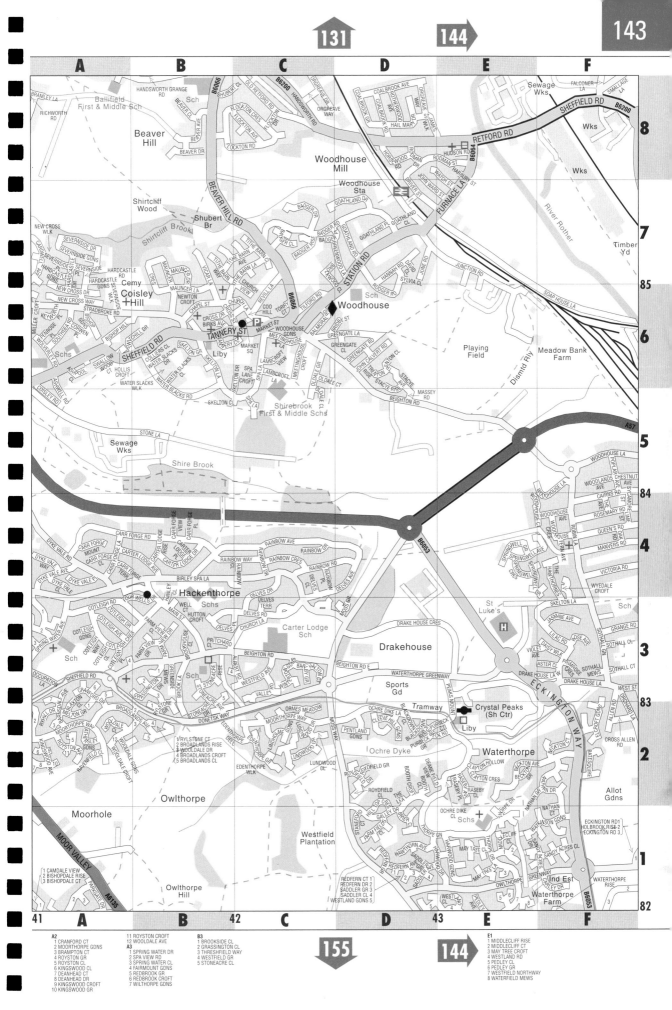

8
7
85
6
5
84
4
83
2
1
82

A2
1 CRANFORD CT
2 MOORTHORPE GDNS
3 BRAMPTON CT
4 ROYSTON GR
5 ROYSTON CL
6 KINGSWOOD CL
7 DEANHEAD CT
8 DEANHEAD DR
9 KINGSWOOD CROFT
10 KINGSWOOD GR
11 ROYSTON CROFT
12 ROYSTON AVE

A3
1 SPRING WATER DR
2 SPA VIEW RD
3 SPRING WATER CL
4 FAIRMOUNT GDNS
5 REDBROOK GR
6 REDBROOK CROFT
7 WILTHORPE GDNS

B3
1 BROOKSIDE CL
2 GRASSINGTON CL
3 THRESHFIELD WAY
4 WESTFIELD GR
5 STONEACRE CL

E1
1 MIDDLECLIFF RISE
2 MIDDLECLIFF CT
3 MAY TREE CROFT
4 WESTLAND RD
5 PEDLEY CL
6 PEDLEY GR
7 WESTFIELD NORTHWAY
8 WATERFIELD MEWS

Grid references: A B C D E F (top and bottom), rows 8 7 85 6 5 84 4 3 83 2 1 82

Aston Fence Junior & Infant Sch
Fence Farm
B6200
Park Hill Farm
Liby
Aston Swallownest Jun & Inf Sch
Nursery
Aston Comprehensive Sch
Cemy
Aston Springwood Jun & Inf Sch
New South Farm
Cemy
Sheffield Rd
Park Hill
Sorby Rd
Great Bridge
Swallownest
Mill Stone Hill
Aston Lodge Jun & Inf Sch
Aston
Aston Pk
Aughton Court
Aston Hall Junior & Infant Sch
Collingham Rd
Works
Mansfield Rd
Aston Common
Sewage Works
Hepworth Pond
Beighton Mill Tail Golf
Beighton Colliery
Chesterfield Rd
Sewage Works
Sewage Works
Works
Pigeon Bridge Brook
A57
Works
Opencast Workings
Waleswood Colliery (dis)
Tulip Tree Cl
Cairns Rd
Rosemary Rd
Rothervale Cl
Queen's Elm
Manvers Rd
Victoria Rd
Sports Gd
New Rd
Sports Ground
Wales Common
Waleswood
The Green
Wales Bar
Beighton
Sothall
River Rother
Rother Valley Country Pk
Bedgreave Mill
Rother Valley Lake
Sewage Works
Meadow Gate La
Dismtd Rly
Meadowgate Lake
County Dike
Ind Est
Holbrook Rise
Owlthorpe Greenway
Longacre Way
Rother Valley Way

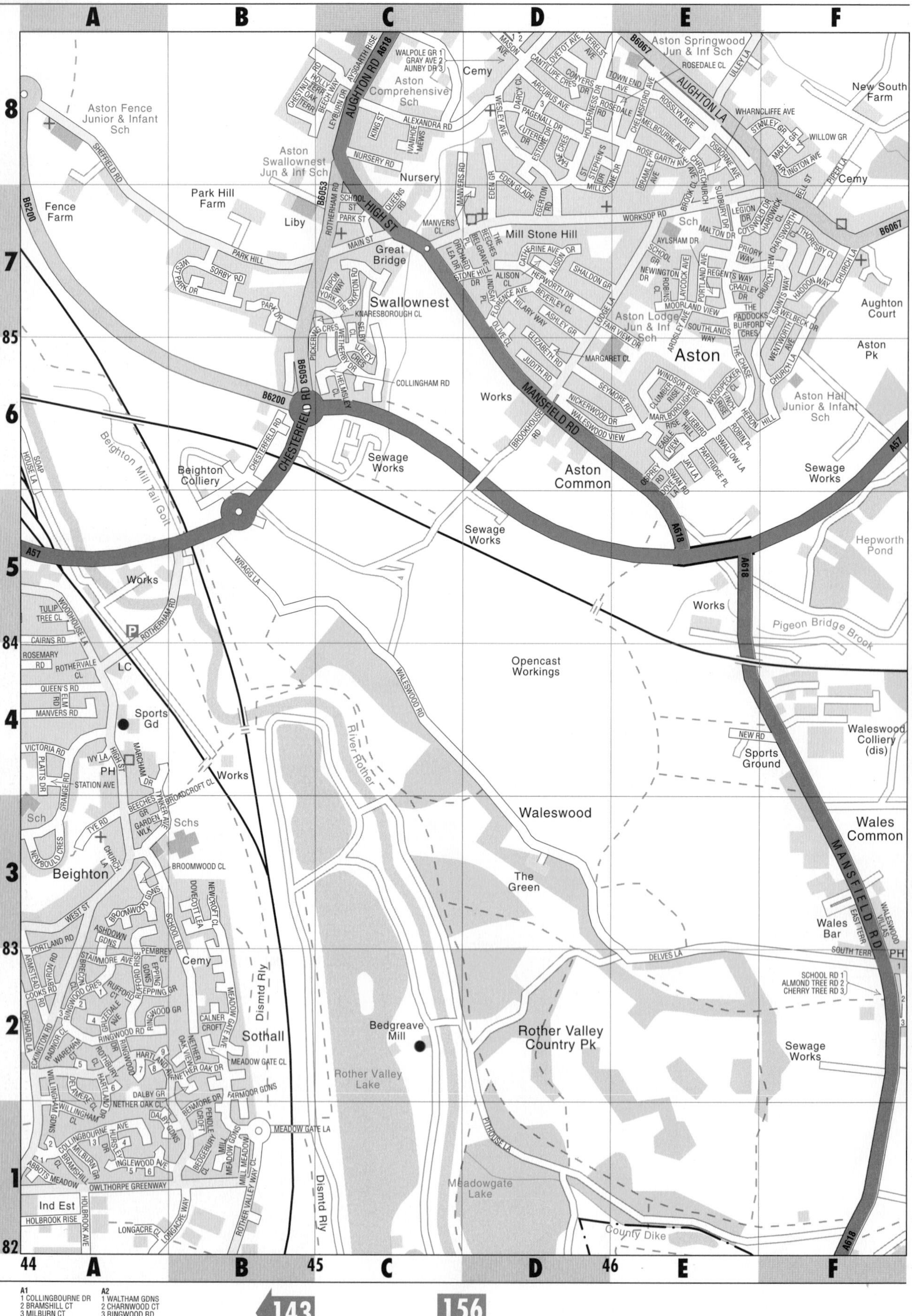

A1
1 COLLINGBOURNE DR
2 BRAMSHILL CT
3 MILBURN CT
4 HURSLEY CL
5 INGLEWOOD CT
6 INGLEWOOD DELL

A2
1 WALTHAM GDNS
2 CHARNWOOD CT
3 RINGWOOD RD
4 GRIZEDALE CL
5 ROTHBURY CT
6 HARTLAND CT
7 WYCHWOOD GLENN
8 WYCHWOOD CROFT
9 WYCHWOOD GR

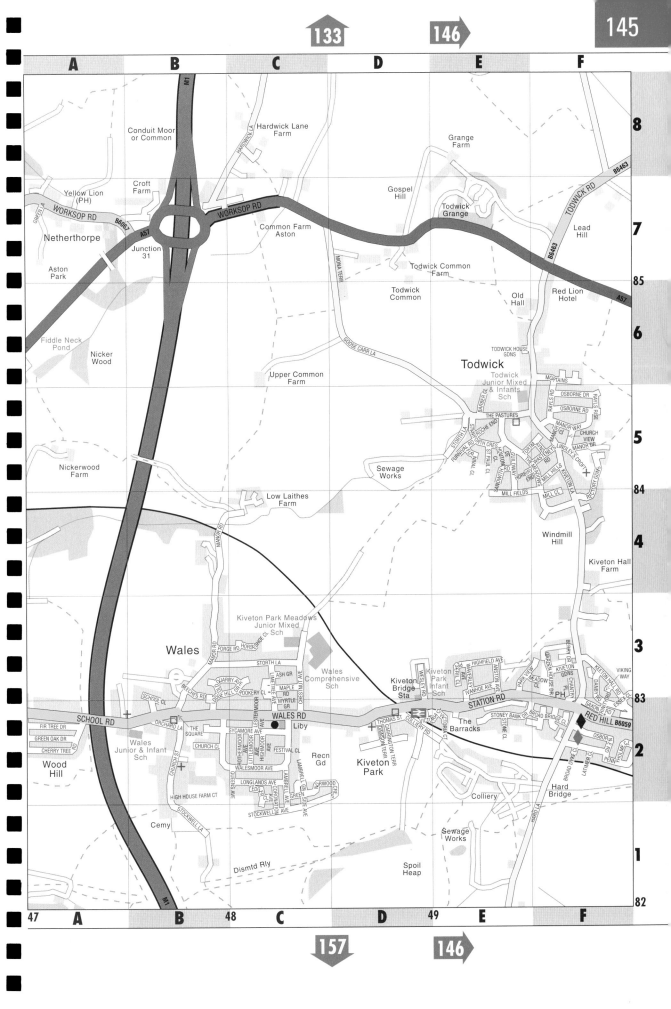

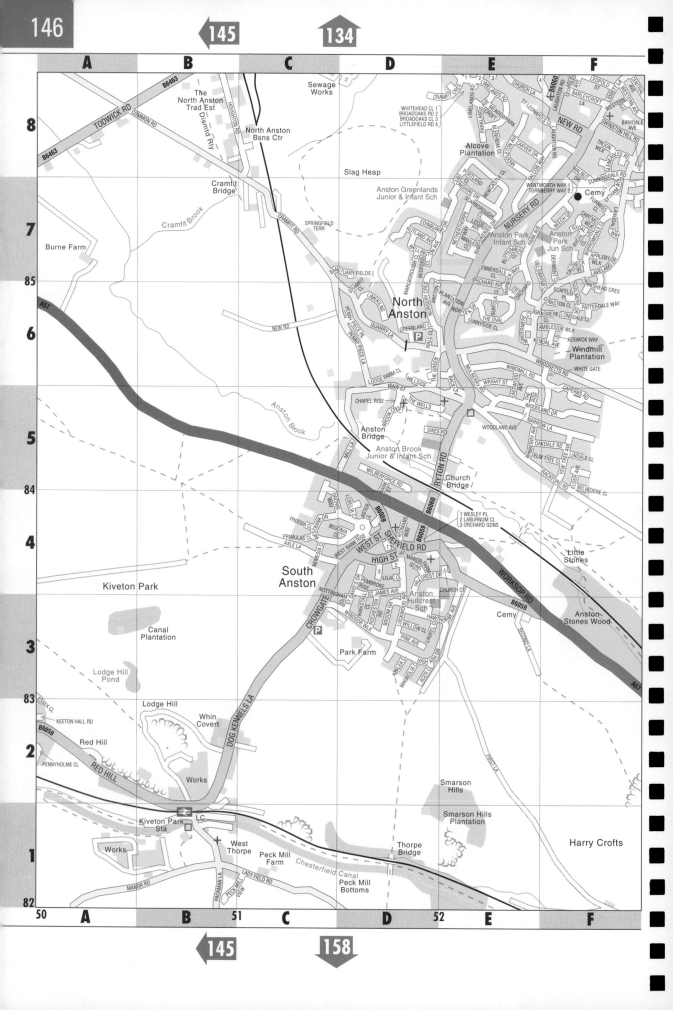

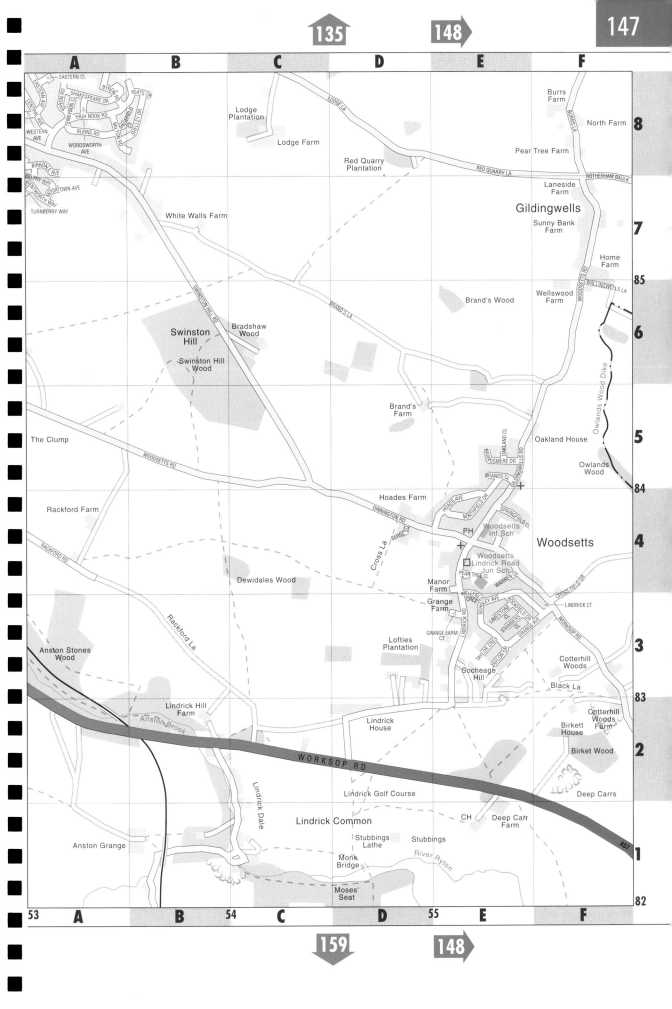

A   B   C   D   E   F

EASTERN CL

Lodge
Plantation

Lodge Farm

Burrs
Farm

North Farm   8

LODGE LA

Red Quarry
Plantation

Pear Tree Farm

BURRS LA

RED QUARRY LA

ROTHERHAM BAULK

Laneside
Farm

White Walls Farm

Gildingwells

Sunny Bank
Farm

7

Home
Farm

WOODSETTS RD

85

WALLINGWELLS LA

BRAND'S LA

Brand's Wood

Wellswood
Farm

Swinston
Hill

Bradshaw
Wood

6

Owlands Wood Dike

SWINSTON HILL RD

Swinston Hill
Wood

Brand's
Farm

5

The Clump

WOODSETTS RD

OAKLAND CL

Oakland House

BEANOSMERE DR

Owlands
Wood

GILDINGWELLS RD

84

Rackford Farm

Hoades Farm

DINNINGTON RD

BRANDS CL

SPRINGFIELD CL

HOADS AVE

NORTHFIELD DR

RACKFORD RD

Cross La

BENNET RD

PH

Woodsetts
Inf Sch

Woodsetts   4

Woodsetts
Lindrick Road
Jun Sch

Dewidales Wood

Manor
Farm

PEAR TREE CL

WELLFIELD CL

WARREN CL

Rackford La

Grange
Farm

CROSS FIELD DR

LINDRICK CT

LINDLEY AVE

SOCKEY LA

Lofties
Plantation

GRANGE FARM
CT

LINDRICK RD

LIMESTONE
CL

STAMBERS
CL

ROCKFIELD DR

GRANGE AVE

WORKSOP RD

Cotterhill
Woods

3

Anston Stones
Wood

Socheage
Hill

TAYLOR CRES

TAYLOR DR

Black La

83

Lindrick Hill
Farm

Anston Brook

Lindrick
House

Birkett
House

Cotterhill
Woods
Farm

Birket Wood

2

WORKSOP RD

Lindrick Golf Course

Deep Carrs

CH

Deep Carr
Farm

A57

Anston Grange

Lindrick Dale

Lindrick Common

Stubbings
Lathe

Stubbings

River Ryton

1

Monk
Bridge

Moses'
Seat

82

53   A   B   54   C   D   55   E   F

A B C D E F

8

Acorn Piece
Miller Lands
Costhorpe Ind Est
Sports Field
Woodland Farm
Langold Holt
Costhorpe
Riddell Arms (PH)

1 WEST VIEW
2 INGHAM BGLWS
3 HIGHFIELD VILLAS

DONCASTER RD
A60

7
Buckwood Farm
ROTHERHAM BAULK

PENTLAND DR 1
HAMBLETON CT 2
CHILTERN WAY 3
LOWTHER SQ 4
BEVERLEY WLK 5
CHICHESTER WLK 6
SALISBURY WLK 7
CANTERBURY WLK 8
CHEVIOT CT 9
MENDIP CT 10
LICHFIELD WLK 11
COTSWOLD CT 12

LAWN RD
NORTHUMBERLAND AVE
SUTHERLAND CL
CUMBERLAND CL
WES CL
NORTH WAY
DADLEY RD

WILLOW AVE
HAWTHORN WAY
BEECH GR
SYCAMORE RD
LIME
TREE AVE
LILAC
CLEVLAND CL
BECKETT AVE
QUEENS RD
RAMSDEN CRES
MULBERRY CRES
OXFORD RD
LINDRICK CL
Liby

85

KNATON RD
STEWART
KINGSTON RD
AMANDA AVE
LONG LA
STEWART RD

6
WALLINGWELLS LA

Carlton Park Infants Sch
Kingston Junior Sch

CARISBROOK RD
CRAITHIE RD
CRAIGSTON RD
FINTHLBS DR
GLAMIS RD
PEMBROKE DR
RICHMOND RD
CONWAY DR
BALMORAL
STRATHMORE RD
STRATHAVON DR
KENILWORTH
WARWICK AVE
WINDSOR GDNS
WINDSOR RD
ARUNDEL DR

Castle Garden

Carlton in Lindrick

Wallingwells Wood
Carlton Wood

CARLTON HALL LA

5
Wallingwells Park
Hollin Hills

The Lawns
A60

84
Owlands Wood
Owlands Wood

The Ashes
Holme Wood
Carlton Lake
CHURCH LA
Field House Farm

4
Sewage Works
The Bottoms
Corn Mill Farm

Owlands Wood Dike
Holme House Farm

Hardwick Ashes

3
OWDAY LA

83

Owday Wood
Broom Farm

2
WORKSOP RD
The Homestead
Owday Plantation
Little Broom Wood

Rough Piece
Nab's Ashes Wood
Sand Hill Plantation

Whipman Wood
CARLTON RD
A60

1
WORKSOP RD
WOODSETTS LA
Fox Covert
Cocked Hat Wood

A57
GATEFORD RD
Ashes Wood
Dog Kennel Plantation
ASHES PARK AVE
EDINSON PARK AVE
EASTWOOD CT

82

56 A B 57 C D 58 E F

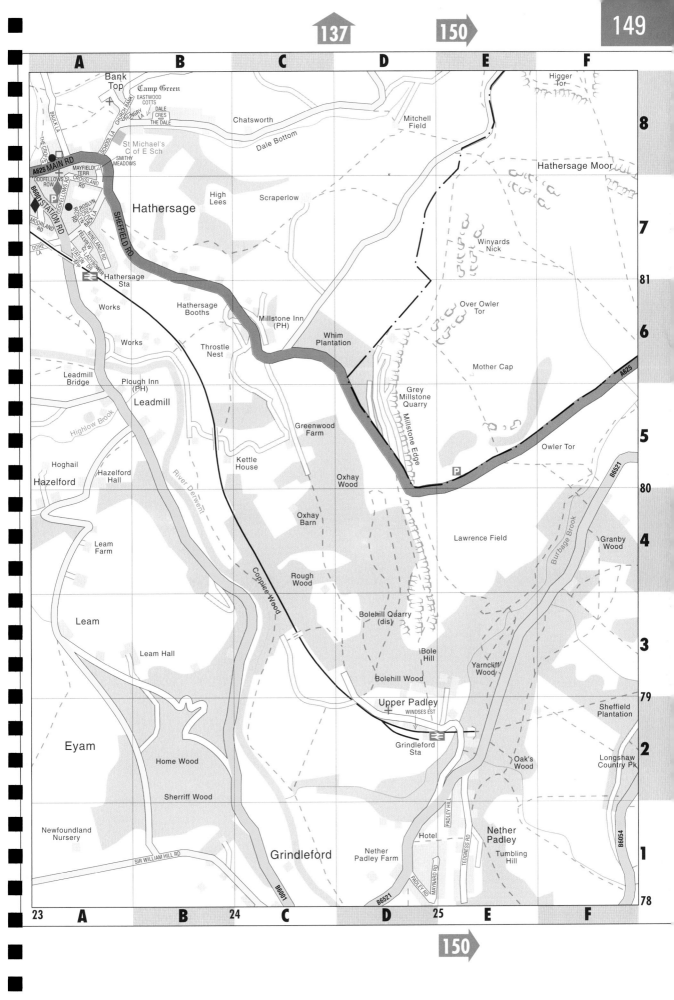

137 150

A B C D E F

8
Higger Tor
Bank Top
Camp Green
EASTWOOD COTTS
Chatsworth
DALE CRES THE DALE
Mitchell Field
Hathersage Moor
St Michael's C of E Sch
SMITHY MEADOWS
Dale Bottom

A625 MAIN RD
MAYFIELD TERR
ODDFELLOWS ROW
CROSSLAND RD
High Lees
Scraperlow
Winyards Nick
7
RD ROSLYN
ROSLYN CRES BACK LA
Hathersage
SHEFFIELD RD
NINELANDS RD
STATION DR
FELLOWER

DORE LA
Hathersage Sta
Works
Hathersage Booths
Millstone Inn (PH)
Whim Plantation
Over Owler Tor
81
6
Works
Throstle Nest
Millstone Inn (PH)
Grey Millstone Quarry
Mother Cap

Leadmill Bridge
Plough Inn (PH)
Leadmill
Greenwood Farm
Millstone Edge
A625
Owler Tor
5
Highlow Brook
River Derwent
Kettle House
Oxhay Wood
P
B6521

Hoghail
Hazelford Hall
Oxhay Barn
Lawrence Field
Burbage Brook
Granby Wood
4
Hazelford
Leam Farm
Coppice Wood
Rough Wood
Bolehill Quarry (dis)
80

Leam
Bole Hill
Yarncliff Wood
3
Leam Hall
Bolehill Wood
79
Upper Padley
WINDSES EST
Sheffield Plantation
Eyam
Home Wood
Grindleford Sta
Oak's Wood
PADLEY HILL
Longshaw Country Pk
2
Sherriff Wood
TEDGNESS RD
Nether Padley
MAYNARD RD
PADLEY RD
Newfoundland Nursery
SIR WILLIAM HILL RD
Grindleford
Nether Padley Farm
Hotel
Tumbling Hill
B6054
1
B6001
B6521

78
23 A B 24 C D 25 E F

150

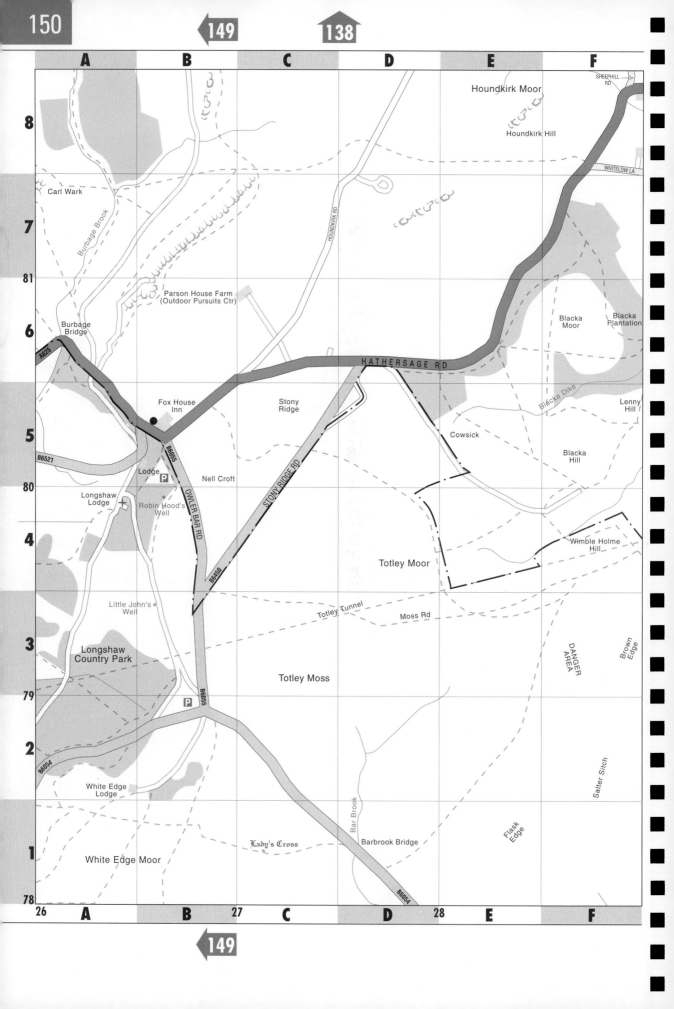

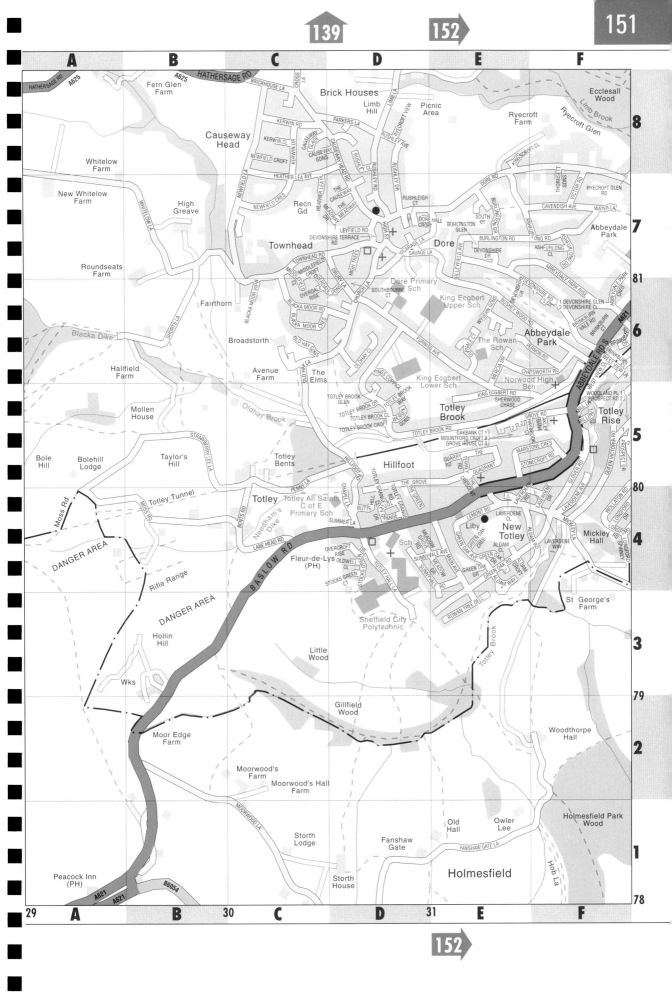

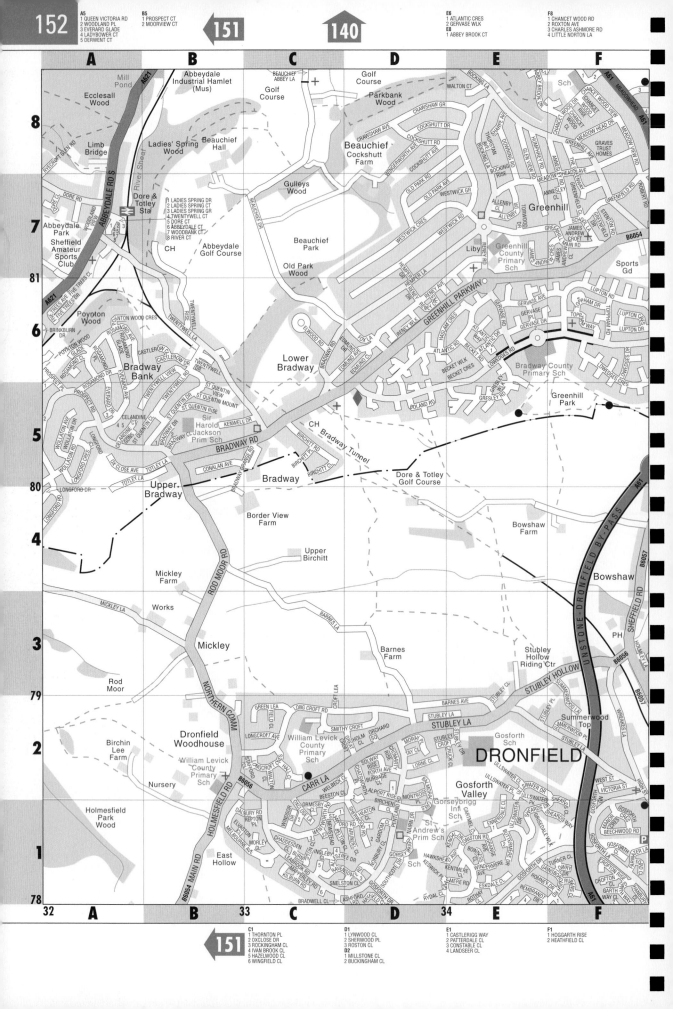

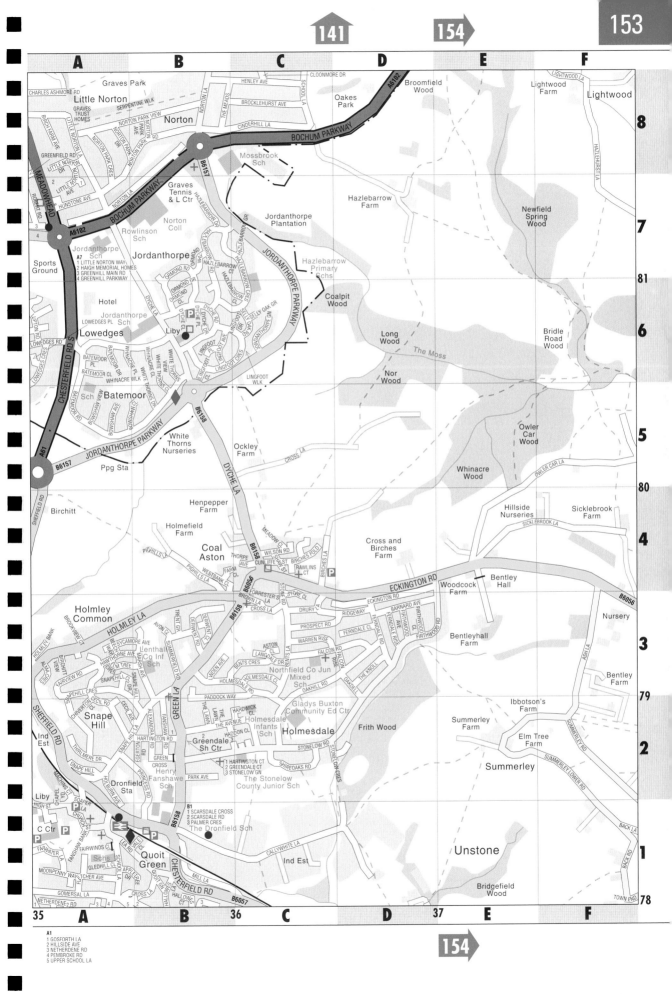

A1
1 GOSFORTH LA
2 HILLSIDE AVE
3 NETHERDENE RD
4 PEMBROKE RD
5 UPPER SCHOOL LA

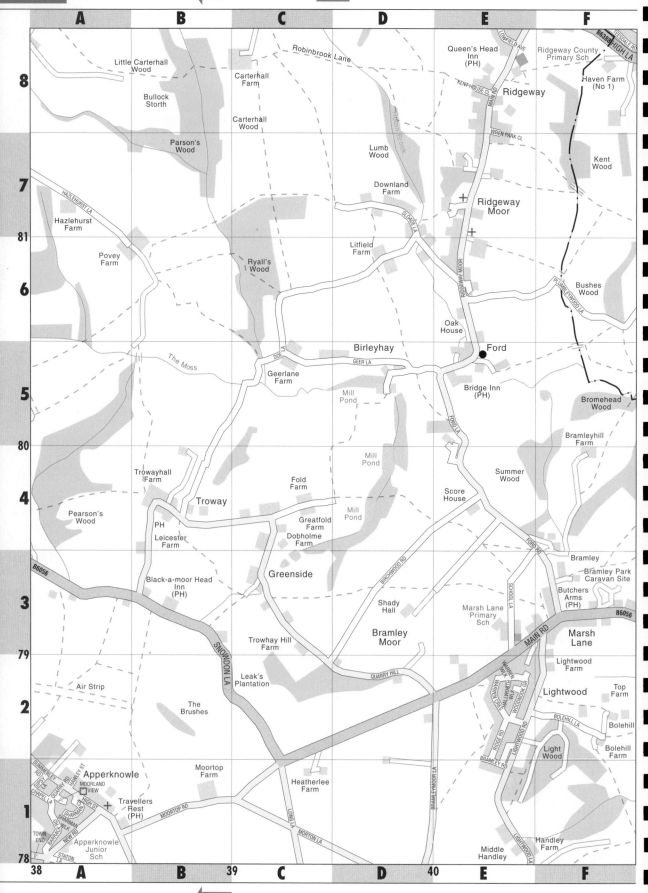

153
142

A   B   C   D   E   F

8

Little Carterhall Wood

Bullock Storth

Parson's Wood

Robinbrook Lane

Carterhall Farm

Carterhall Wood

Queen's Head Inn (PH)

Ridgeway

Ridgeway County Primary Sch

Haven Farm (No 1)

B6384 HIGH LA

LOXFIELD AVE

KENT HOUSE CL

MAIN RD

7

HAZLEHURST LA

Hazlehurst Farm

Povey Farm

Ryall's Wood

Lumb Wood

Downland Farm

WREN PARK CL

Ridgeway Moor

Kent Wood

Adam Brook

SLOADE LA

RIDGEWAY MOOR

81

6

Litfield Farm

Bushes Wood

PLUMBLEYWOOD LA

The Moss

DOE LA

Geerlane Farm

Birleyhay

GEER LA

Oak House

Ford

5

Mill Pond

Bridge Inn (PH)

FORD LA

Bromehead Wood

80

Mill Pond

Summer Wood

Bramleyhill Farm

4

Pearson's Wood

Trowayhall Farm

Troway

Fold Farm

Mill Pond

Score House

PH

Leicester Farm

Greatfold Farm

Dobholme Farm

Greenside

BIRCHWOOD RD

FORD RD

Bramley

Bramley Park Caravan Site

Butchers Arms (PH)

3

B6056

Black-a-moor Head Inn (PH)

Shady Hall

Bramley Moor

Marsh Lane Primary Sch

SCHOOL LA

MAIN RD

Marsh Lane

B6056

79

SNOWDON LA

Trowhay Hill Farm

Leak's Plantation

QUARRY HILL

Lightwood Farm

WARREN WALK

WARREN CRES

WOODNOOK GR

Lightwood

Top Farm

2

Air Strip

The Brushes

BOLEHILL LA

Bolehill

RIDGE RD

LIGHTWOOD RD

Light Wood

Bolehill Farm

1

SUMMERLEY RD

GIPSY LA

CHAPEL LA

HAWLEY ST

HIGH ST

Apperknowle

MOORLAND VIEW

SHARMAN

Travellers Rest (PH)

Moortop Farm

Heatherlee Farm

BRAMLEYMOOR LA

BRAMLEY RD

Handley Farm

78

TOWN END

OSB WALK

NEW RD

GARRICK LA

STATON LA

Apperknowle Junior Sch

MOORTOP RD

LONG LA

MORTON LA

Middle Handley

LIGHTWOOD LA

38   A   B   **39**   C   D   **40**   E   F

153

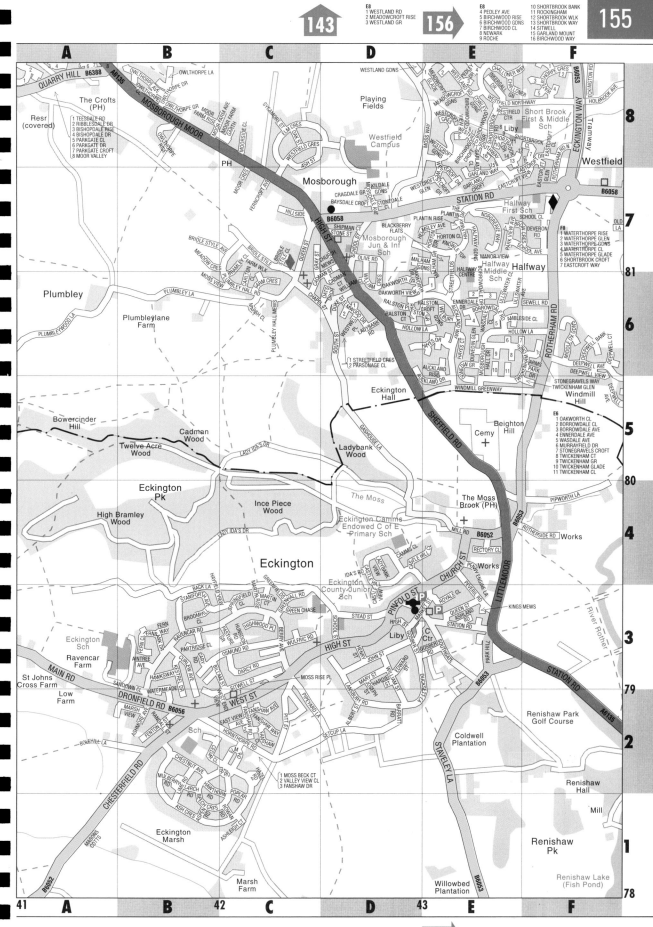

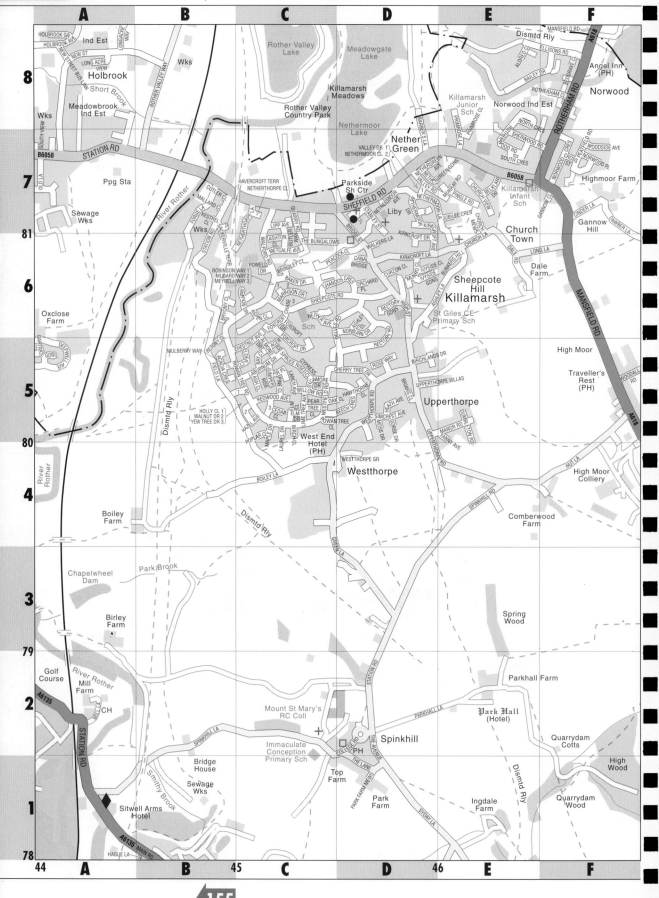

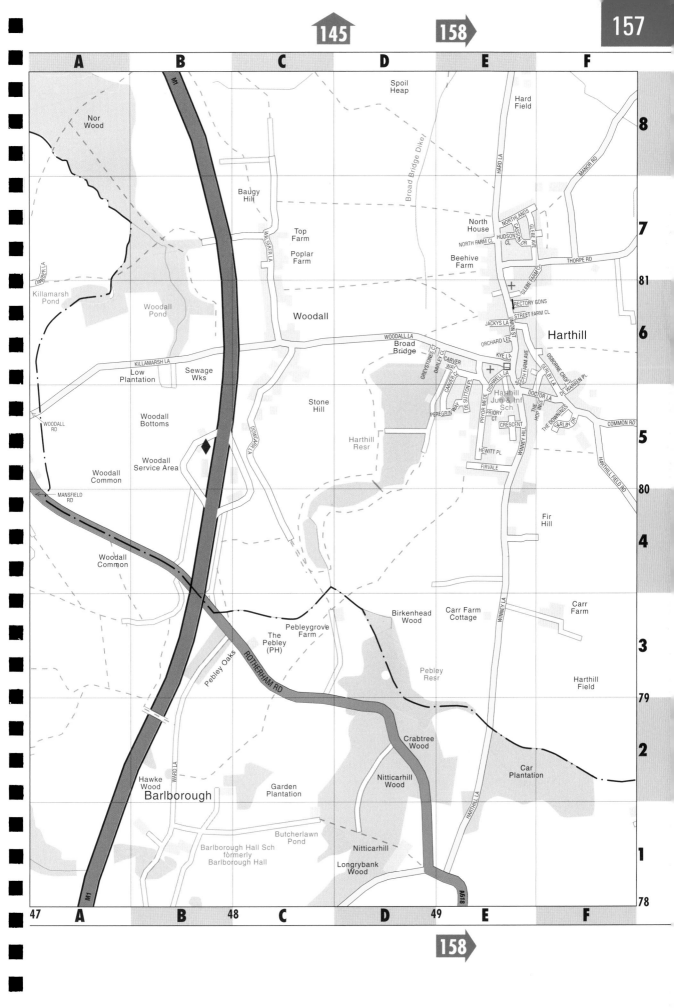

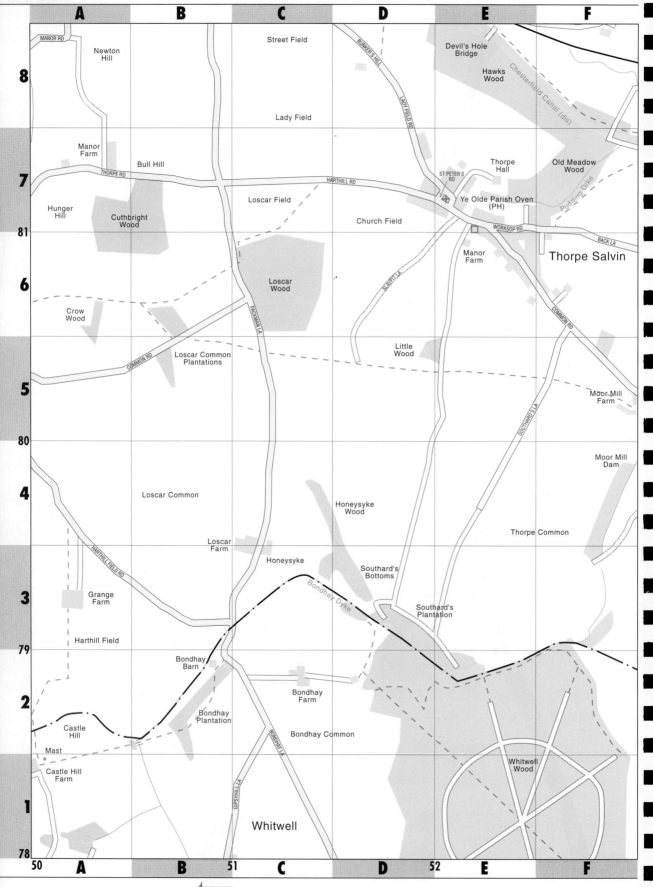

A B C D E F

8

7

81

6

5

80

4

3

79

2

1

78

MANOR RD
Newton Hill
Street Field
Devil's Hole Bridge
Hawks Wood
Chesterfield Canal (dis)
Manor Farm
Bull Hill
THORPE RD
Lady Field
BUNKER'S HILL
St PETER'S RD
Thorpe Hall
Old Meadow Wood
Puddling Dike
Hunger Hill
Cuthbright Wood
HARTHILL RD
Loscar Field
LADY FIELD RD
Church Field
Ye Olde Parish Oven (PH)
WORKSOP RD
Thorpe Salvin
BACK LA
Manor Farm
Crow Wood
Loscar Wood
COMMON RD
PACKMAN LA
Loscar Common Plantations
SLAYPIT LA
Little Wood
COMMON RD
Moor Mill Farm
Loscar Common
Honeysyke Wood
SOUTHARD'S LA
Thorpe Common
Moor Mill Dam
HARTHILL FIELD RD
Loscar Farm
Honeysyke
Bondhay Dyke
Southard's Bottoms
Southard's Plantation
Grange Farm
Harthill Field
Bondhay Barn
Bondhay Farm
Bondhay Plantation
Castle Hill
Mast
BONDHAY LA
Bondhay Common
GIPSYHILL LA
Whitwell Wood
Castle Hill Farm
Whitwell

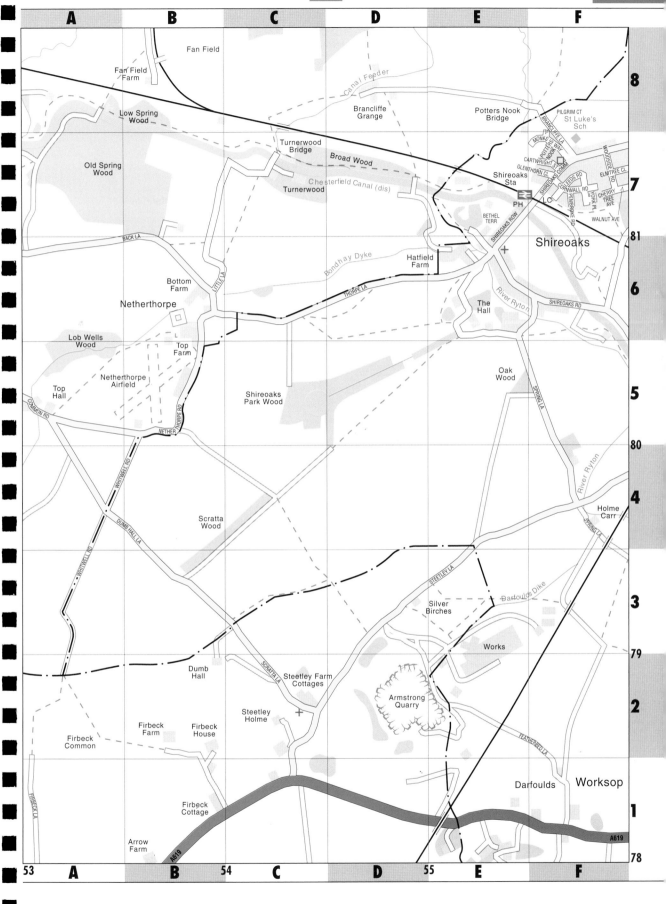

EXPLANATION OF THE STREET INDEX REFERENCE SYSTEM

Street names are listed alphabetically and show the locality, the Post Office Postcode District, the page number and a reference to the square in which the name falls on the map page.

Example: Norfolk Ct. Roth S65......................................115 E7 8

Norfolk Ct   This is the full street name, which may have been abbreviated on the map.

Roth   This is the abbreviation for the town, village or locality in which the street falls.

S65   This is the Post Office Postcode District for the street name.

115   This is the page number of the map on which the street name appears.

E7   The letter and figure indicate the square on the map in which the centre of the street falls. The square can be found at the junction of the vertical column carrying the appropriate letter and the horizontal row carrying the appropriate figure.

8   In congested areas numbers may have been used to indicate the location of a street. In certain circumstances, the number used to represent a street will follow the reference in the gazetteer entry.

ABBREVIATIONS USED IN THE INDEX
Road Names

Approach .... App	Corner .... Cnr	Heights .... Hts	Road .... Rd
Arcade .... Arc	Cottages .... Cotts	Industri al Estate .... Ind Est	Roundabout .... Rdbt
Avenue .... Ave	Court .... Ct	Interchange .... Intc	South .... S
Boulevard .... Bvd	Courtyard .... Ctyd	Junction .... Junc	Square .... Sq
Buildings .... Bldgs	Crescent .... Cres	Lane .... La	Stairs .... Strs
Business Park .... Bsns Pk	Drive .... Dr	North .... N	Steps .... Stps
Business Centre .... Bsns Ctr	Drove .... Dro	Orchard .... Orch	Street,Saint .... St
Bungalows .... Bglws	East .... E	Parade .... Par	Terrace .... Terr
Causeway .... Cswy	Embankment .... Emb	Park .... Pk	Trading Estate .... Trad Est
Centre .... Ctr	Esplanade .... Espl	Passage .... Pas	Walk .... Wlk
Circle .... Circ	Estate .... Est	Place .... Pl	West .... W
Circus .... Cir	Gardens .... Gdns	Precinct .... Prec	Yard .... Yd
Close Cl	Green .... Gn	Promenade .... Prom	
Common .... Comm	Grove .... Gr	Retail Park .... Ret Pk	

Key to abbreviations of Town, Village and Rural locality names used in the index of street names.

Adwick le Street .... Ad le S 40 A6	Dinnington .... Din 134 E1	Killamarsh .... Kill 156 E6	Sykehouse .... Syke 7 C6
Armthorpe .... Arm 64 A5	Dodworth .... Dod 53 F7	Kirk Bramwith .... K Bram 24 A4	Snaith .... Snaith 1 A8
Askern .... Askern 22 A7	Doncaster .... Don 62 E3	Kirk Smeaton .... K Smea 3 D5	South Anston .... S Anst 146 C4
Aston .... Aston 144 E6	Dronfield .... Dron 152 E2	Kirkburton .... Kirkb 28 B8	South Elmsall .... S Elm 19 A2
Auckley .... Auck 86 B7	Dunford Bridge .... Dun Br 48 D1	Langold .... Lan 136 E4	South Hiendley .... S Hie 16 D6
Austerfield .... Aust 105 C2	Eckington .... Eck 155 C4	Langsett .... Lang 71 C6	South Kirkby .... S Kirk 18 C1
Balne Moor .... Bal M 5 F8	Emley .... Emley 12 A6	Laughton en le Morthen Laugh 134 E5	Sprotbrough .... Sprot 61 C1
Bamford .... Bam 124 B1	Epworth .... Epw 67 F6	Letwell .... Let 136 A3	Stainforth .... Stai 24 F3
Barlborough .... Barl 157 B2	Everton .... Ever 123 F3	Maltby .... Maltby 119 C5	Stainton .... Ston 119 F8
Barnby Dun .... B Dun 42 F8	Eyam .... Eyam 149 A2	Mapplewell .... Mapp 14 C1	Stocksbridge .... Stock 73 C2
Barnburgh .... Bnbur 59 D3	Fenwick .... Fenw 6 B5	Marr .... Marr 60 D7	Styrrup .... Styr 121 D1
Barnsley .... Barn 33 C1	Finningley .... Finn 86 E2	Mattersey .... Matt 123 E1	Swinton .... Swint 79 C2
Bawtry .... Bawtry 123 B7	Firbeck .... Fir 136 A6	Mexborough .... Mex 80 B7	Thorne .... Thorne 26 C8
Belton .... Belton 46 F4	Fishlake .... Fish 25 B7	Midhopestones .... Midhop 72 A3	Thorpe in Balne .... T in B 23 B2
Bentley .... Ben 62 B8	Gildingwells .... Gild 147 F7	Misson .... Misson 105 F2	Thorpe Salvin .... Th Sa 158 F6
Bircotes .... Bir 122 D4	Glossop .... Glos 68 A1	Moss .... Moss 6 B1	Thurcroft .... Thurcr 133 D6
Blaxton .... Blax 86 E6	Goole Fields .... G Field 11 B8	Netherton .... Neth 12 A8	Thurgoland .... Thurgo 73 F7
Bradfield .... Bfield 110 B5	Great Houghton .... Gt Hou 36 E3	New Edlington .... N Edl 82 C1	Tickhill .... Tick 121 B6
Braithwell .... Braith 101 A2	Grimethorpe .... Grime 36 B7	North Anston .... N Anst 146 D6	Tintwistle .... Tint 68 A7
Branton .... Bran 85 D8	Grindleford .... Grin 149 C1	Norton .... Norton 4 C3	Todwick .... Tod 145 E6
Brierley .... Bri 17 A3	Hallam Moors .... Hal M 137 E8	Notton .... Notton 14 F6	Treeton .... Treet 131 E4
Brinsworth .... Brin 131 C8	Hampole .... Ham 20 B1	Oldcotes .... Old 136 F6	Ulley .... Ulley 132 F3
Brodsworth .... Brod 39 B4	Harthill .... Hart 157 F6	Oughtibridge .... Ought 111 E7	Unstone .... Uns 153 E1
Burghwallis .... Burg 21 B4	Harworth .... Har 121 E4	Oxspring .... Oxspr 52 B1	Upton .... Upton 19 A8
Cadeby .... Cade 81 D5	Hatfield .... Hat 44 C8	Penistone .... Pen 51 C3	Wadworth .... Wad 102 C7
Carlecotes .... Carl 49 B3	Hathersage .... Hath 149 B7	Pilley .... Pilley 75 D5	Walden Stubbs .... W Stub 4 E6
Carlton in Lindrick .... C in L 148 F5	Hemsworth .... Hem 17 C8	Pollington .... Poll 6 C8	Wales .... Wales 145 B3
Cawthorne .... Caw 31 D4	Hickleton .... Hick 59 B7	Rawcliffe .... Rawcl 2 A8	Wath upon Dearne .... W up D 78 E7
Chapeltown .... Chap 95 B5	High Hoyland .... H Hoy 12 C1	Rawmarsh .... Rawm 97 E5	Wentworth .... Went 77 B1
Clayton .... Clay 37 C4	High Melton .... H Mel 81 C8	Rossington .... Ross 85 B1	West Bretton .... W Bret 12 E8
Clayton West .... Clay W 12 A3	High Peak .... H Pk 106 B1	Rotherham .... Roth 115 F6	Wharncliffe Side .... Wharn 93 B2
Clifton .... Clift 100 E5	Holme .... Holme 47 A8	Royston .... Roy 15 D3	Whitley Common .... Wh Com 49 E7
Conisbrough .... Con 81 B3	Holmesfield .... Hol 151 E1	Ryhill .... Ryhill 16 B8	Whitwell .... Whit 158 C1
Crowle .... Crowle 11 F1	Holmfirth .... Holmfi 28 A5	Scrooby .... Scro 123 A2	Wombwell .... Wombw 56 D2
Cudworth .... Cud 35 C6	Hood Green .... Hd Gr 53 E2	Shafton .... Shaf 16 B3	Womersley .... Womer 4 B8
Darfield .... Dar 57 B5	Hooton Pagnell .... H Pag 38 C5	Sheffield .... Shef 129 D3	Woodsetts .... Woods 147 F4
Dearne .... Dearne 58 D5	Hooton Roberts .... H Rob 99 D7	Shepley .... Shep 28 F8	Woolley .... Wool 13 F7
Denby Dale .... D Dale 30 B6	Hoyland .... Hoy 76 C6	Shireoaks .... Shire 159 F1	Worksop .... Work 159 F1
Derwent .... Derw 124 A5	Ingbirchworth .... Ingb 29 E1	Silkstone .... Silk 52 F8	Wortley .... Wort 74 D3
	Kexbrough .... Kex 32 C7	Skelmanthorpe .... Skel 30 A8	Wroot .... Wroot 67 B3

Abbe's Cl The. Burg DN6 ... 21 B5
Abbe's Wlk The. Burg DN6 ... 21 D4
Abbey Brook Ct. Shef S8 ... 140 E1
Abbey Brook Dr. Shef S8 ... 152 E8
Abbey Brook Gdns. Shef S8 ... 140 E1
Abbey Cl. Holmfi HD7 ... 48 B7
Abbey Cl. Laugh S31 ... 134 D5
Abbey Cl. Shef S8 ... 140 E1
Abbey Cres. Shef S7 ... 140 B1
Abbey Croft. Shef S7 ... 140 B1
Abbey Dr. Hat DN7 ... 44 A8
Abbey Farm Dr. Shep HD8 ... 28 F8
Abbey Fields. Finn DN9 ... 86 E3
Abbey Gdns. Hat DN7 ... 44 A7
Abbey Gn. Dod S75 ... 54 A6
Abbey Gn. Hat DN7 ... 44 A8
Abbey Gr. Barn S71 ... 34 E3
Abbey Gr. Hat DN7 ... 44 A8
Abbey Grange. Shef S7 ... 140 B1
Abbey La. Barn S71 ... 34 E1
Abbey La. Barn S71 ... 34 E2
Abbey La. Laugh S31 ... 135 A8
Abbey La. Shef S11, S7, S8 ... 140 B1
Abbey Lane Jun & Inf Sch. Shef ... 140 E2
Abbey Rd. Hat DN7 ... 44 A8
Abbey Rd S. Shep HD8 ... 28 F8
Abbey Sch The. Roth ... 114 D7
Abbey View Rd. Shef S8 ... 141 A3
Abbey Way. Hat DN7 ... 25 A1
Abbey Way. N Anst S31 ... 134 B1
Abbey Wlk. Ben DN5 ... 61 E6
Abbeydale Ct. Dron S17 ... 152 A7
Abbeydale First & Mid Sch & Language Sch. Shef ... 140 E6
Abbeydale Golf Course. Shef ... 152 B7
Abbeydale Grange Sch. Shef ... 140 D4
Abbeydale Industrial Hamlet (Mus). Shef ... 152 B8
Abbeydale Park Cres. Shef S17 ... 151 F6
Abbeydale Park Rise. Shef S17 ... 151 F6
Abbeydale Rd S. Shef S17, S7 ... 152 A7
Abbeydale Rd. Shef S7 ... 140 E5
Abbeyfield Rd. Hat DN7 ... 43 F8
Abbeyfield Rd. Shef S4 ... 129 B8
Abbot La. Wool WF4 ... 14 B6
Abbots Meadow. Shef S19 ... 144 A1
Abbots Rd. Barn S71 ... 34 F3
Abbotsford Dr. Thurcr S66 ... 133 E6
Abbott St. Don DN4 ... 62 B2
Abdy Rd. Roth S61 ... 96 D2
Abdy Rd. W up D S62 ... 78 D2
Aberconway Cres. Ross DN11 ... 103 F8
Abercorn Rd. Don DN2 ... 63 C4
Aberford Gr. Hoy S74 ... 77 B6
Abingdon Gdns. Roth S61 ... 97 B2
Abingdon Rd. Don DN2 ... 63 B5
Abney Cl. Shef S14 ... 141 C6
Abney Dr. Shef S14 ... 141 C6
Abney Rd. Shef S14 ... 141 C6
Abney St. Shef S1 ... 128 F3
Acacia Ave. Chap S30 ... 94 F4
Acacia Ave. Maltby S66 ... 118 D5
Acacia Ave. Roth S66 ... 117 C5
Acacia Cres. Kill S31 ... 156 B5
Acacia Ct. Ben DN5 ... 41 A2
Acacia Gr. Con DN12 ... 100 A8
Acacia Gr. Shaf S72 ... 16 C2
Acacia Rd. Ad le S DN6 ... 21 A2
Acacia Rd. Don DN4 ... 84 F8
Acacia Rd. Shef S5 ... 113 E4
Acaia Cl. S Elm WF9 ... 19 A4
Ace Bsns Ctr. Shef ... 129 B4 8
Acer Cl. Kill S31 ... 156 C5
Acer Cl. S Anst S31 ... 146 D3
Ackworth Dr. Shef S9 ... 114 F1
Acomb Common Rd. Hat DN7 ... 44 F8
Acorn Croft. Roth S61 ... 97 B2
Acorn Dr. Shef S6 ... 127 C7
Acorn Hill. Shef S6 ... 127 D7
Acorn St. Shef S3 ... 129 A5
Acorn Way. Shef S6 ... 127 B6
Acre Cl. Don DN3 ... 42 F2
Acre Cl. Maltby S66 ... 118 E7
Acre Gate. Chap S30 ... 94 D6
Acre La. Holmfi HD7 ... 28 B6
Acre La. Pen S30 ... 51 D6
Acre La. Wharn S30 ... 111 A8
Acre Rd. Cud S72 ... 35 C4
Acres Hill First Sch. Shef ... 130 B3
Acres Hill La. Shef S9 ... 130 B4
Acres Hill Mid Sch. Shef ... 130 B3
Acres Hill Rd. Shef S9 ... 130 C4
Acres La. Wroot DN9 ... 67 B5
Acton Cl. Aston S31 ... 132 D1
Adam La. Caw S75 ... 32 A2
Adastral Ave. Shef S12 ... 142 A2
Addison Rd. Maltby S66 ... 118 D5
Addison Rd. Mex S64 ... 80 A6
Addison Rd. Shef S5 ... 113 D2
Addy Cl. Shef S6 ... 128 E5
Addy Cres. S Elm WF9 ... 18 F3
Addy Dr. Shef S6 ... 128 E5
Addy St. Shef S6 ... 128 E5
Adelaide Rd. Norton DN6 ... 4 D3
Adelaide Rd. Shef S7 ... 140 D6
Adelaide St. Maltby S66 ... 119 B3
Adelphi St. Shef S6 ... 128 E5
Adkin Royd. Silk S75 ... 52 F8
Adkins Dr. Shef S5 ... 112 E3
Adkins Rd. Shef S5 ... 112 E3
Adlard Rd. Don DN2 ... 63 B6
Adlington Cres. Shef S5 ... 112 F4
Adlington Rd. Shef S5 ... 112 F5
Admirals Crest. Roth S61 ... 96 B2
Adrian Cres. Shef S5 ... 113 A4
Adsetts St. Shef S4 ... 113 E1
Adwick Ave. Ben DN5 ... 40 F5
Adwick Ct. Mex S64 ... 80 B4
Adwick La. Ad I S DN5 ... 40 E6
Adwick La. Ben DN5 ... 40 E6
Adwick Park Mid Sch. Ad le S ... 40 B5
Adwick Rd. Mex S64 ... 80 B6
Adwick Sch. Ad ... 40 B5
Adwick St. Ben DN5 ... 40 F5
Adwick Sta. Ad ... 40 C6
Adwick Washi... Ad le S ... 40 C4
Aeron Wilkinson Ct. S Kirk WF9 ... 18 A2
Agden Rd. Shef S7 ... 140 E8
Agden Side Rd. Bfield S30 ... 109 E8
Agnes Rd. Barn S70 ... 54 E8
Agnes Rd. Kex S75 ... 32 E8
Agnes Terr. Barn S70 ... 54 E8 6
Ainsdale Ave. Dearne S63 ... 58 D4
Ainsdale Cl. Roy S71 ... 15 B5
Ainsdale Ct. Barn S71 ... 34 D6
Ainsdale Rd. Roy S71 ... 15 B5
Ainsley Cl. Bran DN9 ... 86 A7
Ainsley Rd. Shef S10 ... 128 C4
Ainsty Rd. Shef S7 ... 140 F7 3
Aintree Ave. Don DN4 ... 63 D2
Aintree Ave. Eck S31 ... 155 B3
Aintree Cl. Ben DN5 ... 61 D5
Aintree Dr. Mex S64 ... 80 B6
Air Mount Cl. Roth S66 ... 117 A4
Aire Cl. Chap S30 ... 94 F6
Airedale Ave. Tick DN11 ... 121 A8
Airedale Rd. Kex S75 ... 32 D8
Airedale Rd. Shef S6 ... 112 A2
Aireton Cl. Roth S66 ... 117 A5
Aireton Rd. Barn S70 ... 33 E2 7
Airey La. T in B DN6 ... 23 A2
Airstone Rd. Askern DN6 ... 21 F7
Aisby Dr. Ross DN11 ... 85 A2
Aisthorpe Rd. Shef S8 ... 140 F3
Aitken Rd. Swint S62 ... 98 E8
Aizlewood Rd. Shef S8 ... 140 F7
Akley Bank Cl. Shef S17 ... 151 F5
Alan Rd. Kex S75 ... 32 E8
Alba Cl. Dar S73 ... 56 E6
Albanus Croft. Shef S6 ... 127 C6
Albanus Ridge. Shef S6 ... 127 C6
Albany Ave. Shef S30 ... 95 A1
Albany Cl. Barn S73 ... 56 A6
Albany Cres. S Elm WF9 ... 18 F2
Albany La. Ross DN11 ... 84 E1
Albany Pl. S Elm WF9 ... 18 F2 5
Albany Rd. Don DN4 ... 83 B8
Albany Rd. Shef S7 ... 140 F7
Albany Rd. Stock S30 ... 73 B1
Albany Rd. Swint S64 ... 79 D1
Albany St. Roth S65 ... 115 E6
Albany St. S Elm WF9 ... 18 F2
Albert Cres. G Hou S72 ... 57 D7
Albert Rd. Dearne S63 ... 58 E5
Albert Rd. Mex S64 ... 80 A5
Albert Rd. Rawm S62 ... 97 F4
Albert Rd. Shef S8 ... 141 A6
Albert Rd. Shef S12 ... 143 C3
Albert Rd. W up D S63 ... 78 D7
Albert St. Barn S70 ... 33 F1
Albert St. Cud S72 ... 16 C1
Albert St. Dearne S63 ... 58 C8
Albert St E. Barn S70 ... 33 F1 9
Albert St. Eck S31 ... 155 D2
Albert St. Maltby S66 ... 119 B4
Albert St. Roth S60 ... 115 C6
Albert St. Swint S64 ... 79 D4
Albert St. Thorne DN8 ... 26 C8
Albert Terrace Rd. Shef S6 ... 128 E5
Albert Villas. Thorne DN8 ... 26 C8
Albion Dr. Dearne S63 ... 58 F8
Albion House. Barn S70 ... 54 F8 10
Albion Pl. Don DN1 ... 62 E3
Albion Pl. S Elm WF9 ... 19 A3
Albion Rd. Roth S60 ... 115 E6
Albion Rd. Roy S71 ... 34 C8
Albion Row. Shef S6 ... 127 D4
Albion St. Shef S6 ... 128 E4
Albion Terr. Barn S70 ... 55 A8 12
Albion Terr. Don DN4 ... 62 B1
Alcester Rd. Shef S7 ... 140 F7
Aldam Cl. Roth S65 ... 116 D7
Aldam Cl. Shef S17 ... 151 E4
Aldam Croft. Shef S17 ... 151 E4
Aldam Rd. Don DN4 ... 82 F6
Aldam Rd. Shef S17 ... 151 F4
Aldam Way. Shef S17 ... 151 E4
Aldbury Cl. Barn S71 ... 34 B6
Aldcliffe Cres. Don DN4 ... 82 F4
Aldene Ave. Shef S6 ... 111 F1
Aldene Glade. Shef S6 ... 111 F1
Aldene Rd. Shef S6 ... 111 F2
Alder Cl. Mapp S75 ... 14 A1
Alder Gr. Dar S73 ... 56 F4
Alder Gr. Don DN4 ... 83 A7
Alder Gr. Thorne DN8 ... 9 C3
Alder La. Shef S9 ... 130 E3
Alder Mews. Hoy S74 ... 76 E5
Aldergate Cl. Maltby S66 ... 119 C4
Alderney Rd. Shef S8 ... 141 A7 3
Alderns Cl. Braith S66 ... 100 D2
Alders Gn. Shef S6 ... 111 D1
Aldersgate Cl. Ross DN11 ... 104 A7
Alderson Ave. Rawm S62 ... 97 F7
Alderson Cl. Tick DN11 ... 121 B8
Alderson Dr. Barn S71 ... 34 A6
Alderson Dr. Don DN2 ... 62 F3
Alderson Dr. Tick DN11 ... 121 B7
Alderson Pl. Shef S2 ... 141 A8
Alderson Rd N. Shef S2 ... 141 A8
Alderson Rd. Shef S2 ... 141 A8
Aldervale Cl. Swint S64 ... 98 D8
Aldesworth Rd. Don DN4 ... 63 F2
Aldfield Way. Shef S5 ... 113 B2
Aldham Cotts. Wombw S73 ... 56 C5
Aldham Cres. Barn S73 ... 56 A5
Aldham House La. Wombw S73 ... 56 B4
Aldlne Ct. Shef S1 ... 129 B4 3
Aldred Cl. Kill S31 ... 156 E8
Aldred Cl. Roth S66 ... 117 B5
Aldred Rd. Shef S10 ... 128 C5
Aldred St. Roth S65 ... 115 E5
Aldrin Way. Maltby S66 ... 118 E6
Aldwarke La. Rawm S65 ... 98 B2
Aldwarke La. Roth S65 ... 98 C1
Aldwarke Rd. Rawm S62 ... 97 F3
Alexander St. Ben DN5 ... 41 C1
Alexandra Cl. Roth S61 ... 114 E8
Alexandra Ctr. Roth S62 ... 97 F2
Alexandra Rd. Ad I S DN6 ... 40 D6
Alexandra Rd. Aston S31 ... 144 C8
Alexandra Rd. Ben DN5 ... 41 B1
Alexandra Rd. Bir DN11 ... 122 B4
Alexandra Rd. Don DN4, ... 83 B8
Alexandra Rd. Dron S18 ... 153 B2
Alexandra Rd. Mex S64 ... 80 B5
Alexandra Rd. Shef S2 ... 141 B7
Alexandra Rd. Thorne DN8 ... 9 D4
Alexandra St. Maltby S66 ... 119 B3
Alexandra St. Thorne DN8 ... 9 B1
Alexandra Terr. Barn S71 ... 55 F8
Alford Ave. Ought S30 ... 111 D7
Alfred Rd. Askern DN6 ... 21 F7
Alfred Rd. Shef S9 ... 129 F7
Alfred Rd. Shef S9 ... 130 A8
Alfred St. Roy S71 ... 15 E4
Algar Cl. Shef S2 ... 141 E7
Algar Cres. Shef S2 ... 141 F7
Algar Dr. Shef S2 ... 141 E7
Algar Pl. Shef S2 ... 141 E7
Algar Rd. Shef S2 ... 141 E7
Alhambra Sh Ctr. Barn ... 33 F1
Alice Rd. Roth S61 ... 115 B7
Alison Cl. Aston S31 ... 144 D7
Alison Dr. Aston S31 ... 144 D7
All Hallows Dr. Tick DN11 ... 120 F7
All Hallows Dr. Maltby S66 ... 118 E4
All Saints Aston (C of E Aided Jun & Mix Inf Sch). Aston ... 144 E7
All Saints C of E (Aided) Prim Sch. Laugh ... 134 D5
All Saints Cl. Silk S75 ... 32 A1
All Saints Cl. W up D S63 ... 78 E6
All Saints RC Comp Sch. Shef ... 129 C1
All Saints Sq. Con DN12 ... 81 A3
All Saints' Sq. Roth S60 ... 115 D6
All Saints Way. Aston S31 ... 144 F7
Allan St. Roth S65 ... 115 E6
Allas La. Bfield S30 ... 91 E4
Allatt Cl. Barn S70 ... 54 F8
Alldred Cres. Swint S64 ... 79 D1
Allen Rd. Shef S19 ... 143 F2
Allen St. Shef S3 ... 128 F4
Allenby Cl. Shef S8 ... 152 E7
Allenby Cres. Ross DN11 ... 103 E8
Allenby Dr. Shef S8 ... 152 E7
Allendale. Barn S70 ... 55 C5
Allendale Ct. Barn S70 ... 55 C5
Allendale Dr. Hoy S74 ... 76 D5
Allendale Gdns. Ben DN5 ... 61 F3
Allendale Rd. Barn S75 33 E3
Allendale Rd. Ben DN5 ... 61 F3
Allendale Rd. Hoy S74 ... 76 D5
Allendale Rd. Kex S75 ... 32 D8
Allendale Rd. Roth S65 ... 116 C4
Allende Way. Shef S9 ... 130 B6
Allerton St. Don DN1 ... 62 D4
Allestree Dr. Dron S18 ... 152 C1
Alliance St. Shef S4 ... 129 D7
Alliss Rd. Bran DN3 ... 85 E8
Allott Cl. Roth S65 ... 117 D8
Allott Cl. S Elm WF9 ... 18 F3
Allott Cres. Hoy S74 ... 77 A7
Allott St. Hoy S74 ... 76 B5
Allott St. Hoy S74 ... 77 A5
Allsopps Yd. Hoy S74 ... 55 D1
Allt St. Rawm S62 ... 97 F4
Alma Cres. Dron S18 ... 153 A3
Alma Rd. Chap S30 ... 94 D7
Alma Rd. Roth S60 ... 115 D5
Alma Row. Roth S60 ... 116 C1
Alma St. Barn S70 ... 33 D1
Alma St. Shef S3 ... 129 A5
Alma St. Wombw S73 ... 56 E2
Almholme La. Ben DN5 ... 41 E4
Almond Ave. Arm DN3 ... 64 B7
Almond Ave. Cud S72 ... 35 B7
Almond Cl. Finn DN9 ... 86 C4
Almond Cl. Maltby S66 ... 118 D5
Almond Cl. S Elm WF9 ... 19 A5
Almond Dr. Kill S31 ... 156 C5
Almond Glade. Roth S66 ... 117 C3
Almond Pl. W up D S63 ... 78 F5
Almond Rd. Don DN4 ... 84 F8
Almond Tree Rd. Wales S31 ... 144 F2
Alms Hill Glade. Shef S11 ... 139 F3
Alms Hill Rd. Shef S11 ... 139 F3
Almshill Cres. Shef S11 ... 139 F3
Almshill Dr. Shef S11 ... 139 F3
Almshouses. Ben DN5 ... 41 D2
Alney Pl. Shef S6 ... 112 D4
Alnwick Dr. Shef S12 ... 142 C5
Alnwick Rd. Shef S12 ... 142 B5
Alperton Cl. Barn S71 ... 34 F5
Alpha Rd. Roth S65 ... 116 B7
Alpha St. Ben DN5 ... 40 F5
Alpine Cl. Stock S30 ... 73 A1
Alpine Rd. Shef S6 ... 128 D5
Alpine Rd. Stock S30 ... 73 B1
Alport Ave. Shef S12 ... 142 E5
Alport Dr. Shef S12 ... 142 E5
Alport Gr. Shef S12 ... 142 E5
Alport Pl. Shef S12 ... 142 E4
Alport Rd. Shef S12 ... 142 E5
Alport Rise. Dron S18 ... 152 D2
Alric Dr. Brin S60 ... 115 B1
Alsing Rd. Shef S9 ... 114 C3
Alston Cl. Don DN4 ... 84 D7
Alston Cl. Silk S75 ... 52 F8
Alston Rd. Don DN4 ... 84 D6
Alton Cl. Shef S11 ... 140 A2
Alton Way. Mapp S75 ... 14 A1
Alvaston Wlk. Con DN12 ... 81 A3
Alverley La. Don DN4 ... 83 A4
Alverley View. Don DN11 ... 83 A3
Alwyn Ave. Ben DN5 ... 61 E7
Alwyn Rd. Thorne DN8 ... 26 C7
Amalfi Cl. Dar S73 ... 56 F5
Amanda Ave. C in L S81 ... 148 E6
Amanda Dr. Hat DN7 ... 44 C7
Amanda Rd. Har DN11 ... 121 F4
Ambassador Gdns. Arm DN3 ... 64 C5
Amberley Rise. Ad le S DN6 ... 20 F2
Amberley St. Shef S9 ... 130 A8
Ambler Rise. Aston S31 ... 132 C1
Ambleside Cl. Brin S60 ... 131 A8
Ambleside Cl. Shef S19 ... 155 E6
Ambleside Cres. Sprot DN5 ... 61 A1
Ambleside Gr. Barn S71 ... 56 A8
Ambleside Wlk. N Anst S31 ... 146 F6
Ambrose Ave. Hat DN7 ... 44 C8
Amen Cnr. Roth S60 ... 115 C7 4
America La. W up D S73 ... 78 C3
Amersall Cres. Ben DN5 ... 61 E8
Amersall Rd. Ben DN5 ... 61 E7
Amory's Holt Cl. Maltby S66 ... 118 E7
Amory's Holt Dr. Maltby S66 ... 118 E7
Amory's Holt Rd. Maltby S66 ... 118 E7
Amory's Holt Way. Maltby S66 ... 118 E7
Amos Rd. Shef S9 ... 114 B2
Amwell Gn. Hat DN7 ... 44 A6
Amy Rd. Ben DN5 ... 41 C3
Anchorage Cres. Ben DN5 ... 62 A4
Anchorage La. Ben DN5 ... 61 F4
Anchorage Sch The. Ben ... 61 E6
Ancient La. Hat DN7 ... 44 E5
Ancona Rise. Dar S73 ... 56 F6
Andover Dr. Shef S3 ... 129 A6
Andover St. Shef S3 ... 129 B6
Andrew La. Shef S3 ... 129 B5
Andrew St. Shef S3 ... 129 B5
Andwell La. Shef S10 ... 138 F6
Anelay Rd. Don DN4 ... 82 F7
Anfield Rd. Don DN4 ... 84 E8
Angel St. Dearne S63 ... 58 D1
Angel St. Shef S3 ... 129 B4
Angerford Ave. Shef S8 ... 141 A4
Angleton Ave. Shef S2 ... 142 C8
Angleton Cl. Shef S2 ... 142 C8
Angleton Gdns. Shef S2 ... 142 C8
Angleton Gn. Shef S2 ... 142 C8
Angleton Mews. Shef S2 ... 142 C8
Angram Bank Inf Sch. Chap ... 94 C7
Angram Bank Jun Sch. Chap ... 94 D7
Angram Rd. Chap S30 ... 94 D8
Ann St. Rawm S62 ... 97 F3
Annan Cl. Barn S75 ... 32 F5
Annat Pl. Chap S30 ... 94 C7
Annat Royd La. Ingb S30 ... 50 C8
Anne Cres. S Hie S72 ... 16 E5
Anne St. Din S31 ... 134 F3
Annesley Cl. Shef S8 ... 152 F7
Annesley Rd. Shef S8 ... 152 F7
Annet La. Bfield S6 ... 109 F4
Anns Rd N. Shef S2 ... 141 B7
Anns Rd. Shef S2 ... 141 A7
Anns Road Primary Schs. Shef ... 141 A7
Ansdell Rd. Ben DN5 ... 41 B2
Ansell Rd. Shef S11 ... 140 A6
Anson St. Shef S2 ... 129 C3
Ansten Cres. Don DN4 ... 84 E8
Anston Ave. Wales S31 ... 145 E3
Anston Brook Jun & Inf Sch. N Anst ... 146 D5
Anston Cl. N Anst S31 ... 146 D6
Anston Dr. S Elm WF9 ... 19 A5
Anston Greenlands Jun & Inf Sch. N Anst ... 146 E7
Anston Hillcrest Sch. S Anst ... 146 D3
Anston Park Inf Sch. N Anst ... 146 E7
Anston Park Jun Sch. N Anst ... 146 F7
Antrim Ave. Shef S10 ... 128 D2
Anvil Cl. Shef S6 ... 127 E6
Anvil Cres. Shef S30 ... 113 B8
Apley Rd. Don DN1 ... 62 D2
Apollo St. Rawm S62 ... 98 B7
Apostle Cl. Don DN4 ... 82 E6
Apperknowle Jun Sch. Uns ... 154 A1
Apple Gr. Finn DN9 ... 86 A4
Appleby Pl. Ad le S DN6 ... 20 F2
Appleby Rd. Don DN2 ... 63 D4
Appleby Wlk. Din S31 ... 146 F7
Applegarth Cl. Shef S12 ... 142 A6
Applegarth Dr. Shef S12 ... 142 A6
Applehaigh Gr. Roy S71 ... 15 A4
Applehaigh La. Notton WF4 ... 15 A6
Applehaigh View. Roy S71 ... 15 A4
Applehurst La. T in B DN6 ... 23 A1
Appleton Way. Barn S70 ... 55 A5
Appleton Way. Ben DN5 ... 62 A8
Appletree Dr. Dron S18 ... 153 A1
April Cl. Barn S71 ... 34 D4
April Dr. Barn S71 ... 34 D4
Apy Hill La. Ston S66 ... 102 B1
Apy Hill La. Tick DN11 ... 120 D8
Aqueduct St. Barn S71 ... 33 F3
Arbour Cres. Thurcr S66 ... 133 F6
Arbour Dr. Thurcr S66 ... 133 F6
Arbour La. Roth S65 ... 99 E3
Arbourthorne Cotts. Shef S2 ... 141 D8
Arbourthorne Fst & Mid Schs. Shef ... 141 D6
Arbourthorne Rd. Shef S2 ... 141 E6
Arcade The. Barn S70 ... 33 F1
Archdale Cl. Shef S2 ... 142 B8
Archdale Pl. Shef S2 ... 142 A8
Archdale Rd. Shef S2 ... 142 A8
Archer Gate. Shef S6 ... 111 D1
Archer House. Roth S65 ... 115 E7 1
Archer La. Shef S7 ... 140 D5
Archer Rd. Shef S8 ... 140 E3
Archery Cl. Roth S66 ... 117 B3
Archibald Rd. Shef S7 ... 140 E6
Arcon Pl. Rawm S62 ... 98 A6
Arcubus Ave. Aston S31 ... 144 D8
Ardeen Rd. Don DN2 ... 63 A4
Arden Cl. Roth S65 ... 116 B8 10
Arden Gate. Don DN4 ... 82 F4
Ardmore St. Shef S9 ... 130 A5
Ardsley Ave. Aston S31 ... 144 E7
Ardsley Cl. Shef S19 ... 142 F2
Ardsley Dr. Shef S19 ... 142 F2
Ardsley Gr. Shef S19 ... 142 F2
Ardsley Jun Sch. Barn ... 55 F8
Ardsley Mews. Barn S71 ... 56 A8
Ardsley Rd. Barn S70 ... 55 D5
Argosy Cl. Bawtry DN10 ... 122 F8
Argyle Cl. Shef S8 ... 141 B5
Argyle La. Ross DN11 ... 84 E1
Argyle Rd. Shef S8 ... 141 B5
Argyle St. Mex S64 ... 80 A5
Argyll Ave. Don DN2 ... 63 B5
Arklow Rd. Don DN2 ... 63 A5
Arksey First & Mid Sch. Ben ... 41 D2
Arksey La. Ben DN5 ... 41 C1
Arkwright Rd. Ben DN5 ... 61 F5
Arley St. Shef S2 ... 129 A1
Arlington Ave. Aston S31 ... 144 F8
Armer St. Roth S60 ... 115 C5
Armitage Rd. Don DN4 ... 82 F7
Armitage Rd. Stock S30 ... 92 D8
Armley Rd. Shef S9 ... 130 A8
Armroyd La. Hoy S74 ... 76 F4
Arms Park Dr. Shef S19 ... 155 F6
Armstead Rd. Shef S19 ... 144 A2
Armstrong Wlk. Maltby S66 ... 118 E6
Armthorpe C of E Inf Sch. Arm ... 64 B6
Armthorpe Comp Sch. Arm ... 64 A7
Armthorpe La. Don DN3 ... 43 B4
Armthorpe La. Don DN2, DN3 ... 63 A5
Armthorpe Rd. Don DN2 ... 63 C6
Armthorpe Rd. Shef S11 ... 139 F8
Armthorpe Southfield Prim Sch. Arm ... 64 B5
Armthorpe Tranmoor Lane Inf Sch. Arm ... 64 B5
Armytage Wlk. S Kirk WF9 ... 18 C3
Arncliffe Dr. Barn S70 ... 54 B8
Arncliffe Dr. Chap S30 ... 94 F6
Arnold Ave. Barn S71 ... 33 F7
Arnold Ave. Shef S12 ... 142 B1
Arnold Cres. Mex S64 ... 80 A6
Arnold Rd. Roth S65 ... 116 B6
Arnold St. Shef S6 ... 128 C6
Arnside Rd. Maltby S66 ... 119 A6
Arnside Rd. Shef S8 ... 140 E5 1
Arran Hill. Roth S65 ... 98 F3
Arran Rd. Shef S10 ... 128 B3
Arras St. Shef S9 ... 129 F5
Arren Cl. B Dun DN3 ... 42 F8
Arrowsmith House. Roth S65 ... 115 E7 3
Arthington St. Shef S8 ... 141 A6
Arthur Ave. Ben DN5 ... 41 B2
Arthur Pl. Ben DN5 ... 41 C2
Arthur Rd. Stock S30 ... 73 A1
Arthur St. Barn S70 ... 55 A5
Arthur St. Ben DN5 ... 41 C2
Arthur St. Rawm S62 ... 98 A7
Artisan View. Shef S8 ... 141 A6
Arundel Ave. Roth S65 ... 98 D1
Arundel Ave. Treet S60 ... 131 E4
Arundel Cl. Dron S18 ... 152 D1
Arundel Cotts. Treet S60 ... 131 E4
Arundel Cres. Treet S60 ... 131 E4
Arundel Ct. Shef S11 ... 139 F4
Arundel Dr. C in L S81 ... 148 F6
Arundel Gate. Shef S1 ... 129 B3
Arundel Gdns. Ben DN5 ... 61 F8
Arundel La. Shef S1 ... 129 B2
Arundel Rd. Chap S30 ... 95 A6
Arundel Rd. Norton DN6 ... 4 D3
Arundel Rd. Roth S60, S65 ... 115 F5
Arundel Rd. Treet S60 ... 131 E4
Arundel St. Shef S1 ... 129 A2
Arundel St. Stai DN7 ... 24 E3
Arundel St. Treet S60 ... 131 E4
Arundel View. Hoy S74 ... 77 A7
Arundel Wlk. Har DN11 ... 122 B5
Arundell Dr. Barn S71 ... 34 F5
Ascension Cl. Maltby S66 ... 119 B4
Ascot Ave. Don DN4 ... 63 D2
Ascot Cl. Mex S64 ... 80 B6
Ascot Dr. Ben DN5 ... 61 D6
Ascot St. Shef S1 ... 129 A1
Ash Cl. Kill S31 ... 156 C5
Ash Cl. Roth S65 ... 116 D4
Ash Cres. Eck S31 ... 155 B1
Ash Cres. Mex S64 ... 79 F6
Ash Cres. Stock S30 ... 73 D1
Ash Ct. Maltby S66 ... 118 D6
Ash Ct. Sprot DN5 ... 61 D1
Ash Dale Rd. Don DN4 ... 82 C4
Ash Dyke Cl. Kex S75 ... 32 D7
Ash Field Rd. T in B DN5 ... 42 B8
Ash Gr. Arm DN3 ... 64 C7
Ash Gr. Barn S70 ... 55 D7
Ash Gr. Con DN12 ... 81 A1
Ash Gr. Finn DN9 ... 86 B4
Ash Gr. Maltby S66 ... 119 B6
Ash Gr. Rawm S62 ... 98 B5
Ash Gr. Roth S66 ... 117 C5
Ash Gr. S Elm WF9 ... 19 A4
Ash Gr. Shef S10 ... 128 D2
Ash Gr. Wales S31 ... 145 C3
Ash Hill Cres. Hat DN7 ... 44 B7
Ash Hill Rd. Hat DN7 ... 44 B7
Ash Hill Rd. Syke DN14 ... 7 A5
Ash House La. Shef S17 ... 139 D1
Ash La. Eck S18 ... 153 F3
Ash La. Stock S30 ... 73 E1
Ash La. Uns S18 ... 153 F3
Ash Rd. Ad le S DN6 ... 21 B2
Ash Rd. Shaf S72 ... 16 D2
Ash Rd. T in B DN3 ... 42 C8
Ash Rd. W up D S63 ... 79 A5
Ash Ridge. Swint S64 ... 79 D2
Ash St. Barn S73 ... 56 A6
Ash St. Shef S6 ... 128 E6
Ash St. Shef S19 ... 155 C8
Ash Tree Ave. Bawtry DN10 ... 122 F7
Ash Tree Ct. Shef S9 ... 114 B4
Ash Tree Rd. Thorne DN8 ... 26 C6
Ash View. Chap S30 ... 94 F4
Ash View. Roth S61 ... 97 B3
Ashberry Cl. Dearne S63 ... 58 D8
Ashberry Gdns. Shef S6 ... 128 D5
Ashberry Rd. Shef S6 ... 128 D5
Ashbourne Cl. Ought S30 ... 111 E6
Ashbourne Gr. Shef S13 ... 130 F1 1
Ashbourne Rd. Barn S71 ... 34 A7
Ashbourne Rd. Shef S13 ... 130 F1
Ashburnham Cl. Norton DN6 ... 4 E3
Ashburnham Gdns. Ben DN5 ... 61 E3
Ashburnham Rd. Thorne DN8 ... 26 A7
Ashburnham Wlk. Norton DN6 ... 4 E3
Ashburton Cl. Ad I S DN6 ... 40 A6
Ashbury Dr. Shef S8 ... 141 C2
Ashbury La. Shef S8 ... 141 C2
Ashby Ct. Barn S70 ... 54 D8
Ashcroft Cl. N Edl DN12 ... 82 A1
Ashdale Cl. Don DN3 ... 42 F1
Ashdell La. Shef S10 ... 128 C2
Ashdell Rd. Shef S10 ... 128 C2
Ashdell. Shef S10 ... 128 C2
Ashdene Ct. Swint S62 ... 98 D8
Ashdown Gdns. Shef S19 ... 144 A3
Ashdown Pl. Ben DN5 ... 61 F8
Asher Rd. Shef S7 ... 140 F8 14
Ashes La. Went S62 ... 95 F8
Ashes Park Ave. Work S81 ... 148 E1
Ashfield Ave. Thorne DN8 ... 26 A6
Ashfield Cl. Arm DN3 ... 64 C5
Ashfield Cl. Barn S75 ... 33 C3
Ashfield Cl. Shef S12 ... 141 F4
Ashfield Dr. Shef S12 ... 141 F4
Ashfield Gr. Stai DN7 ... 24 F4
Ashfield Rd. Don DN4 ... 83 A6
Ashfield Rd. Hat DN7 ... 43 F7
Ashfield Rd. Hem WF9 ... 17 D5

Beaumont Ave. Barn S70 33 B1
Beaumont Ave. S Elm WF9 18 F3
Beaumont Ave. Shef S2 130 B2
Beaumont Cl. Shef S2 130 B2
Beaumont Cres. Shef S2 130 B2
Beaumont Dr. Roth S65 116 B5
Beaumont Dr. W Bret S65 12 F6
Beaumont Mews. Shef S2 130 B1
Beaumont Rd. Kex S75 32 C8
Beaumont Rd N. Shef S2 130 B1
Beaumont St. Hoy S74 76 B5
Beaumont Way. Shef S2 130 A2
Beaver Ave. Shef S13 143 B8
Beaver Cl. Shef S13 143 B8
Beaver Dr. Shef S13 143 B8
Beaver Hill Comp Sch. Shef 143 B8
Beaver Hill Rd. Shef S13 143 B7
Beccles Way. Roth S66 117 E5
Beck Cl. Shef S5 113 E7
Beck Cl. Swint S64 79 D1
Beck Fst & Mid Sch. Shef 113 D7
Beck Rd. Shef S5 113 D7
Beck Rise. Hem WF9 17 D7
Beck View. Notton WF4 15 A6
Becket Cres. Roth S61 96 D2
Becket Cres. Shef S8 152 E6
Becket Rd. Shef S8 152 E6
Becket Wlk. Shef S8 152 E6
Beckett Ave. C in L S81 148 F7
Beckett Hospl Terr. Barn S70 54 F8 15
Beckett Rd. Don DN2 62 F5
Beckett St. Barn S71 33 F2
Beckfield Gr. Dearne S63 58 B3
Becknoll Rd. W up D S73 78 A8
Beckton Ave. Shef S19 143 E2
Beckton Ct. Shef S19 143 F2
Beckton Gr. Shef S19 143 E2
Beckwith Rd. Laugh S31 134 C2
Beckwith Rd. Roth S65 116 D7
Bedale Ct. Roth S60 115 F4
Bedale Rd. Ben DN5 61 D7
Bedale Rd. Shef S8 140 F6
Bedale Wlk. Shaf S72 16 C3
Bedding Edge Rd. Holmfi HD7 49 A7
Bedford Cl. N Anst S31 146 D7
Bedford Ct. Bawtry DN10 122 F7
Bedford Rd. Ought S30 111 D8
Bedford St. Barn S70 54 F7
Bedford St. Grime S72 36 A5
Bedford St. Maltby S66 119 B4
Bedford St. Shef S6 128 F5
Bedford Terr. Barn S71 34 A5
Bedgebury Cl. Shef S19 144 B1
Bedgrave Cl. Kill S31 156 F8
Beech Ave. Cud S72 35 B8
Beech Ave. Finn DN9 86 A4
Beech Ave. Rawm S62 98 B5
Beech Ave. Roth S65 116 E4
Beech Ave. Silk S75 53 A5
Beech Ave. Tick DN11 121 B7
Beech Cl. Bri S72 17 A3
Beech Cl. Hoy S73 77 D8
Beech Cl. Maltby S66 118 D5
Beech Cl. S Kirk WF9 18 B2
Beech Cres. Eck S31 155 B1
Beech Cres. Kill S31 156 D5
Beech Cres. Mex S64 79 E5
Beech Cres. Stai DN7 24 F4
Beech Dr. Bran DN3 64 E1
Beech Gr. Barn S70 54 D7
Beech Gr. Ben DN5 62 B8
Beech Gr. C in L S81 148 E7
Beech Gr. Con DN12 81 B1
Beech Gr. Din S31 146 F7
Beech Gr. Don DN4 82 C6
Beech Gr. Roth S66 117 C5
Beech Hill. Con DN12 81 C2
Beech Hill Rd. Shef S10 128 D2
Beech House Rd. Hoy S73 77 D7
Beech Rd. Ad le S DN6 21 A1
Beech Rd. Arm DN3 64 B7
Beech Rd. Har DN11 122 A5
Beech Rd. Maltby S66 118 D5
Beech Rd. Norton DN6 4 D1
Beech Rd. Ross DN11 104 A8
Beech Rd. Shaf S72 16 D2
Beech Rd. Upton WF9 19 B7
Beech Rd. W up D S63 79 A6
Beech St. Barn S70 54 F8
Beech St. S Elm WF9 18 E1
Beech Tree Ave. Thorne DN8 26 C6
Beech Tree Cl. Bran DN3 64 B1
Beech Way. Aston S31 144 C8
Beech Way. Dron S18 153 A3
Beecham Ct. Swint S64 79 C1
Beechcroft Rd. Don DN4 82 E5
Beeches Ave. Shef S2 141 C8
Beeches Dr. Shef S2 141 C8
Beeches Gr. Shef S19 144 A3
Beeches Rd. Wales S31 145 B3
Beeches The. Aston S31 144 D7
Beeches The. Don DN3 42 F4
Beeches The. Swint S64 79 C2
Beechfern Cl. Chap S30 94 D8
Beechfield Rd. Don DN1 62 D2
Beechfield Rd. Hat DN7 43 F7
Beechville Ave. Swint S64 79 C1
Beechwood Cl. Don DN3 43 A1
Beechwood Cl. Rawm S62 98 C7
Beechwood Cl. Swint S63 78 F3
Beechwood Cres. Hem WF9 17 C6
Beechwood Mount. Hem WF9 17 D6
Beechwood Rd. Chap S30 94 D6
Beechwood Rd. Dron S18 152 F1
Beechwood Rd. Roth S60 116 A4
Beechwood Rd. Shef S6 128 B8
Beechwood Rd. Stock S30 92 B8
Beechwood. Roth S65 115 F7
Beechwood Wlk. N Edl DN12 82 A1
Beehive Rd. Shef S10 128 D4
Beeley St. Shef S3 128 F1
Beeley Wood La. Shef S6 112 A4
Beeley Wood Rd. Shef S6 112 C3
Beeley Wood Senior Sch. Shef 112 C3
Beely Rd. Ought S30 111 E6
Beeston Cl. Dron S18 152 C2
Beeston Sq. Barn S71 33 F8
Beet St. Shef S3 128 F3
Beeton Gn. Shef S6 126 C5
Beeton Rd. Shef S8 140 F5
Beever La. Barn S75 33 A3
Beevers Rd. Roth S61 96 D2
Beeversleigh. Roth S65 115 E6 3
Beevor St. Barn S71 34 B1
Begonia Cl. S Anst S31 146 D4
Beighton Inf Sch. Shef 144 A3
Beighton Rd E. Shef S19 143 D3
Beighton Rd. Shef S12 143 C3
Beighton Rd. Shef S12, S13 143 D5
Beighton Rd. Swint S62 98 E8
Belcourt Rd. Roth S65 116 D4
Beldon Cl. Shef S2 141 D7
Beldon Pl. Shef S2 141 D7
Beldon Rd. Shef S2 141 D7
Belford Cl. Roth S66 117 C6
Belford Dr. Roth S66 117 C6
Belfry Gdns. Don DN4 85 A7
Belfry Way. Din S31 147 A7
Belgrave Ct. Bawtry DN10 122 F7
Belgrave Dr. Shef S10 127 D1
Belgrave Pl. Aston S31 144 D7
Belgrave Rd. Barn S71 34 A1
Belgrave Rd. Shef S10 127 E1
Belgrave Sq. Shef S2 141 A8 6
Belklane Dr. Kill S31 156 E7
Bell Bank View. Barn S70 54 F5
Bell Butts La. Auck DN9 85 F6
Bell Gn. Fish DN14 7 D4
Bell St. Aston S31 144 F7
Bell St. Upton WF9 19 E8
Bell's Cl. Finn DN9 86 E4
Bellbrooke Pl. Dar S73 56 F7
Belle Green Cl. Cud S72 35 C7
Belle Green Gdns. Cud S72 35 C7
Belle Green La. Cud S72 35 C7
Belle Vue Ave. Don DN4 63 A2
Belle Vue Rd. Mex S64 80 A5
Belle Vue Terr. Thorne DN8 26 B7
Bellerby Pl. Ad le S DN6 20 F2
Bellerby Rd. Ad le S DN6 20 F2
Bellfield Ave. Kex S75 32 C8
Bellhagg Rd. Shef S6 128 B6
Bellhouse Rd. Shef S5 113 E5
Bellis Ave. Don DN4 83 B8
Bellmont Cres. Hem WF9 17 E6
Bellows Rd. Rawm S62 97 F5
Bellrope Acre. Arm DN3 64 B5
Bells Sq. Shef S1 129 A3
Bellscroft Ave. Roth S65 98 E2
Bellwood Cres. Hoy S74 76 C5
Bellwood Cres. Thorne DN8 26 A8
Belmont Ave. Barn S71 34 B5
Belmont Ave. Chap S30 95 A5
Belmont Ave. Don DN4 83 C8
Belmont Cl. Bran DN3 85 E8
Belmont Cres. G Hou S72 57 E7
Belmont. Cud S72 35 C4
Belmont. Cud S72 35 C5
Belmont Dr. Stock S30 73 C1
Belmont St. Mex S64 79 F4
Belmont St. Roth S61 115 A6
Belmont Terr. Thorne DN8 26 B7
Belmont Terr. Thurgo S30 74 A7
Belmont Way. S Elm WF9 19 B3
Belmonte Gdns. Shef S2 129 C2
Belper Rd. Shef S7 140 F6 4
Belsize Rd. Shef S10 139 E7
Beltoft Way. Con DN12 81 E3
Belton Cl. Dron S18 152 C1
Belvedere Cl. Askern DN6 22 B8
Belvedere Cl. N Anst S31 146 F5
Belvedere Cl. Shaf S72 16 C2
Belvedere. Don DN4 82 F6
Belvedere Dr. Dar S73 56 F7
Belvedere Dr. Thorne DN8 9 C3
Belvedere Par. Roth S66 117 C6
Belvoir Ave. Bnbur DN5 59 C3
Ben Bank Rd. Dod S75 53 C6
Ben Cl. Shef S6 111 F1
Bence Cl. Kex S75 32 E7
Bence La. Kex S75 32 D7
Benita Ave. Mex S64 80 C4
Benmore Dr. Shef S19 144 B1
Bennett Cl. Rawm S62 98 B7
Bennett St. Roth S61 114 E6
Bennett St. Shef S2 140 F8 3
Bennetthorpe. Don DN2 62 F2
Benson Rd. Shef S2 129 E2
Bent Hills La. Wharn S30 92 E1
Bent La. Holmfi HD7 48 B8
Bent Lathes Ave. Roth S60 116 C3
Bent Rd. Holmfi HD7 48 D7
Bent St. Pen S30 51 C4
Bentfield Ave. Roth S60 116 C3
Bentham Dr. Barn S71 34 D4
Bentham Way. Mapp S75 14 A2
Bentinck Cl. Don DN1 62 D2
Bentinick St. Con DN12 81 D2
Bentley Ave. Don DN4 82 D6
Bentley Cl. Barn S71 34 E5
Bentley Common La. Ben DN5 62 D8
Bentley High Street Fst & Middle Schs. Ben 62 B7
Bentley Kirkby Ave Fst Sch. Ben 62 A6
Bentley Kirkby Ave Mid Sch. Ben 62 B6
Bentley Moor La. Ad l S DN6 40 E7
Bentley New Village Fst Sch. Ben 41 B2
Bentley RC Sch. Ben 41 B1
Bentley Rd. Ben DN5 62 B6
Bentley Rd. Chap S30 95 B3
Bentley Rd. Roth S66 117 E5
Bentley Rd. Shef S6 128 A5
Bentley St. Roth S60 115 D3
Bentley Sta. Ben 62 A8
Benton Terr. Swint S64 79 D1
Benton Way. Roth S61 114 F7
Bents Cl. Chap S30 95 A5
Bents Cl. Shef S11 139 E5
Bents Cres. Dron S18 153 C3
Bents Cres. Shef S11 139 F5
Bents Dr. Shef S11 139 F5
Bents Green Ave. Shef S11 139 E6
Bents Green Pl. Shef S11 139 E5
Bents Green Rd. Shef S11 139 F5
Bents Green Sch. Shef 139 E5
Bents La. Dron S18 153 C3
Bents La. Shef S6 126 D6
Bents Rd. Carl S30 49 D4
Bents Rd. Roth S61 96 F1
Bents Rd. Shef S11 139 F5
Bents Rd. Shef S17 151 C4
Bents View. Shef S11 139 E5
Benty La. Shef S10 127 F3
Beresford Rd. Maltby S66 119 B4
Beresford St. Ben DN5 41 C1
Berkeley Croft. Roy S71 15 B4
Berkeley Prec. Shef S11 140 D8
Berkley Cl. Barn S70 54 F5
Bernard Gdn. Shef S2 129 C4
Bernard Rd. N Edl DN12 82 C1
Bernard Rd. Shef S2, S4 129 D4
Bernard St. Rawn S62 98 B7
Bernard St. Roth S60 115 E5
Bernard St. Shef S2 129 C3
Berne Sq. Woods S81 147 D4
Berners Cl. Shef S2 141 E6
Berners Dr. Shef S2 141 E6
Berners Pl. Shef S2 141 E6
Berners Rd. Shef S2 141 E6
Berneslai Cl. Barn S70 33 E2
Berneslai Ct. Barn S70 33 E2 2
Bernshall Cres. Shef S5 113 B7
Berresford Rd. Shef S11 140 D8 8
Berrington Cl. Don DN4 83 A4
Berry Ave. Eck S31 155 C3
Berry Dr. Wales S31 145 F3
Berry Holme Cl. Chap S30 95 A5
Berry Holme Ct. Chap S30 95 A5
Berry Holme Dr. Chap S30 95 A5
Berry La. Wort S30 94 A8
Berry Moor Cotts. Thurgo S75 53 A3
Berrydale. Barn S70 55 B5
Berrywell Ave. Pen S30 51 E2
Bertram Rd. Ought S30 111 E6
Bessacarr Fst Sch. Don 84 C8
Bessacarr La. Don DN4 84 E5
Bessemer Pl. Shef S9 129 E5
Bessemer Rd. Shef S9 129 E6
Bessemer Terr. Stock S30 73 B2
Bessemer Way. Roth S60 115 A4
Bessingby Rd. Shef S6 128 C7
Bethel Rd. Roth S65 115 F8
Bethel St. Hoy S74 76 F6
Bethel Terr. Shire S81 159 F7
Bethel Wlk. Shef S1 129 A3 16
Betjeman Gdns. Shef S10 128 C1
Betony Cl. Kill S31 156 B5
Between Rivers La. Snaith DN14 1 C4
Beulah Rd. Shef S6 112 D1
Bevan Ave. Ross DN11 84 F1
Bevan Cl. Hoy S74 77 A6
Bevan Cres. Maltby S66 118 F6
Bevan Way. Chap S30 94 F4
Bever St. Dearne S63 58 F5
Bevercotes Rd. Shef S5 113 E3
Beverley Ave. Barn S70 54 F5
Beverley Cl. Aston S31 144 D7
Beverley Cl. Barn S71 33 E7
Beverley Gdns. Ben DN5 61 D5
Beverley Rd. Don DN2 63 A6
Beverley Rd. Har DN11 122 A4
Beverley St. Shef S9 130 A6 2
Beverley Wlk. C in L S81 148 E7
Beverleys Rd. Shef S8 141 A4
Bevin Pl. Rawm S62 98 B6
Bevre Rd. Arm DN3 64 B7
Bewdley Ct. Roy S71 15 D4
Bewicke Ave. Ben DN5 61 D6
Bib La. Thurcr S31 134 C7
Bickerton Rd. Shef S6 112 C2
Bierlow Cl. W up D S73 78 A8
Bigby Way. Roth S66 117 D7
Bignor Pl. Shef S6 112 D5
Bignor Rd. Shef S6 112 D4
Bilham La. H Pag DN5 38 D2
Bilham Rd. Clay W HD8 12 A2
Bilham Row. H Pag DN5 38 F3
Billam Pl. Roth S61 96 E1
Billam St. Eck S31 155 B3
Billingley Dr. Dearne S63 58 C7
Billingley Green La. G Hou S72 57 F5
Billingley La. G Hou S72 57 F8
Billingley View. Dearne S63 58 B3
Billy Wright's La. Wad DN11 102 F4
Bilston St. Shef S6 128 D7
Binders Rd. Roth S61 96 E1
Binfield Rd. Shef S8 140 F5
Bingham Ct. Shef S11 139 F8
Bingham Park Cres. Shef S11 140 A8
Bingham Park Rd. Shef S11 140 A8
Bingham Rd. Shef S8 140 F2
Bingley La. Shef S6 127 A4
Bingley St. Barn S75 33 D2
Binsted Ave. Shef S5 112 D3
Binsted Cl. Shef S5 112 D3
Binsted Cres. Shef S5 112 D3
Binsted Croft. Shef S5 112 D3
Binsted Dr. Shef S5 112 D3
Binsted Gdns. Shef S5 112 D3
Binsted Glade. Shef S5 112 D3
Binsted Gr. Shef S5 112 D3
Binsted Rd. Shef S5 112 D3
Binsted Way. Shef S5 112 D3
Birch Ave. Ad le S DN6 21 A1
Birch Ave. Chap S30 95 A5
Birch Ave. Finn DN9 86 A4
Birch Cl. Kill S31 156 C5
Birch Cres. Roth S66 117 C5
Birch Farm Ave. Shef S8 153 A8
Birch Gr. Con DN12 81 D2
Birch Gr. Ought S30 111 E6
Birch Green Cl. Maltby S66 118 D6
Birch House Ave. Ought S30 111 D6
Birch Park Ct. Roth S61 115 A6
Birch Rd. Barn S70 55 D7
Birch Rd. Don DN4 84 F8
Birch Rd. Shef S9 129 E6
Birch Tree Cl. B Dun DN3 43 A7
Birch Tree Rd. Stock S30 92 B7
Birchall Ave. Roth S60 116 B1
Birchdale Cl. Don DN3 42 F1
Birchen Cl. Don DN4 84 E5
Birchen Cl. Dron S18 152 D1
Birches Fold. Dron S18 153 C4
Birches La. Dron S18 153 C4
Birchfield Cres. Dod S75 54 A8
Birchfield Rd. Maltby S66 119 B5
Birchfield Wlk. Barn S75 33 B2
Birchitt Cl. Shef S17 152 C5
Birchitt Pl. Shef S17 152 C5
Birchitt Rd. Shef S17 152 C5
Birchitt View. Dron S18 153 A3
Birchlands Dr. Kill S31 156 D5
Birchtree Rd. Roth S61 95 F3
Birchvale Rd. Shef S12 142 D3
Birchwood Ave. Rawm S62 97 F7
Birchwood Cl. Maltby S66 118 D6
Birchwood Cl. Shef S19 155 E8 7
Birchwood Cl. Thorne DN8 9 B1
Birchwood Croft. Shef S19 155 E8
Birchwood Ct. Ross DN4 85 B5
Birchwood Dell. Ross DN4 85 C5
Birchwood Dr. Roth S65 117 D8
Birchwood Gdns. Shef S19 155 E8 6
Birchwood Gr. Shef S19 155 E8
Birchwood Rd. Eck S31 154 D3
Birchwood Rise. Shef S19 155 E8 5
Birchwood View. Shef S19 155 E8
Birchwood Way. Shef S19 155 E8 16
Bircotes Wlk. Ross DN11 85 B1
Bird Ave. Wombw S73 56 C2
Bird La. Thurgo S30 52 E2
Birds Edge La. D Dale HD8 28 F4
Birdsedge Farm Mews. D Dale HD8 29 A4
Birdsedge Fst Sch. D Dale 29 A4
Birdsnest La. Wh Com HD7 28 D2
Birdwell Prim Sch. Barn 75 F7
Birdwell Rd. Dod S75 54 B6
Birdwell Rd. Shef S4 113 F1
Birdwell Rd. Swint S64 79 D1
Birk Ave. Barn S70 55 C7
Birk Cres. Barn S70 55 C7
Birk Gn. Barn S70 55 D7
Birk Hill County Inf Sch. Eck 155 B2
Birk House La. Barn S70 55 D7
Birk House La. Shep HD8 29 B8
Birk Rd. Barn S70 55 C7
Birk Terr. Barn S70 55 C7
Birkbeck Ct. Chap S30 94 D8
Birkdale Ave. Din S31 147 A8
Birkdale Cl. Cud S72 35 C8
Birkdale Cl. Don DN4 85 B6
Birkdale Preparatory Sch. Shef 128 D1
Birkdale Rd. Roy S71 15 B5
Birkdale Rise. Swint S64 79 D2
Birkdale Sch. Shef 128 C2
Birkendale Rd. Shef S6 128 D5
Birkendale. Shef S6 128 D5
Birkendale View. Shef S6 128 D5
Birklands Ave. Shef S13 130 E1
Birklands Cl. Shef S13 130 E1
Birklands Dr. Shef S13 130 E1
Birks Ave. Pen S30 50 E3
Birks Ave. Shef S13 143 B6
Birks Cotts. Pen S30 50 E3
Birks Holt Dr. Maltby S66 119 C3
Birks La. Pen S30 50 E3
Birks Rd. Roth S61 96 E1
Birks Wood Dr. Ought S30 111 D6
Birkwood Ave. Cud S72 35 C4
Birkwood Terr. Braith S66 101 B1
Birley Cty Inf Sch. Shef 142 D3
Birley Cty Prim Sch. Shef 142 D3
Birley Cty Secondary Sch. Shef 142 D3
Birley Ct. Shef S6 112 C6
Birley La. Shef S12 142 D2
Birley Moor Ave. Shef S12 142 E3
Birley Moor Cl. Shef S12 142 E3
Birley Moor Cres. Shef S12 142 E2
Birley Moor Dr. Shef S12 142 E2
Birley Moor Pl. Shef S12 142 E2
Birley Moor Rd. Shef S12 142 E4
Birley Moor Way. Shef S12 142 E2
Birley Rise Cres. Shef S6 112 C4
Birley Rise Rd. Shef S6 112 C4
Birley Spa Jun & Inf Sch. Shef 142 F4
Birley Spa La. Shef S12 143 B4
Birley Vale Ave. Shef S12 142 C5
Birley Vale Cl. Shef S12 142 C4
Birley View. Ought S30 111 D5
Birley Wood Golf Course. Shef 142 E2
Birthwaite Rd. Kex S75 13 B1
Bisby Rd. Rawm S62 98 A6
Biscay Way. W up D S63 78 F6
Bishop Gdns. Shef S13 143 A6
Bishop Hill. Shef S13 143 A6
Bishop St. Shef S3 128 F2
Bishopdale Ct. Shef S19 143 A1
Bishopdale Dr. Shef S19 155 A8
Bishopdale Rise. Shef S19 143 A1
Bishops Ct. Shef S8 141 B5
Bishops Way. Barn S71 34 C3
Bishopscourt Rd. Shef S8 141 A5
Bishopsgate La. Ross DN11 104 A7
Bishopsholme Rd. Shef S5 113 B2
Bishopstoke Ct. Roth S65 116 A7 1
Bishopston Wlk. Maltby S66 118 E6
Bisley Cl. Roy S71 15 E4
Bismarck St. Barn S70 54 F7
Bitholmes Gate. Wharn S30 93 B3
Bittern View. Roth S61 96 A6
Black Bull Cotts. Hat DN8 27 B2
Black Carr Rd. Roth S66 117 A4
Black Hill Rd. Roth S65 116 D4
Black Horse Cl. Silk S75 53 A5
Black Horse Dr. Silk S75 53 A5
Black La. Chap S74 76 B2
Black La. Hoy S74 76 B2
Black La. Shef S6 127 D7
Black Swan Wlk. Shef S1 129 A3 11
Black Syke La. Fish DN14 8 C4
Blacka Moor Cres. Shef S17 151 C6
Blacka Moor Rd. Shef S17 151 C6
Blacka Moor View. Shef S17 151 C6
Blackamoor Rd. Swint S64 78 F1
Blackberry Flats. Shef S19 155 E7
Blackbird Ave. Brin S60 131 D8
Blackbrook Ave. Shef S10 127 A1
Blackbrook Dr. Shef S10 127 A1
Blackbrook Rd. Shef S10 139 A8
Blackburn Cres. Chap S30 94 F6
Blackburn Croft. Chap S30 94 F6
Blackburn Dr. Chap S30 94 E6
Blackburn Jun & Inf Sch. Roth 114 B6
Blackburn La. Barn S75 33 D2
Blackburn La. Barn S70 55 A5
Blackburn La. Roth S61 114 B6
Blackburn Rd. Shef S61 114 B5
Blackburn St. Barn S70 55 A5
Blackburne St. Shef S6 128 D7 1
Blackdown Ave. Shef S19 143 D2
Blackdown Cl. Shef S19 143 D2
Blacker Green La. Askern DN5 22 D4
Blacker La. Barn S70 55 B2
Blacker La. Shaf S72 16 C3
Blacker Rd. Mapp S75 33 C8
Blackergreen La. Silk S75 52 E5
Blackheath Cl. Barn S71 34 B7
Blackheath Rd. Barn S71 34 B7
Blackheath Wlk. Barn S71 34 B7
Blackmoor Cres. Brin S60 115 B1
Blackmore St. Shef S4 129 D5
Blacksmith La. Shef S30 112 C8
Blacksmith's La. Marr DN5 60 C7
Blackstock Cl. Shef S14 141 D2
Blackstock Cres. Shef S14 141 D2
Blackstock Dr. Shef S14 141 D2
Blackstock Rd. Shef S14 141 D4
Blackthorn Ave. Roth S66 117 C5
Blackthorn Cl. Chap S30 94 D8
Blackthorne Cl. N Edl DN12 82 A1
Blackwell Cl. Shef S2 129 C3 3
Blackwell Ct. Shef S2 129 C3 2
Blackwell Pl. Shef S2 129 C3
Blackwood Ave. Don DN4 82 F6
Blagden St. Shef S2 129 C2
Blair Athol Rd. Shef S11 140 B7
Blake Ave. Don DN2 62 F6
Blake Ave. W up D S63 78 C7
Blake Cl. Roth S66 117 E4
Blake Grove Rd. Shef S6 128 E5
Blake St. Shef S6 128 D5
Blakeley Cl. Barn S71 34 B7
Blakeney Rd. Shef S10 128 C3
Bland La. Shef S6 111 F1
Bland St. Shef S4 129 E8
Blast La. Shef S2, S4 129 C4
Blaxton Cl. Shef S19 143 A2
Blayton Rd. Shef S4 129 C8
Bleachcroft Way. Barn S73 55 E7
Bleak Ave. Shaf S72 16 C2
Bleakley Ave. Notton WF4 15 B6
Bleakley Cl. Shaf S72 16 C2
Bleakley La. Notton WF4 15 B6
Bleakley Terr. Notton WF4 15 B6
Bleasdale Gr. Barn S71 34 A4
Blenheim Ave. Barn S70 54 E8
Blenheim Cl. Din S31 146 E8
Blenheim Cl. Hat DN7 44 A6
Blenheim Cl. Roth S66 117 C7
Blenheim Cres. Mex S64 79 E5
Blenheim Ct. Roth S66 117 B6
Blenheim Gdns. Shef S11 140 A5
Blenheim Gr. Barn S70 54 D8
Blenheim Rd. Barn S70 54 E8
Blenheim Rd. Hat DN7 66 A8
Blenheim Rise. Bawtry DN10 122 F6
Blindside La. Bfield S6 109 C3
Bloemfontein Rd. Cud S72 35 A6
Bloemfontein St. Cud S72 35 B6
Blonk St. Shef S1 129 B4
Bloomfield Rd. Mapp S75 13 F1
Bloomfield Rise. Mapp S75 13 F1
Bloomhill Cl. Thorne DN8 9 D4
Bloomhill Ct. Thorne DN8 9 C4
Bloomhill Rd. Thorne DN8 9 B3
Bloomhouse La. Mapp S75 13 F1
Blossom Ave. Askern DN6 22 B7
Blossom Cres. Shef S12 142 B3
Blow Hall Cres. N Edl DN12 82 C2
Blucher St. Barn S70 33 E1
Blue Bell Ct. Blax DN9 86 E5
Blue Boy St. Shef S3 128 F4 12
Bluebell Ave. Pen S30 51 C2
Bluebell Cl. Shef S5 113 F3
Bluebell Rd. Shef S5 113 F3
Bluebell Rd. Wool S75 13 E3
Bluebird Hill. Aston S31 144 E6
Bluestone Cty Prim Sch. Shef 141 D8
Blundell Cl. Don DN4 84 E7
Blundell Ct. Barn S71 34 D5
Blundell St. S Elm WF9 18 E3
Bly Rd. Dar S73 56 F6
Blyde Rd. Shef S5 113 C1
Blyth Ave. Rawm S62 97 F5
Blyth Cl. Roth S60 116 D1
Blyth Gate La. Tick DN11 120 E3
Blyth Rd. Har DN11 121 F2
Blyth Rd. Maltby S66 119 A4
Blyth Rd. Old S81 136 F6
Blyth Rd. Styr DN11 121 F2
Blyth Rd. Tick DN11 121 E6
Blythe St. Wombw S73 56 D3
Boardman Ave. Rawm S62 97 C8
Boat La. Sprot DN5 82 B8
Boating Dyke Way. Thorne DN8 26 A7
Bochum Parkway. Shef S8 153 C8
Bocking Cl. Shef S8 140 D1
Bocking Hill. Stock S30 73 D1
Bocking La. Shef S8 140 D1
Bocking La. Shef S8 152 E8
Bocking Rise. Shef S8 152 E8
Boden La. Shef S1 128 F3
Boden Pl. Shef S9 130 C5
Bodmin Ct. Barn S71 34 B3
Bodmin St. Shef S9 129 F6
Boggard La. Ought S30 111 C6
Boggard La. Pen S30 51 C2
Boiley La. Kill S31 156 C4
Boland Rd. Shef S8 152 D5
Bold St. Shef S9 130 A8
Bole Cl. Dar S73 56 F4
Bole Hill Prim Sch. Shef 128 B6
Bole Hill Rd. Shef S6 128 A5
Bole Hill. Treet S60 131 F5
Bolehill La. Eck S31 154 F2
Bolehill La. Shef S10 128 B4
Bolsover Rd E. Shef S5 113 D1
Bolsover Rd. Shef S5 113 D2
Bolsover St. Shef S3 128 E3
Bolsterstone C of E Jun & Inf Sch. Stock 92 C6
Bolsterstone Rd. Bfield S30 92 C1
Bolton Hill Rd. Don DN4 84 E7
Bolton on Dearne Sta. Dearne 58 C2
Bolton Rd Managed Workshops. W up D S63 79 C7
Bolton Rd. W up D S63 79 C7
Bolton St. Con DN12 80 F3
Bolton St. Shef S3 128 F2

Bolton-on-Dearne Inf Sch. Dearne 58 C2
Bolton-on-Dearne Jun Mix Sch. Dearne 58 C2
Bond Cl. Don DN1 62 C2
Bond Rd. Barn S75 33 D3
Bond St. Ross DN11 104 A7
Bond St. Wombw S73 56 D3
Bondfield Ave. Ross DN11 104 A8
Bondfield Cres. Wombw S73 56 D2
Bondhay La. Whit S80 158 C2
Bone La. Norton DN6 21 C8
Bonet La. Brin S60 115 A1
Bonington Rise. Maltby S66 118 E6
Bonville Gdns. Shef S3 128 F4 2
Booker Rd. Shef S8 140 E2
Booker's La. N Anst S31 134 B1
Bookers Way. N Anst S31 134 B1
Booth Cl. Shef S19 143 D2
Booth Cl. Thurcr S66 134 A6
Booth Croft. Shef S19 143 D2
Booth Pl. Rawm S62 97 E7
Booth Rd. Chap S30 94 C7
Booth St. Hoy S74 76 E6
Booth St. Roth S61 97 B4
Bootham Cl. Hat DN7 44 B8
Bootham Cres. Stai DN7 24 F3
Bootham La. Hat DN7 25 A2
Bootham Rd. Stai DN7 24 F3
Bootle St. Shef S9 130 A6 3
Borough Rd. Shef S6 128 D8
Borrowdale Ave. Shef S19 155 E6 3
Borrowdale Cl. Ad le S DN6 21 C1
Borrowdale Cl. Barn S71 56 A8
Borrowdale Cl. Din S31 146 F7
Borrowdale Cl. N Anst S31 146 F7
Borrowdale Cl. Shef S19 155 E6 2
Borrowdale Dr. Shef S19 155 E6
Borrowdale Rd. Shef S19 155 E6
Boston Castle Gr. Roth S60 115 E4
Boston Castle Terr. Roth S60 115 E4
Boston St. Shef S2 129 A1
Bosvile Cl. Roth S65 99 D3
Bosville Rd. Shef S10 128 B3
Bosville St. Pen S30 51 E2
Bosville St. Roth S65 116 D8
Boswell Cl. Chap S30 94 C8
Boswell Cl. Ross DN11 103 E8
Boswell Cl. Roy S71 15 B4
Boswell Rd. Don DN4 84 D7
Boswell Rd. W up D S63 78 F4
Boswell St. Roth S65 115 F5
Bosworth Cl. Hat DN7 44 A5
Bosworth Rd. Ad I S DN6 40 A6
Bosworth St. Shef S10 128 B4 2
Botanical Rd. Shef S11 128 C1
Botany Bay La. B Dun DN7 43 C7
Botham St. Shef S4 129 E8
Botsford St. Shef S3 129 A6
Boulder Bridge La. Roy S71 15 F1
Boulevard The. Don DN3 42 E2
Boulton Dr. Bran DN3 64 B1
Boundary Ave. Don DN2 63 C7
Boundary Cl. N Edl DN12 82 C3
Boundary Gn. Rawm S62 98 A4
Boundary Rd. Shef S2 129 E2
Boundary St. Barn S70 55 B8
Boundary Wlk. Brin S60 131 A8
Bourne Ct. Mapp S75 14 C2
Bourne Rd. Barn S70 55 A4
Bourne Rd. Shef S5 113 C4
Bourne Wlk. Mapp S75 14 C2
Bow St. Cud S72 35 B7
Bowbridge Cl. Roth S60 115 C4
Bowden Gr. Dod S75 53 F7
Bowden Wood Ave. Shef S9 130 C2
Bowden Wood Cl. Shef S9 130 C2
Bowden Wood Cres. Shef S9 130 C2
Bowden Wood Dr. Shef S9 130 C2
Bowden Wood Pl. Shef S9 130 C2
Bowden Wood Rd. Shef S9 130 C2
Bowdon St. Shef S1 128 F2
Bowen Dr. Roth S65 98 F2
Bowen Rd. Roth S65 115 F8
Bower Cl. Roth S61 96 E1
Bower Hill. Oxspr S30 52 C1
Bower La. Shef S30 94 B1
Bower Rd. Shef S10 128 D4
Bower Rd. Swint S64 79 D4
Bower Spring. Shef S3 129 A4 3
Bower St. Shef S3 129 A4
Bower Vale. N Edl DN12 82 A1
Bowfell View. Barn S71 34 A4
Bowfield Ct. Shef S5 113 C4
Bowfield Rd. Shef S5 113 D4
Bowland Cl. Ben DN5 61 F8
Bowland Cres. Barn S70 54 F4
Bowland Dr. Chap S30 94 E5
Bowlease Gdns. Don DN4 84 E8
Bowling Green St. Shef S3 129 A5
Bowman Cl. Shef S12 141 F2
Bowman Dr. Maltby S66 118 E6
Bowness Cl. Dron S18 152 E1
Bowness Dr. Askern DN6 22 C8
Bowness Rd. Shef S6 128 C7
Bowood Rd. Shef S11 140 D8
Bowshaw Ave. Shef S8 153 A5
Bowshaw Cl. Shef S8 153 A5
Bowshaw View. Shef S8 153 A5
Boyce St. Shef S6 128 D5
Boycott Way. S Elm WF9 19 A4
Boyd Rd. Swint S63 78 F3
Boyland St. Shef S3 128 F6
Boynton Cres. Shef S5 113 A2
Boynton Rd. Shef S5 113 A2
Brabbs Ave. Hat DN7 44 C8
Bracken Ct. Har DN11 121 E4
Bracken Ct. Roth S66 117 B3
Bracken Heen Cl. Hat DN7 44 B8
Bracken Hill. Chap S30 94 D4
Bracken Hill Prim Sch. Shef 113 E3
Bracken Hill. S Kirk WF9 18 D4
Bracken Moor La. Stock S30 92 C8
Bracken Rd. Shef S5 113 E3
Bracken Way. Har DN11 121 E4
Brackenbury Cl. Cade DN5 81 D6
Brackenfield Gr. Shef S12 142 D3
Brackley St. Shef S3 129 B6
Bradberry Balk La. Dar S73 56 D5
Bradberry Balk La. Wombw S73 56 C4
Bradbury St. Barn S70 33 D1
Bradbury St. Shef S8 141 A6
Bradbury's Cl. Rawm S62 97 F3
Bradfield Rd. Shef S6 128 C8
Bradford Rd. Don DN2 63 C8
Bradford Row. Don DN1 62 D3
Bradford Sch. Ought 111 C5
Bradgate Cl. Roth S61 115 A7
Bradgate Cl. Roth S61 114 F7
Bradgate La. Roth S61 114 F7
Bradgate Pl. Roth S61 115 A8
Bradgate Rd. Roth S61 115 A7
Bradlea Rise. Rawm S62 98 A7
Bradley Ave. Wombw S73 56 C3
Bradley Carr Terr. S Elm WF9 37 E8
Bradley St. Shef S10 128 C5
Bradshaw Ave. Treet S60 131 F3
Bradshaw Cl. Barn S75 33 A2
Bradshaw Way. Treet S60 131 F3
Bradstone Rd. Roth S65 116 C8
Bradway Cl. Shef S17 152 B5
Bradway Cty Prim Sch. Shef 152 E6
Bradway Dr. Shef S17 152 B5
Bradway Grange Rd. Shef S17 152 C5
Bradway Rd. Shef S17 152 B5
Bradway Rd. Shef S17 152 C6
Bradwell Ave. Dod S75 54 A6
Bradwell Cl. Dron S18 152 C1
Bradwell St. Shef S2 141 B6 1
Braemar Croft. S Hie S72 16 D7
Braemar Rd. Ben DN2 63 A3
Braemar Rise. S Hie S72 16 D7
Braemore Rd. Shef S6 112 A1
Brailsford Ave. Shef S5 113 A8
Brailsford Rd. Shef S5 113 A8
Braithwaite La. K Bram DN7 23 F7
Braithwaite St. Mapp S75 14 C1
Braithwell Ct. Ben DN5 41 A3
Braithwell Fst & Mid Sch. Braith 101 A2
Braithwell Rd. Ben DN5 41 A3
Braithwell Rd. Maltby S66 118 F5
Braithwell Rd. Roth S65, S66 117 E8
Braithwell Way. Maltby S66 118 A7
Braithwell Wlk. Con DN12 80 F4
Bramah St. Roy S71 15 C1
Bramall La. Shef S2 141 A8
Bramall La. Stock S30 72 F3
Bramall Lane Football Gd. Shef 129 A1
Bramar Rd. Hat DN7 44 A8
Bramble Cl. Roth S66 117 B3
Bramble Way. Finn DN9 86 A4
Bramble Way. Har DN11 121 E4
Bramble Way. W up D S63 78 B6
Brambles The. Shef S30 95 B1
Bramcote Ave. Barn S71 33 E8
Brameld Rd. Rawm S62 97 F5
Brameld Rd. Swint S64 79 B3
Bramham Ct. Shef S9 130 B5
Bramham Rd. Don DN4 63 F1
Bramham Rd. Shef S9 130 B5
Bramley Ave. Aston S31 144 E8
Bramley Ave. Shef S13 142 F8
Bramley Cl. Shef S19 155 C7
Bramley Ct. Con DN12 80 F3 3
Bramley Dr. Shef S13 130 F1
Bramley Grange Cres. Roth S66 117 E5
Bramley Grange Dr. Roth S66 117 E5
Bramley Grange Jun Mix & Inf Sch. Roth 117 E6
Bramley Grange Rise. Roth S66 117 F5
Bramley Grange View. Roth S66 117 E6
Bramley Grange W. Roth S66 117 F5
Bramley Hall Rd. Shef S13 142 F8
Bramley La. Roth S65 118 A8
Bramley La. W Bret S75 13 B8
Bramley Park Cl. Shef S13 142 F8
Bramley Park Rd. Shef S13 130 F1
Bramley Rd. Eck S31 154 E1
Bramley Sunnyside Inf Sch. Roth 117 C6
Bramley Sunnyside Jun Sch. Roth 117 B6
Bramley Way. Maltby S66 118 B6
Bramleymoor La. Eck S31 154 E1
Brampton Ave. Thurcr S66 133 D6
Brampton Bierlow Cortonwood County Inf Sch. W up D 78 A8
Brampton Cl. Arm DN3 64 A5
Brampton Cres. Wombw S73 56 F1
Brampton Ct. S Elm WF9 19 A5
Brampton Ct. Shef S19 143 A2 3
Brampton Ellis Inf Sch. W up D 78 C6
Brampton La. Arm DN3 64 A5
Brampton La. Ulley S31 133 B5
Brampton Meadows. Thurcr S66 133 D6
Brampton Rd. G Hou S73 57 A1
Brampton Rd. Thurcr S66 133 D6
Brampton Rd. W up D S63 78 B7
Brampton St. W up D S73 78 B8
Brampton The Ellis C of E (Aided) Jun Sch. W up D 78 B7
Brampton View. Wombw S73 56 F1
Bramshill Cl. Shef S19 144 A1
Bramshill Ct. Shef S19 144 A1 2
Bramwell Gdns. Shef S3 128 E4
Bramwell St. Roth S65 115 E7
Bramwell St. Shef S3 128 E4
Bramwith La. B Dun DN3 42 E8
Bramwith La. K Bram DN3 23 F2
Bramwith Rd. Shef S11 139 F8
Bramworth Rd. Don DN4 61 F1
Brancliffe La. Shire S81 159 F8
Brancroft Cl. Don DN4 84 D6
Brand La. Sprot DN5 60 F4
Brand's La. Din S81 147 D6
Brandeth Rd. Shef S6 128 E5
Brandfield Cotts. Sprot DN5 61 A4
Brandon St. Shef S3 129 B7
Brandreth Cl. Shef S6 128 E5
Brands Cl. Woods S81 147 E5
Brandsmere Dr. Woods S81 147 E5
Branksome Ave. Barn S70 33 C1
Bransby St. Shef S6 128 D5
Branstone Rd. Sprot DN5 61 B2
Branton C of E Sch. Bran 85 D8
Branton Gate Rd or Whiphill Top La. Bran DN3 64 E1
Brantwood Cres. Don DN4 63 F1
Brathay Cl. Shef S4 113 F1
Brathay Rd. Shef S4 113 F1
Bray St. Shef S9 130 A5
Bray Wlk. Roth S61 96 C2
Brayton Gdns. Norton DN6 21 C8
Brearley Ave. Stock S30 92 D8
Breck La. Din S31 134 F2
Brecklands. Roth S65 116 C4
Brecklands. Roth S66 117 A4
Brecks Cres. Roth S65 116 E4
Brecks La. Don DN3 43 A4
Brecks La. Roth S65 116 D7
Brecks La. Roth S65 116 E6
Brecon Cl. Shef S19 144 A2
Bredon Cl. Hem WF9 17 F7
Breezemount Ct. Stai DN7 24 F4
Brendon Cl. Wombw S73 77 F8
Brentwood Ave. Shef S11 140 D6
Brentwood Cl. Hoy S74 76 C4
Brentwood Rd. Shef S11 140 D6
Bressingham Cl. Shef S4 129 C6
Bressingham Rd. Shef S4 129 C6
Bretby Cl. Don DN4 85 A6
Brett Cl. Rawm S62 97 C8
Brettegate. Hem WF9 17 C7
Bretton Cl. Hat DN7 44 A6
Bretton Cl. Kex S75 32 C8
Bretton Country Park. W Bret 12 F7
Bretton Gr. Shef S12 142 D3
Bretton Hall Coll of High Ed W Bret 12 E6
Bretton House. Don DN1 62 C2 11
Bretton La. W Bret WF4 12 F8
Bretton Rd. Kex S75 32 D8
Bretton View. Cud S72 35 A5
Brewery Rd. W up D S63 78 F7
Breydon Ave. Ben DN5 61 E5
Briar Cl. Finn DN9 86 A4
Briar Croft. Don DN4 83 A8
Briar Ct. Har DN11 121 E4
Briar Ct. Roth S66 117 B3
Briar Gr. Bri S72 17 A3
Briar Rd. Ad le S DN6 21 A1
Briar Rd. Arm DN3 64 A7
Briar Rd. Shef S7 140 E6
Briar Rise. Barn S70 55 A4
Briarfield Ave. Shef S12 142 A3
Briarfield Cres. Shef S12 142 A2
Briarfield Rd. Shef S12 142 A3
Briarfields La. Ought S30 111 C5
Briars Cl. Kill S31 156 D5
Briars La. Stai DN7 24 F5
Briary Ave. Chap S30 94 D7
Briary Cl. Brin S60 131 C7
Brick Kiln La. Moss DN6 23 B8
Brick Row. Thurgo S30 74 B7
Brick St. Shef S10 128 B3
Brickhouse La. Shef S17 151 C8
Bridby St. Shef S13 143 C6
Bride Church La. Tick DN11 121 A7
Bridge Gdns. Barn S71 33 F3
Bridge Gr. Ben DN5 61 F5
Bridge Hill. Ought S30 111 D7
Bridge Inn Rd. Chap S30 95 A6
Bridge La. Rawcl DN14 2 C7
Bridge Rd. Don DN4 63 C1
Bridge St. Barn S71 33 F2
Bridge St. Barn S71 55 E8
Bridge St. Dearne S63 58 D3
Bridge St. Don DN4 62 B2
Bridge St. Kill S31 156 D6
Bridge St. Mapp S75 13 E1
Bridge St. Pen S30 51 C4
Bridge St. Roth S60 115 D7
Bridge St. Shef S3 129 B4
Bridge St. Swint S64 79 E3
Bridge St. Thorne DN8 26 B7
Bridge Terr. Rawcl DN14 2 D7
Bridgegate. Roth S60 115 D7
Bridgehouses. Shef S3 129 A5
Bridgewater Park Dr. Ad le S DN6 20 F2
Bridle Cl. Chap S30 95 A6
Bridle Cres. Chap S30 95 A6
Bridle Stile Cl. Shef S19 155 C7
Bridle Stile. Shef S19 155 C7
Bridle Style Ave. Shef S19 155 B7
Bridleway The. Rawm S62 98 C7
Bridport Rd. Shef S9 130 B5
Brier Cl. Shef S19 143 D1
Brier La. Ryhill WF4 16 C8
Brier St. Shef S6 128 C8
Brierfield Cl. Barn S75 33 C2
Brierholme Carr Rd. Hat DN7 25 F1
Brierholme Cl. Hat DN7 25 E1
Brierholme Ings Rd. Hat DN7 44 F8
Brierley Cres. S Kirk WF9 18 C3
Brierley Grimethorpe Springvale Fst & Mid Schs. Grime 36 A6
Brierley Rd. Don DN4 84 D7
Brierley Rd. Grime S72 36 A8
Brierley Rd. S Hie S72 16 E5
Brierley Rd. Shaf S72 16 D2
Brierly Rd. Roth S65 98 E1
Briers House La. Bfield S6 110 D1
Briery Wlk. Roth S61 97 B3
Briggs Rd. Roy S71 15 C1
Brightholmlee Ct. Wharn S30 93 B2
Brightholmlee Rd. Wharn S30 92 E2
Brightmore Dr. Shef S3 128 E3
Brighton St. Grime S72 36 A7
Brighton Terrace Rd. Shef S10 128 C4
Brightside Fst Sch. Shef 114 B2
Brightside La. Shef S9 129 F7
Brimmesfield Cl. Shef S2 141 F7
Brimmesfield Dr. Shef S2 141 E8
Brimmesfield Rd. Shef S2 141 E7
Brinckman St. Barn S70 55 A8
Brincliffe Cres. Shef S11 140 C7
Brincliffe Ct. Shef S7 140 E6
Brincliffe Edge Cl. Shef S11 140 C6
Brincliffe Edge Rd. Shef S11, S7 140 C6
Brincliffe Gdns. Shef S11 140 C7
Brincliffe Hill. Shef S11 140 B7
Brindley Cl. Shef S8 141 A4
Brindley Cres. Shef S8 141 A4
Brindley Ct. Kill S31 156 C6
Brinkburn Cl. Shef S17 151 F6
Brinkburn Ct. Shef S17 151 F6
Brinkburn Vale Rd. Shef S17 151 F6
Brinsford Rd. Brin S60 115 C1
Brinsworth Comp Sch. Brin 131 A8
Brinsworth Hall Ave. Brin S60 131 B8
Brinsworth Hall Cres. Brin S60 131 B8
Brinsworth Hall Dr. Brin S60 131 B8
Brinsworth Hall Gr. Brin S60 131 B7
Brinsworth Howarth Jun & Inf Sch. Brin 131 C7
Brinsworth La. Brin S60 131 B8
Brinsworth Manor Jun & Inf Sch. Brin 115 C1
Brinsworth Rd. Brin S60 131 B7
Brinsworth Rd. Treet S60 131 C6
Brinsworth Rd. Treet S60 131 B7
Brinsworth St. Roth S60 115 C6
Brinsworth St. Shef S9 129 F6
Brinsworth Whitehill Jun Mix & Inf Sch. Brin 131 C7
Bristol Gr. Don DN2 63 A6
Bristol Rd. Shef S11 128 C1
Britain St. Mex S64 79 F4
Britannia Cl. Barn S70 54 F8
Britannia House. Barn S70 54 F8 11
Britannia Rd. Shef S9 130 C4
Britland Cl. Barn S75 33 A2
Britnall St. Shef S9 130 A6
Briton Sq. Dearne S63 37 E1
Briton St. Dearne S63 37 E1
Brittain St. Shef S2 129 B2
Britten House. Don DN2 63 A6
Broachgate. Ben DN5 61 E8
Broad Balk. H Pag DN5 38 E6
Broad Bridge Cl. Wales S31 145 F2
Broad Carr La. Holmfi HD7 28 A2
Broad Dyke Cl. Wales S31 145 F2
Broad Elms Cl. Shef S11 139 F4
Broad Elms La. Shef S11 139 E3
Broad Elms Sch. Shef 139 F4
Broad Gates. Silk S75 52 F8
Broad Inge Cres. Chap S30 94 E5
Broad Ings La. K Bram DN3 23 E1
Broad La. S Elm WF9 18 E1
Broad La. S Kirk WF9 37 C8
Broad La. Shef S1, S3 128 F3
Broad La. Syke DN14 7 B6
Broad Lane Ct. Shef S1 128 F3 3
Broad Oak La. Ingb S30 30 D2
Broad Oaks. Shef S9 129 F5
Broad Riding. Ston S66 101 F1
Broad St. Rawm S62 97 F3
Broad St. Shef S2 129 B4
Broad St. Shef S2 129 C4
Broad Street La. Shef S2 129 C4
Broadbent Gate Rd. Thorne DN8 9 D1
Broadcarr Rd. Hoy S74 76 E3
Broadcroft Cl. Shef S19 144 B3
Broadfield Rd. Shef S8 140 F6
Broadgate House Cl. Roth S61 115 A7
Broadhead Rd. Stock S30 92 D8
Broadland Cres. Roth S66 117 E4
Broadlands Ave. Shef S19 143 B2
Broadlands Cl. Hat DN7 44 A7
Broadlands Cl. Shef S19 143 B2
Broadlands Croft. Shef S19 143 B2
Broadlands Rise. Shef S19 143 B2
Broadlands. Roth S66 117 E4
Broadley Rd. Shef S13 142 C7
Broadoaks Cl. Din S31 134 E1
Broadoaks Rd. Din S31 134 E1
Broadstone Rd. D Dale HD8 28 F3
Broadwater. Dearne S63 58 B1
Broadwater Dr. Hat DN7 44 A6
Broadway Ave. Chap S30 95 B4
Broadway. Barn S70 54 C8
Broadway. Brin S60 131 B7
Broadway Cl. Swint S64 79 B2
Broadway Ct. Barn S70 33 B1 2
Broadway E. Roth S65 116 B7
Broadway. Hat DN7 43 F7
Broadway. Mapp S75 14 B1
Broadway Nook. Hat DN7 43 F6
Broadway. Roth S65 116 B7
Broadway. S Elm WF9 18 E2
Broadway. Swint S64 79 B2
Broadway Terr. S Elm WF9 18 E1
Broadway The. Don DN4 82 F5
Broc-O-Bank. Norton DN6 4 C3
Brocco Bank. Shef S11 128 C1
Brocco La. Shef S1, S3 128 F4 11
Brocco St. Shef S1, S3 128 F4
Brockenhurst Rd. Hat DN7 44 C7
Brockfield Cl. Barn S70 55 A5 4
Brockhole Cl. Don DN4 84 F7
Brockholes La. Bran DN3 85 D7
Brockholes La. Lang S30 72 A8
Brockholes La. Pen S30 72 A8
Brockhurst Way. Roth S65 98 F2
Brocklehurst Ave. Barn S70 55 D6
Brocklehurst Ave. Shef S8 153 C8
Brockwood Cl. Shef S13 143 C7
Brodsworth C of E (controlled) Fst & Mid Sch. Brod 39 C3
Bromfield Ct. Roy S71 15 D4
Bromley Carr Rd. Wort S30 75 B2
Brompton Rd. Shef S9 130 A7
Brompton Rd. Sprot DN5 61 C1
Bromwich Rd. Shef S8 140 F2
Bronte Ave. Don DN4 82 F6
Bronte Cl. Barn S71 34 B3
Bronte Gr. Hem WF9 17 C6
Bronte Gr. Mex S64 80 B6
Bronte Pl. Rawm S62 98 B7
Brook Cl. Aston S31 144 E7
Brook Cl. Shef S30 94 C1
Brook Croft. N Anst S31 146 D5
Brook Dr. Shef S3 128 F4
Brook Farm Mews. W up D S63 78 E6
Brook Hill La. Carl S30 49 B3
Brook Hill La. Dun Br S30 48 F2
Brook Hill. Roth S61 95 F4
Brook Hill. Shef S3 128 E3
Brook House Jun Sch. Shef 144 B3
Brook House La. Lang S30 70 F7
Brook La. Ought S30 111 C7
Brook La. Roth S66 117 D6
Brook La. Shef S3 128 F3
Brook La. Shef S12 143 B3
Brook La. Shef S30 94 C1
Brook Rd. Chap S30 94 E6
Brook Rd. Con DN12 81 D2
Brook Rd. Con DN12 81 E2
Brook Rd. Roth S65 116 B8
Brook Rd. Shef S8 140 F5
Brook Row. Stock S30 73 C1
Brook Sch. Shef 142 D8
Brook St. Rawm S62 98 A4
Brook St. Roth S60 116 B1
Brook Terr. Wroot DN9 67 A3
Brook Way. Ben DN5 41 D1
Brooke Dr. W up D S43 78 D6
Brooke St. Don DN1 62 D5
Brooke St. Hoy S74 76 D5
Brooke St. Thorne DN8 26 A8
Brookfield Ave. Swint S64 79 D2
Brookfield Cl. Arm DN3 64 B5
Brookfield Cl. Roth S65 98 D1
Brookfield Cl. Thorne DN8 26 A8
Brookfield Jun Mix & Inf Sch. Swint 79 D2
Brookfield Rd. Shef S7 140 F7
Brookfield Terr. Roy S71 34 C8
Brookhaven Way. Roth S66 117 E4
Brookhill Rd. Kex S75 32 B8
Brookhouse Cl. Shef S12 143 B3
Brookhouse Hill. Shef S10 139 C7
Brookhouse La. Laugh S31 134 C6
Brookhouse Rd. Aston S31 144 D6
Brooklands Ave. Shef S10 139 C7
Brooklands Cres. Shef S10 139 C7
Brooklands Dr. Shef S10 139 B7
Brooklands Rd. Ad I S DN6 40 D7
Brooklyn Pl. Shef S8 141 A5 2
Brooklyn Rd. Shef S8 141 A5 5
Brooksfield. S Kirk WF9 18 D4
Brookside Bank Rd. Shef S6 126 F6
Brookside Cl. Shef S12 143 B3 1
Brookside. Con DN12 81 C1
Brookside Cres. W up D S63 78 B6
Brookside Ct. Roth S61 97 E2
Brookside. D Dale HD8 29 F6
Brookside Dr. Barn S70 55 D6
Brookside. Hem WF9 17 E7
Brookside La. Shef S6 126 F6
Brookside. Roth S65 116 C5
Brookside St. S Elm WF9 18 F3
Brookside. Swint S64 79 B1
Brookside Terr. S Elm WF9 18 F3
Brookside Wlk. Bir DN11 122 B4
Brookvale. Barn S71 34 D3
Brookview Ct. Dron S18 153 A3
Broom Ave. Roth S60 116 B3
Broom Chase. Roth S60 115 F4
Broom Cl. Barn S70 55 D6
Broom Cl. Dearne S63 58 B3
Broom Cl. Shef S11 128 F1
Broom Cl. Tick DN11 121 C7
Broom Cl. W up D S63 79 A4
Broom Cres. Roth S60 115 F4
Broom Ct. Hat DN7 44 A7
Broom Ct. Roth S60 116 A4
Broom Dr. Roth S60 116 B3
Broom Gn. Shef S3 128 F2
Broom Gr. Roth S60 115 F5
Broom Gr. S Anst S31 146 D3
Broom Grange. Roth S60 116 A4
Broom Hill Dr. Don DN4 84 F7
Broom La. Roth S60 116 B3
Broom Rd. Roth S60 115 F5
Broom Riddings. Roth S61 97 B2
Broom Royd. Wharn S30 93 B3
Broom St. Shef S10 128 E2
Broom Terr. Roth S60 115 F5
Broom Valley County Sch. Roth 115 F4
Broom Valley Rd. Roth S60 116 A3
Broom Wlk. Shef S3 128 F2 1
Broombank. D Dale HD8 29 F5
Broomcroft. Dod S75 54 B6
Broome Ave. Swint S64 79 D3
Broomfield Cl. Barn S70 54 B8
Broomfield Ct. Stock S30 92 D8
Broomfield Gr. Roth S60 115 F5
Broomfield Gr. Stock S30 92 D8
Broomfield La. Matt DN10 123 C1
Broomfield La. Stock S30 92 C8
Broomfield Rd. Shef S10 128 D2
Broomfield Rd. Stock S30 92 D8
Broomgrove Cres. Shef S10 128 D2
Broomgrove La. Shef S10 128 D1
Broomgrove Rd. Shef S10 128 D1
Broomhall Pl. Shef S10 128 E1
Broomhall Rd. Shef S10 128 E1
Broomhall St. Shef S3 128 E2
Broomhead Ct. Mapp S75 33 B8
Broomhead Rd. Wombw S73 56 F1
Broomhill Cl. Eck S31 155 B3
Broomhill. Con DN12 80 E3
Broomhill Inf Sch. Shef 128 C2
Broomhill La. Dearne S73 57 C3
Broomhill View. Dearne S63 58 B1
Broomhouse Cl. D Dale HD8 30 A5
Broomhouse La. Don DN12, DN4 82 D3
Broomhouse La. N Edl DN12 82 D3
Broomroyd. Barn S70 55 B4
Broomspring Cl. Shef S3 128 E2 4
Broomspring La. Shef S10 128 E2
Broomvale Wlk. N Edl DN12 82 A1
Broomville St. Swint S64 79 E3
Broomwood Cl. Shef S19 144 A3
Broomwood Gdns. Shef S19 144 A3
Brosley Ave. B Dun DN3 43 A7
Brotherton St. Shef S3 129 B6
Brough Gn. Dod S75 54 B5
Broughton Ave. Ben DN5 62 A7
Broughton La. Shef S9 130 B8
Broughton Rd. Don DN4 84 E6
Broughton Rd. Shef S6 112 C1
Brow Cl. Barn S70 54 F6
Brow Cres. Shef S19 155 F7
Brow La. D Dale HD8 30 D6
Brow The. Roth S65 116 E4
Brow View. Dearne S63 58 B2
Browhill Rd. Maltby S66 118 E6
Brown Hills La. Shef S10 138 E8
Brown House La. Bfield S6 110 B6
Brown La. Dron S18 153 C3
Brown La. Shef S1 129 A2 2
Brown St. Roth S60 115 C7
Brown St. Shef S1 129 B2
Brown's Edge La. Lang S30 71 B7
Brown's Edge Rd. Wh Com S30 49 E8
Brownell St. Shef S3 128 F4 7
Brownhill La. Holme HD7 47 B8
Browning Ave. Don DN4 83 B6
Browning Cl. Barn S71 34 B5
Browning Cl. Shef S6 112 D5
Browning Dr. Roth S65 116 B6
Browning Dr. Shef S6 112 D5
Browning Rd. B Dun DN3 42 F8
Browning Rd. Mex S64 80 A6

Browning Rd. Roth S65 ... 116 B5
Browning Rd. Shef S6 ... 112 D5
Browning Rd. W up D S63 ... 78 C7
Brownroyd Ave. Roy S71 ... 15 C2
Browns La. Thorne DN8 ... 26 A7
Broxbourne Gdns. Ben DN5 ... 41 B1
Broxholme La. Don DN1 ... 62 D4
Broxholme Rd. Shef S8 ... 140 F3
Bruce Ave. Barn S70 ... 54 F7
Bruce Cres. Don DN2 ... 63 B5
Bruce Rd. Shef S11 ... 140 D8
Brunel Cl. Styr DN11 ... 121 F2
Brunel Gate. Styr DN11 ... 121 F2
Brunel Rd. Ben DN5 ... 61 F5
Bruni Way. Ross DN11 ... 103 F7
Brunswick Cl. Barn S71 ... 34 A6
Brunswick Fst & Mid Schs. Shef ... 143 D6
Brunswick Rd. Roth S60 ... 115 F4
Brunswick Rd. Shef S3 ... 129 B5
Brunswick Sq. Stai DN7 ... 24 E3
Brunswick St. Dearne S63 ... 37 F1
Brunswick St. Shef S10 ... 128 E2
Brunt Rd. Rawm S62 ... 98 B6
Brushfield Gr. Shef S12 ... 142 D4
Bryans Close La. Misson DN10 ... 105 F3
Bryony Cl. Kill S31 ... 156 B6
Bubup Hill. Wad DN11 ... 83 C2
Bubwith Rd. Shef S9 ... 114 B2
Buchanan Cres. Shef S5 ... 112 E5
Buchanan Dr. Shef S5 ... 112 E5
Buchanan Rd. Shef S5 ... 112 F5
Buck Wood View. Shef S14 ... 141 D5
Buckden Rd. Barn S70 ... 33 D2 7
Buckenham Dr. Shef S4 ... 129 C6
Buckenham St. Shef S4 ... 129 C6
Buckingham Cl. Dron S18 ... 152 D2 2
Buckingham Rd. Con DN12 ... 81 B3
Buckingham Rd. Don DN2 ... 62 F4
Buckingham Way. Brin S60 ... 131 D8
Buckingham Way. Maltby S66 ... 119 A6
Buckingham Way. Roy S71 ... 15 B4
Buckleigh Rd. W up D S63 ... 78 F4
Buckley Ct. Barn S70 ... 54 F8
Buckley House. Barn S70 ... 54 F8 13
Buckthorn Cl. Swint S64 ... 98 C8
Bud La. Wharn S30 ... 92 E3
Bude Ct. Barn S71 ... 34 C3
Bude Rd. Don DN4 ... 83 B8
Bull Haw La. Silk S75 ... 52 F8
Bull La. S Kirk WF9 ... 18 C2
Bull Moor Rd. Hat DN7 ... 45 B7
Bullen Rd. Shef S6 ... 112 C5
Bullenshaw Rd. Hem WF9 ... 17 D6
Bullfinch Cl. Brin S60 ... 131 D8
Bullhouse La. Pen S30 ... 50 C2
Bullivant Rd. Hat DN7 ... 44 C8
Bungalow Rd. N Edl DN12 ... 82 B2
Bungalows The. Kill S31 ... 156 C6
Bungalows The. Treet S60 ... 131 E4
Bunker's Hill. Th Sa S31 ... 158 D8
Bunkers Hill. Kill S31 ... 156 E6
Bunting Cl. Shef S8 ... 141 B2
Bunting Nook. Shef S8 ... 141 B1
Burbage Cl. Dron S18 ... 152 D2
Burbage Gr. Shef S12 ... 142 D5
Burcot Rd. Shef S8 ... 140 F5
Burcroft Cl. Hoy S74 ... 76 B5
Burcroft Hill. Con DN12 ... 81 D3
Burden Cl. Don DN1 ... 62 C2
Burford Ave. Don DN4 ... 82 E5
Burford Cres. Aston S31 ... 144 E7
Burgar Rd. Thorne DN8 ... 26 B5
Burgen Rd. Roth S61 ... 96 E1
Burgess Rd. Shef S9 ... 129 F6
Burgess St. Shef S1 ... 129 A3
Burghwallis La. Burg DN6 ... 21 C6
Burghwallis Rd. Burg DN6 ... 21 B6
Burgoyne Cl. Shef S6 ... 128 D6
Burgoyne Rd. Shef S6 ... 128 D6
Burkinshaw Ave. Rawm S62 ... 97 F8
Burleigh Ct. Barn S70 ... 33 F1 12
Burleigh St. Barn S70 ... 54 F8 3
Burlington Arc. Barn S70 ... 33 F1 2
Burlington Ct. Shef S6 ... 128 E5 1
Burlington Glen. Shef S17 ... 151 E7
Burlington Gr. Shef S17 ... 151 E7
Burlington Rd. Shef S17 ... 151 E7
Burlington St. Shef S6 ... 128 E5
Burman Rd. W up D S63 ... 78 F6
Burn Gr. Chap S30 ... 95 C4
Burn Pl. Barn S71 ... 33 E7
Burn's Villas. Stai DN7 ... 24 F4
Burnaby Cres. Shef S6 ... 128 D7
Burnaby Ct. Shef S6 ... 128 D7
Burnaby Gn. Shef S6 ... 128 D6
Burnaby St. Don DN1 ... 62 C3 1
Burnaby St. Shef S6 ... 128 D7
Burnaston Cl. Dron S18 ... 152 C1
Burnaston Wlk. Con DN12 ... 81 A3
Burncross Jun & Inf Sch. Chap ... 94 F5
Burncross Rd. Chap S30 ... 94 E5
Burnell Rd. Shef S6 ... 112 C1
Burnett Cl. Pen S30 ... 51 E2
Burngreave Bank. Shef S4 ... 129 B6
Burngreave Mid Sch. Shef ... 129 C7
Burngreave Rd. Shef S3 ... 129 B6
Burngreave St. Shef S3 ... 129 B6
Burngrove Pl. Shef S3 ... 129 B7
Burnham Ave. Mapp S75 ... 14 B1
Burnham Cl. Don DN4 ... 84 B7
Burnham Gr. Ben DN5 ... 61 F8
Burnham Way. Dar S73 ... 56 F5
Burns Ave. S Kirk WF9 ... 17 F1
Burns Dr. Chap S30 ... 94 F5
Burns Dr. Roth S65 ... 116 B6
Burns Rd. B Dun DN3 ... 42 F8
Burns Rd. Din S31 ... 147 A8
Burns Rd. Don DN4 ... 83 B6
Burns Rd. Maltby S66 ... 119 A4
Burns Rd. Roth S65 ... 116 B6
Burns Rd. Shef S6 ... 128 D4
Burns St. Ben DN5 ... 41 C1
Burns Way. Don DN4 ... 83 A8
Burns Way. W up D S63 ... 78 C7
Burnsall Cres. Brin S60 ... 131 C7
Burnsall Gr. Barn S70 ... 55 D6
Burnside Ave. Shef S8 ... 141 A5
Burnside. Dearne S63 ... 37 C1
Burnt Hill La. Ought S30 ... 111 A5
Burnt Stones Cl. Shef S10 ... 127 D2
Burnt Stones Dr. Shef S10 ... 127 D2
Burnt Stones Gr. Shef S10 ... 127 D2
Burnt Tree La. Shef S3 ... 128 F5
Burnt Wood Cres. S Kirk WF9 ... 18 C2
Burnt Wood La. S Kirk WF9 ... 17 E1
Burntwood Ave. S Kirk WF9 ... 18 C2
Burntwood Bank. Hem WF9 ... 17 D5
Burntwood Cl. Shef S9 ... 130 B7
Burntwood Cres. Treet S60 ... 131 E5
Burntwood Dr. S Kirk WF9 ... 18 C1
Burntwood Gr. S Kirk WF9 ... 18 C1
Burntwood Inf Sch. S Kirk ... 18 C1
Burntwood Inf Sch. S Kirk ... 18 C2
Burntwood Rd. Grime S72 ... 36 B6
Burntwood Sports & L Ctr. Bri ... 17 C2
Burrell St. Roth S60 ... 115 D6
Burrowlee Rd. Shef S6 ... 112 C1
Burrows Dr. Shef S5 ... 113 A2
Burrows Gr. Wombw S73 ... 56 B3
Burrs La. Gild S81 ... 147 F8
Burton Ave. Barn S71 ... 34 D4
Burton Ave. Don DN4 ... 83 B8
Burton Bank Rd. Barn S71 ... 34 B4
Burton Cres. Barn S71 ... 34 E5
Burton La. Ought S30 ... 111 C6
Burton Rd. Barn S71 ... 34 B3
Burton Rd. Barn S71 ... 34 D5
Burton Rd. Shef S3 ... 128 F6
Burton Road Prim Sch. Barn ... 34 A3
Burton St. Barn S71 ... 33 E3
Burton St. S Elm WF9 ... 18 F2
Burton St. Shef S6 ... 128 D7
Burton Terr. Barn S70 ... 55 B8 3
Burton Terr. Don DN4 ... 83 B8
Burtonlees Ct. Don DN4 ... 84 E7
Burying La. Hoy S74 ... 76 F3
Bush St. Hem WF9 ... 17 E6
Bushey Wood Rd. Shef S17 ... 151 E6
Bushfield Rd. W up D S63 ... 78 D6
Busk Knoll. Shef S5 ... 113 A2
Busk Meadow Fst Sch. Shef ... 113 A1
Busk Meadow. Shef S5 ... 113 A2
Busk Pk. Shef S5 ... 113 A2
Busley Gdns. Ben DN5 ... 62 A8
Butcher Hill. Hem WF9 ... 17 E8
Butcher St. Dearne S63 ... 58 C8
Butchill Ave. Shef S5 ... 113 A8
Bute St. Shef S10 ... 128 B3
Butler Rd. Shef S6 ... 128 A6
Butler Way. Kill S31 ... 156 C6
Butt Hole Rd. Con DN12 ... 81 E2
Butt La. H Pag DN5 ... 38 E4
Butten Meadow. Aust DN10 ... 105 C2
Butterbusk. Con DN12 ... 81 E2
Buttercross. Ad le S DN6 ... 21 A1
Buttercross Cl. Ad le S DN6 ... 21 A2
Buttercross Dr. G Hou S72 ... 57 E6
Butterfield Cl. Snaith DN14 ... 1 C7
Butterill Dr. Arm DN3 ... 64 D5
Butterley Dr. Barn S70 ... 55 D6
Butterleys. Dod S75 ... 54 A7
Buttermere Cl. Ad le S DN6 ... 21 C1
Buttermere Cl. Dearne S63 ... 58 C1
Buttermere Cl. Mex S64 ... 80 C6
Buttermere Cl. N Anst S31 ... 146 E7
Buttermere Dr. Dron S18 ... 152 E1
Buttermere Rd. Shef S7 ... 140 E4
Buttermere Way. Barn S71 ... 56 B8
Butterthwaite Cres. Shef S5 ... 113 E7
Butterthwaite Rd. Shef S5 ... 113 D8
Butterton Cl. Mapp S75 ... 14 C1
Button Hill. Shef S11 ... 140 B5
Button Row. Stock S30 ... 73 C1
Butts Hill. Shef S17 ... 151 D4
Buxton Rd. Barn S71 ... 34 A7
Byland Way. Barn S71 ... 34 D2
Byrley Rd. Roth S61 ... 96 E1
Byrne Cl. Barn S75 ... 32 E4
Byron Ave. Ben DN5 ... 61 F4
Byron Ave. Chap S30 ... 94 F4
Byron Ave. Don DN4, ... 83 A6
Byron Ave. Norton DN6 ... 4 C1
Byron Cres. W up D S63 ... 78 C7
Byron Dr. Barn S71 ... 34 B4
Byron Dr. Roth S65 ... 116 A6
Byron Rd. Din S31 ... 147 A8
Byron Rd. Maltby S66 ... 119 A4
Byron Rd. Mex S64 ... 80 C5
Byron Rd. Shef S7 ... 140 E6
Byron Rd. Shef S19 ... 144 A2
Byron St. G Hou S72 ... 36 E1

Cabb La. S Kirk WF9 ... 18 D4
Cadeby Ave. Con DN12 ... 81 A2
Cadeby La. Cade DN5 ... 81 D6
Cadman Ct. Shef S19 ... 155 D6
Cadman La. Shef S1 ... 129 B3
Cadman Rd. Shef S12 ... 142 C6
Cadman St. Shef S4 ... 129 C4
Cadman St. Shef S19 ... 155 D6
Cadman St. W up D S63 ... 79 A6
Cadwell Cl. Cud S72 ... 35 C8
Caernarvon Cres. Dearne S63 ... 58 B2
Caernarvon Dr. Bnbur DN5 ... 59 C3
Caine Gdns. Roth S61 ... 114 E6
Cairns Rd. Shef S10 ... 128 A2
Cairns Rd. Shef S19 ... 143 F4
Caister Ave. Chap S30 ... 94 F5
Caistor Ave. Barn S70 ... 54 C7
Calcot Gn. Swint S64 ... 79 D2
Calcot Park Ave. Swint S64 ... 79 D2
Caldbeck Gr. Chap S30 ... 94 D8
Caldbeck Pl. N Anst S31 ... 146 F7
Calder Ave. Roy S71 ... 15 E3
Calder Cres. Barn S70 ... 55 D7
Calder Rd. Dearne S63 ... 58 D1
Calder Rd. Roth S61 ... 96 F3
Calder Terr. Con DN12 ... 81 C3
Calder Way. Shef S5 ... 113 C2
Caldervale. Roy S71 ... 15 E4
Calf Hey La. Wh Com S30 ... 49 D7
California Cres. Barn S70 ... 54 F7
California Dr. Chap S30 ... 95 A4
California Dr. Treet S60 ... 131 C5
California Gdns. Barn S70 ... 54 F8 18
California St. Barn S70 ... 54 E7
California Terr. Barn S70 ... 54 E7
Calladine Way. Swint S64 ... 79 D1
Callander Ct. Don DN4 ... 84 E7
Callis La. Pen S30 ... 51 E1
Callow Dr. Shef S14 ... 141 D5
Callow Mount. Shef S14 ... 141 D5
Callow Rd. Shef S14 ... 141 C5
Callywhite La. Dron S18 ... 153 C1
Calner Croft. Shef S19 ... 144 B2
Calver Cl. Dod S75 ... 54 A5
Calvert Rd. Shef S9 ... 130 C6
Cam Height. Hath S10 ... 137 F2
Camborne Cl. Shef S6 ... 112 C5
Camborne Rd. Shef S6 ... 112 C5
Camborne Way. Barn S71 ... 34 B3
Cambourne Cl. Ad I S DN6 ... 40 B6
Cambria Dr. Don DN4 ... 82 E6
Cambrian Cl. Sprot DN5 ... 61 A1
Cambridge Cl. Bnbur DN5 ... 59 C2
Cambridge Cres. Roth S65 ... 116 A7
Cambridge Pl. Roth S65 ... 116 A7
Cambridge Rd. Har DN11 ... 121 F4
Cambridge Rd. Shef S8 ... 141 B6
Cambridge Rd. Stock S30 ... 92 F8
Cambridge St. Mex S64 ... 79 E5
Cambridge St. Ross DN11 ... 84 E2
Cambridge St. Roth S65 ... 116 A7
Cambridge St. S Elm WF9 ... 18 E3
Cambridge St. Shef S1 ... 129 A3
Cambron Gdns. Roth S66 ... 117 D6
Camdale Rise. Shef S12 ... 142 F1
Camdale View. Shef S12 ... 143 A1
Camden Pl. Don DN1 ... 62 C2
Camellia Cl. Con DN12 ... 81 D1
Camellia Dr. Don DN3 ... 42 F3
Camm St. Shef S6 ... 128 C6
Cammell Rd. Shef S5 ... 113 D2
Camms Cl. Eck S31 ... 155 D4
Camp Rd. S Kirk WF9 ... 17 F1
Campbell Dr. Roth S65 ... 116 B6
Campbell St. Roth S61 ... 97 C4
Camping La. Shef S8 ... 140 E2
Camping La. Shef S8 ... 140 E3
Campion Cl. Dearne S63 ... 58 B3
Campion Dr. Kill S31 ... 156 C6
Campion Dr. Swint S64 ... 98 D8
Campo La. Shef S1 ... 129 A4
Campsall Balk. Norton DN6 ... 4 D2
Campsall Dr. Shef S10 ... 128 A3
Campsall Field Cl. W up D S63 ... 78 E4
Campsall Field Rd. W up D S63 ... 78 E5
Campsall Hall Rd. Norton DN6 ... 4 D1
Campsall Park. Norton ... 21 D8
Campsall Park Rd. Norton DN6 ... 4 D1
Campsall Rd. Askern DN6 ... 21 F8
Campsmount High Sch. Norton ... 4 B2
Campsmount. Norton DN6 ... 21 C8
Canada St. Barn S70 ... 54 E7
Canada St. Shef S4 ... 129 D7
Canal Bridge. Kill S31 ... 156 D6
Canal St. Barn S71 ... 33 F3
Canal St. Shef S4 ... 129 D4
Canberra Ave. Hat DN7 ... 66 A7
Canberra Rise. Dearne S63 ... 58 B2
Candy Bank. Blax DN9 ... 66 D2
Canklow Hill Rd. Roth S60 ... 115 D3
Canklow Meadows Ind Est. Roth ... 115 D1
Canklow Rd. Roth S60 ... 115 D4
Canklow Woods Prim Sch. Roth ... 115 D2
Canning St. Shef S1 ... 128 F3 14
Cannock St. Shef S6 ... 128 C8
Cannon Hall Ctry Pk. Caw ... 31 D5
Cannon Hall Rd. Shef S5 ... 113 C1
Canon Popham Sch. Don ... 42 F3
Canons Way. Barn S71 ... 34 C3
Cantello Ct. Ross DN11 ... 103 E7
Canterbury Ave. Shef S10 ... 139 C8
Canterbury Cl. Ben DN5 ... 61 E6
Canterbury Cres. Shef S10 ... 139 C8
Canterbury Dr. Shef S10 ... 139 C8
Canterbury Rd. Don DN2 ... 62 F6
Canterbury Rd. Hat DN7 ... 44 A8
Canterbury Rd. Shef S8 ... 141 B5
Canterbury Wlk. C in L S81 ... 148 E7
Cantilupe Cres. Aston S31 ... 144 D8
Cantley La. Don DN4 ... 84 E8
Cantley Manor Ave. Don DN4 ... 85 A7
Cantley Riding. Don DN2 ... 63 E5
Canyards Hills La. Bfield S30 ... 91 F3
Capel St. Shef S6 ... 128 D7
Caperns Rd. N Anst S31 ... 146 F5
Capri Ct. Dar S73 ... 56 E6
Car Hill. Roth S61 ... 97 C2
Car Vale Dr. Shef S13 ... 142 C8
Car Vale View. Shef S13 ... 142 C8
Caraway Gr. Swint S64 ... 98 D8
Carbis Cl. Barn S71 ... 34 B3
Carbrook Hall Ind Est. Shef ... 114 B1
Carbrook Hall Rd. Shef S9 ... 114 B1
Carbrook St. Shef S9 ... 114 B1
Cardew Cl. Rawm S62 ... 98 A5
Cardiff St. Shef S9 ... 130 A8
Cardigan Rd. Don DN2 ... 63 C5
Cardinal Cl. Ross DN11 ... 85 B1
Cardoness Dr. Shef S10 ... 127 E2
Cardoness Rd. Shef S10 ... 127 F2
Cardwell Ave. Shef S13 ... 143 A7
Cardwell Dr. Shef S13 ... 142 F7
Carey Ave. Barn S71 ... 34 A2
Carfield Ave. Shef S8 ... 141 B5
Carfield County Sch. Shef ... 141 B5
Carfield La. Shef S8 ... 141 C5
Carfield Pl. Shef S8 ... 141 B5
Carisbrook Rd. C in L S81 ... 148 E6
Carisbrooke Rd. Don DN2 ... 63 A4
Carlby Rd. Shef S6 ... 128 A7
Carley Dr. Shef S19 ... 143 F1
Carlin St. Shef S13 ... 142 E6
Carlingford Rd. Roth S60 ... 116 A3
Carlisle Pl. Roth S65 ... 115 E7 5
Carlisle Rd. Don DN2 ... 63 B7
Carlisle Rd. Shef S4 ... 129 E8
Carlisle St E. Shef S4 ... 129 E7
Carlisle St. Roth S65 ... 115 E7
Carlisle St. Shef S4 ... 129 C5
Carlisle St. Swint S64 ... 79 E1
Carlisle Terr. Din S31 ... 134 F1
Carlthorpe Gr. Chap S30 ... 94 C7
Carlton Ave. Roth S65 ... 115 F5
Carlton Cl. Bran DN3 ... 85 E8
Carlton Cl. Hem WF9 ... 17 C5
Carlton Cl. Shef S19 ... 155 C6
Carlton Dr. Bawtry DN10 ... 122 F6
Carlton Fst Sch. S Elm ... 18 F2
Carlton Gdns. S Elm WF9 ... 18 F3
Carlton Hall La. C in L S81 ... 148 F4
Carlton Ind Est. Roy ... 34 C7
Carlton Inf Sch. Roy ... 34 D8
Carlton Jun Sch. Roy ... 34 D8
Carlton Marsh Nature Reserve. Cud ... 16 A1
Carlton Park Inf Sch. C in L ... 148 F6
Carlton Rd. Barn S71 ... 34 B7
Carlton Rd. C in L S81 ... 148 F1
Carlton Rd. Don DN1 ... 62 E5
Carlton Rd. Roy S71 ... 34 B7
Carlton Rd. S Elm WF9 ... 18 F3
Carlton Rd. Shef S6 ... 112 B2
Carlton Rise. Wharn S30 ... 93 B3
Carlton St. Barn S71 ... 33 F4
Carlton St. Cud S72 ... 35 B7
Carlton St. Grime S72 ... 36 A6
Carlyle Rd. Maltby S66 ... 119 A4
Carlyle St. Mex S64 ... 80 A5
Carnaby Rd. Shef S6 ... 128 C7
Carnarvon St. Shef S6 ... 128 E5
Carnforth Rd. Barn S71 ... 34 D5
Carnley St. W up D S63 ... 78 B6
Carnoustie Cl. Swint S64 ... 79 E2
Carpenter Croft. Shef S12 ... 142 C6
Carpenter Gdns. Shef S12 ... 142 C6
Carpenter Mews. Shef S12 ... 142 C6
Carr Bank Cl. Shef S11 ... 139 F8
Carr Bank Dr. Shef S11 ... 139 F8
Carr Bank La. Shef S11 ... 139 E8
Carr Bank. Wad DN11 ... 103 A7
Carr Cl. Brin S60 ... 131 A8
Carr Field La. Dearne S63 ... 58 C3
Carr Forge Cl. Shef S12 ... 143 A4
Carr Forge La. Shef S12 ... 143 A4
Carr Forge Mount. Shef S12 ... 143 A4
Carr Forge Pl. Shef S12 ... 143 B4
Carr Forge Rd. Shef S12 ... 143 B4
Carr Forge Terr. Shef S12 ... 143 A4
Carr Forge View. Shef S12 ... 143 B4
Carr Gn. Dearne S63 ... 58 C3
Carr Gr. Stock S30 ... 92 E8
Carr Green La. Mapp S75 ... 33 C8
Carr Head La. Dearne S63 ... 58 B2
Carr Head Rd. Wort S30 ... 75 B1
Carr Hill. Don DN4 ... 83 B8
Carr Hill Rd. D Dale HD8 ... 29 A6
Carr House La. Wharn S30 ... 92 E3
Carr House Rd. Don DN1, DN4 ... 62 E2
Carr La. Clift DN12 ... 100 E7
Carr La. Don DN4 ... 62 D1
Carr La. Don DN4 ... 84 E5
Carr La. Dron S18 ... 152 C2
Carr La. H Rob S65 ... 99 A6
Carr La. Ingb S30 ... 51 B8
Carr La. Maltby S66 ... 118 D4
Carr La. Pen S30 ... 51 B7
Carr La. Pilley S75 ... 75 C4
Carr La. Shef S1 ... 128 F3
Carr La. Shep HD8 ... 28 F6
Carr La. Thurcr S31 ... 134 D8
Carr La. Ulley S31 ... 133 A3
Carr La. Wad DN11 ... 102 D7
Carr Mount. D Dale HD8 ... 29 A6
Carr Rd. N Edl DN12 ... 82 B1
Carr Rd. Shef S6 ... 128 C6
Carr Rd. Stock S30 ... 92 E8
Carr Rd. W up D S63 ... 79 A6
Carr Side La. Hat DN7 ... 44 C5
Carr St. Barn S71 ... 34 D5
Carr View Ave. Don DN4 ... 83 B8
Carr View Rd. Roth S61 ... 114 D8
Carr View. S Kirk WF9 ... 18 C3
Carrcroft Cl. Stock S30 ... 92 F8
Carrfield Cl. Kex S75 ... 32 D7
Carrfield Ct. Shef S8 ... 141 B6 6
Carrfield Dr. Shef S8 ... 141 B6
Carrfield La. Shef S8 ... 141 B6
Carrfield Prim Sch. Dearne ... 58 C3
Carrfield Rd. Shef S8 ... 141 B6
Carrfield St. Shef S8 ... 141 B6
Carriage Way The. Ross DN11 ... 85 B1
Carrill Dr. Shef S6 ... 112 C6
Carrill Rd. Shef S6 ... 112 C6
Carrington Ave. Barn S75 ... 33 E3
Carrington Rd. Shef S11 ... 140 B8
Carrington St. Barn S75 ... 33 D3
Carrington St. Roth S65 ... 115 F5
Carrington Terr. Wales S31 ... 145 D2
Carroll Ct. S Elm WF9 ... 18 E3
Carrs La. Cud S72 ... 35 B4
Carrville Dr. Shef S6 ... 112 D4
Carrville Rd. Shef S6 ... 112 D4
Carrville Rd W. Shef S6 ... 112 C4
Carrwell La. Shef S6 ... 112 C3
Carrwood Rd. Barn S71 ... 34 E1
Carsick Gr. Shef S10 ... 127 D1
Carsick Hill Cres. Shef S10 ... 127 E1
Carsick Hill Dr. Shef S10 ... 127 E1
Carsick Hill Rd. Shef S10 ... 127 E2
Carsick Hill Way. Shef S10 ... 127 D1
Carsick View Rd. Shef S10 ... 127 D1
Carson Mount. Shef S12 ... 142 B3
Carson Rd. Shef S10 ... 128 B3
Carter Hall La. Shef S12 ... 142 C1
Carter Knowle Ave. Shef S11 ... 140 C5
Carter Knowle Jun Sch. Shef ... 140 D5
Carter Knowle Rd. Shef S11, S7 ... 140 C5
Carter Lodge Ave. Shef S12 ... 143 B4
Carter Lodge Dr. Shef S12 ... 143 B4
Carter Lodge Pl. Shef S12 ... 143 B4
Carter Lodge Rise. Shef S12 ... 143 B4
Carter Lodge Sch. Shef ... 143 C3
Carter Pl. Shef S8 ... 141 B6
Carter Rd. Shef S8 ... 141 A6
Carterhall Rd. Shef S12 ... 142 B2
Cartmel Cl. Dron S18 ... 152 E1
Cartmel Cl. Maltby S66 ... 119 A6
Cartmel Ct. Barn S71 ... 34 D7
Cartmel Wlk. Din S31 ... 146 F7
Cartmell Cres. Shef S8 ... 140 F3
Cartmell Rd. Shef S8 ... 140 E4
Cartworth Moor Rd. Holme HD7 ... 47 E8
Cartwright St. Shire S81 ... 159 F7
Carver Cl. Hart S31 ... 157 E6
Carver Dr. Din S31 ... 146 E8
Carver La. Shef S1 ... 129 A3
Carver St. Shef S1 ... 129 A3
Carver Way. Hart S31 ... 157 E6
Carwood Cl. Shef S4 ... 129 D7
Carwood Gn. Shef S4 ... 129 D7
Carwood Gr. Shef S4 ... 129 D7
Carwood Rd. Shef S4 ... 129 D7
Carwood Way. Shef S4 ... 129 D7
Cary Rd. Eck S31 ... 155 B3
Cary Rd. Shef S2 ... 142 A8
Casson Dr. Hart S31 ... 157 E7
Casson's Rd. Thorne DN8 ... 26 A8
Castell Cres. Don DN4 ... 63 E1
Castle Ave. Con DN12 ... 81 C2
Castle Ave. Roth S60 ... 115 D3
Castle Cl. Barn S71 ... 34 B3
Castle Cl. Ben DN5 ... 61 E2
Castle Cl. Dod S75 ... 54 A6
Castle Cl. Pen S30 ... 51 E2
Castle Cl. Tick DN11 ... 121 A7
Castle Coll. Shef ... 129 C2
Castle Cres. Con DN12 ... 81 C3
Castle Dr. Hd Gr S75 ... 53 E2
Castle Gate. Tick DN11 ... 121 A6
Castle Gate. Tick DN11 ... 121 A7
Castle Gn. Laugh S31 ... 134 D4
Castle Gn. Shef S3 ... 129 B4
Castle Gr. Sprot DN5 ... 61 B1
Castle Grove Terr. Con DN12 ... 81 D3
Castle Hill Ave. Mex S64 ... 80 D4
Castle Hill Cl. Eck S31 ... 155 D4
Castle Hill. Con DN12 ... 81 C2
Castle Hill. Eck S31 ... 155 D4
Castle Hill Fold. Hick DN5 ... 59 C7
Castle Hills Fst & Mid Schs. Ben ... 40 F1
Castle Hills Rd. Ben DN5 ... 40 E1
Castle La. Pen S30 ... 51 E2
Castle Sq. Shef S1 ... 129 B3
Castle St. Barn S70 ... 54 E8
Castle St. Con DN12 ... 81 C2
Castle St. Pen S30 ... 51 E2
Castle St. Shef S3 ... 129 B4
Castle Terr. Con DN12 ... 81 C2
Castle View. Dod S75 ... 53 F8
Castle View. Eck S31 ... 155 D3
Castle View. Hd Gr S75 ... 53 E2
Castle View. N Edl DN12 ... 82 B1
Castle Wlk. Shef S2 ... 129 D4
Castlebeck Croft. Shef S2 ... 130 C1
Castlebeck Ct. Shef S2 ... 130 C1
Castlebeck Dr. Shef S2 ... 142 B8
Castledale Croft. Shef S2 ... 142 B8
Castledale Gr. Shef S2 ... 142 C8
Castledale Pl. Shef S2 ... 142 B8
Castledine Croft. Shef S9 ... 114 B2
Castledine Gdns. Shef S9 ... 114 B2
Castlegate. Shef S3 ... 129 B4
Castlereagh St. Barn S70 ... 33 E1 9
Castlerigg Way. Dron S18 ... 152 E1 1
Castlerow Cl. Shef S17 ... 152 B6
Castlerow Dr. Shef S17 ... 152 B6
Castlewood Cres. Shef S10 ... 139 B8
Castlewood Ct. Shef S10 ... 139 C8
Castlewood Dr. Shef S10 ... 139 B8
Castlewood Rd. Shef S10 ... 139 B8
Castor Rd. Shef S9 ... 129 F7
Cat Hill La. Pen S30 ... 51 D8
Cat La. Shef S2, S8 ... 141 C5
Catania Rise. Dar S73 ... 56 E6
Catch Bar La. Shef S6 ... 112 C2
Catcliffe Jun & Inf Sch. Treet ... 131 D6
Catcliffe Rd. Shef S9 ... 130 C4
Catherine Ave. Aston S31 ... 144 D7
Catherine McAuley Upper Sch. Don ... 85 A8
Catherine Rd. Shef S4 ... 129 C6
Catherine St. Don DN1 ... 62 D2
Catherine St. Mex S64 ... 79 E5
Catherine St. Roth S65 ... 115 E6 2
Cathill Rd. Dearne S73 ... 57 D4
Catley Rd. Shef S9 ... 130 D5
Catling La. B Dun DN3 ... 42 F7
Catshaw La. Pen S30 ... 50 B3
Cattal St. Shef S9 ... 130 A5 6
Catterick Cl. Con DN12 ... 80 F2
Catterick House. Roth S65 ... 115 F7
Caulk La. Barn S73 ... 55 F5
Causeway Gdns. Shef S17 ... 151 D8
Causeway Glade. Shef S17 ... 151 C8
Causeway Head Rd. Shef S17 ... 151 D8
Causeway The. Shef S17 ... 151 D7
Cave St. Shef S9 ... 129 F5
Cavendish Ave. Shef S17 ... 151 F7
Cavendish Ave. Shef S6 ... 111 E1
Cavendish Cl. Bawtry DN10 ... 122 F6
Cavendish Cl. Roth S65 ... 116 D4
Cavendish Ct. Shef S3 ... 128 F2 3
Cavendish Pl. Maltby S66 ... 119 A6
Cavendish Rd. Barn S75 ... 33 E3
Cavendish Rd. Ben DN5 ... 41 A4
Cavendish Rd. Roth S61 ... 115 A6
Cavendish Rd. Shef S11 ... 140 C7
Cavendish St. Shef S3 ... 128 F3
Cavill Rd. Shef S8 ... 141 A3
Cawdor Rd. Shef S2 ... 141 F6
Cawdor St. Ben DN5 ... 41 B1
Cawdron Rise. Brin S60 ... 131 C7
Cawley Pl. Barn S71 ... 34 A4
Cawston Rd. Shef S4 ... 129 C8
Cawthorne C of E Prim Sch. Caw ... 31 E4
Cawthorne Cl. Dod S75 ... 54 A6
Cawthorne Cl. Roth S65 ... 116 C7
Cawthorne Cl. Shef S8 ... 140 E3
Cawthorne Gr. Shef S8 ... 140 E3
Cawthorne La. Caw S75 ... 32 B6
Cawthorne La. Kex S75 ... 32 B6
Cawthorne Rd. Barn S75 ... 32 D5
Cawthorne Rd. Roth S65 ... 116 C7
Cawthorne View. Pen S30 ... 51 F6
Caxton La. Shef S10 ... 128 C2
Caxton Rd. Ad I S DN6 ... 40 B5
Caxton Rd. Shef S10 ... 128 C2
Caxton St. Barn S70 ... 33 E2
Caythorpe Cl. Cud S71 ... 35 A5
Cayton Cl. Barn S71 ... 33 F7
Cecil Ave. Don DN4 ... 82 C5
Cecil Ave. Dron S18 ... 153 A2
Cecil Rd. Dron S18 ... 153 A2
Cecil Sq. Shef S2 ... 140 F8
Cedar Ave. Mex S64 ... 79 F6
Cedar Ave. Roth S66 ... 117 C5
Cedar Ave. Stai DN7 ... 25 A4
Cedar Cl. Don DN4 ... 82 E5
Cedar Cl. Eck S31 ... 155 B2

Crescent The. Hat DN7 25 A1
Crescent The. N Edl DN12 82 B3
Crescent The. Shef S10 151 E5
Crescent The. Swint S64 79 B2
Crescent The. Thurcr S66 134 A6
Crescent W The. Roth S66 117 B7
Cresswell Rd. Shef S9 130 C4
Cresswell Rd. Swint S64 79 D4
Cresswell St. Barn S75 33 C2
Cresswell St. Mex S64 79 F4
Crest Rd. Shef S5 113 C4
Crestwood Ct. Shef S5 113 C4
Crestwood Gdns. Shef S5 113 C4
Creswick Ave. Shef S5 112 F7
Creswick Cl. Roth S65 116 D8
Creswick Greave Cl. Shef S5 112 E7
Creswick Greave. Shef S30 112 E7
Creswick La. Shef S30 112 E7
Creswick Rd. Roth S65 116 D8
Creswick St. Shef S6 128 D6
Creswick Way. Shef S6 128 D6
Crevesford Sch. Barn 34 B6
Crewe Rd. Bir DN11 122 B4
Crich Ave. Barn S71 34 A7
Cricket Inn Cres. Shef S2 129 E3
Cricket Inn Rd. Shef S2 129 D4
Cricket View Rd. Went S62 76 D1
Cricketers Wlk. Shef S2 129 D4
Cridling Gdns. Norton DN6 4 E3
Crimicar Ave. Shef S10 139 B8
Crimicar Cl. Shef S10 139 C7
Crimicar Dr. Shef S10 139 B8
Crimicar La. Shef S10 139 B8
Crimpsall Rd. Don DN4 62 B2
Cripps Ave. Ross DN11 85 A1
Cripps Cl. Maltby S66 119 B4
Crispin Cl. Shef S12 142 A4
Crispin Dr. Shef S12 142 A4
Crispin Gdns. Shef S12 142 A4
Crispin Rd. Shef S12 142 A4
Croasdale Gdns. Ad le S DN6 21 C1
Crochley Cl. Don DN4 63 F1
Croft Ave. Roy S71 15 B3
Croft Bldgs. Shef S1 129 A4 12
Croft Cl. Shef S11 139 F3
Croft Ct. Don DN3 43 A3
Croft Ct. Finn DN9 86 E3
Croft Dr. Pen S30 50 E3
Croft Dr. Tick DN11 121 A8
Croft La. Shef S11 139 F3
Croft Lea. Dron S18 152 C2
Croft Rd. Barn S70 55 C7
Croft Rd. Brin S60 115 B1
Croft Rd. Don DN4 82 E5
Croft Rd. Finn DN9 87 A1
Croft Rd. Hoy S74 76 D7
Croft Rd. Shef S6 127 D6
Croft Rd. Shef S12 142 B5
Croft St. Barn S70 55 A5
Croft St. Roth S61 97 B4
Croft The. Barn S74 32 E5
Croft The. Ben DN5 41 E3
Croft The. Con DN12 81 C1
Croft The. Hoy S74 77 A5
Croft The. Pen S30 51 F6
Croft The. Swint S64 79 B2
Croft The. Thorne DN8 26 C5
Croft The. Treet S60 131 C5
Croft The. W Bret WF4 12 F8
Crofton Ave. Shef S6 112 B2
Crofton Cl. Dron S18 152 F1
Crofton Dr. Dearne S63 58 C3
Crofton Rise. Chap S30 94 D6
Crofton Rise. Dron S18 152 F1
Crofts Dr. Roth S65 98 E2
Crofts La. Stai DN7 24 D4
Crofts The. Hath S30 149 A8
Crofts The. Roth S60 115 D6
Crofts The. Roth S66 117 B3
Cromarty Rise. Dron S18 152 D2
Cromer Cl. Rawm S62 97 F6
Cromer Rd. Don DN2 63 C4
Cromer St. Grime S72 36 A7
Cromford Ave. Barn S71 34 B6
Cromford Cl. Don DN4 85 A6
Cromford St. Shef S2 129 B1
Crompton Ave. Barn S70 54 D8
Crompton Ave. Ben DN5 61 F4
Crompton Rd. Don DN2 63 B8
Cromwell Ct. Ad le S DN6 20 F1
Cromwell Dr. Ben DN5 61 F2
Cromwell Gr. Ad le S DN6 21 A2
Cromwell Mount. Barn S70 54 E6
Cromwell Rd. Ben DN5 62 B5
Cromwell Rd. Mex S64 80 A4
Cromwell St. Dearne S63 37 E1
Cromwell St. Shef S6 128 C5
Cronkhill La. Roy S71 15 D1
Crook Tree La. Hat DN7 25 E2
Crooke House La. Dar S71 36 A1
Crooked La. H Rob DN12 99 D8
Crooked Lane Head. Tick DN11 120 F5
Crookes Broom Ave. Hat DN7 44 B7
Crookes Broom La. Hat DN7 44 A7
Crookes Endowed Jun Mix & Inf Sch. Shef 128 B3
Crookes La. Roy S71 15 C1
Crookes Rd. Don DN4 83 B6
Crookes Rd. Shef S10 128 C3
Crookes. Shef S10 128 B3
Crookes St. Barn S70 33 D1
Crookes Valley Rd. Shef S10 128 D4
Crookesmoor Bldgs (Univ of Sheffield). Shef 128 C3
Crookesmoor Dr. Shef S6 128 D4
Crookesmoor Mid Sch. Shef 128 D4
Crookesmoor Rd. Shef S10, S6 128 D4
Crookhill Park Municipal Golf Course. Clift 100 E7
Crookhill Rd. Con DN12 81 E2
Cropton Rd. Roy S71 15 B3
Crosby Ave. Roth S66 117 E5
Crosby Ct. Barn S71 34 D5
Crosby Rd. Shef S8 140 F3
Crosby St. Cud S72 35 B8
Cross Allen Rd. Shef S19 143 F2
Cross Bank. Don DN4 83 B8
Cross Bedford St. Shef S6 128 F5
Cross Burgess St. Shef S1 129 A3 15
Cross Butcher St. Dearne S63 58 C8
Cross Chantrey Rd. Shef S8 141 A3
Cross Dr. Shef S13 143 B6
Cross Field Dr. Woods S81 147 F4
Cross Gate. Ben DN5 62 A6
Cross Gate. Mex S64 80 C4
Cross Gilpin St. Shef S6 128 E6 6
Cross Hill. Ad le S DN6 20 F1
Cross Hill. Bri S72 16 F3
Cross Hill Cl. Shef S30 113 C7
Cross Hill Ct. Ad le S DN6 20 F2
Cross Hill. Hem WF9 17 D7
Cross Hill. Shef S30 113 C7
Cross House Rd. Shef S30 112 C8
Cross Keys La. Hoy S74 76 A6
Cross La. Aust DN10 105 C5
Cross La. Dron S18 153 B1
Cross La. Dron S18 153 C3
Cross La. Dron S18 153 C5
Cross La. Oxspr S30 73 A7
Cross La. Pen S30 51 A1
Cross La. Pen S30 51 F8
Cross La. Roy S71 15 E3
Cross La. Shef S10 128 B3
Cross La. Shef S17 139 C1
Cross La. Shep HD8 28 E6
Cross La. Wort S30 74 C5
Cross La. Wort S30 75 B2
Cross Love St. Shef S3 129 A4 4
Cross Myrtle Rd. Shef S2 141 B7
Cross Park Rd. Shef S8 141 A5 1
Cross Rd. Hat DN7 45 C7
Cross Riding. Don DN2 63 E4
Cross Road Banner. Shef S11 140 B5
Cross Smithfield. Shef S3 128 F4
Cross South St. Roth S61 97 C3
Cross St. Barn S75 32 D4
Cross St. Barn S75 33 D3
Cross St. Barn S71 34 C3
Cross St. Barn S70 55 B6
Cross St. Ben DN5 41 B1
Cross St. Dearne S63 58 F5
Cross St. Don DN4 83 A7
Cross St. G Hou S72 36 E1
Cross St. Grime S72 36 B6
Cross St. Hem WF9 17 C7
Cross St. Hoy S74 76 B5
Cross St. Kill S31 156 F7
Cross St. Lan S81 136 E3
Cross St. Maltby S66 119 A5
Cross St. N Edl DN12 82 B2
Cross St. Rawm S62 97 F3
Cross St. Ross DN11 103 F8
Cross St. Roth S61 115 A6
Cross St. Roth S66 117 D5
Cross St. Roth S61 97 C3
Cross St. Roth S65 98 E2
Cross St. Shef S13 143 B6
Cross St. Thurcr S66 133 E6
Cross St. Upton WF9 19 D8
Cross St. W up D S63 78 E6
Cross Turner St. Shef S2 129 B2
Crosscourt View. Don DN4 84 C8
Crossfield Dr. Ad le S DN6 21 A2
Crossfield Dr. W up D S63 78 E5
Crossfield Gdns. Chap S30 94 D7
Crossfield House Cl. Ad le S DN6 21 A2
Crossfield La. Ad le S DN6 21 A2
Crossfield La. Ad le S DN6 21 C1
Crossgate. Dearne S63 58 D7
Crossgate. Mapp S75 14 B1
Crossgates. Wad DN11 102 C6
Crossland Dr. Shef S12 142 A3
Crossland Pl. Shef S12 142 A4
Crossland Rd. Hath S30 149 A7
Crossland St. Swint S64 79 D3
Crossland Way. Ben DN5 61 E7
Crossley Cl. Maltby S66 118 E6
Crossway. Swint S64 79 B2
Crossways. Dearne S63 58 C2
Crossways. Don DN2 63 B7
Crossways N. Don DN2 63 B7
Crossways S. Don DN2 63 B6
Crossways. Stai DN7 24 F4
Crossways The. Shef S2 130 B1
Crow Tree Bank. Hat DN8 46 B8
Crow Tree La. Mex S64 79 F7
Crowden Wlk. Barn S75 33 A1
Crowder Ave. Shef S5 113 A4
Crowder Cl. Shef S5 113 A3
Crowder Cres. Shef S5 113 A3
Crowder Rd. Shef S5 113 B3
Crowgate. S Anst S31 146 C3
Crowland Rd. Shef S5 113 B4
Crowley Dr. W up D S63 78 F4
Crown Ave. Barn S70 55 A7
Crown Ave. Cud S72 35 C4
Crown Cl. Barn S70 55 A7
Crown Cl. Roth S61 114 E8
Crown Hill Rd. Barn S70 33 A1
Crown Pl. Shef S2 129 C3
Crown Rd. Tick DN11 120 F7
Crown St. Barn S70 55 A7
Crown St. Hoy S74 76 D6
Crown St. Swint S64 79 D3
Crownhill Rd. Brin S60 115 B1
Crowther Pl. Shef S7 141 A8 7
Croydon St. Shef S11 140 F8
Cruck Cl. Dron S18 152 E2
Cruise Rd. Shef S11 139 F8
Crummock Rd. Shef S7 140 E5 4
Crummock Way. Barn S71 56 B8
Crumpsall Dr. Shef S5 112 F1
Crumpsall Rd. Shef S5 112 F1
Crusader Dr. Ben DN5 61 E3
Crystal Peaks (Sh Ctr). Shef 143 E2
Cubley Rise Rd. Pen S30 51 C1
Cuckoo La. Hat DN7 25 C2
Cuckstool Rd. D Dale HD8 30 A6
Cudworth Birkwood Fst Sch. Cud 35 C5
Cudworth Churchfield Prim Sch. Cud 35 B7
Cudworth Churchfield Prim Sch. Grime 35 F7
Cudworth Pontefract Rd Fst Sch. Cud 35 B8
Cudworth View. Grime S72 36 A6
Cullabine Rd. Shef S2 142 A7
Cumberland Ave. Don DN2 63 B4
Cumberland Cl. Barn S70 54 F5
Cumberland Cl. Bir DN11 122 D4
Cumberland Cl. C in L S81 148 F7
Cumberland Cl. Hoy S74 76 E7
Cumberland Cres. Chap S30 95 B4
Cumberland Dr. Barn S71 56 A8
Cumberland House. Bir DN11 122 D4
Cumberland Pl. Con DN12 80 F3 4
Cumberland Rd. Hoy S74 76 E7
Cumberland St. Shef S1 129 A2 8
Cumberland Way. Dearne S63 58 C1
Cumberland Way. Shef S1 129 A2
Cumberworth La. D Dale HD8 28 F6
Cumbrian Wlk. Barn S75 33 B2 1
Cundy St. Shef S6 128 D6
Cunliffe St. Dron S18 153 C4
Cunningham Rd. Don DN1 62 D2
Cunningham Rd. Hat DN7 66 A8
Cupola La. Shef S30 94 C1
Cupola. Shef S3 129 A4
Cupola Yd. Roth S60 115 C6
Curlew Ave. Eck S31 155 B3
Curlew Ct. Ross DN11 85 A1
Curlew Mid Sch. Don 42 D1
Curlew Ridge. Shef S2 129 D2
Curlew Rise. Roth S61 96 A6
Curzen Cres. Don DN3 43 A4
Curzon Cl. Kill S31 156 D6
Cusworth Hall (Mus). Ben 61 D4
Cusworth House. Don DN1 62 C2 7
Cusworth La. Ben DN5 61 E5
Cusworth Park Ctry Pk. Ben 61 D4
Cusworth Rd. Ben DN5 62 A7
Cuthbert Bank Rd. Shef S6 128 D7
Cuthbert Rd. Shef S6 128 D7
Cutler Cl. Kill S31 156 B7
Cutlers Ave. Barn S70 54 D8
Cuttlehurst. Clay W HD8 30 D8
Cutts Ave. W up D S63 78 D5
Cutts Terr. Shef S8 140 F7
Cutty La. Barn S75 33 D3
Cyclops St. Shef S4 129 E8
Cypress Ave. Finn DN9 85 F3
Cypress Ave. Shef S8 141 C1
Cypress Cl. Kill S31 156 C5
Cypress Gate. Chap S30 94 F4
Cypress Gr. Con DN12 99 F8
Cypress Rd. Barn S70 55 B7
Cyprus Rd. Shef S8 141 A5

Dadley Rd. C in L S81 148 F7
Dadsley Ct. Tick DN11 120 F8
Dadsley Rd. Tick DN11 121 A8
Daffodil Rd. Shef S5 113 F3
Dagnam Cl. Shef S2 141 F6
Dagnam Cres. Shef S2 141 F6
Dagnam Dr. Shef S2 141 F7
Dagnam Pl. Shef S2 141 F6
Dagnam Rd. Shef S2 141 F7
Daisy Bank. Shef S3 128 E4
Daisy Lee La. Holmfi HD7 48 C7
Daisy Wlk. Shef S3 128 F4 8
Daisy Wlk. Shef S19 143 F3
Dalbury Rd. Dron S18 152 C1
Dalby Gdns. Shef S19 144 A1
Dalby Gr. Shef S19 144 A2
Dale Ave. Roth S65 116 C5
Dale Cl. Barn S71 34 A7
Dale Cl. D Dale HD8 29 F5
Dale Cres. Hath S30 149 B8
Dale Croft. Bfield S6 110 A4
Dale Ct. Rawm S62 97 F5
Dale Gr. Dearne S63 58 B1
Dale Green Rd. Barn S70 54 F7
Dale Hill Cl. Maltby S66 118 F7
Dale Hill Rd. Maltby S66 118 E7
Dale La. S Elm WF9 19 B5
Dale Lane Ind Est. S Elm 19 B5
Dale Pit Rd. Hat DN7 44 F5
Dale Rd. Bfield S6 109 D4
Dale Rd. Con DN12 81 C2
Dale Rd. Kill S31 156 E6
Dale Rd. Rawm S62 97 E6
Dale Rd. Roth S65 116 C4
Dale Rd. Roth S66 117 A4
Dale Side. Shef S10 128 B1
Dale St. Rawm S62 97 F6
Dale The. Hath S30 149 B8
Dale The. Shef S8 140 F3
Dale View. Hem WF9 17 F6
Dalebrook Ct. Shef S10 127 E1
Dalebrook Ct. Shef S10 139 E8
Dalecroft Rd. Ad l S DN6 40 B8
Daleswood Ave. Barn S70 33 B1
Daleswood Dr. Barn S70 55 D5
Daleview Rd. Shef S8 140 F4
Dalewood Ave. Shef S8 140 C2
Dalewood Dr. Shef S8 140 C1
Dalewood Rd. Shef S8 140 C1
Dalmore Rd. Shef S7 140 C5
Dalroyd La. Bfield S6 110 E3
Dalton Ct. Con DN12 80 F3 2
Dalton Ct. Shef S8 140 F7 9
Dalton House. Roth S60 116 B3
Dalton Jun Mix Sch. Roth 98 C1
Dalton La. Roth S65 116 D8
Dalton Listerdale Cty Prim Sch. Roth 116 E4
Dalton Terr. Barn S70 55 A8 10
Dam Rd. Tick DN11 121 A6
Damasel Cl. Wharn S30 93 B1
Damasel La. Wharn S30 93 B1
Damasel Rd. Wharn S30 93 B2
Damer St. Shef S10 128 D3
Damsteads. Dod S75 54 A7
Danby Rd. Wales S31 145 F2
Dance La. Thurgo S30 74 D7
Dane St. Dearne S63 58 E8
Dane St N. Dearne S63 58 E8
Dane St S. Dearne S63 58 E8
Danebrook Cl. Shef S2 130 C1
Danebrook Ct. Shef S2 130 C1
Danebrook Dr. Shef S2 130 C1
Danesthorpe Cl. Don DN2 63 C6
Danesway. Ben DN5 40 F1
Danethorpe Way. Con DN12 100 A8
Danewood Ave. Shef S2 130 C1
Danewood Croft. Shef S2 130 C1
Danewood Gdns. Shef S2 130 C1
Danewood Gr. Shef S2 130 C1
Daniel Hill Ct. Shef S6 128 D5
Daniel Hill. Shef S6 128 E5
Daniel Hill St. Shef S6 128 D5
Daniel Hill Terr. Shef S6 128 E5
Daniel La. Rawm S62 97 B6
Daniels Dr. Aston S31 132 C1
Dannemora Dr. Shef S9 130 C7
Danum Cl. Thorne DN8 26 C7
Danum Ct. Con DN12 80 F3
Danum Dr. Roth S65 115 F7
Danum Grammar Sch. Don 62 F2
Danum Grammar Sch. Don 63 D6
Danum Rd. Don DN4 62 F2
Danum Rd. Hat DN7 44 B6
Danum Sch. Don 63 D4
Dara St. Shef S9 114 B5
Darcy Cl. Aston S31 144 D8
Darcy Rd. Eck S31 155 C3
Daresbury Cl. Shef S2 141 D6
Daresbury Dr. Shef S2 141 D6
Daresbury Pl. Shef S2 141 D6
Daresbury Rd. Shef S2 141 D6
Daresbury View. Shef S2 141 E6
Darfield Ave. Shef S19 142 F2
Darfield C of E (Controlled) Jun Sch. Dar 57 B5
Darfield Cl. Ross DN11 85 B1
Darfield Cl. Shef S19 142 F2
Darfield Foulstone High Sch. Dar 57 B5
Darfield House. Don DN1 62 C2 13
Darfield Jun & Inf Sch. Dar 56 F5
Darfield Rd. Cud S72 35 D4
Darfield Upperwood Jun & Inf Sch. Dar 56 F6
Dargle Ave. Don DN2 63 A5
Darhaven. Dar S73 57 A6
Dark La. Barn S70, S75 54 B7
Dark La. Barn S70 55 B3
Dark La. Caw S75 31 E5
Dark La. Midhop S30 71 E5
Darley Ave. BarnS71 34 A7
Darley Ave. Barn S70 54 F6
Darley. Barn S70 55 C5
Darley Cl. Barn S71 34 A7
Darley Cl. Hart S31 157 E6
Darley Cliff Cotts. Barn S70 55 B5
Darley Gr. Shef S6 127 D6
Darley Terr. Barn S75 33 D2
Darley Yd. Barn S70 55 B5
Darlington Gr. Thorne DN8 9 C4
Darlington Wlk. Thorne DN8 9 C4
Darnall Dr. Shef S9 130 B5
Darnall Rd. Shef S9 130 B5
Darnall Sta. Shef 130 C4
Darrington Dr. Don DN4 82 D5
Darrington Pl. Barn S71 34 E3
Dart Gr. Auck DN9 86 A7
Dart Sq. Shef S3 128 E4
Dartmouth Rd. Don DN4 85 B6
Darton Hall Cl. Mapp S75 13 F1
Darton Hall Dr. Mapp S75 13 F1
Darton High Sch. Kex 32 B8
Darton High Sch. Mapp 32 F8
Darton Kexbrough Inf Sch. Kex 32 B8
Darton La. Mapp S75 33 A8
Darton Mapplewell Cty Inf Sch. Mapp 14 B1
Darton Prim Sch. Mapp 13 F1
Darton Rd. Caw S75 31 F5
Darton St. Barn S70 55 D7
Darton Sta. Mapp 13 E1
Dartree Wlk. Dar S73 56 F6
Darwall Cl. Chap S30 94 D8
Darwent La. Ought S30 111 B4
Darwin Cl. Shef S10 127 F2
Darwin La. Shef S10 127 F2
Darwin Rd. Shef S6 112 B2
Darwynn Ave. Swint S64 79 A3
David Cl. Shef S13 143 D7
David La. Shef S10 139 A7
Davies Dr. Swint S64 79 D1
Davis Rd. Askern DN6 21 E7
Davis St. Roth S65 116 A7
Davy Dr. Maltby S66 118 F6
Davy Rd. Con DN12 80 E3
Daw Croft Ave. Barn S70 55 A5
Daw La. Ben DN5 41 B2
Daw La. Wad DN11 102 D8
Daw Wood. Ben DN5 41 C3
Dawber La. Kill S31 156 F7
Dawlands Cl. Shef S2 130 B1
Dawlands Dr. Shef S2 130 B1
Dawson Ave. Rawm S62 97 C8
Dawson Terr. Wales S31 145 D2
Day St. Barn S70 54 E8
Daykin Cl. Kex S75 32 D8
Daylands Ave. Con DN12 81 B1
De Houton Cl. Tod S31 145 E5
De La Salle Dr. Shef S4 129 C7
De Lacy Dr. Barn S70 55 A5
De Sutton Pl. Hart S31 157 E5
De Warren Pl. Hart S31 157 F5
Deacon Cl. Ross DN11 85 B1
Deacon Cres. Maltby S66 119 A4
Deacon Cres. Ross DN11 84 E1
Deacons Way. Barn S71 34 C3
Deadman's Hole La. Shef S9 114 E3
Deakins Wlk. Shef S10 127 F1
Dean Cl. Ben DN5 61 D2
Dean Cl. Ross DN11 85 B1
Dean Head La. Oxspr S30 73 B5
Dean La. Holmfi HD7 48 D8
Dean La. Roth S65 116 F7
Dean St. Barn S70 33 D1
Deane Field View. Shef S19 143 D2
Deanhead Ct. Shef S19 143 A2 7
Deanhead Dr. Shef S19 143 A2 8
Deans Way. Barn S71 34 C4
Deansfield Cl. Arm DN3 64 B5
Dearden Ct. Shef S30 113 B8
Dearne Cl. Wombw S73 56 F1
Dearne Ct. Shef S9 114 A2
Dearne Dike La. D Dale HD8 28 E5
Dearne Goldthorpe Inf Sch. Dearne 58 E5
Dearne Goldthorpe Jun Schs. Dearne 58 E5
Dearne Hall Rd. Barn S75 32 F6
Dearne Rd. Dearne S63 58 B1
Dearne Rd. W up D S63 79 B8
Dearne Road Flatlets. Dearne S63 58 B1
Dearne St. Con DN12 81 D3
Dearne St. G Hou S72 36 E1
Dearne St. Mapp S75 13 F1
Dearne St. S Elm WF9 18 F3
Dearne St. Shef S9 114 A2
Dearne Thurscoe The Hill Inf Sch. Dearne 37 F1
Dearne View. Dearne S63 58 E5
Dearneside Comp Sch. Dearne 58 E4
Dearneside Rd. D Dale HD8 29 F5
Dearneway. W up D S63 78 F6
Dearnfield. D Dale HD8 29 C6
Dearnley View. Barn S75 33 D4
Decoy Bank N. Don DN4 62 D1
Decoy Bank (S). Don DN4 83 E7
Deep La. Shef S5 113 F8
Deepcar La. Cud S72 35 E3
Deepcar St John's C of E Jun Sch. Stock 92 E8
Deepdale Rd. Roth S61 114 F6
Deepwell Ave. Shef S19 155 F6
Deepwell Bank. Shef S19 155 F6
Deepwell Ct. Shef S19 155 F6
Deepwell View. Shef S19 155 F6
Deer Leap Dr. Roth S65 99 A2
Deer Park Cl. Shef S6 127 E6
Deer Park Pl. Shef S6 127 E6
Deer Park Rd. Roth S65 99 A2
Deer Park Rd. Shef S6 127 F6
Deer Park View. Shef S6 127 E6
Deer Park Way. Shef S6 127 F6
Deerlands Cl. Shef S5 112 F6
Deerlands Mount. Shef S5 112 E6
Deerlands Sch. Shef 113 B5
Deershaw La. Holmfi HD7 28 C5
Deershaw Sike La. Holmfi HD7 28 C5
Deightonby St. Dearne S63 37 E1
Delamere Cl. Shef S19 144 A2
Delf Cotts. Barn S75 54 D5
Delf Rd. Bfield S30 110 C6
Delf St. Shef S2 141 B7
Dell Ave. Grime S72 36 A8
Dell Cres. Don DN4 61 F1
Della Ave. Barn S70 54 D8
Delmar Way. Roth S66 117 B6
Delph Cl. Silk S75 32 A1
Delph Edge. Stock S30 73 E3
Delph House Rd. Shef S10 127 F3
Delta Pl. Roth S65 116 B7
Delta Way. Maltby S66 119 B6
Delves Ave. Shef S12 143 D4
Delves Cl. Shef S12 143 C4
Delves Dr. Shef S12 143 C4
Delves La. Wales S31 144 E2
Delves Pl. Shef S12 143 B3
Delves Rd. Kill S31 156 C6
Delves Rd. Shef S12 143 C3
Delves Terr. Shef S12 143 C3
Den Bank Ave. Shef S10 127 E3
Den Bank Cl. Shef S10 127 F3
Den Bank Cres. Shef S10 127 E3
Den Bank Dr. Shef S10 127 F3
Denaby La. Con DN12 80 C3
Denaby La. H Rob DN12 99 A8
Denaby Lane Ind Est. Con 80 E3
Denaby Main Inf Sch. Con 81 A4
Denaby Main Jun Sch. Con 80 F4
Denby C of E Sch. D Dale 29 F3
Denby Dale Rd. W Bret HD8 12 C8
Denby Dale Sta. D Dale 29 E6
Denby Hall La. D Dale HD8 30 D4
Denby La. D Dale HD8 29 D3
Denby La. D Dale HD8 30 A3
Denby La. D Dale HD8 30 C4
Denby Rd. Barn S71 33 F7
Denby St. Ben DN5 41 B1
Denby St. Shef S2 129 A1
Denby Way. Maltby S66 118 A5
Dene Cl. Roth S66 117 C4
Dene Cres. Roth S65 116 B8
Dene La. Shef S3 128 F2
Dene Rd. Roth S65 116 B8
Denehall Rd. Don DN3 43 A3
Denham Rd. Shef S11 128 E1
Denholme Cl. Shef S3 129 B5
Denholme Meadow. S Elm WF9 18 F4
Denison Ct. Barn S70 54 F8 9
Denison Rd. Don DN4 62 B2
Denman Rd. W up D S63 78 D6
Denman St. Roth S65 115 E8
Denmark Rd. Shef S2 141 B6
Denson Cl. Shef S2 141 B6 2
Dent La. Shef S12 142 F2
Denton Rd. Shef S8 140 F4 2
Denton St. Barn S71 33 F2
Dentons Green La. Don DN3 42 F4
Denver Rd. Norton DN6 4 E3
Derby Pl. Shef S2 141 C6
Derby Rd. Don DN2 63 C8
Derby St. Barn S70 33 D1
Derby St. Shef S2 141 C6
Derby Terr. Shef S2 141 C6
Derbyshire La. Shef S8 141 A3
Derriman Ave. Shef S11 140 B4
Derriman Cl. Shef S11 140 B4
Derriman Dr. Shef S11 140 B4
Derriman Glen. Shef S11 140 A4
Derriman Gr. Shef S11 140 B4
Derry Gr. Dearne S63 58 C7
Derwent Cl. Barn S71 34 B7
Derwent Cl. Dron S18 153 B3
Derwent Cl. N Anst S31 146 F7
Derwent Cres. Barn S71 34 B7
Derwent Cres. Brin S60 131 B7
Derwent Ct. Shef S17 152 A5 5
Derwent Dr. Chap S30 94 E5
Derwent Dr. Don DN3 42 F3
Derwent Dr. Mex S64 80 C6
Derwent Gdns. Dearne S63 58 E4
Derwent Pl. Sprot DN5 61 B1
Derwent Pl. Wombw S73 56 F1
Derwent Rd. Barn S71 34 B7
Derwent Rd. Dron S18 153 B3
Derwent Rd. Mex S64 80 C6
Derwent Rd. Roth S61 97 A3
Derwent St. Shef S2 129 D4
Derwent Terr. Mex S64 80 A6
Derwent Way. W up D S63 78 C8
Deveron Rd. Shef S19 155 F7
Devon Ct. Con DN12 80 F2
Devon Rd. Shef S4 129 C8
Devonshire Cl. Shef S17 151 F6

Egerton Rd. Dron S18 153 B2
Egerton St. Shef S1 128 F2
Egerton Wlk. Shef S3 128 F2 2
Egg La. Wad DN11 102 F7
Eggington Cl. Don DN4 85 B7
Eglins Rd. Thorne DN8 9 D1
Egmanton Rd. Barn S71 14 F1
Eilam Cl. Roth S61 114 E8
Eilam Rd. Roth S61 114 E8
Ekin St. Roth S9 114 F3
Eland Cl. Ross DN11 84 F2
Elcroft Gdns. Shef S19 143 F2
Elder Ave. N Anst S31 146 F5
Elder Ave. Upton WF9 19 C8
Elder Ct. Kill S31 156 C5
Elder Dr. Roth S66 117 C6
Elder Dr. Upton WF9 19 C8
Elder Gr. Con DN12 81 A1
Elder Gr. Finn DN9 86 A5
Eldertree Rd. Roth S61 95 F3
Eldon Arc. Barn S70 33 F1 1
Eldon Ct. Shef S1 128 F3 13
Eldon Gr. Thorne DN8 9 E3
Eldon Rd. Roth S65 115 F8
Eldon St. Barn S70 33 F1
Eldon St N. Barn S71 33 F2
Eldon St. Shef S1 128 F3
Eleanor Ct. Don DN3 42 E1
Eleanor St. Shef S9 130 B6
Elgar Dr. Maltby S66 119 C4
Elgin House Preparatory Sch. Don 62 E4
Elgin St. Shef S10 128 B3
Elgitha Dr. Thurcr S66 133 E6
Elizabeth Ave. Don DN3 43 A3
Elizabeth Ave. S Hie S72 16 E5
Elizabeth Ct. Hem WF9 17 F6
Elizabeth Rd. Aston S31 144 D6
Elizabeth St. Dearne S63 58 E5
Elizabeth St. Grime S72 36 A6
Elizabeth St. Hoy S74 76 E6
Elizabeth Way. Roth S60 115 C6
Ella Rd. Shef S4 129 C7
Elland Cl. Barn S71 33 E7
Ellavale. Hoy S74 77 A6
Ellen Tree Cl. Brin S60 131 B8
Ellenbro Rd. Shef S6 128 B8
Ellerker Ave. Don DN4 62 B2
Ellers Ave. Don DN4 84 D7
Ellers Cres. Don DN4 84 C8
Ellers Dr. Don DN4 84 C7
Ellers High Sch. Don 84 B8
Ellers La. Auck DN9 86 A7
Ellers Rd. Don DN4 84 C8
Ellershaw La. Con DN12 81 A1
Ellershaw Rd. Con DN12 81 B1
Ellerton Gdns. Don DN4 63 E1
Ellerton Rd. Shef S5 113 D2
Ellesmere First Sch. Shef 129 C6
Ellesmere Gr. Stai DN7 25 B4
Ellesmere Rd N. Shef S4 129 C7
Ellesmere Rd. Shef S4 129 C6
Ellesmere Terr. Roth S65 115 F6 4
Ellesmere Wlk. Shef S4 129 C6
Ellin St. Shef S1 129 A1
Ellington Ct. Barn S70 54 C7
Elliot La. Shef S30 94 E3
Elliot Rd. Shef S6 128 D4
Elliott Ave. Wombw S73 56 D1
Elliott Cl. W up D S63 78 C7
Elliott Ct. Roth S65 115 E7 10
Elliott Dr. Roth S61 96 F2
Elliott La. Chap S30 94 D4
Elliottville St. Shef S6 128 C6
Ellis Ave. W up D S63 78 E4
Ellis Cres. Ross DN11 84 E1
Ellis Cres. W up D S73 78 A7
Ellis St. Brin S60 115 C1
Ellis St. Shef S3 128 F4
Ellison St. Shef S3 128 F4
Ellison St. Thorne DN8 26 B6
Ellisons Rd. Kill S31 156 F8
Elliston Ave. Mapp S75 14 C1
Ellorslie Dr. Stock S30 73 C1
Elm Cl. B Dun DN3 42 F7
Elm Cl. Kill S31 156 C5
Elm Cotts. G Hou S72 36 E2
Elm Cres. Ben DN5 41 C2
Elm Cres. Shef S19 155 C8
Elm Ct. Barn S70 55 B4
Elm Dr. Finn DN9 86 F3
Elm Dr. Kill S31 156 C5
Elm Gr. Roth S61 97 B3
Elm Gr. S Elm WF9 18 F3
Elm Green La. Con DN12 81 C2
Elm La. Shef S5 113 B4
Elm Pl. Arm DN3 64 A7
Elm Pl. Barn S71 34 D5
Elm Pl. Rawm S62 98 A5
Elm Rd. Ad le S DN6 21 B2
Elm Rd. Arm DN3 64 A7
Elm Rd. Eck S31 155 C2
Elm Rd. Finn DN9 85 F3
Elm Rd. Hem WF9 17 E7
Elm Rd. Mex S64 79 F6
Elm Rd. Shef S19 144 A4
Elm Rise. Chap S30 94 F4
Elm Row. Barn S71 34 B1
Elm St. Hoy S74 76 B5
Elm Tree Cl. N Anst S31 146 F5
Elm Tree Cres. Dron S18 153 A3
Elm Tree Dr. Bawtry DN10 122 F7
Elm Tree Gr. Thorne DN8 26 B6
Elm Tree Rd. Maltby S66 118 D5
Elm Tree Rd. Roth S66 95 F3
Elm Way. W up D S63 79 A4
Elmdale Cl. Swint S64 98 D8
Elmdale Dr. Don DN3 42 F1
Elmfield Ave. Shef S5 113 B4
Elmfield Rd. Don DN1 62 E2
Elmfield Rd. Ross DN11 104 A8
Elmham Rd. Don DN4 63 E1
Elmham Rd. Shef S9 130 D4
Elmhirst Dr. Roth S65 116 C4
Elmhirst La. Dod S75 32 D1
Elmhirst Rd. Thorne DN8 26 C7
Elmore Rd. Shef S10 128 C3
Elmsall La. H Pag DN6,DN5 38 C7
Elmsall Way. S Elm WF9 19 B5
Elmsdale. Barn S70 55 B4
Elmsdale Cl. S Elm WF9 19 B2
Elmtree Cl. Shire S81 159 F7
Elmview Rd. Shef S9 114 B4
Elmville Ave. Swint S64 79 C1
Elmwood Ave. Ad le S DN6 39 F6
Elmwood Cres. Arm DN3 64 A6
Elmwood Dr. Shef S19 155 D6
Elsecar CE Sch (Jun & Inf). Hoy 77 B5
Elsecar & Hoyland Sta. Hoy 77 A5
Elsecar Rd. W up D S63 78 A6
Elsham Cl. Roth S66 117 D7
Elstead Cl. Barn S75 32 E5
Elstree Dr. Shef S12 142 B4
Elstree Rd. Shef S12 142 B4
Elsworth Cl. Don DN1 62 C1
Elvaston Cl. Dron S18 152 B1
Elwis St. Don DN5 62 B4
Elwood Rd. Shef S17 152 C6
Ely Rd. Don DN2 62 F7
Ely St. Ross DN11 84 E1
Embankment Rd. Shef S10 128 C3
Emerson Ave. Stai DN7 24 F3
Emerson Cl. Shef S5 113 B5
Emerson Cres. Shef S5 113 B4
Emerson Dr. Shef S5 113 B4
Emily Cl. Barn S71 34 D2
Emily Rd. Shef S7 140 E6
Emley Dr. Ben DN5 61 C7
Emley House. Don DN1 62 C2 8
Emmanuel Mid Sch. Shef 143 E1
Empire Rd. Shef S7 140 F6
Emsley Ave. Cud S72 35 C4
Endcliffe Ave. Shef S10 128 C1
Endcliffe Cres. Shef S10 128 B1
Endcliffe Edge. Shef S10 128 B1
Endcliffe Glen Rd. Shef S11 128 C1
Endcliffe Grove Ave. Shef S10 128 B1
Endcliffe Hall Ave. Shef S10 128 B1
Endcliffe Rise Rd. Shef S11 128 C1
Endcliffe Terrace Rd. Shef S11 128 C1
Endcliffe Vale Ave. Shef S11 140 C8
Endcliffe Vale Rd. Shef S10 128 B1
Endcliffe Way. Don DN2 63 C7
Endfield Rd. Shef S5 112 F8
Endowood Rd. Shef S7 140 B2
Enfield Pl. Shef S13 130 F2
Engine La. Dearne S63 58 F4
Engine La. Grime S72 35 E7
Ennerdale Ave. Shef S19 155 E6 4
Ennerdale Cl. Dron S18 152 E1
Ennerdale Cl. Mex S64 80 C6
Ennerdale Cl. N Anst S31 146 E7
Ennerdale Dr. Shef S19 155 E6
Ennerdale Rd. Barn S71 56 B8
Ennerdale Rd. Don DN2 63 C7
Ennis Cres. Don DN2 63 A5
Entwhistle Rd. Chap S30 94 E7
Epping Gdns. Shef S19 144 A2
Epping Gr. Shef S19 144 A2
Epsom Cl. Mex S64 80 B6
Epsom Rd. Don DN4 63 D2
Epworth Ct. Ben DN5 62 A6
Epworth Rd. Hat DN7 44 E7
Eric St. S Elm WF9 19 A3
Errington Ave. Shef S2 141 E6
Errington Cl. Shef S2 141 E6
Errington Cres. Shef S2 141 E6
Errington Rd. Shef S2 141 E6
Errington Way. Shef S2 141 E7
Erskine Cres. Shef S2 141 C7
Erskine Rd. Roth S65 115 E8
Erskine Rd. Shef S2 141 C7
Erskine View. Shef S2 141 C7
Eshton Ct. Mapp S75 14 A2
Eshton Wlk. Barn S70 33 D1 3
Eskdale Cl. Dron S18 152 E1
Eskdale Cl. Shef S6 112 C2
Eskdale Dr. Ben DN5 61 F8
Eskdale Rd. Barn S71 56 A8
Eskdale Rd. Roth S61 96 F3
Eskdale Rd. Shef S6 112 C2
Eskdale Wlk. Ben DN5 61 C7
Eskholme La. Syke DN14 7 D8
Esperanto Pl. Shef S1 129 B3
Essendine Cres. Shef S8 141 B3
Essex Ave. Don DN2 63 B4
Essex Cl. Wales S31 145 F3
Essex Dr. Bir DN11 122 D4
Essex Rd. Barn S70 54 F7 1
Essex Rd. Bir DN11 122 D4
Essex Rd. Shef S2 129 D1
Estate Rd. Rawm S62 97 F7
Estfeld Cl. Tick DN11 121 A8
Estfeld Sch. Tick 121 A8
Estone Dr. Aston S31 144 D8
Etwall Way. Shef S5 113 C4
Eunice La. D Dale HD8 29 C6
Europa Link. Treet S60 131 B6
Evans St. Shef S3 128 F2
Evanston Gdns. Don DN4 83 A8
Eveline St. Cud S72 35 B6
Evelyn Ave. Don DN2 63 B4
Evelyn Cl. Don DN2 63 B4
Evelyn Rd. Shef S10 128 B3
Evelyn St. Rawm S62 98 B6
Evelyn Terr. Barn S70 55 B8 2
Everard Ave. Shef S17 152 A5
Everard Dr. Shef S17 152 A5
Everard Glade. Shef S17 152 A5 3
Everdale Mount. Hem WF9 17 C6
Everdale Mount. S Elm WF9 18 E3
Everetts Cl. Tick DN11 120 F7
Everill Cl. Wombw S73 56 F1
Everill Gate La. Dar S73 57 A2
Everill Gate La. Wombw S73 56 F2
Everingham Cl. Shef S5 113 A3
Everingham Rd. Don DN4 63 E1
Everingham Rd. Shef S5 113 A3
Everson Cl. Maltby S66 118 E7
Everton Rd. Shef S11 140 C8
Evesham Cl. Shef S9 114 B3
Ewden Rd. Wombw S73 56 F1
Ewden Village. Stock S30 92 C5
Ewden Way. Barn S75 33 A1
Ewers Rd. Roth S61 114 F7
Ewood Dr. Don DN4 84 E8
Exchange Gateway. Shef S1 129 A3 9
Exchange Pl. Shef S2 129 B4
Exchange St. Don DN1 62 D1
Exchange St. S Elm WF9 18 F3
Exchange St. Shef S2 129 B4
Exeter Dr. Shef S3 128 F1
Exeter Pl. Shef S3 128 E2
Exeter Rd. Don DN2 63 A6
Exeter Way. Shef S3 128 E2 2
Exley Ave. Shef S6 128 D6
Eyam Cl. Dod S75 53 E7
Eyam Rd. Shef S10 128 B3
Eyncourt Rd. Shef S5 113 D3
Eyre Gdns. Chap S30 94 D6
Eyre La. Shef S1 129 A2
Eyre St. Shef S1 129 A2
Fabian Way. Roth S66 117 E4
Factory La. Don DN1 62 C3
Fair Field. Barn S70 54 F1
Fair House La. Bfield S6 110 A4
Fair View Ave. Ad le S DN6 39 F5
Fair View Dr. Aston S31 144 E7
Fairbank Rd. Shef S5 113 B1
Fairbank View. Roth S60 116 C1
Fairbarn Cl. Shef S6 127 E5
Fairbarn Dr. Shef S6 127 E5
Fairbarn Pl. Shef S6 127 E5
Fairbarn Rd. Shef S6 127 E5
Fairbarn Way. Shef S6 127 E5
Fairburn Gr. Hoy S74 77 B6
Fairfax Rd. Don DN2 63 B4
Fairfax Rd. Shef S2 142 B8
Fairfax Way. Tick DN11 120 F7
Fairfield Cl. Don DN4 84 D6
Fairfield Cl. Roth S66 117 C7
Fairfield Ct. Arm DN3 64 B5
Fairfield. Dearne S63 58 B2
Fairfield Manor. Sprot DN5 61 D1
Fairfield. Rawcl DN14 2 D7
Fairfield Rd. Ben DN5 61 F6
Fairfield Rd. Shef S6 128 E6
Fairfields. D Dale HD8 29 F3
Fairford Cl. Don DN4 85 A6
Fairhurst La. Wharn S30 92 D6
Fairleigh Dr. Roth S60 115 E4
Fairleigh. Shef S2 142 A8
Fairmount Gdns. Shef S12 143 A3 4
Fairthorn Rd. Shef S5 113 D4
Fairtree Wlk. Thorne DN8 26 B7
Fairview Cl. Hoy S74 76 C5
Fairview Rd. Dron S18 153 A3
Fairview Terr. B Dun DN3 42 F6
Fairview Villas. B Dun DN3 42 F6
Fairway Ave. Mapp S75 14 C2
Fairway. Dod S75 54 A6
Fairway The. Shef S10 127 D1
Fairway The. Thorne DN8 9 A4
Fairways. Roth S66 117 B4
Fairwinds Cl. Dron S18 153 A1
Faith St. Barn S71 34 F6
Faith St. S Kirk WF9 18 D4
Falcon Cl. Ad l S DN6 40 B6
Falcon Ct. Ross DN11 85 A1
Falcon Dr. Barn S70 75 F8
Falcon Dr. Treet S60 131 F3
Falcon Knowl Ing. Kex S75 13 D1
Falcon Rd. Dron S18 153 C3
Falcon Rise. Dron S18 153 D3
Falcon St. Barn S70 33 E2
Falcon Way. Din S31 146 E8
Falconer Cl. Kex S75 13 D1
Falconer La. Aston S13 131 F1
Falding St. Chap S30 95 B5
Falding St. Roth S60 115 C6
Falkland Rd. Shef S11 140 A6
Fall Bank Ind Est. Dod 53 D8
Fall Head La. Silk S75 32 B1
Fall View. Silk S75 53 A8
Falledge La. D Dale HD8 29 E2
Fallon Rd. Shef S6 127 D6
Falmouth Cl. Barn S71 34 B3
Falmouth Rd. Shef S7 140 E5
Falstaff Cres. Shef S5 112 F4
Falstaff Rd. Shef S5 112 F5
Falthwaite Green La. Hd Gr S75 53 D3
Fane Cres. Aston S31 144 D8
Fanny Ave. Kill S31 156 E5
Fanshaw Ave. Eck S31 155 C2
Fanshaw Bank. Dron S18 153 A1
Fanshaw Cl. Eck S31 155 C2
Fanshaw Dr. Eck S31 155 C2
Fanshaw Gate La. Hol S17 151 E1
Fanshaw Rd. Dron S18 153 B2
Fanshaw Rd. Eck S31 155 C2
Fanshaw Way. Eck S31 155 C2
Far Bank La. Fish DN7 24 F7
Far Common Rd. Hat DN7 45 B7
Far Cres. Roth S65 116 B7
Far Croft. Dearne S63 58 C2
Far Dalton La. Roth S65 116 F8
Far Field Cl. Don DN3 43 A3
Far Field La. Barn S71 34 E6
Far Field La. W up D S63 79 B6
Far Field Rd. Don DN3 43 A3
Far Field Rd. Roth S65 116 C5
Far La. Holmfi HD7 48 F8
Far La. Roth S65 116 B7
Far La. Shef S6 112 B1
Far Moor Cl. Bnbur DN5 59 C2
Far Pl. Roth S65 116 B7
Far View Rd. Shef S5 113 B4
Far Well La. Holmfi HD4 28 B8
Faraday Rd. Shef S9 129 E6
Faranden Rd. Shef S9 130 A5 5
Farcliff. Sprot DN5 61 B1
Farcroft Gr. Shef S4 113 F1
Fargate. Shef S1 129 A3
Farish Pl. Shef S2 141 B6 3
Farlow Croft. Chap S30 94 C8
Farm Bank Rd. Shef S2 129 C2
Farm Cl. Barn S71 34 C4
Farm Cl. Barn S70 55 B6
Farm Cl. Brin S60 131 B7
Farm Cl. Don DN3 43 A1
Farm Cl. Dron S18 153 B4
Farm Cl. Shef S12 142 A2
Farm Cres. Shef S19 155 C6
Farm Ct. Ad l S DN6 40 C6
Farm Fields Cl. Shef S19 143 D1
Farm House La. Barn S75 33 A2
Farm Rd. Barn S70 55 C6
Farm Rd. Shef S2 129 B1
Farm View Cl. Roth S61 114 D8
Farm View Cl. Shef S12 143 B3
Farm View Dr. Shef S12 143 B3
Farm View Rd. Roth S61 114 D8
Farm Way. Dar S73 57 A6
Farm Wlk. Shef S19 155 C7
Farmhill Cl. Ben DN5 61 E5
Farmoor Gdns. Shef S19 144 B2
Farmstead Cl. Shef S14 141 D5
Farnaby Gdns. Chap S30 94 D8
Farnborough Dr. Don DN4 85 A6
Farndale Rd. Ben DN5 61 D7
Farndale Rd. Shef S6 112 C2
Farnley Ave. Shef S6 112 D4
Farnworth Rd. Roth S65 116 C7
Farquhar Rd. Maltby S66 119 B5
Farrar Rd. Shef S7 140 F7 2
Farrar St. Barn S70 33 D1
Farrier Gate. Chap S30 94 E6
Farringdon Dr. Ross DN11 104 A7
Farrow Cl. Dod S75 54 A7
Farthing Gale Mews. Ben DN5 61 F5
Farwater La. Dron S18 152 F1
Favell Rd. Roth S65 116 D7
Favell Rd. Shef S3 128 E3
Fawcett St. Shef S3 128 E4
Fearn House Cres. Hoy S74 76 C5
Fearnehough St. Shef S9 130 A5 1
Fearnley Rd. Hoy S74 76 C5
Fearnville Gr. Roy S71 15 C3
Featherbed La. Work S80 159 F2
Felkirk Mid Sch. S Hie 16 C7
Felkirk View. Shaf S72 16 B3
Fell Rd. Shef S9 130 A7
Fell St. Shef S9 129 F8
Fellbrigg Rd. Shef S2 141 D7
Fellows Wlk. Wombw S73 56 B4
Fellowsfield Way. Roth S61 114 E8
Fellview Cl. Hath S30 149 A7
Fenland Rd. Thorne DN8 26 C6
Fenn Rd. Pilley S75 75 F5
Fenney La. Shef S11 139 E2
Fensome Way. Dar S73 57 A6
Fenton Cl. Arm DN3 64 B5
Fenton Cl. S Kirk WF9 18 B1
Fenton Croft. Roth S61 115 A8
Fenton Fields. Roth S61 115 A8
Fenton Rd. Roth S61 97 A2
Fenton St. Barn S70 33 E1 4
Fenton St. Eck S31 155 B2
Fenton St. Roth S61 114 F7
Fenton Way. Roth S61 97 B2
Fentonville St. Shef S11 140 E8
Fenwick Common La. Fenw DN6 6 A4
Fenwick Common La. Moss DN6 5 F2
Fenwick La. Norton DN6 5 E2
Feoffees Rd. Shef S30 113 B8
Ferguson St. Shef S9 129 F6
Ferham Cl. Roth S61 115 A6
Ferham Jun & Inf Sch. Roth 115 B6
Ferham Park Ave. Roth S61 115 A6
Ferham Rd. Roth S61 115 A6
Fern Ave. Ben DN5 62 A7
Fern Ave. Shef S19 143 F4
Fern Bank. Ad l S DN6 40 B6
Fern Cl. Dar S73 57 A5
Fern Cl. Don DN2 63 C6
Fern Cl. Eck S31 155 B3
Fern Hollow. Roth S66 117 C3
Fern Lea Gr. Dearne S63 58 B2
Fern Rd. Shef S6 128 B6
Fern Way. Eck S31 155 B3
Fernbank Dr. Arm DN3 64 B8
Fernbank Dr. Eck S31 155 B3
Fernbank Special Sch. Ad le S 40 C6
Ferncroft Ave. Shef S19 155 C7
Ferndale Cl. Dron S18 153 D3
Ferndale Dr. Roth S66 117 C6
Ferndale Dr. Thorne DN8 9 C2
Ferndale Pl. Hem WF9 17 D6
Ferndale Rd. Con DN12 81 B2
Ferndale Rd. Dron S18 153 D3
Ferndale Rise. Dron S18 153 D3
Ferndale View. Ben DN5 61 F5
Fernhall Cl. Don DN3 43 A3
Fernhurst Rd. Don DN2 63 C6
Fernlea Cl. Ben DN5 61 F5
Fernlea Gr. Shef S30 113 B8
Fernleigh Dr. Brin S60 115 B2
Fernvale Wlk. Swint S62 98 D8
Ferrand St. Barn S70 75 F7
Ferrara Cl. Dar S73 56 E6
Ferrars Cl. Shef S9 114 F2
Ferrars Dr. Shef S9 114 F1
Ferrars Rd. Shef S9 114 F2
Ferrars Way. Shef S9 114 F1
Ferrers Rd. Don DN2 62 F5
Ferriby Rd. Shef S6 112 B2
Ferry Boat La. Con DN12 80 C3
Ferry La. Con DN12 81 C3
Ferry Moor La. Cud S72 35 D6
Ferry Rd. Fish DN7 8 E2
Ferry Terr. Con DN12 81 C3
Ferrymore House. Don DN1 62 C2 14
Fersfield St. Shef S4 129 D5
Festival Ave. Har DN11 122 A4
Festival Cl. Wales S31 145 C2
Festival Rd. W up D S63 78 F5
Field Cl. Dar S73 57 A6
Field Cl. Dron S18 152 C2
Field Cres. S Elm WF9 18 F2 2
Field Dr. Cud S72 35 C5
Field Gate. Ross DN11 85 A2
Field Head Rd. Hoy S74 76 E5
Field House Rd. Sprot DN5 82 B8
Field La. Barn S70 55 E7
Field La. Kill S31 156 B5
Field La. Pen S30 50 D1
Field La. Roth S60 133 A7
Field La. S Elm WF9 19 C4
Field La. Ulley S60 132 F7
Field La. Upton WF9 19 A8
Field La. Wroot DN9 67 B1
Field Rd. Stai DN7 24 E4
Field Rd. Thorne DN8 26 B8
Field Side. Thorne DN8 26 A8
Field Station Rd. T in B DN5 42 A8
Field View. Brin S60 131 C8
Field Way. Roth S60 115 D8
Field Way. Shep HD8 28 E8
Fieldhead Farm Cotts. Dod S75 53 C8
Fieldhead Rd. Shef S8 141 A7
Fieldhouse Way. Shef S4 129 D7
Fielding Dr. Roth S66 117 D5
Fielding Gr. Rawm S62 97 F7
Fielding Rd. Shef S6 112 C2
Fields End. Oxspr S30 73 B8
Fieldsend Ct. Upton WF9 19 A7
Fieldsend Gdns. Shef S30 113 B8
Fieldside. Don DN3 42 F1
Fife Cl. Shef S9 114 A4
Fife Gdns. Shef S9 114 A4
Fife St. Barn S70 54 D8
Fife St. Shef S9 114 A4
Fife Way. Shef S9 114 A4
Fifth Ave. Ad l S DN6 40 C3
Fifth Sq. Stai DN7 24 E4
Fiftyeights Rd. Finn DN9 87 C2
Fig Tree La. Shef S1 129 A4 19
Filby Rd. Don DN5 61 E5
Filey Ave. Roy S71 15 D4
Filey La. Shef S3 128 E2
Filey St. Shef S10 128 E2
Finch Cl. Roth S65 99 A2
Finch Rd. Don DN4 82 F6
Finch Rise. Aston S31 144 E6
Finchwell Cl. Shef S13 130 F2
Finchwell Cres. Shef S13 130 F2
Finchwell Rd. Shef S13 130 F2
Findon Cres. Shef S6 128 A8
Findon Pl. Shef S6 128 A8
Findon Rd. Shef S6 128 A8
Findon St. Shef S6 128 B8
Finghall Rd. Ad le S DN6 20 F2
Finkle Cl. Wool WF4 13 F7
Finkle St. Ben DN5 62 B8
Finkle St. Stai DN7 24 E5
Finkle St. Thorne DN8 26 B7
Finkle St. Wool WF4 13 F7
Finkle Street La. Wort S30 74 C3
Finlay Rd. Roth S65 116 A8
Finlay St. Shef S3 128 E4
Finningley C of E Control Jun & Inf Sch. Finn 86 F3
Finningley Camp Cty Prim Sch. Finn 85 F4
Finningley Sta. Finn 86 E4
Finnley's La. Snaith DN14 1 A7
Fir Cl. W up D S63 79 A5
Fir Pl. Kill S31 156 C5
Fir Rd. Eck S31 155 C2
Fir St. Shef S6 128 C5
Fir Tree Ave. Finn DN9 86 A4
Fir Tree Cl. Hick DN5 59 C7
Fir Tree Dr. Norton DN6 4 C3
Fir Tree Dr. Wales S31 145 A2
Fir Tree. Thurgo S30 74 A7
Fir Vale Pl. Shef S5 113 C1
Fir Vale Rd. Shef S5 113 C1
Fir View Gdns. Shef S4 129 D8
Fir Wlk. Maltby S66 118 C5
Firbeck Ave. Lough S31 134 E4
Firbeck Cres. Lan S81 136 F3
Firbeck House. Don DN1 62 C2 5
Firbeck La. Laugh S31 134 E5
Firbeck La. Whit S80 159 A1
Firbeck Rd. Don DN4 62 F2
Firbeck Rd. Shef S8 140 E3
Firbeck Rehabilitation Unit. Fir 136 B6
Firbeck Way. Ross DN11 85 B1
Fircroft Ave. Shef S5 113 D5
Fircroft Rd. Shef S5 113 E6
Firham Cl. Roy S71 15 A4
Firs Hill First Sch. Shef 129 B8
Firs Hill Mid Sch. Shef 129 B8
Firs La. Pen S30 51 D7
Firs The. Barn S70 55 C6
Firs The. Roy S71 15 A4
Firsby La. H Rob DN12 99 E6
Firshill Ave. Shef S4 129 B8
Firshill Cl. Shef S4 129 B8
Firshill Cres. Shef S4 129 A8
Firshill Croft. Shef S4 129 A8
Firshill Gdns. Shef S4 129 A8
Firshill Glade. Shef S4 129 A8
Firshill Mews. Shef S4 129 B8
Firshill Rd. Shef S4 129 B8
Firshill Rise. Shef S4 129 B8
Firshill Way. Shef S4 129 A8
Firshill Wlk. Shef S4 129 A8
First Ave. Ad l S DN6 40 C4
First Ave. Roth S65 116 A7
First Ave. Roy S71 15 D4
First Ave. S Kirk WF9 17 F1
First Ave. Upton WF9 19 A7
First La. S Anst S31 146 E2
First Sq. Stai DN7 24 E4
Firth Ave. Cud S72 35 A6
Firth Cres. Maltby S66 119 A4
Firth Cres. Ross DN11 84 E1
Firth Field Rd. Hat DN7 44 E8
Firth La. Wroot DN9 67 A3
Firth Park Ave. Shef S5 113 E3
Firth Park Cres. Shef S5 113 D3
Firth Park Rd. Shef S5 113 E2
Firth Park Sch. Shef 113 D5
Firth Park Sch. Shef 113 C3
Firth Rd. W up D S63 78 C6
Firth St. Barn S71 33 F2 4
Firth St. Don DN4 62 B1
Firth St. Roth S61 97 C3
Firth St. Shep HD8 28 E8
Firth's Homes. Shef S11 139 F8
Firthwood Ave. Dron S18 153 D3
Firthwood Cl. Dron S18 153 D3
Firthwood Rd. Dron S18 153 D3
Firtree Rise. Chap S30 95 A4
Firvale. Hart S31 157 E5
Fish Dam La. Barn S71 34 D7
Fish Dam La. Roy S71 34 D7
Fish Pond La. Ston S66 119 B8
Fisher Cl. Roth S60 115 C7
Fisher La. Shef S9 130 C5
Fisher Rd. Maltby S66 119 B5
Fisher St. Ben DN5 41 B2
Fisher Terr. Ben DN5 62 A5
Fishlake Endowed Fst Sch. Fish 25 A7
Fishlake Nab. K Bram DN7 24 E6
Fishponds Rd. Shef S13 142 C7
Fishponds Rd W. Shef S13 142 C7
Fitzalan Rd. Shef S13 130 F1
Fitzalan. Shef S1 129 B3
Fitzgerald Rd. Shef S10 128 B4

Goodwin Athletics Ctr
(Univ of Sheffield) The. Shef 128 D3
Goodwin Ave. Rawm S62 .... 97 F6
Goodwin Cres. Swint S64 .... 79 D4
Goodwin Rd. Roth S61 .... 97 A4
Goodwin Rd. Shef S8 .... 141 A6 7
Goodwin Way. Roth S61 .... 97 A4
Goodwood Gdns. Don DN4 .... 63 D2
Goodyear Cres. Wombw S73 .... 56 D2
Goore Ave. Shef S9 .... 130 B2
Goore Dr. Shef S9 .... 130 B3
Goore Rd. Shef S9 .... 130 B2
Goose Carr La. Tod S31 .... 145 D6
Goose La. Roth S66 .... 117 C4
Gooseacre Ave. Dearne S63 .... 37 C1
Goosebutt House. Rawm S62 .... 97 F4
Goosebutt St. Rawm S62 .... 97 F4
Goosecroft Ave. Roth S65 .... 98 E2
Goosehole La. S Elm WF9 .... 19 B1
Gordon Ave. Shef S8 .... 141 A2
Gordon Pl. S Elm WF9 .... 18 F2
Gordon Rd. N Edl DN12 .... 82 B2
Gordon Rd. Shef S11 .... 140 D8 6
Gordon Sq. Stai DN7 .... 24 E3
Gordon St. Barn S70 .... 55 E8
Gordon St. Don DN1 .... 62 C3
Gordon Terr. Roth S65 .... 115 F6 5
Gorse Cl. Hat DN7 .... 43 F5
Gorse Dr. Kill S31 .... 156 D5
Gorse La. Shef S10 .... 138 F7
Gorse The. Roth S65 .... 116 C5
Gorse The. Roth S66 .... 117 B3
Gorseland Ct. Roth S66 .... 117 A4
Gorsey Brigg. Dron S18 .... 152 D1
Gorseybrigg Cty Jun Sch. Dron 152 D1
Gorseybrigg Inf Sch. Dron 152 D1
Gosber Rd. Eck S31 .... 155 E3
Gosber St. Eck S31 .... 155 D3
Gosforth Cl. Dron S18 .... 152 F1
Gosforth Cres. Dron S18 .... 152 F1
Gosforth Dr. Dron S18 .... 152 D1
Gosforth Dr. Dron S18 .... 152 E1
Gosforth Gn. Dron S18 .... 152 F1
Gosforth La. Dron S18 .... 152 F1
Gosforth Sch. Dron 152 E2
Gosling Gate Rd. Dearne S63 .... 58 E6
Gossips Wood Rd. Rawcl DN14 .... 2 D7
Gotham Rd. Brin S60 .... 115 C2
Gough Cl. Roth S65 .... 116 C4
Goulding St. Mex S64 .... 79 F4
Gowdall Gn. Ben DN5 .... 41 A3
Gower St. Shef S4 .... 129 C6
Gower St. Wombw S73 .... 56 E2
Grace Rd. N Edl DN12 .... 82 C3
Grace St. Barn S71 .... 34 F6
Graftdyke Cl. Ross DN11 .... 85 B1
Grafton St. Barn S70 .... 33 D1
Grafton St. Shef S2 .... 129 C2
Grafton Way. Roth S65 .... 115 E7
Graham Ave. Brin S60 .... 131 D7
Graham Ave. Upton WF9 .... 19 D8
Graham Knoll. Shef S11 .... 139 F8
Graham Rd. Don DN3 .... 42 F3
Graham Rd. Shef S10 .... 139 F8
Graham's Orch. Barn S70 .... 33 E1
Grainger Ct. N Edl DN12 .... 82 A1
Grainger Ct. Shef S10 .... 127 E1
Grammar St. Shef S6 .... 128 D7
Grampian Cl. Barn S75 .... 33 B2
Grampian Cl. Ben DN5 .... 61 E5
Grampian Way. Thorne DN8 .... 26 A5
Granby Cres. Don DN2 .... 62 F2
Granby Ct. S Elm WF9 .... 19 A5
Granby La. Ross DN11 .... 84 D1
Granby Rd. N Edl DN12 .... 82 C2
Granby Rd. Shef S5 .... 113 D2
Grange Ave. Aston S31 .... 132 C1
Grange Ave. Bawtry DN10 .... 122 F8
Grange Ave. Don DN4, ... 83 A7
Grange Ave. Dron S18 .... 152 E1
Grange Ave. Hat DN7 .... 44 C8
Grange Ave. S Elm WF9 .... 19 A3
Grange Ave. Woods S81 .... 147 E3
Grange Cl. Askern DN6 .... 22 C8
Grange Cl. Bri S72 .... 16 F3
Grange Cl. Don DN4 .... 84 F6
Grange Cl. Hat DN7 .... 44 B8
Grange Cl. Thurcr S66 .... 133 D5
Grange Cliffe Cl. Shef S11 .... 140 B4
Grange Cres. Barn S71 .... 34 E2
Grange Cres. Dearne S63 .... 58 E8
Grange Cres. Shef S11 .... 140 E8
Grange Crescent Rd. Shef S11 .... 140 E8
Grange Ct. Don DN5 .... 62 B6
Grange Ct. Don DN4 .... 84 F6
Grange Ct. Roth S66 .... 117 B4
Grange Dr. Har DN11 .... 122 A5
Grange Dr. Maltby S66 .... 118 B4
Grange Dr. Roth S61 .... 96 D1
Grange Farm Ct. Woods S81 .... 147 E3
Grange Farm. Don DN4 .... 83 B4
Grange Farm Dr. Ought S30 .... 111 D4
Grange Gate Cty Jun Sch. Barn 34 E2
Grange Gr. Thorne DN8 .... 9 D4
Grange House. Bri S72 .... 16 F3
Grange La. BarnS71 .... 34 E1
Grange La. Brin S60 .... 115 A2
Grange La. Burg DN6 .... 21 A4
Grange La. Don DN4 .... 82 F4
Grange La. Maltby S66 .... 119 B6
Grange La. Ross DN11 .... 103 D8
Grange Mill La. Roth S9 .... 114 B4
Grange Park Golf Course. Roth 96 B1
Grange Pk. Don DN3 .... 43 A4
Grange Rd. Ad I S DN6 .... 40 C3
Grange Rd. Ben DN5 .... 41 A4
Grange Rd. Bri S72 .... 16 F2
Grange Rd. Don DN4 .... 84 F6
Grange Rd. Norton DN6 .... 4 D1
Grange Rd. Rawm S62 .... 98 B7
Grange Rd. Ross DN11 .... 84 F1
Grange Rd. Roth S60 .... 116 B2
Grange Rd. Roy S71 .... 15 B3
Grange Rd. Shef S11 .... 140 E8
Grange Rd. Shef S19 .... 144 A4
Grange Rd. Snaith DN14 .... 1 A8
Grange Rd. Swint S64 .... 79 B2
Grange Rd. Thorne DN8 .... 9 D4
Grange Rd. W up D S63 .... 78 E5
Grange Sq. Thorne DN8 .... 9 D4
Grange St. Dearne S63 .... 58 E8
Grange Terr. Dearne S63 .... 58 E8
Grange The. Roth S61 .... 96 C2
Grange View Cres. Roth S61 .... 114 D8
Grange View. Don DN4 .... 83 A8
Grange View. Har DN11 .... 122 A5
Grange View. Hem WF9 .... 17 D6
Grange View Rd. Roth S61 .... 114 D8
Grange Way. Con DN12 .... 80 F3
Grangefield Ave. Ross DN11 .... 84 F1
Grangefield Cres. Ross DN11 .... 84 F1
Grangefield Terr. Ross DN11 .... 84 F1
Grangeway. Hem WF9 .... 17 D7
Grangewood Rd. Laugh S31 .... 134 E4
Grantham St. Ross DN11 .... 84 E1
Grantley Cl. Wombw S73 .... 77 F8
Granville Cres. Stai DN7 .... 24 F3
Granville Rd. Shef S2 .... 129 C1
Granville Sq. Shef S2 .... 129 B2
Granville St. Barn S75 .... 33 D3
Granville St. Shef S2 .... 129 B2
Granville Terr. Roth S65 .... 115 F6 2
Grasby Ct. Roth S66 .... 117 D7
Grasmere Ave. Don DN2 .... 63 C4
Grasmere Cl. N Anst S31 .... 146 D6
Grasmere Cl. Pen S30 .... 51 D4
Grasmere Cres. Mapp S75 .... 14 A3
Grasmere Rd. Ad le S DN6 .... 21 C1
Grasmere Rd. Barn S71 .... 34 A1
Grasmere Rd. Con DN12 .... 81 C2
Grasmere Rd. Dron S18 .... 152 D1
Grasmere Rd. Shef S8 .... 140 E5
Grassdale View. Shef S12 .... 142 F3
Grassington Cl. Shef S12 .... 143 B3 2
Grassington Dr. Shef S12 .... 143 B3
Grassington Way. Chap S30 .... 94 F6
Grassmoor Cl. Shef S12 .... 141 F5
Grassthorpe Rd. Shef S12 .... 142 B4
Grattan St. Roth S61 .... 114 E6
Graven Cl. Shef S30 .... 112 B8
Graves Art Gal. Shef 129 B3
Graves Tennis & L Ctr. Shef 153 B7
Graves Trust Homes. Shef S10 .... 128 A3
Graves Trust Homes. Shef S12 .... 142 A5
Graves Trust Homes. Shef S8 .... 152 F8
Graves Trust Homes. Shef S8 .... 153 A8
Gray Ave. Aston S31 .... 132 D1
Gray Gdns. Don DN4 .... 83 B6
Gray St. Hoy S74 .... 77 B5
Gray St. Shef S3 .... 129 B6
Gray St. Shef S19 .... 155 C7
Gray's Rd. Roy S71 .... 15 C1
Grays Ct. Con DN12 .... 81 A4
Grayson Cl. Roth S65 .... 117 D8
Grayson Cl. Stock S30 .... 92 C8
Grayson Rd. Roth S61 .... 97 A4
Greasbro Rd. Shef S9 .... 114 D2
Greasbrough Inf Sch. Roth 97 B3
Greasbrough Jun Sch. Roth 97 B3
Greasbrough La. Rawm S62 .... 97 E5
Greasbrough Prim Sch. Roth 97 B4
Greasbrough Rd. Rawm S62 .... 97 E3
Greasbrough St. Roth S60 .... 115 C7
Greasebrough Rd. Roth S60,S61 .. 115 D8
Greasebrough Rd. Roth S60 .... 115 D7 3
Great Bank Rd. Roth S65 .... 116 C4
Great Central Ave. Don DN4 .... 83 B8
Great Croft. Dron S18 .... 152 D2
Great Eastern Way. Rawm S62 .... 97 F3
Great Houghton Cty Prim Sch.
G Hou 36 E1
Great North Rd. Ad I S DN6 .... 40 B3
Great North Rd. Bawtry DN10 .... 104 F5
Great North Rd. Ross DN11 .... 104 F5
Great Park Rd. Roth S61 .... 114 E8
Greave Rd. Holmfi HD7 .... 48 A8
Greaves Cl. Shef S6 .... 127 C6
Greaves Fold. Barn S75 .... 33 B2 4
Greaves La. Chap S30 .... 75 D2
Greaves La. Shef S6 .... 127 D7
Greaves Rd. Roth S61 .... 115 A7
Greaves Rd. Shef S5 .... 113 A8
Greaves Sike La. Braith S66 .... 100 C2
Greaves St. Shef S6 .... 128 D7
Green Abbey. Holmfi HD7 .... 48 B7
Green Acres. Hoy S74 .... 76 E5
Green Acres. Rawm S62 .... 98 A5
Green Arbour Rd. Thurcr S66 .... 133 F5
Green Arbour Sch. Thurcr 133 E6
Green Balk. Clift S66 .... 100 F5
Green Bank. Thorne DN8 .... 27 B3
Green Bvd. Don DN4 .... 84 E8
Green Chase. Eck S31 .... 155 C3
Green Cross. Dron S18 .... 153 B2
Green Dyke La. Don DN1 .... 62 C1
Green Finch Cl. Brin S60 .... 131 D8
Green Gate Cl. Dearne S63 .... 58 D3
Green House Rd. Don DN2 .... 63 B6
Green Ings La. W up D S63 .... 79 A7
Green La. Ad I S DN6 .... 40 A4
Green La. Ad le S DN6 .... 20 E3
Green La. Askern DN6 .... 21 F7
Green La. Aston S31 .... 145 A7
Green La. Barl S31 .... 156 C3
Green La. Barn S75 .... 54 C5
Green La. Ben DN5 .... 40 B1
Green La. Bnbur DN5 .... 59 A3
Green La. Bran DN3 .... 64 B1
Green La. Brin S60 .... 131 B7
Green La. D Dale HD8 .... 29 B2
Green La. Dod S75 .... 54 A6
Green La. Dron S18 .... 153 B2
Green La. Hat DN7 .... 44 C2
Green La. Hoy S74 .... 76 A5
Green La. Kill S31 .... 156 C3
Green La. Notton WF4 .... 15 A5
Green La. Ought S30 .... 111 B7
Green La. Pen S75 .... 52 C7
Green La. Rawm S62 .... 98 A5
Green La. Roth S61 .... 114 C7
Green La. Roth S60 .... 116 A2
Green La. Roth S66 .... 117 A5
Green La. Roth S66 .... 133 D8
Green La. S Kirk WF9 .... 18 B2
Green La. Shef S3 .... 129 A5
Green La. Shef S30 .... 113 C8
Green La. Ulley S31 .... 132 D4
Green La. Upton WF9 .... 19 C8
Green La. W up D S63 .... 78 D3
Green La. Wad DN11 .... 102 A7
Green La. Wharn S30 .... 92 C2
Green La. Wharn S30 .... 93 B1
Green Lane Mid Sch. Thorne 26 D6
Green Lea. Dron S18 .... 152 C2
Green Moor Rd. Stock S30 .... 73 E3
Green Oak Ave. Shef S17 .... 151 E4
Green Oak Cres. Shef S17 .... 151 E4
Green Oak Dr. Shef S17 .... 151 E4
Green Oak Dr. Wales S31 .... 145 A2
Green Oak Rd. Shef S17 .... 151 E4
Green Rd. Pen S30 .... 51 D2
Green Rise. Rawm S62 .... 97 D7
Green Spring Ave. Barn S70 .... 75 F8
Green St. Barn S70 .... 55 C5
Green St. Don DN4 .... 82 F6
Green St. Hoy S74 .... 76 F6
Green St. Roth S61 .... 97 B4
Green St. Stock S30 .... 73 D1
Green The. Bran DN9 .... 86 A7
Green The. Con DN12 .... 80 C3
Green The. Dearne S63 .... 58 C3
Green The. Finn DN9 .... 86 E3
Green The. Har DN11 .... 121 E3
Green The. N Anst S31 .... 146 D6
Green The. Pen S30 .... 51 D2
Green The. Roth S60 .... 115 F3
Green The. Roth S60 .... 132 B8
Green The. Roy S71 .... 15 C3
Green The. S Kirk WF9 .... 18 C3
Green The. Shef S17 .... 151 D4
Green The. Swint S64 .... 79 B2
Green The. Thorne DN8 .... 9 D4
Green The. Thorne DN8 .... 26 B7
Green The. Wool WF4 .... 14 A7
Green View The. Shaf S72 .... 16 C4
Green's Rd. Hat DN7 .... 43 F5
Greenacre Dr. D Dale HD8 .... 29 E3
Greenacre Rd. Upton WF9 .... 19 C8
Greenbank Wlk. Grime S72 .... 35 F7
Greencroft. Roth S60 .... 115 F4
Greendale Ct. Dron S18 .... 153 B2
Greendale Sh Ctr. Dron 153 B2
Greenfield Cl. Arm DN3 .... 64 C5
Greenfield Cl. B Dun DN3 .... 43 A6
Greenfield Cl. D Dale HD8 .... 29 F3
Greenfield Cl. Roth S65 .... 116 D8
Greenfield Cl. Shef S8 .... 152 F7
Greenfield Cotts. Roy S71 .... 34 C8
Greenfield Ct. Roth S66 .... 117 B6
Greenfield Dr. Shef S8 .... 152 F7
Greenfield Gdns. Don DN4 .... 85 A7
Greenfield Gdns. Roth S66 .... 117 B6
Greenfield La. Don DN4 .... 83 A8
Greenfield. Rawm S62 .... 97 F5
Greenfield Rd. Hem WF9 .... 17 D5
Greenfield Rd. Hoy S74 .... 76 E6
Greenfield Rd. Roth S65 .... 116 D8
Greenfield Rd. Shef S8 .... 152 F7
Greenfields. Eck S31 .... 155 C3
Greenfoot Cl. Barn S75 .... 33 D3
Greenfoot La. Barn S75 .... 33 D3
Greengate Cl. Shef S13 .... 143 D6
Greengate La. Chap S30 .... 94 E7
Greengate La. Shef S13 .... 143 D6
Greengate Lane Jun & Inf Sch.
Chap 94 E7
Greengate Rd. Norton WF8 .... 3 F3
Greengate Rd. Shef S13 .... 143 D6
Greenhall Rd. Eck S31 .... 155 C3
Greenhead La. Chap S30 .... 95 A5
Greenhill Ave. Barn S71 .... 33 F3
Greenhill Ave. Maltby S66 .... 118 B4
Greenhill Ave. Shef S8 .... 152 F8
Greenhill Cty Prim Sch. Shef 152 E7
Greenhill Main Rd. Shef S8 .... 152 F7
Greenhill Parkway. Shef S8 .... 152 D6
Greenhill Rd. Shef S8 .... 140 F2
Greenhouse La. Shef S10, S11 .... 138 F5
Greenhow St. Shef S6 .... 128 C5
Greenland Ave. Maltby S66 .... 119 A7
Greenland Cl. N Anst S31 .... 146 D6
Greenland Cl. Shef S9 .... 130 C5
Greenland Ct. Shef S9 .... 130 C6
Greenland Dr. Shef S9 .... 130 C6
Greenland La. Rawcl DN14 .... 2 B4
Greenland La. Snaith DN14 .... 1 E5
Greenland Rd. Shef S9 .... 130 C6
Greenland View. Barn S70 .... 54 F4
Greenland View. Shef S9 .... 130 C5
Greenland Way. Maltby S66 .... 119 A7
Greenland Way. Shef S9 .... 130 C6
Greenland Way. Shef S9 .... 130 C7
Greenlands Ave. Ross DN11 .... 85 A2
Greenlands Fst & Mid Sch. Shef .. 130 C5
Greenleafe Ave. Don DN2 .... 63 C7
Greenock St. Shef S6 .... 128 B8
Greenpiece Cotts. Rawm S62 .... 97 D8
Greens Rd. Roth S65 .... 116 B6
Greenset View. Barn S71 .... 14 E1
Greenside Ave. Mapp S75 .... 14 C1
Greenside Ave. Wales S31 .... 145 C2
Greenside. D Dale HD8 .... 30 A7
Greenside Gdns. Pen S30 .... 52 A6
Greenside La. Hoy S74 .... 76 E7
Greenside. Mapp S75 .... 14 C1
Greenside Mews. Shef S12 .... 143 B3
Greenside. Pen S30 .... 52 A6
Greenside Pl. Mapp S75 .... 14 C1
Greenside. Roth S61 .... 97 B3
Greenside. Ryhill WF4 .... 16 B8
Greenside. Shaf S72 .... 16 C3
Greensprings Holiday Pk. Hd Gr 75 B8
Greentop Fst Sch. Thorne 26 B6
Greenway The. Shef S8 .... 152 F8
Greenway The. Stock S30 .... 92 E8
Greenwich Ct. Roth11 S65 .... 116 B8
Greenwood Ave. Barn S70 .... 55 B5
Greenwood Ave. Har DN11 .... 121 F5
Greenwood Ave. Shef S9 .... 130 B3
Greenwood Ave. Upton WF9 .... 19 C8
Greenwood Cl. Shef S9 .... 130 C3
Greenwood Cl. Upton WF9 .... 19 C8
Greenwood Cres. Roth S66 .... 117 C5
Greenwood Cres. Roy S71 .... 15 B4
Greenwood Cres. Shef S9 .... 130 A3
Greenwood Dr. Shef S9 .... 130 A3
Greenwood House. Rawm S62 .... 97 F5
Greenwood La. Shef S13 .... 143 D7
Greenwood Rd. Chap S30 .... 94 F7
Greenwood Rd. Shef S9 .... 130 B2
Greenwood Rd. Swint S62 .... 98 E7
Greenwood Terr. Barn S70 .... 33 E2
Greenwood Way. Shef S9 .... 130 A3
Greenwood Wlk. Askern DN6 .... 22 C8
Greeton Dr. Ought S30 .... 111 E6
Gregg House Cres. Shef S5 .... 113 D6
Gregg House Rd. Shef S5 .... 113 D5
Gregory Cres. Har DN11 .... 121 E4
Gregory Rd. Shef S8 .... 141 A6
Gregory's Bldgs. G Hou S72 .... 36 D2
Grenfell Ave. Mex S64 .... 80 B5
Grenfolds Rd. Shef S30 .... 112 D8
Greno Cres. Shef S30 .... 112 D8
Greno Gate. Shef S30 .... 94 C1
Greno Rd. Swint S64 .... 79 D2
Greno View. Hd Gr S75 .... 53 D2
Greno View. Hoy S74 .... 76 C5
Greno View Rd. Chap S30 .... 94 E7
Greno Wood Ct. Shef S30 .... 94 C1
Grenobank Rd. Shef S30 .... 112 D8
Grenomoor Cl. Shef S30 .... 112 C7
Grenoside Jun & Inf Sch. Shef 94 C1
Grenville Pl. Barn S75 .... 33 C3
Grenville Rd. Don DN4 .... 82 F5
Gresham Ave. Brin S60 .... 131 D8
Gresham Rd. Shef S6 .... 128 C6
Gresley Ave. Bawtry DN10 .... 123 A8
Gresley Rd. Don DN4 .... 62 B1
Gresley Rd. Shef S8 .... 152 E5
Gresley Wlk. Shef S8 .... 152 E5
Grey Friars' Rd. Don DN1 .... 62 C4
Grey Stone Cl. Tick DN11 .... 120 F6
Greyfriars. Shef S11 .... 140 A7
Greystock St. Shef S4 .... 129 D5
Greystock St. Shef S4 .... 129 E6
Greystone La. Tick DN11 .... 120 F8
Greystones Ave. Barn S70 .... 54 F4
Greystones Ave. Shef S11 .... 140 B8
Greystones Cl. Shef S11 .... 140 A7
Greystones Cres. Shef S11 .... 140 A7
Greystones Ct. Hart S31 .... 157 D6
Greystones Ct. Shef S11 .... 140 A7
Greystones Dr. Shef S11 .... 140 A7
Greystones Grange Cres.
Shef S11 .... 140 A7 2
Greystones Grange Rd. Shef S11 . 140 A7
Greystones Grange. Shef S11 .... 140 A7 1
Greystones Hall Rd. Shef S11 .... 140 A7
Greystones Prim Sch. Shef 140 B7
Greystones Rd. Roth S60 .... 116 D1
Greystones Rd. Shef S11 .... 140 A7
Greystones Rise. Shef S11 .... 140 A7 3
Grice Cl. Don DN4 .... 63 F2
Griffin Rd. Swint S64 .... 79 B3
Griffiths Cl. Rawm S62 .... 97 F4
Griffiths Rd. Chap S30 .... 94 E6
Grime La. Wh Com HD7 .... 49 D8
Grimesthorpe Rd. Shef S4 .... 129 C6
Grimesthorpe Rd. Shef S4 .... 129 D8
Grimethorpe St. S Elm WF9 .... 18 F2 1
Grimsell Cl. Shef S6 .... 112 D7
Grimsell Cres. Shef S6 .... 112 D7
Grimsell Dr. Shef S6 .... 112 D7
Grimsell Wlk. Shef S6 .... 112 D6
Grindleford Sta. Grin 149 D2
Grindlow Cl. Shef S14 .... 141 C6
Grindlow Dr. Shef S14 .... 141 C6
Grisedale Wlk. Dron S18 .... 152 E1
Grizedale Ave. Shef S19 .... 144 A2
Grizedale Cl. Shef S19 .... 144 A2 4
Grosvenor Ave. Upton WF9 .... 19 A7
Grosvenor Cres. Ben DN5 .... 41 D2
Grosvenor Cres. Don DN4 .... 82 D6
Grosvenor Ct. Fish DN7 .... 25 B7
Grosvenor Dr. Barn S70 .... 33 C1
Grosvenor Rd. Ad I S DN6 .... 40 B5
Grosvenor Rd. Bir DN11 .... 122 B4
Grosvenor Rd. Roth S65 .... 115 F8
Grosvenor Sq. Shef S2 .... 140 F8 7
Grosvenor Terr. Don DN4 .... 82 D6
Grouse Croft. Shef S6 .... 128 D6
Grouse St. Shef S6 .... 128 C6
Grove Ave. Ben DN5 .... 62 A5
Grove Ave. Hem WF9 .... 17 E6
Grove Ave. S Kirk WF9 .... 18 C2
Grove Ave. Shef S6 .... 112 A2
Grove Cl. Pen S30 .... 51 D1
Grove Cl. W up D S63 .... 78 C8
Grove Dr. S Kirk WF9 .... 18 B2
Grove Hall Cl. Don DN3 .... 43 A1
Grove Head. S Kirk WF9 .... 18 B2
Grove Hill Rd. Don DN2 .... 63 C7
Grove House Ct. Shef S17 .... 151 E5
Grove La. Hem WF9 .... 17 E6
Grove La. S Kirk WF9 .... 18 B2
Grove Lea Cl. Hem WF9 .... 17 E6
Grove Mount. S Kirk WF9 .... 18 A8
Grove Pl. Don DN1 .... 62 C2
Grove Pl. Hem WF9 .... 17 E6
Grove Rd. Fish DN7 .... 25 B7
Grove Rd. Mapp S75 .... 14 A1
Grove Rd. Roth S60 .... 115 D5
Grove Rd. Shef S7 .... 140 C3
Grove Rd. Shef S17 .... 151 F5
Grove Rd. Stock S30 .... 92 F8
Grove Rd. W up D S63 .... 78 C8
Grove Sq. Shef S6 .... 128 E7
Grove St. Barn S71 .... 34 A1
Grove St. Barn S70 .... 55 C5
Grove St. S Kirk WF9 .... 18 B2
Grove Street Inf Sch. Barn 34 A1
Grove Street Jun Sch. Barn 34 A1
Grove Terr. Hem WF9 .... 17 E6
Grove The. B Dun DN3 .... 42 E8
Grove The. Cud S72 .... 16 C1
Grove The. Don DN2 .... 63 B6
Grove The. Rawm S62 .... 98 A5
Grove The. Roth S65 .... 116 B7
Grove The. Roth S66 .... 117 B4
Grove The. S Elm WF9 .... 18 F4
Grove The. Shef S6 .... 127 E6
Grove The. Shef S17 .... 151 D5
Grove The. Wharn S30 .... 93 B3
Grove Vale. Don DN2 .... 63 C7
Grove Way. S Kirk WF9 .... 18 B2
Grudgby La. Oxspr S30 .... 73 A6
Gudgeon Hole La. Hd Gr S30 .... 74 E8
Guernsey Rd. Shef S2 .... 141 A7
Guest La. Don DN4 .... 82 D7
Guest La. Silk S75 .... 32 A1
Guest Pl. Hoy S74 .... 76 E7
Guest Pl. Roth S60 .... 115 F4
Guest Rd. Barn S75 .... 33 D3
Guest Rd. Roth S60 .... 115 F4
Guest Rd. Shef S11 .... 140 C8
Guest St. Hoy S74 .... 76 E7
Guilbert Ave. Thurcr S66 .... 133 E5
Guild Rd. Roth S65 .... 116 B6
Guildford Ave. Shef S2 .... 141 D8
Guildford Cl. Shef S2 .... 141 D8
Guildford Dr. Shef S2 .... 141 D8
Guildford Rd. Don DN2 .... 63 B7
Guildford Rd. Roy S71 .... 15 B5
Guildford Rise. Shef S2 .... 141 E8
Guildford View. Shef S2 .... 141 E7
Guildford Way. Shef S2 .... 141 D8
Guildhall Ind Est. Don 42 E3
Guildway. Tod S31 .... 145 E5
Guilthwaite Common La.
Ulley S60 .... 132 D5
Guilthwaite Cres. Roth S60 .... 116 A1
Gullane Dr. Don DN4 .... 82 D6
Gulling Wood Dr. Roth S65 .... 99 A2
Gully The. Holmfi HD7 .... 28 C5
Gun La. Shef S3 .... 129 B4 6
Gunhills La. Arm DN3 .... 64 C7
Gunthwaite La. Ingb HD8 .... 30 B2
Gunthwaite Top. D Dale HD8 .... 29 F3
Gurney Rd. Don DN4 .... 83 B6
Gurth Ave. Don DN3 .... 43 A2
Gurth Dr. Thurcr S66 .... 133 E5
Gyme Cnr. Snaith DN14 .... 1 E8
Gypsy La. Wombw S73 .... 56 E1

Habershon Dr. Chap S30 .... 94 F6
Habershon Rd. Roth S61 .... 96 F1
Hacienda Fun Pk. K Bram 7 A1
Hackenthorpe Village Inf Sch.
Shef 143 B3
Hacking La. S Elm WF9 .... 19 B3
Hackings Ave. Pen S30 .... 51 C1
Hackness La. Brin S60 .... 115 B1
Hackthorn Rd. Shef S8 .... 140 F3
Haddingley La. Holmfi HD7 .... 28 D4
Haddon Cl. Dod S75 .... 53 E7
Haddon Cl. Dron S18 .... 153 B2
Haddon Cl. S Elm WF9 .... 19 A5
Haddon Rd. Barn S71 .... 34 B6
Haddon Rise. Mex S64 .... 80 D6
Haddon St. Shef S3 .... 128 F6
Haddon Way. Aston S31 .... 144 F7
Hadds La. Thorne DN8 .... 8 F6
Hadds Nook Rd. Thorne DN8 .... 8 F4
Hade Edge Sch. Holmfi 48 B8
Haden St. Shef S6 .... 128 C8
Hadfield St. Shef S6 .... 128 C5
Hadfield St. Wombw S73 .... 56 E1
Hadrian Rd. Brin S60 .... 115 C2
Hadrians Cl. Ross DN11 .... 104 A7
Hagg Hill. Shef S10 .... 127 F4
Hagg Hill. Shef S6 .... 112 B5
Hagg La. Misson DN10 .... 123 E8
Hagg La. Shef S10 .... 127 D4
Hagg La. Shef S10 .... 127 E3
Haggard Rd. Shef S6 .... 128 D8
Haggs La. Fenw DN6 .... 6 B3
Haggstones Dr. Ought S30 .... 111 D6
Haggstones Rd. Ought S30 .... 111 E6
Hague Ave. Rawm S62 .... 97 E8
Hague Cres. Hem WF9 .... 17 E5
Hague La. Barl S31 .... 156 B1
Hague La. Chap S30 .... 94 C7
Hague La. Went S62 .... 96 B7
Hague Park La. S Kirk WF9 .... 18 B3
Hague Row. Shef S2 .... 129 C3 7
Hague Terr. Hem WF9 .... 17 E6
Haids Cl. Maltby S66 .... 118 F7
Haids Rd. Maltby S66 .... 118 E7
Haig Cres. Ross DN11 .... 103 E8
Haig Cres. Stai DN7 .... 24 F3
Haig Rd. Thorne DN8 .... 9 D4
Haigh Cl. Pen S30 .... 51 F6
Haigh Croft. Roy S71 .... 15 B4
Haigh Head. Pen S30 .... 51 F7
Haigh Hill. Wool WF4 .... 13 C6
Haigh La. Pen S30 .... 52 A7
Haigh La. Wool S75 .... 13 C5
Haigh Memorial Homes. Shef S8 .. 153 A7
Haigh Mews. Wool S75 .... 13 C5
Haigh Moor Cl. Shef S13 .... 130 F1 2
Haigh Moor Rd. Shef S13 .... 142 F8
Haigh Rd. Don DN4 .... 83 A7
Hail Mary Dr. Shef S13 .... 143 D8
Haise Mount. Mapp S75 .... 14 A1
Hakehill Cl. Don DN4 .... 84 D6
Halcyon Cl. Shef S12 .... 142 F3
Haldane Cl. Bri S72 .... 16 F3
Haldane Rd. Roth S65 .... 116 A8
Haldene. Barn S70 .... 55 B4
Haldynby Gdns. Arm DN3 .... 64 D6
Hale Hill La. Hat DN7 .... 44 E5
Hale St. Shef S8 .... 140 F6
Halesworth Rd. Shef S13 .... 130 F2
Halfway Ctr. Shef S19 .... 155 E7
Halfway Dr. Shef S19 .... 155 E7
Halfway Fst Sch. Shef 155 F7
Halfway Gdns. Shef S19 .... 155 E7
Halfway Mid Sch. Shef 155 E6
Halifax Ave. Con DN12 .... 81 A2
Halifax Cres. Ben DN5 .... 61 F6
Halifax Rd. Pen S30 .... 51 D6
Halifax Rd. Shef S6 .... 112 D5
Halifax Rd. Wort S30 .... 74 C4
Halifax St. Barn S71 .... 33 E4
Hall Ave. Hoy S74 .... 77 A7
Hall Ave. Mex S64 .... 80 B5
Hall Balk La. Barn S75 .... 33 D3
Hall Balk La. Don DN11 .... 83 C3
Hall Brig. Clay DN5 .... 37 C4
Hall Broome Gdns. Dearne S63 .... 58 C3
Hall Cl. Barn S70 .... 55 A2
Hall Cl. Dron S18 .... 152 C2
Hall Cl. N Anst S31 .... 146 D6
Hall Cl. W up D S63 .... 78 B7
Hall Close Ave. Roth S60 .... 116 C1
Hall Cres. Roth S60 .... 116 B2
Hall Croft. Roth S66 .... 117 C4
Hall Cross Comp Sch. Don 62 D3
Hall Cross Hill. Don DN1 .... 62 E2
Hall Dr. W up D S63 .... 78 D5
Hall Farm Cl. Aston S31 .... 132 D2

Hethersett Way. Ross DN11 103 E7
Hewitt Pl. Hart S31 157 E5
Hewitt St. Mex S64 80 D5
Hexthorpe Fst Sch. Don 62 A2
Hexthorpe Mid Sch. Don 62 A1
Hexthorpe Rd. Don DN4 62 B2
Hey Slack La. Wh Com HD7 28 C2
Heyhouse Dr. Chap S30 94 F7
Heyhouse Way. Chap S30 94 F7
Heysham Gn. Barn S71 34 D6
Heyworth La. Moss DN6 22 E8
Hibberd Pl. Shef S6 128 A8
Hibberd Rd. Shef S6 128 B8
Hibbert Terr. Barn S70 54 F7 3
Hickleton Ct. Dearne S63 58 C7
Hickleton Rd. Bnbur DN5 59 C4
Hickleton St. Con DN12 80 F3
Hickleton Terr. Dearne S63 58 E7
Hickmott Rd. Shef S11 140 D8
Hicks La. Shef S3 129 A4 5
Hicks St. Shef S3 129 A6
Hickson Dr. Barn S71 34 E4
Hides St. Shef S9 130 B8
High Alder Rd. Don DN4 84 C8
High Ash Ave. Clay W HD8 12 A2
High Ash Cl. Notton WF4 14 F7
High Ash Dr. S Anst S31 146 D3
High Bank La. Pen S30 50 E4
High Bridge Rd. Thorne DN8 26 F5
High Cl. Kex S75 13 D1
High Common La. Aust DN10 105 B6
High Common La. Tick DN11 121 F8
High Croft. Hoy S74 76 E5
High Ct. Shef S1 129 B4 4
High Field La. Aust DN10 105 B3
High Fisher Gate. Don DN1 62 D4
High Greave Ave. Shef S5 113 C7
High Greave Pl. Roth S65 116 C7
High Greave Rd. Roth S65 116 C8
High Greave Road Prim Sch. Roth 116 C8
High Green Jun & Inf Sch. Chap 94 D8
High Green Sch. Chap 94 E8
High Hazel Cres. Treet S60 131 C6
High Hazel Rd. Thorne DN8 9 D3
High Hazels Cl. Shef S9 130 D4
High Hazels Mead. Shef S9 130 D4
High Hooton Rd. Maltby S66 118 E1
High House Farm Ct. Wales S31 145 B2
High House Terr. Shef S6 128 D7
High Hoyland La. H Hoy S75 31 B8
High La. Eck S12 142 E1
High La. Ingb S30 50 E7
High La. Shef S12 154 F8
High La. Ulley S31 133 C3
High Lee La. Pen S30 52 A4
High Levels Bank. Thorne DN8 27 C1
High Matlock Ave. Shef S6 127 D6
High Matlock Rd. Shef S6 127 D6
High Meadow. Bawtry DN10 122 F7
High Nook Rd. Din S31 147 A8
High Pavement Row. Shef S2 129 C4
High Rd. Don DN4 82 C6
High Rd. Don DN4 83 A7
High Rd. N Edl DN12 82 B1
High Ridge. Barn S70 54 F5
High Royd Ave. Cud S72 35 B6
High Royd La. Pen S30 52 A5
High St. Ad I S DN6 40 C8
High St. Askern DN6 22 A7
High St. Aston S31 144 C7
High St. B Dun DN3 42 F7
High St. Barn S70 33 E1
High St. Barn S71 34 C4
High St. Barn S70 55 B5
High St. Bawtry DN10 123 A6
High St. Ben DN5 41 D2
High St. Ben DN5 62 B8
High St. Bnbur DN5 59 D3
High St. Braith S66 101 A2
High St. Clay W HD8 12 A1
High St. Con DN12 81 C2
High St. Dearne S63 58 C2
High St. Dearne S63 58 C7
High St. Dearne S63 58 E5
High St. Dod S75 53 F7
High St. Don DN1 62 D3
High St. Dron S18 153 A1
High St. Eck S31 155 D3
High St. G Hou S72 36 D2
High St. G Hou S72 57 F6
High St. Grime S72 36 A6
High St. Hat DN7 43 E4
High St. Hat DN7 44 D8
High St. Hoy S74 76 E6
High St. Kill S31 156 D6
High St. Laugh S31 134 D5
High St. Maltby S66 119 A5
High St. Mapp S75 14 A2
High St. Mex S64 80 A4
High St. Norton DN6 4 D3
High St. Norton DN6 21 C8
High St. Pen S30 51 D2
High St. Rawm S62 97 F5
High St. Roth S61 114 E7
High St. Roth S60 115 D6
High St. Roth S60 116 B1
High St. Roy S71 15 B3
High St. S Anst S31 146 D4
High St. S Elm WF9 19 A3
High St. S Hie S72 16 E5
High St. Shaf S72 16 C2
High St. Shef S3 129 B3
High St. Shef S19 144 A4
High St. Shef S17 151 D7
High St. Shef S19 155 D7
High St. Shef S30 113 B8
High St. Silk S75 53 A8
High St. Snaith DN14 1 A7
High St. Snaith DN14 1 C7
High St. Uns S18 154 A1
High St. Upton WF9 19 B7
High St. W up D S63 78 F6
High St. Wad DN11 102 B7
High St. Wombw S73 56 D3
High St. Wool WF4 14 A7
High St. Wroot DN9 67 A3
High Storrs Cl. Shef S11 140 A6
High Storrs Cres. Shef S11 140 A7
High Storrs Dr. Shef S11 140 A7
High Storrs Rd. Shef S11 139 F6
High Storrs Rise. Shef S11 140 A7
High Storrs Sch. Shef 139 F6
High Street La. Shef S2 129 C3 1
High Thorns. Silk S75 52 F8
High Trees. Roth S60 116 B3
High Trees. Shef S17 151 D7
High View Cl. Dar S73 57 B6
High View. Roy S71 15 B3
High Well Hill La. S Hie S72 16 C7
High Wray Cl. Shef S11 140 B4
Higham Common Rd. Barn S75 32 E3
Higham La. Dod S75 32 E1
Higham View. Kex S75 32 D7
Highbury Ave. Don DN4 84 E8
Highbury Cres. Don DN4 84 E8
Highbury Vale. N Edl DN12 82 A1
Highcliffe Ct. Swint S64 79 E3
Highcliffe Dr. Ought S30 111 D6
Highcliffe Dr. Shef S11 139 F7
Highcliffe Dr. Swint S64 79 D3
Highcliffe Pl. Shef S11 139 F6
Highcliffe Rd. Shef S11 139 F6
Highfield Ave. BarnS71 34 A6
Highfield Ave. Barn S70 54 F6
Highfield Ave. D Dale HD8 29 A4
Highfield Ave. Dearne S63 58 D5
Highfield Ave. Wales S31 145 E3
Highfield Bglws. W up D S63 78 F6
Highfield Ct. Shep HD8 28 E6
Highfield Ct. Swint S64 79 C3
Highfield Ctr. Hem WF9 17 D6
Highfield Gr. W up D S63 78 A7
Highfield La. T in B DN6 23 B4
Highfield La. Treet S13, S60 131 C3
Highfield Pk. Maltby S66 119 B6
Highfield Pl. Hem WF9 17 C6
Highfield Pl. Shef S2 141 A8
Highfield Range. Dar S73 57 A7
Highfield Rd. Askern DN6 22 B8
Highfield Rd. Bawtry DN10 123 B8
Highfield Rd. Con DN12 81 D2
Highfield Rd. Dar S73 57 A6
Highfield Rd. Don DN1 62 E4
Highfield Rd. Hem WF9 17 D6
Highfield Rd. Roth S61 97 C3
Highfield Rd. Swint S64 79 B3
Highfield Rise. Shef S6 127 C6
Highfield Sch. Shef 140 F8
Highfield View. Treet S60 131 C6
Highfield Villas. C in L S81 148 F8
Highfields Fst/Mid Sch. Ad le S 40 B2
Highfields. Pen S30 51 F6
Highfields Rd. Kex S75 32 B8
Highgate Cl. Ross DN11 104 A7
Highgate Ct. Dearne S63 58 C4
Highgate. Dar S73 57 B2
Highgate Greyhound Stad. Dearne 58 D6
Highgate Jun Mix & Inf Sch. Dearne 58 C5
Highgate La. Dearne S63 58 C4
Highgate. Shef S9 114 E2
Highgreave. Shef S5 113 C6
Highgrove Ct. Don DN4 85 A6
Highlow View. Brin S60 115 C1
Highmill Ave. Swint S64 79 B3
Highmoor Ave. Wales S31 145 C2
Highnam Crescent Rd. Shef S10 128 C3
Highroyds. Barn S70 54 F6
Highstone Ave. Barn S70 54 F7
Highstone Cres. Barn S70 54 E7
Highstone La. Barn S70 54 F6
Highstone Rd. Barn S70 54 F7
Highstone Vale. Barn S70 54 E7
Highthorn Rd. Swint S62 98 E8
Highton St. Shef S6 128 C6
Highwood Cl. Kex S75 32 C8
Highwood Pl. Eck S31 155 C3
Highwoods Cres. Mex S64 79 E5
Highwoods Inf Sch. Swint 79 E6
Highwoods Rd. Mex S64 79 E6
Hilary Way. Aston S31 144 D7
Hild Ave. Cud S72 35 D4
Hill Cl. Roth S65 116 E4
Hill Cl. Shef S6 127 C6
Hill Crest. Ad le S DN6 20 E1
Hill Crest. Hoy S74 76 C5
Hill Crest Rd. Chap S65 94 F5
Hill Crest Rd. Roth S65 116 B7
Hill End Rd. Mapp S75 33 C7
Hill Estate. Upton WF9 19 B7
Hill Farm Cl. Dearne S63 58 B7
Hill House Sch. Don 62 E4
Hill Park Gr. Dod S75 53 F8
Hill Rd. Har DN11 121 F4
Hill Side La. Pen S30 50 F2
Hill Side. Roth S60 116 C1
Hill St. Barn S71 55 E8
Hill St. Dar S73 57 A5
Hill St. Hoy S74 77 A5
Hill St. Shef S2 129 A1
Hill Top Ave. Barn S71 14 E1
Hill Top. Barn S71 33 F6
Hill Top. Caw S75 31 E5
Hill Top Cl. Brin S60 115 B1
Hill Top Cl. Roth S61 114 D6
Hill Top Cres. Don DN2 63 C7
Hill Top Cres. N Edl DN12 101 B8
Hill Top Cres. Shef S19 143 D2
Hill Top Ct. Har DN11 122 A4
Hill Top La. Barn S75 33 B3
Hill Top La. Roth S61 114 D6
Hill Top La. Roth S65 117 A6
Hill Top La. Shef S30 112 B8
Hill Top La. Stock S30 73 D3
Hill Top Rd. Barn S70 75 F8
Hill Top Rd. Con DN12 80 E2
Hill Top Rd. Shef S6 126 E7
Hill Top Rd. Shef S30 112 D8
Hill Top Rise. Shef S30 112 D8
Hill Top Sch. Maltby 118 D6
Hill Turrets Cl. Shef S11 139 F4
Hill View E. Roth S61 114 D8
Hill View Rd. Roth S61 114 D8
Hillary House. Don DN2 62 F6
Hillcote Cl. Shef S10 127 D1
Hillcote Dr. Shef S10 127 D1
Hillcote Mews. Shef S10 127 D1
Hillcote Rise. Shef S10 127 D1
Hillcrest. Dearne S63 58 C7
Hillcrest Dr. Ought S30 111 C6
Hillcrest Dr. S Anst S31 146 D4
Hillcrest Rd. Don DN2 63 A6
Hillcrest Rd. Stock S30 92 F8
Hillcrest Rise. Stock S30 92 F8
Hillfold. S Elm WF9 19 B3
Hillfoot Rd. Shef S3 128 E6
Hillfoot Rd. Shef S17 151 D5
Hills Cl. Ben DN5 61 E2
Hills Rd. Stock S30 73 D1
Hillsborough Barracks Bsns & Sh Ctr. Shef 128 D8
Hillsborough Ctr Sh Arcade. Shef 128 C8
Hillsborough Fst & Mid Schs. Shef 112 C2
Hillsborough Football Gd. Shef 112 C2
Hillsborough Golf Course. Shef 111 D3
Hillsborough Hall (Public Liby). Shef 112 C1
Hillsborough Pl. Shef S6 128 C8
Hillsborough Rd. Don DN4 84 E8
Hillsborough Rd. Shef S6 128 C8
Hillsborough Sacred Heart Prim Sch. Shef 128 C7
Hillscroft Rd. Blax DN9 86 E5
Hillside Ave. Dron S18 153 A1
Hillside Ave. ShefS5 113 B6
Hillside. Barn S71 56 A8
Hillside Cl. Pen S30 51 F6
Hillside Cres. Bri S72 17 A2
Hillside Ct. Roth S61 97 D1
Hillside Ct. S Elm WF9 19 A4
Hillside Ct. Sprot DN5 82 B8
Hillside. D Dale HD8 30 A6
Hillside Dr. Hoy S74 76 F5
Hillside Dr. N Edl DN12 82 A1
Hillside Gr. Bri S72 17 A2
Hillside Mount. Bri S72 17 A2
Hillside. N Anst S31 146 D6
Hillside Rd. Don DN2 63 C7
Hillside. Shef S19 155 C7
Hillside Way. Wort S30 74 D4
Hilltop. Bri S72 16 F3
Hilltop Cl. Maltby S66 118 D6
Hilltop Dr. Wharn S30 111 B8
Hilltop Est. S Kirk WF9 18 C4
Hilmian Way. Hem WF9 17 F5
Hilton Dr. Shef S30 113 B8
Hilton St. Askern DN6 22 A8
Hilton St. Barn S75 33 D2
Hind Rd. Roth S60 116 C2
Hindburn Cl. Don DN4 84 C7
Hinde House Comp Sch. Shef 113 F4
Hinde House Cres. Shef S4 113 E2
Hinde House Croft. Shef S4 113 E2
Hinde House La. Shef S4 113 E2
Hinde St. Shef S4 113 E1
Hindewood Cl. Shef S4 113 E2
Hindle St. Barn S70 33 D1
Hinds Cres. S Elm WF9 18 F3
Hirst Common La. Shef S6 112 B6
Hirst Dr. Roth S65 116 D7
Hirst Gate. Mex S64 80 C5
Hirst La. Holmfi HD7 28 B5
Hirst La. Ston S66 101 E1
HM Young Offender Inst. Hat 25 F1
Hoads Ave. Woods S81 147 E4
Hoar Stones Rd. Bfield S6 109 D3
Hob La. Wharn S30 92 E2
Hobart St. Shef S11 140 F8
Hobcroft Terr. Ad le S DN6 21 B1
Hobson Ave. Shef S6 128 F7
Hobson Pl. Shef S6 128 E7
Hodder Ct. Chap S30 94 F6
Hoddesdon Cres. Hat DN7 44 A5
Hodge La. K Smea WF8 3 E6
Hodgkinson Ave. Pen S30 51 D3
Hodgson St. Shef S3 128 F2
Hodroyd Cl. Shaf S72 16 D1
Hodroyd Cotts. Bri S72 16 F2
Hodster La. G Hou S72 36 D4
Hog Close La. Wh Com HD7 49 C8
Hoggarth Rise. Dron S18 152 F1 1
Holberry Cl. Shef S10 128 E2
Holberry Gdns. Shef S10 128 E2
Holbourne Gr. Chap S30 94 D8
Holbrook Ave. Shef S19 156 A8
Holbrook Dr. Shef S13 142 B6
Holbrook Gn. Shef S19 156 A8
Holbrook Rd. Shef S13 142 B7
Holbrook Rise. Shef S19 144 A1
Holburn Ave. Dron S18 153 A2
Holderness Cl. Har DN11 122 A4
Holderness Dr. Aston S31 144 D8
Holdings Rd. Shef S2 129 D1
Holdroyd's Yd. Dod S75 53 F6
Holdworth La. Shef S6 110 F4
Hole House La. Stock S30 73 B1
Holgate Ave. Shef S5 112 F6
Holgate Cl. Shef S5 112 F6
Holgate Cres. Hem WF9 17 C7
Holgate Cres. Shef S5 113 A6
Holgate Dr. Shef S5 113 A6
Holgate Gdns. Hem WF9 17 C7
Holgate Hospl. Hem 17 A6
Holgate Mount. Barn S70 54 F6
Holgate Rd. Shef S5 113 A6
Holgate Sch. Barn 33 D1
Holgate View. Bri S72 17 B3
Holgate. Wombw S73 56 B3
Holiwell Cl. Maltby S66 119 B6
Holkham Rise. Shef S11 139 F2
Holland Cl. Rawm S62 97 F7
Holland Pl. Shef S2 141 A8 8
Holland Rd. Chap S30 94 D7
Holland Rd. Shef S2 141 A8
Holland St. Shef S1 128 F3
Hollin Bridge La. Hat DN7 45 A5
Hollin Busk La. Stock S30 92 C7
Hollin Busk Rd. Stock S30 92 C8
Hollin Cl. Ross DN11 85 B2
Hollin Croft. Dod S75 54 A8
Hollin Edge. D Dale HD8 30 A6
Hollin Edge La. Stock S30 92 F5
Hollin Hill La. Roth S66 116 F4
Hollin House La. Clay W HD8 31 A8
Hollin House La. Holmfi HD7 28 A5
Hollin House La. Shef S6 110 F3
Hollin La. Wh Con S30 50 A4
Hollin Moor La. Roth S66 117 A4
Hollin Moor La. Thurgo S30 53 B1
Hollin Rd. Ought S30 111 C6
Hollinberry La. Wort S30 75 B1
Hollindale Dr. Shef S12 142 C5
Holling Croft. Stock S30 73 E1
Holling's La. Roth S65 117 C8
Hollins Cl. Shef S6 127 F5
Hollins Ct. Shef S6 127 F6
Hollins Dr. Shef S6 128 A5
Hollins La. Shef S6 128 A6
Hollins Mount. Hem WF9 17 C7
Hollins The. Dod S75 54 A6
Hollinsend Ave. Shef S12 142 C5
Hollinsend Pl. Shef S12 142 C5
Hollinsend Rd. Shef S12 142 B5
Hollis Cl. Rawm S62 97 D8
Hollis Croft. Shef S1 128 F4
Hollis Croft. Shef S13 143 A6
Hollis Hospl. Shef 139 E2
Hollow Gate. Cade DN5 81 C5
Hollow Gate. Chap S30 94 D5
Hollow Gate. Roth S60 116 B1 2
Hollow La. Shef S19 155 D6
Hollow La. Shef S19 155 E6
Hollowdene. Barn S75 33 C3
Hollowgate Ave. W up D S63 78 C8
Hollowgate. Bnbur DN5 59 C2
Hollowgate. Roth S60 115 E5
Hollows The. Auck DN9 86 A6
Hollows The. Don DN4 84 E6
Holly Ave. Ben DN5 62 A7
Holly Cl. Chap S30 94 F4
Holly Cl. Kill S31 156 C5
Holly Cres. Roth S66 117 C6
Holly Croft Gr. Tick DN11 121 B7
Holly Ct. Har DN11 121 E4
Holly Dene. Arm DN3 64 B8
Holly Dr. Ben DN5 41 B2
Holly Gdns. Shef S12 142 C6
Holly Gr. Bri S72 17 A3
Holly Gr. Ross DN11 85 A2
Holly Gr. W up D S63 78 F4
Holly Hall La. Stock S30 74 A3
Holly La. Shef S1 129 A3 4
Holly Mount. Roth S66 117 C4
Holly Rd. Finn DN9 86 A4
Holly Rd. Thorne DN8 9 C2
Holly St. Don DN1 62 C1
Holly St. Hem WF9 17 D7
Holly St. Shef S1 129 A3
Holly Terr. Aston S31 144 C8
Holly Terr. Don DN4 82 F7
Holly Wlk. Thorne DN8 9 C2
Holly's House Rd. Roth S65 99 F1
Hollybank Ave. D Dale HD8 29 C6
Hollybank Ave. Shef S12 142 C6
Hollybank Cl. Shef S12 142 D6
Hollybank Cres. Shef S12 142 C6
Hollybank Dr. Shef S12 142 D6
Hollybank Rd. Shef S12 142 C6
Hollybank Way. Shef S12 142 D6
Hollybush St. Rawm S62 97 F3
Hollycroft Ave. Roy S71 15 B3
Hollygate. Barn S70 55 B5
Hollythorpe Cres. Shef S8 141 A4
Hollythorpe Rd. Shef S8 141 B4
Hollytree Ave. Maltby S66 118 D6
Hollywell Cl. Rawm S62 97 B7
Holm Cl. Dron S18 152 D2
Holm Flatt St. Rawm S62 97 E3
Holme Cl. Shef S6 128 C8
Holme Ct. Dearne S63 58 C4
Holme Fleet La. K Bram DN3 23 D2
Holme Gdns. Stai DN7 24 F5
Holme Hall La. Ston S66 119 E8
Holme La. Askern DN5 22 B2
Holme La. Shef S6 128 B7
Holme La. Shef S6 112 D7
Holme Oak Way. Shef S6 127 C7
Holme Styes La. Holme HD7 48 A8
Holme View Rd. Kex S75 32 B8
Holme Way. Shef S6 128 B7
Holme Wood Gdns. Don DN4 84 E7
Holme Wood La. Arm DN3 64 E6
Holmefield Cl. Arm DN3 64 C5
Holmefield Croft. Scro DN10 123 A2
Holmeroyd Rd. Ad I S DN6 40 E7
Holmes Carr Cres. Ross DN11 84 D1
Holmes Carr Rd. Don DN4 84 D6
Holmes Carr Rd. Ross DN11 84 D1
Holmes Cres. Treet S60 131 E4
Holmes La. H Rob S65 99 C7
Holmes La. Roth S61 115 B6
Holmes Market The. Don DN1 62 D4
Holmes Rd. Roth S66 117 D4
Holmes The. Don DN1 62 D4
Holmesdale Cl. Dron S18 153 C3
Holmesdale Inf Sch. Dron 153 C2
Holmesdale Rd. Dron S18 153 C3
Holmesfield Rd. Dron S18 152 B1
Holmesfield Rd. Ought S30 111 D7
Holmhirst Cl. Shef S8 140 E2
Holmhirst Dr. Shef S8 140 E3
Holmhirst Rd. Shef S8 140 F2
Holmhirst Way. Shef S8 140 E3
Holmley Bank. Dron S18 153 A3
Holmley La. Dron S18 152 F3
Holmley La. Dron S18 153 A3
Holmoak Cl. Swint S64 79 D1
Holmshaw Dr. Shef S13 142 E8
Holmshaw Gr. Shef S13 142 E8
Holmsley Ave. S Kirk WF9 18 A2
Holmsley Gr. S Kirk WF9 18 A2
Holmsley La. S Kirk WF9 17 F2
Holmsley Mount. S Kirk WF9 18 A2
Holt House Inf Sch. Shef 140 D4
Holtwood Rd. Shef S4 129 B7
Holwick Cl. Silk S75 52 F8
Holwick Ct. Barn S70 33 E1 2
Holy Cross Deanery C of E Prim Sch. Barn 34 B6
Holy Family Prim Sch. Stai 24 F5
Holy Rood RC Prim Sch. Barn 33 D1
Holyoake Ave. Shef S13 142 E8
Holyrood Rd. Don DN2 63 A3
Holyrood Rise. Roth S66 117 D6
Holywell Cres. Braith S66 101 A1
Holywell La. Braith S66 101 A1
Holywell La. Con DN12 81 C1
Holywell Pl. Roth S65 115 E7 7
Holywell Rd. Shef S4, S9 114 A2
Holywell Rd. Swint S64 79 D1
Home Farm Ct. H Pag DN5 38 D5
Home Farm Ct. Hick DN5 59 C7
Home Farm Ct. Wort S30 74 D4
Home Meadows. Tick DN11 121 A6
Homecroft Rd. Dearne S63 58 D5
Homefield Cres. Ben DN5 61 E8
Homestead Cl. Shef S5 113 D5
Homestead Dr. Brin S60 115 B1
Homestead Dr. Rawm S62 97 F7
Homestead Garth. Hat DN7 44 B8
Homestead Rd. Shef S5 113 D5
Homestead The. Ben DN5 41 B1
Honey Lands La. Askern DN5 22 D2
Honeysuckle Ct. Finn DN9 86 E3
Honeysuckle Rd. Shef S5 113 F3
Honeywell Cl. Barn S71 33 F3
Honeywell Gr. Barn S71 33 F4
Honeywell La. Barn S71, S75 33 E3
Honeywell Pl. Barn S71 33 F3
Honeywell St. Barn S71 33 F3
Honister Cl. W up D S63 78 A7
Hoober Ave. Shef S11 140 A5
Hoober Ct. Rawm S62 97 D8
Hoober Field. W up D S62 78 B2
Hoober Hall La. W up D S62 78 B3
Hoober La. Went S62 77 B1
Hoober Rd. Shef S11 140 A5
Hoober St. W up D S63 78 B7
Hoober View. Rawm S62 97 D8
Hoober View. Wombw S73 56 F1
Hood Green Rd. Hd Gr S75 53 E2
Hood St. S Elm WF9 18 E1
Hoole La. Shef S10 128 C2
Hoole Rd. Shef S10 128 C3
Hoole St. Shef S6 128 D6
Hooton Cl. Laugh S31 134 E5
Hooton La. Laugh S31 134 E6
Hooton La. Maltby S66 118 E4
Hooton La. Roth S65 99 C3
Hooton Pagnell C of E Fst & Mid Sch. H Pag 38 C5
Hooton Rd. Swint S62 98 F7
Hop Hills. Hat DN7 25 A1
Hop Hills La. Hat DN7 25 A1
Hop Inge The. Hart S31 157 F5
Hope Ave. Dearne S63 58 D5
Hope Rd. Ought S30 111 E6
Hope St. Barn S75 33 D2
Hope St. Barn S71 34 F6
Hope St. Dar S73 56 F4
Hope St. Mapp S75 33 C8
Hope St. Mex S64 80 A4
Hope St. Roth S60 115 C7
Hope St. Ryhill WF4 16 C8
Hope St. Shef S3 128 E4
Hope St. Stock S30 73 C1
Hope St. Wombw S73 56 E2
Hope Street Extension. Roth S60 115 C7
Hopedale Rd. Shef S12 142 D4
Hopefield Ave. Shef S12 142 D4
Hopewell St. Barn S70 55 D8
Hopping La. Thurgo S30 52 F1
Hopwood La. Shef S6 127 B4
Hopwood St. Barn S70 33 E2
Hopyard La. Tick DN11 103 C1
Horace St. Roth S60 115 E5
Horbiry End. Tod S31 145 E5
Horbury La. Chap S30 94 E4
Horbury Rd. Cud S72 35 B8
Hordron Rd. Lang S30 70 C5
Horn Cote La. Holmfi HD7 28 A6
Horn Croft. Caw S75 31 F5
Horn La. Holmfi HD7 28 A6
Horn La. Ingb S30 29 B1
Hornbeam Cl. Chap S30 94 F4
Hornbeam Rd. Roth S66 117 B6
Hornby Ct. Shef S11 140 A7
Hornby St. Barn S70 55 A7
Horndean Rd. Shef S5 113 D1
Horner Cl. Stock S30 73 B2
Horner Rd. Shef S7 141 A7 1
Hornes La. Mapp S75 14 C1
Horninglow Cl. Don DN4 85 A7
Horninglow Cl. Shef S5 113 C3
Horninglow Rd. Shef S5 113 D3
Hornsby Rd. Arm DN3 64 C5
Hornthorpe Rd. Eck S31 155 C2
Hornthwaite Hill Rd. Pen S30 51 A3
Horse Carr View. Barn S71 56 A8
Horse Croft La. Wharn S30 111 B8
Horse Fair Gn. Thorne DN8 26 B7
Horsehills La. Arm DN3 64 A5
Horsemoor Rd. Dearne S63 58 B8
Horseshoe Cl. Wales S31 145 C3
Horsewood Cl. Barn S70 54 B8
Horsewood Rd. Shef S13 143 D8
Horton Cl. Shef S19 155 E7
Horton Dr. Shef S19 155 E7
Hough La. Wombw S73 56 C2
Houghton Rd. Dearne S63 58 B8
Houghton Rd. N Anst S31 146 B8
Hound Hill La. Barn S75,S70 54 D5
Hound Hill La. Mex S63 79 D8
Houndkirk Rd. Shef S11 138 F2
Hounsfield Cres. Roth S65 116 D7
Hounsfield La. Shef S10 128 E3
Hounsfield Rd. Roth S65 116 D7
Hounsfield Rd. Shef S3 128 E3
Houps Rd. Thorne DN8 26 C7
House Carr La. Hd Gr S75 53 C4
Housley La. Chap S30 94 F5
Housley Pk. Chap S30 95 A6
Houstead Rd. Shef S9 130 D3
Howard La. Shef S2 129 B2
Howard Rd. Bir DN11 122 C4
Howard Rd. Maltby S66 119 B5
Howard Rd. Roth S66 117 E6
Howard Rd. Shef S6 128 D5
Howard St. Barn S70 54 F7 7
Howard St. Dar S73 57 C5
Howard St. Din S31 135 A1
Howard St. Roth S60, S65 115 E6
Howard St. Shef S1 129 B2
Howards Cl. Thurcr S66 134 A6
Howarth Rd. Brin S60 131 D7
Howbeck Dr. N Edl DN12 82 A1
Howbrook Cl. Chap S30 94 C8
Howden Ave. Ad le S DN6 20 E1
Howden Cl. Don DN4 84 C6

Linden Gr. Maltby S66 118 D5
Linden Gr. N Edl DN12 82 B1
Linden Rd. Shef S30 95 B1
Linden Rd. W up D S63 78 B6
Linden Wlk. Ben DN5 41 A4
Lindholme Bank Rd. Hat DN7 45 D2
Lindholme Dr. Ross DN11 85 B1
Lindholme Gdns. Shef S19 143 C2
Lindhurst Rd. Barn S71 33 F8
Lindley Cres. Dearne S63 58 D7
Lindley Rd. Finn DN9 86 E3
Lindley Rd. Shef S5 113 D2
Lindley St. Roth S65 115 E8
Lindley's Croft. Tod S31 145 F5
Lindrick Ave. Swint S64 79 E2
Lindrick Cl. C in L S81 148 F6
Lindrick Cl. Con DN12 81 E3
Lindrick Cl. Cud S72 16 C1
Lindrick Cl. Don DN4 84 D6
Lindrick Cl. Tick DN11 120 F6
Lindrick Ct. Woods S81 147 F3
Lindrick Dr. Arm DN3 64 B5
Lindrick Golf Course. Woods 147 D2
Lindrick La. Tick DN11 120 F6
Lindrick Rd. Hat DN7 44 F6
Lindrick Rd. Woods S81 147 E3
Lindrick. Tick DN11 121 A6
Lindsay Ave. Shef S5 113 B5
Lindsay Cl. Shef S5 113 B5
Lindsay Cres. Shef S5 113 B5
Lindsay Dr. Shef S5 113 B5
Lindsay Pl. Aston S31 144 D7
Lindsay Rd. Shef S5 113 B5
Lindsay Road Infant & Jun Sch. Shef 113 B5
Lindsey Cl. Don DN4 84 D5
Lindsey Rd. Har DN11 122 A5
Lindum Dr. Roth S66 117 C4
Lindum St. Don DN4 62 B2
Lindum Terr. Roth S65 115 E6 1
Ling Field Rd. Brod DN5 39 B3
Ling House La. B Dun DN7 24 C2
Lingamore Leys. Dearne S63 37 D1
Lingard Ct. Barn S75 33 D2
Lingard St. Barn S75 33 D2
Lingfield Dr. Ben DN5 61 D5
Lingfield Wlk. Mex S64 80 C6
Lingfoot Ave. Shef S8 153 B6
Lingfoot Cl. Shef S8 153 B6
Lingfoot Cres. Shef S8 153 C6
Lingfoot Dr. Shef S8 153 C6
Lingfoot Pl. Shef S8 153 B6
Lingfoot Wlk. Shef S8 153 C6
Lingmoor Cl. Don DN4 82 E6
Lingodell Cl. Laugh S31 134 E4
Lings La. Hat DN7 44 B5
Lings La. Roth S66 117 C4
Lings La. Upton DN6 20 A8
Lings The. Arm DN3 64 D5
Lings The. Roth S66 117 E4
Link Rd. Roth S65 99 A2
Link Row. Shef S2 129 C4
Link The. Dod S75 54 A6
Links View. Mapp S75 14 B2
Linkswood Ave. Don DN2 63 C6
Linkthwaite. Dod S75 54 A7
Linkway. Don DN2 63 B6
Linkway. Hat DN7 44 F6
Linkway. Norton DN6 4 D3
Linley La. Shef S12, S13 142 E5
Linnet Mount. Roth S61 95 F5
Linscott Rd. Shef S8 140 E2
Linshaws Rd. Dun Br HD7 47 E5
Linthwaite La. Hoy S62 77 C4
Linton Cl. Barn S70 54 B8
Lion Cott. Caw S75 31 E4
Lipp Ave. Kill S31 156 C7
Liskeard Pl. Ad I S DN6 40 A5
Lisle Rd. Roth S60 116 A4
Lismore Rd. Shef S8 141 B5
Lister Ave. Don DN4 83 B8
Lister Ave. Rawm S62 97 E7
Lister Ave. Shef S12 142 B3
Lister Cl. Shef S12 142 B3
Lister Cres. Shef S12 142 B3
Lister Ct. Don DN2 63 A5
Lister Dr. Shef S12 142 B3
Lister La. Shef S3 128 F5 2
Lister Pl. Shef S12 142 B3
Lister Rd. Shef S6 128 C7
Lister Row. G Hou S72 36 D3
Lister St. Roth S65 115 F6
Lister Way. Shef S12 142 B3
Listerdale Sh Ctr. Roth S65 116 E4
Litherop La. Emley HD8 12 C5
Litherop Rd. H Hoy S75 12 D3
Little Attercliffe. Shef S9 130 B5
Little Common La. Roth S61 114 D7
Little Common La. Roth S60 116 E1
Little Common La. Shef S11 139 F3
Little Haynooking La. Maltby S66 118 F5
Little Hemsworth. Hem WF9 17 E6
Little La. Don DN2 42 C1
Little La. K Smea WF8 4 A7
Little La. S Elm WF9 18 F3
Little La. S Elm WF9 19 B3
Little La. Shef S12 142 B6
Little La. Shef S4 113 F1
Little La. Sprot DN5 61 A4
Little La. Th Sa S80 159 B6
Little La. Upton WF9 19 B7
Little La. Went S30 95 E6
Little Leeds. Hoy S74 76 E6
Little London La. Snaith DN14 1 A7
Little London Pl. Shef S8 140 F6
Little London Rd. Shef S8 140 F5
Little Matlock Gdns. Shef S6 127 D6
Little Matlock Way. Shef S6 127 D6
Little Norton Ave. Shef S8 153 A8
Little Norton Dr. Shef S8 153 A8
Little Norton La. Shef S8 153 A8
Little Norton Way. Shef S8 153 A7
Little Wood Dr. Shef S12 142 A3
Little Wood Rd. Shef S12 142 A3
Littledale Rd. Shef S9 130 C2
Littlefield La. Dar S73 56 D3
Littlehey Cl. Maltby S66 118 D6
Littlemoor Ave. Wales S31 145 C2
Littlemoor. Eck S31 155 E4
Littlemoor La. Don DN4 62 B1
Littlemoor St. Don DN4 62 B1
Littlewood Rd. Thorne DN8 26 C7
Littlewood St. Don DN4 62 B2
Littlewood Way. Maltby S66 119 B6
Littleworth Cl. Ross DN11 85 B1
Littleworth La. Barn S71 34 D3
Littleworth La. Ross DN11 85 C1
Littleworth Lane Inf Sch. Barn 34 D3
Litton Wlk. Barn S70 33 D2 2
Liverpool Ave. Don DN2 62 F6
Liverpool Pl. Shef S9 129 F7
Liverpool St. Shef S9 130 A7
Livingston Rd. Shef S9 129 E6
Livingstone Ave. Don DN2 42 D1
Livingstone Cres. Barn S71 34 B5
Livingstone Rd. Chap S30 94 E5
Livingstone Terr. Barn S70 54 E8 4
Llewelyn Cres. Askern DN6 21 F7
Lloyd St. Rawm S62 97 F3
Lloyd St. Shef S4 113 E1
Lloyds Terr. Hat DN7 24 F1
Load Field Rd. Bfield S30 91 F2
Loakfield Dr. Shef S5 112 F7
Lobelia Cres. Don DN3 42 F3
Lobelia Ct. S Anst S31 146 D4
Lobwood. Barn S70 55 B5
Lobwood La. Barn S70 55 B5
Locarno Rd. Thorne DN8 9 D3
Lock Hill. Thorne DN8 26 A7
Lock House Rd. Shef S9 114 C1
Lock La. Shef S9 114 E3
Lock La. Thorne DN8 26 A7
Lock St. Shef S6 128 E6
Locke Ave. Barn S70 54 E8
Locke Ave. Barn S70 54 F6
Locke Rd. Dod S75 54 A6
Locke St. Barn S70 54 D7
Lockeaflash Cres. Barn S70 55 D7
Lockesley Ave. Con DN12 81 A1
Lockgate Rd. Bal M DN6 5 F8
Locking Dr. Arm DN3 64 D5
Locksley Ave. Don DN3 42 F2
Locksley Dr. Thurcr S66 133 E6
Locksley Gdns. Norton DN6 4 C1
Lockton Cl. Chap S30 94 C8
Lockton Way. Con DN12 81 D3
Lockwood Ave. S Anst S31 146 D3
Lockwood Cl. Roth S65 116 C7
Lockwood Cl. Thorne DN8 26 D7
Lockwood La. Barn S70 54 F7 11
Lockwood La. Dearne S63 58 F6
Lockwood Rd. Dearne S63 58 E6
Lockwood Rd. Don DN1 62 E5
Lockwood Rd. Roth S65 116 C7
Lodge Ct. Hat DN7 44 B7
Lodge Dr. Went S62 76 D1
Lodge Farm Cl. N Anst S31 146 D6
Lodge Hill Dr. Wales S31 145 B3
Lodge La. Aston S31 144 D7
Lodge La. Din S31 135 B1
Lodge La. K Bram DN7 24 B6
Lodge La. Roth S61 95 F3
Lodge La. Shef S10, S6 127 A2
Lodge La. Snaith DN14 1 A8
Lodge La. Wort S30 93 D5
Lodge Moor Hospl. Shef 126 F1
Lodge Moor Rd. Shef S10 138 F8
Lodge Rd. Ad le S DN6 21 C2
Lodge St. Hem WF9 17 D8
Lodge The. Shef S11 140 A5
Lodge Way. Brin S60 115 C1
Logan Rd. Shef S9 130 D4
Loicher La. Shef S30 95 D1
Lomas Cl. Shef S6 127 C7
Lomas Lea. Shef S6 127 B6
Lombard Cl. Barn S75 33 E3
Lombard Cres. Dar S73 56 E5
London La. Moss DN6 6 B1
London Rd. Shef S2 140 F8
London Way. Roth S61 95 E4
Long Acre View. Shef S19 156 A8
Long Cl. Don DN4 84 E6
Long Close La. Holmfi HD8 28 C7
Long Close La. S Elm WF9 19 C6
Long Croft. Mapp S75 14 B1
Long Croft Rd. Dron S18 152 C2
Long Cswy. Barn S71 34 D3
Long Cswy. Hath S10 137 C5
Long Edge La. Ben DN5 40 E1
Long Field Dr. Don DN3 43 B3
Long Field Rd. Don DN3 43 A3
Long Gate. Wad DN12 101 F5
Long Gr. Stai DN7 24 E4
Long Henry Row. Shef S2 129 C3 6
Long Ing Rd. Holmfi HD7 48 A7
Long La. C in L S81 148 F6
Long La. K Smea WF8 3 D3
Long La. Kill S31 156 F6
Long La. Ought S30 111 C7
Long La. Ought S30 111 D2
Long La. Oxspr S30 72 F8
Long La. Roth S60 132 A7
Long La. Shef S6 126 D5
Long La. Shef S10 127 F4
Long La. Shef S6 111 D2
Long La. Shep HD8 28 D4
Long La. Sprot DN5 61 B4
Long La. Stock S30 91 E8
Long La. Treet S60 132 A7
Long La. Uns S31 154 C1
Long Lands La. Ad le S DN5 39 E5
Long Leys La. Braith S66 101 A5
Long Line. Shef S11 139 B2
Long Rd. Thurcr S66 133 E2
Long Royd La. Shep HD8 29 B8
Longacre Cl. Shef S19 144 A1
Longacre Way. Shef S19 144 B1
Longcar Jun & Inf Sch. Barn 54 D8
Longcar La. Barn S70 54 D8
Longcroft Ave. Dron S18 152 C2
Longcroft Cres. Dron S18 152 C2
Longdale Dr. S Elm WF9 18 E4
Longfellow Dr. Roth S65 116 B5
Longfellow Rd. Don DN4 83 C6
Longfield Cl. Wombw S73 56 B2
Longfield Dr. Don DN4 84 D6
Longfield Dr. Mapp S75 14 B1
Longfield Dr. Roth S65 117 D8
Longfield Rd. Shef S10 128 B5
Longfields Cres. Hoy S74 76 D6
Longford Cl. Shef S17 152 A5
Longford Cres. Shef S17 152 A5
Longford Dr. Shef S17 151 F4
Longford Rd. Shef S17 152 A4
Longford Spinney. Shef S17 151 F4
Longlands Ave. Wales S31 145 C2
Longlands Dr. Mapp S75 33 B8
Longlands Dr. Roth S65 99 A3
Longley Ave W. Shef S5 112 F2
Longley Cl. Barn S75 32 E4
Longley Cl. Shef S5 113 B2
Longley Cres. Shef S5 113 B3
Longley Dr. Shef S5 113 B2
Longley Edge Rd. Holmfi HD7 48 B8
Longley Hall Gr. Shef S5 113 C2
Longley Hall Rd. Shef S5 113 C2
Longley Hall Rise. Shef S5 113 B3
Longley Hall Way. Shef S5 113 C2
Longley Jun & Inf Sch. Shef 113 A2
Longley La. Holmfi HD7 48 A8
Longley La. Shef S5 113 B3
Longley St. Barn S75 32 E4
Longman Rd. Barn S70 33 E2
Longridge Rd. Barn S71 34 D6
Longshaw Ctry Pk. Grin 150 A3
Longside Way. Barn S75 33 A1
Longsight Rd. Mapp S75 14 A1
Longstone Cres. Shef S12 142 D4
Longthwaite Cl. Lough S31 134 E4
Longton Rd. Don DN3 43 A4
Lonsbrough Way. S Elm WF9 19 A4
Lonsdale Ave. Barn S71 56 B8
Lonsdale Ave. Don DN2 63 D4
Lonsdale Cl. N Anst S31 146 F6
Lonsdale House. Don DN2 63 C5
Lonsdale Rd. Shef S6 128 C7
Loosemore Dr. Shef S12 141 F5
Lopham St. Shef S3 129 B5
Lord St. Barn S71 34 C2
Lord St. Roth S65 116 A7
Lord St. Stai DN7 24 E3
Lord's Head La. Don DN4 82 D4
Lordens Hill. Din S31 135 A1
Lords Cl. N Edl DN12 82 C3
Lorna Rd. Mex S64 80 A5
Lorne Cl. Dron S18 152 D2
Lorne Rd. Dearne S63 58 C8
Lothian Rd. Don DN2 63 C5
Louden Cl. Roth S61 96 B2
Louden Rd. Roth S61 96 B2
Lound Inf Sch. Chap 94 F6
Lound Jun Sch. Chap 95 A6
Lound La. H Pag DN5 38 F5
Lound Rd. Shef S9 130 D3
Lound Side. Chap S30 95 A5
Lounde Cl. Sprot DN5 61 C1
Louth Rd. Shef S11 140 B8
Love La. Shef S3 129 A4
Love St. Shef S3 129 A4
Lovell St. Shef S4 129 D5
Loversall Cl. Don DN4 83 C5
Loversall. Don 83 C5
Lovetot Ave. Aston S31 144 D8
Lovetot Rd. Roth S61 96 E2
Lovetot Rd. Shef S9 129 E5
Low Bradfield Cty Prim Sch. Bfield 110 A4
Low Cudworth. Cud S72 35 B5
Low Cudworth Gn. Cud S72 35 B5
Low Deeps La. Misson DN10 87 E1
Low Field La. Aust DN10 105 C1
Low Fisher Gate. Don DN1 62 D4
Low Gate. S Elm WF9 19 A3
Low Grange Sq. Dearne S63 58 C8
Low La. K Bram DN7 23 F4
Low La. Maltby S66 118 C2
Low La. Roth S61 115 A8
Low La. Thurcr S66 118 C2
Low Laithes View. Wombw S73 56 B4
Low Levels Bank. Hat DN8 46 C6
Low Matlock La. Shef S6 127 E8
Low Moor La. Midhop S30 71 D3
Low Pastures Cl. Dod S75 54 A7
Low Rd. Con DN12 81 D3
Low Rd. Don DN4 83 A7
Low Rd E. Don DN4 82 D6
Low Rd. Ought S30 111 D7
Low Rd. Scro DN10 123 A2
Low Rd. Shef S6 128 A6
Low Rd. Thurgo S30 52 D1
Low Rd W. Don DN4 82 C6
Low Row. Mapp S75 13 E3
Low St. Dod S75 54 B6
Low View. Dod S75 53 F7
Lowburn Rd. Shef S13 142 C7
Lowe La. Hd Gr S75 53 F3
Lowedges Cres. Shef S8 152 F6
Lowedges Dr. Shef S8 152 F6
Lowedges Pl. Shef S8 153 A6
Lowedges Rd. Shef S8 152 E6
Lowell Ave. Don DN4 83 B6
Lower Boundary Rd. T in B DN5 42 B7
Lower Castlereagh St. Barn S70 33 E1 6
Lower Common La. Clay W HD8 30 D8
Lower Denby La. D Dale HD8 30 B4
Lower Dolcliffe Rd. Mex S64 79 F5
Lower Kenyon St. Thorne DN8 26 B8
Lower Malton Rd. Ben DN5 61 E6
Lower Maythorn La. Wh Com HD7 49 D8
Lower Mill Cl. Dearne S63 58 C4
Lower Northcroft. S Elm WF9 19 A3
Lower Northfield La. S Kirk WF9 18 C3
Lower Putting Mill. D Dale HD8 30 B7
Lower Thomas St. Barn S70 54 E8 3
Lower Unwin St. Pen S30 51 D2
Lower York St. Wombw S73 56 D3
Lowfield Ave. Eck S12 154 E8
Lowfield Ave. Roth S61 97 C3
Lowfield Cl. B Dun DN3 43 A6
Lowfield Cres. Hem WF9 17 E7
Lowfield Ct. Shef S2 141 A7 4
Lowfield Jun & Inf Sch. Shef 141 A7
Lowfield Rd. Dearne S63 58 D2
Lowfield Rd. Don DN2 63 C7
Lowfield Wlk. Con DN12 80 F4
Lowgate. Bal M DN6 6 A8
Lowgate. Ben DN5 61 E7
Lowgreave. Roth S65 116 C8
Lowhill. Thorne DN8 8 F1
Lowhouse Rd. Shef S5 113 E7
Lowlands Cl. Barn S71 34 D5
Lowlands Wlk. Askern DN6 22 B7
Lowry Dr. Dron S18 152 F1
Lowther Rd. Don DN1 62 E5
Lowther Rd. Shef S6 112 D1
Lowther Sq. C in L S81 148 E7
Lowton Way. Maltby S66 118 A5
Loxley Ave. Wombw S73 56 C2
Loxley Coll. Stock 73 B2
Loxley Ct. Shef S6 128 C7
Loxley Jun & Inf Sch. Shef 111 E1
Loxley Mount. Norton DN6 4 C1
Loxley New Rd. Shef S6 128 B7
Loxley Rd. Barn S71 34 F3
Loxley Rd. Bfield S6 110 C4
Loxley Rd. Shef S6 127 E8
Loxley View Rd. Shef S10 128 B5
Loy Cl. Roth S61 97 A3
Lucas St. Shef S4 129 C7
Lucknow Ct. Shef S7 140 E6
Ludgate Cl. Ross DN11 104 A7
Ludwell Hill. Bnbur DN5 59 E2
Lugano Gr. Dar S73 56 E6
Luke La. Shef S6 111 F1
Lulworth Cl. Barn S70 55 B8 6
Lumb La. Wharn S30 110 E8
Lumley Cl. Maltby S66 119 C4
Lumley Cres. Maltby S66 119 C4
Lumley Dr. Laugh S31 134 C2
Lumley Dr. Maltby S66 119 C4
Lumley Dr. Tick DN11 121 B7
Lumley St. Shef S4, S9 129 D4
Lumley St. Shef S9 129 F4
Lump La. Shef S30 94 C1
Luna Croft. Shef S12 141 F2
Lunbreck Rd. Don DN4 82 C5
Lund Ave. Barn S71 34 F3
Lund Cl. Barn S71 34 F3
Lund Cres. Barn S71 34 F3
Lund Hill La. Roy S71 15 F5
Lund Hill La. Ryhill S71 15 F5
Lund La. Barn S71 34 F3
Lund Rd. Ought S30 111 D5
Lundhill Cl. Wombw S73 56 E1
Lundhill Gr. Wombw S73 56 E1
Lundhill Rd. Wombw S73 56 E1
Lundwood Cl. Shef S19 143 C2
Lundwood Dr. Shef S19 143 C2
Lundwood Gr. Shef S19 143 C2
Lundwood House. Don DN1 62 C2 18
Lunn Rd. Cud S72 35 B6
Lupton Bdlgs. Swint S64 79 D4
Lupton Cres. Shef S8 152 F6
Lupton Dr. Shef S8 152 F6
Lupton Rd. Shef S8 152 F6
Luterel Dr. Aston S31 144 D8
Lutterworth Dr. Ad I S DN6 40 A6
Lych Gate Cl. Don DN4 85 A7
Lydgate Cty Jun Sch. Shef 128 A3
Lydgate Ct. Shef S10 128 B3
Lydgate Hall Cres. Shef S10 128 A3
Lydgate La. Shef S10 128 B3
Lydgate Mid Sch. Shef 128 A2
Lydgate Rd. Shep HD8 28 F8
Lyme St. Roth S60 115 C6
Lyme Terr. Ad le S DN6 20 E1
Lyminster Rd. Shef S6 112 D4
Lymister Ave. Roth S60 115 F1
Lyndale Ave. Don DN3 42 F1
Lynden Ave. Ad I S DN6 40 A6
Lyndhurst Cl. Norton DN6 4 E3
Lyndhurst Cl. Shef S11 140 C6
Lyndhurst Cl. Thorne DN8 25 F8
Lyndhurst Cres. Don DN3 42 E3
Lyndhurst Dr. Norton DN6 4 E3
Lyndhurst Rd. Shef S11 140 D6
Lyndhurst Rise. Norton DN6 4 E3
Lynmouth Rd. Shef S7 140 E5
Lynn Pl. Shef S9 130 B8
Lynton Ave. Roth S60 116 B3
Lynton Dr. Don DN3 42 E2
Lynton Pl. Kex S75 32 D8
Lynton Rd. Shef S11 140 D8 9
Lynwood Cl. Dron S18 152 D1 1
Lynwood Dr. Roy S71 15 C2
Lynwood La. Roy S71 15 C2
Lyons Rd. Shef S4 129 C7
Lyons St. Shef S4 129 D7
Lytham Ave. Barn S71 34 D5
Lytham Ave. Din S31 146 F7
Lytham Cl. Don DN4 85 B6
Lyttleton Cres. Pen S30 51 C1
Lytton Ave. Shef S5 112 E5
Lytton Cl. Don DN4 83 B6
Lytton Cres. Shef S5 112 E5
Lytton Dr. Shef S5 112 F5
Lytton Rd. Shef S5 112 E5

Mabel St. Roth S60 115 F5
Macaulay Cres. Arm DN3 64 C6
Machin Dr. Rawm S62 97 D8
Machin La. Stock S30 72 E2
Machins Ct. Dron S18 153 A2
Machon Bank Rd. Shef S7 140 E6
Machon Bank. Shef S7 140 E6
Mackenzie Cres. Chap S30 94 E4
Mackenzie Cres. Shef S10 128 E2
Mackenzie St. Shef S11 140 E8
Mackey Cres. Bri S72 16 F3
Macmanus Ave. Rawm S62 97 F8
Macnaghten Rd. Pilley S75 75 F5
Macro Rd. Wombw S73 56 F2
Madam La. B Dun DN3 42 E8
Madehurst Gdns. Shef S2 141 B7
Madehurst Rd. Shef S2 141 B7
Madehurst Rise. Shef S2 141 B7
Madehurst View. Shef S2 141 B7
Madingley Cl. Don DN4 83 A5
Mafeking Pl. Chap S30 95 A6
Magellan Rd. Maltby S66 118 E6
Maggot La. Thurgo S75 52 D2
Magna Cl. Roth S66 117 B6
Magna Cres. Roth S66 117 A6
Magna La. Roth S65 98 E1
Magnolia Cl. Don DN3 42 F3
Magnolia Cl. S Anst S31 146 D3
Magnolia Cl. Shaf S72 16 D2
Magnolia Ct. Shef S10 139 E8
Magpie Gr. Shef S2 129 E2
Mahon Ave. Rawm S62 97 F6
Maidstone Rd. Shef S6 112 D4
Main Ave. N Edl DN12 82 B3
Main Ave. Shef S17 151 E4
Main Rd. Dron S18 152 B1
Main Rd. Eck S31 154 F3
Main Rd. Eck S12 154 E8
Main Rd. Eck S31 156 B1
Main Rd. Hath S30 149 A8
Main Rd. Shef S9 130 C4
Main Rd. Shef S9 130 D4
Main Rd. Shef S6 110 D1
Main Rd. Wharn S30 93 B2
Main St. Aston S31 132 C2
Main St. Aston S31 144 C7
Main St. Auck DN9 86 A6
Main St. Bran DN3 64 B1
Main St. Dearne S63 58 E6
Main St. Fish DN7 25 A7
Main St. Ham DN6 20 B1
Main St. Har DN11 121 E4
Main St. Hat DN7 44 F6
Main St. K Smea WF8 3 D6
Main St. Mex S64 79 F4
Main St. N Anst S31 146 D6
Main St. Old S81 136 F6
Main St. Rawm S62 98 A6
Main St. Roth S60 115 D6
Main St. Roth S66 117 D5
Main St. Roth S61 97 C3
Main St. Roth S65 99 D2
Main St. S Hie S72 16 D6
Main St. Shef S12 143 B3
Main St. Shef S30 112 C8
Main St. Sprot DN5 82 B8
Main St. Styr DN11 121 D1
Main St. Treet S60 131 D6
Main St. Ulley S31 132 E4
Main St. Upton WF9 19 D8
Main St. Wad DN11 102 C7
Main St. Went S62 77 B1
Main St. Wombw S73 56 C3
Main View. Stai DN7 25 B4
Makin St. Mex S64 80 C4
Malcolm Cl. Barn S70 55 D8
Malham Cl. Bawtry DN10 122 F8
Malham Cl. Shaf S72 16 C3
Malham Ct. Barn S70 33 D2 3
Malham Gdns. Shef S19 155 D7
Malham Gr. Shef S19 155 E7
Malham Pl. Chap S30 94 F6
Malin Bridge Jun & Inf Schs. Shef 128 B8
Malin Rd. Roth S65 116 D8
Malin Rd. Shef S6 128 A7
Malinda St. Shef S3 128 F5
Mallard Ave. B Dun DN3 42 F6
Mallard Cl. Don DN4 82 F6
Mallard Cl. Kill S31 156 B7
Mallard Cl. Roth S61 96 A5
Mallin Dr. N Edl DN12 82 B1
Mallory Ave. Rawm S62 97 E6
Mallory Dr. Mex S64 80 D6
Mallory Rd. Roth S65 116 C8
Mallory Way. Cud S72 35 C7
Malpas Hill. Don DN11 120 F1
Maltas Ct. Barn S70 55 C5
Maltby Comp Sch. Maltby 118 F5
Maltby Crags Jun Mix & Inf Sch. Maltby 119 A4
Maltby Hall Inf Sch. Maltby 118 E5
Maltby House. Don DN1 62 C2 17
Maltby La. Maltby S66 118 F8
Maltby Rd. Old S81 136 E6
Maltby St. Shef S9 130 A7
Malthouse Rd. Barn S70 33 F1 18
Malting La. Shef S4 129 C4
Maltings The. Roth S60 115 D5
Maltkiln St. Roth S60 115 D5
Maltkin Cotts. Don DN3 42 F5
Maltkin Dr. W Bret WF4 12 F8
Malton Dr. Aston S31 144 E7
Malton Pl. Barn S71 33 E7
Malton Rd. Ben DN5 61 D7
Malton Rd. Don DN2 63 B5
Malton Rd. Upton WF9 19 D8
Malton St. Shef S4 129 C7
Maltravers Cl. Shef S2 129 E2
Maltravers Cres. Shef S2 129 E3
Maltravers Pl. Shef S2 129 E3
Maltravers Rd. Shef S2 129 E3
Maltravers St. Shef S4 129 C4
Maltravers Terr. Shef S2 129 E2
Maltravers Way. Shef S2 129 E3
Malvern Ave. Ben DN5 61 E5
Malvern Cl. Barn S75 33 B2
Malvern Cl. Thorne DN8 26 A6
Malvern Rd. Don DN2 63 C4
Malvern Rd. Shef S9 130 B5
Malwood Way. Maltby S66 119 B6
Manchester Rd. Pen S30 50 D3
Manchester Rd. Shef S10 127 D3
Manchester Rd. Stock S30 73 B2
Manchester Rd. Stock S30 73 E1
Mandale Rd. B Dun DN3 42 F8
Mandeville St. Shef S9 130 C5
Mangham La. Tick DN11 121 A8
Mangham Rd. Roth S61, S62 97 E2
Mangham Way. Roth S61 97 D1
Mannering Rd. Don DN4 82 E6
Manners St. Shef S3 128 F6
Manor App. Roth S61 114 F7
Manor Ave. Dearne S63 58 E5
Manor Cl. B Dun DN3 42 E7
Manor Cl. K Smea WF8 3 D5
Manor Cl. Maltby S66 118 F5
Manor Cl. Norton DN6 4 C3
Manor Cl. Notton WF4 14 F7
Manor Cl. Rawm S62 97 C8
Manor Cl. Tod S31 145 F5
Manor Cl. W up D S63 78 B7
Manor Cl. Wad DN11 102 C6
Manor Cres. Brin S60 131 B8
Manor Cres. Dron S18 152 F1
Manor Cres. Grime S72 36 A8
Manor Croft. S Hie S72 16 D6
Manor Ct. Con DN12 80 E3
Manor Dr. Cade DN5 81 D5
Manor Dr. Don DN2 62 F3
Manor Dr. Roth S60 116 C1
Manor Dr. Roy S71 15 B3
Manor Dr. S Hie S72 16 D6
Manor Dr. Tod S31 145 F5

Nethergreen Ave. Kill S31 156 D7
Nethergreen Gdns. Kill S31 156 D7
Nethergreen Rd. Shef S11 139 F8
Nethermoor Ave. Kill S31 156 D7
Nethermoor Cl. Kill S31 156 D7
Nethermoor Dr. Kill S31 156 D7
Nethermoor Dr. Roth S66 117 C2
Nethermoor La. Kill S31 156 D7
Netherthorpe Airfield. Th Sa 159 B5
Netherthorpe Cl. Kill S31 156 C7
Netherthorpe Fst Sch. Shef 128 F4
Netherthorpe La. Kill S31 156 C7
Netherthorpe Pl. Shef S3 128 F4
Netherthorpe Rd. Shef S3 128 F4
Netherthorpe St. Shef S3 128 F4 5
Netherthorpe Way. N Anst S31 146 E7
Netherthorpe Wlk. Shef S3 128 F4 4
Netherwood Rd. Dar S73 56 D5
Nettle Croft. Tick DN11 121 C7
Nettleham Rd. Shef S8 140 F3
Nettleholme. Hat DN7 44 B8
Nettleton House. Hem WF9 17 D6
Neville Ave. Barn S70 55 C7
Neville Cl. Barn S70 55 D7
Neville Cl. S Kirk WF9 18 C3
Neville Cl. Shef S3 129 B5
Neville Cl. Wombw S73 56 B4
Neville Cres. Barn S70 55 D7
Neville Ct. Wombw S73 56 B4
Neville Dr. Shef S3 129 B6
Neville La. K Bram DN7 24 A8
Neville Pits La. Bal M DN6 5 C8
Neville Rd. Roth S61 96 F1
Neville St. Roth S60 115 D7
New Brighton. D Dale HD8 29 B3
New Chapel Ave. Pen S30 51 C1
New Cl. Silk S75 52 F8
New Close La. Norton DN6 20 E7
New Cotts. Rawcl DN8 2 E6
New Cross Dr. Shef S13 143 A6
New Cross Way. Shef S13 143 A6
New Cross Wlk. Shef S13 143 A7
New Droppingwell Rd. Roth S61 114 B6
New Hall Cres. Stock S30 72 F2
New Hall La. Stock S30 72 F1
New Hill. Con DN12 81 C2
New House. Holmfi HD7 48 D7
New Ings. Arm DN3 64 A6
New Ings La. K Bram DN3 23 D2
New Inn La. Stai DN7 24 E5
New La. Rawcl DN14 2 A8
New La. Ross DN11 85 A1
New La. Sprot DN5 61 B1
New La. Upton WF9 19 A7
New Lane Cres. Upton WF9 19 A7
New Lodge Cres. Barn S71 33 E7
New Mill Bank. Stock S30 92 C5
New Mill Field Rd. Hat DN7 44 D7
New Orchard La. Thurcr S66 133 E7
New Orchard Rd. Thurcr S66 133 E7
New Park Est. Stai DN7 25 A5
New Rd. Bfield S6 92 B3
New Rd. Bfield S6 110 C3
New Rd. Braith S66 100 E3
New Rd. Caw S75 31 B5
New Rd. Din S31 146 F8
New Rd. Fir S81 136 A6
New Rd. G Field DN14 11 E7
New Rd. Hoy S73 77 D7
New Rd. K Smea WF8 3 D8
New Rd. Mapp S75 14 B1
New Rd. N Anst S31 146 C6
New Rd. Norton DN6 4 F3
New Rd. Norton DN6 21 B8
New Rd. Pen S30 30 E1
New Rd. Pilley S75 75 E5
New Rd. Roth S61 114 B5
New Rd. Shef S6 110 E2
New Rd. Stock S30 73 D1
New Rd. Tick DN11 121 A7
New Rd. Uns S18 154 A1
New Rd. W up D S63 78 F6
New Rd. Wad DN11 102 C6
New Rd. Wales S31 144 E4
New Rd. Wool WF4 14 B6
New Row La. Ingb S30 50 E8
New Royd. Pen S30 50 E3
New Smithy Ave. Pen S30 51 A4
New Smithy Dr. Pen S30 51 A4
New St. Ad le S DN6 21 D1
New St. Barn S70 33 F1
New St. Barn S70 54 E8
New St. Barn S70 55 A4
New St. Barn S70 55 C4
New St. Barn S71 55 E8
New St. Ben DN5 62 B8
New St. Blax DN9 86 E5
New St. Chap S30 94 D8
New St. Dar S73 57 A5
New St. Dearne S63 58 D1
New St. Din S31 134 F1
New St. Dod S75 53 F6
New St. Don DN1 62 C1
New St. G Hou S72 36 E1
New St. Grime S72 36 A7
New St. Hoy S73 77 B7
New St. Laugh S31 134 E4
New St. Mapp S75 14 B1
New St. Mex S64 80 D5
New St. Rawm S62 97 F5
New St. Roth S61 95 F4
New St. Roth S61 97 B4
New St. Roy S71 15 C3
New St. S Elm WF9 18 E3
New St. S Hie S72 16 D6
New St. Shef S1 129 A4
New St. Shef S19 156 A8
New St. Treet S60 131 D6
New St. Wombw S73 56 E3
New Station Rd. Swint S64 79 E3
New Street Bus Link. Shef S19 156 A8
New Street La. Shef S2 129 C4
New Winterwell. W up D S63 78 D7
New Wortley Rd. Roth S60,S61 115 B7
Newark Cl. Mapp S75 14 B2
Newark Rd. Mex S64 79 E5
Newark. Shef S19 155 E8 8
Newark St. Ross DN11 84 E1
Newark St. Shef S9 130 A7
Newbiggin Cl. Rawm S62 97 E4
Newbiggin Dr. Rawm S62 97 E4
Newbold Terr. Ben DN5 61 F5
Newbolt Rd. Don DN4 83 B6
Newbould Cres. Shef S19 144 A3
Newbould La. Shef S10 128 D2
Newbridge Gr. N Edl DN12 82 C2
Newburn Dr. Shef S9 114 E2
Newbury Dr. S Elm WF9 19 A5
Newbury Rd. Shef S10 128 B4
Newbury Way. Ben DN5 61 D6
Newby Cres. Don DN4 83 A5
Newcastle Cl. N Anst S31 146 E7
Newcastle St. Shef S1 128 F3
Newcomen Rd. Ben DN5 62 A5
Newcroft Cl. Shef S19 144 B3
Newdale Ave. Cud S72 35 A5
Newent La. Shef S10 128 B4
Newfield Ave. Barn S71 34 D4
Newfield Cres. Shef S17 151 C7
Newfield Cres. W up D S63 78 D5
Newfield Croft. Shef S17 151 C8
Newfield Ct. Shef S10 139 D8
Newfield Farm Cl. Shef S14 141 E5
Newfield Green Rd. Shef S2 141 D6
Newfield La. Shef S17 151 C7
Newfield Sec Sch (Boys). Shef 141 C3
Newfield Sec Sch (Girls). Shef 141 C3
Newfields Ave. Thorne DN8 9 D2
Newfields Cl. Thorne DN8 9 C2
Newfields Dr. Thorne DN8 9 C2
Newgate Cl. Chap S30 94 E7
Newhall Ave. Roth S66 117 C2
Newhall La. Thurcr S66 118 A2
Newhall Rd. Don DN3 43 A3
Newhall Rd. Shef S9 129 F7
Newhill Rd. Barn S71 34 A4
Newhill Rd. W up D S63 78 D5
Newhill. S Kirk WF9 18 B1
Newholme Dr. Thorne DN8 9 C3
Newington Ave. Cud S72 35 B8
Newington Cl. Don DN4 84 F7
Newington Dr. Aston S31 144 E7
Newington Rd. Aust DN10 123 C8
Newington Rd. Shef S11 140 C8
Newland Ave. Cud S72 35 A5
Newland Ave. Maltby S66 118 F6
Newland Rd. Barn S71 33 F7
Newlands Ave. Ad le S DN6 20 F2
Newlands Ave. Shef S12 142 A6
Newlands Cl. Don DN4 84 F7
Newlands Dr. Ben DN5 61 F6
Newlands Dr. Shef S12 142 A6
Newlands Gr. Shef S12 142 B6
Newlands Rd. Shef S12 142 A6
Newlyn Dr. Barn S71 34 B3
Newlyn Pl. Shef S8 141 A3
Newlyn Rd. Shef S8 140 F3
Newman Ave. Roy S71 15 C1
Newman Cl. Shef S9 114 B4
Newman Ct. Roth S60 116 A2
Newman Ct. Shef S9 114 B4
Newman Dr. Shef S9 114 A4
Newman Rd. Roth S60 116 B2
Newman Rd. Shef S9 114 A4
Newman Sch. Roth 116 A1
Newmarch St. Shef S9 114 E3
Newmarche Dr. Askern DN6 22 C8
Newmarket Rd. Don DN4 63 D2
Newsam Rd. Swint S64 79 E1
Newsham Rd. Shef S8 140 F4
Newsome Ave. Wombw S73 56 C3
Newstead Ave. Ought S30 111 D8
Newstead Ave. Shef S12 142 E3
Newstead Cl. Dron S18 152 C1
Newstead Cl. Roth S65 116 B8 9
Newstead Cl. Shef S12 142 E3
Newstead Dr. Shef S12 142 E3
Newstead Gr. Shef S12 142 E3
Newstead Pl. Shef S12 142 E2
Newstead Rd. Barn S71 33 E8
Newstead Rd. Ben DN5 61 F8
Newstead Rd. Shef S12 142 F3
Newstead Rise. Shef S12 142 F2
Newstead Way. Shef S12 142 E2
Newthorpe Rd. Norton DN6 4 C3
Newton Ave. Stock S30 72 F2
Newton Croft. Shef S13 143 B6
Newton Dr. Ben DN5 61 F3
Newton Dr. Roth S65 116 A6
Newton La. Ben DN5 61 E3
Newton La. Shef S1 129 A2
Newton La. Stock S30 72 F2
Newton Pl. Roth S61 95 F3
Newton Rd. Chap S30 94 E7
Newton St. Barn S70 33 D2
Newton St. Roth S65 116 A6
Newtown Ave. Cud S72 35 B5
Newtown Ave. Roy S71 15 B4
Newtown Gn. Cud S72 35 B5
Newtree Dr. Wad DN11 102 B6
Newven House. Roth S65 115 F7
Niagara Rd. Shef S6 112 C3
Nicholas La. Dearne S63 58 C6
Nicholas Rd. Shef S6 128 A5
Nicholas St. Barn S70 33 D1
Nicholson Ave. Barn S75 32 E4
Nicholson Ave. W up D S63 78 D5
Nicholson Pl. Shef S8 141 B6 5
Nicholson Rd. Don DN4 62 A1
Nicholson Rd. Shef S8 141 A6
Nickerwood Dr. Aston S31 144 D6
Nidd Rd E. Shef S9 130 B5
Nidd Rd. Shef S9 130 A5
Nidderdale Pl. Roth S66 117 C6
Nidderdale Rd. Roth S61 96 F3
Nightingale Cl. Roth S60 115 E5
Nightingale Croft. Roth S61 96 A6
Nightingale Ct. Roth S60 115 E5
Nightingale Rd. Shef S30 112 D8
Nile St. Shef S10 128 C2
Nine Trees Trad Est. Roth 133 D8
Ninelands Rd. Hath S30 149 A7
Ninescores La. Finn DN9 87 E7
Ninian Gr. Don DN4 84 E7
Noble St. Hoy S74 76 F5
Noblethorpe La. Silk S75 52 F7
Noblethorpe Rd. Swint S62 98 F7
Nodder Rd. Shef S13 142 C7
Noehill Pl. Shef S2 130 B1
Noehill Rd. Shef S2 130 B1
Nook End. Shef S6 127 D6
Nook La. Pen S30 51 E1
Nook La. Shef S6 127 C6
Nook Lane Jun Sch. Shef 127 C6
Nook The. Pen S30 52 A6
Nook The. Shef S10 128 D4
Nookery Cl. Maltby S66 119 B6
Nooking Cl. Arm DN3 64 C7
Nor Wood Rd. Hem WF9 17 D5
Nora St. Dearne S63 58 F6
Norborough Rd. Don DN2 62 F5
Norborough Rd. Shef S9 114 E3
Norbreck Cres. Don DN4 82 C4
Norbreck Rd. Askern DN6 22 C7
Norbreck Rd. Don DN4 82 C5
Norbrook Way. Roth S60 116 D1
Norburn Dr. Kill S31 156 D6
Norbury Cl. Dron S18 152 D1
Norcroft. Barn S70 54 F6
Norcroft La. Caw S75 31 F3
Norfolk Ave. Bir DN11 122 D4
Norfolk Cl. Barn S71 34 B4
Norfolk Ct. Roth S65 115 E7 8
Norfolk Dr. Bir DN11 122 C4
Norfolk Dr. N Anst S31 146 E6
Norfolk Fst Sch. Shef 141 E7
Norfolk Gr. Bir DN11 122 C4
Norfolk Hill Croft. Shef S30 94 C1
Norfolk Hill. Shef S30 94 C1
Norfolk La. Shef S1 129 A3
Norfolk Mid Sch. Shef 141 E7
Norfolk Park Ave. Shef S2 141 D8
Norfolk Park Dr. Shef S2 129 C1
Norfolk Park Rd. Shef S2 129 C1
Norfolk Park Sch. Shef 129 C1
Norfolk Park Students Residence.
Shef S2 129 D1
Norfolk Pl. Maltby S66 119 A5
Norfolk Rd. Bir DN11 122 C4
Norfolk Rd. Don DN4 83 B6
Norfolk Rd. G Hou S72 36 F1
Norfolk Rd. Shef S2 129 C2
Norfolk Row. Shef S1 129 A3
Norfolk Sch. Shef 141 E7
Norfolk St. Roth S65 115 E7
Norfolk St. Shef S1 129 B3
Norfolk Way. Roth S60 116 A2
Norgreave Way. Shef S19 155 E7
Norman Cl. Barn S71 34 C4
Norman Cl. Barn S70 55 A5
Norman Cres. Ben DN5 61 D7
Norman Cres. Ross DN11 84 E1
Norman Dr. Hat DN7 44 B6
Norman Rd. D Dale HD8 29 F5
Norman Rd. Hat DN7 44 B6
Norman St. Dearne S63 58 E8
Norman St. Shef S9 130 A7
Normancroft Cres. Shef S2 130 C1
Normancroft Ct. Shef S2 130 B1 4
Normancroft Dr. Shef S2 130 B1
Normancroft Way. Shef S2 130 C1
Normandale Ave. Shef S6 127 E8
Normandale Rd. G Hou S72 36 E2
Normandale Rd. Shef S6 128 D7 2
Normanton Gdns. Shef S4 129 C7
Normanton Gr. Shef S13 142 F6
Normanton Hill. Shef S13 142 D6
Normanton Spring Ct. Shef S13 142 F6
Normanton Spring Rd. Shef S13 142 F5
Normanville Ave. Brin S60 115 B1
Norrel's Croft. Roth S60 115 F4
Norris Rd. Shef S6 128 B8
Norroy St. Shef S4 129 D6
Norstead Cres. Roth S66 117 E5
North Anston Bsns Ctr. N Anst 146 C8
North Anston Trad Est The.
N Anst 146 B8
North Ave. Bawtry DN10 123 A8
North Ave. S Elm WF9 18 F2
North Border Comp Sch. Bir 122 C5
North Border Inf Sch. Har 122 B4
North Border Jun Sch. Har 122 B4
North Bridge Rd. Don DN5 62 C4
North Church St. Shef S1 129 A4
North Cl. Roy S71 15 C3
North Cliff Rd. Con DN12 81 B2
North Common Rd. Thorne DN8 9 B4
North Cres. Kill S31 156 E8
North Cres. Roth S65 116 A7
North Cres. S Elm WF9 19 B4
North Dr. Roth S60 115 D8
North Eastern Rd. Thorne DN8 26 A8
North End Dr. Bnbur DN5 59 C2
North Farm Cl. Hart S31 157 E7
North Field. Dod S75 53 F8
North Field Rd. H Pag DN6 38 D7
North Field. Silk S75 52 F8
North Gate. Mex S64 80 C5
North Gate. Tick DN11 121 A8
North Hill Rd. Shef S5 112 F4
North Ings Rd. Hat DN7 44 D8
North La. Caw S75 31 A2
North La. Syke DN14 7 C7
North La. Syke DN14 7 E8
North Park La. Ad le S DN6 21 D3
North Pitt St. Roth S61 114 F6
North Pl. Barn S75 33 B3
North Pl. Roth S65 116 A7
North Quadrant. Shef S5 113 D4
North Rd. Roth S65 116 B8
North Rd. Roy S71 15 D4
North Rd. T in B DN3 42 C8
North Row. Shep HD8 28 D8
North Sq. N Edl DN12 82 C2
North St. Dar S73 57 A6
North St. Don DN4 62 E1
North St. N Edl DN12 82 C2
North St. Rawm S62 98 B7
North St. Roth S60 115 C7
North St. S Kirk WF9 18 B3
North St. Shef S6 128 F5
North St. Swint S64 79 E3
North View. Grime S72 35 F6
North Way. C in L S81 148 F7
North Wlk. Hem WF9 17 D8
Northampton Rd. Don DN2 63 C5
Northcliffe Comp Sch. Con 81 B2
Northcote Ave. Shef S2 141 B6
Northcote Rd. Shef S2 141 B6
Northcote Terr. Barn S75 33 C2 4
Northcroft Ave. S Elm WF9 19 A4
Northcroft. S Elm WF9 19 A3
Northern Ave. Shef S2 141 E7
Northern Coll Wentworth Castle.
Hd Gr 53 F3
Northern Comm. Dron S18 152 B2
Northern General. Shef 113 C2
Northfield Ave. Rawm S62 97 F7
Northfield Ave. S Kirk WF9 18 C3
Northfield Ave. Shef S10 128 B5
Northfield Cl. Shef S10 128 C5
Northfield Cty Jun Mix Sch. Dron 153 C3
Northfield Ct. Roth S66 117 B4
Northfield Ct. Woods S81 147 E4
Northfield Gr. S Kirk WF9 18 C3
Northfield La. Roth S66 117 B5
Northfield La. S Kirk WF9 18 C3
Northfield Mid Sch. S Kirk 18 C3
Northfield Rd. Ben DN5 62 A5
Northfield Rd. Roth S60 115 D8
Northfield Rd. Shef S10 128 B5
Northfield St. S Kirk WF9 18 B3
Northgate. Barn S75 33 C3
Northgate. S Hie S72 16 E6
Northgate. Thorne DN8 9 D4
Northlands. Ad l S DN6 40 A6
Northlands. Hart S31 157 E7
Northlands Rd. Shef S5 112 F4
Northlands. Roy S71 15 C4
Northmoor Rd. Crowle DN17 11 F2
Northorpe. Dod S75 54 B6
Northpoint Ind Est. Shef 114 B3
Northside Rd. W up D S63 78 F6
Northumberland Ave. C in L S81 148 E8
Northumberland Ave. Don DN2 63 C4
Northumberland Ave. Hoy S74 76 E7
Northumberland La. Con DN12 80 F3
Northumberland Rd. Shef S10 128 D3
Northumberland Way. Barn S71 56 A8
Norton and Kirk Smeaton Rd.
Norton WF8 3 E4
Norton Ave. Shef S14 141 E2
Norton Church Rd. Shef S8 141 B1
Norton Coll. Shef 153 B7
Norton Common La. Norton DN6 4 E2
Norton Common Rd. Norton DN6 5 A2
Norton Free Sch. Shef 141 C1
Norton Fst Sch. Norton 4 C3
Norton Green Cl. Shef S8 141 C1
Norton Hammer La. Shef S8 140 E4 1
Norton La. Shef S8 153 A7
Norton Lawns. Shef S8 141 C1
Norton Lees Cl. Shef S8 141 A3
Norton Lees Cres. Shef S8 141 A4
Norton Lees La. Shef S8 141 A4
Norton Lees Rd. Shef S8 141 A4
Norton Lees Sq. Shef S8 141 A3
Norton Mid Sch. Norton 4 D3
Norton Mill La. Norton DN6 4 C4
Norton Park Ave. Shef S8 153 B8
Norton Park Cres. Shef S8 153 A8
Norton Park Dr. Shef S8 153 A8
Norton Park Rd. Shef S8 153 B8
Norton Park View. Shef S8 153 B8
Norton Rd. Don DN2 63 B5
Norton Rd. Shef S12 142 A3
Norton Rd. W up D S63 78 D7
Norville Cres. Dar S73 57 B6
Norwich Rd. Don DN2 63 A7
Norwich Row. Shef S2 129 C3 5
Norwith Rd. Don DN4 84 D6
Norwood Ave. Auck DN9 86 A7
Norwood Ave. Maltby S66 118 F6
Norwood Ave. Shef S5 113 B2
Norwood Cl. Maltby S66 118 F6
Norwood Cl. Shef S5 113 B1
Norwood Cres. Kill S31 156 F7
Norwood Cres. Wales S31 145 D2
Norwood Dr. Barn S75 32 E5
Norwood Dr. Ben DN5 41 B3
Norwood Dr. Bri S72 17 A3
Norwood Dr. Shef S5 113 B1
Norwood Grange Dr. Shef S5 113 B2
Norwood High Sch. Shef 151 F6
Norwood Ind Est. Kill 156 E8
Norwood La. Pen S30 50 F6
Norwood Pl. Kill S31 156 F7
Norwood Rd. Con DN12 81 B2
Norwood Rd. Hat DN7 24 F1
Norwood Rd. Shef S5 113 B1
Norwood St. Roth S65 98 D1
Nostell Fold. Dod S75 53 F6
Nostell Pl. Don DN4 84 D6
Notre Dame High Sch. Shef 128 A1
Nottingham Cl. Barn S71 56 A7
Nottingham Cl. Ben DN5 61 D6
Nottingham Cl. S Anst S31 146 D3
Nottingham Cliff. Shef S3 129 B6
Nottingham St. Roth S65 115 E7
Nottingham St. Shef S3 129 B6
Notton La. Notton WF4 15 B6
Novello St. Maltby S66 119 C4
Nowill Ct. Shef S8 141 A6 2
Nowill Pl. Shef S8 141 A6 3
Nunnery Cres. Treet S60 131 C6
Nunnery Dr. Shef S2 129 F3
Nunnery Terr. Shef S2 129 F3
Nunthorne Cl. Hat DN7 44 B7
Nursery Cres. N Anst S31 146 D6
Nursery Dr. Shef S30 113 B8
Nursery Dr. Treet S60 131 C6
Nursery Gdns. Barn S70 55 E7
Nursery Gr. Shef S30 113 B8
Nursery La. Shef S3 129 B5
Nursery La. Sprot DN5 82 A7
Nursery Rd. Aston S31 144 C8
Nursery Rd. Din S31 146 E7
Nursery Rd. N Anst S31 146 E7
Nursery St. Barn S70 54 E8
Nursery St. Shef S3 129 B5
Nutfields Gr. Stai DN7 24 F4
Nuttall Pl. Shef S2 129 D3
Nutwell Cl. Don DN4 84 E6
Nutwell La. Arm DN3 64 C3
Nutwell La. Bran DN3 64 C3
Nutwood Trad Est. Shef 112 B5

Oak Ave. W up D S63 79 A5
Oak Cl. Hoy S74 76 D5
Oak Cl. Kill S31 156 C5
Oak Cl. Mex S64 79 E5
Oak Cl. Roth S66 117 B6
Oak Dale Rd. Don DN4 82 C4
Oak Gr. Arm DN3 64 A8
Oak Gr. Con DN12 81 B1
Oak Grove Gn. Shef S17 151 E4
Oak Haven Ave. G Hou S72 36 E1
Oak Lea Ave. W up D S63 78 C7
Oak Lea. Roth S61 97 B3
Oak Leigh. Caw S75 31 E4
Oak Lodge Rd. Chap S30 94 C7
Oak Pk. Shef S10 128 B2
Oak Rd. Arm DN3 64 A8
Oak Rd. Dearne S63 58 D8
Oak Rd. Maltby S66 118 D5
Oak Rd. Mex S64 79 E5
Oak Rd. Shaf S72 16 D2
Oak Rd. Shef S12 142 A2
Oak Rd. Shef S19 143 F4
Oak Rd. Thorne DN8 9 B1
Oak Rd. W up D S63 79 A5
Oak St. Barn S70 33 D1
Oak St. Grime S72 36 B5
Oak St. S Elm WF9 18 F1
Oak St. Shef S8 141 A7
Oak St. Shef S19 155 C8
Oak Terr. Aston S31 144 B8
Oak Terr. Don DN1 62 C1
Oak Tree Ave. Cud S72 35 B7
Oak Tree Ave. Finn DN9 85 F4
Oak Tree Cl. Kex S75 32 D8
Oak Tree Gr. Hem WF9 17 F6
Oak Tree Rd. Bawtry DN10 122 F7
Oak Tree Rd. Bran DN3 64 E1
Oak Well La. Barn S70 55 A8
Oakbank Cl. Swint S64 98 D8
Oakbank Ct. Shef S17 151 E5
Oakbrook Ct. Shef S11 139 F8
Oakbrook Rd. Shef S11 139 F8
Oakburn Ct. Shef S10 128 D1
Oakcrest. Ross DN4 85 B4
Oakdale. Barn S70 55 B4
Oakdale Cl. Barn S70 55 B4
Oakdale Cl. Don DN3 42 F1
Oakdale Pl. Roth S61 114 F6
Oakdale Rd. N Anst S31 146 F5
Oakdale Rd. Roth S61 114 F6
Oakdale Rd. Shef S7 140 D6
Oakdell. Dron S18 153 D3
Oakdene. Ross DN11 103 F8
Oaken Wood Cl. Roth S61 96 A5
Oaken Wood Rd. Roth S61 95 F5
Oakes Gn. Shef S9 129 F6
Oakes Park Sch. Shef 141 C2
Oakes Park View. Shef S14 141 D1
Oakes St. Shef S9 114 B4
Oakfern Gr. Chap S30 94 D8
Oakfield Ct. Mapp S75 14 A1
Oakfield Jun Sch. Wombw 56 D2
Oakfield Wlk. Barn S75 33 B2
Oakham Dr. Shef S3 128 F6
Oakham Pl. Barn S75 33 C3
Oakhill Rd. Don DN2 63 B6
Oakhill Rd. Dron S18 153 C3
Oakhill Rd. Shef S7 140 D6
Oakholme Mews. Shef S10 128 C1
Oakholme Rd. Shef S10 128 C1
Oakland Ave. Hat DN7 44 A7
Oakland Cl. Woods S81 147 E5
Oakland Ct. Shef S6 128 B8
Oakland Rd. Shef S6 128 B8
Oakland Terr. N Edl DN12 82 B2
Oaklands Ave. Barn S71 34 D4
Oaklands Dr. Don DN4 84 D8
Oaklands Dr. Styr DN11 121 D2
Oaklands Gdns. Don DN4 84 D7
Oaklands Pl. W up D S63 78 E5
Oaklea. Barn S70 55 C4
Oaklea Cl. Mapp S75 14 B2
Oakley Rd. Shef S13 130 E2
Oakmoor Gr. Thorne DN8 9 D4
Oakmoor Rd. Thorne DN8 9 D5
Oaks Ave. Stock S30 73 A1
Oaks Cl. W up D S63 79 A4
Oaks Cres. Barn S70 55 C8
Oaks Farm Cl. Mapp S75 13 F1
Oaks Farm Dr. Mapp S75 13 F1
Oaks Fold Ave. Shef S5 113 E5
Oaks Fold Rd. Shef S5 113 E6
Oaks Fold. Shef S5 113 E6
Oaks La. Barn S71 34 D1
Oaks La. Barn S70 55 C8
Oaks La. Bfield S6 110 C2
Oaks La. Midhop S30 72 C3
Oaks La. Roth S61 96 D2
Oaks La. Shef S5 113 E5
Oaks Sch The. W up D S63 79 A4
Oaks The. Shef S10 128 B2
Oaks Wood Dr. Mapp S75 14 A1
Oakwell Cl. Maltby S66 119 A6
Oakwell Dr. Askern DN6 22 C8
Oakwell Football Gd. Barn 34 A1
Oakwell Terr. Barn S71 34 A1
Oakwood Ave. Roy S71 15 C4
Oakwood Ave. Shef S5 112 F7
Oakwood Cl. Barn S70 55 C4
Oakwood Cres. Ought S30 111 D5
Oakwood Cres. Rawm S62 97 E7
Oakwood Cres. Roy S71 15 B4
Oakwood Dr. Arm DN3 64 A5
Oakwood Dr. Bran DN3 85 D8
Oakwood Dr. Hem WF9 17 E6
Oakwood Dr. Roth S60 116 A4
Oakwood Flats. Shef S5 113 B1
Oakwood Gr. Roth S60 116 A3
Oakwood Hall Dr. Roth S60 115 F2
Oakwood Rd. Don DN4 82 F7
Oakwood Rd E. Roth S60 116 A3
Oakwood Rd. Roy S71 15 B4
Oakwood Rd W. Roth S60 115 F3
Oakwood Sch The. Roth 115 F3
Oakwood Sq. Kex S75 32 B8
Oakworth Cl. Barn S75 33 B3
Oakworth Cl. Shef S19 155 E6 1
Oakworth Dr. Shef S19 155 D6
Oakworth Gr. Shef S19 155 D6
Oakworth View. Shef S19 155 D6
Oates Ave. Rawm S62 98 A5
Oates Cl. Roth S61 115 A7
Oates St. Roth S61 115 A7
Oats Orch. Shef S19 155 D6

Pear Tree La. K Bram DN7 24 A7
Pear Tree Rd. Shef S5 113 D6
Pearce Rd. Shef S9 130 C3
Pearce Wlk. Shef S9 130 C4
Pearl St. Shef S11 140 E8
Pearson Bldg
(Sheffield Hallam Univ). Shef 128 D1
Pearson Cres. Wombw S73 56 B4
Pearson Pl. Shef S8 140 F4
Pearson St. Stock S30 73 B2
Pearson's Cl. Roth S65 116 C4
Pearson's Field. Wombw S73 56 D3
Peartree Ave. Dearne S63 58 C8
Peartree Mews. Wad DN11 83 C2
Pearwood Cres. Don DN4 82 F5
Peashill St. Rawm S62 97 F5
Peastack La. Tick DN11 102 F1
Peat Carr Bank. Finn DN9 87 E7
Peat Pits La. Bfield S30 110 C8
Peatfield Rd. Kill S31 156 F7
Peck Hall La. Bfield S6 110 C4
Peck Mill View. Th Sa S31 146 B1
Peckham Rd. Chap S30 94 F6
Pedley Ave. Shef S19 155 E8 4
Pedley Cl. Shef S19 143 E1 5
Pedley Dr. Shef S19 155 E8
Pedley Gr. Shef S19 143 E1 6
Peel Castle Rd. Thorne DN8 26 C6
Peel Cl. Maltby S66 118 E6
Peel Hill Rd. Thorne DN8 26 C6
Peel Par. Barn S70 33 E1
Peel Pl. Barn S71 34 A3
Peel Sq. Barn S70 33 E1
Peel St Arc. Barn S70 33 E1
Peel St. Barn S70 33 E1
Peel St. Barn S70 54 F7
Peel St. Shef S10 128 C2
Peet Wlk. Hoy S74 76 F7
Pell's Cl. Don DN1 62 C3
Pembrey Ct. Shef S19 144 A2
Pembridge Ct. Roy S71 15 C4
Pembroke Ave. Don DN4 83 B6
Pembroke Cres. Chap S30 94 E6
Pembroke Dr. C in L S81 148 E6
Pembroke Rd. Dron S18 153 A1
Pembroke Rd. Shire S81 159 F7
Pembroke Rise. Ben DN5 61 D6
Pembroke Rise. S Anst S31 146 D4
Pembroke St. Roth S61 114 F6
Pembroke St. Shef S11 128 E1
Pen Nook Cl. Stock S30 92 E7
Pen Nook Ct. Stock S30 92 E7
Pen Nook Dr. Stock S30 92 E7
Pen Nook Gdns. Stock S30 92 E7
Penarth Ave. Upton WF9 19 A7
Penarth Terr. Upton WF9 18 F7
Pendeen Rd. Shef S11 139 F8
Pendennis Ave. S Elm WF9 18 F4
Pendle Croft. Shef S19 144 B1
Pendlebury Gr. Hoy S74 76 C5
Pengeston Rd. Pen S30 51 C2
Penistone Grammar Sch. Pen 51 C5
Penistone La. Holmfi HD8 28 D6
Penistone La. Midhop S30 71 D5
Penistone Rd. Bfield S30 91 E1
Penistone Rd. Chap S30 94 D4
Penistone Rd. D Dale HD8 29 C3
Penistone Rd. Holmfi HD7 28 C6
Penistone Rd. Holmfi HD7 48 D7
Penistone Rd N. Shef S6 112 C2
Penistone Rd. Shef S30, S6 128 E7
Penistone Rd. Shef S30, S6 94 D4
Penistone Rd. Shep HD8 28 C6
Penistone Springvale Prim Sch.
Pen 51 F3
Penistone St. Don DN1 62 D4
Penistone Sta. Pen 51 E3
Penley St. Shef S11 140 F8
Penlington Cl. Hem WF9 17 D5
Pennine Ctr The. Shef 129 A4 20
Pennine Rd. Thorne DN8 26 A6
Pennine View. Mapp S75 14 A2
Pennine View. Stock S30 92 B7
Pennine View. Upton WF9 19 A8
Pennine Way. Barn S75 33 B2
Pennine Way. Hem WF9 17 F7
Penns Rd. Shef S2 141 C6
Penny Engine La. Eck S31 155 E4
Penny Hill. Fir S81 135 E4
Penny Hill La. Ulley S31 133 B4
Penny La. Shef S17 151 C5
Penny Piece La. N Anst S31 146 D6
Penny Piece Pl. N Anst S31 146 D6
Pennyholme Cl. Wales S31 145 F2
Penrhyn Rd. Shef S11 140 C7
Penrhyn Wlk. Barn S71 56 A8
Penrith Cl. Shef S5 112 E2
Penrith Cres. Shef S5 112 E2
Penrith Gr. Barn S71 56 A8
Penrith Rd. Don DN2 63 C4
Penrith Rd. Shef S5 112 E2
Penrose Pl. Shef S13 143 A6
Penthorpe Cl. Shef S12 142 B5
Pentland Dr. C in L S81 148 F7
Pentland Gdns. Shef S19 143 D2
Pentland Rd. Dron S18 152 D1
Penton St. Shef S1 129 A3 1
Penyghent Cl. Chap S30 94 F6
Pepper Cl. Roth S61 96 D2
Pepper St. Hoy S74 76 E8
Percy St. Roth S65 115 E6
Percy St. S Kirk WF9 18 B2
Percy St. Shef S3 128 F5
Peregrin Way. Hart S31 157 E5
Peregrine Dr. Barn S70 75 F8
Perigree Rd. Shef S8 140 E3
Periwood Ave. Shef S8 140 E3
Periwood Cl. Shef S8 140 E3
Periwood Dr. Shef S8 140 E3
Periwood Gr. Shef S8 140 E3
Perkyn Rd. Shef S5 113 D7
Perkyn Terr. Shef S5 113 D7
Perran Gr. Ben DN5 61 F5
Perseverance St. Barn S70 33 D1
Persimmon Cl. Ross DN11 103 F7
Perth Cl. Mex S64 80 C6
Petal Cl. Maltby S66 119 B6
Peter St. Roth S61 114 E7
Peter St. Thurcr S66 133 E7
Peter's Rd. N Edl DN12 82 B1
Peterborough Cl. Shef S10 139 A8
Peterborough Dr. Shef S10 127 A1
Peterborough Rd. Shef S10 127 A1
Petersgate. Ben DN5 61 F8
Petre Dr. Shef S4 129 E8
Petre St. Shef S4 129 D8
Petunia Rd. Don DN3 42 F3
Petworth Croft. Roy S71 15 B4
Petworth Dr. Shef S11 139 F2
Peveril Cl. Wales S31 145 E3
Peveril Cres. Barn S71 34 A7
Peveril Rd. Don DN4 82 E6
Peveril Rd. Eck S31 155 E3
Peveril Rd. Shef S11 140 B8
Pexton Rd. Shef S4 129 C8
Pheasant Bank. Ross DN11 85 A1
Philip Rd. Barn S70 55 D7
Phillimore Rd. Shef S9 130 B6
Phillimore Rd Jun & Inf Sch. Shef 130 B6
Phillips Rd. Shef S6 111 D1
Phoenix Ct. Eck S12 142 E1
Phoenix Gr. Brin S60 115 B1
Phoenix Rd. Eck S12 142 E1
Phoenix Rd. Roth S9 114 E4
Piccadilly. Ben DN5 62 A8
Piccadilly Rd. Swint S64 79 C1
Pickburn La. Brod DN5 39 D3
Pickering Cres. Aston S31 144 C7
Pickering Gr. Thorne DN8 26 B6
Pickering Rd. Ben DN5 41 B3
Pickering Rd. Shef S3 128 F7
Pickering St. Shef S9 130 B8
Pickhill's Ave. Dearne S63 58 F5
Pickmere Rd. Shef S10 128 B4
Pickup Cres. Wombw S73 56 D2
Piece End. Chap S30 94 D8
Piece End Cl. Chap S30 94 D8
Pieces N The. Roth S60 132 B8
Pieces S The. Roth S60 132 B8
Pighills La. Dron S18 153 B4
Pike Lowe Gr. Mapp S75 33 D8
Pike Rd. Brin S60 115 C1
Pilgrim Ct. Shire S81 159 F7
Pilgrim Rise. Aust DN10 105 C1
Pilgrim St. Shef S3 129 B7
Pilley Gn. Pilley S75 75 D5
Pilley Hill. Dod S70 53 F6
Pilley La. Pilley S75 75 D6
Pinch Mill La. Roth S60 116 F1
Pincheon Green La. Syke DN14 8 B7
Pinchfield Ct. Roth S66 117 B3
Pinchfield Holt. Roth S66 117 B3
Pinchfield La. Roth S66 117 B3
Pinchmill Hollow. Roth S66 117 C2
Pindar Oaks Cotts. Barn S70 55 B8
Pindar Oaks St. Barn S70 55 A8
Pinder St. Barn S70 55 B8
Pine Ave. S Anst S31 146 D3
Pine Cl. Barn S70 55 C6
Pine Cl. Hoy S74 76 E5
Pine Cl. Kill S31 156 C5
Pine Cl. Roth S66 117 C6
Pine Croft. Chap S30 95 A4
Pine Gr. Con DN12 100 A8
Pine Hall Rd. B Dun DN3 42 F6
Pine Rd. Don DN4 84 F8
Pine St. S Elm WF9 18 E1
Pine Wlk. Swint S64 98 D8
Pinecroft Way. Chap S30 95 A4
Pinefield Ave. B Dun DN3 43 A6
Pinefield Rd. B Dun DN3 43 A6
Pinehall Dr. Barn S71 34 D4
Pinehurst Rise. Swint S64 79 D2
Pines The. Shef S10 139 A8
Pinewood Ave. Arm DN3 64 B8
Pinewood Ave. Don DN4 82 E5
Pinewood Cl. G Hou S72 36 D3
Pinfield Cl. G Hou S72 36 E2
Pinfold Cl. Barn S71 55 E8
Pinfold Cl. Finn DN9 86 E3
Pinfold Cl. Swint S64 79 C2
Pinfold Cl. Tick DN11 121 A7
Pinfold Cotts. Cud S72 35 C6
Pinfold Cross. K Smea WF8 3 D5
Pinfold Ct. B Dun DN3 42 F6
Pinfold Gdns. Fish DN7 25 A8
Pinfold Hill. Barn S70 55 A6
Pinfold La. Dar S73 57 B6
Pinfold La. Fish DN7 25 A8
Pinfold La. K Smea WF8 3 D5
Pinfold La. Moss DN6 6 B1
Pinfold La. Norton DN6 4 D3
Pinfold La. Roth S60 115 E5
Pinfold La. Roy S71 15 C2
Pinfold La. Shef S3 129 B7
Pinfold La. Styr DN11 121 D1
Pinfold La. Styr DN11 121 E1
Pinfold La. Thorne DN8 26 A8
Pinfold La. Thurgo S75 53 A2
Pinfold La. Tick DN11 120 F7
Pinfold Lands. Mex S64 80 B4
Pinfold Pl. Tick DN11 120 F7
Pinfold St. Eck S31 155 D3
Pinfold St. Shef S1 129 A3
Pinfold The. Bnbur DN5 59 C4
Pinfold. W up D S63 78 E6
Pingle Ave. Shef S7 140 C3
Pingle La. Roth S65 99 C2
Pingle Rd. Kill S31 156 E7
Pingle Rd. Shef S7 140 C3
Pingle Rise. D Dale HD8 30 A7
Pingles Cres. Roth S65 98 F2
Pinner Rd. Shef S11 140 C8
Pinstone St. Shef S1 129 A3
Pipe House La. Rawm S62 97 F7
Piper Cl. Shef S5 113 A3
Piper Cres. Shef S5 113 A3
Piper La. Aston S31 144 F8
Piper Rd. Shef S5 113 B2
Piper Well La. Shep HD8 28 E6
Pipering Lane (E). Ben DN5 61 F8
Pipering Lane (W). Ben DN5 61 E7
Pipeyard La. Eck S31 155 C2
Pipworth Fst Sch. Shef 130 B1
Pipworth Gr. Shef S2 130 C1
Pipworth La. Eck S31 155 F4
Pipworth Mid Sch. Shef 130 B1
Pipworth Rd. Shef S2 130 B1
Pisgah House Rd. Shef S10 128 C3
Pit La. Roth S61 95 F3
Pit La. Shef S12 142 A6
Pit La. Treet S60 131 F4
Pit Row. Hoy S73 77 C6
Pitchford La. Shef S10 127 D1
Pithouse La. Wales S31 144 D1
Pitman Rd. Con DN12 80 E3
Pitsmoor Rd. Shef S3 129 A6
Pitsmoor Rd. Shef S3 129 B8
Pitt Cl. Shef S1 128 F3 6
Pitt La. Shef S1 128 F3
Pitt St. Barn S70 33 E1
Pitt St. Dar S73 56 E5
Pitt St. Eck S31 155 C2
Pitt St. Mex S64 80 C5
Pitt St. Roth S61 114 F6
Pitt St. Shef S1 128 F3
Pitt St W. Barn S70 33 E1 10
Pittam Cl. Arm DN3 64 B6
Plains La. Belton DN8 46 E6
Plane Cl. Don DN4 84 F8
Plane Dr. Roth S66 117 C4
Plane Tree Way. Finn DN9 85 F3
Planet Rd. Ad I S DN6 40 C7
Plank Gate. Stock S30 93 C4
Plank Gate. Wharn S30 93 C4
Plank Gate. Wort S30 74 B2
Plantation Ave. Din S31 134 F1
Plantation Ave. N Anst S31 146 E6
Plantation Ave. Ross DN4 85 B4
Plantation Ave. Roy S71 15 D3
Plantation Cl. Askern DN6 22 C7
Plantation Cl. Maltby S66 118 F6
Plantation Rd. Shef S8 141 A6 8
Plantation Rd. T in B DN5 42 B7
Plantation Rd. Thorne DN8 26 B7
Plantin Rise. Shef S19 155 E7
Plantin The. Shef S19 155 E7
Plaster Pits La. Sprot DN5 61 B4
Platt St. Shef S3 129 A6
Platts Common Ind Est. Hoy 76 D7
Platts Dr. Shef S19 144 A4
Platts La. Bfield S6 109 F1
Platts La. Wharn S30 111 E8
Playford Yd. Hoy S74 76 D8
Pleasant Ave. G Hou S72 36 E2
Pleasant Cl. Shef S12 142 B6
Pleasant Rd. Shef S12 142 B6
Pleasant View. Cud S72 35 C4
Pleasley Rd. Aston S60 132 C6
Pleasley Rd. Roth S60 132 C6
Pleasley Rd. Ulley S31 132 C6
Plimsoll St. Hem WF9 17 D7
Plover Croft. Roth S61 96 A6
Plover Ct. Ross DN11 85 A1
Plover Ct. Shef S2 129 E2
Plover Dr. Barn S70 75 F8
Plover Prim Sch. Don 63 C4
Plowmans Way. Roth S61 96 F3
Plowright Cl. Shef S14 141 D5
Plowright Dr. Shef S14 141 D5
Plowright Mount. Shef S14 141 D5
Plowright Way. Shef S14 141 D5
Plum La. Shef S3 129 A4
Plum St. Shef S3 129 A4
Plumber St. Barn S70 33 D1 4
Plumbley Hall Mews. Shef S19 155 C6
Plumbley Hall Rd. Shef S19 155 C6
Plumbley La. Shef S19 155 B6
Plumbleywood La. Eck S12, S19 154 F6
Plumper's Rd. Shef S9 114 D2
Plumpton Ave. Mex S64 80 C6
Plumpton Gdns. Don DN4 85 A6
Plumpton La. Bfield S6 110 A4
Plumpton Park Rd. Don DN4 85 A6
Plumtree Farm Ind Est. Bir 122 C5
Plumtree Hill Rd. K Bram DN7 24 E6
Plumtree Rd. Bir DN11 122 C5
Plunket Rd. Don DN2 62 F4
Plymouth Rd. Shef S7 140 E5
Poffinder Wood Rd. Stai DN8 25 D5
Pog La. Thurgo S30 74 B7
Pog Well La. Barn S75 32 E3
Pogmoor La. Barn S75 33 A1
Pogmoor Rd. Barn S75 33 B2
Pole Hill. Shef S8 141 A2
Poles Bank. Wroot DN9 67 D3
Polka Ct. Shef S3 129 A6
Pollard Ave. Shef S5 112 E3
Pollard Cres. Shef S5 112 E3
Pollard Rd. Shef S5 112 E3
Pollard St. Roth S61 114 E6
Pollitt St. Barn S75 33 D3
Pollyfox Way. Dod S75 53 F7
Polton Cl. Stai DN7 25 A5
Polton Toft. Stai DN7 25 A5
Pomona St. Shef S11 128 E1
Pond Cl. Shef S6 127 D6
Pond Common La. Oxspr S30 73 B6
Pond Hill. Shef S1 129 B3
Pond Rd. Shef S6 127 D6
Pond St. Barn S70 54 E8
Pond St. Shef S1 129 B3
Ponds Forge International
Sports Ctr. Shef 129 B3
Ponker La. Skel HD8 29 E8
Pontefract Rd. Barn S71 34 D2
Pontefract Rd. Cud S72 16 C1
Pontefract Rd. W up D S73 78 B8
Pontefract Terr. Hem WF9 17 E6
Pool Ave. Askern DN6 22 A8
Pool Dr. Don DN4 85 B5
Pool Hill La. D Dale HD8 30 D6
Pool Sq. Shef S1 129 A3 6
Poole Pl. Shef S9 130 C4
Poole Rd. Shef S9 130 C4
Pools La. Roy S71 15 E3
Pope Ave. Con DN12 81 A2
Pope Pius RC Sec Sch. W up D 78 F4
Poplar Ave. Dearne S63 58 E5
Poplar Ave. Roth S65 98 E2
Poplar Ave. Shaf S72 16 C2
Poplar Ave. Shef S19 143 F5
Poplar Ave. Stock S30 92 B8
Poplar Cl. Bran DN3 64 E1
Poplar Cl. Kill S31 156 C5
Poplar Cl. Mex S64 79 F6
Poplar Cl. Ought S30 111 C7
Poplar Dr. Brin S60 131 B8
Poplar Dr. Don DN2 63 C6
Poplar Dr. W up D S63 79 A4
Poplar Glade. Roth S66 117 B4
Poplar Gr. Askern DN6 22 A8
Poplar Gr. Con DN12 100 B8
Poplar Gr. Don DN4 82 C4
Poplar Gr. Roth S65 117 E8
Poplar Gr. Swint S64 79 D3
Poplar Pl. Arm DN3 64 B6
Poplar Rd. Ad le S DN6 21 B1
Poplar Rd. Eck S31 155 C2
Poplar Rd. Hat DN7 43 F8
Poplar Rd. Ought S30 111 C7
Poplar Rd. Wombw S73 56 E2
Poplar Rise. Maltby S66 118 D6
Poplar St. Grime S72 36 B6
Poplar Terr. Ben DN5 62 B8
Poplar Terr. Roy S71 15 D4
Poplar Terr. S Elm WF9 19 A2
Poplar Terr. Thurgo S30 74 C8
Poplar Way. Finn DN9 86 A5
Poplar Way. Treet S60 131 B5
Poplars Rd. Barn S70 55 B7
Poplars The. Bnbur DN5 59 C3
Popple St. Shef S4 113 D1
Porter Ave. Barn S75 33 C2 1
Porter Brook View. Shef S11 140 D8
Porter Croft C of E Prim Sch. Shef 128 E1
Porter Terr. Barn S75 33 B2 5
Portland Ave. Aston S31 144 E7
Portland Cl. N Anst S31 146 E8
Portland La. Shef S1 128 F3 7
Portland Pl. Don DN1 62 C3 2
Portland Pl. Maltby S66 119 A5
Portland Pl. Upton WF9 19 A7
Portland Rd. Ross DN11 103 F7
Portland Rd. Shef S19 144 A3
Portland St. Barn S70 55 B8
Portland St. Rawcl DN14 2 C7
Portland St. Shef S6 128 E5 3
Portland St. Swint S64 79 D3
Portland Wlk. Shef S6 128 E6 3
Portman Ct. Bawtry DN10 122 F7
Portobello La. Shef S1 128 F3 5
Portobello. Shef S1 128 F3
Portobello St. Shef S1 128 F3
Portsea Rd. Shef S6 128 B8
Pot House La. Stock S30 73 B1
Potter Hill La. Chap S30 94 C7
Potter Hill. Roth S61 97 C3
Potterdyke Ave. Rawm S62 97 F8
Potters Gate. Chap S30 94 C7
Potters Gate. Wh Com HD8 28 E1
Potters Nook. Shire S81 159 F7
Pottery Cl. Rawm S62 97 F5
Pottery Row. Roth S61 115 A6
Potts Cres. G Hou S72 36 E2
Poucher St. Roth S61 114 D6
Poulton St. Barn S71 34 D6
Powder Mill La. Barn S70 55 C3
Powell Dr. Kill S31 156 C6
Powell St. Barn S70 55 B4
Powell St. S Kirk WF9 18 D3
Powell St. Shef S3 128 E4
Power Station Rd. Don DN5 62 B4
Powley Rd. Shef S6 112 D5
Poxton Gr. S Elm WF9 18 E1
Poynton Ave. Ulley S31 132 E3
Poynton Way. Ulley S31 132 E3
Poynton Wood Cres. Shef S17 152 A6
Poynton Wood Glade. Shef S17 152 A6
Prescott Gr. Hat DN7 44 A8
Prescott Rd. Shef S6 112 A2
Preston Ave. Hoy S74 77 A7
Preston St. Shef S8 141 A7
Preston Way. Barn S71 34 D6
Prestwich St. Shef S9 114 B4
Prestwood Gdns. Chap S30 94 E5
Priest Croft La. Dar S73 56 F8
Priestley Ave. Rawm S62 98 B7
Priestley Cl. Don DN4 82 F5
Priestley St. Shef S2 129 B1
Priestly Ave. Kex S75 32 C8
Primrose Ave. Brin S60 131 D7
Primrose Ave. Dar S73 56 F5
Primrose Ave. Shef S5 113 E4
Primrose Circ. Ross DN11 104 A8
Primrose Cl. Dearne S63 58 B3
Primrose Cl. Kill S31 156 E7
Primrose Cres. Shef S19 143 F3
Primrose Dr. Shef S30 113 B8
Primrose Hill. Roth S60 115 D8
Primrose Hill. Shef S6 128 D6
Primrose La. Kill S31 156 E7
Primrose Way. Hoy S74 76 E5
Primulas Cl. S Anst S31 146 C4
Prince Arthur St. Barn S75 33 D2
Prince Edward Fst & Mid Schs.
Shef 142 A7
Prince Of Wales Rd. Shef S2, S9 130 C2
Prince St. Swint S64 79 D4
Prince's Cres. N Edl DN12 82 B3
Prince's Rd. Don DN4 63 B1
Prince's Sq. Don DN3 42 F4
Prince's St. Don DN1 62 D3
Princegate. Don DN1 62 D3
Princes St. Roth S60 115 B6
Princess Ave. S Elm WF9 18 F2
Princess Ave. Stai DN7 24 E4
Princess Cl. Dearne S63 58 B2
Princess Ct. Shef S2 142 B8
Princess Dr. Stock S30 92 C8
Princess Gdns. Wombw S73 56 D2
Princess Gr. Pilley S75 75 C5
Princess Rd. Dearne S63 58 E5
Princess Rd. Dron S18 153 B2
Princess Rd. Mex S64 80 B5
Princess St. Ad I S DN6 40 B4
Princess St. Barn S70 54 E8
Princess St. Cud S72 16 C1
Princess St. Grime S72 36 A6
Princess St. Hoy S74 76 B5
Princess St. Laugh S31 134 C2
Princess St. Mapp S75 14 A1
Princess St. Shef S4 129 D6
Princess St. W up D S63 78 D7
Princess St. Wombw S73 56 C3
Pringle Rd. Brin S60 131 B8
Printing Office St. Don DN1 62 C3
Prior Rd. Con DN12 81 B1
Priory Ave. Shef S7 140 F8
Priory Cl. Barn S70 54 F2
Priory Cl. Con DN12 81 C3
Priory Cl. Shef S30 95 A1
Priory Comp Sch. Barn 34 E3
Priory Cres. Barn S71 34 E3
Priory Ct. Hart S31 157 E5
Priory Estate. S Elm WF9 19 B3
Priory Pl. Barn S71 34 E4
Priory Pl. Don DN1 62 C3
Priory Pl. Shef S7 140 F8
Priory Rd. Barn S71 34 E4
Priory Rd. Dearne S63 58 C2
Priory Rd or Hall La. Norton DN6 4 D4
Priory Rd. Shef S7 140 F8
Priory Rd. Shef S30 95 A1
Priory Terr. Shef S7 140 F8 10
Priory Way. Aston S31 144 E7
Pritchard Cl. Shef S12 143 B3
Probert Ave. Dearne S63 58 D5
Proctor Pl. Shef S6 128 C8
Progress Dr. Roth S66 117 D5
Prospect Cl. Roth S66 117 D4
Prospect Cotts. S Elm WF9 18 E3
Prospect Ct. Shef S17 152 B5 1
Prospect Dr. Shef S17 151 F5
Prospect. Pen S30 51 A3
Prospect Pl. Don DN1 62 D2
Prospect Pl. Shef S17 152 A5
Prospect Rd. Ben DN5 41 A4
Prospect Rd. Cud S72 35 B6
Prospect Rd. Dearne S63 58 C3
Prospect Rd. Dron S18 153 C3
Prospect Rd. Rawcl DN14 2 D8
Prospect Rd. Shef S2 141 A7
Prospect Rd. Shef S17 152 A5
Prospect St. Barn S70 33 D2
Prospect St. Cud S72 35 B7
Prospect St. Norton DN6 4 C3
Prospect Terr. S Kirk WF9 18 B2
Providence Ct. Barn S70 54 F8
Providence Rd. Shef S6 128 B6
Providence St. Dar S73 56 F4
Providence St. Roth S60 115 C6
Providence St. Roth S61 97 C3
Pryor Mede. Hart S31 157 E5
Psalter La. Shef S11 140 C7
Psalters Dr. Oxspr S30 52 B1
Psalters La. Roth S61 114 F6
Psalters La. Roth S61 115 A6
Pudding And Dip La. Hat DN7 44 B8
Pump St. D Dale HD8 29 B3
Purbeck Ct. Shef S19 143 D2
Purbeck Gr. Shef S19 143 D2
Purbeck Rd. Shef S19 143 D2
Purcell Cl. Maltby S66 119 C4
Pye Ave. Cud S72 35 D4
Pye Ave. Mapp S75 33 B8
Pye Bank Cl. Shef S3 129 A6
Pye Bank Dr. Shef S3 129 A6
Pye Bank Fst Sch. Shef 129 A6
Pye Bank Rd. Shef S3 129 A6
Pye Bank Trinity Mid Sch. Shef 129 B6
Pym Rd. Mex S64 80 A5

Quadrant The. Shef S17 151 E5
Quail Rise. Shef S2 129 E2
Quaker Cl. W up D S63 78 D5
Quaker La. Barn S71 55 F8
Quaker La. Barn S71 56 A8
Quaker La. Don DN4 82 D6
Quantock Cl. Thorne DN8 26 A5
Quarry Cl. Brin S60 131 A8
Quarry Cl. Kex S75 32 D8
Quarry Field La. Roth S66 117 B3
Quarry Hill. Eck S31 154 D2
Quarry Hill Rd. W up D S63 78 E4
Quarry Hill. Roth S60 115 D6
Quarry Hill. Shef S19 155 B8
Quarry La. Ad I S DN6 40 A4
Quarry La. Bran DN3 85 D8
Quarry La. N Anst S31 146 D8
Quarry La. Roth S61 115 C8
Quarry La. Shef S11 140 C6
Quarry La. Upton WF9 19 A8
Quarry Pl. Din S31 135 A1
Quarry Rd. Hoy S74 55 D1
Quarry Rd. Kill S31 156 C7
Quarry Rd. Norton DN6 4 F3
Quarry Rd. Shef S13 130 E3
Quarry Rd. Shef S17 151 E5
Quarry Rd. Uns S18S18 154 A1
Quarry St. Barn S71 34 A5
Quarry St. Barn S70 54 F8 4
Quarry St. Cud S72 35 B7
Quarry St. Mex S64 80 B4
Quarry St. Rawm S62 97 F6
Quarry Vale Gr. Shef S12 142 C4
Quarry Vale Rd. Shef S12 142 C4
Quarryfield La. Maltby S66 118 F6
Quay Rd. Thorne DN8 8 F1
Quayside. Thorne DN8 8 E1
Queen Ave. Maltby S66 119 A4
Queen Ave. Ross DN11 84 E1
Queen Elizabeth Ct. Thorne DN8 26 B7
Queen Gdns. Wombw S73 56 D2
Queen Mary Cl. Shef S2 142 A7
Queen Mary Cres. Don DN3 42 F4
Queen Mary Cres. Shef S2 142 A8
Queen Mary Mews. Shef S2 142 A7
Queen Mary Rd. Shef S2 142 B7
Queen Mary St. Maltby S66 119 A3
Queen Mary's Rd. Ross DN11 84 E1
Queen St. Barn S70 33 F1 4
Queen St. Chap S30 95 A5
Queen St Cty Prim Sch. Swint 79 D3
Queen St. Dar S73 57 B6
Queen St. Dearne S63 58 E5
Queen St. Dearne S63 58 F7
Queen St. Din S31 134 F2
Queen St. Don DN4, 83 C8
Queen St. Eck S31 155 E3
Queen St. Pen S30 51 E3
Queen St. Rawm S62 98 A7
Queen St. Roth S65 116 A7
Queen St S. Barn S70 33 F1 5
Queen St. S Elm WF9 18 F2
Queen St. Shef S1 129 A4 16
Queen St. Shef S19 155 C7
Queen St. Swint S64 79 D4
Queen St. Thorne DN8 26 A7
Queen Victoria Rd. Shef S17 151 F5
Queen's Ave. Barn S75 33 D2

Queen's Ave. G Hou S72 57 D7
Queen's Ave. Swint S64 79 D4
Queen's Cres. Bawtry DN10 123 A7
Queen's Cres. N Edl DN12 82 B3
Queen's Cres. Stai DN7 24 E3
Queen's Ct. Ben DN5 62 A6
Queen's Ct. Thorne DN8 26 A7
Queen's Dr. Ben DN5 62 A6
Queen's Dr. Cud S72 16 C1
Queen's Dr. Dod S75 54 A7
Queen's Dr. Shaf S72 16 B3
Queen's Rd. Ad I S DN6 40 C8
Queen's Rd. Askern DN6 22 B8
Queen's Rd. Cud S72 16 C1
Queen's Rd. Don DN1 62 E4
Queen's Rd. Shef S19 143 F4
Queen's Row. Shef S3 128 F4
Queen's Terr. Mex S64 80 A5
Queens Ave. Wales S31 145 C2
Queens Cres. Hoy S74 76 A5
Queens Dr. Barn S75 33 C3
Queens Gdns. Barn S75 33 C3
Queens Gdns. Hoy S74 76 B5
Queens Rd. Aston S31 144 C7
Queens Rd. C in L S81 148 F7
Queens Rd. Grime S72 36 B6
Queens Rd. Shef S2 141 B8
Queens Retail Pk. Shef 141 B8
Queens St. Hoy S74 76 B5
Queensberry Rd. Don DN2 63 C5
Queensgate. Shef S30 112 D8
Queensway. Barn S75 33 C3
Queensway. Barn S70 55 B5
Queensway. Hoy S74 76 F6
Queensway. Roth S60 115 F2
Queensway. Roy S71 15 C4
Quern Way. Dar S73 57 A6
Quest Ave. Hoy S73 77 C7
Quiet La. Shef S10 139 C6
Quilter Rd. Maltby S66 119 C4
Quintec Ct. Roth S61 97 E1
Quoit Gn. Dron S18 153 B1

Raby Rd. Don DN2 62 F5
Raby St. Shef S9 114 E3
Race Common Ave. Pen S30 72 C8
Race La. Stock S30 92 D5
Race St. Barn S70 33 E1
Racecommon La. Barn S70 54 E7
Racecommon Rd. Barn S70 54 D8
Racecourse Rd. Swint S64 79 A3
Racker Way. Shef S6 128 B7
Rackford Rd. N Anst S31 146 F5
Radburn Rd. Ross DN11 103 E7
Radcliffe Mount. Ben DN5 41 A2
Radcliffe Rd. Barn S71 34 A8
Radcliffe Rd. Ben DN5 41 A2
Radford Cl. Roth S65 117 E8
Radford Park Ave. S Kirk WF9 18 B1
Radford St. Shef S3 128 F4
Radiance Rd. Don DN1 62 E5
Radley Ave. Roth S66 117 B5
Radnor Cl. Shef S19 144 A2
Radnor Way. Don DN2 63 C5
Raeburn Cl. Shef S14 141 E2
Raeburn Pl. Shef S14 141 E3
Raeburn Rd. Shef S14 141 E3
Raeburn Way. Shef S14 141 E2
Rag La. Thurgo S30 73 F7
Ragusa Dr. Ross DN11 103 F7
Raikes St. Mex S64 79 E4
Rail Mill Way. Roth S62 97 F2
Rails Rd. Shef S6 127 A3
Railway Ave. Treet S60 131 C5
Railway Cotts. Dod S75 53 E7
Railway Cotts. Dod S75 54 B5
Railway Cotts. Don DN3 42 D3
Railway Cotts. Dun Br S30 48 F2
Railway Cotts. S Elm WF9 19 E7
Railway Cotts. Treet S60 131 C6
Railway Terr. Dearne S63 58 D5
Railway Terr. Roth S60 115 C6
Railway View. Dearne S63 58 E5
Rainborough Mews. W up D S63 78 B7
Rainborough Rd. W up D S63 78 B6
Rainbow Ave. Shef S12 143 C4
Rainbow Cl. Shef S12 143 C4
Rainbow Cres. Shef S12 143 C4
Rainbow Dr. Shef S12 143 C4
Rainbow Forge Inf Sch. Shef 143 B4
Rainbow Forge Jun Sch. Shef 143 B4
Rainbow Gr. Shef S12 143 C4
Rainbow Pl. Shef S12 143 C4
Rainbow Rd. Shef S12 143 C4
Rainbow Way. Shef S12 143 C4
Rainford Dr. Barn S71 34 D6
Rainford Sq. Don DN3 42 F5
Rainsbutt Rd. Crowle DN17 11 F1
Rainton Gr. Barn S75 33 B4
Raintree Rd. Don DN1 62 E2
Raintree Ct. Ben DN5 61 F5
Raisen Hall Pl. Shef S5 113 A2
Raisen Hall Rd. Shef S5 113 A3
Rake Bridge Bank. Hat DN7 44 B3
Rake's La. Wad DN11 83 E2
Rake's La. Wad DN11 84 A3
Rakes La. N Edl DN12 101 C5
Raleigh Ct. Don DN2 63 B3
Raleigh Dr. Chap S30 94 D5
Raleigh Rd. Shef S2 141 B6
Raleigh Terr. Don DN4 82 E6
Raley St. Barn S70 54 D8
Ralph Ellis Dr. Stock S30 92 B8
Ralston Croft. Shef S19 155 E6
Ralston Ct. Shef S19 155 D6
Ralston Gr. Shef S19 155 D6
Ralston Pl. Shef S19 155 D6
Ramper Rd. Let S81 136 A3
Ramper Rd. Thurcr S66 118 B1
Rampton Rd. Shef S7 140 F7 1
Ramsay Cres. Ben DN5 62 A5
Ramsden Ave. Lan S81 136 F3
Ramsden Cres. C in L S81 148 F7
Ramsden La. Holme HD7 47 B7
Ramsden Rd. Don DN4 62 B2
Ramsden Rd. Holme HD7 47 C7
Ramsden Rd. Roth S60 115 E5
Ramsey Rd. Shef S10 128 C4
Ramsker Dr. Arm DN3 64 B5
Ramskir La. Stai DN7 24 F5
Ramskir View. Stai DN7 24 F4
Ramsworth Cl. Ben DN5 61 E5
Ranby Rd. Shef S11 140 B8
Randall Pl. Shef S2 140 F8 4
Randall St. Eck S31 155 B2
Randall St. Shef S2 129 A1
Randerson Dr. Swint S64 79 E1
Rands La. Arm DN3 64 D7
Ranelagh Dr. Shef S11 140 B5
Ranfield Ct. Roth S65 117 E8
Rangeley Rd. Shef S6 128 A5
Ranmoor Cliffe Rd. Shef S10 127 F1
Ranmoor Cres. Shef S10 127 F1
Ranmoor Ct. Shef S11 140 A8
Ranmoor House
(Univ of Sheffield). Shef 128 A2
Ranmoor Park Rd. Shef S10 127 F1
Ranmoor Rd. Shef S10 127 F1
Ranmoor Rise. Shef S10 127 F1
Ranskill Ct. Shef S9 130 C7
Ranworth Rd. Roth S66 117 E5
Ranyard Rd. Don DN4 82 F7
Raseby Ave. Shef S19 143 E2
Raseby Cl. Shef S19 143 E2
Raseby Pl. Shef S19 143 E2
Rasen Cl. Mex S64 80 C6
Ratcliffe Rd. Shef S11 140 D8 7
Ratten Row. Dod S75 53 E6
Ratten Row. Wad DN11 102 C7
Rattigan House. Don DN2 63 A6
Raven Dr. Roth S61 96 A6
Raven La. Ryhill S72 16 A6
Raven Meadows. Swint S64 98 C8
Raven Rd. Shef S7 140 D6
Ravencar Rd. Eck S31 155 B3
Ravencarr Pl. Shef S2 130 A1
Ravencarr Rd. Shef S2 130 A1
Ravenfield Cl. Shef S19 143 A2
Ravenfield Cty Prim Sch. Roth 99 D1
Ravenfield Dr. Barn S71 34 A5
Ravenfield La. H Rob S65 99 C5
Ravenfield Rd. Arm DN3 64 C5
Ravenholt. Barn S70 55 A4
Ravens Cl. Mapp S75 33 B8
Ravens Wlk. Con DN12 81 E2
Ravenscar Cl. Con DN12 80 F3
Ravenscourt. Barn S70 55 B4
Ravenscroft Ave. Shef S13 142 E8
Ravenscroft Cl. Shef S13 142 E8
Ravenscroft Cres. Shef S13 142 E8
Ravenscroft Ct. Shef S13 142 E8
Ravenscroft Dr. Shef S13 142 E7
Ravenscroft Oval. Shef S13 142 E8
Ravenscroft Pl. Shef S13 142 E8
Ravenscroft Rd. Shef S13 142 E7
Ravenscroft Way. Shef S13 142 E8
Ravensdale Rd. Dron S18 152 D1
Ravensfield St. Con DN12 80 F4
Ravenshaw Cl. Barn S75 33 B3
Ravensmead Ct. Dearne S63 58 C1
Ravenswood Dr. Auck DN9 86 A7
Ravensworth Rd. Don DN1 62 E2
Ravine The. Shef S5 113 E7
Raw La. Ston S66 119 E8
Rawcliffe Bridge Cty Prim Sch.
Rawcl 2 D7
Rawlins Ct. Dron S18 153 C4
Rawmarsh Ashwood Jun & Inf Sch.
Rawm 97 F3
Rawmarsh High Sch. Rawm 97 E6
Rawmarsh Hill. Rawm S62 97 F4
Rawmarsh House. Rawm S62 97 F4
Rawmarsh Monkwood Cty Prim Sch.
Rawm 97 E7
Rawmarsh Monkwood Inf Sch.
Rawm 97 E7
Rawmarsh Rd. Roth S60 115 D8
Rawmarsh Rosehill Jun Mix Sch.
Rawm 98 A7
Rawmarsh Sandhill Jun Mix & Inf
Sch. Rawm 98 C6
Rawmarsh Sh Ctr. Rawm 97 F5
Rawmarsh St Mary's C of E
Jun & Inf Sch. Rawm 97 F5
Rawmarsh Thorogate Prim Sch.
Rawm 97 F7
Rawson Cl. Don DN4 63 F1
Rawson Rd. Roth S65 115 E7
Rawson Rd. Tick DN11 120 F6
Rawson Spring Rd. Shef S6 112 D2
Rawson Spring Way. Shef S6 112 D2
Rawson St. Shef S6 128 E7
Rawsons Bank. Shef S30 113 B8
Raybould Rd. Roth S61 96 F1
Rayls Rd. Tod S31 145 F5
Rayls Rise. Tod S31 145 F5
Raymond Ave. Grime S72 36 A6
Raymond Rd. Barn S70 55 D8
Raymond Rd. Ben DN5 61 F6
Raynald Rd. Shef S2 130 A1
Raynor Sike La. Wharn S30 111 A8
Rayton Ct. Bir DN11 122 A4
Reader Cres. Swint S64 79 D3
Reading Gate. G Field DN14 11 F7
Reading Room La. Wort S30 74 D3
Reaper Cres. Chap S30 94 E6
Reasbeck Terr. Barn S71 33 F5
Reasby Ave. Roth S65 117 D8
Rebecca Row. Barn S70 54 F8
Recreation Ave. Thurcr S66 133 F6
Recreation La. Ross DN11 84 E1
Recreation Rd. Ad I S DN6 40 B4
Recreation Rd. W up D S63 78 F7
Rectory Cl. Dearne S63 58 B8
Rectory Cl. Eck S31 155 E4
Rectory Cl. Roy S71 15 D1
Rectory Cl. Stock S30 73 C1
Rectory Cl. Wombw S73 56 D3
Rectory Garth. Hem WF9 17 D7
Rectory Gdns. Don DN1 62 E4
Rectory Gdns. Hart S31 157 E6
Rectory Gdns. Kill S31 156 D6
Rectory Gdns. N Edl DN12 101 A7
Rectory Gdns. Tod S31 145 F5
Rectory La. Dearne S63 58 B8
Rectory La. Finn DN9 86 E3
Rectory Mews. Sprot DN5 82 B8
Rectory Rd. Kill S31 156 D5
Rectory St. Rawm S62 97 F4
Rectory Way. Barn S71 34 D3
Red Fern Gr. Stock S30 92 B8
Red Hill La. Hick DN5 59 C8
Red Hill. Shef S1 128 F3
Red Hill. Wales S31 146 A2
Red House Caravan Pk. Hat 44 F2
Red House La. Ad I S DN6 40 A7
Red House La. Brod DN6 39 D6
Red La. Shef S10 128 C1
Red Quarry La. Gild S81 147 E8
Redbourne Rd. Ben DN5 41 B1
Redbrook Bsns Pk. Barn 33 B5
Redbrook Croft. Shef S19 143 A3 6
Redbrook Ct. Barn S75 33 C4
Redbrook Gr. Shef S19 143 A3 5
Redbrook Rd. Barn S75 33 B3
Redbrook View. Barn S75 33 C4
Redcar Cl. Con DN12 80 E2
Redcar Rd. Shef S10 128 C3
Redcliffe Cl. Barn S75 33 B4
Redfearn St. Barn S71 33 F2 2
Redfern Ave. Shef S19 143 D1
Redfern Ct. Shef S19 143 D1
Redfern Dr. Shef S19 143 D1
Redfern Gr. Shef S19 143 D1
Redgrave Pl. Roth S66 117 B6
Redhall Cl. Don DN3 43 A4
Redhill Ave. Barn S70 55 C8
Redhill Ct. Wad DN11 102 B7
Redland Cres. Thorne DN8 9 C1
Redland Gr. Mapp S75 14 B2
Redland Way. Maltby S66 118 E6
Redmarsh Ave. Rawm S62 97 E7
Redmires La. Shef S10 126 D1
Redmires Rd. Hal M S10 138 B8
Redmires Rd. Shef S10 127 B1
Redrock Rd. Roth S60 116 A2
Redscope Cty Prim Jun Mix Sch.
Roth 96 E1
Redscope Cres. Roth S61 96 D1
Redscope Rd. Roth S61 96 D1
Redthorn Rd. Shef S13 142 F8
Redthorne Way. Shaf S72 16 C3
Redthorpe Crest. Barn S75 33 A4
Redwood Ave. Kill S31 156 C5
Redwood Ave. Roy S71 15 C3
Redwood Cl. Hoy S74 76 D5
Redwood Dr. Maltby S66 118 C5
Redwood Glen. Chap S30 94 F4
Redwood Prim Sch. Maltby 118 C5
Reed Cl. Dar S73 57 A5
Reedham Dr. Roth S66 117 E5
Reedholme La. Thorne DN8 8 E8
Regent Ave. Arm DN3 64 C5
Regent Cres. Barn S71 33 F7
Regent Cres. S Hie S72 16 E5
Regent Ct. Barn S75 33 C4
Regent Ct. Shef S6 128 C8
Regent Gdns. Barn S70 33 E2
Regent Gr. Ben DN5 61 F5
Regent Gr. Ross DN11 104 A7
Regent Sq. Don DN1 62 E3
Regent St. Barn S70 33 F2
Regent St. Don DN4 83 A7
Regent St. Hem WF9 17 C7
Regent St. Hoy S74 76 A5
Regent St. Roth S61 114 F6
Regent St S. Barn S70 33 F2 5
Regent St. S Elm WF9 18 E3
Regent St. S Hie S72 16 E5
Regent St. Shef S1 128 F3
Regent Terr. Shef S3 128 F3
Regents Way. Aston S31 144 E7
Regina Cres. Bri S72 16 E2
Regina Cres. Ryhill WF4 16 C8
Reginald Rd. Barn S70 55 D7
Reginald Rd. Wombw S73 56 F2
Reignhead Prim Sch. Shef 144 A3
Rembrandt Dr. Dron S18 152 E1
Remington Ave. Shef S5 112 F7
Remington Dr. Shef S5 112 F7
Remington Rd. Shef S5 112 F7
Remount Rd. Roth S61 96 E2
Remount Way. Roth S61 96 D2
Remple Ave. Hat DN7 45 A6
Remple Common Rd. Hat DN7 44 F5
Remple La. Hat DN7 45 A6
Renald La. Pen S30 51 E7
Renathorpe Rd. Shef S5 113 D6
Rencliffe Ave. Roth S60 115 F3
Reneville Cl. Roth S60 115 E4
Reneville Cres. Shef S5 113 A8
Reneville Ct. Shef S5 113 A8
Reneville Dr. Shef S5 113 A8
Reneville Rd. Roth S60 115 E4
Reney Ave. Shef S8 152 D6
Reney Cres. Shef S8 152 D6
Reney Dr. Shef S8 152 D6
Reney Rd. Shef S8 152 E7
Reney Wlk. Shef S8 152 D6
Renishaw Ave. Roth S60 116 B2
Renshaw Cl. Chap S30 94 C8
Renshaw Rd. Shef S11 140 A6
Renville Cl. Rawm S62 97 E7
Renway Rd. Roth S60 116 A3
Repton Pl. Dron S18 152 C1
Repton Rd. Ad I S DN6 40 B8
Reresby Cres. Roth S60 116 C2
Reresby Dr. Roth S60 116 C2
Reresby Rd. Roth S60 116 C2
Reresby Rd. Roth S65 99 A2
Reresby Wlk. Con DN12 80 F4
Reservoir Rd. Shef S10 128 C3
Reservoir Rd. Ulley S31 132 D4
Retail World Sh Ctr & Trad Est.
Roth 97 F1
Retford Rd. Aston S13 143 E8
Retford Rd. Shef S13 131 B1
Retford Rd. Shef S13 143 E8
Retford Wlk. Ross DN11 85 B1
Revel Garth. D Dale HD8 30 A5
Revell Cl. Roth S65 116 D7
Revill Cl. Maltby S66 118 F6
Revill La. Shef S13 143 C6
Rex Ave. Shef S7 140 C4
Reynard La. Shef S6 127 B5
Reynolds Cl. Roth S66 117 B6
Rhodes Ave. Roth S61 96 E2
Rhodes Dr. Roth S60 116 C2
Rhodes St. Shef S2 129 C3
Rhodes Terr. Barn S70 55 A8 7
Rhodesia Ct. Don DN4 84 D8
Ribble Croft. Chap S30 95 A6
Ribble Way. Shef S5 113 C3
Ribblesdale Dr. Shef S12 142 F1
Riber Ave. Barn S71 34 A7
Riber Cl. Shef S6 127 D6
Ribston Cl. Shef S9 130 B4
Ribston Rd. Shef S9 130 B4
Rich Farm Cl. Ben DN5 41 D3
Richard Ave. Barn S71 34 A6
Richard La. Ross DN11 84 E1
Richard Newman Inf Sch. Barn 33 F7
Richard Rd. Barn S71 34 A6
Richard Rd. Kex S75 32 E8
Richard Rd. Roth S60 115 E5
Richard St. Barn S70 33 D1 5
Richards Rd. Shef S2 141 B6
Richards Way. Rawm S62 98 A6
Richardson Wlk. Wombw S73 56 B4
Richmond Ave. Kex S75 32 D7
Richmond Ave. Shef S13 142 F8
Richmond Coll of F Ed. Shef 142 D8
Richmond Dr. Askern DN6 22 C8
Richmond Gr. Shef S13 142 E8
Richmond Hall Ave. Shef S13 142 D8
Richmond Hall Cres. Shef S13 142 D7
Richmond Hall Dr. Shef S13 142 D8
Richmond Hall Rd. Shef S13 142 D8
Richmond Hall Way. Shef S13 142 D7
Richmond Hill Fst Sch. Ben DN5 61 E3
Richmond Hill Mid Sch. Ben 61 E2
Richmond Hill Rd. Ben DN5 61 E2
Richmond Hill Rd. Shef S13 142 D7
Richmond La. Bawtry DN10 122 F6
Richmond Park Ave. Roth S61 114 D6
Richmond Park Ave. Shef S13 130 E2
Richmond Park Cl. Shef S13 130 E1
Richmond Park Cres. Shef S13 130 E2
Richmond Park Croft. Shef S13 130 E1
Richmond Park Dr. Shef S13 130 E1
Richmond Park Gr. Shef S13 130 E1
Richmond Park Rd. Shef S13 130 E1
Richmond Park Rise. Shef S9 130 D2
Richmond Park View. Shef S13 130 E1
Richmond Park Way. Shef S13 130 E1
Richmond Pl. Shef S13 142 D7
Richmond Rd. Ben DN5 61 D7
Richmond Rd. C in L S81 148 F6
Richmond Rd. Dearne S63 58 C8
Richmond Rd. Roth S61 114 E6
Richmond Rd. Shef S13 142 D7
Richmond Rd. Thorne DN8 9 D4
Richmond Rd. Upton WF9 19 A7
Richmond St. Barn S70 33 D1 1
Richmond St. Shef S3 129 B6
Richworth Rd. Shef S13 142 F8
Ricknald Cl. Aston S31 132 D1
Ridal Ave. Stock S30 73 A2
Ridal Cl. Stock S30 73 A2
Ridal Croft. Stock S30 73 A2
Riddell Ave. Lan S81 136 E3
Riddings Cl. Hem WF9 17 D5
Riddings Cl. Shef S2 142 A7
Riddings Cl. Thurcr S66 133 F6
Riddings La. Aust DN10 105 A4
Rider Rd. Shef S6 128 C8
Ridge Balk La. Ad le S DN6 39 F5
Ridge Cl. Roth S65 115 E7
Ridge Ct. Shef S10 127 C2
Ridge Rd. Ad I S DN6 40 B2
Ridge Rd. Eck S31 154 E2
Ridge Rd. Roth S65 115 F7
Ridge The. Shef S10 127 C1
Ridge View Cl. Shef S9 114 A3
Ridge View Dr. Shef S9 114 A3
Ridgehill Ave. Shef S12 142 B5
Ridgehill Gr. Shef S12 142 B5
Ridgestone Ave. Hem WF9 17 E7
Ridgewalk Way. Barn S70 54 F6
Ridgeway Cl. Maltby S66 118 A4
Ridgeway Cl. Roth S65 116 D7
Ridgeway Cty Prim Sch. Eck 154 E8
Ridgeway Cres. Roy S71 15 C1
Ridgeway Cres. Shef S12 142 A6
Ridgeway Dr. Shef S12 142 A6
Ridgeway. Dron S18 153 D3
Ridgeway Moor. Eck S12 154 E6
Ridgeway Rd. Brin S60 131 C8
Ridgeway Rd. Shef S12 142 A5
Ridgeway. Roth S65 116 D7
Ridgewood Ave. Don DN3 42 F1
Ridgill Ave. Ad I S DN6 21 A1
Ridgway Ave. Dar S73 57 A6
Riding Cl. Don DN4 85 B6
Riding Cl. Roth S66 117 A5
Ridings Ave. Barn S71 34 B5
Ridings The. Barn S71 34 C5
Rig Cl. Roth S61 96 F1
Rig Dr. Swint S64 79 A3
Riggs High Rd. Shef S6 126 F5
Riggs Low Rd. Shef S6 127 A5
Riley Ave. Don DN4 82 F6
Rimington Rd. Wombw S73 56 D3
Rimini Rise. Dar S73 56 E5
Ringinglow Rd. Shef S11 139 D5
Ringstead Ave. Shef S10 127 E3
Ringstead Cres. Shef S10 127 F3
Ringstone Gr. Bri S72 17 B3
Ringway. Dearne S63 58 B3
Ringwood Cres. Shef S19 144 A2
Ringwood Dr. Shef S19 144 A2
Ringwood Gr. Shef S19 144 A2
Ringwood Rd. Shef S19 144 A2 3
Ringwood Way. Hem WF9 17 F7
Ripley Gr. Barn S75 33 B4
Ripley St. Shef S6 128 C7
Ripon Ave. Don DN2 62 F6
Ripon St. Shef S9 129 F5
Ripon Way. Aston S31 144 C7
Rippon Cres. Shef S6 128 B8
Rippon Ct. Rawm S62 97 F7
Rippon Rd. Shef S6 128 B8
Rise The. N Anst S31 146 E5
Rise The. Swint S64 79 B2
Risedale Rd. Dearne S63 58 F4
Rising St. Shef S3 129 B6
Rivelin Bank. Shef S6 128 B7
Rivelin Fst Sch. Shef 128 C7
Rivelin Glen Cotts. Shef S6 127 E4
Rivelin Park Cres. Shef S6 128 A6
Rivelin Park Dr. Shef S6 127 F6
Rivelin Park Rd. Shef S6 128 A6
Rivelin Rd. Shef S6 128 A6
Rivelin St. Shef S6 128 B6
Rivelin Terr. Shef S6 128 A6
Rivelin Valley Rd. Shef S6 127 C4
River Cotts. Rawcl DN14 2 E7
River Ct. Dron S17 152 A7
River La. Fish DN7 25 B7
River Terr. Shef S6 128 C8
River Valley View. D Dale HD8 30 A6
River View Rd. Ought S30 111 E7
River Way. Auck DN9 85 F7
Riverdale Ave. Shef S10 140 A8
Riverdale Dr. Shef S10 128 A1
Riverdale Rd. Ben DN5 61 E8
Riverdale Rd. Shef S10 140 A8
Riverside Cl. Dar S73 57 C6
Riverside Cl. Shef S6 127 F8
Riverside Dr. Sprot DN5 82 C8
Riverside Gdns. Dearne S63 58 D1
Riverside Mews. Shef S6 128 C8 3
Riverside Park. Shef 129 C2
Riverside. Sprot DN5 61 B1
Riverside Way. Roth S60 115 C5
Riviera Mount. Ben DN5 62 B5
Riviera Par. Ben DN5 62 B5
Rix Rd. Swint S62 98 D8
Roach Rd. Shef S11 140 C7
Roache Dr. Dearne S63 58 C4
Rob Roy La. Barn S70 54 D6
Rob Royd. Dod S75 53 F6
Robert Ave. Barn S71 34 D2
Robert Rd. Shef S8 153 A7
Robert St. Barn S70 55 A4 3
Robert St. Roth S60 115 B6
Roberts Ave. Con DN12 81 D1
Roberts Rd. Don DN4 62 B1
Roberts Rd. N Edl DN12 82 C1
Roberts St. Cud S72 35 B7
Robertshaw Cres. Stock S30 73 D1
Robertson Dr. Shef S6 128 A6
Robertson Rd. Shef S6 128 B6
Robertson Sq. Stai DN7 24 E4
Robey St. Shef S4 113 E1
Robin Hood Ave. Roy S71 15 D4
Robin Hood Chase. Shef S6 127 C7
Robin Hood Cres. Don DN3 43 A1
Robin Hood Rd. Don DN3 43 A1
Robin Hood Rd. Shef S9 114 A4
Robin La. Hem WF9 17 A5
Robin La. Roy S71 15 D4
Robin La. Shef S19 143 F4
Robin Pl. Aston S31 144 E6
Robinets Rd. Roth S61 97 A3
Robins Cl. Aston S31 144 E7
Robinson Rd. Shef S2 129 C2 3
Robinson St. Roth S60 115 D4
Robinson Way. Kill S31 156 C6
Roche Cl. Barn S71 34 B3
Roche End. Tod S31 145 E5
Roche. Shef S19 155 E8 9
Rocher Ave. Shef S30 112 E7
Rocher Cl. Shef S30 112 E7
Rocher Gr. Shef S30 112 E7
Rocher La. Wharn S30 92 C4
Rochester Cl. Shef S10 127 A1
Rochester Dr. Shef S10 127 A1
Rochester Rd. Barn S71 34 B4
Rochester Rd. S Anst S31 146 D3
Rochester Rd. Shef S10 127 A1
Rochester Row. Ben DN5 61 D5
Rock Mount. Hoy S74 76 F6
Rock Mount Rd. Shef S9 114 B4
Rock Pl. Stock S30 73 D1
Rock Side Rd. Pen S30 51 A3
Rock St. Barn S70 33 E2
Rock St. Shef S3 129 B6
Rockcliffe Dr. Wad DN11 102 B7
Rockcliffe Rd. Rawm S62 97 F5
Rockfield Dr. Woods S81 147 E3
Rockingham Cl. Barn S70 75 F6
Rockingham Cl. Dron S18 152 C1 3
Rockingham Cl. Shef S1 129 A2
Rockingham Coll Annexe. W up D 78 C8
Rockingham Coll. W up D 78 E6
Rockingham Gate. Shef S1 129 A2 4
Rockingham House. Don DN1 62 C1 4
Rockingham House. Rawm S62 98 A6
Rockingham Inst of F Ed. Rawm 97 F4
Rockingham Jun & Inf Sch. Roth 96 F3
Rockingham La. Shef S1 129 A3
Rockingham Rd. Dod S75 54 A5
Rockingham Rd. Don DN2 62 E5
Rockingham Rd. Rawm S62 98 A6
Rockingham Rd. Swint S64 79 B3
Rockingham Row. Barn S70 75 F6
Rockingham. Shef S19 155 E8 11
Rockingham St. Barn S71 33 E4
Rockingham St. Barn S70 75 F6
Rockingham St. Grime S72 36 A7
Rockingham St. Hoy S74 76 B6
Rockingham St. Shef S1 128 F3
Rockingham Way. Roth S61 96 F3
Rockingham Way. Shef S1 129 A2
Rockland Villas. Roth S65 98 E2
Rocklea Cl. Swint S64 79 C2
Rockley Ave. Barn S70 75 F8
Rockley Ave. Hoy S71 56 B1
Rockley Cres. Barn S70 75 E7
Rockley La. Askern DN5 22 B3
Rockley La. Barn S70, S75 75 D8
Rockley La. Hd Gr S75 54 C2
Rockley Mount Sch. Barn 54 C7
Rockley Nook. Don DN2 63 B7
Rockley Old Hall. Barn S70 54 E2
Rockley Rd. Shef S6 112 B2
Rockley View. Pilley S75 75 D6
Rockleys. Dod S75 54 A6
Rockwood Cl. Chap S30 94 E5
Rockwood Cl. Mapp S75 13 F1
Rockwood Rise. D Dale HD8 30 A7
Rod Moor Rd. Dron S18 152 B4
Rod Side. Hal M S6 126 B5
Roden Way. Rawm S62 97 C8
Rodes Ave. G Hou S72 36 E1
Rodger Rd. Shef S13 143 D6
Rodger St. Roth S61 115 C7
Rodman Dr. Shef S13 143 D8
Rodman St. Shef S13 143 E8

Rodney Hill. Shef S6 111 E1
Roe Croft Cl. Sprot DN5 61 B2
Roe La. Shef S3 129 B8
Roe Wood Mid Sch. Shef 129 B8
Roebuck Hill. Hoy S74 76 F8
Roebuck Rd. Shef S6 128 D4
Roebuck St. Wombw S73 56 E1
Roeburn Cl. Mapp S75 14 A2
Roehampton Rise. Barn S71 56 A7
Roehampton Rise. Ben DN5 61 E5
Roehampton Rise. Brin S60 115 A1
Roewood Ct. Shef S3 129 B8
Roger Rd. Barn S71 34 E2
Rojean Rd. Shef S30 112 D8
Rokeby Dr. Shef S5 113 B6
Rokeby Rd. Shef S5 113 A6
Rolleston Ave. Maltby S66 118 E5
Rolleston Rd. Ad I S DN6 40 B8
Rolleston Rd. Shef S5 113 D4
Rollet Cl. Shef S2 142 A8
Rollin Dr. Shef S6 112 B1
Rolling Dales Cl. Maltby S66 118 E6
Rolls Cres. Rawm S62 97 C8
Roman Cres. Brin S60 115 C2
Roman Cres. Rawm S62 97 E6
Roman Ct. Roth S61 114 E6
Roman Rd. Don DN4 62 E2
Roman Rd. Kex S75 32 D8
Roman Ridge. Ad I S DN5 40 A4
Roman Ridge Rd. Shef S9 114 B3
Roman St. Dearne S63 37 E1
Romandale Gdns. Shef S2 130 C1
Romney Cl. Roth S66 117 B6
Romney Dr. Dron S18 152 E1
Romney Gdns. Shef S2 141 B6
Romsdal Rd. Shef S10 128 C4
Romwood Ave. Swint S64 79 A3
Ronald Rd. Don DN4 83 A7
Ronald Rd. Shef S9 130 C4
Ronksley Cres. Shef S5 113 D6
Ronksley La. Hal M S6 126 C3
Ronksley Rd. Shef S5 113 D6
Rook Hill. Barn S70 55 C5
Rookdale Cl. Barn S75 33 B4
Rookery Cl. Wales S31 145 C3
Rookery Rd. Swint S64 79 B3
Rookery Way. Thurgo S30 74 A6
Rope Wlk. Thorne DN8 26 A7
Roper Hill. Shef S10 138 D7
Roper La. Thurgo S30 73 F7
Rosa Rd. Shef S10 128 C4
Rosamond Ave. Shef S17 152 A6
Rosamond Cl. Shef S17 152 A6
Rosamond Dr. Shef S17 152 A6
Rosamond Glade. Shef S17 152 A6
Rosamond Pl. Shef S17 152 A6
Roscoe Bank Jun & Inf Sch. Shef 127 E5
Roscoe Bank. Shef S6 127 E5
Roscoe Dr. Shef S6 127 F5
Roscoe Mount. Shef S6 127 F5
Roscoe Rd. Shef S3 128 F5
Rose Ave. Dar S73 57 A7
Rose Ave. Don DN4 83 B8
Rose Ave. Shef S19 143 F3
Rose Ave. Upton WF9 19 A7
Rose Cl. Brin S60 131 D7
Rose Cl. Upton WF9 19 A7
Rose Cres. Ben DN5 61 E7
Rose Cres. Rawm S62 98 B6
Rose Ct. Don DN4 83 A8
Rose Ct. Roth S66 117 A4
Rose Dr. Roth S66 117 C5
Rose Garth Ave. Aston S31 144 E8
Rose Gr. Arm DN3 64 A6
Rose Gr. Upton WF9 19 A7
Rose Gr. Wombw S73 56 C4
Rose Hill Cl. Pen S30 51 D2
Rose Hill Ct. Don DN4 63 C2
Rose Hill. Don DN4 63 D1
Rose Hill Dr. Dod S75 53 F7
Rose Hill Rise. Don DN4 63 C2
Rose La. Laugh S31 134 C6
Rose Pl. Wombw S73 56 C4
Rose Tree Ave. Cud S72 35 B7
Rose Tree Ct. Cud S72 35 B7
Rose Way. Kill S31 156 D5
Roseberry Ave. Hat DN7 44 B7
Roseberry Cl. Hoy S74 76 E4
Rosebery St. Barn S70 55 D8
Rosebery St. Roth S61 115 A6
Rosebery Terr. Barn S70 55 A8 2
Rosedale Ave. Rawm S62 97 F6
Rosedale Cl. Aston S31 144 E8
Rosedale Cl. Upton WF9 19 B7
Rosedale Gdns. Barn S70 33 C1
Rosedale Gdns. Shef S11 140 D8
Rosedale Rd. Aston S31 144 E8
Rosedale Rd. Ben DN5 41 A2
Rosedale Rd. Ben DN5 61 D7
Rosedale Rd. Shef S11 140 D8
Rosedale Way. Roth S66 117 C6
Rosegarth Cl. Ben DN5 61 E7
Rosehill Ave. Hem WF9 17 C6
Rosehill Ave. Rawm S62 98 A7
Rosehill Ct. Barn S70 33 E2
Rosehill. Rawcl DN14 2 C7
Rosehill Rd. Rawm S62 97 F6
Rosehill Terr. Rawcl DN14 2 D7
Roselle St. Shef S6 128 C8
Rosemary Ct. Shef S6 128 C5
Rosemary Gr. Cade DN5 81 D5
Rosemary Rd. Roth S66 117 A5
Rosemary Rd. Shef S19 143 F4
Rosewood Dr. B Dun DN3 42 E8
Roslin Rd. Shef S10 128 C3
Roslyn Cres. Hath S30 149 A7
Roslyn Rd. Hath S30 149 A7
Ross St. Shef S9 130 D4
Rosser Ave. Shef S12 141 F2
Rossetti Mount. Roth S66 117 B6
Rossington Comp Sch & Don Valley Inst for F Ed. Ross 104 A7
Rossington Grange Lane Fst Sch. Ross 103 D8
Rossington Hall Sch. Ross 104 D6
Rossington Holmescarr Mid Sch. Ross 84 E1
Rossington House. Don DN1 62 C1 5
Rossington Pheasant Bank Mid Sch. Ross 84 E1
Rossington Rd. Shef S11 140 C8
Rossington St. Con DN12 80 F4
Rossington Tornedale Fst Sch. Ross 84 F1
Rossiter Rd. Roth S61 97 C4
Rosslyn Ave. Aston S31 144 E8
Rosslyn Cres. Ben DN5 41 B2
Rossmoor Cl. Auck DN9 86 A7
Rosston Rd. Maltby S66 119 B5
Rostholme Sq. Ben DN5 41 B2
Roston Cl. Dron S18 152 D1 3
Rothay Cl. Dron S18 152 E1
Rothay Rd. Shef S4 113 F1
Rothbury Cl. Shef S19 144 A2
Rothbury Ct. Shef S19 144 A2 5
Rothbury Way. Brin S60 115 C1
Rother Cres. Treet S60 131 E4
Rother Rd. Roth S60 115 D3
Rother St. W up D S73 78 B8
Rother Terr. Roth S60 115 D3
Rother Valley Ctry Pk. Wales 144 D2
Rother Valley Way. Shef S19 156 B8
Rother View Rd. Roth S60 115 D4
Rother Way. Maltby S66 118 A6
Rotherham Baulk. C in L S81 148 C7
Rotherham Baulk. Gild S81 148 C7
Rotherham Central Sta. Roth 115 D7
Rotherham Cl. Kill S31 156 F8
Rotherham Coll of Arts and Technology. Roth 115 E7
Rotherham District Gen Hospl. Roth 115 F2
Rotherham La. Lough S31 134 C5
Rotherham Rd. Aston S19 144 A5
Rotherham Rd. Aston S31 144 C7
Rotherham Rd. Barl S31 157 C3
Rotherham Rd. Barn S71, S72 34 B4
Rotherham Rd. Eck S19, S31 155 F6
Rotherham Rd. G Hou S72 57 E7
Rotherham Rd. Kill S31 156 F8
Rotherham Rd. Laugh S31 134 C2
Rotherham Rd. Maltby S66 118 D4
Rotherham Rd N. Shef S19 155 F8
Rotherham Rd. Roth S62 97 E2
Rotherham Rd. Shef S13 131 B1
Rotherham Rd. Shef S19 144 A5
Rotherham Rd. Shef S19, S31 155 F6
Rotherham Rd. Tick DN11 120 E6
Rotherham Rd. Treet S60 131 D6
Rotherham Rd. W up D S63 78 B6
Rotherham St. Shef S9 130 A7
Rotherhill Cl. Roth S65 116 A7
Rothermoor Ave. Wales S31 145 C2
Rotherside Rd. Eck S31 155 F4
Rotherstoke Cl. Roth S60 115 E4
Rothervale Cl. Shef S19 144 A4
Rotherway. Roth S60 131 E8
Rotherwood Ave. Shef S13 143 D8
Rotherwood Cl. Ben DN5 61 D6
Rotherwood Cres. Thurcr S66 133 E6
Rotherwood Rd. Kill S31 156 E7
Rothesay Cl. Ben DN5 61 F5
Rotunda Bsns Ctr. Chap 95 A7
Rough La. Shef S30 94 B1
Rough La. Wort S30 74 D1
Roughbirchworth La. Oxspr S30 52 C1
Roughwood Cty Prim Sch. Roth 96 E2
Roughwood Gn. Roth S61 97 A3
Roughwood Rd. Roth S61 96 E2
Roughwood Way. Roth S61 96 E2
Round Close Rd. Holme HD7 48 B6
Round Green La. Hd Gr S75 54 C3
Roundel St. Shef S9 129 F5
Roundwood Ct. Barn S70 55 A4 2
Roundwood Gr. Rawm S62 98 B5
Roundwood Way. Dar S73 56 F6
Row Gate. Shep HD8 28 D6
Row The. Bran DN3 64 B1
Rowan Cl. Barn S70 54 F7
Rowan Cl. Chap S30 95 A4
Rowan Cl. Finn DN9 86 A4
Rowan Cl. Thorne DN8 9 C3
Rowan Ct. Don DN2 63 C6
Rowan Dr. Barn S75 33 B3
Rowan Dr. Roth S66 117 C5
Rowan Garth. Ben DN5 62 A6
Rowan Mount. Don DN2 63 B6
Rowan Rd. Eck S31 155 C1
Rowan Rise. Maltby S66 118 D5
Rowan Sch The. Shef 151 E6
Rowan Tree Cl. Kill S31 156 C5
Rowan Tree Dell. Shef S17 151 E3
Rowan Tree Rd. Kill S31 156 C5
Rowborn Dr. Shef S30 111 F4
Rowdale Cres. Shef S12 142 D5
Rowe Cl. S Elm WF9 19 A4
Rowel La. Shef S6 127 C8
Rowena Ave. Don DN3 42 F1
Rowena Cty Inf Sch. Con 81 B2
Rowena Dr. Ben DN5 61 D6
Rowena Dr. Thurcr S66 133 E7
Rowena Rd. Con DN12 81 B2
Rowgate. D Dale HD8 29 B6
Rowland Pl. Don DN1 62 C2 10
Rowland Rd. Barn S75 33 C3
Rowland Rd. Shef S2 141 A8 3
Rowland St. Roy S71 15 D4
Rowland St. Shef S3 129 A5
Rowlands Ave. Upton WF9 19 A7
Rowley La. S Elm WF9 19 A2
Rowlinson Sch. Shef 153 A7
Rowms La. Swint S64 79 E3
Rowsley St. Shef S2 129 B1
Roxby Cl. Don DN4 84 D6
Roxton Ave. Shef S8 152 F8 2
Roxton Rd. Shef S8 140 E1
Roy Kilner Rd. Wombw S73 56 B4
Roy Kilner Rd. Wombw S73 56 C4
Royal Ave. Don DN1 62 E4
Royal Hallamshire Hospl. Shef 128 D2
Royal Hospl Annexe. Shef 139 D7
Royal St. Barn S70 33 E2
Royale Cl. Eck S31 155 E3
Royd Ave. Cud S72 35 B6
Royd Ave. Mapp S75 14 B1
Royd Ave. Pen S30 50 D3
Royd Cl. Barn S70 54 F4
Royd Field La. Pen S30 72 D8
Royd Inf Sch. Stock 92 E8
Royd La. Barn S75 32 D3
Royd La. Caw S75 32 C3
Royd La. Pen S30 50 D4
Royd La. Stock S30 92 D7
Royd Moor La. Hem WF9 18 B8
Royd Moor Rd. Pen S30 50 E5
Royd The. Stock S30 92 D7
Roydfield Cl. Shef S19 143 D2
Roydfield Dr. Shef S19 143 D2
Roydfield Gr. Shef S19 143 D2
Royds Ave. Roth S60 116 C2
Royds Close Cres. Roth S65 98 E2
Royds La. Hoy S74 77 C5
Royds La. Shef S4 129 E6
Royds Moor Hill. Roth S60 116 F1
Royds Pk. D Dale HD8 30 A6
Royds The. Clay W HD8 12 A3
Royles Cl. S Kirk WF9 18 C2
Royston Ave. Ben DN5 62 A7
Royston Ave. Shef S19 143 A2
Royston C of E School. Roy 15 C3
Royston Cl. Shef S19 143 A2 5
Royston Comp Sch. Roy 15 C4
Royston Croft. Shef S19 143 A2 11
Royston Gr. Shef S19 143 A2 4
Royston Hill. Hoy S74 76 D6
Royston Inf School. Roy 15 C3
Royston La. Roy S71 15 C2
Royston Medstead Jun & Inf Sch. Roy 15 B3
Royston Rd. Cud S72 16 B1
Royston Summer Fields Jun & Inf Sch. Roy 15 A4
Rubens Cl. Dron S18 152 F1
Rubens Row. Shef S2 129 C4
Rud Broom Cl. Pen S30 51 C2
Rud Broom La. Pen S30 51 C3
Ruddle La. Clift S66 100 E4
Ruddle Mill La. Ston S66 101 C1
Rudgate La. Syke DN14 8 C6
Rudyard Rd. Shef S6 128 C8
Rufford Ave. Barn S71 34 A8
Rufford Ct. Shef S19 144 A2
Rufford Pl. Roth S65 116 B8 3
Rufford Rd. Don DN4 62 F1
Rufford Rise. Dearne S63 58 C4
Rufford Rise. Shef S19 144 A2
Rufus La. Ross DN11 84 E1
Rugby St. Shef S3 129 A6
Rugged Butts La. Misson DN10 105 F5
Rundle Dr. Shef S7 140 E7
Rundle Rd. Shef S7 140 E7
Rundle Rd. Stock S30 73 B1
Runnymede Rd. Don DN2 63 B4
Rupert Rd. Shef S7 140 E6
Rural Cres. Bran DN3 85 D8
Rural La. Shef S6 111 F2
Rushby St. Shef S4 113 D1
Rushdale Ave. Shef S8 141 B5
Rushdale Mount. Shef S8 141 A5 4
Rushdale Rd. Shef S8 141 B5
Rushdale Terr. Shef S8 141 A5 3
Rushey Cl. Rawm S62 97 E8
Rushleigh Ct. Shef S17 151 D7
Rushley Ave. Shef S17 151 D8
Rushley Cl. Auck DN9 86 A6
Rushley Cl. Shef S17 151 D8
Rushley Dr. Shef S17 151 D7
Rushley Rd. Shef S17 151 D7
Rushworth Cl. Kex S75 32 C8
Rushy La. Bfield S30 91 F4
Rushy Moor Ave. Askern DN6 22 B7
Rushy Moor La. Askern DN6 22 B7
Rushy Moor Rd. Askern DN5 22 D6
Ruskin Ave. Mex S64 80 A6
Ruskin Cl. W up D S63 78 C7
Ruskin Dr. Arm DN3 64 C6
Ruskin Rd. Don DN4 83 A6
Ruskin Sq. Shef S8 141 A6
Russell Ave. Har DN11 121 F4
Russell Cl. Barn S71 34 B5
Russell Cl. Shef S11 140 A2
Russell Pl. Maltby S66 119 A6
Russell Rd. Swint S62 98 E7
Russell St. Roth S65 115 E8
Russell St. Shef S3 129 A5
Russet Gr. Bawtry DN10 123 A7
Rustlings Ct. Shef S11 139 F8
Rustlings Rd. Shef S11 140 B8
Ruth Sq. Shef S10 128 E2
Ruthin St. Shef S4 129 E8
Ruthven Dr. Don DN4 82 D7
Rutland Ave. N Anst S31 146 D7
Rutland Cres. Har DN11 121 F5
Rutland Dr. Har DN11 121 F5
Rutland La. Ross DN11 84 D1
Rutland Pk. Shef S10 128 C2
Rutland Pl. Wombw S73 56 B2
Rutland Rd. Shef S3 129 A6
Rutland St. Don DN1 62 E4
Rutland St. Shef S3 129 A6
Rutland Way. Barn S75 33 C3
Rutland Way. Shef S3 128 F5
Ryan Pl. Rawm S62 97 F4
Rydal Cl. Dearne S63 58 C1
Rydal Cl. Din S31 146 F7
Rydal Cl. Dron S18 152 D1
Rydal Cl. Pen S30 51 D4
Rydal Rd. Ad le S DN6 21 C1
Rydal Rd. Din S31 146 F7
Rydal Rd. Shef S8 140 E5
Rydal Terr. Barn S71 34 A1
Rydal Way. Mex S64 80 C6
Rydalhurst Ave. Shef S6 112 A2
Rydall Pl. Ben DN5 61 F8
Rye Bank. Roth S60 116 D1
Rye Croft. Barn S71 34 A6
Rye Croft. Con DN12 81 E2
Rye Croft. Tick DN11 121 A8
Rye La. Shef S6 126 E7
Ryecroft Ave. Norton DN6 4 C3
Ryecroft Cty Prim Sch. Rawm 98 A6
Ryecroft Glen Rd. Shef S17 152 A8
Ryecroft Rd. Norton DN6 4 C2
Ryecroft Rd. Rawm S62 98 C6
Ryecroft View. Shef S17 151 D8
Ryedale Wlk. Ben DN5 61 C7
Ryefield Gdns. Shef S11 140 A5
Ryegate Cres. Shef S10 128 B3
Ryegate Hospl. Shef 128 B2
Ryegate Rd. Shef S10 128 B3
Ryeview Gdns. Roth S61 97 B2
Ryhill Dr. Shef S19 143 A2
Ryhill Pits La. Ryhill WF4 15 F8
Ryle Rd. Shef S7 140 E7
Rylstone Ct. Shef S12 143 B2
Rylstone Gr. Shef S12 143 B2
Rylstone Wlk. Barn S70 55 D6
Ryton Ave. Wombw S73 56 F1
Ryton Cl. Maltby S66 119 A5
Ryton Rd. N Anst S31 146 D5
Ryton Rd. S Anst S31 146 D5
Ryton Way. Don DN4 85 A6

Sackerville Terr. Kill S31 156 B7
Sackup La. Mapp S75 13 F1
Sackville Rd. Shef S10 128 B4
Sackville St. Barn S70 33 E2
Sacred Heart Sch. Dearne 58 E6
Saddler Ave. Shef S19 143 D1
Saddler Cl. Shef S19 143 D1
Saddler Gn. Shef S19 143 D1
Saddler Gr. Shef S19 143 D1
Sadler Gate. Barn S70 33 E2 5
Sadler's Gate. Wombw S73 56 C4
Saffron Cl. Tick DN11 120 F7
Saffron Cres. Tick DN11 120 F7
Saffron Rd. Tick DN11 120 F7
St Agnes' Rd. Don DN4 63 A2
St Aidan's Ave. Shef S2 141 D8
St Aidan's Cl. Shef S2 141 E8
St Aidan's Dr. Shef S2 141 E8
St Aidan's Mount. Shef S2 141 E8
St Aidan's Pl. Shef S2 141 E8
St Aidan's Rd. Shef S2 141 E8
St Aidan's Way. Shef S2 141 E8
St Alban's RC Sch. Con 81 A3
St Alban's Way. Roth S66 117 B4
St Albans Cl. Shef S10 127 C1
St Albans Ct. Roth S66 117 B4
St Albans Dr. Shef S10 127 B1
St Albans Jun Mix & Inf Sch (C of E). Roth 117 B4
St Albans Rd. Shef S10 127 C1
St Andrew Rd. Stock S30 92 E8
St Andrew's Cl. Shef S11 140 D7
St Andrew's Cl. Swint S64 79 D1
St Andrew's Prim Sch. Dron 152 D1
St Andrew's Rd. Con DN12 81 B1
St Andrew's Rd. Shef S11 140 D7
St Andrew's Sq. Dearne S63 58 C2
St Andrew's Terr. Don DN4 62 E1
St Andrew's Way. B Dun DN3 43 A6
St Andrews Cl. Don DN4 85 B6
St Andrews Cl. Roth S66 117 C7
St Andrews Cres. Hoy S74 76 E6
St Andrews Dr. Mapp S75 14 A1
St Andrews Gr. Hat DN7 44 B7
St Andrews Rd. Hoy S74 76 E6
St Andrews Way. Barn S71 56 A7
St Andrews Wlk. Brin S60 115 A1
St Ann's Jun & Inf Sch. Roth 115 F7
St Ann's RC Jun & Inf Sch. Stock 92 B8
St Ann's Rd. Roth S65 115 E7
St Ann's Rd. Stock S30 73 D1
St Anne's Dr. Barn S71 34 D6
St Anne's Rd. Don DN4 63 A2
St Anthony Rd. Shef S10 128 A4
St Augustine's Rd. Don DN4 63 C1
St Austell Dr. Barn S75 32 E4
St Barbara's Cl. Maltby S66 118 E4
St Barbara's Rd. Dar S73 56 F5
St Barnabas La. Shef S2 141 A8 4
St Barnabas Rd. Shef S2 141 A8 5
St Barnabas Sch. Shef 141 A8
St Bart's Terr. Barn S70 54 F8 14
St Bartholomew's Cl. Maltby S66 118 E4
St Bede's Catholic Schs. Roth 114 E8
St Bede's Rd. Roth S60 115 C6
St Bernard's Cath Sec Sch. Roth 116 C5
St Catherine's Ave. Don DN4 83 C8
St Catherine's Dr. Hat DN7 43 E4
St Catherine's Hospl. Don 83 B5
St Catherine's RC Fst & Mid Sch. Shef 129 B8
St Catherines Way. Barn S75 33 B1
St Cecilia's Rd. Don DN4 63 A1
St Chad's Sq. Con DN12 80 F4
St Chad's Way. Sprot DN5 61 D1
St Charles' Sch. Shef 129 F6
St Charles St. Shef S9 129 E6
St Christopher's Cres. Ben DN5 61 E6
St Christopher's. Don DN4 83 A7
St Christophers Cl. Barn S71 56 A7
St Clement's Cl. Ben DN5 61 D6
St Clements Cl. Barn S71 56 A7
St David Rd. Stock S30 92 E8
St David's Dr. Barn S71 55 F8
St David's Dr. Ben DN5 61 D6
St David's Dr. S Anst S31 146 D4
St David's Rd. Con DN12 81 B2
St Davids Dr. Brin S60 115 A1
St Dominic's Cl. Sprot DN5 82 B8
St Edmund's Ave. Thurcr S66 133 E6
St Edwards Ave. Barn S70 54 D8
St Edwins Cl. Hat DN7 44 A8
St Edwins Dr. Hat DN7 44 A7
St Elizabeth Cl. Shef S2 141 B8
St Eric's Rd. Don DN4 63 D1
St Francis Bvd. Barn S71 34 D7
St Francis Cl. Roth S66 117 C7
St Francis Xavier Prim Sch. Don 62 C1
St George Gate. Don DN1 62 C3
St George Rd. Stock S30 92 E8
St George's Ave. Hat DN7 43 F5
St George's Ave. Swint S64 79 C3
St George's Cl. Shef S3 128 E3
St George's Ct. Shef S1 128 F3 4
St George's Rd. Barn S70 54 E8
St George's Rd. Don DN4 63 C1
St George's Sch (Inf). Don 42 D1
St George's Terr. Shef S1 128 F3
St Georges Cl. Thorne DN8 26 D5
St Georges Dr. Brin S60 131 A8
St Georges Dr. Thorne DN8 26 D5
St Gerard's RC Sch (Mix & Inf). Roth 98 E2
St Giles CE Prim Sch. Kill 156 D6
St Giles Gate. Ben DN5 61 D6
St Giles Sq. Chap S30 94 F5
St Helen Rd. Stock S30 92 E7
St Helen's Ave. Barn S71 34 B5
St Helen's Ave. Hem WF9 17 C7
St Helen's Bvd. Barn S71 34 B6
St Helen's Jun & Inf Sch. Barn 34 D5
St Helen's La. Bnbur DN5 59 E3
St Helen's RC Sch. Hoy 76 D6
St Helen's Rd. Don DN4 63 A2
St Helen's Sch. Barn 34 C7
St Helen's Sq. Don DN3 42 F4
St Helen's St. Hoy S74 77 A6
St Helens Cl. Dearne S63 58 B8
St Helens Cl. Treet S60 131 F3
St Helens Ct. Hoy S74 77 A6
St Helens Way. Barn S71 34 D5
St Helier Dr. Barn S75 33 B2
St Hilda Ave. Barn S70 33 C1
St Hilda Cl. Stock S30 92 E7
St Hilda's Jun Sch. Barn 33 F7
St Hilda's Rd. Don DN4 63 A2
St Hildas Cl. Dearne S63 37 E1
St James Ave. Hat DN7 43 F5
St James Ave. S Anst S31 146 D4
St James' Cl. Barn S70 55 A4
St James Cl. Don DN3 42 F4
St James Cl. W up D S63 79 A6
St James' Dr. Roth S65 99 D3
St James' Gdns. Don DN4 62 B1
St James' Row. Shef S1 129 A3 10
St James St. Don DN1 62 D1
St James' St. Shef S1 129 A3
St James' View. Roth S65 99 D3
St James Wlk. Shef S13 143 D8
St James's Bridge. Don DN4 62 C2
St Joan Ave. Stock S30 92 E7
St John C of E Jun & Inf Sch. Shef 129 D3
St John Fisher RC Jun & Inf Sch. Shef 143 A3
St John the Baptist C of E Inf Sch. Pen 51 C2
St John the Baptist C of E School. Pen 51 C2
St John's Ave. Barn S75 32 E4
St John's Ave. Roth S60 115 B7
St John's Cl. Dod S75 53 E6
St John's Cl. Pen S30 51 C2
St John's Cl. Roth S65 116 A8
St John's Ct. Laugh S31 134 E4
St John's Ct. Roth S66 117 C6
St John's Gn. Roth S61 96 E1
St John's Rd. Barn S70 54 E8
St John's Rd. Cud S72 35 B6
St John's Rd. Don DN4 83 A8
St John's Rd. Lough S31 134 E4
St John's Rd. N Edl DN12 82 B2
St John's Rd. Roth S65 116 A8
St John's Rd. Shef S2 129 D4
St John's Rd. Swint S64 79 C3
St John's Wlk. Roy S71 15 D4
St Johns Ave. Roth S66 117 C6
St Johns Ct. Roth S60 115 B6
St Johns. Pen S30 51 F6
St Joseph's Ct. Din S31 134 F1
St Joseph's Prim Sch. Din 134 F1
St Joseph's RC Prim Sch. Ross 84 F1
St Joseph's RC Sch (Jun Mix & Infant). Rawm 98 A5
St Joseph's Rd. Shef S13 130 F1
St Joseph's Sch. Barn 55 B8
St Julien's Mount. Caw S75 31 E4
St Julien's Way. Caw S75 31 E4
St Lawrence Rd. Hat DN7 43 F7
St Lawrence Rd. Shef S9 114 E2
St Lawrence's Terr. Ad I S DN6 40 C6
St Leger Ave. Laugh S31 134 C2
St Leonard's Cl. Din S31 146 F8
St Leonard's Croft. Roth S65 98 F3
St Leonard's La. Roth S65 115 F7
St Leonard's Lea. Ben DN5 61 E6
St Leonard's Pl. Roth S65 115 F7
St Leonard's Rd. Roth S65 115 F7
St Leonard's. Tick DN11 121 A7
St Leonards Ave. Roth S65 99 A2
St Leonards Ct. Shef S5 113 B3
St Leonards Way. Barn S71 56 A7
St Luke's Cl. Hat DN7 43 E4
St Luke's Hospice. Shef 139 F3
St Luke's Hospice. Shef 143 E3
St Luke's Sch. Shire 159 F7
St Lukes Way. Barn S71 34 C3
St Margaret Ave. Stock S30 92 E8
St Margaret's Dr. Swint S64 79 B3
St Margaret's Rd. Don DN4 63 A1
St Margaret's Rd. Shef S5 113 B7
St Margarets Ave. Bnbur DN5 59 C3
St Maries RC Sch. Shef 128 A1
St Mark Rd. Stock S30 92 E8
St Mark's Cres. Shef S10 128 D2
St Martin Cl. Stock S30 92 E8
St Martin's Ave. Bawtry DN10 123 A8
St Martin's Ave. Ben DN5 61 F6
St Martin's Cl. Fir S81 136 A6
St Martins Cl. Barn S75 33 B1
St Mary Cres. Stock S30 92 F7
St Mary's C of E Jun & Inf Sch. Shef 128 D6
St Mary's C of E Prim Sch. Barn 33 C2
St Mary's Catholic Sch. N Edl 82 B2
St Mary's Cl. S Elm WF9 19 A2
St Mary's Cl. Shef S30 95 A1
St Mary's Cres. Don DN1 62 E4
St Mary's Cres. Swint S64 79 C4
St Mary's Cres. Tick DN11 121 A7
St Mary's Dr. Arm DN3 64 C6
St Mary's Dr. Hat DN7 43 E4
St Mary's Dr. Treet S60 131 C6
St Mary's Garden. Barn S70 55 A2
St Mary's Gate. Barn S70 33 E2 4
St Mary's Gate. Shef S11 128 F1
St Mary's Gate. Tick DN11 121 A7
St Mary's Pl. Barn S70 33 E2
St Mary's RC Jun & Inf Sch. Chap 94 E8
St Mary's RC Prim Sch. Maltby 119 B4
St Mary's RC Sch. Roth 116 C6
St Mary's Rd. Dar S73 57 B5
St Mary's Rd. Dearne S63 58 F6
St Mary's Rd. Don DN1 62 E4
St Mary's Rd. Hat DN7 43 E4
St Mary's Rd. N Edl DN12 82 C1
St Mary's Rd. Rawm S62 98 A5
St Mary's Rd. Shef S2 129 B1
St Mary's Rd. Tick DN11 121 A7

St Mary's Sch. Don 84 D8
St Mary's St. Pen S30 51 D3
St Mary's View. Roth S61 97 B3
St Marys Cl. Cud S72 35 B6
St Marys Rd. Wombw S73 56 C2
St Matthew's Inf Sch. Barn 33 C2
St Matthews Way. Barn S71 34 C3
St Matthias Rd. Stock S30 92 E8
St Michael's Ave. Barn S71 34 D6
St Michael's Ave. Swint S64 79 D4
St Michael's C of E Sch. Hath 149 A8
St Michael's C of E Sch. Ross 85 B1
St Michael's Cl. Shef S5 113 B8
St Michael's Cl. Thorne DN8 26 D6
St Michael's Cres. Shef S5 113 B7
St Michael's Dr. Thorne DN8 26 D6
St Michael's RC Prim Sch. Dar 56 F4
St Michael's Rd. Don DN4 63 B1
St Michael's Rd. Shef S5 113 B7
St Michael's Sch. Barn 34 B7
St Michaels Ave. Ross DN11 85 A2
St Michaels Cl. Dearne S63 58 D5
St Nicholas Cl. Don DN3 42 E2
St Nicholas Rd. Thorne DN8 26 B7
St Nicolas Rd. Rawm S62 98 A6
St Nicolas Wlk. Rawm S62 98 B6
St Oswald's Cl. Finn DN9 86 D3
St Oswald's Dr. Don DN3 42 F2
St Oswald's Dr. Finn DN9 86 E3
St Oswald's RC Sch. Shef 129 E2
St Owens Dr. Barn S75 33 B2
St Patrick Rd. Stock S30 92 E8
St Patrick's Jun & Inf Sch. Shef 113 C4
St Patrick's RC Prim Sch. Har 122 B4
St Patrick's Rd. Don DN2 63 A5
St Patrick's Way. Ben DN5 61 D6
St Paul Cl. Stock S30 92 E8
St Paul Cl. Tod S31 145 E5
St Paul's C of E Fst Sch. Bri 17 A3
St Paul's Cl. Upton WF9 19 D8
St Paul's Par. Barn S71 55 F8
St Paul's Par. Barn S71 56 A7
St Paul's Par. Ben DN5 61 E5
St Paul's Par. Shef S1 129 A3 13
St Peter and St Paul's Cath. Shef 129 A3
St Peter Ave. Stock S30 92 F8
St Peter's Cl. Bnbur DN5 59 C4
St Peter's Cl. Brin S60 131 A8
St Peter's Cl. Shef S1 129 A4 18
St Peter's Dr. Con DN12 81 C1
St Peter's Gate. Dearne S63 37 C1
St Peter's High Sch. Don 85 A8
St Peter's Rd. Con DN12 81 B1
St Peter's Rd. Don DN4 82 E7
St Peter's Rd. Th Sa S80 158 E7
St Peter's R C Prim Sch. Don 63 A1
St Peter's Terr. Barn S70 55 A8 1
St Peters R C Sch. Shef 113 A7
St Philip's La. Shef S3 128 F5 1
St Philip's Rd. Shef S3 128 E4
St Philip's Rd. Shef S3 128 F5
St Phillip's Cl. Maltby S66 118 E4
St Quentin Cl. Shef S17 152 B5
St Quentin Dr. Shef S17 152 B5
St Quentin Mount. Shef S17 152 B5
St Quentin Rise. Shef S17 152 B5
St Quentin View. Shef S17 152 B5
St Ronan's Rd. Shef S7 140 F7
St Sepulchre Gate. Don DN1 62 C3
St Sepulchre Gate W.
Don DN1, DN4 62 C2
St Stephen's Dr. Aston S31 144 D8
St Stephen's Rd. Roth S65 115 E7
St Stephen's Wlk. Shef S3 128 E4
St Theresa's RC Prim Schs. Shef 142 B7
St Thomas More's R C Sch. Shef 112 E7
St Thomas of Canterbury Prim Sch.
Shef 152 F8
St Thomas Rd. Shef S10 128 B3
St Thomas St. Shef S1 128 F3 2
St Thomas's Cl. Don DN4 82 E6
St Thomas's Rd. Barn S75 33 A4
St Ursula's Rd. Don DN4 63 A2
St Veronica Rd. Stock S30 92 F7
St Vincent Ave. Ad le S DN6 39 F6
St Vincent Ave. Don DN1 62 E4
St Vincent Rd. Don DN1 62 E4
St Vincent's Ave. Bran DN3 85 C8
St Vincent's RC Jun & Inf Sch.
Shef 128 F4
St Wandrilles Cl. Shef S30 95 B1
St Wilfrid's Gdns. Don DN4 84 E7
St Wilfrid's RC Jun & Inf Sch.
Shef 140 C4
St Wilfrid's Rd. Don DN4 84 D8
St Wilfrid's Rd. Shef S2 141 A8 11
St Withold Ave. Thurcr S66 133 E6
Salcombe Gr. Bawtry DN10 122 F8
Sale Hill. Shef S10 128 B2
Sale St. Hoy S74 76 A5
Salerno Way. Dar S73 56 E6
Sales La. Syke DN14 7 D5
Salisbury Rd. Don DN4 62 A1
Salisbury Rd. Maltby S66 119 A6
Salisbury Rd. Shef S10 128 B4
Salisbury St. Barn S75 33 D3
Salisbury Wlk. C in L S81 148 E7
Salmon St. Shef S11 140 F8 5
Salt Box La. Shef S30 112 D7
Salt Hill. Fir S81 136 B5
Salt Hill Rd. Fir S81 136 C4
Salter Hill La. Stock S30 72 F6
Salter's Way. Pen S30 51 D2
Saltersbrook. Dearne S63 58 D5
Saltersbrook Rd. Dar S73 57 A7
Samson St. Shef S2 129 C2 5
Samuel Cl. Shef S2 141 D7
Samuel Dr. Shef S2 141 D7
Samuel Pl. Shef S2 141 D7
Samuel Rd. Barn S75 33 B3
Samuel Rd. Shef S2 141 D8
Samuel Sq. Barn S75 33 B3
Samuel St. Don DN4 83 A6
Sanctuary Fields. N Anst S31 146 D7
Sand La. Wroot DN9 66 F4
Sandal Rd. Con DN12 81 B1
Sandall Beat La. Don DN2 63 D5
Sandall Beat Rd. Don DN2 63 C3
Sandall Carr Rd. Don DN3 42 E3
Sandall La. Don DN3 42 E4
Sandall Park Dr. Don DN2 63 C7
Sandall Rise. Don DN2 63 B6
Sandall Stones Rd. Don DN3 42 D3
Sandall View. Lough S31 134 C3
Sandall Wood Sch. Don 63 D5
Sandalwood Cl. Don DN2 63 C8
Sandalwood Rise. Swint S62 98 D8
Sandbeck Cl. Barn S71 33 F3
Sandbeck Ct. Con DN12 80 F3
Sandbeck House. Don DN1 62 C2 4
Sandbeck La. Maltby DN11 120 B2
Sandbeck La. Tick DN11 120 B3
Sandbeck Pl. Shef S11 140 D8
Sandbeck Rd. Don DN4 62 F2
Sandbeck Way. Maltby S66 118 A5
Sandbed Rd. Shef S3 128 E7
Sandbergh Rd. Roth S61 96 E2
Sandby Croft. Shef S14 141 E2
Sandby Ct. Shef S14 141 E2
Sandby Dr. Shef S14 141 E2
Sandcliffe Rd. Don DN2 63 B6
Sandcroft Cl. Hoy S74 76 C5
Sandeby Dr. Roth S65 117 D7
Sanderson St. Shef S9 129 F7
Sanderson's Bank. Misson DN10 87 F4
Sandford Ct. Barn S70 54 D8
Sandford Grove Rd. Shef S7 140 E6
Sandford Rd. Don DN4 83 A7
Sandford Rd. S Elm WF9 19 A5
Sandhill Cl. Rawm S62 98 B7
Sandhill Gr. Grim S72 17 A1
Sandhill Rd. Rawm S62 98 B7
Sandhill Rise. Auck DN9 86 A7
Sandhurst Rd. Don DN4 85 A6
Sandown Cl. Eck S31 155 B2
Sandown Gdns. Don DN4 63 D2
Sandown Rd. Mex S64 80 B6
Sandpiper Rd. Roth S61 95 F6
Sandpit Hill. Bran DN3 85 D8
Sandringham Ave. Roth S60 116 B1
Sandringham Cl. Pen S30 51 A4
Sandringham Ct. Har DN11 122 B5
Sandringham Fst Sch. Don 63 B6
Sandringham Pl. Roth S65 117 D8
Sandringham Rd. Don DN2 63 B4
Sandringham Rd. Shef S9 114 A4
Sandrock Dr. Don DN4 84 E7
Sandrock Rd. Har DN11 121 F5
Sands Cl. Shef S14 141 E4
Sands The. Bfield S6 110 A4
Sandstone Ave. Shef S9 113 F2
Sandstone Cl. Shef S9 114 A3
Sandstone Dr. Shef S9 113 F2
Sandstone Rd. Shef S9 114 A3
Sandtoft Rd. Hat DN7 45 C8
Sandwith Rd. Tod S31 145 E5
Sandy Acres Cl. Shef S19 143 F1
Sandy Acres Dr. Shef S19 143 F1
Sandy Flat La. Roth S66 117 B2
Sandy La. Don DN4 63 A1
Sandy La. Hoy S73 55 F2
Sandy La. Roth S66 117 F3
Sandy La. Thurcr S66 133 F7
Sandy Mount E. Har DN11 122 A4
Sandy Mount W. Har DN11 122 A4
Sandybridge La. Shaf S72 16 B4
Sandyfields View. Ad le S DN6 21 B1
Sandygate Cres. W up D S63 78 F4
Sandygate Gr. Shef S10 127 D2
Sandygate La. Hem WF9 17 C7
Sandygate Park Cres. Shef S10 127 D2
Sandygate Park Rd. Shef S10 127 D2
Sandygate Pk. Shef S10 127 D2
Sandygate Rd. Shef S10 127 E2
Sandygate. W up D S63 78 F4
Sandygate. W up D S63 78 F5
Sandymount E. Har DN11 122 A4
Sandymount. Har DN11 122 A5
Sandymount Rd. W up D S63 79 A6
Sandymount W. Har DN11 122 A4
Sankey Sq. Dearne S63 58 D5
Saracens La. Scro DN10 122 F2
Sarah St. Mex S64 80 A4
Sarah St. Roth S61 115 B6
Sark Rd. Shef S2 141 A7
Saundby Cl. Don DN4 84 C7
Saunders Pl. Shef S2 129 E3
Saunders Rd. Shef S2 129 E3
Saunders Row. Wombw S73 56 C2
Saunderson Rd. Pen S30 51 B4
Savage La. Shef S17 151 D7
Savile La. Pen S30 51 A3
Savile St E. Shef S4 129 D6
Savile St. Shef S4 129 C5
Savile Wlk. Bri S72 17 B3
Saville Ct. Hoy S74 76 F7
Saville Hall La. Dod S75 53 F6
Saville La. Pen S30 50 F3
Saville Rd. Dod S75 54 A6
Saville Rd. Roth S60 116 B1
Saville Rd. W up D S63 78 E6
Saville St. Cud S72 35 B7
Saville St. Roth S65 98 C1
Saville Terr. Barn S70 54 E8 7
Sawdon Rd. Shef S11 128 E1
Sawn Moor Ave. Thurcr S66 133 F6
Sawn Moor Rd. Thurcr S66 133 F5
Sawston Cl. Don DN4 83 A4
Saxon Ave. S Kirk WF9 17 F2
Saxon Cl. Upton WF9 19 E7
Saxon Cres. Barn S70 55 A5
Saxon Gr. S Kirk WF9 18 A1
Saxon Mount. S Kirk WF9 17 F1
Saxon Rd. Roth S61 114 D6
Saxon Rd. Shef S2 141 A7 5
Saxon Rd. Wales S31 145 F2
Saxon St. Cud S72 35 B6
Saxon St. Dearne S63 58 E8
Saxon Way. Har DN11 121 F4
Saxonlea Ave. Shef S2 130 C1
Saxonlea Cres. Shef S2 130 C1
Saxonlea Ct. Shef S2 130 C1
Saxonlea Dr. Shef S2 130 B1 3
Saxton Ave. Don DN4 63 C1
Saxton Cl. Hoy S74 77 B6
Saxton Dr. Roth S60 115 F1
Sayers Cl. Bnbur DN5 59 C2
Scafell Pl. N Anst S31 146 F6
Scaftworth Cl. Don DN4 84 C7
Scaly Gate. Holmfi HD7 28 A2
Scaly Gate. Holmfi HD7 28 A5
Scammadine Cl. Brin S60 131 D8
Scampton Lodge. Shef S5 113 B2
Scar Hole La. Holmfi HD7 28 A3
Scar La. Barn S71 55 F8
Scarborough Cl. N Anst S31 146 E7
Scarborough La. Ross DN11 84 E1
Scarborough Rd. Roth S66 117 B5
Scarborough Rd. Shef S9 130 C5
Scarbrough Cres. Maltby S66 119 A4
Scarfield Cl. Barn S71 55 F8
Scargill Croft. Shef S3 129 B6
Scarlett Oak Meadow. Shef S6 127 C6
Scarll Rd. Don DN4 62 A1
Scarsdale Cross. Dron S18 153 B1
Scarsdale Rd. Dron S18 153 B1
Scarsdale Rd. Shef S8 140 F3
Scarsdale St. Din S31 135 A1
Scarth Ave. Don DN4 83 B8
Scawsby La. Ben DN5 61 B8
Scawsby Ridgewood Comp Sch.
Ben 61 C7
Scawsby Rosedale Fst Sch. Ben 61 D7
Scawsby Rosedale Mid Sch. Ben 61 D7
Scawsby Saltersgate Fst Sch. Ben 61 E6
Scawthorpe Ave. Ben DN5 40 D1
Scawthorpe Cotts. Ben DN5 61 C8
Sceptone Gr. Shaf S72 16 C3
Sceptre Gr. Ross DN11 103 E7
Schofield Dr. Dar S73 57 A6
Schofield Pl. Dar S73 57 A6
Schofield Rd. Dar S73 57 A6
Schofield Rd. Stock S30 92 D8
Schofield St. Mex S64 79 E5
Schofield Technical Coll. Mex 80 A6
Schole Ave. Pen S30 51 C3
Schole Hill La. Pen S30 51 B2
Scholes Gn. Roth S61 96 C3
Scholes La. Roth S61 96 B4
Scholes Moor Rd. Holmfi HD7 48 B8
Scholes Sch. Roth 96 B3
Scholes View. Hoy S74 76 E5
Scholes View. Hoy S74 76 F7
Scholes View. Shef S30 95 B1
Scholey Ave. Woods S81 147 E3
Scholey Rd. Roth S66 117 B5
Scholey St. Shef S3 129 B5
Scholfield Cres. Maltby S66 119 B4
School Ave. Shef S19 155 F7
School Cl. Shef S19 155 F7
School Cl. Wales S31 145 B2
School Gr. Aston S31 144 E7
School Green La. Shef S10 139 B7
School Hill. Cud S72 35 B7
School Hill. Roth S60 116 B1
School La. Auck DN9 86 A6
School La. D Dale HD8 30 A6
School La. Dron S18 153 A1
School La. Eck S31 154 E3
School La. Hath S30 149 A8
School La. Rawm S62 97 E3
School La. Roth S65 98 F3
School La. Shef S6 127 C5
School La. Shef S2 129 C3
School La. Shef S8 152 F7
School La. Shef S30 94 C1
School La. Ston S66 119 E8
School La. Wharn S30 93 B1
School Lane Cl. Shef S8 141 C1
School Rd. Chap S30 94 F6
School Rd. Lan S81 136 E3
School Rd. Lough S31 134 D4
School Rd. Shef S10 128 C4
School Rd. Shef S19 144 B3
School Rd. Thurcr S66 133 F6
School Rd. Wales S31 145 A2
School St. Aston S31 144 C7
School St. Barn S75 33 D3
School St. Barn S70 55 E8
School St. Cud S72 35 B8
School St. Dar S73 57 B6
School St. Dearne S63 58 C2
School St. Dearne S63 58 D8
School St. Din S31 134 F1
School St. Eck S31 155 D3
School St. G Hou S72 36 E2
School St. Hoy S73 77 C8
School St. Mapp S75 13 E1
School St. Mapp S75 14 C1
School St. Roth S65 98 E2
School St. Shef S19 155 D7
School St. Upton WF9 19 D8
School St. Wombw S73 56 D3
School Terr. Con DN12 81 B2
School Wlk. Bawtry DN10 123 A7
School Wlk. Con DN12 81 A4
School Wlk. Maltby S66 119 A5
School Wlk. N Edl DN12 101 A7
Schoolfield Dr. Rawm S62 97 F7
Scorah's La. Swint S64 79 A3
Scorcher Hills La. Burg DN6 20 E5
Scot La. Bawtry DN10 123 A7
Scot La. Don DN1 62 D3
Scotch Spring La. Ston S66 119 E7
Scotia Cl. Shef S2 141 F8
Scotia Dr. Shef S2 141 F8
Scotland St. Shef S3 129 A4
Scott Ave. Bnbur DN5 59 C2
Scott Ave. Con DN12 81 A2
Scott Cl. Thurcr S66 133 E6
Scott Cres. Don DN3 42 E3
Scott Hill. Sprot DN5 82 B8
Scott Rd. Shef S4 129 C8
Scott St. Shef S4 129 E8
Scott Way. Chap S30 94 F4
Scott Wlk. Maltby S66 118 D6
Scout Dike Outdoor Ed Ctr Pen 51 B6
Scovell Ave. Rawm S62 97 D7
Scovell House. Rawm S62 97 D7
Scowerdons Cl. Shef S12 142 F5
Scowerdons Dr. Shef S12 142 F5
Scraith Wood Dr. Shef S5 112 E2
Scratta La. Whit S80 159 C2
Scrooby Dr. Roth S61 97 C3
Scrooby La. Roth S62 97 D3
Scrooby Pl. Roth S61 97 C3
Scrooby Rd. Bir DN11 122 C4
Scrooby Rd. Har DN11 121 F3
Scrooby St. Roth S61 97 C3
Seabrook Rd. Shef S2 129 D2
Seagrave Ave. Shef S12 142 B4
Seagrave Cres. Shef S12 142 B4
Seagrave Dr. Shef S12 142 B4
Seagrave Rd. Shef S12 142 B4
Searby Rd. Roth S66 117 D7
Seaton Cl. Shef S2 129 F2
Seaton Cres. Shef S2 129 F2
Seaton Gdns. Ross DN11 103 F7
Seaton Pl. Shef S2 129 F2
Seaton Way. Shef S2 129 F2
Sebastion View. Brin S60 115 C2
Seckar La. Wool WF4 14 B8
Second Ave. Ad l S DN6 40 C4
Second Ave. S Kirk WF9 17 F1
Second Ave. Upton WF9 19 A8
Second La. Roth S66 117 D2
Second La. S Anst S31 146 E3
Second Sq. Stai DN7 24 E4
Sedan St. Shef S4 129 C7
Sedge Cl. Roth S66 117 E4
Sedgefield Way. Mex S64 80 B6
Sedgley Rd. Shef S6 128 D8
Sefton Ct. Shef S10 139 D7
Sefton Rd. Shef S10 139 E7
Selborne Rd. Shef S10 128 A3
Selborne St. Roth S65 115 E8
Selbourne Cl. Barn S75 32 E5
Selby Cl. Aston S31 144 C7
Selby Rd. Askern DN6 5 A4
Selby Rd. Barn S71 33 F7
Selby Rd. Don DN2 63 A5
Selby Rd. Norton DN6 5 A4
Selby Rd. Shef S4 113 D1
Selby Rd. Thorne DN8 8 E5
Selby Rd. W Stub DN6 5 A4
Selby Rd. Womer DN6 5 A4
Selhurst Cres. Don DN4 84 E7
Selkirk Ave. Don DN4 82 D6
Selkirk Rd. Don DN2 63 C6
Sellars Rd. Roth S61 96 E1
Sellers St. Shef S8 140 F7
Selly Oak Gr. Shef S8 153 C6
Selly Oak Rd. Shef S8 153 C6
Selwood. Roth S65 115 F7
Selwyn St. Roth S65 115 E8
Senior Rd. Don DN4 62 A2
Senior Rd. Shef S9 130 C4
Sennen Croft. Barn S71 34 B3
Serlby Dr. Hart S31 157 F5
Serlby House. Don DN1 62 C2 6
Serlby La. Hart S31 157 F6
Serlby Rd. Styr DN11 121 E2
Serpentine Wlk. Shef S8 153 B8
Setcup La. Eck S31 155 D2
Seth Terr. Barn S70 55 A8
Sevenfields Ct. Shef S6 112 A1
Sevenfields La. Shef S6 112 A1
Severn Ct. Shef S10 128 D3
Severn Rd. Shef S10 128 D3
Severnside Dr. Shef S13 143 A7
Severnside Gdns. Shef S13 143 A7
Severnside Pl. Shef S13 143 A7
Severnside Wlk. Shef S13 143 A6
Sewell Rd. Shef S19 155 F6
Sexton Dr. Roth S66 117 D4
Seymore Rd. Aston S31 144 E6
Seymour Rd. Maltby S66 119 B5
Shackleton Rd. Don DN2 42 D1
Shackleton View. Pen S30 51 D2
Shady Side. Don DN4 62 A1
Shaftesbury Ave. Don DN2 63 B4
Shaftesbury Dr. Hoy S74 76 D5
Shaftesbury St. Barn S70 55 E8
Shaftholme La. Ben DN5 41 C6
Shaftholme Rd. Ben DN5 41 D4
Shafton Hall Dr. Shaf S72 16 B3
Shafton Rd. Roth S60 116 B2
Shafton Two Gates Fst Sch. Shaf 16 C2
Shaftsbury Ave. Ad le S DN6 39 F5
Shaftsbury Sq. Roth S65 115 E7
Shakespeare Ave. Ben DN5 61 F4
Shakespeare Ave. Norton DN6 4 C1
Shakespeare Dr. Din S31 147 A8
Shakespeare Rd. Ben DN5 41 B1
Shakespeare Rd. Roth S65 115 F8
Shakespeare Rd. W up D S63 78 D7
Shaldon Gr. Aston S31 144 D7
Shalesmoor. Shef S3 128 F5
Shambles St. Barn S70 33 E1
Shardlow Gdns. Don DN4 84 F6
Sharlston Gdns. Ross DN11 85 B1
Sharman Cl. Uns S18 154 A1
Sharman Wlk. Uns S18 154 A1
Sharp Royd Nook. Oxspr S30 73 C5
Sharpe Ave. Shef S8 152 E8
Sharpfield Ave. Rawm S62 97 F8
Sharrard Cl. Shef S12 142 B5
Sharrard Dr. Shef S12 142 B5
Sharrard Gr. Shef S12 142 B6
Sharrard Rd. Shef S12 142 B5
Sharrow Inf Sch. Shef 140 F8
Sharrow La. Shef S11 140 F8
Sharrow Lane Inf & Jun Schs.
Shef 140 F8
Sharrow St. Shef S11 140 F8
Sharrow Vale Rd. Shef S11 140 D8
Sharrow View. Shef S7 140 E8
Shaw Cl. S Elm WF9 19 A4
Shaw Ct. Arm DN3 64 C5
Shaw La. Barn S70 33 D1
Shaw La. Cud S71 15 E1
Shaw La. Don DN2 63 D8
Shaw La. Fenw DN6 6 A4
Shaw La. Mapp S75 14 C2
Shaw La. Midhop S30 71 D3
Shaw La. Roy S71 15 E1
Shaw Lane Ind Est. Don 63 D8
Shaw Rd. N Edl DN12 82 C3
Shaw Rd. Roth S65 116 A8
Shaw St. Barn S70 54 D8
Shaw St. Dron S18 153 C4
Shaw Wood Jun & Inf Sch. Arm 64 A7
Shawfield Cl. B Dun DN3 43 A6
Shawfield Rd. Barn S71 34 C6
Shawlands Jun & Inf Sch. Barn 54 D8
Shawsfield Rd. Roth S60 115 F3
Shay House La. Stock S30 92 B8
Shay Rd. Stock S30 73 C1
Shay The. Don DN4 84 E7
Sheaf Bank. Shef S2 141 A7
Sheaf Cl. Con DN12 81 D1
Sheaf Cres. Dearne S63 58 D1
Sheaf Ct. Barn S70 55 D7
Sheaf Gdns. Shef S2 129 B1
Sheaf Sq. Shef S1 129 B2
Sheaf St. Shef S1 129 B3
Sheardown St. Don DN4 62 B2
Sheards Cl. Dron S18 152 F1
Sheards Dr. Dron S18 152 E1
Sheards Way. Dron S18 152 F1
Shearman Ave. Roth S61 96 E2
Shearwood Rd. Shef S10 128 E3
Sheep Bridge La. Ross DN11 85 B2
Sheep Cote La. Hat DN7 44 C4
Sheep Cote Rd. Roth S60 116 E3
Sheep Dike La. Roth S66 133 C7
Sheep Dip La. Hat DN7 44 A7
Sheep La. H Mel DN5 60 D3
Sheepcote Rd. Kill S31 156 C6
Sheephill Rd. Shef S11 139 A2
Sheepwalk La. Upton WF9 19 E8
Sheepwash La. Tick DN11 103 D1
Sheerien Cl. Barn S71 33 E8
Sheffield Amateur Sports Club.
Shef 152 A7
Sheffield Arena. Shef 130 B7
Sheffield Childrens Hospl. Shef 128 D3
Sheffield City Polytechnic. Shef 140 C7
Sheffield City Polytechnic. Shef 151 D4
Sheffield Hallam Univ. Shef 129 B3
Sheffield High Sch (girls). Shef 128 C2
Sheffield La. Treet S60 131 C5
Sheffield Laboratories. Roth 116 A3
Sheffield Parkway. Shef S9 130 D2
Sheffield Parkway. Treet S60 131 B6
Sheffield Polytechnic. Shef 128 F1
Sheffield Rd. Aston S31 144 A8
Sheffield Rd. Barn S70 75 F7
Sheffield Rd. Con DN12 81 C1
Sheffield Rd. Con DN12 81 F3
Sheffield Rd. Don DN12 82 B4
Sheffield Rd. Dron S18 152 F3
Sheffield Rd. Eck S31 155 E5
Sheffield Rd. Hath S30 149 A7
Sheffield Rd. Holmfi HD7 28 A1
Sheffield Rd. Hoy S74 76 B4
Sheffield Rd. Kill S31 156 D7
Sheffield Rd. Oxspr S30 52 B1
Sheffield Rd. Roth S60 115 B4
Sheffield Rd. S Anst S31 146 D4
Sheffield Rd. Shef S9 114 E3
Sheffield Rd. Shhef S 114 C1
Sheffield Rd. Shef S12, S9 143 A3
Sheffield Rd. Shef S13 143 B6
Sheffield Rd. Shef S31 155 E5
Sheldon Ave. Con DN12 81 D1
Sheldon La. Shef S6 127 C6
Sheldon Rd. Shef S7 140 E6
Sheldon Rd. Stock S30 73 C1
Sheldon Row. Shef S3 129 B4
Sheldon St. Shef S2 129 A1
Sheldrake Cl. Roth S61 95 F5
Shelley Ave. Don DN4 83 B6
Shelley Cl. Pen S30 51 D4
Shelley Dr. Arm DN3 64 C6
Shelley Dr. Barn S71 34 B3
Shelley Dr. Din S31 147 B8
Shelley Dr. Roth S65 116 B6
Shelley Gr. Ben DN5 61 F4
Shelley Rd. Roth S65 116 C6
Shelley Rise. Ad l S DN6 40 A5
Shelley Way. W up D S63 78 C7
Shelley Woodhouse La. Skel HD8 29 E8
Shenley Cl. Hat DN7 44 A6
Shenstone Dr. Roth S65 116 B4
Shenstone Rd. Roth S65 116 B4
Shenstone Rd. Shef S6 112 C2
Shepcote La. Shef S9 130 C8
Shepcote Way. Shef S9 130 D7
Shephard's Cl. Con DN12 80 F3
Shepherd Dr. Chap S30 94 E6
Shepherd La. Dearne S63 58 D7
Shepherd St. Shef S3 128 F4
Shepherds Croft. Blax DN9 86 F6
Shepley Croft. Chap S30 94 E6
Shepley Fst Sch. Shep 28 E8
Sheppard Rd. Don DN4 83 A7
Shepperson Rd. Shef S6 112 B1
Sherburn Cl. Ad le S DN6 20 E2
Sherburn Gate. Chap S30 94 F6
Sherburn Rd. Barn S71 33 E7
Sherde Rd. Shef S6 128 E5
Sheridan Ave. Don DN4 83 C6
Sheridan Ct. Barn S71 34 B3
Sheridan Dr. Roth S65 116 C6
Sheridan Rd. B Dun DN3 42 F8
Sheringham Cl. Chap S30 94 D7
Sheringham Gdns. Chap S30 94 D7
Sherwood Ave. Askern DN6 21 E7
Sherwood Ave. Ben DN5 61 D6
Sherwood Ave. Con DN12 81 A1
Sherwood Ave. Don DN3 42 F2
Sherwood Chase. Shef S17 151 E5
Sherwood Cl. Norton DN6 21 C8
Sherwood Cres. Roth S60 115 E6
Sherwood Dr. Ad le S DN6 20 E2
Sherwood Dr. Don DN4 82 E5
Sherwood Glen. Shef S7 140 A1
Sherwood Pl. Dron S18 152 D1 2
Sherwood Rd. Dron S18 152 D1
Sherwood Rd. Har DN11 121 F5
Sherwood Rd. Kill S31 156 E7
Sherwood Rd. Ross DN11 104 A8
Sherwood St. Barn S71 33 F1 15
Sherwood Way. Cud S72 16 A1
Shetland Gdns. Don DN2 63 B5
Shield Ave. Barn S70 55 A5
Shildon Gr. Thorne DN8 9 E3
Shinwell Dr. Upton WF9 19 D8
Ship Hill. Roth S60 115 D6
Shipcroft Cl. Wombw S73 56 E2
Shipman Balk. Clift S66 100 E5
Shipman Ct. Shef S19 155 D7
Shipton St. Shef S6 128 E5
Shirburn Gdns. Don DN4 63 F1
Shirebrook Fst & Mid Schs. Shef 143 C5
Shirebrook Rd. Shef S8 141 A6
Shirecliffe Cl. Shef S3 129 B7
Shirecliffe Coll of F Ed. Shef 129 A8
Shirecliffe Inf Sch. Shef 112 E2
Shirecliffe Jun Sch. Shef 112 E2

Stafford La. Shef S2 129 D2
Stafford Mews. Shef S2 129 D2
Stafford Pl. Con DN12 80 F3 5
Stafford Rd. Ad l S DN6 40 C4
Stafford Rd. Shef S2 129 D2
Stafford St. Shef S2 129 C2 7
Stafford Way. Chap S30 94 F5
Staffordshire Cl. Maltby S66 119 B5
Stag Cl. Roth S60 116 C3
Stag Cres. Roth S60 116 C3
Stag La. Roth S60 116 B3
Stainborough Cl. Dod S75 53 F6
Stainborough La. Hd Gr S75 53 F1
Stainborough Rd. Dod S75 53 F6
Stainborough View. Barn S70 54 F5
Stainborough View. Pilley S75 75 D6
Staincross Comm. Mapp S75 14 B2
Staindrop View. Chap S30 95 A6
Stainforth Eastgate First Sch. Stai 24 E4
Stainforth Kirton Lane Fst Sch. Stai 25 A5
Stainforth Mid Sch. Stai 24 E4
Stainforth Moor Rd. Hat DN7,DN8 45 C5
Stainforth Rd. B Dun DN3 43 A8
Stainforth Sta. Stai 24 F2
Stainforth Westgate Fst Sch. Stai 24 E4
Stainley Cl. Barn S75 33 B4
Stainmore Ave. Shef S19 144 A2
Stainmore Cl. Silk S75 52 F8
Stainton Cl. Barn S71 33 E6
Stainton Cty Prim Sch. Ston 119 E8
Stainton La. Ston S66 119 D7
Stainton La. Ston S66 101 E3
Stainton Rd. Shef S11 140 B8
Stainton St. Con DN12 80 F3
Stair Rd. Shef S4 129 C8
Staithes Wlk. Con DN12 81 A4
Stake Hill Rd. Bfield S6 125 B6
Stalker Lees Rd. Shef S11 140 D8
Stambers Cl. Woods S81 147 E3
Stamford St. Shef S9 129 F7
Stamford Way. Mapp S75 14 B2
Stampers Hill. Hd Gr S75 54 D2
Stan Valley. K Smea WF8 3 E6
Stanage Rise. Shef S12 142 E5
Stanbury Cl. Barn S75 33 B4
Stancil La. Wad DN11 103 B6
Stancil La. Wad DN11 103 C4
Stand House Fst Sch. Shef 142 A8
Standhill Cres. Barn S71 33 E7
Standish Ave. Shef S5 129 A8
Standish Cl. Shef S5 113 A1
Standish Cres. S Kirk WF9 18 C4
Standish Dr. Shef S5 113 A1
Standish Rd. Shef S5 113 A1
Standon Cres. Shef S9 114 A5
Standon Dr. Shef S9 114 A5
Standon Rd. Shef S9 114 A5
Standwel House. Ben DN5 61 E5
Staneford Ct. Shef S19 143 D1
Stanford Rd. Dron S18 152 C1
Stanford Rd. Maltby S66 119 C4
Stanhope Ave. Caw S75 31 F5
Stanhope Gdns. Barn S75 33 C3
Stanhope Rd. Don DN4 62 E5
Stanhope Rd. Shef S12 142 C5
Stanhope St. Barn S70 33 D1 2
Stanhurst La. Hat DN7 26 A1
Staniforth Ave. Eck S31 155 B3
Staniforth Cres. Tod S31 145 E5
Staniforth Rd. Shef S9 130 B5
Stanley Ct. Maltby S66 118 D5
Stanley Gdns. Don DN4 62 B1
Stanley Gdns. Stai DN7 24 E3
Stanley Gr. Aston S31 144 F8
Stanley Gr. Hat DN7 25 A1
Stanley La. Shef S3 129 B5
Stanley Rd. Barn S70 55 E7
Stanley Rd. Ben DN5 61 D7
Stanley Rd. Chap S30 94 E6
Stanley Rd. Shef S8 141 B5
Stanley Rd. Stai DN7 24 E3
Stanley Rd. Stock S30 73 C1
Stanley Sq. Don DN3 42 F4
Stanley St. Barn S70 33 D1
Stanley St. Cud S72 35 C4
Stanley St. Kill S31 156 D7
Stanley St. Roth S60 115 D6
Stanley St. Shef S3 129 B5
Stanley Terr. Maltby S66 118 D5
Stannington Coll of F Ed. Shef 127 F7
Stannington Inf Sch. Shef 127 C6
Stannington Rd. Shef S6 127 D6
Stannington View Rd. Shef S10 128 B4
Stanton Cres. Shef S12 142 D4
Stanwell Ave. Shef S9 114 A4
Stanwell Cl. Shef S9 114 A4
Stanwell St. Shef S9 114 A4
Stanwell Wlk. Shef S9 114 A4
Stanwood Ave. Shef S6 127 F6
Stanwood Cres. Shef S6 128 A6
Stanwood Dr. Shef S6 127 F6
Stanwood Mews. Shef S6 127 F6
Stanwood Rd. Shef S6 127 F6
Staple Gn. Roth S65 99 A2
Stapleton Rd. Don DN4 82 D5
Star La. Barn S70 33 E1
Starkbridge La. Syke DN14 7 B6
Starling House. Hem WF9 17 D6
Starling Mead. Shef S2 129 E2
Starnhill Cl. Shef S30 95 C1
Station App. Hath S30 149 A7
Station Ave. Shef S19 144 A4
Station Cl. Finn DN9 86 E4
Station La. Ought S30 111 D7
Station La. Shef S9 114 A2
Station Rd. Ad l S DN6 40 D7
Station Rd. Askern DN6 22 A8
Station Rd. B Dun DN3 42 F6
Station Rd. Barl S31 156 D2
Station Rd. Barn S70 33 D2
Station Rd. Barn S71 34 F5
Station Rd. Barn S70, S73 55 F4
Station Rd. Bawtry DN10 123 A7
Station Rd. Ben DN5 41 D2
Station Rd. Chap S30 95 B6
Station Rd. Con DN12 81 C3
Station Rd. Dar S73 56 E3
Station Rd. Dearne S63 58 C2
Station Rd. Dearne S63 58 D8
Station Rd. Dod S75 53 E7
Station Rd. Eck S31 156 A2
Station Rd. Finn DN9 86 E4
Station Rd. Hat DN7 24 F1
Station Rd. Hat DN7 44 B8
Station Rd. Hath S30 149 A7
Station Rd. Hem WF9 17 E7
Station Rd. Laugh S31 134 C3
Station Rd. Mapp S75 13 E1
Station Rd. Mex S64 80 A4
Station Rd. Norton DN6 4 E3
Station Rd. Rawcl DN14 2 B8
Station Rd. Ross DN11 85 A1
Station Rd. Roth S60 115 C6
Station Rd. Roy S71 15 B4
Station Rd. S Elm WF9 19 A3
Station Rd. Scro DN10 123 A2
Station Rd. Shef S9 130 C4
Station Rd. Shef S13 143 D7
Station Rd. Shef S19 155 E7
Station Rd. Shef S30 95 C1
Station Rd. Stock S30 74 A1
Station Rd. Treet S60 131 C6
Station Rd. Treet S60 131 E4
Station Rd. W up D S63 79 A7
Station Rd. Wales S31 145 E2
Station St. Swint S64 79 D3
Station Terr. Roy S71 15 E4
Station Way. Laugh S31 134 C3
Staton La. Uns S18 154 A1
Statutes The. Roth S60 115 D6
Staunton Rd. Don DN4 85 A7
Staveley La. Eck S31 155 E2
Staveley Rd. Shef S8 141 A7
Staveley St. N Edl DN12 82 B3
Stead La. Hoy S74 76 C4
Stead St. Eck S31 155 D3
Steade Rd. Shef S7 140 F7
Steadfield Rd. Hoy S74 76 C5
Steadfolds Cl. Thurcr S66 134 A6
Steadfolds La. Thurcr S66 134 B6
Steadfolds Rise. Thurcr S66 134 A6
Steadlands The. Rawm S62 97 D7
Steel Hill. Shef S6 112 C7
Steel Rd. Shef S11 140 C8
Steel St. Roth S61 115 A5
Steele St. Hoy S74 76 A5
Steelhouse La. Shef S3 129 A4 7
Steep La. Pen S30 52 A4
Steetley La. Whit S80 159 E3
Steetley La. Work S80 159 E3
Steeton Ct. Hoy S74 77 A6
Stemp St. Shef S11 140 F8
Stenton Rd. Shef S8 152 F7
Stephen Dr. Shef S10 127 F3
Stephen Dr. Shef S30 112 B8
Stephen Hill Rd. Shef S10 128 A3
Stephen Hill. Shef S10 127 F3
Stephen La. Shef S30 112 B8
Stepney Row. Shef S2 129 C4
Stepney St. Shef S2 129 C4
Stepping La. Shef S30 94 B1
Sterndale Rd. Shef S7 140 C3
Steven Cl. Chap S30 94 F4
Steven Cres. Chap S30 94 F5
Stevens Rd. Don DN4 62 B1
Stevenson Dr. Barn S65 32 E4
Stevenson Dr. Roth S65 116 B5
Stevenson Rd. Don DN4 83 B6
Stevenson Rd. Shef S9 129 E6
Stevenson Way. Shef S9 129 F6
Steventon Rd. Roth S65 99 A2
Stewart Cl. C in L S81 148 E6
Stewart Rd. C in L S81 148 E6
Stewart Rd. Shef S11 140 D8
Stewart St. Don DN1 62 C2
Stewarts Rd. Rawm S62 98 B6
Sticking La. Mex S63 79 E7
Stirling Ave. Bawtry DN10 123 A8
Stirling Cl. Hoy S74 77 A6
Stirling Dr. C in L S81 148 E6
Stirling Inf Sch. Don 62 C2
Stirling Jun Sch. Don 62 C2
Stirling St. Don DN1 62 C1
Stock Rd. Shef S2 129 E1
Stock's La. Barn S75 33 D2
Stock's La. Rawm S62 97 F5
Stockarth Cl. Shef S30 111 F4
Stockarth La. Shef S30 111 F4
Stockbridge Ave. Ben DN5 62 A7
Stockbridge La. Ad le S DN5 21 E3
Stockil Rd. Don DN4 62 E2
Stockingate. S Kirk WF9 18 B2
Stocks Dr. Rawcl DN14 2 C7
Stocks Dr. Shep HD8 28 E8
Stocks Green Ct. Shef S17 151 D4
Stocks Green Dr. Shef S17 151 D4
Stocks Hill Cl. Roy S71 15 C1
Stocks Hill. Shef S30 95 A1
Stocks La. Midhop S30 71 D4
Stocks Way. Shep HD8 28 D8
Stocksbridge Inf Sch. Stock 73 A1
Stocksbridge Jun Sch. Stock 92 B8
Stocksbridge La. Ben DN5 41 C2
Stocksbridge Sch. Stock 73 B1
Stocksbridge Sch. Stock 92 B8
Stockton Cl. Shef S3 129 B5
Stockton Pl. Shef S3 129 B5
Stockwell Ave. Wales S31 145 C1
Stockwell La. Wales S31 145 B1
Stockwith La. Hoy S74 76 B7
Stocthorn Gr. Wharn S30 93 C2
Stoke St. Shef S9 129 E5
Stoket La. Ulley S60 132 F5
Stokewell Rd. W up D S63 78 C7
Stone Cl. Dron S18 153 C3
Stone Cl. Roth S65 117 D7
Stone Cl. Wales S31 145 E2
Stone Close Ave. Don DN4 62 B2
Stone Cres. Roth S66 117 B5
Stone Crest Rise. Thurgo S30 73 F7
Stone Cross Dr. Sprot DN5 61 B2
Stone Ct. S Hie S72 16 E5
Stone Delf. Shef S10 127 D1
Stone Font Gr. Don DN4 85 A7
Stone Gr. Shef S10 128 D2
Stone Hill Dr. Aston S31 144 D7
Stone Hill. Hat DN7 45 A7
Stone Hill Rd. Hat DN7 44 F7
Stone La. Shef S13 143 B5
Stone Moor Rd. Stock S30 92 B7
Stone Park Cl. Maltby S66 119 B5
Stone Rd. Dron S18 153 C3
Stone Riding. N Edl DN12 82 A1
Stone St. Barn S71 33 E4
Stone St. Shef S19 155 D7
Stoneacre Ave. Shef S12 143 B3
Stoneacre Cl. Shef S12 143 B3 5
Stoneacre Dr. Shef S12 143 B2
Stoneacre Rise. Shef S12 143 B3
Stonebridge La. G Hou S72 36 F2
Stonecliff Wlk. Con DN12 81 A4
Stonecliffe Cl. Shef S2 130 A1
Stonecliffe Dr. Stock S30 92 B7
Stonecliffe Pl. Shef S2 130 A1
Stonecliffe Rd. Shef S2 130 A1
Stonecliffe Wlk. Shef S2 130 B1 1
Stonecroft Gdns. Shep HD8 28 F8
Stonecroft Rd. Shef S17 151 F5
Stonecross Gdns. Don DN4 85 A7
Stonedale Cl. Shef S19 155 D7
Stonegarth Cl. Cud S72 35 B6
Stonegate Cl. Blax DN9 86 E6
Stonegate. Thorne DN8 26 B7
Stonegravels Croft. Shef S19 155 E6 7
Stonegravels Way. Shef S19 155 F6
Stonehill Rise. Ben DN5 61 E7
Stonehill Rise. Cud S72 35 B6
Stonehill Rise. Pen S30 51 C1
Stonelea Cl. Silk S75 52 F8
Stoneleigh Croft. Barn S70 54 F7 9
Stoneley Cl. Shef S12 142 B1
Stoneley Cres. Shef S12 142 B1
Stonelow Cty Jun Sch The. Dron 153 C2
Stonelow Cres. Dron S18 153 C2
Stonelow Gn. Dron S18 153 B2
Stonelow Rd. Dron S18 153 C2
Stonely Brook. Roth S65 117 D6
Stonerow Way. Roth S60 97 F1
Stones Ings. Chap S30 94 D7
Stonewood Ct. Shef S10 127 D2
Stonewood Gr. Hoy S74 76 E4
Stonewood Gr. Shef S10 127 D2
Stoney Bank Dr. Wales S31 145 E2
Stoney Gate. Chap S30 94 D8
Stoney La. Tick DN11 120 F6
Stoney Well La. Maltby S66 119 E4
Stoneybrook Cl. W Bret WF4 12 F8
Stony Croft La. Burg DN6 21 A3
Stony Croft La. Midhop S30 72 A3
Stony La. Ought S30 111 B7
Stony La. Shef S6 110 F3
Stony La. Tick DN11 102 E2
Stony Ridge Rd. Shef S17 150 C5
Stonyford Rd. Dar S73 56 F4
Stoops La. Don DN4 84 C6
Stoops Rd. Don DN4 84 D7
Stopes Rd. Shef S6 127 A6
Store St. Shef S2 129 B1
Storey St. Swint S64 79 D3
Storey's Gate. Wombw S73 56 B4
Storm House Sch for Autistic Children. W up D 78 D7
Storrs Bridge La. Shef S6 111 A1
Storrs Carr. Shef S6 126 F8
Storrs Gn. Shef S6 126 F8
Storrs Hall Rd. Shef S6 128 B6
Storrs La. Askern DN5 22 C4
Storrs La. Oxspr S30 52 C4
Storrs La. Shef S6 127 A7
Storrs La. Wort S30 75 B2
Storrs Mill. Cud S72 35 D3
Storrs Mill La. Dar S72 35 E2
Storth Ave. Shef S10 139 E8
Storth La. Shef S10 127 E1
Storth La. Tod S31 145 E5
Storth La. Wales S31 145 C3
Storth La. Wharn S30 93 A2
Storth Pk. Shef S10 139 D7
Stortholme Mews. Shef S10 127 E1
Storthwood Ct. Shef S10 127 E1
Stotfold Dr. Dearne S63 58 C8
Stotfold Rd. Clay DN5 37 E3
Stothard Rd. Shef S10 128 B4
Stottercliffe Rd. Pen S30 51 C3
Stour La. Shef S6 111 F2
Stovin Cl. Shef S9 130 C7
Stovin Dr. Shef S9 130 B7
Stovin Gdns. Shef S9 130 C7
Stow Bridge La. Ulley S60 132 E6
Stowe Ave. Shef S7 140 C4
Stradbroke Ave. Shef S13 142 D7
Stradbroke Cl. Shef S13 142 E7
Stradbroke Cres. Shef S13 142 E7
Stradbroke Dr. Shef S13 142 E7
Stradbroke Pl. Shef S13 142 E7
Stradbroke Prim Sch. Shef 142 D7
Stradbroke Rd. Shef S13 142 E6
Stradbroke Way. Shef S13 142 E7
Stradbroke Wlk. Shef S13 142 D7
Strafford Ave. Barn S70 54 F6
Strafford Ave. Hoy S74 77 B6
Strafford Pl. Roth S61 95 E5
Strafford Rd. Don DN2 62 E5
Strafford Rd. Roth S61 96 E2
Strafford St. Kex S75 32 C8
Strafford Wlk. Dod S75 53 F6
Strafforth House. Con DN12 80 E3
Straight La. Dearne S63 58 E5
Straight La. Ham DN6 20 B4
Strait La. W up D S63 78 E6
Stratford Rd. Shef S10 127 D1
Strathavon Rd. C in L S81 148 F6
Strathmore Ct. Har DN11 122 B5
Strathmore Dr. C in L S81 148 F6
Strathmore Gdns. S Elm WF9 19 B4
Strathmore Gr. W up D S63 78 F6
Strathmore Rd. Don DN2 63 A3
Strathtay Rd. Shef S11 140 B7
Strauss Cres. Maltby S66 119 B4
Straw La. Shef S6 128 E5
Strawberry Ave. Shef S5 113 B6
Strawberry Gdns. Roy S71 15 D4
Strawberry Lee La. Shef S17 151 B5
Streatfield Cres. Ross DN11 84 E1
Street Farm Cl. Hart S31 157 E6
Street La. H Pag DN5 38 F3
Street La. W up D S62 77 E2
Streetfield Cres. Shef S19 155 D6
Streetfields. Shef S19 155 E6
Strelley Ave. Shef S8 140 E1
Strelley Rd. Barn S71 33 E8
Strelley Rd. Shef S8 140 E1
Stretton Cl. Don DN4 85 A8
Stretton Rd. Barn S71 34 A5
Stretton Rd. Shef S11 140 C7
Strickland Rd. Upton WF9 19 D8
Strines Moor Rd. Holmfi HD7 48 C8
Stringers Croft. Roth S60 116 D1
Stripe Rd. Ross DN11 104 B5
Stripe Rd. Tick DN11 103 F1
Struan Rd. Shef S7 140 D5
Strutt Rd. Shef S3 129 A7
Stuart Gr. Chap S30 95 B4
Stuart Rd. Chap S30 95 B4
Stuart St. Dearne S63 58 E8
Stubbin Cl. Rawm S62 97 D7
Stubbin La. D Dale HD8 30 B6
Stubbin La. Rawm S62 97 D8
Stubbin La. Shef S5 113 D4
Stubbin Rd. Rawm S62 97 B7
Stubbing House La. Shef S30 112 B7
Stubbing La. Ought S30 111 C3
Stubbins Hill. N Edl DN12 82 C1
Stubbs Cres. Roth S61 96 F1
Stubbs La. Norton DN6 4 D4
Stubbs Rd. K Smea DN6 4 A5
Stubbs Rd. Wombw S73 56 C2
Stubbs Wlk. Roth S61 96 F1
Stubley Cl. Dron S18 152 E2
Stubley Croft. Dron S18 152 D2
Stubley Dr. Dron S18 152 E2
Stubley Hollow. Dron S18 152 F3
Stubley Hollow Riding Ctr. Dron 152 E3
Stubley La. Dron S18 152 D2
Stubley Pl. Dron S18 152 E2
Studfield Cres. Shef S6 127 F8
Studfield Dr. Shef S6 111 F1
Studfield Gr. Shef S6 127 F8
Studfield Hill. Shef S6 127 F8
Studfield Rd. Shef S6 127 F8
Studfield Rise. Shef S6 127 F8
Studley Ct. Shef S9 130 C4
Studmoor Rd. Roth S61 96 D2
Stump Cross Gdns. Dearne S63 58 B2
Stump Cross La. Tick DN11 120 D3
Stump Cross Rd. W up D S63 78 E5
Stumperlowe Ave. Shef S10 139 E8
Stumperlowe Cl. Shef S10 139 E8
Stumperlowe Crescent Rd. Shef S10 139 E8
Stumperlowe Croft. Shef S10 127 D1
Stumperlowe Hall Chase. Shef S10 127 D1
Stumperlowe Hall Rd. Shef S10 139 D8
Stumperlowe La. Shef S10 139 D8
Stumperlowe Park Rd. Shef S10 139 E8
Stumperlowe View. Shef S10 127 D1
Stupton Rd. Shef S9 114 A2
Sturton Cl. Don DN4 84 D6
Sturton Croft. Roth S65 98 E1
Sturton Rd. Shef S4 129 C8
Stygate La. Norton DN6 4 C2
Styrrup La. Old DN11 121 B1
Styrrup La. Styr DN11 121 B1
Styrrup Rd. Har DN11 121 E3
Styrrup Rd. Styr DN11 121 E3
Sudbury Dr. Aston S31 144 E7
Sudbury St. Shef S3 128 F5
Suffolk Ave. Bir DN11 122 D4
Suffolk Cl. N Anst S31 146 E6
Suffolk Gr. Bir DN11 122 D4
Suffolk Rd. Bir DN11 122 D4
Suffolk Rd. Don DN4 83 B6
Suffolk Rd. Shef S2 129 B2
Suffolk View. Con DN12 80 F2
Sugworth Rd. Bfield S6 125 A7
Sulby Gr. Barn S70 55 D6
Sullivan Gr. S Kirk WF9 18 B1
Summer La. Barn S70,S75 33 D2
Summer La. Roy S71 15 B4
Summer La. Shef S17 151 D4
Summer La. Wombw S73 56 C3
Summer Rd. Roy S71 15 B4
Summer St. Barn S70 33 D2
Summer St. Shef S3 128 E4
Summerdale Rd. Cud S72 35 A5
Summerfield Rd. Dron S18 153 B3
Summerfield. Roth S65 115 E6
Summerfield St. Shef S11 128 E1
Summerfields Dr. Blax DN9 86 E6
Summerley Lower Rd. Uns S18 153 F2
Summerley Rd. Uns S18 153 F2
Summerwood La. Dron S18 152 F3
Summerwood Pl. Dron S18 152 F2
Sumner Rd. Roth S65 115 F8
Sunderland Pl. Tick DN11 121 B7
Sunderland St. Shef S11 128 E1
Sunderland St. Tick DN11 121 B7
Sunderland Terr. Barn S70 55 A8
Sundew Croft. Chap S30 94 D8
Sundew Gdns. Chap S30 94 D8
Sundown Pl. Shef S13 142 F8
Sundown Rd. Shef S13 142 F8
Sunlea Flats. Roth S65 115 F7
Sunningdale Ave. Mapp S75 14 A1
Sunningdale Cl. Don DN4 85 B6
Sunningdale Cl. Swint S64 79 D2
Sunningdale Dr. Cud S72 16 C1
Sunningdale Mount. Shef S11 140 C5
Sunningdale Rd. Din S31 146 F8
Sunningdale Rd. Don DN2 63 A5
Sunningdale Rd. Hat DN7 44 F6
Sunny Ave. S Elm WF9 19 B2
Sunny Ave. Upton WF9 19 A7
Sunny Bank. Chap S30 94 D7
Sunny Bank Dr. Cud S72 35 C5
Sunny Bank Rd. Silk S75 52 F8
Sunny Bank Rd. Stock S30 92 D6
Sunny Bank Rise. Hoy S74 77 A6
Sunny Bank. Shef S10 128 E1
Sunny Bar. Don DN1 62 D3
Sunnybank Cres. Brin S60 131 C8
Sunnybank. D Dale HD8 29 F5
Sunnybank Cl. Hoy S74 76 E4
Sunnymede Ave. Askern DN6 22 B8
Sunnymede Cres. Askern DN6 22 B8
Sunnymede Terr. Askern DN6 22 B8
Sunnyside. Bran DN3 85 E8
Sunnyside Cl. N Anst S31 146 E6
Sunnyside. Don DN3 42 E2
Sunnyvale Ave. Shef S17 151 E4
Sunnyvale Mount. S Elm WF9 18 E3
Sunnyvale Rd. Shef S17 151 D4
Sunrise Manor. Hoy S74 76 E8
Surbiton St. Shef S9 130 B8
Surrey Cl. Barn S70 54 F7
Surrey La. Shef S1 129 B2
Surrey Pl. Shef S1 129 B3
Surrey St. Don DN4 83 B7
Surrey St. Shef S1 129 A3
Surtees Cl. Maltby S66 118 E7
Sussex Cl. Hem WF9 17 D8
Sussex Gdns. Con DN12 80 F3
Sussex Rd. Chap S30 95 A5
Sussex Rd. Shef S4 129 C5
Sussex St. Don DN4 83 B7
Sussex St. Shef S4 129 C4
Suthard Cross Rd. Shef S10 128 B4
Sutherland Cl. C in L S81 148 F8
Sutherland House. Don DN2 63 A6
Sutherland Rd. Shef S4 129 C6
Sutherland St. Shef S4 129 D5
Sutton Ave. Barn S71 33 F8
Sutton Rd. Askern DN6 21 E5
Sutton Rd. Don DN3 43 A5
Sutton Rd. Norton DN6 21 C8
Sutton St. Shef S3 128 E3
Suttonfield Rd. Askern DN6 21 D6
Suzanne Cres. S Elm WF9 18 E3
Swaith Ave. Ben DN5 61 F7
Swaithe View. Barn S70 55 D5
Swaithedale. Barn S70 55 C5
Swale Cl. Dearne S63 58 D2
Swale Dr. Chap S30 94 E5
Swale Gdns. Shef S9 130 C4
Swale Rd. Roth S61 97 A3
Swaledale Rd. Shef S7 140 D5
Swallow Cl. Barn S70 75 F8
Swallow Cl. Kex S75 32 D8
Swallow Ct. Ross DN11 85 A1
Swallow Hill Rd. Mapp S75 33 B7
Swallow La. Aston S31 144 E6
Swallow Wood Ct. Shef S13 143 A6
Swamp Wlk. Shef S6 128 D7
Swan Rd. Aston S31 144 E6
Swan St. Bawtry DN10 123 A6
Swan St. Ben DN5 41 B1
Swan St. Roth S60 115 D5
Swan Syke Dr. Norton DN6 4 E3
Swanbourne Pl. Shef S5 113 C4
Swanbourne Rd. Shef S5 113 C5
Swanee Rd. Barn S70 55 C7
Swannington Cl. Don DN4 85 B7
Swarcliffe Rd. Shef S9 130 A5
Swawthorpe Sunnyfields Prim Sch. Ben 61 E7
Sweeny House. Stock S30 73 A1
Sweet La. Wad DN11 102 C7
Sweyn Croft. Barn S70 55 A5
Swift Rd. Shef S30 112 D8
Swift Rise. Roth S61 96 A6
Swift St. Barn S75 33 D2
Swift Way. Shef S2 129 E1
Swifte Rd. Roth S60 116 A3
Swinburne Ave. Ad l S DN6 40 A5
Swinburne Ave. Don DN4 83 B6
Swinburne Cl. B Dun DN3 42 F8
Swinburne Pl. Roth S65 116 B5
Swinburne Rd. Roth S65 116 B5
Swinnock La. Wharn S30 93 A2
Swinnow Rd. Bir DN11 122 C4
Swinston Hill Rd. Din S31 147 B6
Swinton Comp Sch. Swint 79 C2
Swinton Meadows Bsns Pk. Swint 79 F3
Swinton Meadows Ind Est. Swint 79 F3
Swinton Rd. Mex S64 79 F4
Swinton St. Shef S3 129 A5
Swinton Sta. Swint 79 E3
Swithen Hill. Kex S75 13 B3
Sycamore Ave. Arm DN3 64 C7
Sycamore Ave. Cud S72 35 B7
Sycamore Ave. Dron S18 153 A3
Sycamore Ave. Grime S72 36 B5
Sycamore Ave. Roth S66 117 C5
Sycamore Ave. Wales S31 145 C2
Sycamore Cres. Bawtry DN10 122 F7
Sycamore Cres. W up D S63 78 F5
Sycamore Dr. Finn DN9 86 A4
Sycamore Dr. Kill S31 156 C5
Sycamore Dr. Roy S71 15 A3
Sycamore Farm Cl. Roth S66 117 B3
Sycamore Flats. W up D S63 78 F5
Sycamore Gr. Con DN12 81 A1
Sycamore Gr. Don DN4 84 F8
Sycamore Hall Prep Sch. Don 83 A7
Sycamore House Rd. Shef S5 113 F6
Sycamore La. W Bret WF4 12 F8
Sycamore Primary Schs. Don 84 E7
Sycamore Rd. B Dun DN3 42 F7
Sycamore Rd. C in L S81 148 E7
Sycamore Rd. Hem WF9 17 C6
Sycamore Rd. Mex S64 79 E5
Sycamore Rd. Roth S65 98 B1
Sycamore Rd. Shef S30 113 B8
Sycamore Rd. Stock S30 92 A8
Sycamore St. Barn S75 33 C2
Sycamore St. Shef S19 143 F4
Sycamore St. Shef S19 155 C8
Sycamore View. Sprot DN5 61 D1
Sycamore Wlk. Dearne S63 37 D1
Sycamore Wlk. Pen S30 51 D3
Sycamores The. Ben DN5 61 D8
Syday La. Barl S31 156 D1
Sydney Rd. Shef S6 128 D4
Sydney Terr. Barn S70 55 A8
Sykehouse La. Shef S6 126 D7
Sykehouse Prim Sch. Syke 7 C7
Sykehouse Rd. Syke DN14 7 E7
Sykes Ave. Barn S75 33 D2
Sykes Ct. Swint S64 79 D1
Sykes St. Barn S70 54 D7
Sylvan Cl. Maltby S66 119 B6
Sylvester Ave. Don DN4 62 C1
Sylvester Gdns. Shef S1 129 A2
Sylvester St. Shef S1 129 A2
Sylvestria Cl. Ross DN11 85 A1
Sylvia Cl. Shef S13 143 D7
Symes Gdns. Don DN4 63 F1
Symonds Ave. Rawm S62 97 C8
Symons Cres. Shef S5 112 F4

Union St. Hem WF9 17 E6
Union St. Roth S61 115 B6
Union St. Shef S1 129 A2
Unity Pl. Roth S60 115 D6
Univ of Sheffield. Shef 128 E3
Unsliven Rd. Stock S30 72 F3
Unstone St. Shef S1 129 A1
Unstone-Dronfield By-Pass. Dron S18 152 F3
Unwin Cres. Pen S30 51 D2
Unwin St. Pen S30 51 D2
Uplands Ave. Kex S75 32 C8
Uplands Rd. Arm DN3 64 C6
Uplands Way. Rawm S62 97 E6
Upper Albert Rd. Shef S8 141 B5
Upper Allen St. Shef S3 128 F4
Upper Ash Gr. S Elm WF9 19 B3
Upper Clara St. Roth S61 114 F6
Upper Cliffe Rd. Dod S75 53 E8
Upper Common La. Clay W HD8 12 A1
Upper Common La. Clay W HD8 30 F8
Upper Cumberworth C of E Aided Fst Sch. D Dale 29 B6
Upper Field La. H Hoy S75 12 E1
Upper Field La. Kex S75 12 E1
Upper Folderings. Dod S75 53 F7
Upper Gate Rd. Shef S6 127 C6
Upper Hanover St. Shef S3 128 E2
Upper Hanover St. Shef S3 128 E3
Upper House Rd. Holmfi HD7 48 C8
Upper Hoyland Rd. Hoy S74 76 C7
Upper Kenyon St. Thorne DN8 26 B8
Upper Ley Cl. Chap S30 95 A5
Upper Ley Dell. Chap S30 95 A5
Upper Maythorn La. Wh Com HD7 49 D8
Upper Mill Gate. Roth S60 115 D6
Upper New St. Barn S70 54 F8 1
Upper Norcroft. Caw S75 31 F3
Upper Rye Cl. Roth S60 116 D1
Upper School La. Dron S18 153 A1
Upper Sheffield Rd. Barn S70 55 A6
Upper Valley Rd. Shef S8 141 B5
Upper Whiston La. Ulley S60 132 D7
Upper Wortley Rd. Roth S61 96 B2
Upperfield Cl. Maltby S66 118 F6
Upperfield Rd. Maltby S66 118 E6
Upperthorpe Fst Sch. Shef 128 E5
Upperthorpe Glen. Shef S6 128 D5
Upperthorpe Mid Sch. Shef 128 E5
Upperthorpe Rd. Kill S31 156 D4
Upperthorpe Rd. Shef S6 128 E5
Upperthorpe. Shef S6 128 D5
Upperthorpe Villas. Kill S31 156 D5
Upperwood Hall. Dar S73 56 E6
Upperwood Rd. Dar S73 56 E6
Upton Cl. Maltby S66 118 F7
Upton Cl. Wombw S73 56 B4
Upton Mid Sch. Upton 18 F7
Upwell Hill. Shef S4 113 E1
Upwell La. Shef S4 113 E1
Upwell St. Shef S4 113 F1
Upwood Rd. Shef S6 112 B1
Urban Rd. Don DN4 62 A1
Urch Cl. Con DN12 81 C1
Uttley Cl. Shef S9 130 B6
Uttley Croft. Shef S9 130 B6
Uttley Dr. Shef S9 130 B6
Uttoxeter Ave. Mex S64 80 C6

Vaal St. Barn S70 55 B8
Vainor Rd. Shef S6 112 A2
Vale Ave. Roth S65 98 F2
Vale Cl. Dron S18 153 B1
Vale Cres. Roth S65 98 F2
Vale Gr. Shef S6 127 E8
Vale Rd. Roth S65 99 A2
Vale Rd. Shef S3 128 F7
Valentine Cl. Shef S5 113 C5
Valentine Cres. Shef S5 113 C5
Valentine Rd. Shef S5 113 C5
Valestone Ave. Hem WF9 17 E7
Valetta House. Rawm S62 97 F4
Valiant Gdns. Ben DN5 61 E3
Valley Ave. S Elm WF9 19 B3
Valley Dr. Bran DN3 85 D8
Valley Dr. Kill S31 156 D7
Valley Dr. W up D S63 78 E6
Valley Rd. Chap S30 94 E6
Valley Rd. Dar S73 56 E3
Valley Rd. Kill S31 156 D7
Valley Rd. Mapp S75 14 A1
Valley Rd. Shef S8 141 A6
Valley Rd. Shef S12 143 C3
Valley Rd. Swint S64 79 B1
Valley St. S Elm WF9 18 F2
Valley View Cl. Eck S31 155 C2
Valley View. S Elm WF9 19 B3
Valley Way. Hoy S74 76 E5
Vancouver Dr. Dearne S63 58 B2
Varley Gdns. Roth S66 117 B6
Varney Rd. W up D S63 78 E4
Varsity Cl. Hat DN7 66 A7
Vaughan Rd. Barn S75 33 B3
Vaughan Rd. Norton DN6 4 D1
Vaughan St. Don DN1 62 D4
Vaughan Terr. G Hou S72 36 E2
Vaughton Hill. Shef S30 73 F1
Vauxhall Cl. Shef S9 114 B4
Vauxhall Rd. Shef S9 114 B4
Velvet Wood Cl. Barn S75 33 A3
Venetian Cres. Dar S73 56 F5
Ventnor Cl. Don DN4 82 F7
Ventnor Ct. Shef S7 140 F8 13
Ventnor Pl. Shef S7 140 F8
Venus Ct. Brin S60 115 C2
Verdant Way. Shef S5 113 D5
Verdon St. Shef S3 129 B5
Vere Rd. Shef S6 112 C2
Verelst Ave. Aston S31 144 D8
Verger Cl. Ross DN11 85 B1
Vermuyden Rd. Thorne DN8 9 D3
Vernon Cl. Barn S70 54 F7
Vernon Cres. Barn S70 54 F5
Vernon Delph. Shef S10 127 F3
Vernon Dr. Chap S30 95 A5
Vernon Rd. Barn S70 55 A4
Vernon Rd. Roth S60 116 B3
Vernon Rd. Shef S17 151 F6
Vernon St. Barn S71 33 F2
Vernon St. Barn S70 75 F6
Vernon St. Hoy S74 76 C5
Vernon St N. Barn S71 33 F2 3
Vernon Terr. Shef S10 128 A2
Vernon Way. Barn S75 33 B3
Vernon Way. Maltby S66 118 E6
Vervena Rise. Dar S73 57 A5
Vesey St. Rawm S62 97 F4
Vicar Cres. Dar S73 57 B5
Vicar La. Shef S1 129 A3
Vicar La. Shef S13 143 B7
Vicar Rd. Dar S73 57 B5
Vicar Rd. W up D S63 78 E7
Vicarage Cl. Don DN4 85 A7
Vicarage Cl. Hoy S74 76 E6
Vicarage Cl. Mex S64 80 C4
Vicarage Cl. Roth S65 116 D8
Vicarage Cl. S Kirk WF9 18 C3
Vicarage Cres. Shef S30 112 C8
Vicarage Dr. Wad DN11 102 B7
Vicarage La. Roth S60 115 D6
Vicarage La. Roy S71 15 C3
Vicarage La. Shef S17 151 D7
Vicarage Rd. Shef S9 129 F6
Vicarage Rd. Shef S30 112 C8
Vicarage Way. Ben DN5 41 E2
Vicarage Wlk. Pen S30 51 D3
Vickers Ave. S Elm WF9 18 E1
Vickers Dr. Shef S5 113 D3
Vickers Rd. Chap S30 94 D7
Vickers Rd. Shef S5 113 D2
Victor Rd. S Kirk WF9 18 C2
Victor Rd. Shef S17 151 F7
Victor St. Ad I S DN6 40 B8
Victor St. S Elm WF9 18 F2
Victor St. Shef S6 128 D7
Victor Terr. Barn S70 55 A8 3
Victoria Ave. Barn S70 33 E2 1
Victoria Ave. Hat DN7 44 C8
Victoria Ave. Roth S65 115 F6
Victoria Cl. Stai DN7 24 F2
Victoria Cl. Stock S30 73 B1
Victoria Cl. Wales S31 145 E2
Victoria Cres. Barn S70, S75 33 D2
Victoria Cres. Barn S70 75 E7
Victoria Cres W. Barn S75 33 D2
Victoria Ct. Ben DN5 41 B3
Victoria Ct. Upton WF9 19 A7
Victoria Ct. Wales S31 145 E2
Victoria La. Ross DN11 84 E1
Victoria Rd. Ad I S DN6 40 D6
Victoria Rd. Askern DN6 21 F6
Victoria Rd. Barn S70 33 E2
Victoria Rd. Ben DN5 41 B3
Victoria Rd. Don DN4, 83 B8
Victoria Rd. Mex S64 80 A5
Victoria Rd. N Edl DN12 82 B3
Victoria Rd. Norton DN6 4 C3
Victoria Rd. Rawm S62 97 F4
Victoria Rd. Rawm S62 98 A4
Victoria Rd. Roy S71 15 D4
Victoria Rd. Shef S10 128 E1
Victoria Rd. Shef S19 143 F4
Victoria Rd. Stock S30 73 C1
Victoria Rd. W up D S63 78 D7
Victoria Rd. Wombw S73 56 D3
Victoria St. Barn S70 33 E2
Victoria St. Barn S70 55 D8
Victoria St. Cud S72 35 B7
Victoria St. Dar S73 57 B6
Victoria St. Dearne S63 58 E5
Victoria St. Din S31 135 A1
Victoria St. Dron S18 152 F2
Victoria St. Hem WF9 17 E6
Victoria St. Hoy S74 76 F6
Victoria St. Maltby S66 119 A3
Victoria St. Mex S64 79 E5
Victoria St. Pen S30 51 D3
Victoria St. Roth S60 115 B6
Victoria St. Shef S3 128 F3
Victoria St. Stock S30 73 C1
Victoria St. Swint S62 98 E7
Victoria St. Treet S60 131 D6
Victoria Station Rd. Shef S4 129 C4
Victoria Terr. Barn S70 55 A8 11
Victoria Way. Maltby S66 118 D6
Victorian Cres. Don DN2 62 F4
View Rd. Pen S30 51 A4
View Rd. Roth S65 116 A8
View Rd. Shef S2 141 A7
Viewland Cl. Cud S72 35 C5
Viewlands Cl. Pen S30 51 D5
Viewlands. Silk S75 53 A5
Viewtree Cl. Went S62 76 D1
Viking Way. Wales S31 145 F3
Vikinglea Cl. Shef S2 142 B8
Vikinglea Dr. Shef S2 142 B8
Vikinglea Glade. Shef S2 130 B1
Vikinglea Rd. Shef S2 130 B1
Villa Gdns. Ben DN5 41 A5
Villa Park Rd. Don DN4 84 E8
Villa Rd. Ad I S DN6 40 B5
Village St. Ad I S DN6 40 C6
Village St. Ben DN6 61 D5
Villiers Cl. Shef S2 141 E6
Villiers Dr. Shef S2 141 E6
Vincent Rd. Barn S71 34 F3
Vincent Rd. Roth S65 117 D7
Vincent Rd. Shef S7 140 F8
Vincent Terr. Dearne S63 58 F7
Vine Cl. Barn S71 34 C4
Vine Cl. Roth S60 115 C6
Vine Rd. Tick DN11 121 C7
Vineyard Cl. Tick DN11 120 F8
Viola Bank. Stock S30 73 B1
Violet Ave. N Edl DN12 82 B1
Violet Ave. Shef S19 143 F3
Violet Bank Rd. Shef S7 140 E6
Vissett Cl. Hem WF9 17 B6
Vissitt La. Hem WF9 17 B6
Vivian Rd. Shef S5 113 D2
Vizard Rd. Hoy S74 76 F6
Vizard Rd. Hoy S74 77 A6
Vulcan House. Roth S65 116 A7 2
Vulcan Rd. Shef S9 114 B2
Vulcan Rd. Shef S9 114 D2
Vulcan Way. Hat DN7 44 F1
Vulcan Way. Hat DN7 45 A1

Wadbrough Rd. Shef S11 128 D1
Waddington Rd. Barn S75 33 B2
Wade Cl. Roth S60 115 F4
Wade Meadow. Shef S6 112 A1
Wade St. Barn S75 33 B2
Wade St. Shef S4 113 E1
Wadsley La. Shef S6 112 B2
Wadsley Park Cres. Shef S6 112 A1
Wadsworth Ave. Shef S12 142 D5
Wadsworth Cl. Shef S12 142 D5
Wadsworth Dr. Rawm S62 97 C8
Wadsworth Dr. Shef S12 142 D5
Wadsworth Rd. Roth S66 117 D4
Wadsworth Rd. Shef S12 142 C5
Wadworth Ave. Ross DN11 85 B1
Wadworth Cl. Bnbur DN5 59 C3
Wadworth Hill. Wad DN11 102 C8
Wadworth Jun & Inf Sch. Wad 102 C6
Wadworth Rise. Roth S65 98 E1
Wadworth St. Con DN12 81 A4
Waggon La. Upton WF9 19 C8
Wagon Rd. Roth S61 97 B2
Waingate. Shef S3 129 B4
Wainwright Ave. Shef S13 142 D8
Wainwright Ave. Wombw S73 56 C3
Wainwright Cres. Shef S13 142 D8
Wainwright Pl. Wombw S73 56 B3
Wainwright Rd. Don DN4 62 E2
Wainwright Rd. Roth S61 96 F1
Wake Rd. Shef S7 140 E7
Wakefield District Coll. Hem 17 E7
Wakefield Rd. Barn S71, S75 33 E2
Wakefield Rd. Barn S71 34 A5
Wakefield Rd. D Dale HD8 30 B7
Wakefield Rd. Hem WF9 17 D8
Wakefield Rd. Mapp S75 14 C2
Walbank Rd. Arm DN3 64 C6
Walbert Ave. Dearne S63 58 C7
Walbrook. Barn S70 55 B4
Walden Ave. Ben DN5 40 E1
Walden Rd. Shef S2 141 B7
Walden Stubbs Rd. Norton DN6 4 D4
Walders Ave. Shef S6 112 A2
Wales Comp Sch. Wales 145 C3
Wales Jun & Inf Sch. Wales 145 B2
Wales Pl. Shef S6 128 D6
Wales Rd. Wales S31 145 C2
Walesmoor Ave. Wales S31 145 C2
Waleswood Rd. Wales S31 144 C4
Waleswood View. Aston S31 144 D6
Waleswood Villas. Wales S31 144 F3
Walford Rd. Kill S31 156 C6
Walk Royd Hill. Kex S75 13 B2
Walk The. Barn S70 75 E6
Walker Cl. Shef S30 112 C8
Walker Edge. Bfield S30 92 A3
Walker La. Roth S65 115 E7
Walker Rd. Pilley S75 75 F5
Walker Rd. Roth S61 96 F1
Walker St. Rawm S62 98 B6
Walker St. Shef S3 129 B5
Walker St. Swint S64 79 E3
Walker View. Rawm S62 98 B6
Walkers La. Kill S31 156 D6
Walkers Terr. Barn S71 34 C5
Walkley Bank Cl. Shef S6 128 C7
Walkley Bank Rd. Shef S6 128 B7
Walkley Crescent Rd. Shef S6 128 B6
Walkley Inf Sch. Shef 128 D6
Walkley Jun Sch. Shef 128 D6
Walkley La. Shef S6 128 C7
Walkley Rd. Shef S6 128 C6
Walkley St. Shef S6 128 D5
Walkley Terr. Shef S6 128 A6
Wall Nook La. Holmfi HD8 28 D6
Wall St. Barn S70 54 E8
Wallace Rd. Don DN4 82 E6
Wallace Rd. Shef S3 128 F7
Walled Garden The. Wool WF4 14 A7
Waller Rd. Shef S6 128 A5
Walling Cl. Shef S9 114 B2
Walling Rd. Shef S9 114 B2
Wallingwells La. Gild S81 147 F6
Wallroyds. D Dale HD8 29 F5
Walmsley Dr. Upton WF9 19 B7
Walney Fold. Barn S71 34 D6
Walnut Ave. Finn DN9 86 A4
Walnut Ave. Shire S81 159 F7
Walnut Ave. Tick DN11 121 B7
Walnut Dr. Din S31 146 F8
Walnut Dr. Kill S31 156 C5
Walnut Gr. Mex S64 79 F6
Walnut Pl. Chap S30 94 F4
Walnut St. S Elm WF9 18 F1
Walnut Tree Hill. Wad DN11 102 C7
Walpole Cl. Don DN4 82 F5
Walpole Gr. Aston S31 132 D1
Walseker La. Hart S31 157 C7
Walsham Dr. Ben DN5 61 E5
Walshaw Rd. Ought S30 111 D5
Walter St. Roth S60 115 C7
Walter St. Shef S6 128 D7
Walters Rd. Maltby S66 119 B5
Waltham Dr. Ad le S DN6 20 E2
Waltham Gdns. Shef S19 144 A2 1
Waltham St. Barn S70 54 F8 7
Waltheof Rd. Shef S2 142 A8
Waltheof Sch Darnall Road Annexe. Shef 130 B5
Waltheof Sch. Shef 130 B2
Walton Cl. Chap S30 94 C8
Walton Cl. Dron S18 152 C2
Walton Ct. Shef S8 152 E8
Walton Rd. Shef S11 128 D1
Walton Rd. Upton WF9 19 D8
Walton St. Barn S75 33 C3
Walton St N. Barn S75 33 C3
Wannop St. Rawm S62 97 F3
Wansfell Rd. Shef S4 113 F1
Wansfell Terr. Barn S71 34 A1
Wapping The. H Rob S65 99 D7
Warburton Cl. Shef S2 141 C7
Warburton Gdns. Shef S2 141 C7
Warburton Rd. Shef S2 141 C7
Ward Green Prim Sch. Barn 54 F5
Ward La. Barl S43 157 B2
Ward Pl. Shef16 S7 140 F8
Ward St. Pen S30 51 D2
Ward St. Shef S3 129 A5
Warde Ave. Don DN4 82 F6
Warde-Aldam Cres. Roth S66 117 A5
Warden Cl. Don DN4 85 A8
Warden St. Roth S60 115 D3
Wardlow Rd. Shef S12 142 D5
Wardsend Rd N. Shef S6 112 C3
Wardsend Rd. Shef S6 112 D2
Wareham Ct. Shef S19 144 A2
Wareham Gr. Dod S75 54 A8
Warehouse La. W up D S63 78 E6
Warminster Cl. Shef S8 141 A4
Warminster Dr. Shef S8 141 B3
Warminster Gdns. Shef S8 141 B4
Warminster Pl. Shef S8 141 B2
Warminster Rd. Shef S8 141 A3
Warmsworth C of E Fst Sch. Don 82 D5
Warmsworth Ct. Don DN4 82 D6
Warmsworth Halt. Don DN12 82 B4
Warmsworth Halt Ind Est. Don 82 C4
Warmsworth Mid Sch. Don 82 C6
Warmsworth Rd. Don DN4 82 E6
Warner Ave. Barn S75 33 B2
Warner Pl. Barn S75 33 C2
Warner Rd. Barn S75 33 B2
Warner Rd. Shef S6 112 B1
Warning Tongue La. Don DN4 85 B6
Warning Tongue La. Ross DN4 85 B6
Warnington Dr. Ross DN4 85 B5
Warren Ave. Rawm S62 97 E7
Warren Cl. Don DN2 63 A4
Warren Cl. Roy S71 15 D5
Warren Cl. Woods S81 147 E4
Warren Cres. Barn S70 54 F7
Warren Cres. Eck S31 154 E2
Warren Dr. Roth S61 114 F8
Warren Gdns. Chap S30 95 B8
Warren Hill. Roth S61 114 F8
Warren House Cl. Roth S66 117 D5
Warren La. Chap S30 75 F1
Warren La. Chap S30 95 B8
Warren La. Don DN4 84 F5
Warren La. Mapp S75 14 C4
Warren La. Ross DN11 85 A3
Warren La. Wool S75 14 C4
Warren Mount. Roth S61 114 F8
Warren Pl. Barn S70 54 F7 14
Warren Quarry La. Barn S70 54 F7
Warren Rd. Con DN12 81 B1
Warren Rd. Roth S66 117 B5
Warren Rd. Thorne DN8 26 C6
Warren Rise. Dron S18 153 C3
Warren St. Shef S4 129 D5
Warren St. Shef S4 129 E5
Warren Vale. Rawm S62 98 A7
Warren Vale Rd. Swint S64 79 A2
Warren Vale. Swint S64 79 A1
Warren View. Hoy S74 76 C4
Warren Wlk. Eck S31 154 E2
Warreners Dr. Roth S65 99 A2
Warrenne Cl. Hat DN7 44 A7
Warrenne Rd. Hat DN7 44 A8
Warrington Rd. Shef S10 128 D4
Warris Cl. Roth S61 96 E1
Warris Pl. Shef S2 129 D3
Warsop Rd. Barn S71 14 E1
Warwick Ave. C in L S81 148 F6
Warwick Cl. Hat DN7 45 A6
Warwick Rd. Barn S71 34 B4
Warwick Rd. Don DN2 63 B5
Warwick St. Roth S60 115 E5
Warwick St S. Roth S60 115 E5
Warwick St. Shef S10 128 C4
Warwick Terr. Shef S10 128 C4
Warwick Way. N Anst S31 146 E7
Wasdale Ave. Shef S19 155 E6 5
Wasdale Cl. Shef S19 155 E6
Washfield La. Treet S60 131 E4
Washford Rd. Shef S9 129 E5
Washheld Cres. Treet S60 131 E4
Washington Ave. Con DN12 81 A2
Washington Ave. Wombw S73 56 B2
Washington Gr. Ben DN5 62 A7
Washington Rd. Ad I S DN6 40 C5
Washington Rd. Dearne S63 58 D4
Washington Rd. Shef S11 140 F8
Washington Rd. Shef S30 95 B1
Washington St. Mex S64 80 B5
Wasteneys Rd. Tod S31 145 F5
Watch House La. Ben DN5 62 A7
Watch St. Shef S13 143 E8
Watchley La. H Pag DN5 38 B3
Water Bank. Wroot DN9 67 C2
Water Hall La. Pen S30 51 D4
Water La. Hoy S74 77 A3
Water La. K Smea WF8 3 E6
Water La. Roth S60 115 D5
Water La. S Kirk WF9 17 F4
Water La. Shef S17 151 F7
Water La. Stai DN7 24 E5
Water La. Tick DN11 121 A5
Water La. Wool WF4 14 A8
Water Royd Dr. Dod S75 54 A7
Water Slacks Cl. Shef S13 143 B6
Water Slacks Dr. Shef S13 143 B6
Water Slacks Rd. Shef S13 143 B5
Water Slacks Wlk. Shef S13 143 B6
Water St. Shef S3 129 A4
Waterdale. Don DN1 62 D3
Waterdale Rd. Barn S70 54 F4
Waterfield Mews. Shef S19 143 E1 8
Waterfield Pl. Barn S70 55 E8
Waterford Rd. Shef S3 128 E7
Waterhall View. Pen S30 51 D4
Waterhouse Cl. Roth S65 98 E1
Watering Place Rd. Pen S30 51 A3
Waterloo Rd. Barn S70 33 D1 7
Waterloo Wlk. Shef S3 128 F5
Watermead. Dearne S63 58 D1
Watermead Fst Sch. Shef 112 F2
Watermeade. Eck S31 155 B2
Waterside Gdns. Ought S30 111 D7
Waterside. Thorne DN8 25 E8
Waterslack Rd. Bir DN11 122 B4
Watersmeet Rd. Shef S6 128 B7
Waterthorpe Cl. Shef S19 155 F8 4
Waterthorpe Cres. Shef S19 155 F8
Waterthorpe Fst Sch. Shef 143 E1
Waterthorpe Gdns. Shef S19 155 F8 3
Waterthorpe Glade. Shef S19 155 F8 5
Waterthorpe Glen. Shef S19 155 F8 2
Waterthorpe Greenway. Shef S19 143 D3
Waterthorpe Rise. Shef S19 155 F8 1
Waterton Cl. S Kirk WF9 18 D3
Waterton La. Hat DN7 44 C3
Watery St. Shef S3 128 F5
Wath C of E Jun & Inf Sch. W up D 78 E7
Wath Comp Sch Park Rd Annexe. W up D 78 E5
Wath Golf Course. W up D 78 D3
Wath Rd. Dearne S63 58 C1
Wath Rd. Hoy S74 77 C5
Wath Rd. Mex S64 79 D5
Wath Rd. Shef S7 140 E6
Wath Rd. W up D S73 57 A1
Wath Rd. W up D S64 79 E5
Wath Rd. Wombw S73 56 F1
Wath upon Dearne Central Sch. W up D 78 F5
Wath upon Dearne Grammar Sch. W up D 78 F5
Wath Victoria Jun Mix & Inf Sch. W up D 79 A6
Wath West Ind Est. W up D 78 C8
Wath Wood Bottom. W up D S63 78 F3
Wath Wood Dr. Swint S64 78 F3
Wath Wood Rd. Swint S63 78 F3
Wathwood Hospl. Swint 78 F3
Watkinson Gdns. Shef S19 143 F1
Watnall Rd. Barn S71 33 F8
Watson Cl. Roth S61 114 F8
Watson Glen. Roth S61 114 C8
Watson Rd. Roth S61 114 F8
Watson Rd. Shef S10 128 D2
Watson St. Hoy S74 76 B5
Watt La. Shef S10 127 F2
Waulkmill Cl. Upton WF9 19 A7
Waveney Dr. Barn S75 32 E3
Waverley Ave. Con DN12 81 C2
Waverley Ave. Don DN4 82 E7
Waverley Ave. Thurcr S66 133 F6
Waverley Ave. Wales S31 145 E3
Waverley Cotts. Shef S13 130 F3
Waverley Ct. Ben DN5 41 A4
Waverley Rd. Shef S9 130 C4
Waverley View. Treet S60 131 C5
Waycliffe. Barn S71 34 C3
Wayford Ave. Roth S66 117 E6
Wayland Ave. Barn S70 54 F5
Wayland Rd. Shef S11 140 D8
Weakland Cl. Shef S12 142 F3
Weakland Cres. Shef S12 142 F3
Weakland Dr. Shef S12 142 F3
Weakland Way. Shef S12 142 F3
Weather Hill La. Holme HD7 47 E8
Weatherall Pl. Ad le S DN6 20 F2
Weaver Cl. Barn S75 32 E3
Weavers Cl. Shef S30 94 C1
Weavers Wlk. D Dale HD8 30 B7
Webb Ave. Stock S30 92 E8
Webbs Ave. Shef S6 127 E6
Webster Cl. Roth S61 114 D8
Webster Cres. Roth S61 114 D8
Webster St. Shef S9 114 B1
Wedgewood Cl. Rawm S62 97 F5
Weedon St. Shef S9 114 B1
Weet Shaw La. Cud S72 16 B1
Weetwood Dr. Shef S11 140 B5
Weetwood Rd. Roth S60 116 A2
Weigh La. Shef S2 129 C3 4
Weir Cl. Hoy S74 76 F4
Weir Head. Shef S9 114 B1
Weirside. Old S81 136 F6
Welbeck Cl. Dron S18 152 C2
Welbeck Dr. Aston S31 144 F7
Welbeck Pl. Roth S65 116 B8 4
Welbeck Rd. Don DN4 62 F2
Welbeck Rd. Har DN11 122 A5
Welbeck Rd. Shef S6 128 B6
Welbeck St. Barn S75 33 D2
Welbury Gdns. Shef S19 155 E6
Welby Pl. Shef S8 140 F5
Welfare Ave. Con DN12 81 A2
Welfare Rd. Ad I S DN6 40 C4
Welfare Rd. Dearne S63 58 D8
Welfare View. Dearne S63 58 D4
Welfare View. Dod S75 53 F8
Welham Dr. Roth S60 115 E4
Well Croft. Chap S30 94 D7
Well Ct. Shef S12 143 B3
Well Dr. Roth S65 99 A2
Well Green Rd. Shef S6 127 B5
Well Hill Gr. Roy S71 15 C4
Well Hill Rd. Stock S30 73 F4
Well House La. Pen S30 51 D5
Well Houses La. Wort S30 74 D5
Well La. Aston S31 132 C2
Well La. Barn S71 34 C5
Well La. Roth S60 116 B1
Well La. Shef S6 111 F2
Well La. Treet S60 131 E5
Well La. Ulley S60 132 D7
Well La. Wad DN11 102 C7
Well Lane Ct. G Hou S72 57 F6
Well Meadow Dr. Shef S3 128 F4 6
Well Meadow St. Shef S3 128 F4
Well Pl. Shef S8 141 A6
Well Rd. Shef S8 141 A6
Well St. Barn S70 33 D1 6
Well View Rd. Roth S61 114 D8
Welland Cl. Shef S3 128 F6
Welland Cres. Hoy S74 77 B6
Welland Ct. Barn S75 32 E3
Wellbourne Cl. Chap S30 95 C4
Wellcarr Rd. Shef S8 141 A2
Wellcliffe Cl. Roth S66 117 C6
Wellcroft Cl. Don DN2 63 C6
Wellesley Rd. Shef S10 128 D3
Wellfield Cl. Eck S12 142 E1
Wellfield Cl. Shef S6 128 D5
Wellfield Cres. Woods S81 147 E3
Wellfield Gr. Pen S30 51 D5
Wellfield Rd. Barn S75 33 D3
Wellfield Rd. Roth S61 96 E2
Wellfield Rd. Shef S6 128 D5
Wellgate. Con DN12 81 C2
Wellgate. Mapp S75 14 B1
Wellgate Mount. Roth S60 115 E6
Wellgate. Roth S60 115 E6
Wellgate Terr. Roth S60 115 E6 4
Wellhead Rd. Shef S8 141 A6 4
Wellhouse Way. Pen S30 51 D5
Welling Way. Roth S61 114 E7
Wellingley La. Tick DN11 102 F2

Wellingley La. Wad DN11 102 E5
Wellington Ave. N Anst S31 146 D7
Wellington Cl. Barn S71 34 B4
Wellington Cres. Barn S70 55 C5
Wellington Gr. Bawtry DN10 122 F8
Wellington Gr. Ben DN5 62 A7
Wellington Pl. Barn S70 33 D1 8
Wellington Pl. Shef S9 130 C4
Wellington Rd. Hat DN7 66 A8
Wellington Rd. N Edl DN12 82 B2
Wellington Rd. Shef S6 127 E6
Wellington St. Barn S70 33 E1
Wellington St. Dearne S63 58 E5
Wellington St. Mex S64 80 A5
Wellington St. Shef S1 128 F2
Wellington St. Shef S1 129 A3
Wellington St. Stai DN7 24 F4
Wellingtonia Dr. Norton DN6 4 C1
Wells Mount. D Dale HD8 29 A6
Wells Rd. Don DN2 62 F6
Wells St. Cud S72 35 B6
Wells St. Kex S75 32 E8
Wells The. N Anst S31 146 D5
Wellsyke Rd. Ad l S DN6 40 D7
Wellthorne Ave. Ingb S30 29 E1
Wellthorne La. Ingb S30 29 D1
Wellway The. Roth S66 117 C7
Welney Pl. Shef S6 112 C4
Welton Cl. Don DN4 84 C6
Welwyn Cl. Shef S12 142 B4
Welwyn Rd. Shef S12 142 B4
Wembley Ave. Con DN12 81 A2
Wembley Cl. Don DN2 63 C5
Wembley Rd. Lan S81 136 F3
Wembley Rd. Thorne DN8 9 D3
Wenchirst La. Fish DN7 8 A2
Wendan Rd. Thorne DN8 26 B5
Wendel Gr. Hoy S74 77 B6
Wenlock St. Shef S13 130 F1
Wensley Cl. Shef S4 113 E1
Wensley Cres. Don DN4 84 F7
Wensley Croft. Shef S4 113 E2
Wensley Ct. Shef S4 113 E2
Wensley Dale Dr. Brin S60 131 D7
Wensley Gdns. Shef S4 113 E2
Wensley Gn. Shef S4 113 E2
Wensley Rd. Barn S71 33 E7
Wensley St. Dearne S63 58 B8
Wensley St. Shef S4 113 E2
Wensleydale Rd. Ben DN5 61 D7
Wensleydale Rd. Roth S61 96 F3
Went Edge Rd. K Smea WF8 3 B6
Wentdale. K Smea WF8 3 E6
Wentworth Ave. Aston S31 144 F7
Wentworth Ave. Shef S11 140 A2
Wentworth Cl. Roth S61 95 E5
Wentworth Cl. Wool WF4 13 F7
Wentworth Cres. Mapp S75 33 D8
Wentworth Cres. Pen S30 51 D3
Wentworth Ct. Roth S61 97 B4
Wentworth Dr. S Kirk WF9 18 C3
Wentworth Gdns. Swint S64 79 C1
Wentworth Hospl (Almshouses).
Went S74 77 A1
Wentworth House. Don DN1 62 C2 9
Wentworth Ind Pk. Pilley 75 D4
Wentworth Pl. Roth S61 96 C2
Wentworth Rd. Don DN2 62 F5
Wentworth Rd. Dron S18 152 C1
Wentworth Rd. Hoy S74 55 D2
Wentworth Rd. Hoy S74 77 A4
Wentworth Rd. Hoy S74 77 A7
Wentworth Rd. Kex S75 32 D8
Wentworth Rd. Mapp S75 33 C8
Wentworth Rd. Pen S30 51 D4
Wentworth Rd. Rawm S62 97 D8
Wentworth Rd. Roth S61 96 A5
Wentworth Rd. Swint S64 98 C8
Wentworth St. Barn S71 33 E3
Wentworth St. Barn S70 75 F7
Wentworth View. Hoy S74 76 E5
Wentworth View. Wombw S73 56 D1
Wentworth Way. Din S31 147 A7
Wentworth Way. Dod S75 53 F6
Wentworth Way. Pilley S75 75 D4
Wescoe Ave. G Hou S72 36 F1
Wesley Ave. Aston S31 144 D8
Wesley Ct. Roth S61 95 F5
Wesley La. Shef S10 128 B3
Wesley Pl. S Anst S31 146 D4
Wesley Rd. Chap S30 94 C7
Wesley Rd. Wales S31 145 D3
Wesley St. Barn S70 33 F1
Wesley St. S Elm WF9 18 E2
Wesley Terr. D Dale HD8 29 F6
Wessenden Cl. Barn S75 33 A1
Wessex Gdns. Shef S17 151 D5
West Ave. Ad le S DN6 39 F4
West Ave. Dearne S63 58 B1
West Ave. Don DN4 83 A7
West Ave. Rawm S62 97 F6
West Ave. Roy S71 15 D4
West Ave. S Elm WF9 19 B4
West Ave. Stai DN7 24 F4
West Ave. Wombw S73 56 B3
West Bank. K Bram DN7 24 D5
West Bank Rise. S Anst S31 146 D4
West Bar. Shef S3 129 A4
West Bawtry Rd. Roth S60 115 D1
West Bretton Jun & Inf School.
W Bret 12 F8
West Circuit. T in B DN3 42 C8
West Cl. Roth S61 114 E8
West Cres. Oxspr S30 52 A2
West Cres. Stock S30 73 A1
West Don St. Shef S6 128 E6
West End Ave. Ben DN5 62 A7
West End Ave. Pen S30 50 D3
West End Ave. Roy S71 15 A3
West End Cres. Roy S71 15 A3
West End La. Ross DN11 84 E1
West End Rd. Norton DN6 4 C3
West End Rd. W up D S63 78 B7
West End View. Eck S31 155 C2
West Garth Cl. Din S31 134 F1
West Gate. Holme HD7 47 F8
West Gate. Mex S64 80 C5
West Gate. Tick DN11 120 F6
West Gr. Don DN2 63 A5
West Gr. Roy S71 15 A4
West Hill. Roth S61 114 C6
West Kirk La. G Hou S72 57 F7
West La. Aston S31 132 B1
West La. Bfield S6 109 F1
West La. Shef S6 111 A2
West La. Syke DN14 6 F4
West La. Thurcr S66 118 B1
West Laith Gate. Don DN1 62 C3 4
West Melton Jun & Inf Sch.
W up D 78 C7
West Moor Cres. Barn S75 33 A1
West Moor La. Arm DN3 64 D8
West Moor La. Hat DN3 43 E1
West Park Dr. Aston S31 144 B7
West Pinfold. Roy S71 15 C2
West Pl. Ben DN5 41 B1
West Quadrant. Shef S5 113 D3
West Rd. Barn S75 33 C2
West Rd. Mex S64 79 F5
West Rd. Thorne DN8 9 D3
West Service Rd. T in B DN3 42 C8
West St. Barn S70 55 B4
West St. Con DN12 81 C2
West St. Dar S73 57 A5
West St. Dearne S63 58 E5
West St. Don DN1 62 C3
West St. Dron S18 152 F2
West St. Eck S31 155 C2
West St. Har DN11 122 A5
West St. Hoy S74 76 D6
West St. Mex S64 80 A6
West St. Roy S71 15 D4
West St. S Anst S31 146 D4
West St. S Elm WF9 19 B4
West St. S Hie S72 16 E5
West St. S Kirk WF9 18 A2
West St. Shef S1 128 F3
West St. Shef S19 144 A3
West St. Thorne DN8 26 B6
West St. Thurcr S66 133 F6
West St. W up D S63 78 E6
West St. Wombw S73 56 C3
West Street La. Shef S1 129 A3 3
West Vale Gr. Roth S65 98 F2
West View. Barn S70 54 E7
West View. C in L S81 148 F6
West View Cl. Shef S17 151 F8
West View Cres. Dearne S63 58 D4
West View. Cud S72 35 C5
West View La. Shef S17 151 F6
West View Rd. Mex S64 80 A4
West View Rd. Roth S61 114 C6
West View. Silk S75 53 A6
West View Terr. Barn S70 55 B4
West Way. Barn S70 33 E1
West Wood Est. Bawtry DN10 122 F6
Westbank Cl. Dron S18 153 B4
Westbank Dr. S Anst S31 146 C4
Westbar Gn. Shef S1, S3 129 A4
Westbourne Gdns. Don DN4 82 F5
Westbourne Gr. Barn S75 33 D3
Westbourne Prep Sch. Shef 128 C2
Westbourne Rd. Shef S10 128 C2
Westbourne Terr. Barn S70 33 C1
Westbrook Bank. Shef S11 140 D8
Westbrook Rd. Chap S30 95 A5
Westbury Ave. Chap S30 95 B4
Westbury Cl. Barn S75 33 B4
Westbury St. Shef S9 129 F5
Westby Cl. Roth S65 117 E8
Westby Cres. Roth S60 116 B1
Westby Wlk. Roth S66 117 E5
Westcroft Cres. Shef S19 155 E8
Westcroft Dr. Shef S19 155 E7
Westcroft Gdns. Shef S19 155 E8
Westcroft Glen. Shef S19 155 E7
Westcroft Gr. Shef S19 155 E7
Westcroft Rd. Hem WF9 17 D7
Westerdale Rd. Ben DN5 61 D6
Western Ave. Din S31 146 F8
Western Bank. Shef S10 128 D3
Western Cl. Din S31 146 F8
Western Rd. Roth S65 116 B6
Western Rd. Shef S10 128 C4
Western St. Barn S70 33 E2
Western Terr. Wombw S73 56 C3
Westfield Ave. Aston S31 132 C1
Westfield Ave. Pen S30 51 A4
Westfield Ave. Shef S12 143 C3
Westfield Bglws. S Elm WF9 19 A2
Westfield Campus. Shef 155 D8
Westfield Cl. Tick DN11 120 F7
Westfield Cres. Askern DN6 22 B8
Westfield Cres. Dearne S63 37 C1
Westfield Cres. Shef S19 155 C8
Westfield Ctr. Shef S19 155 E7
Westfield Gr. Ingb S30 29 D1
Westfield Gr. Shef S12 143 B3 4
Westfield La. Bnbur DN5 59 B3
Westfield La. Fish DN7 7 C1
Westfield La. Norton WF8 3 F3
Westfield La. Pen S30 50 F4
Westfield La. S Elm WF9 18 F2
Westfield Northway. Shef S19 155 E8
Westfield Rd. Arm DN3 64 A6
Westfield Rd. Don DN4 83 B8
Westfield Rd. Fish DN7 24 D8
Westfield Rd. Hat DN7 44 C8
Westfield Rd. Hem WF9 17 D7
Westfield Rd. Kill S31 156 C5
Westfield Rd. Rawm S62 97 E4
Westfield Rd. Roth S66 117 D5
Westfield Rd. Tick DN11 120 F7
Westfield Rd. W up D S63 78 A7
Westfield Southway. Shef S19 155 E8
Westfield St. Barn S70 33 D1
Westfield Terr. Shef S1 128 F3
Westfield Villas. Hat DN7 44 C8
Westfields. Barn S70 55 A4
Westfields. Roy S71 15 A4
Westgate. Barn S70 33 E1
Westgate. Barn S71 34 B4
Westgate. Hem WF9 17 C6
Westgate. Pen S30 51 E2
Westgate. Roth S60 115 D6
Westhaven. Cud S72 35 C5
Westhill La. Shef S3 128 F3
Westholme Rd. Don DN4 62 B1
Westland Cl. Shef S19 143 E1
Westland Gdns. Shef S19 143 D1
Westland Gr. Shef S19 155 E8 3
Westland Rd. Shef S19 155 E8 1
Westminster Ave. Shef S10 127 B1
Westminster Cl. Shef S10 127 B1
Westminster Cres. Don DN2 63 C5
Westminster Cres. Shef S10 127 B1
Westminster House. Don DN2 63 C5
Westmoreland St. Shef S6 128 E5 2
Westmorland Ct. Bir DN11 122 D4
Westmorland Dr. C in L S81 148 F8
Westmorland La. Con DN12 80 F3
Westmorland St. Don DN4 82 F6
Westmorland Way. Sprot DN5 61 B1
Westmount Ave. W up D S63 78 C8
Westnall Rd. Shef S5 113 D7
Westnall Terr. Shef S5 113 D7
Westoff La. S Hie S72 16 D7
Weston Park Hospl. Shef 128 D3
Weston Park Mus. Shef 128 D3
Weston Rd. Don DN4 83 B6
Weston St. Shef S3 128 E4
Westover Rd. Shef S10 127 E2
Westpit Hill. W up D S63 78 A7
Westside Grange. Don DN4 83 A8
Westthorpe Gr. Kill S31 156 D4
Westthorpe Rd. Kill S31 156 D5
Westville Rd. Barn S75 33 D3
Westways Prim Sch. Shef 128 C4
Westwell Pl. Shef S19 155 D6
Westwick Cres. Shef S8 152 D7
Westwick Gr. Shef S8 152 E7
Westwick Rd. Shef S8 152 E7
Westwood Ct. Barn S70 33 E2
Westwood Ctry Pk. Chap 75 E2
Westwood La. Wort S75 75 C3
Westwood New Rd. Chap S30 94 C7
Westwood New Rd. Pilley S75 75 D3
Westwood New Rd. Pilley S75 75 E5
Westwood Rd. Chap S30 94 D8
Westwood Rd. Shef S11 139 F8
Wet Moor La. W up D S63 78 D7
Wet Moor La. W up D S63 78 F7
Wet Shaw La. Bfield S6 109 E1
Wetherby Cl. Ben DN5 61 D5
Wetherby Ct. Shef S9 130 C4
Wetherby Dr. Aston S31 144 C6
Wetherby Dr. Mex S64 80 B6
Whaley Rd. Barn S75 33 A5
Whams Rd. Carl S30 49 F2
Wharf Cl. Swint S64 79 E3
Wharf Rd. Don DN1 62 D5
Wharf Rd. Shef S9 114 D3
Wharf Rd. Swint S62 98 E7
Wharf St. Barn S71 34 A3
Wharf St. Bawtry DN10 123 A7
Wharf St. Shef S2 129 B4
Wharf St. Swint S64 79 E3
Wharfedale Dr. Chap S30 94 E5
Wharfedale Rd. Barn S75 33 B2
Wharncliffe Ave. Aston S31 144 E8
Wharncliffe Ave. W up D S63 78 F6
Wharncliffe Ave. Wharn S30 93 B3
Wharncliffe Cl. Hoy S74 76 D4
Wharncliffe Cl. Rawm S62 97 D8
Wharncliffe. Dod S75 54 A6
Wharncliffe Rd. Chap S30 94 D7
Wharncliffe Rd. Shef S10 128 E2
Wharncliffe Side Cty Prim Sch.
Wharn 93 B1
Wharncliffe Side Jun & Inf Sch.
Wharn 93 B2
Wharncliffe St. Barn S70 33 D1
Wharncliffe St. Don DN4 62 A2
Wharncliffe St. Roth S65 115 E6
Wharncliffe St. Roy S71 34 D8
Wharton Ave. Aston S31 132 D1
Wheat Croft. Con DN12 81 E2
Wheat Holme La. Askern DN5 41 D8
Wheata Dr. Shef S5 113 B7
Wheata Pl. Shef S5 113 A7
Wheata Rd. Shef S5 113 A7
Wheatacre Rd. Stock S30 73 C1
Wheatcroft Rd. Rawm S62 98 B6
Wheatfield Cl. B Dun DN3 43 A6
Wheatfield Cres. Shef S5 113 D6
Wheatfield Dr. Dearne S63 58 D7
Wheatfield Dr. Tick DN11 121 B8
Wheatfields. Thorne DN8 26 B7
Wheathill St. Roth S60 115 D5
Wheatley Cl. Barn S71 33 F4
Wheatley Golf Course. Don 63 D7
Wheatley Gr. Shef S13 130 E1
Wheatley Hall Rd. Don DN2 62 F6
Wheatley High Sch for Girls. Don 62 E5
Wheatley Hill La. Clay W HD8 30 E8
Wheatley Hills Mid Sch. Don 63 D7
Wheatley La. Don DN1 62 D4
Wheatley Pl. Con DN12 80 F3 7
Wheatley Rd. Barn S70 55 E7
Wheatley Rd. Ben DN5 41 A2
Wheatley Rd. Roth S61 96 E1
Wheatley Rd. Swint S62 98 E7
Wheatley Rise. Mapp S75 14 B2
Wheatley St. Con DN12 80 F3
Wheats La. Shef S1 129 A4 17
Wheel La. Ought S30 111 C7
Wheel La. Ought S30 111 D6
Wheel La. Shef S30 112 D8
Wheel The. Shef S30 112 F8
Wheeldon St. Shef S1 128 F3
Wheldrake Rd. Shef S5 113 D2
Whernside Ave. Chap S30 94 F6
Whih Moor La. Silk S75 52 C7
Whin Cl. Hem WF9 17 D5
Whin Gdns. Dearne S63 37 D1
Whin Hill Rd. Don DN4 84 D8
Whinacre Cl. Shef S8 153 B6
Whinacre Pl. Shef S8 153 A6
Whinacre Wlk. Shef S8 153 A6
Whinby Croft. Dod S75 53 F7
Whinfell Cl. Ad l S DN6 40 B6
Whinfell Ct. Shef S11 139 E2
Whinmoor Cl. Silk S75 31 F1
Whinmoor Ct. Silk S75 31 F1
Whinmoor Dr. Silk S75 31 F1
Whinmoor Rd. Chap S30 94 C7
Whinmoor Rd. Shef S5 113 F3
Whinmoor Sch. Barn 32 D4
Whinmoor View. Silk S75 31 F1
Whinmoor Way. Silk S75 31 F1
Whins The. Rawm S62 97 C5
Whinside Cres. Dearne S63 37 C1
Whiphill Cl. Don DN4 84 E7
Whiphill La. Arm DN3 64 C5
Whirlow Brook Sch. Shef 139 D1
Whirlow Court Rd. Shef S11 139 F2
Whirlow Gr. Shef S11 139 F2
Whirlow La. Shef S11 139 F3
Whirlow Mews. Shef S11 139 F3
Whirlow Park Rd. Shef S11 139 F1
Whirlowdale Cl. Shef S11 139 F2
Whirlowdale Cres. Shef S7 140 B3
Whirlowdale Rd. Shef S11, S7 140 B3
Whirlowdale Rise. Shef S11 139 F2
Whiston Brook View. Roth S60 116 D1
Whiston Gr. Roth S60 115 F4
Whiston Grange. Roth S60 116 A1
Whiston Grange Sch. Roth 116 B1
Whiston Jun & Inf Sch. Roth 116 B1
Whiston Vale. Roth S60 132 B8
Whiston Worrygate Prim Sch.
Roth 116 D1
Whitaker Cl. Ross DN11 103 F7
Whitbeck Cl. Wad DN11 102 B7
Whitburn Rd. Don DN1 62 E2
Whitby Rd. Har DN11 122 A5
Whitby Rd. Ross DN11 103 F8
Whitby Rd. Shef S9 130 C5
Whitcomb Dr. Ross DN11 103 F7
White Apron St. S Kirk WF9 18 B2
White Ave. Lan S81 136 E3
White Croft. Shef S1 129 A4
White Cross Gdns. S Hie S72 16 D6
White Cross La. Barn S70 55 D5
White Cross La. Don DN11 83 B1
White Cross La. Wad DN11 102 B8
White Cross Rd. Cud S72 35 B5
White Cross Rise. Barn S70 55 D5
White Gate. N Anst S31 146 F6
White Gate Rd. Holme HD7 47 D7
White Hill Ave. Barn S70 33 B1
White Hill Gr. Barn S70 33 B1
White Hill Terr. Barn S70 33 B1
White House Cl. Hat DN7 44 A7
White House Cl. Stai DN7 24 E5
White House Dr. Bir DN11 122 C4
White House Rd. Bir DN11 122 C4
White La. Chap S30 95 B7
White La. Eck S12 142 C2
White La. H Pag DN5 38 E4
White La. Shef S12 142 B3
White La. Thorne DN8 25 F8
White Lee La. Bfield S6 92 B3
White Ley Bank. Holmfi HD7 28 A7
White Ley Rd. Norton WF8 3 E1
White Rose Ct. Ben DN5 41 C1
White Rose Way. Don DN4 83 F7
White Thorns Cl. Shef S8 153 B5
White Thorns Dr. Shef S8 153 B5
White Thorns View. Shef S8 153 B6
White's La. Shef S2 129 D3
Whitecroft Cres. Brin S60 131 C8
Whitegate Wlk. Roth S61 96 F3
Whitehall Rd. Roth S61 97 A3
Whitehall Way. Roth S61 97 A3
Whitehead Ave. Stock S30 73 D1
Whitehead Cl. Din S31 134 E1
Whitehill Ave. Brin S60 131 C8
Whitehill Dr. Brin S60 131 C7
Whitehill La. Brin S60 131 D7
Whitehill La. Treet S60 131 D7
Whitehill Rd. Brin S60 131 C8
Whitehouse Ct. Bir DN11 122 C4
Whitehouse La. Shef S6 128 D6
Whitehouse Rd. Shef S6 128 D6
Whitelea Gr. Mex S64 79 F4
Whitelee Rd. Swint S64 79 E4
Whiteley La. Shef S10 139 C7
Whiteley Wood Cl. Shef S11 139 F7
Whiteley Wood Rd. Shef S11 139 E7
Whiteleys Ave. Rawm S62 97 E7
Whitelow La. Shef S17 151 B7
Whiteways Cl. Shef S4 129 D8
Whiteways Dr. Shef S4 129 D8
Whiteways Gr. Shef S4 129 D8
Whiteways Mid Sch. Shef 129 D8
Whiteways Rd. Shef S4 129 D8
Whitewood Cl. Roy S71 15 B3
Whitfield Rd. Rawm S62 97 D7
Whitfield Rd. Shef S10 139 C7
Whiting St. Shef S8 141 A6 9
Whitley Carr. Shef S30 94 E2
Whitley La. Shef S30 94 E2
Whitley Terr. Wh Com S30 49 D5
Whitley View Rd. Roth S61 114 B6
Whitney Cl. Don DN4 82 E5
Whittier Rd. Don DN4 83 A6
Whittington St. Don DN1 62 D5
Whitton Cl. Don DN4 84 C6
Whitwell Cres. Stock S30 73 B1
Whitwell La. Stock S30 92 A8
Whitwell Rd. Th Sa S80 159 A4
Whitwell St. Shef S9 130 D4
Whitwell View. Ross DN11 85 B1
Whitworth La. Shef S9 130 A7
Whitworth Rd. Shef S10 127 F2
Whitworth St. Dearne S63 58 E5
Whitworth Way. W up D S63 78 E7
Whitworth's Terr. Dearne S63 58 E8
Whybourne Gr. Roth S60 115 E5
Whybourne Terr. Roth S60 115 E6 5
Whyn View. Dearne S63 58 D6
Wicker La. Shef S3 129 B4
Wicker. Shef S3 129 B4
Wickersley High Sch. Roth 117 C4
Wickersley Northfield Inf Sch.
Roth 117 B5
Wickersley Northfield Jun Sch.
Roth 117 B5
Wickersley Rd. Roth S60 116 C4
Wicket Way. N Edl DN12 82 C3
Wickett Hern Rd. Arm DN3 64 C6
Wickfield Cl. Shef S12 142 F5
Wickfield Dr. Shef S12 142 F5
Wickfield Gr. Shef S12 142 E4
Wickfield Pl. Shef S12 142 F5
Wickfield Rd. Shef S12 142 F5
Wicklow Rd. Don DN2 63 B5
Widdop Cl. Shef S13 142 D8
Widdop Croft. Shef S13 142 D8
Widford Gn. Hat DN7 44 A6
Wigfield Dr. Barn S70 54 F5
Wigfull Rd. Shef S11 128 C1
Wignall Ave. Roth S66 116 F4
Wike Gate Cl. Thorne DN8 26 D6
Wike Gate Gr. Thorne DN8 26 D6
Wike Gate Rd. Thorne DN8 26 D6
Wike Rd. Barn S71 34 E2
Wilberforce Rd. Don DN2 42 D1
Wilberforce Rd. S Anst S31 146 D5
Wilbrook Rise. Barn S75 33 A4
Wilby Carr High Sch. Don 63 E1
Wilby La. Barn S70 55 A8
Wilcox Cl. Shef S6 112 D5
Wilcox Rd. Shef S6 112 D5
Wild Ave. Rawm S62 97 C7
Wildflower Cl. Ross DN11 103 F7
Wilding Cl. Roth S61 114 E8
Wilding Way. Roth S61 114 E8
Wilford Rd. Barn S71 14 E1
Wilfred Cl. Shef S9 130 A5
Wilfred Dr. Shef S9 130 A5
Wilfred St. Roth S60 115 D6
Wilfrid Rd. Shef S9 130 A5
Wilkinson Ave. Ross DN11 104 A8
Wilkinson Ave. Thorne DN8 9 C2
Wilkinson La. Shef S10 128 E3
Wilkinson Rd. Hoy S74 77 A5
Wilkinson St. Barn S70 54 F8 17
Wilkinson St. Shef S10 128 E3 3
Willan Dr. Treet S60 131 C5
Willbury Dr. Shef S12 142 A6
Willey St. Shef S3 129 B4
William Bradford Cl. Aust DN10 105 C1
William Cl. Shef S19 155 D6
William Cres. Shef S19 155 D6
William La. Ross DN11 84 E1
William Levick Cty Prim Sch.
Dron 152 B2
William Nuttall Cott Homes.
Don DN2 62 F2
William St. Barn S70 55 A5
William St. Dearne S63 58 C5
William St. Eck S31 155 D3
William St. Rawm S62 98 A4
William St. Roth S60 115 E6
William St. Shef S10 128 E2
William St. Swint S64 79 E3
William St. W up D S63 78 F6
William St. Wombw S73 56 C3
Williams Rd. Ben DN5 61 F6
Williams St. Lan S81 136 E3
Williamson Rd. Shef S11 140 D7
Willingham Cl. Shef S19 144 A1
Willingham Gdns. Shef S19 144 A2
Willington Rd. Ad le S DN6 21 B1
Willington Rd. Shef S5 113 C4
Willis Rd. Shef S6 112 B1
Willman Rd. Barn S71 34 F3
Willoughby St. Shef S4 113 E2
Willow Ave. C in L S81 148 E7
Willow Ave. Don DN4 84 F8
Willow Ave. Rawm S62 98 A6
Willow Ave. Thorne DN8 9 B2
Willow Bank. Barn S75 33 E4
Willow Beck. Notton WF4 15 A6
Willow Bridge La. K Bram DN6 23 E6
Willow Bridge La. T in B DN6 23 E6
Willow Bridge Rd. Ben DN5 62 B5
Willow Brook Rd. Mapp S75 33 A8
Willow Cl. Brin S60 131 D7
Willow Cl. Cud S72 35 B7
Willow Cl. Hoy S74 76 C5
Willow Cl. Roth S66 117 C6
Willow Cl. S Anst S31 146 D3
Willow Cotts. Fish DN7 24 E8
Willow Cres. Braith S66 101 A2
Willow Cres. Chap S30 95 A4
Willow Cres. Finn DN9 85 F4
Willow Cres. Thorne DN8 9 C1
Willow Dene Rd. Grime S72 36 A7
Willow Dr. Hem WF9 17 D5
Willow Dr. Mex S64 79 F5
Willow Dr. Roth S66 117 C6
Willow Dr. Shef S9 130 E3
Willow Garth La. Norton DN6 5 C1
Willow Garth. Rawm S62 98 A6
Willow Garth. S Elm WF9 19 B2
Willow Gr. Aston S31 144 F8
Willow Gr. Thorne DN8 9 C1
Willow Inf Sch. Don 84 D6
Willow La. Dearne S63 58 D1
Willow La. Ross DN11 85 A2
Willow Pl. Braith S66 101 A2
Willow Rd. Arm DN3 64 C7
Willow Rd. Dearne S63 37 D1
Willow Rd. Kill S31 156 C5
Willow Rd. Maltby S66 118 D5
Willow Rd. Norton DN6 4 D1
Willow Rd. Stock S30 92 B7
Willow Rd. Thorne DN8 9 B1
Willow Rd. W up D S63 79 A4
Willow St. Barn S70 54 D8
Willow St. Con DN12 81 C2
Willow Wlk. Ben DN5 41 A3
Willowbridge Rd. K Smea WF8 4 A6
Willowbrook. Ad le S DN6 20 F2
Willowdale Cl. Sprot DN5 82 D8
Willowgarth Ave. Brin S60 131 C8
Willowgarth High Sch. Grim 17 A1
Willowgarth House. Rawm S62 98 A6
Willowlees Ct. Don DN4 84 E7
Willows The. Oxspr S30 52 B1
Willows The. Roth S61 96 D2
Wilsden Gr. Barn S75 33 B4
Wilsic Hall Sch. Wad 102 A4
Wilsic La. Wad DN11 102 D2
Wilsic Rd. Tick DN11 120 F8
Wilsic Rd. Wad DN11 102 A5
Wilson Ave. Pen S30 51 D2
Wilson Ave. Rawm S62 97 E6
Wilson Dr. Roth S65 98 E1
Wilson Gr. Barn S71 34 F4
Wilson Pl. Shef S8 141 A7 6
Wilson Rd. Dron S18 153 C4
Wilson Rd. Shef S11 140 C8
Wilson Rd. Stock S30 92 F8
Wilson St. Shef S3 129 A6
Wilson St. Wombw S73 56 B4
Wilson Wlk. Dod S75 54 A6
Wilthorpe Ave. Barn S75 33 C4

STREET ATLASES ORDER FORM

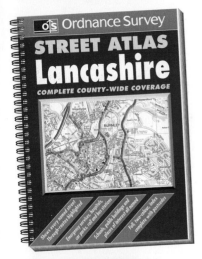

All Street Atlases contain Ordnance Survey mapping and provide the perfect solution for the driver who needs comprehensive, detailed regional mapping in a choice of compact and easy-to-use formats. They are indispensable and are ideal for use in the car, the home or the office.

The series is available from all good bookshops or by mail order direct from the publisher. Before placing your order, please check by telephone that the complete range of titles are available. Payment can be made in the following ways:

By phone Phone your order through on our special Credit Card Hotline on **01733 371999** (Fax: **01733 370585**). Speak to our customer service team during office hours (9am to 5pm) or leave a message on the answering machine, quoting your full credit card number plus expiry date and your full name and address.

By post Simply fill out the order form (you may photocopy it) and send it to: **Reed Books Direct, 43 Stapledon Road, Orton Southgate, Peterborough** PE2 6TD.

NEW COLOUR EDITIONS

	HARDBACK	SPIRAL	POCKET	£ Total
BERKSHIRE	Quantity @ £10.99 each ☐ 0 540 06170 0	Quantity @ £8.99 each ☐ 0 540 06172 7	Quantity @ £4.99 each ☐ 0 540 06173 5	➤
MERSEYSIDE	Quantity @ £10.99 each ☐ 0 540 06480 7	Quantity @ £8.99 each ☐ 0 540 06481 5	Quantity @ £3.99 each ☐ 0 540 06482 3	➤
SURREY	Quantity @ £12.99 each ☐ 0 540 06435 1	Quantity @ £8.99 each ☐ 0 540 06436 X	Quantity @ £4.99 each ☐ 0 540 06438 6	➤
DURHAM	Quantity @ £12.99 each ☐ 0 540 06365 7	Quantity @ £9.99 each ☐ 0 540 06366 5	Quantity @ £4.99 each ☐ 0 540 06367 3	➤
HERTFORDSHIRE	☐ 0 540 06174 3	☐ 0 540 06175 1	☐ 0 540 06176 X	➤
EAST KENT	☐ 0 540 07274 5	☐ 0 540 07276 1	☐ 0 540 07287 7	➤
WEST KENT	☐ 0 540 07366 0	☐ 0 540 07367 9	☐ 0 540 07369 5	➤
GREATER MANCHESTER	☐ 0 540 06485 8	☐ 0 540 06486 6	☐ 0 540 06487 4	➤
TYNE AND WEAR	☐ 0 540 06370 3	☐ 0 540 06371 1	☐ 0 540 06372 X	➤
SOUTH YORKSHIRE	☐ 0 540 06330 4	☐ 0 540 06331 2	☐ 0 540 06332 0	➤
WEST YORKSHIRE	☐ 0 540 06329 0	☐ 0 540 06327 4	☐ 0 540 06328 2	➤
LANCASHIRE	Quantity @ £14.99 each ☐ 0 540 06440 8	Quantity @ £9.99 each ☐ 0 540 06441 6	Quantity @ £4.99 each ☐ 0 540 06443 2	➤

BLACK AND WHITE EDITIONS

	HARDBACK	SOFTBACK	POCKET	£ Total
BRISTOL AND AVON	Quantity @ £12.99 each ☐ 0 540 06140 9	Quantity @ £9.99 each ☐ 0 540 06141 7	Quantity @ £4.99 each ☐ 0 540 06142 5	➤

NEW AUGUST

NEW AUGUST

STREET ATLASES ORDER FORM

BLACK AND WHITE EDITIONS	HARDBACK	SOFTBACK	POCKET	
	Quantity @ £12.99 each	Quantity @ £9.99 each	Quantity @ £4.99 each	£ Total
BUCKINGHAMSHIRE	☐ 0 540 05989 7	☐ 0 540 05990 0	☐ 0 540 05991 9	➤ ☐
CARDIFF, SWANSEA & GLAMORGAN	☐ 0 540 06186 7	☐ 0 540 06187 5	☐ 0 540 06207 3	➤ ☐
CHESHIRE	☐ 0 540 06143 3	☐ 0 540 06144 1	☐ 0 540 06145 X	➤ ☐
DERBYSHIRE	☐ 0 540 06137 9	☐ 0 540 06138 7	☐ 0 540 06139 5	➤ ☐
EDINBURGH & East Central Scotland	☐ 0 540 06180 8	☐ 0 540 06181 6	☐ 0 540 06182 4	➤ ☐
GLASGOW & West Central Scotland	☐ 0 540 06183 2	☐ 0 540 06184 0	☐ 0 540 06185 9	➤ ☐
SOUTH HAMPSHIRE	☐ 0 540 05855 6	☐ 0 540 05856 4	☐ 0 540 05857 2	➤ ☐
NOTTINGHAMSHIRE	☐ 0 540 05858 0	☐ 0 540 05859 9	☐ 0 540 05860 2	➤ ☐
OXFORDSHIRE	☐ 0 540 05986 2	☐ 0 540 05987 0	☐ 0 540 05988 9	➤ ☐
STAFFORDSHIRE	☐ 0 540 06134 4	☐ 0 540 06135 2	☐ 0 540 06136 0	➤ ☐
WEST SUSSEX	☐ 0 540 05876 9	☐ 0 540 05877 7	☐ 0 540 05878 5	➤ ☐
	Quantity @ £10.99 each	Quantity @ £8.99 each	Quantity @ £4.99 each	£ Total
WARWICKSHIRE	☐ 0 540 05642 1	—	—	➤ ☐
	Quantity @ £12.99 each	Quantity @ £8.99 each	Quantity @ £4.99 each	£ Total
EAST ESSEX	☐ 0 540 05848 3	☐ 0 540 05866 1	☐ 0 540 05850 5	➤ ☐
WEST ESSEX	☐ 0 540 05849 1	☐ 0 540 05867 X	☐ 0 540 05851 3	➤ ☐
NORTH HAMPSHIRE	☐ 0 540 05852 1	☐ 0 540 05853 X	☐ 0 540 05854 8	➤ ☐
EAST SUSSEX	☐ 0 540 05875 0	☐ 0 540 05874 2	☐ 0 540 05873 4	➤ ☐

Post to: **Reed Books Direct, 43 Stapledon Road, Orton Southgate, Peterborough** PE2 6TD

◆ Free postage and packing

◆ All available titles will normally be dispatched within 5 working days of receipt of order but please allow up to 28 days for delivery

☐ Please tick this box if you do not wish your name to be used by other carefully selected organisations that may wish to send you information about other products and services

Registered Office: Michelin House, 81 Fulham Road, London SW3 6RB. Registered in England number:1974080

I enclose a cheque / postal order, for a **total** of ☐

made payable to *Reed Book Services*, or please debit my

☐ Access ☐ American Express ☐ Visa ☐ Diners

account by ☐

Account no ☐☐☐☐ ☐☐☐☐ ☐☐☐☐ ☐☐☐☐

Expiry date ☐☐ ☐☐

Signature...

Name...

Address...

....

....

....POSTCODE

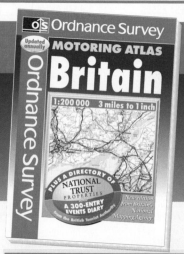